W9-CZK-622

SIMONSEN'S NAVIGATION

SIMONSEN'S

by Captain Svend T. Simonsen

NAVIGA-
TION

COASTWISE
AND
BLUE WATER
NAVIGATION

PRENTICE-HALL, INC., Englewood Cliffs, N.J.

Simonsen's Navigation: Coastwise and Blue Water Navigation,
by Captain Svend T. Simonsen

Printed in the United States of America

Prentice-Hall International, Inc., London
Prentice-Hall of Australia, Pty. Ltd., North Sydney
Prentice-Hall of Canada, Ltd., Toronto
Prentice-Hall of India Private Ltd., New Delhi
Prentice-Hall of Japan, Inc., Tokyo

Library of Congress Cataloging in Publication Data

Simonsen, Svend T.
Simonsen's navigation.
1. Navigation. I. Title.
VK145.S57 623.89 72-8426
ISBN 0-13-809970-7

Portions of this book were originally published as *Blue Water Navigation* by Captain Svend T. Simonsen; copyright 1947 by Cornell Maritime Press.

To my wife
JUNE
and my children
Orlene, Christina, and Debbie
who were my inspiration

Introduction

This book was written to provide the navigator and the would-be navigator with a complete text on the best methods in modern navigation, coastwise, celestial, and electronic. To a large extent it is based on the methods of explanation and demonstration that have been used so successfully with thousands of students in the Coast Navigation School and the government navigation schools of which I was previously in charge, but the material in this book is a completely new and fresh explanation and arrangement.

Certain time-honored procedures that are still useful have been included, but all unnecessary and obsolete material has been eliminated. In the last twenty years, many marine navigators have come to prefer N.O. 249, *Sight Reduction Tables for Air Navigation,* in preference to H.O. 214, *Tables of Computed Altitude and Azimuth,* and the question is still being argued. Many have also expressed a preference for the *Air Almanac* over the *Nautical Almanac.* In 1971, a new set of tables, N.O. 229, *Sight Reduction Tables for Marine Navigation,* was published and slated to replace H.O. 214 which will be phased out by 1975. (However, if public demand exists, it will be continued indefinitely.) Whereas the volumes of H.O. 214 and N.O. 229 never change, the first volume of N.O. 249 must be replaced with an updated volume every five years. The *Nautical Almanac* is good for an entire year, but the *Air Almanac* covers only 4 months in each issue.

My personal preference in navigating large or small vessels is to use N.O. 249 with the *Air Almanac.* There is a slight loss of accuracy as compared to the other sets of tables and the *Nautical Almanac,* but in practical navigation it is negligible, especially when we consider the limitations of our other tools, the timepiece and the sextant. However, because H.O. 214 is so well liked and familiar to many navigators, I have included an explanation of its use also, together with the use of the *Nautical Almanac.*

Likewise, an explanation of the new N.O. 229 has been included, although I do not recommend it. This is contrary to my belief that we should teach only one method, but because we are in a period of transition, it is necessary to include all three approaches. The student can study one or all three methods, according to individual preference, since there is really very little difference among them, and once he has learned to use a particular set of tables, he will have no difficulty learning to use the others if he wants to.

The basic principle pervading this book, as it does our courses at Coast Navigation School, is to provide the student with a solid understanding of the basic principles of navigation and then teach him to apply common sense and reason in his work, based on this knowledge. If he understands what he is doing, he will avoid those senseless errors that result from a mere knowledge of formula. The very few rules I give in this book will be for the purpose of checking your work. Rules require memory. Reason is superior to memory every time.

At this point it is necessary to clear up, insofar as possible, the confusion that exists in the numbering of government nautical publications. Originally, all such publications, except those from the U.S. Coast and Geodetic Survey, were published by the HYDROGRAPHIC OFFICE, and all had the prefix H.O., followed by the number of the chart or publication. In 1971, the name was changed to THE U.S. NAVAL OCEANOGRAPHIC OFFICE, and beginning January 1, 1972, all charts were given the prefix N.O. and a new number. Navigation Tables, however, were still carried with the prefix H.O. and the old numbers. As of July 1, 1972, by presidential order, all government mapping and charting functions were reorganized under a completely new and separate agency, THE DEFENSE MAPPING AGENCY (DMA). However, the network of chart sales offices remains the same, and chart agents know how and by what numbers to order specific charts and publications, regardless of the designation used by the customer.

Needless to say, this has caused some confusion in this book. However, where H.O. or N.O. are used to designate certain charts and publications, it means the same. Generally speaking, the policy has been to use H.O. 214, as it is being phased out, but to label the other sets of tables N.O. 249 and N.O. 229, and all charts are presently bearing an N.O. prefix and number.

In this volume I have included a number of usable short-cuts along with an explanation of the "Multiple Sights System" that I have never seen in any other text. We teach this system at the school because I believe it provides an extraordinary accuracy in celestial navigation. I hope you will enjoy using this book as much as I have enjoyed writing it.

Captain Svend T. Simonsen
Santa Barbara, California

To All Those Who Helped to Make This Book Possible

Every book is the result of the efforts and talents of many people, and this book is no exception. It all began with that remarkable man, Clyde Vandeburg of Vandeburg-Linkletter Associates, who suggested I write the book in the first place and introduced me to Bob Howland, crack navigator on Buddy Ebsen's *Polynesian Concept* and West Coast representative for Prentice-Hall. Bob's father, Raymond Howland, who has a solid background of U.S. Power Squadron teaching and experience, agreed to give a critical review of each chapter as it was written. To each of these men I want to express my profound gratitude for his valuable contribution.

Closer to home, I am most appreciative of the excellent drawings contributed by Robert Falck, Art Director of Coast Navigation School. With his patient work of producing easy-to-understand illustrations, the text has been immeasurably enriched. Michael B. Pyzel, Brandon C. McClintock, and Robert J. Thompson, my right-hand assistants at CNS, contributed their excellent thinking to our discussions, and my grateful thanks go to Elaine Offutt, my secretary, for her gracious and cheerful participation. Everyone who has had to work with the manuscript is truly appreciative of the excellent manner in which it was prepared by Marianne O'Donnell and Judy Lund, and my deepest appreciation goes to Tina McDonald, George Kuhl, and Victor Young for their loyal support, their interest, and their unsparing efforts on my behalf.

I owe a great debt of gratitude to James L. Jespersen, Chief, Frequency-Time Dissemination Research Section, Time and Frequency Division, National Bureau of Standards, Boulder, Colorado, for his expert help and friendly advice in matters pertaining to time signals, and especially for making it possible to include storm warnings on WWV and WWVH broadcasts. Like every author, I have drawn on the thinking of experts too numerous to name in every field relating to the subject of navigation, and I wish to thank those who have contributed photographs and diagrams and permitted me to include them. Credit has been given, where possible, for all such material. My thanks also to an old friend and my one-time chief mate on a school ship, Don Mueller, for allowing me to use his picture illustrating the taking of sights with an artificial horizon. Above all, it is time I paid my respects and expressed a lifelong gratitude to my first teacher and mentor in navigation, Bill Smith, the grand old "Mr. Power Squadron" himself, who more years ago than I care to reveal made navigation simple and easy to understand, and for me a delightful experience that eventually became my profession.

Last of all I wish to thank our thousands of students around the world who over the years have written me letters of interest, appreciation, and encouragement. Their warm friendship has been the real reward of my career as a teacher of navigation.

Captain Svend T. Simonsen
Santa Barbara, California

Contents

PART I

Blue Water Navigation

Chapter 1

The Earth and Its Coordinates

The Earth is an imperfect sphere, being somewhat flattened at the poles, but for practical purposes in navigation we consider it a sphere. Actually, the radius to the equator is 3,444 nautical miles and the radius to the pole is 3,432 nautical miles, a difference of 12 miles, approximately.

The Earth is one of the several planets revolving around the sun. It spins on its axis once every 24 hours, and at the same time travels in an elliptical orbit around the sun once every 365¼ solar days.

The imaginary axis about which the Earth spins is called the *polar axis,* and the two points where this axis cuts the surface of the Earth are called the *North Pole* and *South Pole,* respectively.

The Circle

Because the Earth is round, its outline forms a circle, so in navigation we deal with circles and measure them in terms of *angular distance.* A circle is divided into 360 pie-shaped segments called *degrees,* so there are 360 degrees, written 360°, in a circle. For finer measurement we divide each degree into 60 equal parts, called *minutes,* which have no relation to minutes of time. Thus, half a degree is 30 minutes, written 30′. For further refinement, each minute is divided into 60 *seconds.* Three-fourths of a minute is, then, 45 seconds, written 45″. In modern practice we do not use seconds, preferring to work in tenths of a minute. One-tenth of a minute is 6″, the closest tolerance we work to in marine navigation. Thus, if you had an angle of 45 degrees, 15 minutes, and 42 seconds, you would write it 45°15.7′. You have just learned most of the mathematics you will ever use in navigation.

Geographical Position

A circle on the surface of the Earth that has its center at the center of the Earth is called a *great circle*. The great circle that is everywhere the same distance from the poles is called the *equator*. Since the angular distance from pole to pole is a half-circle, or 180°, the angular distance from the equator to either pole is always 90°. If you are located between the equator and the North Pole anywhere on Earth, you are said to be in the northern hemisphere, or in *north latitude*. If you are between the equator and the South Pole, you are in the southern hemisphere, or in *south latitude*.

All great circles that pass through the North and South poles are called *meridians*. The meridian that passes through an arbitrarily selected point in Greenwich, England, is called the *Greenwich meridian*, or *the prime meridian*. If you are located *east* of this meridian, you are said to be in *east longitude*, and if you were *west* of this meridian, you are in *west longitude*. In this manner we establish the eastern and the western hemispheres of the Earth.

The location of a place on Earth is determined in terms of latitude and longitude.

The *latitude* of a position is the *angle*, at the center of the Earth, between a line drawn to the equator and a line, in the same plane, drawn to that position. It is expressed in degrees and minutes. For example, the latitude of Santa Barbara in Fig. 1–1 is 34°24′ N. Latitude is labeled *north* (N) or *south* (S), depending on whether we are north or south of the equator, and is measured *from* the equator toward the pole. Thus, the latitude of the North Pole is 90° N. The latitude of a point on the equator is 0°—neither north nor south.

Longitude is measured as the *angle* at the pole between the Greenwich meridian and the meridian that passes through a particular position on Earth. Longitude is labeled *east* (E) or *west* (W), depending on whether the place is east or west of Greenwich. Again, since the outline of the Earth at the equator is a circle, we measure longitude in degrees and minutes, from 0° at Greenwich to 180° E in the eastern hemisphere and 180° W in the western

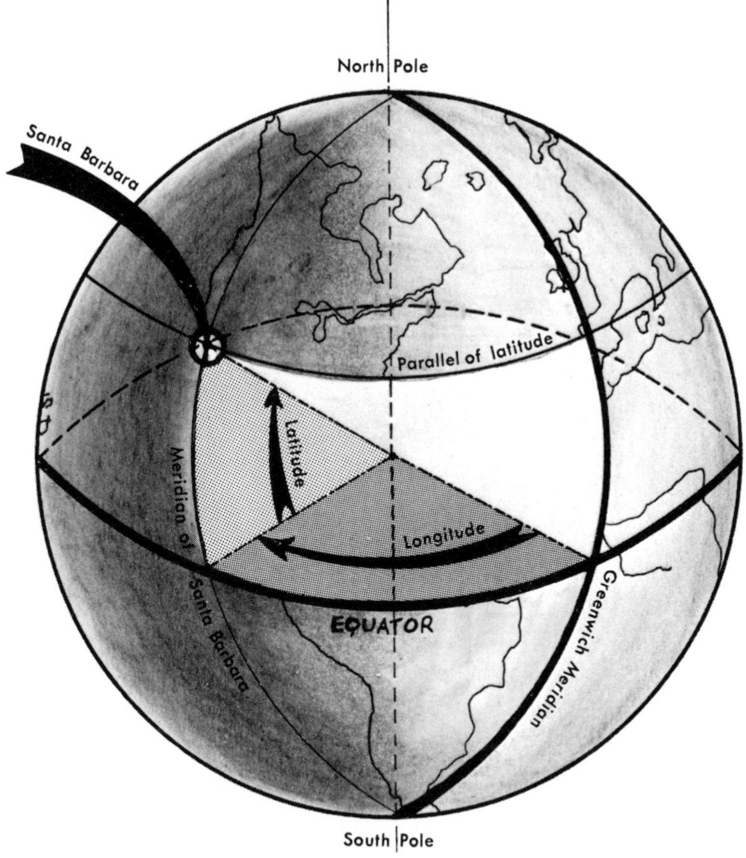

FIG. 1-1

hemisphere. Thus, at the 180° meridian, on the opposite side of the Earth from Greenwich, we again have a dividing line between the eastern and western hemispheres. Longitude has a maximum value of 180°, latitude a maximum value of 90°.

A circle on the surface of the Earth that has its center in the polar axis and lies in a plane perpendicular to the polar axis is called a *parallel of latitude*. None of the parallels of latitude, except the equator, is a great circle. All points on a parallel of latitude have the same latitude because they are the same distance from the equator. Fig. 1–1 shows the parallel of latitude that passes through Santa Barbara, California.

All geographical positions are given in terms of their latitude, north or south, and their longitude, east or west. As shown in Fig. 1–1, the position of Santa Barbara is latitude 34°24′ N, longitude 119°40′ W.

Chapter 2

Charts

A *chart* is a visual representation on a flat surface of a portion of the Earth's surface. If it is designed for marine navigation, it is called a chart, but if it is for land use mostly, it is called a map.

The surface of the Earth is represented most accurately on a globe, but since it would be impractical to practice navigation with a globe, we transfer a part of the curved surface of a globe to a flat surface. Whenever you flatten out a curved surface you introduce distortions of one kind or another that must be compensated for. It is not the purpose of this book to go into details of chart construction or projection, except to mention the features of the most common types in use.

Types of Charts

In marine navigation the most commonly used type of chart is known as a *Mercator projection,* where parallels of latitude are shown as straight lines running east and west across the chart, and meridians of longitude as parallel straight lines perpendicular to the parallels of latitude. North is always at the top of the chart and south is at the bottom. East is to the right and west to the left.

Since the meridians of longitude on the globe actually converge between the equator and the pole, we create east-to-west distortion of a given area when we make the meridians parallel on a Mercator chart. To overcome this, the chart is constructed so that each area is elongated in the north-south direction also. In this manner a more nearly correct proportion is maintained, but it means that land and water areas that are some distance from the equator are shown larger by comparison with areas at the equator. For example, Greenland appears on a Mercator chart to be much larger than it actually is. For navigation purposes, this does not matter so long as we have the right proportion in the area in which we are navigating.

On a Mercator chart the longitude scale runs east and west across the chart at the top and bottom, and the latitude scale runs north and south at the left- and right-hand edges of the chart. Both scales show the degrees, and on some charts parts of degrees, of latitude and longitude. As will be explained in the next chapter, we use the latitude scale at the side of the chart for measuring distances, 1 minute of latitude being equal to 1 nautical mile.

Occasionally in marine navigation, but nearly always in air navigation, we use what is called a gnomonic chart, usually a special form called the Lambert conformal projection. This chart will show parallels of latitude as curved lines, and meridians of longitude as straight lines that converge toward the pole. There is less distortion on this type of chart, and it is hoped that eventually all marine charts will be available in this projection. We shall come back to this later in the book.

Marine charts show the details of the water and adjacent land, the depth of water, sometimes the character of the bottom, reefs, shoals, and other dangers as well as aids to navigation, such as lighthouses, buoys, beacons, radio aids, and much more. Certain charts are prepared for electronic navigation, showing loran, Consolan, Decca, and Omega lines of position.

Sources

In the United States, charts showing U.S. coastlines, harbors, and other inland waters are published by the National Ocean Survey, a branch of the Department of Commerce. Charts of the Great Lakes and inland rivers are published by the Army Corps of Engineers. Charts of foreign waters are produced by the Naval Oceanographic Office in the Department of the Navy. Many of these charts are obtained from foreign countries and republished here, and it is well to remember that many charts of remote areas date back to such early explorers as Captains Cook and Bligh and have had little revision since, and should therefore be used with caution. If you are cruising in foreign waters and have an opportunity to obtain locally published charts, you are likely to have more up-to-date and detailed local information than you would find on American charts.

Charts are available to various scales and in varying degrees of detail. A chart catalog is published by the Oceanographic Office, which lists National Ocean Survey charts as well as world charts, plus many other publications pertaining to marine navigation, such as *Sailing Directions, Pilot Charts, Tide and Current Tables, Light Lists,* etc. The National Ocean Survey and the Army Corps of Engineers both publish catalogs of the charts they produce, as well as their other publications, such as light lists of domestic waters. All chart catalogs carry a list of authorized chart agents from whom the charts can be ordered.

Chart Scales

Generally speaking, charts fall into certain main categories:

1. *Sailing charts,* which cover a large section of the ocean—for example, the entire Pacific coast of the United States. The scale would probably be 1:1,200,000, which means that 1 inch on this chart represents about 20 miles.
2. *General coastal charts,* used in coastwise navigation, usually to a scale of around 1:200,000.
3. *Coast charts,* showing details of inlets, entrances to harbors and waterways, buoys, and other information needed for inshore navigation. Scale is usually 1:80,000.
4. *Harbor charts,* each covering a specific harbor with all detail using a scale as large as 1:12,000.
5. *Special charts* used to convey specific information, such as pilot charts, current charts, weather charts, temperature charts, great circle route charts, magnetic charts, and even a whale chart are available from the Oceanographic Office.

Data on Charts

Every chart has a legend or description which gives the number of the chart, its scale, the area covered, and much important information, such as the basis for the soundings given (usually mean low water) and whether soundings are given in feet, in fathoms (a fathom is 6 feet), or in both fathoms and feet.* Mean low water is the average height of low tide as observed over a number of years; in areas where the tides are irregular, the basis for the soundings is mean lower low water. The chart may or may not have a mileage scale; if it does not, you can use the latitude scale for measuring distances in the manner described above. There will be an indication of the last date to which the chart was updated. On the chart will be one or more *compass rose,* which shows direction of true north and (usually) magnetic north.

It is of the utmost importance that you know what each figure and symbol on the chart means. It is too late to look it up when you need it. The Naval Oceanographic Office's publication N.O. chart #1, "Nautical Chart Symbols and Abbreviations," is one of the most useful publications you can have. It is not a chart at all, but a booklet which describes in detail all symbols used on American charts. Keep it aboard, study it often, and get to know it by heart.

American charts are updated by information published weekly in *Notices to Mariners,* a free publication put out by the U.S. Coast Guard.

The Naval Oceanographic Office prior to 1971 was known as the Hydrographic Office. All their charts and publications were identified by the letters H.O. plus a number —for example, H.O. 9, the famous *American Practical Navigator* by Nathaniel Bowditch. In 1971 the entire numbering system of charts was modernized and streamlined, and charts and publications are now identified by the letters N.O. and a new number.

* Plans are underway to give all soundings in meters to conform with international usage.

Chapter 3

The Elements of Navigation

Marine navigation is the practice of the knowledge that enables us to determine the position of a vessel and safely conduct the vessel from one point to another on the surface of the Earth.

Coastwise navigation and piloting involve the methods by which we navigate a vessel within sight of land, making use of available landmarks, visible and radio aids to navigation, and soundings.

Dead reckoning (DR) is the method of determining the approximate position of a vessel by accounting for the direction and distance sailed in a given time from a known position. The method was originally called deduced reckoning, often shortened to ded. reckoning, pronounced "dead reckoning," and now universally so called.

Celestial navigation is the practice of the knowledge that enables us to fix the position of a vessel by observations of the sun; of the planets Venus, Jupiter, Mars, and Saturn; and of about fifty-seven selected stars, known as navigation stars.

Electronic navigation involves the use of various special electronic receivers such as radio direction finders, loran, omega, and Decca. Another method, consolan, requires only a standard radio receiver. Radar sends and receives electrical impulses that portray coastlines and objects on the water on an electronic screen.

Tools Used in Navigation

Dividers Hinged pointers used for measuring and transferring distances on a chart.

Parallel Rulers An instrument consisting of two straightedges connected by hinges in such a way that the two edges always remain parallel. They are used for laying down courses or bearings on a chart and transferring these to or from the compass rose on the chart.

Protractor A circular or semicircular plastic device graduated in degrees and sometimes half-degrees. Used for measuring angles in chart work.

Three-armed Protractor A protractor on which are mounted three movable arms. It is used for plotting courses and bearings and sometimes for plotting a position from known horizontal angles.

Compass An instrument that indicates the direction of north, south, east, west, and all points in between. On smaller vessels we use a *magnetic compass,* which consists essentially of one or more magnetized needles mounted on the underside of a circular *compass card* on which is printed the degrees and/or points of the directions from 0° at North through 90° at East, 180° at South, and 270° at West. The card is pivoted on a jeweled bearing at the center to eliminate as much friction as possible, and for steadiness it is usually floated in liquid and kept enclosed in a compass bowl. On larger vessels we may find a *gyrocompass,* a high-speed electrical machine that has a free-spinning gyro wheel, the axis of which tends to align itself with the axis of the Earth and thus is able to point to the direction of the geographical North Pole.

Pelorus A device for sighting at landmarks to determine bearing or direction. It may be aligned with the compass or with the ship's keel. In either case it gives the direction of a landmark with respect to the north direction shown by the ship's compass. In celestial navigation, a pelorus is used for taking bearings on the sun, usually for the purpose of checking the accuracy of the compass.

Hand-Lead A weighted line, marked every 6 feet, used to measure the depth of the water. "Arming the Lead" means to smear grease or tallow on the bottom of the lead weight so that material on the bottom of the sea—e.g. sand or mud—will adhere to the weight and give an indication of the nature of the bottom.

Depth-Finder An electrical device that emits and receives electrical impulses which in turn indicate the depth of the water. Some instruments record the depth on a moving strip of graph paper, others have a flashing indicator, and some give a digital readout.

Radio Direction Finder (RDF) An instrument that shows the direction, on a ship, of a radio station or radio beacon with respect to north.

Taffrail Log Consists of a rotating device towed behind the vessel on a line, called the *log line,* which turns an indicator mechanism that registers the distance the vessel has moved through the water. The log can be read at any time, but is always read at the end of every watch.

Chronometer A very accurate clock which is set to Greenwich Mean Time (GMT). It should be compared daily to a radio time signal to find out whether it has gained or lost, and the rate of loss or gain recorded in the chronometer logbook. So long as the rate is uniform, the chronometer is satisfactory, but if it has an uneven rate of gain or loss, it must be repaired. The older chronometers were wound by hand daily at a certain hour, but the newer crystal oscillator clocks are run by electricity and are much more accurate. The celestial navigator needs Greenwich Mean Time for his observations. In recent years the tendency has been to compare a navigation watch to a radio time signal before taking sights, thus eliminating the use of the chronometer. In navigation and, in fact, in all nautical activity, we use a 24-hour time system. The day begins with *zero hours,* 0000, at midnight, which is the beginning of the new day, as well as the ending of the previous day. For the next twelve hours, until noon, time progresses in the conventional manner, except that the even hour, i.e. 9 A.M., is written 0900, referred to as *oh nine hundred hours;* 10 A.M. would be *ten hundred hours,* 1000, but half past nine would be written 0930, *oh nine thirty.* At noon, instead of beginning all over again, as in a twelve-hour system, we continue on. That is, 1 P.M. is 1300, 8 P.M. is 2000, and so on until 2400, which is midnight of that day as well as 0000 of the next day. When we are very precise, time is written in hours, minutes, and seconds, i.e. 13-47-23, which is 47 minutes and 23 seconds after 1 P.M.

Sextant An instrument for measuring the angle between

FIG. 3-1
Compass

FIG. 3-2
Pelorus

COURTESY DAVIS INSTRUMENTS

a celestial body and the horizon just below it. This angle, when accurately timed, can then be translated into a line of position on the chart.

Star Finder Known usually as the Rude or Simex Star Finder, it is a series of plastic disks which, when properly aligned, will give the altitude and bearing of any navigation star or planet for any instant of time at any place in the world. By predicting this information before taking sights, the navigator can frequently observe the evening stars in his sextant before he can see them with his naked eye, thus having a longer interval for taking sights before his horizon becomes too dark to use.

There are other miscellaneous instruments that can be used in navigation, such as barometers or barographs that register atmospheric pressure, anemometers that register wind velocity, and speedometers of various kinds, but those mentioned above are most commonly used.

Terms Used in Coastwise Navigation

If you understand the precise meaning of the terms we use in navigation, your work will become much easier and you will always know the significance of what you are doing; in short, you will be an intelligent navigator.

The Earth A spherical body, slightly flattened at the poles, but for practical purposes in navigation having the outline of a circle. It spins about its axis once in 24 hours and travels around the sun once every 365¼ solar days.

Circle Because the earth is nearly a sphere, circular measurements are important in navigation. The circle has radius, diameter, and circumference as well as a center. The circle is divided into 360 degrees, each degree into 60 minutes, and each minute into 60 seconds. Half a circle is 180°, a quarter-circle is 90°. We express seconds as tenths of minutes; therefore, $\frac{1}{10}$ minute equals 6″.

Great Circle Any circle on the surface of the Earth that has its center at the center of the Earth. As will be shown later, a route along a great circle is the shortest distance between two points. On long ocean or air voyages we therefore frequently follow a *great circle route.*

Equator That great circle on the surface of the Earth that is everywhere 90° from either pole. The equator is the only parallel of latitude which is also a great circle.

Latitude The angular distance of a place on Earth, north or south of the equator, measured in degrees, minutes, and seconds.

Parallel of Latitude A circle on the surface of the Earth that has its center in the polar axis and lies in a plane perpendicular to the polar axis. The plane of any parallel of latitude is always parallel to the plane of the equator. All points on a parallel of latitude have the same latitude.

Longitude The angle at the pole (or at the equator) between the Greenwich meridian and the meridian that passes through a given position on Earth.

Meridians of Longitude Great circles on the surface of the Earth that pass through both poles.

Greenwich Meridian Also called the *prime meridian,* is that meridian of longitude that passes through Greenwich, England. We use this as a reference meridian for measuring longitude east or west of Greenwich.

Position The position of any place on Earth is always expressed in terms of latitude and longitude. *Example:* The position of Santa Barbara, California, is latitude 34°24′ N, longitude 119°40′ W.

Mercator Chart The type of chart most commonly used in marine navigation. Meridians are vertical and parallels of latitude cross the meridians at a 90° angle. North is up, south is down, east to the right, and west to the left.

Direction On the surface of the Earth, and therefore also on the chart, direction is always measured from north, *clockwise,* or to the right, through east, south, and west, using the entire circle. Therefore, we can measure direction in degrees, beginning with 0° at north. East is 90°, south is 180°, and west is 270°.

Course The track that we wish the ship to follow from

one point to another on the chart. To find the course between two points, we draw a line between them. Placing the parallel rulers on this line, we walk it over to the compass rose on the chart, placing one edge through the center of the rose. The course is now read as the angle between north (or 0°) and the marking at the ruler. Thus, *course is expressed as an angle,* the angle between north and the direction in which we wish to move the vessel.

Course Line The line, drawn between two points on the chart, along which we intend to sail.

Track The actual path followed by a vessel with respect to the bottom of the sea. Although we steer the vessel along an intended course line, conditions of wind and current may be such that the vessel does not follow the intended line, but actually moves along a different path which we call the *track.* The actual track is sometimes called *the course made good.*

Heading When we start out to follow a certain course line between two points, being aware of winds and currents that may set us off the course, we often point the vessel into the wind or current to overcome their effect. The vessel is pointed to one side or the other of the intended direction, but if the allowance is correctly made, the vessel will not leave the intended course line. This direction in which the bow is pointed, with respect to north, is called the *heading.*

Distance In marine navigation we measure disance in *nautical miles.* The circumference of the Earth is 360° of arc, a full circle, or 21,600 minutes. Dividing 21,600 into the circumference of the Earth established arbitrarily the length of a nautical mile. Therefore, in practical navigation 1 minute of arc on the surface of the Earth is equal to 1 nautical mile.* Since there are 60 minutes in a degree, it follows that there are 60 nautical miles in a degree measured along a great circle, such as a meridian of longitude or the equator. For this reason we can always use the latitude scale at the side of a chart to measure mileage, since this

* By international agreement a nautical mile is 1,852 meters exactly, or approximately 6,076 U.S. feet. A land mile is 5,280 ft.

scale follows a meridian of longitude up and down. *Never measure distance on the longitude scale at the top or bottom of chart.*

Practice Problems • Reading about something is very good, but we learn best by doing in addition to reading. To make sure you have understood the material presented, I suggest that you take any atlas or world map you have handy and look up the position of the places listed below and see if *on your own* you get the correct answers. Since you won't have accurate charts available, the answers (in the Appendix) are to the nearest degree, which is close enough for practice purposes. This is purely an exercise in geographical orientation for learning to use latitude and longitude correctly.

Location	Latitude—N or S	Longitude—E or W
Hong Kong		
New York		
Sydney		
Ottawa		
Buenos Aires		
Singapore		
Honolulu		
New Orleans		
Berlin		
Johannesburg		
San Francisco		
Cairo		

Chapter 4
The Compass

Since the early days of seafaring, the compass in one form or another has been the basis for navigation. Admittedly, the greatest navigators of all, the Polynesians, did not know the compass, but the early Mediterranean navigators and the Vikings used it. Even today, with all our electronic equipment, the compass is still the cornerstone of our navigational knowledge and practice.

The Vikings found that if they floated a piece of a certain rock called a lodestone (known to us as magnetite) on a sliver of wood in a tub of water, it would always turn in a certain direction. Today we attach a bundle of magnetic wires to the underside of a compass card, pivot it at the center on a jeweled bearing, and float it in an enclosed bowl filled with a light oil or similar substance, and we have the same principle.

Principle Without going into a great deal of technical detail, we can simply state that the magnetic compass is effective because the Earth has a magnetic field. This field surrounds the Earth and can be considered as consisting of many magnetic lines of force which tend to converge at a magnetic North Pole and a magnetic South Pole. Place a freely suspended magnet anywhere in this field, and it will align itself approximately parallel to the local lines of force; usually one end of the magnet will point in the direction of the magnetic North Pole and the other toward the magnetic South Pole.

Unfortunately, the magnetic and geographical poles are located several hundred miles apart on the Earth's surface. But they are close enough for the purposes of navigation, since the discrepancies can be compensated for in calculating courses and bearings.

Construction The modern magnetic compass is a precision instrument. The bowl, which is hermetically sealed, has an expansion chamber to allow for contraction and expan-

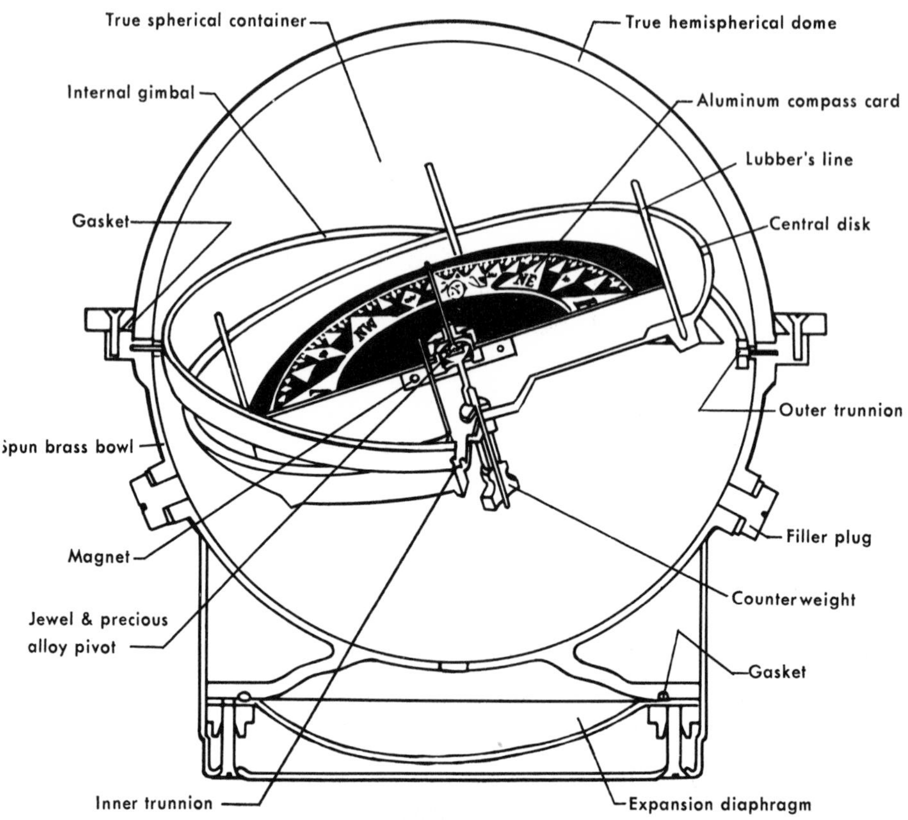

FIG. 4-1
Diagram of magnetic compass

(COURTESY DANFORTH)

sion of the liquid within the bowl due to temperature variations; thus, the bowl is always full. The liquid in the bowl serves to dampen, or steady, the motion of the compass card. On later compasses the card is flared up at the edges for easier reading. Below the card are two sets of movable adjusting magnets used to counteract undesired magnetic influences existing in the vessel.

The compass card itself is marked in degrees from 0° to 360° and is so made that the magnets under the card follow the line from 0° to 180°. The 0° mark will always point toward north and the 180° mark toward south. The compass bowl is suspended in gimbals so it will remain level as the vessel rolls or pitches. The inside rim of the bowl has two guide marks, the *lubber's line,* 180° apart. When the compass is installed on the vessel, these marks are aligned with the keel of the ship. The entire compass installation, except for the compass card, is fixed to the ship and turns with the ship, but the freely suspended card remains more or less stationary and keeps itself aligned with the direction of the magnetic poles. When the ship turns, the card remains still while the ship, and the compass bowl with it, turns around the card.

Using the Compass Since the ship's heading, as previously defined, is the angle between the keel and the direction of north, we can always read the heading on the compass card opposite the lubber's line. Because the card points to magnetic north, this direction is called the *magnetic heading*.

A *gyrocompass* is something else again. It aligns itself with the Earth's axis and therefore indicates the direction of geographic north, also known as *true north*. On the gyrocompass we therefore read what is called a *true heading*.

Variation When a magnetic compass is used, it indicates the direction of magnetic north, rather than true, geographical north. The angle between these two north directions at any place on Earth is called *variation*. Since it is an angle, it is expressed in degrees. When magnetic north lies to the east of true north, we say that we have so many degrees of *easterly variation*. When it lies to the left, or west, of true north, we have *westerly variation*. Variation is always measured in degrees and is always labeled either east or west.

FIG. 4-2

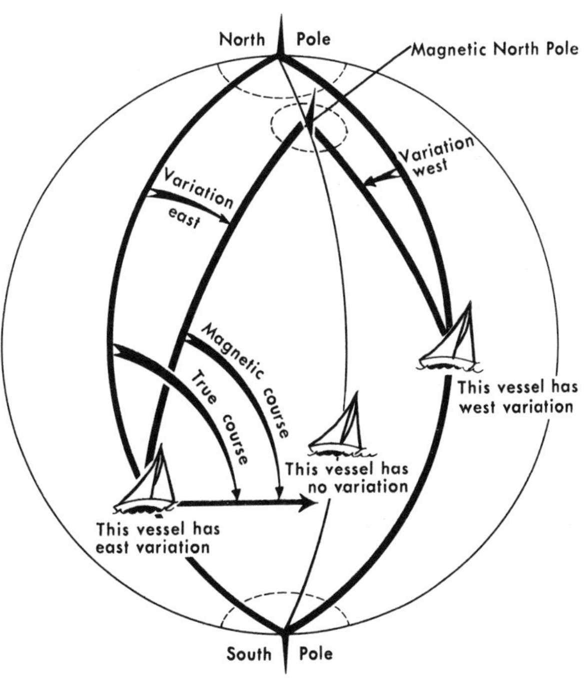

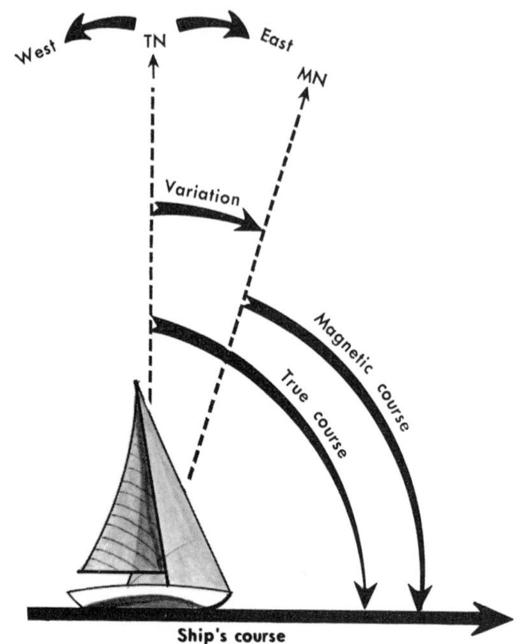

FIG. 4-3A

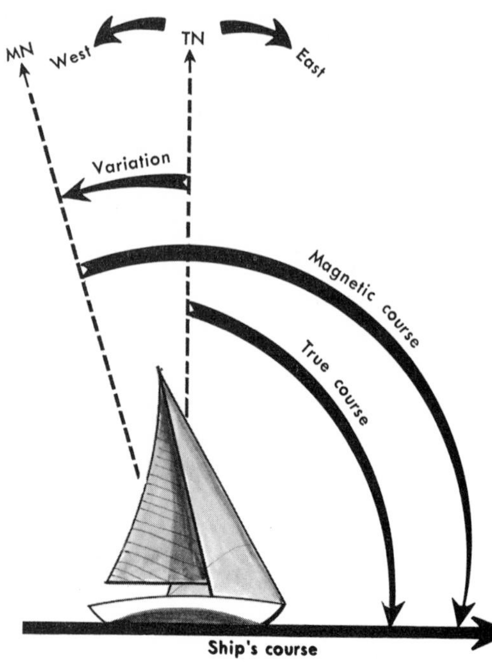

FIG. 4-3B

A course angle or heading measured from magnetic north is called a *magnetic course* or *magnetic heading,* and if measured from true north it is called a *true course* or *true heading.* When measured from the north point of the ship's compass, it is called a *compass course* or *compass heading.* It is best shown on a *compass diagram,* as illustrated above.

Variation depends on the vessel's location on the surface of the Earth. Magnetic north is nearly stationary but does vary a little from year to year. It can always be found on the chart of a given locality, printed inside the compass rose as so many degrees east or west in a given year, together with the amount of annual change. You always use the nearest whole degree of variation in practical navigation, just as we also use the nearest whole degree for courses and bearings. It is not practical, on a boat, to measure or steer any closer.

Deviation On a wood- or plastic-hulled vessel containing no magnetic metals or wiring that can set up a magnetic field, the compass will always point to magnetic north. However, when you add an engine or have a steel hull or superstructure or have electrical wiring in the vicinity of the compass, additional magnetic forces are introduced that usually cause the compass card to swing either to the right or to the left of magnetic north. The new direction to which the north point on the compass card points is called *compass north,* and the influence which causes it to swing either right or left of magnetic north is called *deviation.*

Note that we are now dealing with a total of three north directions: true (geographical) north, magnetic north, and compass north.

If deviation causes the compass card's 0°, or north mark, to swing to the right, or *east,* of magnetic north, we say we have *easterly deviation.* If the card swings to the left, or *west,* of magnetic north, we have *westerly deviation.* Like variation, deviation is an angle and is therefore measured in degrees also. It must always be labeled *east* or *west.*

As the ship turns, the compass card remains steady, but the deviation-producing influences, being inherent in the structure of the vessel, also turn and now attack the compass needle from a different angle. As a result, we have a different amount and direction of deviation on the new heading, and must allow for this fact.

Variation depends on locality and can be found on the chart. It does not change materially while you are in that area. Deviation, on the other hand, changes every time you change the ship's heading. It is determined by placing the vessel on different headings, usually 15° apart, and comparing the actual heading read on the compass card with a correct magnetic heading, as explained in Chapter 28. The difference is the deviation for that heading. It is either removed by adjustment of the magnets in or around the compass, or it is recorded in a *deviation table.* This table, kept handy at the chart table, shows the deviation for different headings 15° apart, and is consulted every time the course is changed.

Like variation, deviation is best explained on a compass diagram, as shown in Fig. 4–4. When we know the variation and the deviation, we can convert a true course to a compass course and vice versa. This is important because the course you plot on the chart, in terms of degrees, will not be the same as the compass course which you steer on your boat's compass.

Compass Diagrams There are rules for applying variation and deviation, but they are difficult to remember. It is

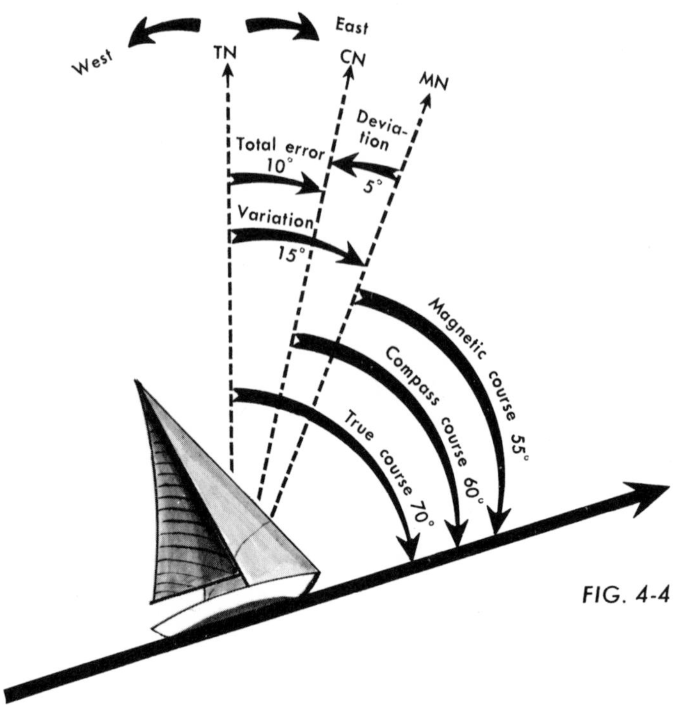

FIG. 4-4

much better to draw a compass diagram and inspect it carefully to see how these compass errors affect the courses, so you will know what to add and what to subtract. Again, *reason* is better than *memory*. The algebraic sum of variation and deviation is called *total compass error*. For example, if the variation is 15° E and the deviation is 5° W, the total compass error is 10° E.

To draw a compass diagram always draw true north straight up and then insert in the diagram the other angles you know or which are given. Then solve for the remaining values you need.

Never apply deviation to a true course or bearing and never apply variation to a compass bearing or course. Never apply total error to a magnetic course or bearing.

Many navigators will suggest to you that it is much easier to remember the rules by reciting certain jingles that suggest correct procedure. Don't believe them! However, so that you will not know less than they do, I will quote a couple of the funnier ones:

CAN	DEAD	MEN	VOTE	TWICE	AT	ELECTION
Compass	Deviation	Magnetic	Variation	True	Add	East

This means that if you work from compass to true, you *add easterly error* and *subtract westerly error.*

TRUE	VIRGINS	MAKE	DULL	COMPANIONS	ADD	WHISKEY
True	Variation	Magnetic	Deviation	Compass	Add	West

Which cheerful nonsense means that when you work the other way, from true to compass, you *add westerly error* and *subtract easterly error.* My advice is to forget it!

The Simex Course Converter In Figure 4–5, there is an illustration of the Simex Course Converter, an ingenious device. It consists of three dials and a movable arm. In effect, the outer dial repesents the *true* compass rose, the middle dial is the *magnetic* compass rose, and the inner dial is the ship's *compass card.* The arm represents a course line or a bearing.

To use the converter, simply set the middle dial to the correct variation, set the inner dial to the correct deviation, and set the arm to either the true course on the outer dial or the compass course on the inner dial. On the arm you now read the *true course* on the *outer dial,* the *magnetic course* on the *middle dial,* and the *compass course* on the *inner dial.* It is simple and almost foolproof. If you compare it with a compass diagram, you will see that it is essentially the same thing.

In later chapters we shall discuss bearings for fixing our position. Since bearings are almost invariably based on the ship's compass, they, too, need to be adjusted for deviation and variation, and the Course Converter offers a ready solution for these problems as well.

Figure 4–5 shows the manner in which the Simex Course Converter is used. The navigator has laid down a true course of 100° on the chart. His variation from the chart is 15° W, the deviation from the deviation table is 5° E. He wants to know the compass course to steer.

Note that he has set the two arrows to the correct variation and deviation, and that the arm is set to 100° on the outer scale. The middle dial reads a magnetic course of 115° and the inner scale shows a compass course of 110°.

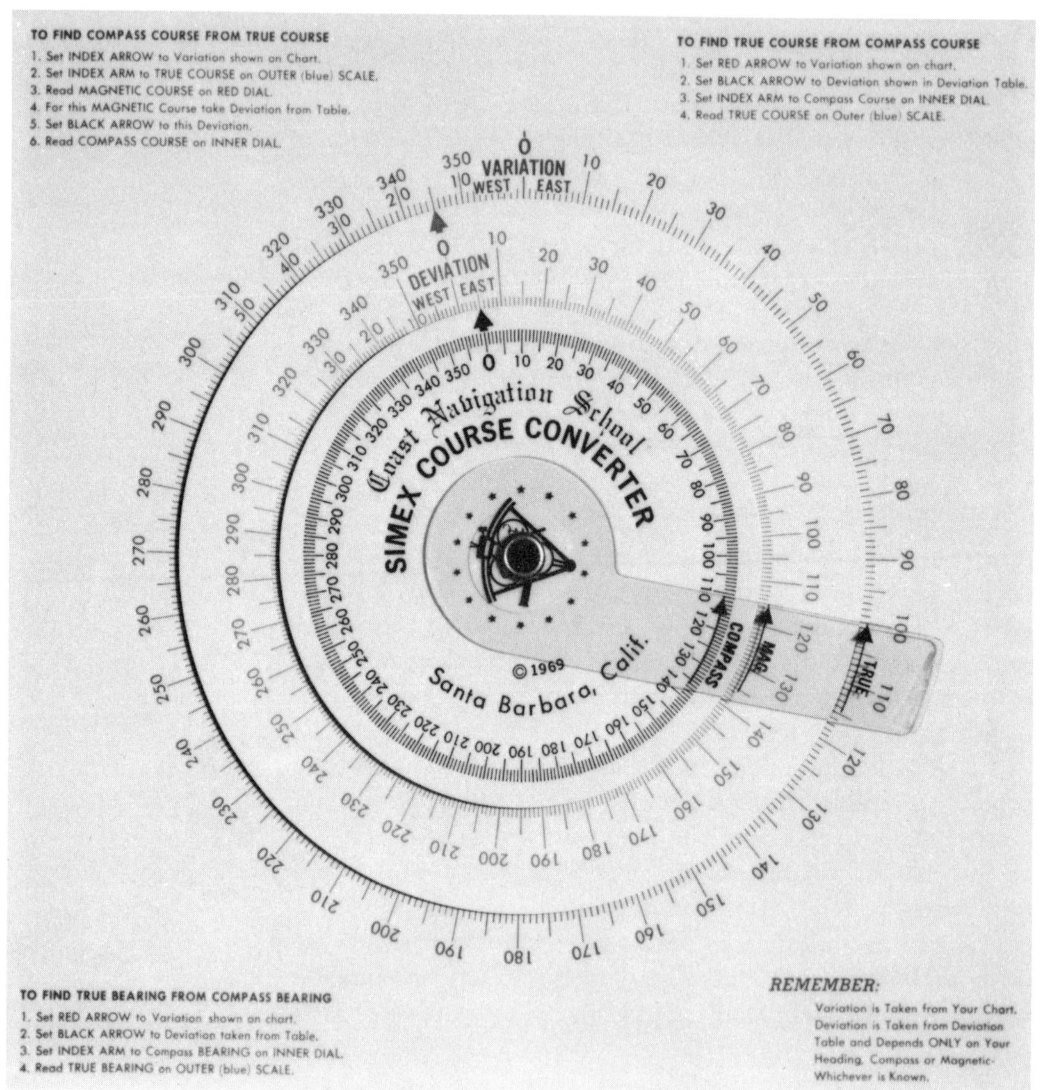

FIG. 4-5
Simex Course Converter, speed-time-distance computer on reverse side
(COURTESY COAST NAVIGATION SCHOOL)

If, with the same variation and deviation, he had obtained a compass bearing of 110° on a lighthouse and wanted to plot it on the chart, he would set the arm to 110° on the inner (compass) dial and read a true bearing of 100° on the outer dial.

Practice Problems • Some people have difficulty drawing compass diagrams. My experience with thousands of students shows that until a person can do this correctly, he will never really understand variation and deviation and will always have trouble getting the right answer. I once gave an impromptu test to thirty seasoned cruising and racing skippers and found that only seven out of the thirty could give the right answer to a simple compass problem. Ten of them made the same mistake and came up with a course that was 20° off! I suggest you work the problems below, draw a diagram of each one, using a protractor, and check your figures against the angles you measure in the diagram.

COMPASS COURSE	DEVIATION	MAGNETIC COURSE	VARIATION	TRUE COURSE	TOTAL ERROR
________	10°	________	15° E	100°	25° E
________	5° W	________	10° W	180°	15° W
________	10° W	________	20° E	270°	10° E
________	5° E	________	18° W	355°	13° W
197°	8° W	________	3° E	________	5° W
050°	12° E	________	12° W	________	0°
277°	________	290°	________	270°	________

Chapter 5

Chart Navigation

When you plan your trip, you know where you are and you know where you want to go, and you must have a chart that shows both places. You then draw a line from the point of departure to the point of destination, if a single straight line can be drawn. If you have to cruise around islands or shoals, you must plot a series of legs that will clear the obstacles and ultimately take you to your destination.

Plotting Courses

To plot any course, simply draw a straight line on the chart from where you are to where you want to go. Place your parallel rulers on this line and walk it over to the center of the compass rose. You move parallel rulers across a chart by alternately holding one ruler and moving the other. Accuracy will improve with practice.

On the outside scale of the compass rose you read the true course, with respect to true north, and on the inside scale you can read the magnetic course. You can also apply the variation to the true course to find the magnetic course, but you need the magnetic course in order to consult the deviation table.

The deviation table is set up with two parallel columns, one for *compass heading,* and one for *magnetic heading.* In between you will find the deviation, east or west, that applies to each heading. Sometimes you may have to interpolate a little if you have large deviations, because the table is usually set up for every 15° of compass heading. In any case, you will always be able to pick the nearest value. You thus enter the table with the magnetic heading, pick the nearest deviation, and apply it to your magnetic heading to find the compass heading you must steer on your own ship's compass.

DEVIATION TABLE

YACHT ______________

DATE ______________

Compass Heading	Deviation W	Deviation E	Magnetic Heading	Compass Heading	Deviation W	Deviation E	Magnetic Heading
0	8		352°	180		6	186°
15	6		009°	195		5	200°
30	4		026°	210		4	214°
45	3		042°	225		3	228°
60	2		058°	240		2	242°
75	1		074°	255		1	256°
90	0		90°	270	0		270°
105		1	106°	285	1		284°
120		2	122°	300	2		298°
135		3	138°	315	3		312°
150		4	154°	330	4		326°
165		5	170°	345	6		339°
180		6	186°	360	8		352°

FIG. 5-1

Next, you will probably want to know when you will arrive at your destination, so you must understand the problems of *time, speed,* and *distance.*

Time-Speed-Distance In navigation, distance is measured in *nautical miles.* One nautical mile is about 6,080 feet and is equal to 1 minute of latitude on a chart. (A land or statute mile is only 5,280 feet.)

Time, of course, is measured in hours, minutes, and seconds. Speed is measured in *knots.* A knot is a rate of speed of 1 nautical mile per hour. A speed of 10 knots is a rate of speed of 10 nautical miles per hour. A knot is not a distance. If you ever say that a distance is 15 knots, or use the expression "knots per hour," seamen will know you for a landlubber.

Time, speed, and distance problems can be conveniently solved on a calculator, such as the *Simex Navigator,* which has a Course Converter on one side and a nautical slide rule for time, speed, and distance problems on the other. However, you should be able to solve all such problems without any mechanical help. It just requires some common sense and a little simple arithmetic.

If you travel 10 nautical miles in 1 hour, your speed is 10 knots. If your speed is 10 knots and you travel for 20 minutes at this speed, you will cover a distance of:

$$\frac{10 \text{ knots} \times 20 \text{ min.}}{60 \text{ min.}} = 3.3 \text{ miles}$$

By dividing 10 by 60, you find out how far you travel in 1 minute, and if you then multiply by 20 you find out how far you travel in 20 minutes, or in any other number of minutes you want to work with.

If you have traveled 20 miles in 2 hours, you can determine what your speed is by dividing the time in hours into the distance in miles. The answer is obviously 10 knots. If you have traveled 27.2 miles in 3 hours 24 minutes, your speed is:

$$\frac{27.2 \text{ miles}}{3.4 \text{ hours}} = 8 \text{ knots}$$

Here you take advantage of the fact that 6 minutes is $\frac{1}{10}$ of an hour, so 24 minutes is 0.4 hour. There are many ways of solving these problems, but if you use reason and common sense, you won't go wrong.

If you have a distance of 42 miles to go and your speed is 7 knots, it will obviously take you 6 hours to get there. You simply divide the speed in knots into the distance in miles. Thus, if you must sail 24.5 miles and your speed is $5\frac{1}{2}$ knots, the time will be:

$$\frac{24.5 \text{ miles}}{5.5 \text{ knots}} = 4.45 \text{ hours}$$

To sum up:

$$\text{speed} \times \text{time} = \text{distance}$$

$$\frac{\text{distance}}{\text{time}} = \text{speed}$$

$$\frac{\text{distance}}{\text{speed}} = \text{time}$$

Remember that 0.1 hour is 6 minutes, so 0.05 hours is 3 minutes, and the total time is 4 hours, 27 minutes.

This kind of arithmetic is awkward for many sailors. Take comfort in the fact that you will never know your actual speed under all circumstances, so always allow a safe margin on your predictions. Figuring such problems to the exact minute is usually a waste of time, unless it is on some examination. If you predict your estimated time of arrival (ETA) to the nearest half-hour, you are being practical.

Finding Speed It is, however, important to know the speed of your vessel as closely as possible under all conditions. With a sailboat it is often a matter of judgment, unless you have a good speedometer aboard, and then it measures speed through the water and not over the bottom. With a power boat, the skipper should set up a speed table for different rpm's. This is best done by running over a measured mile at the various speeds. Because of currents, however, the course must be run twice—once each in opposite directions. The speed is calculated for each run separately and then the two results are averaged together. Do not just add the times of the two runs and then take the average. This will not give the correct answer.

Bearings and Fixes The fact that you set out on a given course line on the chart is no guarantee that you will remain on that course line. The odds, in fact, are overwhelmingly against your remaining on that line after some period of sailing. Winds, currents, leeway, bad steering, etc., are almost sure to set you off course. For this reason it is important for you to check your position periodically to maintain a reliable course line on the chart.

In coastwise navigation we establish position by taking bearings on landmarks, such as mountains, buildings, and points of land, or on aids to navigation such as lighthouses, buoys, radio beacons, etc. You can take a bearing on anything you can see and which can be located on the chart.

A *bearing* is a line of sight from the ship to the landmark, and it is also an angle, given as so many degrees from north. If you are sighting at the landmark over the ship's compass, you obtain a *compass bearing,* reading from compass north.

In order to plot such a bearing on the chart, you must correct it for deviation and variation, to obtain the *true bearing,* measured from true north. The deviation to be applied is determined by the compass heading of the boat. While you are on a certain heading you may take many different bearings, but the deviation to be applied will be the same in all cases. Only when you change the ship's heading will you have a new deviation.

If you are on a large ship having gyrocompass, a sighting device called a *pelorus* is mounted on the compass, and since a gyro is oriented to true north, the bearing read on the pelorus will be a true bearing.

We cannot plot a compass bearing, because the chart does not indicate where compass north is. We can plot a true or a magnetic bearing, because the chart does indicate the direction of true and magnetic north. Hence a compass bearing is always converted to a true bearing for plotting. (Some navigators prefer to work with magnetic north exclusively. It is entirely correct and acceptable. My personal preference is to convert everything to true courses or bearings for my chart work.)

The chart shows the location of the landmark. Since a bearing is a line of sight from the ship to the landmark, it follows that at the same instant the bearing is taken, it is also identical with a line of sight from the landmark to the ship, except that the observer on land looks in the opposite direction, and his bearing with respect to north will be 180° different. This is called a *reverse* or *reciprocal bearing.* We can plot such a reverse bearing from the landmark, in the direction of the ship, and this plotted line of bearing thus becomes a *line of position. At the instant the bearing was observed, the ship was on this line of position.*

A single line of position merely tells us that the ship is somewhere on that line, but it does not show how far away from the landmark we are. If we are able to obtain simultaneous bearings on two separate landmarks, we can establish two lines of position on the chart. If we are on both of these lines at the same time, we must obviously be at the place where they intersect. This is called a *fix* and is considered an absolute determination of your position.

The vessel shown in Fig. 5–2 is cruising along the coast.

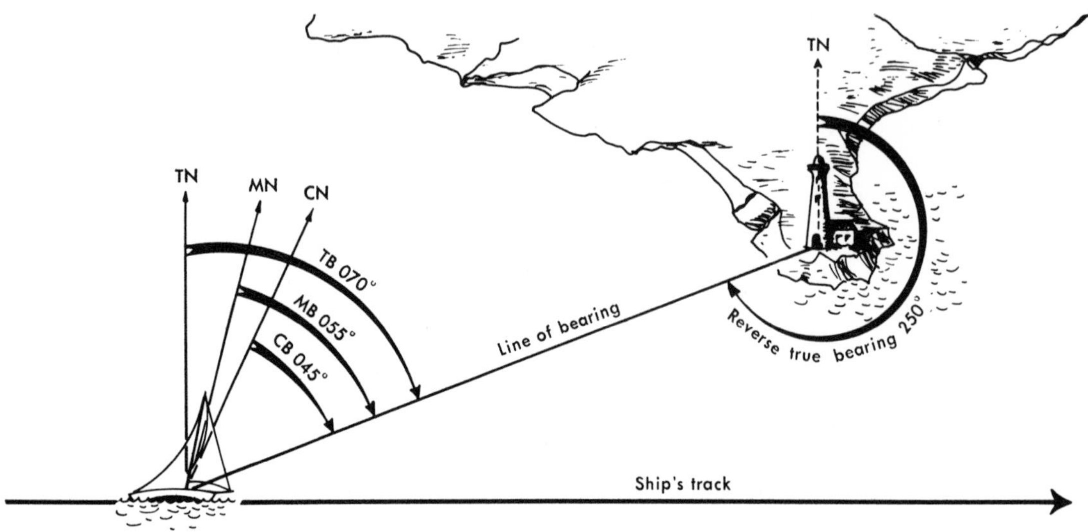

FIG. 5-2

A bearing on a lighthouse is taken over the ship's compass, reading 045°. The variation for the vicinity is given on the chart as 15° E. On the particular heading, the compass has a deviation of 10° E. Total compass error (TE) is thus 25° E. We now calculate the *reciprocal true bearing* (RTB) as follows:

Compass Bearing	045°	
Deviation	10° E	or simply:
Magnetic Bearing	055°	CB = 045°
Variation	15° E	TE = 25° E
True Bearing	070°	TB = 070°
	+ 180°	+ 180°
Reciprocal True Bearing	250°	RTB = 250°

When we plot this bearing on the chart from the lighthouse, your chart will look like this:

FIG. 5-3

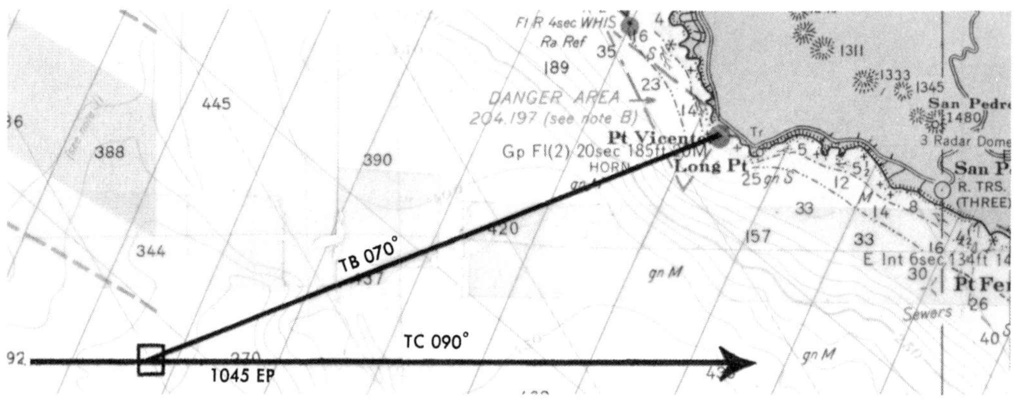

Note that you do not really know how far away from the landmark you are. Since in most cases you will have drawn an intended course line on the chart, in the absence of better information you could say that your position is at the intersection of the bearing line and the course line; but this is always open to much doubt. We shall discuss this in more detail later, along with methods for labeling courses, bearings, and positions.

To obtain an absolute fix you must have two or more bearings taken almost simultaneously. On a fairly slow-moving boat it is not necessary to allow for the motion of the vessel between consecutive bearings. Supposing that when you obtained the bearing shown you had also observed a second bearing on another landmark on an outlying island, as indicated in Fig. 5–4. Here the compass bearing (CB) is 135°. You now get:

CB	=	135°
TE	=	25° E
TB	=	160°
		+ 180°
RTB	=	340°

When this is plotted, you have a fix as shown in Fig. 5–4.

FIG. 5-4

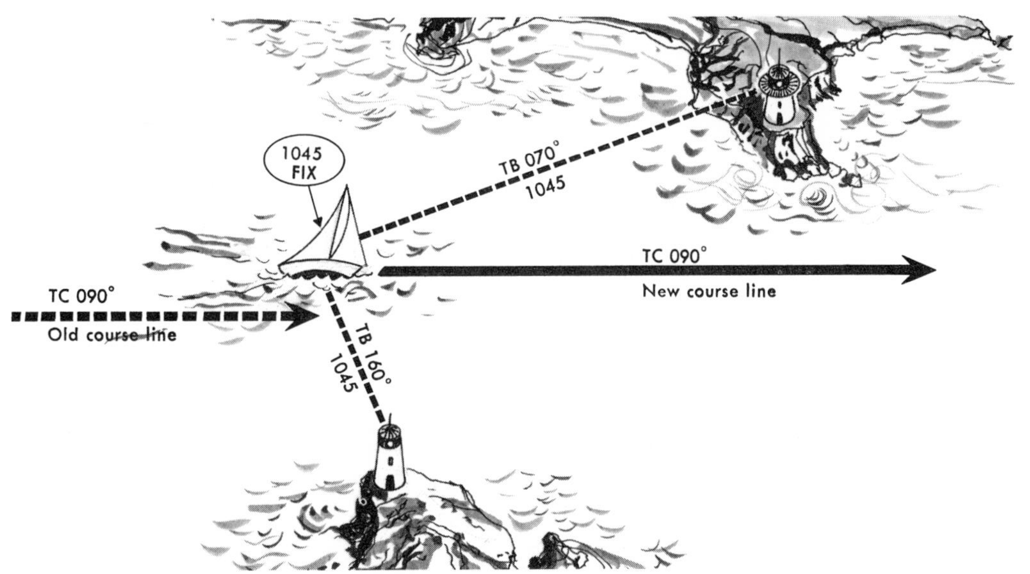

This is by far the simplest and best way of determining your position in coastwise navigation and should be used whenever possible. If you do not have two visible landmarks, you might use one landmark and a radio direction finder bearing (to be discussed later) on a radio beacon or other radio station, or you might obtain two radio bearings if visibility is poor.

Running Fix However, there are times when only one landmark is available, in which case we take a bearing on that landmark, keep on the same course for some suitable distance, and then obtain a second bearing on the same landmark. We can then construct a fairly approximate position which is called a *running fix,* obtained from two bearings on a single object, with a run between. This is illustrated in Fig. 5–5.

At 1100 you are on true course 100°, speed 10 knots. You

FIG. 5-5

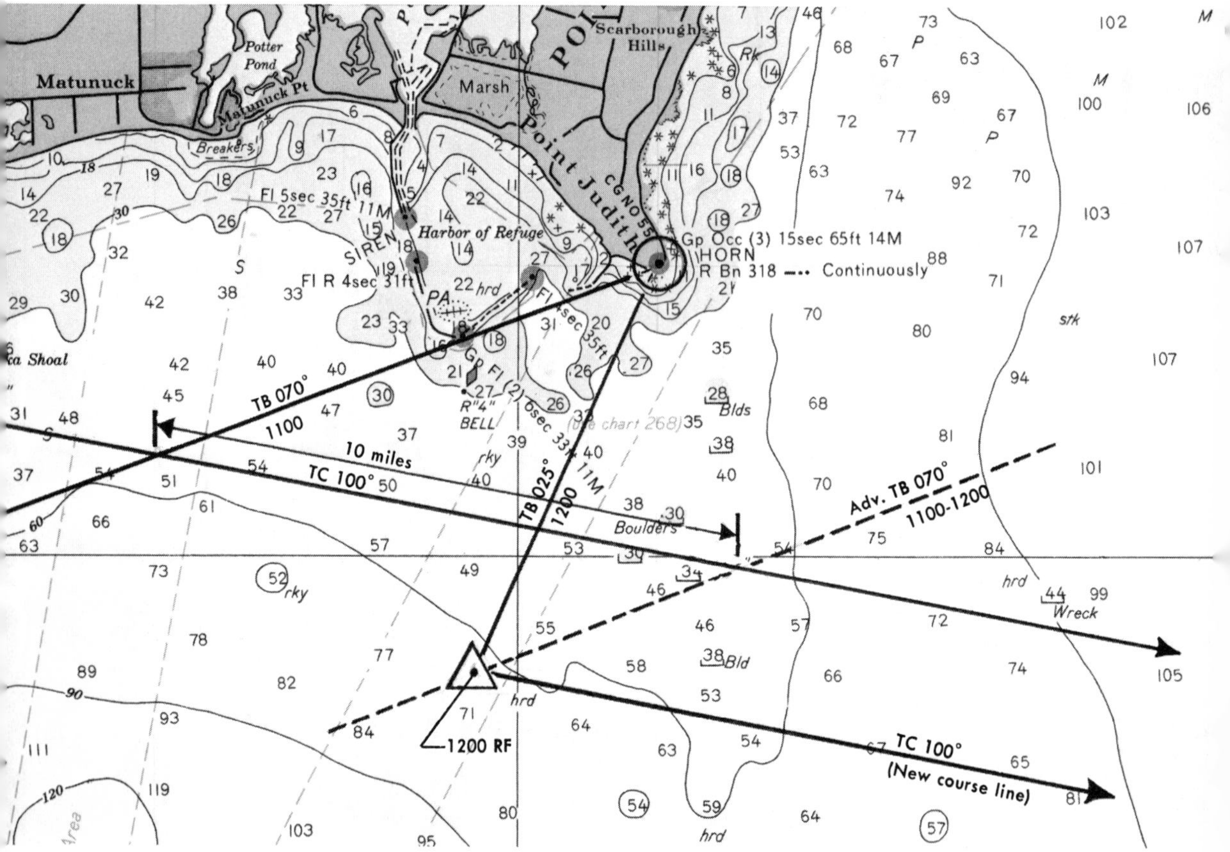

take a compass bearing on a landmark, reading 75°. At 1200 you take another bearing on the same landmark, now reading 30° by compass. Variation is 10° W, deviation on this heading is 5° E, so total compass error is 5° W. You now compute the true bearings:

CB	75°	CB	30°	Distance traveled from 1100 to 1200 is 10 nautical miles.
TE	5° W	TE	5° W	
TB	70°	TB	25°	
	+ 180°		+ 180°	
RTB	250°	RTB	205°	

At 1100 you plot the first bearing as shown. It crosses the intended course line at point *A*. After taking the second bearing at 1200, you plot it as shown and label it.

From point *A* set down a distance of 10 miles, the distance you have sailed between the two bearings, along the intended course line. This establishes point *B*. If you had been at point *A* at 1100 and had sailed 10 miles on TC 110°, you would be at point *B* at 1200. The trouble is that you could not be sure you were at point *A*.

Through point *B* draw a dotted line parallel to the first bearing. This is called *advancing a bearing.* This line represents all the possible places you might be after having sailed 1 hour on this course. This line is everywhere 10 miles ahead of the first line of position (LOP) in the direction of 110° true, and it gives you, in effect, a new LOP at 1200. Since you must be somewhere on this dotted line at 1200 and also on the second line of bearing, your real position must be where they intersect. We call this position the 1200 *running fix* and it is so marked. It shows that we are considerably further offshore than we had intended to be. A running fix is not as accurate as a fix, but it is the best available to us, so we plot a new course from that position toward our destination.

Position from Soundings The navigation chart indicates the depth of water, usually based on mean low water, for most places. These depth measurements are called *soundings,* and they can be used to determine position when other means are not available, as for instance, during thick fog.

There are two recognized methods in use, one being to combine a bearing, particularly one obtained from a radio direction finder (RDF), with a sounding, and the other to obtain a series, or chain, of soundings which can be identified on the chart.

Fix from Bearing and Sounding Obtaining a fix from a bearing and a sounding is a simple and easy method. Obtain a bearing on a landmark, either visually or by radio. At the same time take a sounding with a lead line or a depth finder. Correct the sounding for height of tide, as described in Chapter 7, and note the time. Now plot the bearing on the chart from the landmark toward the vessel. Look along this line on the chart until you find the correct sounding, making sure that there is only one such depth indicated along the line. This point will be your fix. Indicate it as such on the chart and note the time, as shown in Fig. 5–6.

FIG. 5-6

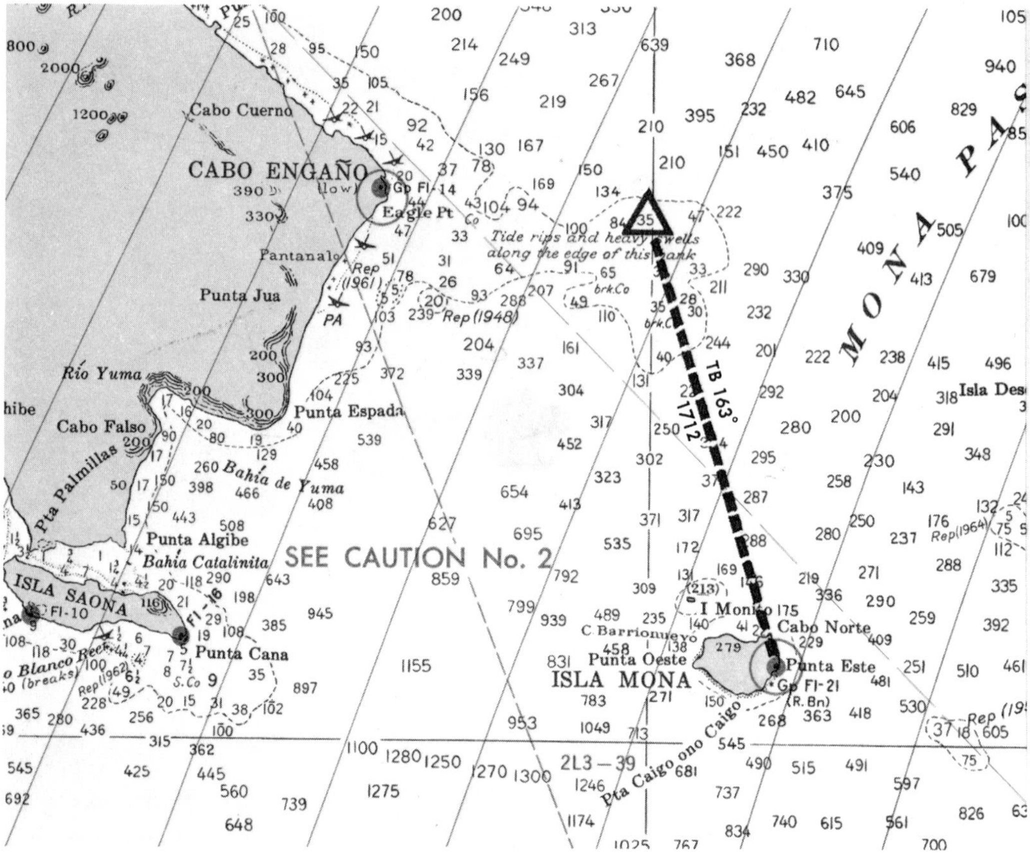

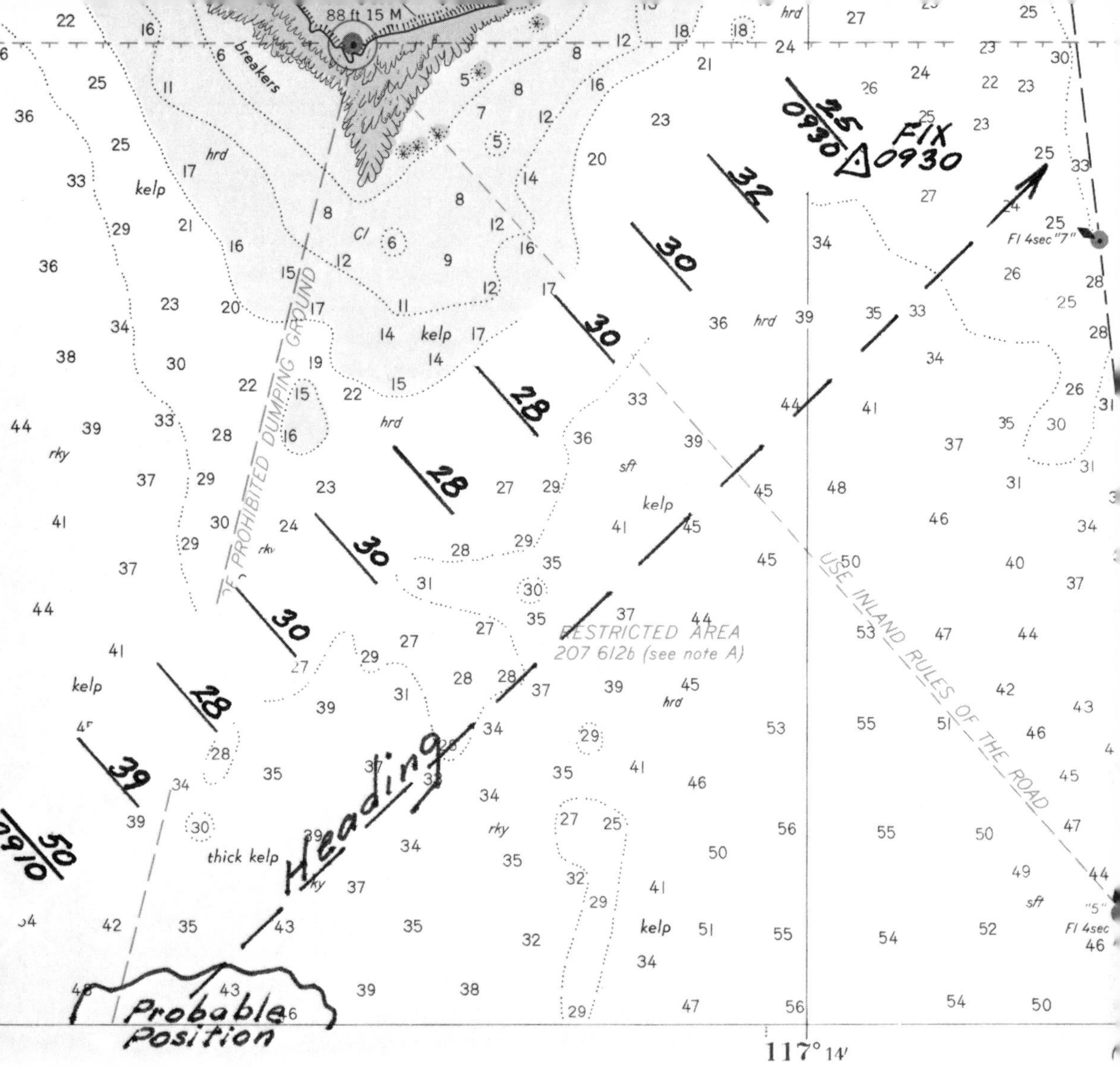

FIG. 5-7

Chain of Soundings Obtaining a chain of soundings requires a fairly accurate knowledge of the speed you are making, and is therefore best suited to a power vessel where you have a table of speeds for various rpm's of the engine. You now examine your chart and mark your *most probable position* (MPP), then select a course that will give the most marked change in depth as you proceed, such as toward shore or across a bank, making sure you have enough sea room for a safe run of at least a mile. You adjust the rpm for a slow speed, say 3 knots. This means that in 20 minutes you will cover 1 mile. Using a watch, you now take soundings every 2 minutes, if you have a depth finder, or every 4 minutes if you use a lead line, which is a slower process. On a strip of paper equal to 1 mile on the chart you note the depth of the water, which is corrected for height of tide, if necessary. By moving this strip across the chart, parallel to the course steered, in the area of your most probable position, you can often locate the only possible place on the chart where such a series of soundings exists and thus obtain a close approximation to your position. If you wish to confirm the position, head back at an angle of 45° to your previous course and repeat the process. Needless to say, this method is used mostly when you are close to land and have a large-scale chart available.

Contour Navigation Contour navigation is the method often used in thick fog, when you are trying to find a harbor entrance. Usually there is a sea buoy somewhere off the harbor entrance, and the chart gives the depth of water at the buoy. Coming in from the sea you deliberately head well to one or the other side of the harbor entrance, so there can be no doubt which side you are on. Proceed toward shore, taking soundings as you go, until you reach the depth indicated under the sea buoy. Now make a right-angle turn toward the direction in which the harbor lies, continuing taking soundings and making sure you change course as necessary to remain at the same depth of water. This will help you locate the sea buoy in short order and keep you out of trouble.

Taking Bearings Up to now we have talked about compass bearings, magnetic bearings, and true bearings. On large ships having gyrocompasses, there is no problem about taking bearings. There will be a repeater compass on either wing of the bridge. The navigator mounts on this a special type of pelorus, called an *azimuth ring,* through which he can sight for bearings on landmarks. He also uses this for taking bearings on the sun for the purpose of checking his compass error—we shall discuss this under celestial navigation (Section III).

On a smaller vessel, however, it is often difficult to take bearings because the compass is frequently located in a place near the steering apparatus where you cannot simultaneously look at the compass and the landmark. To overcome this, many small boats carry a special hand-held bearing compass with which the navigator can walk to any part of the boat and take his bearings. In using such a compass, it is important that he does not stand close to any metal or electrical wiring which can create magnetism and induce deviation in the compass. Usually, if you are 4 or 5 feet away you will have no trouble, except on a steel-hulled vessel, where it is impossible to get away from deviation and a hand-held compass should not be used.

FIG. 5-8
Hand bearing compass
(COURTESY HEATH NAVIGATION)

Many smaller vessels carry a portable pelorus. It consists of sighting vanes mounted over a printed compass card which can be rotated. This type of pelorus can be mounted in a place where it is possible to see the landmarks clearly, such as atop the cabin or in the open on the flying bridge of power boats. The pelorus is sometimes called a "dumb" compass, because it has a compass card and lubber lines, but no magnets or direction of its own. To use it, you align the lubber's line with the keel, or parallel to the keel, and usually set the card to read the same as the compass. You then sight through the vanes at the landmark and obtain your bearings. Because the card was made to simulate the compass card, the reading will be a compass bearing—*but* you must be sure that the helmsman is exactly on course when you make the reading. The best way to effect this is to have him sing out, "On—on—on," while he is on course, and "Off—off—off," when he is off course. It is difficult to hold small boats on an accurate course continuously, and if the reading is made when the helmsman is 5° off course, the bearing will be in error. Always remember that a compass bearing must be converted to a true bearing before it can be plotted. *The simplest way of getting a compass bearing is to head the boat directly for the landmark. The compass course is now identical with the compass bearing:*

$$\text{CC} = \text{CB}$$

Relative Bearings There may be times when it is preferable to use a different kind of bearing called a *relative bearing,* taken relative to the ship's heading, or bow, or keel, whichever way you want to look at it. If the pelorus is set so the 0° mark points dead ahead, and the 0°–180° line is parallel to the keel, a relative bearing is read from 0° clockwise on the starboard side to 180°, which is dead astern, or counterclockwise on the port side from 0° to 180°. This is the most common way. Such bearings are expressed as so many degrees "on the starboard bow," or so many degrees "on the port bow." Although the bearing may well be to an object abaft the beam, and in a sense behind the vessel, we still use the phrase "on the bow."

In the U.S. Navy a somewhat different system prevails. Relative bearings are read from 0°, dead ahead, clockwise through 360°. Thus relative bearing 270° would be the same as 90° on the port bow, or abeam to port. A relative bearing, like a compass bearing, cannot be plotted on the chart without conversion to a true bearing, but the operation is quite simple. It is important that you study the next diagram in order to see the relationship and the basis for the simple conversion.

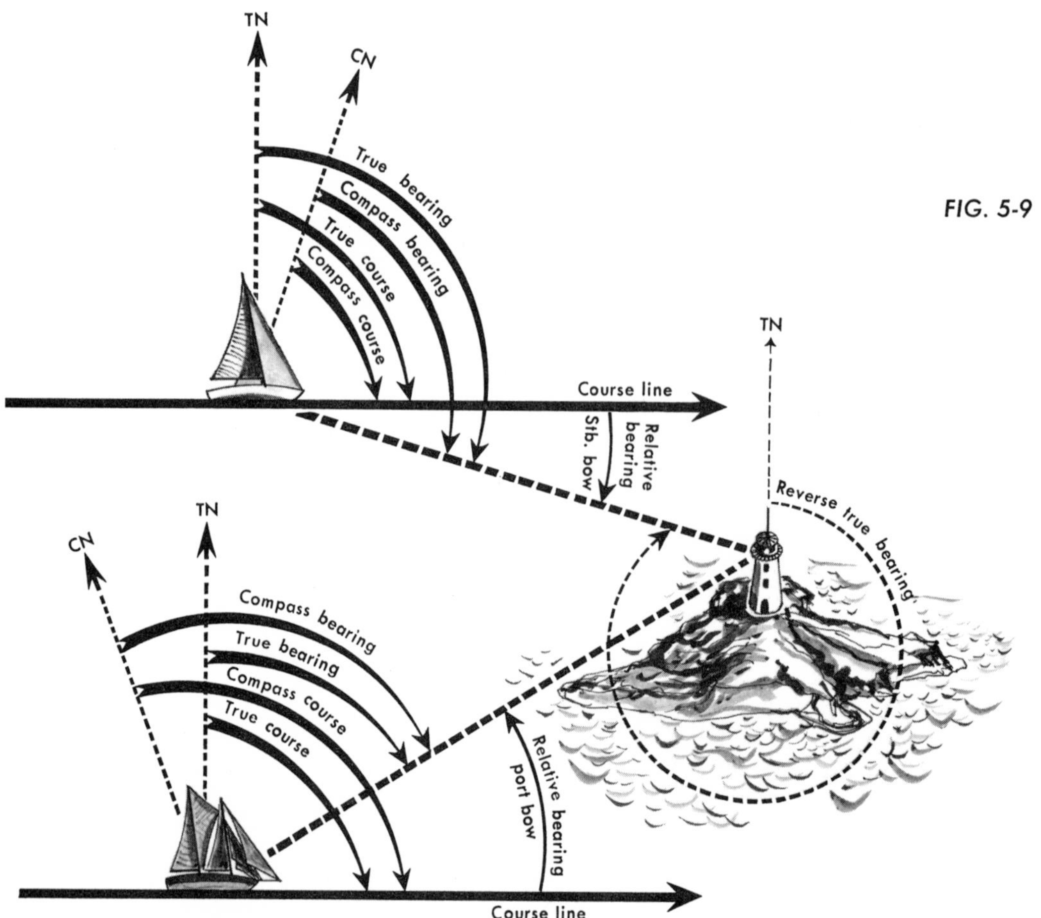

FIG. 5-9

From the diagram you can recognize that the following simple statement holds true:

A relative bearing to starboard, added to the course, gives the bearing.

A relative bearing to port, subtracted from the course, gives the bearing.

If you apply a relative bearing to a true course, you get the true bearing. If you apply a relative bearing to a compass course, you get a compass bearing. That is really all there is to it, so please don't make it complicated.

If you are using the Navy system, all bearings are added to the course, never subtracted. Again, if added to the true course, it gives a true bearing, etc. If the addition comes to more than 360°, just subtract 360°.

In navigation you sometimes hear the term *abeam*. This simply means at right angles to the keel. Other terms used are *broad on the bow,* which means 45° off the bow, and *broad on the quarter,* which means 45° abaft the beam. In the old days, a compass card was marked not in degrees, but in *points*. One point is 11¼°. This is rarely used nowadays except in the Rules of the Road, that archaic set of hard-to-read traffic rules. Light sectors of navigation lights, for example, are expressed as "from dead ahead to 2 points abaft the beam," or a light "must be visible for 32 points," which means all around the horizon, or 360°.

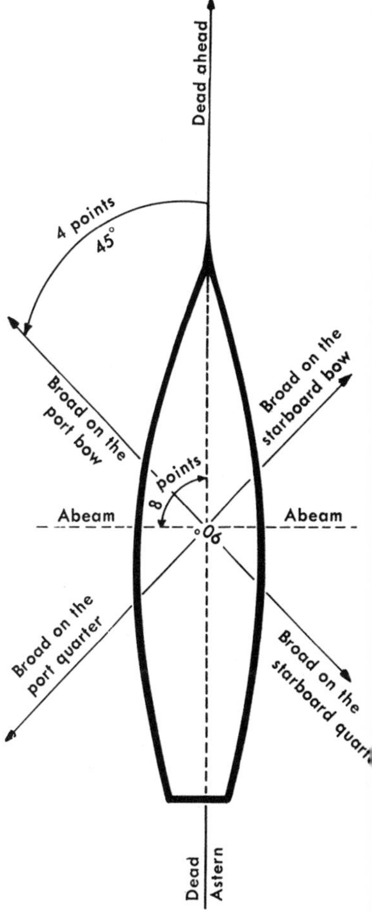

FIG. 5-10

Special Situations Sometimes, when you are sailing singlehanded and cannot leave the tiller to do chart navigation, you can make use of special bearings that will tell you how far offshore you are, although they are not plotted on the chart. The advantage is that with a simple mental calculation you will know in advance whether you will clear certain outlying shoals up ahead.

If you have a landmark on the coast up ahead, such as a point with hidden reefs a mile or two off that you want to be sure to avoid, you note the time when the angle between a bearing to the landmark and the direction dead ahead in which you are sailing is 26½°, i.e. a relative bearing of 26½° on the bow. Note again the time when that point is 45° off your bow and then calculate the distance you have sailed between the two observations. This distance is the distance by which you will clear the

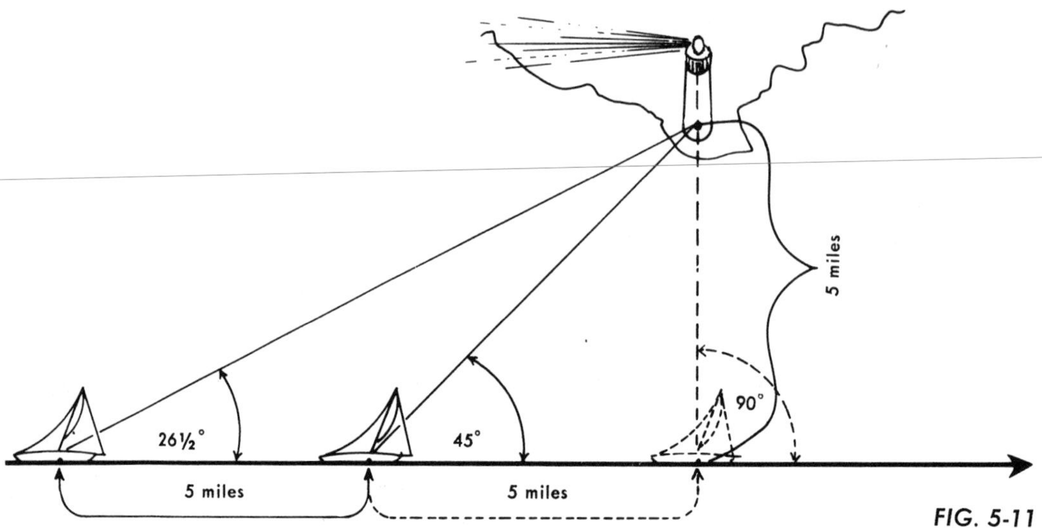

FIG. 5-11

point when you come abeam, and it is also the distance you must go until you are abeam of the point. This type of thing is useful if there is a possibility of fog ahead and you want to make sure you are far enough out.

If you are simply cruising along a coast and want to know how far out you are, note the time when a certain landmark is 45° off your bow, and then take the time when you have the landmark abeam. The distance you have sailed between the two bearings is the distance you will be off when you are abeam.

These special angles are developed from simple geometry and should be used only when you are unable to do

FIG. 5-12

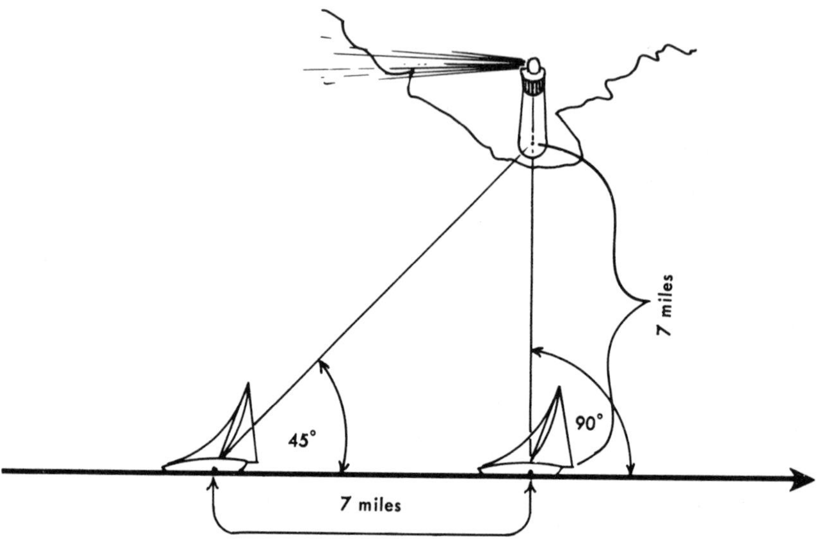

regular chart work. There are many other combinations of angles that can be used, but mostly this is a waste of time and not worth remembering—if you could. The safest procedure is to plot your progress neatly and continuously on the chart, using the standard methods described.

Chart Work

It is of utmost importance that your chart work be neat, legible, and labeled according to a uniform system. This helps you avoid the errors that come from sloppy chart work, and also enables the next man on watch to understand what you have done. Never erase your chart work until the end of the trip. It is a valuable record of your navigation, and it could prove important evidence if you had been in trouble and had to appear in admiralty court.

Always do your chart work with a sharp, soft pencil. Use a fairly heavy line for course lines and lighter lines for plotting bearings and current diagrams. Label everything immediately, neatly, and clearly, preferably following the few simple rules given below.

Courses Write the true course in three digits above the course line, and indicate distance and speed, if any, below the line, as shown.

TC 090°

S10 32.2Mi.

Bearings Write the true bearing in three digits above the line and show the time the bearing was taken in four digits below the line, using the 24-hour system, as shown.

TB 085°

1027

Advanced Bearing Show the line dotted and write the true bearing in three digits above the line. Below the line indicate the time the first bearing was taken, followed by the time of the second bearing to which it was advanced.

TE 085°
1027 – 1127

Fixes Indicate a fix as a small triangle surrounding the dot of the fix, and write the word FIX, followed by the time of the fix alongside.

FIX 0245

Running Fixes Show the running fix as a small circle surrounding the dot of the position and write RF and the time alongside.

RF 1127

Dead Reckoning Position Dead reckoning position is the position set down on the chart based on direction and distance sailed since the last fix. It is indicated by a half-circle, without a dot, the letters DR, and the time in four digits.

TC 090° DR 1430

Estimated Position *Estimated position* generally is used where a single line of position is obtained that does not agree with the DR position for the same instant of time. A perpendicular dropped from the DR point to the line of position intersects at a point called the estimated position. It is marked with a small square, the letters EP, and the time, as shown below. This method of obtaining a position should not be taken too seriously, as it is subject to possible error.

TC 090° DR 1430

TB 045°
1430

EP 1430

Of course, you can use symbols of your own making, but the important thing is that your system be consistent and familiar to fellow navigators who may take over the watch after you.

Alternate Methods There are many more methods of fixing a position at sea, but those given here will cover all the situations you may encounter in coastwise navigation. Sailors and navigators are inclined to be tradition-bound and hate to give up the old methods. I have presented the methods used most frequently by myself and other experienced navigators in recent years. Aboard ship we have many other things to do besides navigation, so a few simple streamlined but dependable procedures will best serve your purpose.

Practice Problems •

Find

1. CB = 275°, var. 10° W, dev. 5° E MB = ______ TB = ______
2. CB = 182°, var. 15° E, dev. 3° W MB = ______ TB = ______
3. Rel.B = 25° on stbd. bow, TC = 090° TB = ______
4. Rel.B = 125° on port bow, TC = 180° TB = ______
5. Rel.B = 75° on port bow, TC = 050° TB = ______
6. Rel.B = 100° on stbd. bow, TC = 270° TB = ______
7. Rel.B = 45° on port bow, CC = 120°
   var. 15° W, dev. 5° W Reverse TB = ______
8. At 1600 lighthouse bears 26.5° on stbd. bow.
   At 1730 lighthouse bears 45° on stbd. bow.
   Speed is 10 knots Distance to go until abeam? ______
   Distance off when abeam? ______
   Time when ship is abeam? ______
9. At 1527 landmark bears 45° on port bow.
   At 1612 landmark is abeam. Speed is 10 knots.
   Distance off at 1612? ______
10. You sail 30 miles in 5 hours. Speed? ______
11. You must sail 56 miles at 6 knots. Time required? ______
12. You travel 4^h20^m (4 hours, 20 minutes) at 12 knots. Distance covered? ______

Chapter 6

Wind and Currents

The force of the wind on the superstructure of any vessel will cause that vessel to drift with the wind. If the vessel is moving along a given heading under either power or sail, the effect of the wind will be to change that track slightly in the direction in which the wind is blowing. This is called *leeway*. Since it changes the angle of the ship's course, it is measured in degrees. To overcome the effect of leeway, we head the vessel slightly into the wind, changing the heading but causing the vessel to move along its intended course line.

Leeway is an uncertain element since it depends on the strength of the wind, the amount of superstructure exposed to the wind, and the depth and shape of the part of the hull that is below the water surface. A flat-bottomed boat with little draft and high superstructure, such as a houseboat, will make a lot of leeway, while a deep-draft sailing vessel with a large keel or a heavily laden freighter will make relatively little leeway. Since it depends on the individual boat, it becomes a matter of judgment and experience to decide how much to compensate for leeway. Under varying circumstances of force and direction of wind, the seasoned skipper who knows his boat well will have little difficulty deciding how far to head into the wind to overcome the effect of leeway. The compensation is made as a correction to the heading and *always in the direction from which the wind blows.*

Example • You are on a course of 050° and estimate you are being set 10° to the right of your course by a northerly wind. You would change the course 10° to the left, steering 040°, in an attempt to remain on your intended track. At the first opportunity you will fix your position to see if your estimate was correct and change the heading again if necessary. *Watch leeway. Many vessels have been lost on a lee shore because a correction was not made in time.*

Current is different from leeway, because current is a horizontal flow of water in a given direction which carries the boat with it while you are sailing through that current. Some currents are caused by the ebb and flood of the tide, to be discussed in Chapter 7, while the great ocean currents are in effect rivers in the ocean with more or less definite boundaries.

The effect of the current is the same as that of leeway. It sets a vessel off its course in the direction in which the current flows. Because a great deal is known about currents, however, we can often predict them fairly accurately and make a reasonably correct change in heading to overcome their effect. Constantly fixing your position on the chart enables you to determine the strength and direction of the current and the correctness of the allowance you have made. Of course, you are often faced with a combination of current and leeway, in which case you must be doubly watchful in keeping track of your position. *The only thing you can take for granted is that the heading you are steering is probably not keeping you exactly on your intended course.*

The speed at which the water in a current moves is called the *drift,* and the direction in which the current flows is called the *set.* Drift is measured in knots and set is measured in degrees from true north. Problems involving current are mainly of two types. One is to determine the set and drift of current by comparing your DR (dead reckoning) position with an accurate fix for the same instant of time; the other is to determine what allowance in heading to make for a known set and drift of current. A third, but not too common, problem is to determine what speed through the water you must make to overcome the effect of a known current in order to meet a certain ETA (estimated time of arrival) at a destination. All such problems are solved by constructing *current diagrams.*

In your work with current diagrams, it is important to distinguish between *course* (or *track*) and *heading.* The course is the path you want the ship to follow. The heading is the direction in which you point the bow to move along the desired path, overcoming the current. In a strong current a vessel can be seen moving practically sidewise along the track to the destination. Two other terms must be distinguished: *Speed* is always the speed at which a vessel would be moving through *still* water, and *effective speed* is the rate at which the ship moves along the intended course line *under the effect of the current.* Effective speed is greater than ship's speed when the current is abaft the beam, less when it is forward of the beam. In working with current diagrams we simplify the procedure by considering what happens in 1 hour, *exactly.*

To Find the Set and Drift of the Current See Fig. 6–1. At 0800 you leave point *A* on a true course of 090°. Vessel's speed is 10 knots through still water. You have thick fog and no wind, so there is no leeway. At 0930 the fog clears and you take bearings on landmarks which determine a *fix* at point *C*. However, had there been no current, you would have been at point *B,* your 0930 DR position, 15 miles due east of point *A*. In 1½ hours the effect of the current was such that you moved not along line *A–B,* but along line *A–C,* and the total effect of the current for 1½ hours is represented by line *B–C*.

To determine drift, we need to know what the current did in 1 hour. We therefore plot the 0900 DR position at point *d,* 10 miles due east of point *A*. Through *d* we draw a dotted line parallel to *B–C,* intersecting the actual track

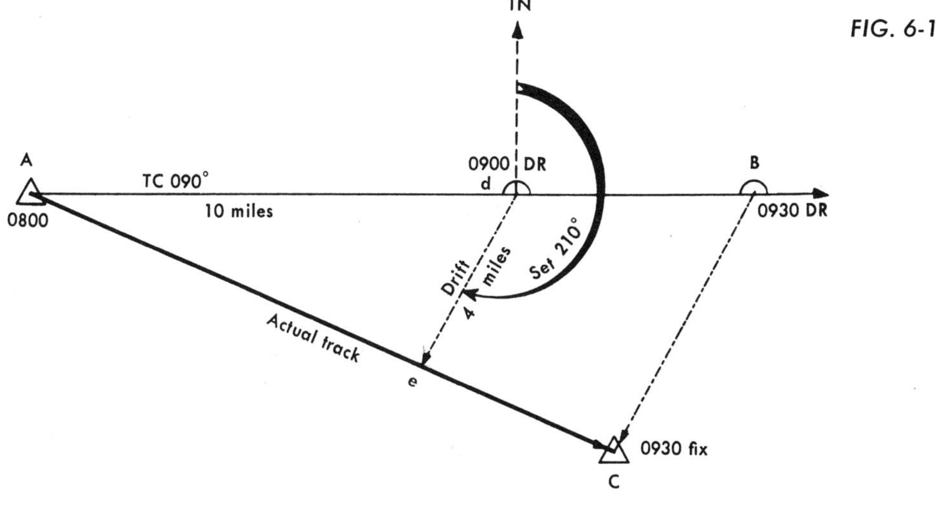

FIG. 6-1

at point *e,* the place where we actually were at 0900. The direction of line *d–e,* measured from true north, is the *set* of the current, and the length of line *d–e* is the *drift,* in this case 4 knots because we have determined, using the scale of the chart, that *d–e* is 4 nautical miles long.

To Allow for Set and Drift of Current Knowing the set and drift, we can apply it to our intended course to find the *heading* we must steer to overcome the current and also the *effective speed* we shall attain along the course line we wish to follow.

At this point it is well to remember—and it will be mentioned several times again—that the *deviation* we shall use to find the *compass heading* we shall steer depends on the heading of the ship, not on the course followed over the bottom. The current diagram will give a *true heading,* which in turn must be converted to a compass heading to be steered by the helmsman.

The approach to this problem is to show in the diagram what the current will do to the vessel in 1 hour if the boat just drifted with the current, and then determine what must be done to overcome this effect.

Example • In the previous example we determined that the set was 210° and the drift was 4 knots. What heading must we steer to *make good* a true course of 090° and what will be our effective speed along that course? See Fig. 6–2.

From the point of departure *A,* set down the intended course line to destination point *B,* due east, or 090° true. From *A* lay out the current vector *A–X* in the direction of 210° true. A vector simply represents direction and speed of current for one hour. Its length is 4 miles, the motion of the current in 1 hour. If we simply drifted with the current from *A* for 1 hour, we would be at point *X.*

Now set your dividers to 10 miles, the ship's speed through the water. Place one point at *X* and the other point back on the course line. Connect the two points of the dividers with a line *X–Y.* This completes the current diagram.

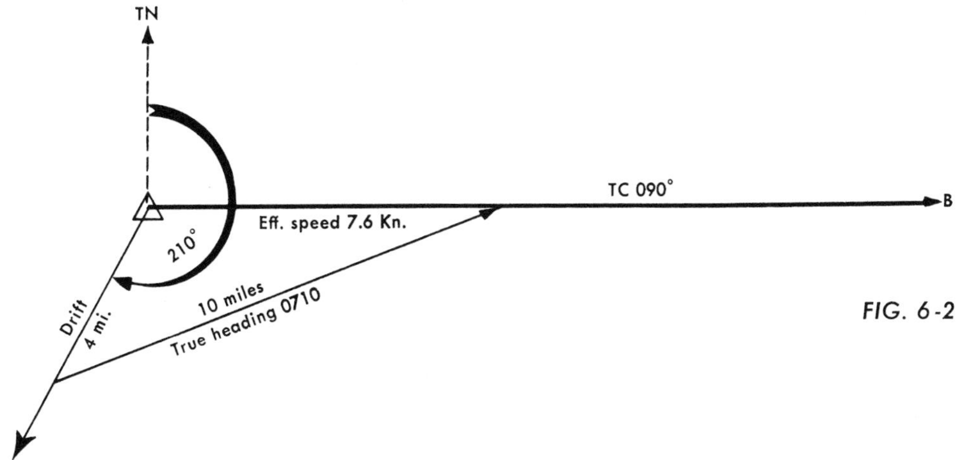

FIG. 6-2

The direction of line *X–Y* is the *true heading to steer from Point A to remain on line A–B.* With a protractor you measure its direction as 071° true. When you leave point *A* you head in the direction of 071° true, but you never leave the track *A–B,* because the current constantly pushes you back on this intended course.

The length of the line *A–Y* is the *effective speed* of the vessel. After leaving point *A* on a heading of 071° true, at a speed through the water of 10 knots, the vessel in 1 hour will move to point *Y,* 7.6 miles distant from *A* along the track *A–Y.*

Having obtained this information, it is necessary to convert this true heading to a compass heading by applying variation and deviation. Assuming there is a 15° E variation in the locality, taken from the compass rose on the chart, and using the deviation table on p. 30 (Fig. 5–1) we find:

True course to make good	090°
True heading to steer	071°
Variation	15° E
Magnetic heading	056°
Deviation	2° W
Compass heading to steer	058°

The following examples demonstrate various current problems.

Example • You take departure at 1500 on true heading 250°, speed 12 knots. At 1700 a fix shows you to be 7 miles northwest of your DR position. What is set and drift of current?

1500 fix
Actual track
TN
Drift
12 miles
1700 fix
1600 DR
Set
TC 250°
1700 DR

FIG. 6-3

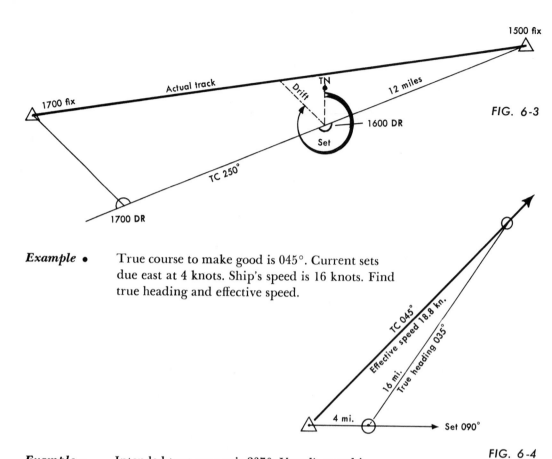

Example • True course to make good is 045°. Current sets due east at 4 knots. Ship's speed is 16 knots. Find true heading and effective speed.

TC 045°
Effective speed 18.8 kn.
True heading 035°
16 mi.
4 mi.
Set 090°

FIG. 6-4

Example • Intended true course is 237°. Vessel's speed is 6 knots. Current sets 070° with drift of 3 knots. Find true heading to make good 237°. What will be effective speed?

FIG. 6-5

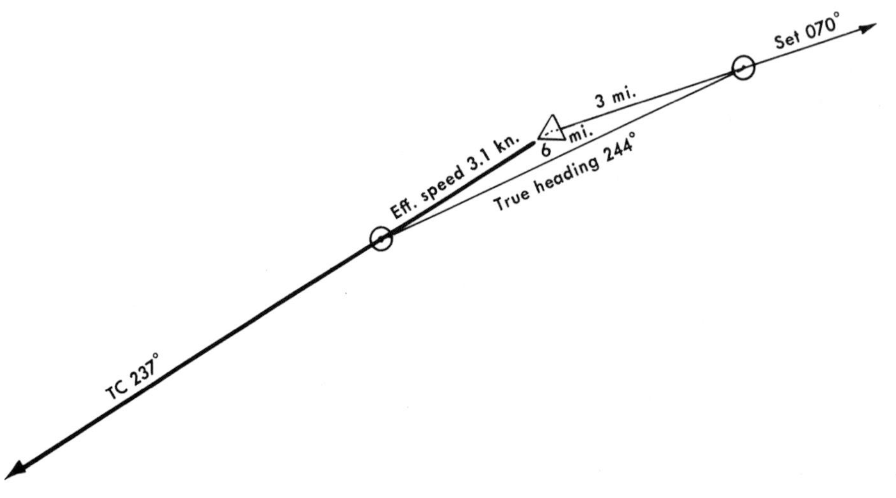

For additional uses of current diagrams, see the Appendix.

Ocean Currents

Most of the water in the world's oceans is in constant motion in one direction or another at various rates of flow. The primary cause of this motion is wind and the secondary cause is difference of density, which in turn is determined by salinity, temperature, and pressure. High-density water has a lower surface elevation than low-density water, with the result that water tends to flow from an area of low density toward an area of high density. The water level difference due to density has a maximum of 1 to 2 feet in 40 miles, sufficient to cause a horizontal flow.

Wind currents are set up where the wind blows steadily in a certain direction for a period of time, such as in the trade wind belts, and the current may attain a speed of 1 to 2 percent of the wind speed. In a general way, the direction of the flow of the current in the ocean is determined by the direction of the wind that is the primary cause of that current, but several factors influence this direction.

The most obvious influence is the location of land masses in the path of the currents, causing deflection along shorelines. The rotation of the Earth on its axis creates a Coriolis force that deflects both winds and currents, to the right in the northern hemisphere and to the left in the southern hemisphere. A wind-driven current moves at an angle to the wind that causes it of about 15° in shallow waters to 45° in deeper waters. Since the currents bring with them water of varying temperatures, they in turn influence the weather, and particularly the winds, around the world, and these winds in turn influence the currents.

Out of these natural forces comes a more or less predictable system of great ocean currents around the world. In general, there is a westerly flow north of the equator that in each ocean turns northward and creates a clockwise circulation. This is called the *north equatorial current,* and when the flow is reversed eastward at higher latitudes it is called the North Pacific and North Atlantic currents respectively. These in turn give rise to other special currents.

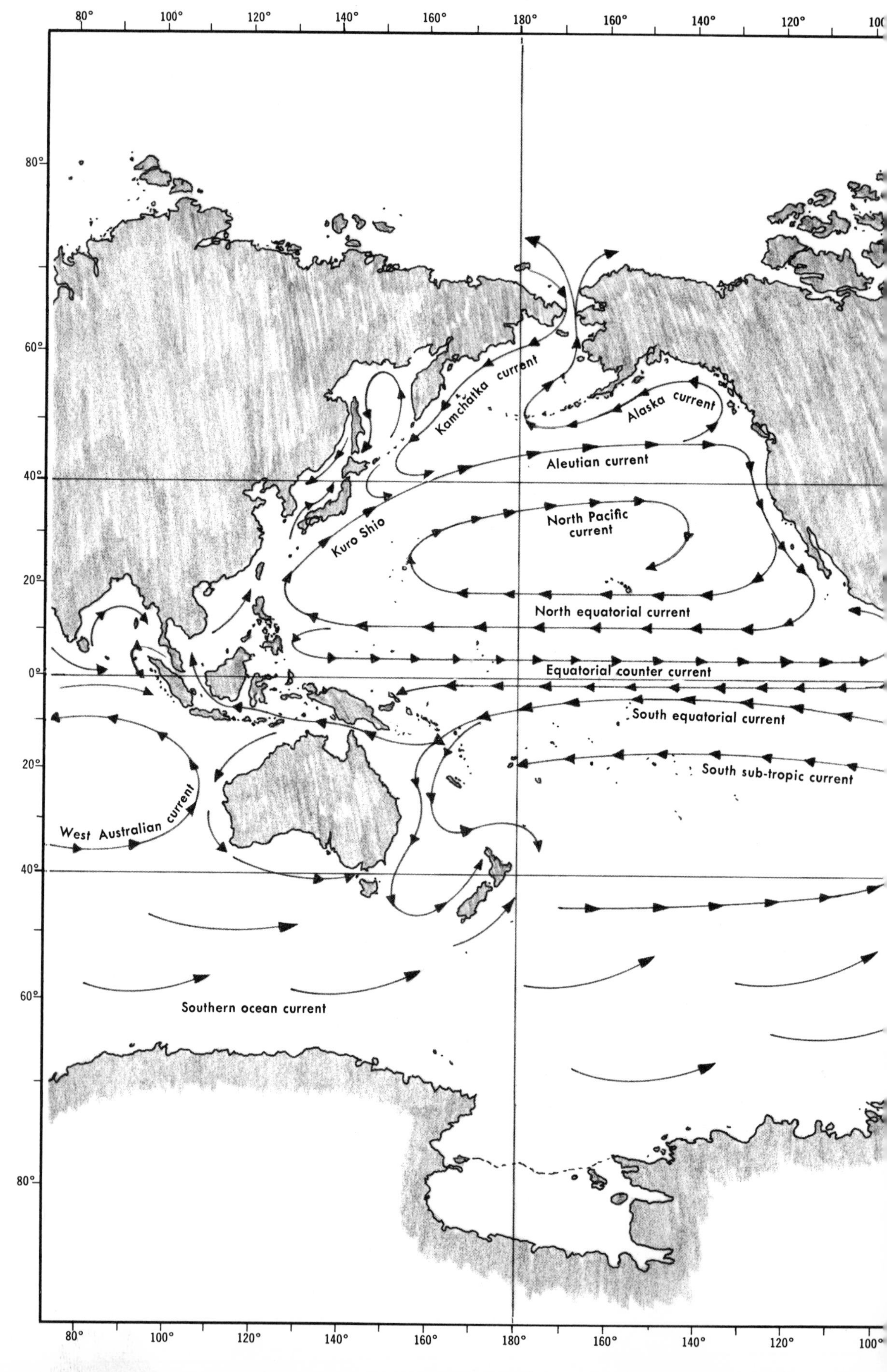

80°
100°
120°
140°
160°
180°
160°
140°
120°
100°
80°
60°
40°
20°
0°
20°
40°
60°
80°
Kamchatka current
Alaska current
Aleutian current
Kuro Shio
North Pacific current
North equatorial current
Equatorial counter current
South equatorial current
South sub-tropic current
West Australian current
Southern ocean current

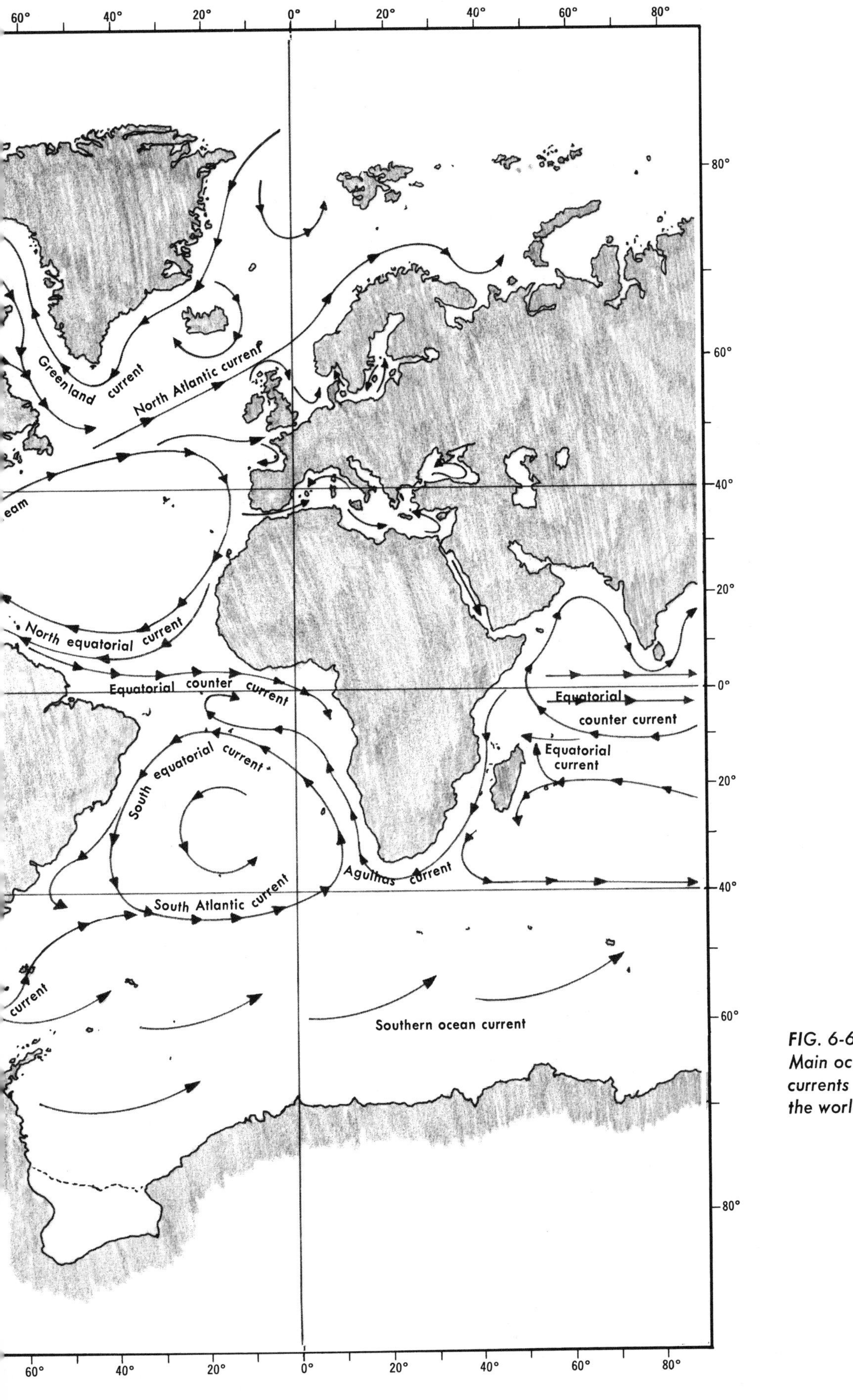

FIG. 6-6
Main ocean currents of the world

Right around the equator and southward is another massive westerly current, the *south equatorial current.* It tends to rotate in a counterclockwise direction and eventually turns back eastward at the higher southern latitudes, and also helps form other currents. In between the north and south equatorial currents flows a rather weak *equatorial countercurrent,* moving eastward.

Although the strength and direction of the large ocean currents vary with the seasons, certain well-defined and quite predictable currents are of interest to the navigator because they are practically rivers in the ocean. Main among these is the *Gulf Stream,* which is formed off the southeast coast of Florida, where it sometimes reaches a strength of 4 knots. It flows in general along the east coast of the United States, broadening and slowing up as it travels past Cape Hatteras and up toward the Grand Banks. The Gulf Stream is known for its warm water of deep blue color, and navigators must make allowance for its set and drift to stay on course.

Along the west coast of the U.S. the *California current* flows southward at about 1 knot during the year, and in winter there is a rather weak north-flowing countercurrent close to shore called the *Davidson current.*

Currents are indicated on the monthly "Pilot Charts" in terms of direction and average strength, and every navigator contemplating a race or a cruise *must* consider their effect on his course and speed.

Practice Problems •

1. You sail at 10 knots for 2 hours on true course 160°. A fix shows you to be 8 miles southeast of the DR position. Find set and drift.
2. Using set and drift found in problem 1, what compass heading must you steer to make good a true course of 045° and what will be your effective speed? Vessel's speed is 10 knots. Variation is 10° W. Use "Polaris" deviation table (Fig. 5–1).

Chapter 7

Tide and Current Tables

The moon exerts a strong gravitational pull on the Earth, and to a lesser extent so does the sun. Since a large portion of the Earth's surface consists of water in the oceans, this gravitational pull regularly moves masses of water in one direction or another, creating the familiar tidal flow of water, or *tides.* When the moon and sun, because of their position, both pull in the same direction, we have a maximum effect, known as *spring tides,* creating very high and very low water; and when they are at quadrature, they oppose each other, and we have the lesser tidal effect known as *neap tide.*

Spring tides occur when the moon is new and when it is full. Neap tides occur in the first and third quarter. *High water* is the maximum height to which the tide rises in a given locality on a given day, and *low water* is the lowest level to which it drops on that day. The *stand* is the stage of the tide when it has reached its maximum high or low—when there is no further vertical movement until the tide begins to reverse itself.

The tides have the effect of constantly changing the depth of water under a vessel and must be reckoned with in marginal situations where there is doubt as to whether there will be enough water under the ship's bottom to pass safely. The charts give soundings in feet or fathoms (and sometimes meters), indicating the lowest water experienced at any given location, and the navigator must constantly consider the stage of the tide over this minimum depth.

Tide tables, published annually in the United States by the National Ocean Survey (formerly known as the Coast and Geodetic Survey), cover most of the world and give the times and amount of tidal rise and fall at more than 6,000 different locations. The information is given directly for a number of key *reference stations,* and indirectly for a large number of secondary locations, for which are given the variations in time and height from the direct data given for the reference stations. For any instant of time under consideration, the stage of the tide must be applied to the soundings on the chart to determine how deep the water really is. Separate tide tables are published each year for the following areas:

East coast of North and South America, including Greenland
West coast of North and South America, including the Hawaiian Islands
Europe and west coast of Africa, including the Mediterranean Sea
Central and western Pacific Ocean and the Indian Ocean

In addition, many other countries publish detailed tide tables for various locations in their own harbors and waterways.

Tidal currents are caused by the horizontal flow of water that accompanies the rise and fall of the tides. When the current flows toward the land, it is called *flood tide,* and when it is flowing away from the coast, it is called *ebb tide.* The period of little or no horizontal flow of water, when the tide is changing from flooding to ebbing, or vice versa, is called *slack water.*

Tidal currents can be felt for miles inland and in some places become so strong that they seriously affect the movement of vessels. In sailing-ship days, ships would anchor and wait for a favorable tide to help them reach open water. Even today vessels of limited power and speed must reckon with the tidal current to enter or leave certain harbors. Because of this, the National Ocean Survey also publishes annually a complete set of *Tidal Current Tables.*

Tidal Current Tables give the time of maximum current during ebb and flood, the time of slack water, the strength of the current, and the direction in which it flows during either ebb or flow, in all navigable waters. Again, since the full effect of the current is not felt at the same time in various waters along the same coast, the tables give specific information for a number of reference stations, and then relate the effect on surrounding waters at many secondary locations to this basic data. The National Ocean Survey publishes two volumes, *Tidal Current Tables,* annually covering the following areas:

Atlantic coast of North America
Pacific coast of North America and Asia

KETCHIKAN, ALASKA

TIMES AND HEIGHTS OF HIGH AND LOW WATERS

APRIL

DAY	TIME H.M.	HT. FT.	DAY	TIME H.M.	HT. FT.
1	0036	15.2	16	0106	16.8
TU	0642	0.7	W	0718	-1.5
	1254	15.4		1336	15.4
	1854	-0.2		1924	0.8
2	0106	16.2	17	0136	16.9
W	0718	-0.6	TH	0754	-1.9
	1330	15.8		1412	15.0
	1930	-0.2		1954	1.5
3	0136	16.9	18	0206	16.7
TH	0754	-1.6	F	0830	-1.8
	1406	15.7		1448	14.4
	2000	0.2		2030	2.3
4	0212	17.4	19	0236	16.2
F	0830	-2.2	SA	0906	-1.3
	1448	15.3		1524	13.6
	2036	0.9		2100	3.2
5	0242	17.4	20	0312	15.4
SA	0912	-2.2	SU	0942	-0.5
	1536	14.5		1606	12.7
	2112	1.8		2136	4.1
6	0324	17.0	21	0342	14.5
SU	1000	-1.8	M	1024	0.4
	1624	13.5		1648	11.7
	2200	3.0		2212	5.1
7	0406	16.2	22	0424	13.5
M	1048	-0.9	TU	1112	1.4
	1718	12.3		1742	10.9
	2248	4.3		2254	6.0
8	0500	15.1	23	0506	12.5
TU	1154	0.2	W	1206	2.3
	1830	11.4		1848	10.4
	2354	5.4			
9	0606	14.0	24	0000	6.7
W	1312	1.0	TH	0606	11.6
	2006	11.2		1318	2.8
				2006	10.4
10	0130	5.9	25	0130	6.8
TH	0730	13.2	F	0730	11.2
	1436	1.2		1424	2.9
	2130	11.9		2112	11.1
11	0306	5.3	26	0300	6.0
F	0906	13.2	SA	0854	11.4
	1548	0.9		1530	2.6
	2230	13.1		2200	12.1
12	0418	3.8	27	0400	4.7
SA	1018	13.8	SU	1000	12.1
	1648	0.4		1618	2.1
	2318	14.4		2242	13.3
13	0512	2.1	28	0448	3.0
SU	1118	14.6	M	1054	12.9
	1730	0.1		1700	1.7
	2354	15.5		2318	14.5
14	0600	0.6	29	0530	1.2
M	1206	15.1	TU	1142	13.8
	1812	0.1		1742	1.3
				2348	15.7
15	0030	16.3	30	0612	-0.5
TU	0642	-0.7	W	1230	14.5
	1254	15.4		1818	1.2
	1848	0.3			

MAY

DAY	TIME H.M.	HT. FT.	DAY	TIME H.M.	HT. FT.
1	0024	16.7	16	0106	16.2
TH	0648	-1.9	F	0736	-1.7
	1312	15.0		1400	13.7
	1854	1.2		1930	3.2
2	0100	17.5	17	0136	16.0
F	0730	-2.9	SA	0812	-1.6
	1354	15.1		1436	13.5
	1936	1.5		2006	3.6
3	0142	17.9	18	0212	15.6
SA	0812	-3.4	SU	0848	-1.3
	1442	14.9		1512	13.1
	2018	2.0		2036	4.1
4	0224	17.8	19	0248	15.1
SU	0900	-3.3	M	0924	-0.8
	1530	14.4		1554	12.6
	2100	2.6		2118	4.6
5	0306	17.3	20	0318	14.4
M	0948	-2.7	TU	1000	-0.1
	1624	13.7		1636	12.1
	2154	3.5		2154	5.2
6	0354	16.3	21	0400	13.6
TU	1042	-1.7	W	1048	0.6
	1724	13.0		1724	11.7
	2248	4.3		2242	5.7
7	0454	15.1	22	0442	12.8
W	1142	-0.6	TH	1136	1.3
	1830	12.6		1812	11.5
				2336	6.0
8	0000	4.9	23	0536	12.0
TH	0600	13.9	F	1224	2.0
	1254	0.4		1906	11.6
	1942	12.6			
9	0124	4.9	24	0048	5.9
F	0724	13.0	SA	0642	11.4
	1406	1.1		1318	2.5
	2048	13.2		2000	12.1
10	0248	4.1	25	0206	5.2
SA	0842	12.6	SU	0800	11.1
	1512	1.5		1418	2.8
	2148	14.0		2054	12.8
11	0354	2.8	26	0312	3.9
SU	1000	12.8	M	0912	11.3
	1606	1.7		1512	2.9
	2236	14.8		2136	13.8
12	0454	1.3	27	0406	2.3
M	1100	13.2	TU	1018	11.9
	1654	1.9		1606	2.9
	2318	15.5		2224	14.9
13	0542	0.1	28	0500	0.5
TU	1154	13.5	W	1118	12.7
	1742	2.2		1654	2.8
	2354	16.0		2306	15.9
14	0618	-0.9	29	0542	-1.1
W	1236	13.8	TH	1206	13.5
	1818	2.5		1742	2.6
				2348	16.9
15	0030	16.2	30	0630	-2.5
TH	0700	-1.5	F	1254	14.1
	1318	13.8		1830	2.5
	1854	2.8			
			31	0036	17.7
			SA	0718	-3.5
				1348	14.5
				1918	2.5

JUNE

DAY	TIME H.M.	HT. FT.	DAY	TIME H.M.	HT. FT.
1	0118	18.0	16	0154	15.3
SU	0800	-4.0	M	0830	-1.3
	1436	14.7		1500	13.0
	2006	2.5		2024	4.4
2	0206	18.0	17	0230	15.0
M	0848	-3.9	TU	0906	-1.1
	1524	14.6		1542	12.9
	2054	2.8		2100	4.5
3	0300	17.5	18	0306	14.6
TU	0942	-3.4	W	0942	-0.7
	1618	14.4		1612	12.8
	2148	3.1		2142	4.6
4	0354	16.6	19	0342	14.0
W	1030	-2.5	TH	1018	-0.2
	1712	14.2		1654	12.8
	2248	3.5		2224	4.7
5	0448	15.4	20	0424	13.3
TH	1124	-1.3	F	1054	0.5
	1806	14.0		1730	12.8
	2354	3.7		2312	4.7
6	0554	14.0	21	0506	12.5
F	1224	0.0	SA	1136	1.3
	1906	14.0		1812	12.9
7	0106	3.6	22	0006	4.5
SA	0700	12.8	SU	0600	11.7
	1324	1.3		1224	2.1
	2006	14.1		1900	13.1
8	0224	3.0	23	0112	4.0
SU	0818	12.0	M	0706	11.0
	1424	2.3		1318	3.0
	2100	14.3		1948	13.5
9	0330	2.1	24	0218	3.0
M	0930	11.7	TU	0824	10.7
	1524	3.2		1412	3.6
	2148	14.7		2042	14.1
10	0424	1.2	25	0324	1.8
TU	1042	11.7	W	0942	11.0
	1618	3.7		1512	4.0
	2236	14.9		2136	14.9
11	0518	0.3	26	0424	0.3
W	1136	12.0	TH	1054	11.6
	1706	4.1		1618	4.0
	2324	15.2		2230	15.8
12	0600	-0.5	27	0524	-1.3
TH	1224	12.3	F	1154	12.5
	1754	4.2		1712	3.7
				2324	16.7
13	0006	15.3	28	0612	-2.6
F	0642	-0.9	SA	1248	13.5
	1312	12.6		1812	3.3
	1830	4.3			
14	0042	15.4	29	0018	17.5
SA	0718	-1.2	SU	0706	-3.6
	1348	12.8		1336	14.3
	1912	4.3		1906	2.7
15	0118	15.4	30	0112	18.1
SU	0754	-1.3	M	0754	-4.2
	1424	12.9		1424	14.9
	1948	4.3		1954	2.3

TIME MERIDIAN 120° W. 0000 IS MIDNIGHT. 1200 IS NOON.
HEIGHTS ARE RECKONED FROM THE DATUM OF SOUNDINGS ON CHARTS OF THE LOCALITY WHICH IS MEAN LOWER LOW WATER.

FIG. 7-1 Excerpt showing reference station in tide table

TABLE 2.—TIDAL DIFFERENCES AND OTHER CONSTANTS

No.	PLACE	POSITION		DIFFERENCES				RANGES		Mean Tide Level
		Lat.	Long.	Time		Height				
				High water	Low water	High water	Low water	Mean	Spring	
		° ′	° ′	h. m.	h. m.	feet	feet	feet	feet	feet
	BRITISH COLUMBIA—Continued	N.	W.	on KETCHIKAN, p.110						
	Prince Rupert—Continued									
				Time meridian, 120°W.						
	Wright Sound									
1151	Hartley Bay	53 26	129 15	-0 38	-0 28	+1.6	+3.4	11.2	14.3	10.5
	Douglas Channel									
1153	Kitimat	53 59	128 42	-0 34	-0 19	+2.4	+3.6	11.8	15.1	11.0
	Gardner Canal									
1154	Kemano Bay	53 31	128 07	-0 34	-0 19	+2.7	+3.6	12.1	15.5	11.2
	Grenville Channel									
1155	Lowe Inlet	53 33	129 35	-0 26	-0 15	+2.8	+4.0	11.8	14.9	11.4
	Principe Channel, etc.									
1157	Port Stephens	53 21	129 43	-0 36	-0 27	+0.5	+3.2	10.3	13.2	9.9
1159	Port Canaveral	53 35	130 09	-0 29	-0 21	+0.5	+3.2	10.3	13.2	9.9
1161	Beaver Passage	53 48	130 21	-0 20	-0 09	+3.7	+3.5	13.2	17.1	11.6
	Chatham Sound									
1163	Porcher Island	54 05	130 24	-0 24	-0 13	+3.6	+4.6	12.0	15.2	12.1
1165	Qlawdzeet Anchorage	54 12	130 46	-0 15	-0 10	+4.2	+4.3	12.9	16.6	12.3
1167	Prince Rupert	54 19	130 20	-0 07	-0 02	+4.6	+4.3	13.3	17.3	12.5
1169	Port Simpson	54 34	130 26	-0 07	-0 02	+3.9	+4.2	12.7	16.5	12.1
	Queen Charlotte Islands									
1171	Skidegate Inlet	53 15	132 04	+0 03	+0 08	+5.5	+4.8	13.7	17.7	13.2
1173	Tasu Sound	52 45	132 01	-0 36	-0 30	(*0.58+3.6)		7.5	9.4	8.2
	BRITISH COLUMBIA and ALASKA									
	Dixon Entrance									
	Graham Island, B.C.									
1175	Parry Passage	54 11	132 59	-0 38	-0 29	(*0.68+4.2)		8.9	11.2	9.6
1177	Wiah Point	54 07	132 19	-0 22	-0 19	(*0.79+3.8)		10.3	12.9	10.1
1179	Masset Harbor	53 59	132 08	+0 03	+0 14	(*0.58+2.0)		7.6	9.5	6.6
								Mean	Diurnal	
1181	Cape Muzon, Dall Island, Alaska	54 40	132 40	-0 13	-0 07	(*0.76+0.3)		9.9	12.1	6.4
1183	Nichols Bay, Alaska	54 43	132 08	-0 07	-0 07	-2.0	-0.1	11.1	13.4	6.9
1185	Cape Chacon, Alaska	54 42	132 01	-0 13	-0 04	-1.9	0.0	11.1	13.6	7.0
1187	Kelp Island Passage, Duke Island	54 53	131 18	-0 03	+0 04	-0.8	0.0	12.2	14.6	7.6
1189	Barren Island, Alaska	54 45	131 21	-0 14	-0 10	-1.4	0.0	11.6	13.9	7.3
1191	Cape Fox, Alaska	54 46	130 51	-0 15	-0 11	-0.8	-0.2	12.4	14.6	7.5
1193	Port Tongass, Tongass I., Alaska	54 46	130 44	-0 15	-0 14	-0.8	-0.2	12.4	14.6	7.5
1195	Nakat Harbor, Alaska	54 49	130 42	+0 02	+0 09	-0.7	-0.1	12.4	14.7	7.6
1197	Haystack Island, B. C	54 43	130 37	-0 13	-0 10	[1]-0.4	[1]0.0	12.6	15.0	7.8
	Port Simpson, B. C. (see No. 1169)	54 34	130 26	------	------	-----	-----	----	----	----
	Portland Canal, etc.									
1201	Wales Island (Cannery), Pearse Canal	54 47	130 33	-0 01	+0 05	[1]-0.1	[1]0.0	12.9	15.3	7.9
1203	Kumeon Bay, B. C	54 43	130 14	-0 05	-0 03	[1]+0.2	[1]0.0	13.2	15.6	8.1
1205	Mill Bay, Nass River, B. C	55 00	129 54	-0 07	+0 18	[1]+0.1	[1]-0.1	13.2	15.5	8.0
1207	Halibut Bay, Alaska	55 14	130 06	-0 05	-0 04	[1]+0.6	[1]+0.2	13.4	16.0	8.4
1209	Fords Cove, B. C	55 37	130 06	-0 02	-0 01	[1]+0.8	[1]+0.1	13.7	16.2	8.4
1211	Davis River entrance, Alaska	55 46	130 11	-0 01	+0 01	[1]+1.2	[1]0.0	14.2	16.6	8.6
1213	Stewart, B. C	55 55	129 48	-0 05	-0 03	[1]+1.4	[1]+0.1	14.3	16.8	8.7
	ALASKA									
	Revillagigedo Channel									
1215	Morse Cove, Duke Island	54 55	131 15	+0 04	+0 15	-0.6	0.0	12.4	14.8	7.7
1217	Kah Shakes Cove	55 03	130 59	-0 02	+0 03	-0.4	0.0	12.6	15.0	7.8
1219	Boca de Quadra	55 07	130 48	+0 01	+0 05	-0.4	-0.1	12.7	15.0	7.7
1221	Mary Island Anchorage	55 06	131 12	+0 01	-0 07	0.0	0.0	13.0	15.4	8.0
1223	Hassler Harbor, Annette Island	55 13	131 26	-0 01	-0 03	+0.1	0.0	13.1	15.5	8.0
1224	Coon Island, George Inlet	55 28	131 30	-0 06	-0 07	-0.1	0.0	12.9	15.3	7.9
1225	Gnat Cove, Carroll Inlet	55 23	131 20	+0 02	-0 06	0.0	0.0	13.0	15.4	8.0

*Ratio. Multiply heights at reference station by this ratio and then apply the accompanying correction.

[1]Heights are referred to mean lower low water, the datum of soundings on Coast and Geodetic Survey charts.

FIG. 7-2 Excerpt showing tidal differences for specific locations

Other governments publish similar tables of tidal currents for their own coasts and waterways.

How to Use the Tide Tables Fig. 7–1 shows an actual page of tide predictions for April, May, and June (the year is unimportant here) for the reference station of Ketchikan, Alaska. Remember that this and other tables in this book are examples only; for actual navigation you must use your own table for the current year. Fig. 7–2 is a sample page from "Table 2," giving data for a number of secondary locations, and Fig. 7–3 is "Table 3" for interpolating the tide at any time between high and low tide. At the back of the actual volume of tide tables is an index, not reproduced here, which gives the name and reference number of all secondary locations.

***Example* •** Find the times and heights of high and low water on April 1 at Porcher Island in Chatham Sound. The following steps are recommended as standard procedure:

Step 1. Look in index at the back for the number of Porcher Island. It is found to be no. 1163.

Step 2. Secondary locations are listed in numerical order. Locate no. 1163 in "Table 2," (Fig. 7–2) and note that the reference station is Ketchikan, Alaska.

Step 3. Go to tide table for Ketchikan (Fig. 7–1), and note that April 1 is found at the top. Copy the data for Ketchikan as shown on the left side of the form below.

Step 4. Go back to "Table 2" (Fig. 7–2) and copy the differences for Porcher Island in the middle section of the form below.

Step 5. Apply the differences for Porcher Island to the data for Ketchikan and complete the right side of the form.

TABLE 3.—HEIGHT OF TIDE AT ANY TIME

Duration of rise or fall, see footnote.	TIME FROM THE NEAREST HIGH WATER OR LOW WATER														
h.m.	*h.m.*	*h.m.*	*h.m.*	*h.m.*	*h.m.*	*h.m.*	*h.m.*	*h.m.*	*h.m.*	*h.m.*	*h.m.*	*h.m.*	*h.m.*	*h.m.*	*h.m.*
4 00	0 08	0 16	0 24	0 32	0 40	0 48	0 56	1 04	1 12	1 20	1 28	1 36	1 44	1 52	2 00
4 20	0 09	0 17	0 26	0 35	0 43	0 52	1 01	1 09	1 18	1 27	1 35	1 44	1 53	2 01	2 10
4 40	0 09	0 19	0 28	0 37	0 47	0 56	1 05	1 15	1 24	1 33	1 43	1 52	2 01	2 11	2 20
5 00	0 10	0 20	0 30	0 40	0 50	1 00	1 10	1 20	1 30	1 40	1 50	2 00	2 10	2 20	2 30
5 20	0 11	0 21	0 32	0 43	0 53	1 04	1 15	1 25	1 36	1 47	1 57	2 08	2 19	2 29	2 40
5 40	0 11	0 23	0 34	0 45	0 57	1 08	1 19	1 31	1 42	1 53	2 05	2 16	2 27	2 39	2 50
6 00	0 12	0 24	0 36	0 48	1 00	1 12	1 24	1 36	1 48	2 00	2 12	2 24	2 36	2 48	3 00
6 20	0 13	0 25	0 38	0 51	1 03	1 16	1 29	1 41	1 54	2 07	2 19	2 32	2 45	2 57	3 10
6 40	0 13	0 27	0 40	0 53	1 07	1 20	1 33	1 47	2 00	2 13	2 27	2 40	2 53	3 07	3 20
7 00	0 14	0 28	0 42	0 56	1 10	1 24	1 38	1 52	2 06	2 20	2 34	2 48	3 02	3 16	3 30
7 20	0 15	0 29	0 44	0 59	1 13	1 28	1 43	1 57	2 12	2 27	2 41	2 56	3 11	3 25	3 40
7 40	0 15	0 31	0 46	1 01	1 17	1 32	1 47	2 03	2 18	2 33	2 49	3 04	3 19	3 35	3 50
8 00	0 16	0 32	0 48	1 04	1 20	1 36	1 52	2 08	2 24	2 40	2 56	3 12	3 28	3 44	4 00
8 20	0 17	0 33	0 50	1 07	1 23	1 40	1 57	2 13	2 30	2 47	3 03	3 20	3 37	3 53	4 10
8 40	0 17	0 35	0 52	1 09	1 27	1 44	2 01	2 19	2 36	2 53	3 11	3 28	3 45	4 03	4 20
9 00	0 18	0 36	0 54	1 12	1 30	1 48	2 06	2 24	2 42	3 00	3 18	3 36	3 54	4 12	4 30
9 20	0 19	0 37	0 56	1 15	1 33	1 52	2 11	2 29	2 48	3 07	3 25	3 44	4 03	4 21	4 40
9 40	0 19	0 39	0 58	1 17	1 37	1 56	2 15	2 35	2 54	3 13	3 33	3 52	4 11	4 31	4 50
10 00	0 20	0 40	1 00	1 20	1 40	2 00	2 20	2 40	3 00	3 20	3 40	4 00	4 20	4 40	5 00
10 20	0 21	0 41	1 02	1 23	1 43	2 04	2 25	2 45	3 06	3 27	3 47	4 08	4 29	4 49	5 10
10 40	0 21	0 43	1 04	1 25	1 47	2 08	2 29	2 51	3 12	3 33	3 55	4 16	4 37	4 59	5 20

Range of tide, see footnote.	CORRECTION TO HEIGHT														
Ft.	*Ft.*	*Ft.*	*Ft.*	*Ft.*	*Ft.*	*Ft.*	*Ft.*	*Ft.*	*Ft.*	*Ft.*	*Ft.*	*Ft.*	*Ft.*	*Ft.*	*Ft.*
0.5	0.0	0.0	0.0	0.0	0.0	0.0	0.1	0.1	0.1	0.1	0.1	0.2	0.2	0.2	0.2
1.0	0.0	0.0	0.0	0.0	0.1	0.1	0.1	0.2	0.2	0.2	0.3	0.3	0.4	0.4	0.5
1.5	0.0	0.0	0.0	0.1	0.1	0.1	0.2	0.2	0.3	0.4	0.4	0.5	0.6	0.7	0.8
2.0	0.0	0.0	0.0	0.1	0.1	0.2	0.3	0.3	0.4	0.5	0.6	0.7	0.8	0.9	1.0
2.5	0.0	0.0	0.1	0.1	0.2	0.2	0.3	0.4	0.5	0.6	0.7	0.9	1.0	1.1	1.2
3.0	0.0	0.0	0.1	0.1	0.2	0.3	0.4	0.5	0.6	0.8	0.9	1.0	1.2	1.3	1.5
3.5	0.0	0.0	0.1	0.2	0.2	0.3	0.4	0.6	0.7	0.9	1.0	1.2	1.4	1.6	1.8
4.0	0.0	0.0	0.1	0.2	0.3	0.4	0.5	0.7	0.8	1.0	1.2	1.4	1.6	1.8	2.0
4.5	0.0	0.0	0.1	0.2	0.3	0.4	0.6	0.7	0.9	1.1	1.3	1.6	1.8	2.0	2.2
5.0	0.0	0.1	0.1	0.2	0.3	0.5	0.6	0.8	1.0	1.2	1.5	1.7	2.0	2.2	2.5
5.5	0.0	0.1	0.1	0.2	0.4	0.5	0.7	0.9	1.1	1.4	1.6	1.9	2.2	2.5	2.8
6.0	0.0	0.1	0.1	0.3	0.4	0.6	0.8	1.0	1.2	1.5	1.8	2.1	2.4	2.7	3.0
6.5	0.0	0.1	0.2	0.3	0.4	0.6	0.8	1.1	1.3	1.6	1.9	2.2	2.6	2.9	3.2
7.0	0.0	0.1	0.2	0.3	0.5	0.7	0.9	1.2	1.4	1.8	2.1	2.4	2.8	3.1	3.5
7.5	0.0	0.1	0.2	0.3	0.5	0.7	1.0	1.2	1.5	1.9	2.2	2.6	3.0	3.4	3.8
8.0	0.0	0.1	0.2	0.3	0.5	0.8	1.0	1.3	1.6	2.0	2.4	2.8	3.2	3.6	4.0
8.5	0.0	0.1	0.2	0.4	0.6	0.8	1.1	1.4	1.8	2.1	2.5	2.9	3.4	3.8	4.2
9.0	0.0	0.1	0.2	0.4	0.6	0.9	1.2	1.5	1.9	2.2	2.7	3.1	3.6	4.0	4.5
9.5	0.0	0.1	0.2	0.4	0.6	0.9	1.2	1.6	2.0	2.4	2.8	3.3	3.8	4.3	4.8
10.0	0.0	0.1	0.2	0.4	0.7	1.0	1.3	1.7	2.1	2.5	3.0	3.5	4.0	4.5	5.0
10.5	0.0	0.1	0.3	0.5	0.7	1.0	1.3	1.7	2.2	2.6	3.1	3.6	4.2	4.7	5.2
11.0	0.0	0.1	0.3	0.5	0.7	1.1	1.4	1.8	2.3	2.8	3.3	3.8	4.4	4.9	5.5
11.5	0.0	0.1	0.3	0.5	0.8	1.1	1.5	1.9	2.4	2.9	3.4	4.0	4.6	5.1	5.8
12.0	0.0	0.1	0.3	0.5	0.8	1.1	1.5	2.0	2.5	3.0	3.6	4.1	4.8	5.4	6.0
12.5	0.0	0.1	0.3	0.5	0.8	1.2	1.6	2.1	2.6	3.1	3.7	4.3	5.0	5.6	6.2
13.0	0.0	0.1	0.3	0.6	0.9	1.2	1.7	2.2	2.7	3.2	3.9	4.5	5.1	5.8	6.5
13.5	0.0	0.1	0.3	0.6	0.9	1.3	1.7	2.2	2.8	3.4	4.0	4.7	5.3	6.0	6.8
14.0	0.0	0.2	0.3	0.6	0.9	1.3	1.8	2.3	2.9	3.5	4.2	4.8	5.5	6.3	7.0
14.5	0.0	0.2	0.4	0.6	1.0	1.4	1.9	2.4	3.0	3.6	4.3	5.0	5.7	6.5	7.2
15.0	0.0	0.2	0.4	0.6	1.0	1.4	1.9	2.5	3.1	3.8	4.4	5.2	5.9	6.7	7.5
15.5	0.0	0.2	0.4	0.7	1.0	1.5	2.0	2.6	3.2	3.9	4.6	5.4	6.1	6.9	7.8
16.0	0.0	0.2	0.4	0.7	1.1	1.5	2.1	2.6	3.3	4.0	4.7	5.5	6.3	7.2	8.0
16.5	0.0	0.2	0.4	0.7	1.1	1.6	2.1	2.7	3.4	4.1	4.9	5.7	6.5	7.4	8.2
17.0	0.0	0.2	0.4	0.7	1.1	1.6	2.2	2.8	3.5	4.2	5.0	5.9	6.7	7.6	8.5
17.5	0.0	0.2	0.4	0.8	1.2	1.7	2.2	2.9	3.6	4.4	5.2	6.0	6.9	7.8	8.8
18.0	0.0	0.2	0.4	0.8	1.2	1.7	2.3	3.0	3.7	4.5	5.3	6.2	7.1	8.1	9.0
18.5	0.1	0.2	0.5	0.8	1.2	1.8	2.4	3.1	3.8	4.6	5.5	6.4	7.3	8.3	9.2
19.0	0.1	0.2	0.5	0.8	1.3	1.8	2.4	3.1	3.9	4.8	5.6	6.6	7.5	8.5	9.5
19.5	0.1	0.2	0.5	0.8	1.3	1.9	2.5	3.2	4.0	4.9	5.8	6.7	7.7	8.7	9.8
20.0	0.1	0.2	0.5	0.9	1.3	1.9	2.6	3.3	4.1	5.0	5.9	6.9	7.9	9.0	10.0

Obtain from the predictions the high water and low water, one of which is before and the other after the time for which the height is required. The difference between the times of occurrence of these tides is the duration of rise or fall, and the difference between their heights is the range of tide for the above table. Find the difference between the time of the nearest high or low water and the time for which the height is required.

Enter the table with the duration of rise or fall, printed in heavy-faced type, which most nearly agrees with the actual value, and on that horizontal line find the time from the nearest high or low water which agrees most nearly with the corresponding actual difference. The correction sought is in the column directly below, on the line with the range of tide.

When the nearest tide is high water, subtract the correction
When the nearest tide is low water, add the correction.

FIG. 7-3 Excerpt from tide table to determine tide at any time

TIDES AT KETCHIKAN		DIFFERENCES			TIDES AT PORCHER ISLAND	
Time	Ht.	Tide	Time	Ht.	Time	Ht.
0036	15.2 ft.	High	-24^m	+3.6 ft.	0012	18.8 ft.
0646	0.7 ft.	Low	-13^m	+4.6 ft.	0633	5.3 ft.
1254	15.4 ft.	High	-24^m	+3.6 ft.	1230	19.0 ft.
1854	−0.2 ft.	Low	-13^m	+4.6 ft.	1841	4.4 ft.

Next find the height of tide at Porcher Island on April 1 at 0400. For this, it is convenient to use "Table 3" (Fig. 7–3), which is self-explanatory:

Time to nearest low water is $0633 - 0400 = 2^h33^m$

Duration of rise or fall is $0633 - 0012 = 6^h21^m$

Range of tide is 18.8 ft. — 5.3 ft. = 13.5 ft.

From "Table 3" (Fig. 7–3), correction to height of tide at low water is 4.7 ft.

Height of tide at 0400 is therefore $5.3 + 4.7 = 10$ ft. Remember that the figures given in both the tide tables and the tidal current tables are projected figures. They can change considerably due to local weather conditions. If your draft is such that 6 inches makes a difference, *don't go that way or wait for a more favorable tide!*

Tidal Current Tables Similar to the tide tables, *Tidal Current Tables* give data for a number of reference stations and auxiliary data for a much larger number of individual locations. Fig. 7–4 shows data for the reference station at Seymour Narrows, British Columbia, for March and April; Fig. 7–5, tidal current differences for a number of individual locations based on Seymour Narrows ("Table 2"); and "Table 3" (Fig. 7–6) for interpolating the current at any time. At the back of the volume itself is an index (not reproduced here) to the reference numbers of individual stations.

Example • Find the currents at Race Point in Georgia Straits on March 1. It helps to follow these steps:

Step 1. Find reference number of Race Point in the index. It is no. 605.

Step 2. Locate no. 605, Race Point, on "Table 2" (Fig. 7–5), and note that the reference station is Seymour Narrows.

Step 3. Write down data for Seymour Narrows for March 1 (Fig. 7–4).

Step 4. Set up differences for Race Point as shown in the following table and determine desired information.

Note that whereas the tide tables usually give an amount in feet to be applied to the tabulated values, except where an asterisk (*) indicates that the correction figure is a *ratio,* the *Tidal Current Tables* always indicate velocity differences as a ratio, found in the column headed "Velocity ratio."

SEYMOUR NARROWS			RACE POINT				
Time	Current, Knots	Flood, Ebb, or Slack	Time Difference: Slack +5m Time	Time Difference: Max. Curr. +5m Time	Velocity Ratio: Flood 0.7 Current, knots	Velocity Ratio: Ebb 0.7 Current, knots	Direction
0025	9.9	F		0030	6.9		125°
0400		S	0405				
0710	8.7	E		0715		6.1	305°
1020		S	1025				
1250	5.5	F		1255	3.9		125°
1530		S	1535				
1855	8.7	E		1900		6.1	305°
2145		S	2150				

Next, find the strength of the current at Race Point at 0200 on March 1. For this we use "Table 3" (Fig. 7–6).

Interval between slack and maximum current = 0400 — 0025 = 3^h35^m

Interval between slack and desired time = 0400 — 0200 = 2^h00^m

From "Table B," the factor f is 0.8

Current at 0200 is therefore $9.9 \times 0.8 = 7.9$ knots

SEYMOUR NARROWS, BRITISH COLUMBIA

F–FLOOD, DIR. 180° TRUE   E–EBB, DIR. 0° TRUE

MARCH

DAY	SLACK WATER TIME H.M.	MAXIMUM CURRENT TIME H.M.	MAXIMUM CURRENT VEL. KNOTS
1		0025	9.9F
SA	0400	0710	8.7E
	1020	1250	5.5F
	1530	1855	8.7E
	2145		
2		0105	10.7F
SU	0430	0740	9.7E
	1045	1325	6.9F
	1610	1935	9.7E
	2225		
3		0140	11.3F
M	0500	0810	10.5E
	1115	1355	8.2F
	1650	2010	10.5E
	2305		
4		0210	11.6F
TU	0530	0840	11.2E
	1145	1430	9.4F
	1730	2045	10.9E
	2345		
5		0245	11.5F
W	0600	0910	11.6E
	1215	1505	10.4F
	1815	2125	11.0E
6	0025	0320	11.0F
TH	0630	0945	11.7E
	1250	1545	11.0F
	1855	2205	10.6E
7	0105	0400	10.0F
F	0700	1020	11.5E
	1325	1630	11.2F
	1945	2250	9.8E
8	0150	0440	8.7F
SA	0735	1100	11.0E
	1405	1715	11.0F
	2040	2340	8.6E
9	0245	0525	7.0F
SU	0810	1140	10.1E
	1455	1810	10.5F
	2145		
10		0040	7.4E
M	0350	0620	5.4F
	0900	1235	9.1E
	1550	1915	10.0F
	2255		
11		0155	6.6E
TU	0510	0735	4.2F
	1000	1340	8.2E
	1700	2030	9.8F
12	0015	0315	6.7E
W	0635	0855	3.9F
	1115	1500	8.0E
	1810	2140	10.2F
13	0125	0430	7.7E
TH	0750	1015	4.7F
	1245	1620	8.6E
	1925	2250	11.1F
14	0225	0530	9.3E
F	0845	1120	6.3F
	1400	1730	9.8E
	2025	2345	12.0F
15	0310	0620	10.8E
SA	0930	1210	8.2F
	1505	1825	11.1E
	2120		

DAY	SLACK WATER TIME H.M.	MAXIMUM CURRENT TIME H.M.	MAXIMUM CURRENT VEL. KNOTS
16		0035	12.7F
SU	0355	0705	12.1E
	1010	1300	10.0F
	1600	1915	12.2E
	2210		
17		0120	12.9F
M	0435	0745	13.0E
	1050	1340	11.4F
	1650	2000	12.7E
	2300		
18		0200	12.6F
TU	0510	0825	13.3E
	1125	1425	12.3F
	1735	2045	12.7E
	2340		
19		0240	11.8F
W	0545	0900	13.2E
	1200	1505	12.6F
	1820	2125	12.0E
20	0025	0315	10.6F
TH	0620	0935	12.5E
	1235	1540	12.2F
	1905	2205	10.9E
21	0110	0355	9.0F
F	0650	1010	11.4E
	1315	1625	11.4F
	1950	2250	9.5E
22	0155	0435	7.2F
SA	0725	1050	10.0E
	1355	1705	10.2F
	2040	2335	7.8E
23	0245	0515	5.4F
SU	0800	1130	8.3E
	1435	1755	8.9F
	2135		
24		0030	6.3E
M	0345	0605	3.6F
	0835	1215	6.7E
	1525	1850	7.6F
	2235		
25		0135	5.2E
TU	0505	0715	2.3F
	0925	1315	5.3E
	1625	2000	6.7F
	2350		
26		0300	4.8E
W	0635	0835	1.8F
	1045	1435	4.6E
	1735	2115	6.6F
27	0100	0415	5.4E
TH	0750	0955	2.3F
	1215	1555	4.8E
	1845	2215	7.1F
28	0155	0510	6.5E
F	0835	1055	3.6F
	1335	1700	5.9E
	1950	2310	8.0F
29	0240	0555	7.7E
SA	0905	1140	5.1F
	1430	1750	7.2E
	2040	2350	8.9F
30	0315	0630	8.9E
SU	0935	1220	6.9F
	1515	1830	8.6E
	2125		
31		0030	9.7F
M	0345	0700	10.0E
	1005	1255	8.6F
	1555	1910	9.8E
	2205		

APRIL

DAY	SLACK WATER TIME H.M.	MAXIMUM CURRENT TIME H.M.	MAXIMUM CURRENT VEL. KNOTS
1		0105	10.3F
TU	0415	0730	11.0E
	1035	1330	10.3F
	1635	1950	10.8E
	2245		
2		0140	10.5F
W	0445	0805	11.7E
	1105	1405	11.7F
	1715	2025	11.4E
	2325		
3		0215	10.4F
TH	0515	0835	12.1E
	1135	1440	12.7F
	1800	2105	11.5E
4	0010	0255	9.8F
F	0550	0910	12.2E
	1210	1520	13.2F
	1845	2150	11.1E
5	0055	0335	8.8F
SA	0620	0945	11.8E
	1250	1605	13.1F
	1930	2235	10.3E
6	0140	0415	7.5F
SU	0700	1025	11.1E
	1335	1650	12.5F
	2025	2325	9.2E
7	0235	0505	6.1F
M	0740	1115	10.0E
	1420	1745	11.5F
	2125		
8		0025	8.2E
TU	0345	0610	4.8F
	0835	1215	8.7E
	1520	1850	10.5F
	2230		
9		0135	7.6E
W	0500	0725	4.1F
	0950	1325	7.7E
	1630	2005	9.8F
	2340		
10		0255	7.8E
TH	0620	0845	4.5F
	1120	1450	7.4E
	1750	2115	9.8F
11	0045	0405	8.7E
F	0720	1000	5.9F
	1245	1610	8.1E
	1905	2220	10.1F
12	0145	0500	9.9E
SA	0815	1100	7.8F
	1400	1715	9.3E
	2010	2320	10.6F
13	0235	0550	11.2E
SU	0855	1155	9.8F
	1500	1810	10.6E
	2105		
14		0010	10.9F
M	0315	0635	12.2E
	0935	1240	11.5F
	1550	1900	11.6E
	2155		
15		0050	10.8F
TU	0355	0715	12.8E
	1015	1320	12.7F
	1640	1945	12.1E
	2245		

DAY	SLACK WATER TIME H.M.	MAXIMUM CURRENT TIME H.M.	MAXIMUM CURRENT VEL. KNOTS
16		0135	10.4F
W	0435	0750	12.9E
	1050	1400	13.4F
	1720	2025	12.0E
	2330		
17		0215	9.6F
TH	0505	0825	12.5E
	1125	1440	13.4F
	1805	2110	11.5E
18	0010	0250	8.5F
F	0540	0905	11.7E
	1200	1515	12.9F
	1845	2150	10.5E
19	0055	0330	7.2F
SA	0615	0940	10.5E
	1240	1555	11.9F
	1930	2230	9.3E
20	0140	0410	5.7F
SU	0645	1015	9.1E
	1315	1635	10.7F
	2015	2315	8.0E
21	0235	0450	4.2F
M	0720	1055	7.5E
	1355	1720	9.3F
	2105		
22		0010	6.8E
TU	0335	0545	3.0F
	0805	1145	6.0E
	1440	1810	7.9F
	2200		
23		0110	6.0E
W	0445	0650	2.1F
	0905	1240	4.8E
	1535	1915	6.9F
	2300		
24		0215	5.7E
TH	0605	0810	2.1F
	1025	1355	4.1E
	1645	2025	6.5F
25	0000	0325	6.1E
F	0700	0925	3.0F
	1200	1515	4.4E
	1800	2130	6.7F
26	0055	0420	6.9E
SA	0740	1020	4.5F
	1310	1625	5.4E
	1910	2225	7.2F
27	0140	0505	8.0E
SU	0815	1105	6.3F
	1410	1720	6.8E
	2010	2310	7.8F
28	0220	0540	9.1E
M	0850	1145	8.2F
	1455	1805	8.2E
	2100	2350	8.4F
29	0255	0615	10.2E
TU	0920	1220	10.2F
	1540	1845	9.5E
	2145		
30		0030	8.8F
W	0330	0650	11.2E
	0955	1300	11.9F
	1620	1930	10.6E
	2230		

TIME MERIDIAN 120° W. 0000 IS MIDNGIHT. 1200 IS NOON.

FIG. 7-4 Excerpt showing reference station in current table

TABLE 2.—CURRENT DIFFERENCES AND OTHER CONSTANTS

No.	PLACE	POSITION		TIME DIFFERENCES		VELOCITY RATIOS		MAXIMUM CURRENTS			
								Flood		Ebb	
		Lat.	Long.	Slack water	Maximum current	Maximum flood	Maximum ebb	Direction (true)	Average velocity	Direction (true)	Average velocity
		° ′	° ′	h. m.	h. m.			deg.	knots	deg.	knots
	GEORGIA STRAIT—Continued	**N.**	**W.**	**on BURRARD INLET, p.76**							
				Time meridian, 120°W.							
588	BURRARD INLET, First Narrows----------	49 19	123 08	Daily predictions				135	3.7	315	3.7
589	Second Narrows, Burrard Inlet---------	49 18	123 01	-0 10	-0 10	0.9	0.9	90	3.3	270	3.3
591	Seechelt Rapids-----------------------	49 45	123 55	+1 25	+1 25	1.8	1.8	150	6.5	330	6.5
				on SEYMOUR NARROWS, p.82							
593	Stevens Pass--------------------------	49 31	124 31	+0 15	+0 15	0.2	0.2	310	2.2	130	2.2
595	Cape Lazo-----------------------------	49 43	124 48	+0 15	+0 15	0.2	0.2	355	2.0	175	2.0
597	Kuhushan Point------------------------	49 53	125 04	+0 10	+0 10	0.2	0.2	325	2.0	145	2.0
599	Shelter Point-------------------------	49 57	125 10	+0 10	+0 10	0.2	0.2	145	2.0	325	2.0
	DISCOVERY PASSAGE										
601	Off Cape Mudge------------------------	50 00	125 14	+0 15	+0 15	0.5	0.5	165	5.0	345	5.0
603	Orange Point--------------------------	50 04	125 17	+0 10	+0 10	0.5	0.5	145	5.0	325	5.0
605	Race Point----------------------------	50 07	125 20	+0 05	+0 05	0.7	0.7	125	6.5	305	6.5
607	SEYMOUR NARROWS-----------------------	50 08	125 21	Daily predictions				180	9.2	0	9.8
609	Separation Head-----------------------	50 11	125 22	-0 05	-0 05	0.4	0.4	170	3.4	350	3.6
611	Otter Point---------------------------	50 16	125 25	-0 10	-0 10	0.3	0.3	170	2.5	350	2.5
613	Chatham Point-------------------------	50 20	125 27	-0 20	-0 20	0.3	0.3	165	2.5	345	2.5
	JOHNSTONE STRAIT										
615	Ripple Point--------------------------	50 22	125 35	-0 40	-0 40	0.4	0.4	105	3.4	285	3.6
617	Camp Point----------------------------	50 24	125 51	-1 00	-1 00	0.4	0.4	90	3.4	270	3.6
619	Race Passage†-------------------------	50 23	125 53	-1 00	-1 00	0.5	0.5	110	4.8	290	5.2
621	Current Passage-----------------------	50 25	125 54	-1 00	-1 00	0.5	0.5	120	4.8	300	5.2
623	Ransom Point--------------------------	50 28	126 06	-1 00	-1 00	0.3	0.3	110	2.5	290	2.5
625	Off Broken Island---------------------	50 30	126 17	-1 00	-1 00	0.3	0.3	100	2.5	280	2.5
627	Off Robson Bight----------------------	50 30	126 35	-1 15	-1 15	0.3	0.3	100	2.5	280	2.5
629	Ella Point, Weynton Passage-----------	50 33	126 48	-1 25	-1 25	0.4	0.4	105	3.9	285	4.1
	BROUGHTON STRAIT										
631	Race Passage, Cormorant Island--------	50 35	126 54	-1 30	-1 30	0.4	0.4	165	3.9	345	4.1
633	Leonard Point, Cormorant Island-------	50 36	126 58	-1 35	-1 35	0.3	0.3	90	2.5	270	2.5
635	Ledge Point---------------------------	50 36	127 04	-1 40	-1 40	0.3	0.3	110	2.5	290	2.5
637	Pulteney Point------------------------	50 37	127 10	-1 45	-1 45	0.3	0.3	120	2.5	300	2.5
	QUEEN CHARLOTTE STRAIT										
639	False Head, 2 miles north from--------	50 41	127 17	-2 20	-2 20	0.3	0.3	130	2.5	310	2.5
641	Dillon Point, 1 mile north from-------	50 46	127 25	-2 30	-2 30	0.3	0.3	110	2.5	290	2.5
643	Gordon Channel------------------------	50 55	127 40	-2 40	-2 40	0.3	0.3	125	2.5	305	2.5
	GOLETAS CHANNEL										
645	Duval Point---------------------------	50 48	127 30	-3 05	-3 05	0.3	0.3	110	2.5	290	2.5
647	Boxer Point---------------------------	50 49	127 39	-3 15	-3 15	0.3	0.3	110	2.5	290	2.5
649	Lemon Point---------------------------	50 51	127 46	-3 20	-3 20	0.3	0.3	110	2.5	290	2.5
651	Heath Point---------------------------	50 53	127 53	-3 25	-3 25	0.3	0.3	110	3.0	290	3.0
653	Nawhitti Bar--------------------------	50 54	128 00	-4 40	-4 40	0.4	0.4	100	4.0	280	4.0
	PASSAGES NORTH of VANCOUVER ISLAND										
655	Surge Narrows, Okisollo Channel-------	50 14	125 10	-0 45	-0 45	0.7	0.7	140	7.0	320	7.0
657	Hole-in-the-Wall, Okisollo Channel----	50 18	125 14	-0 55	-0 55	0.8	0.8	60	7.5	240	7.5
659	Rapids, near Pulton Bay, Okisollo Chan	50 19	125 16	-0 55	-0 55	0.7	0.7	70	6.5	250	6.5
661	Arran Rapids, north of Stuart Island--	50 25	125 09	-0 45	-0 45	0.7	0.7	65	7.0	245	7.0
663	Yuculta Rapids, SW. of Stuart Island--	50 21	125 10	-0 40	-0 40	0.5	0.5	145	5.0	325	5.0
665	Yucluetaw Rapids, Cordero Channel-----	50 25	125 15	-0 55	-0 55	0.6	0.6	125	6.0	305	6.0
667	Godwin Point, Cordero Channel---------	50 28	125 25	-0 55	-0 55	0.2	0.2	50	2.2	230	2.2
669	Shell Point, Blind Channel------------	50 26	125 31	-1 10	-1 10	0.5	0.5	170	5.0	350	5.0
671	Green Point Rapids, Cordero Channel---	50 25	125 32	-1 30	-1 30	0.5	0.5	145	5.0	325	5.0
673	Whirlpool Rapids, Wellbore Channel----	50 27	125 47	-1 50	-1 50	0.6	0.6	185	6.0	5	6.0
675	Shaw Point, Sunderland Channel--------	50 28	125 56	-1 05	-1 05	0.2	0.2	60	1.5	240	1.5
677	Root Point, Chatham Channel-----------	50 35	126 12	-1 05	-1 05	0.6	0.6	110	5.5	290	5.5
679	Littleton Point, Chatham Channel------	50 37	126 17	-1 05	-1 05	0.4	0.4	130	3.5	310	3.5
681	Ripple Bluff, Knight Inlet------------	50 38	126 31	-1 15	-1 15	0.3	0.3	105	2.5	285	2.5
683	Owl Island, main ent. to Knight Inlet-	50 38	126 41	-1 20	-1 20	0.3	0.3	120	2.5	300	2.5

† Dangerous eddy current and tide rips are reported to occur between Helmcken Island and Ripple Shoal around the time of ebb strength.

FIG. 7-5 Excerpt showing current differences for specific locations

TABLE 3.—VELOCITY OF CURRENT AT ANY TIME

Table A

Interval between slack and desired time	Interval between slack and maximum current													
	h. m. 1 20	*h. m.* 1 40	*h. m.* 2 00	*h. m.* 2 20	*h. m.* 2 40	*h. m.* 3 00	*h. m.* 3 20	*h. m.* 3 40	*h. m.* 4 00	*h. m.* 4 20	*h. m.* 4 40	*h. m.* 5 00	*h. m.* 5 20	*h. m.* 5 40
h. m.	*f.*	*f.*	*f.*	*f.*	*f.*	*f.*	*f.*	*f.*	*f.*	*f.*	*f.*	*f.*	*f.*	*f.*
0 20	0.4	0.3	0.3	0.2	0.2	0.2	0.2	0.1	0.1	0.1	0.1	0.1	0.1	0.1
0 40	0.7	0.6	0.5	0.4	0.4	0.3	0.3	0.3	0.3	0.2	0.2	0.2	0.2	0.2
1 00	0.9	0.8	0.7	0.6	0.6	0.5	0.5	0.4	0.4	0.4	0.3	0.3	0.3	0.3
1 20	1.0	1.0	0.9	0.8	0.7	0.6	0.6	0.5	0.5	0.5	0.4	0.4	0.4	0.4
1 40	----	1.0	1.0	0.9	0.8	0.8	0.7	0.7	0.6	0.6	0.5	0.5	0.5	0.4
2 00	----	----	1.0	1.0	0.9	0.9	0.8	0.8	0.7	0.7	0.6	0.6	0.6	0.5
2 20	----	----	----	1.0	1.0	0.9	0.9	0.8	0.8	0.7	0.7	0.7	0.6	0.6
2 40	----	----	----	----	1.0	1.0	1.0	0.9	0.9	0.8	0.8	0.7	0.7	0.7
3 00	----	----	----	----	----	1.0	1.0	1.0	0.9	0.9	0.8	0.8	0.8	0.7
3 20	----	----	----	----	----	----	1.0	1.0	1.0	0.9	0.9	0.9	0.8	0.8
3 40	----	----	----	----	----	----	----	1.0	1.0	1.0	0.9	0.9	0.9	0.9
4 00	----	----	----	----	----	----	----	----	1.0	1.0	1.0	1.0	0.9	0.9
4 20	----	----	----	----	----	----	----	----	----	1.0	1.0	1.0	1.0	0.9
4 40	----	----	----	----	----	----	----	----	----	----	1.0	1.0	1.0	1.0
5 00	----	----	----	----	----	----	----	----	----	----	----	1.0	1.0	1.0
5 20	----	----	----	----	----	----	----	----	----	----	----	----	1.0	1.0
5 40	----	----	----	----	----	----	----	----	----	----	----	----	----	1.0

Table B

Interval between slack and desired time	Interval between slack and maximum current													
	h. m. 1 20	*h. m.* 1 40	*h. m.* 2 00	*h. m.* 2 20	*h. m.* 2 40	*h. m.* 3 00	*h. m.* 3 20	*h. m.* 3 40	*h. m.* 4 00	*h. m.* 4 20	*h. m.* 4 40	*h. m.* 5 00	*h. m.* 5 20	*h. m.* 5 40
h. m.	*f.*	*f.*	*f.*	*f.*	*f.*	*f.*	*f.*	*f.*	*f.*	*f.*	*f.*	*f.*	*f.*	*f.*
0 20	0.5	0.4	0.4	0.3	0.3	0.3	0.3	0.3	0.2	0.2	0.2	0.2	0.2	0.2
0 40	0.8	0.7	0.6	0.5	0.5	0.5	0.4	0.4	0.4	0.4	0.3	0.3	0.3	0.3
1 00	0.9	0.8	0.8	0.7	0.7	0.6	0.6	0.5	0.5	0.5	0.4	0.4	0.4	0.4
1 20	1.0	1.0	0.9	0.8	0.8	0.7	0.7	0.6	0.6	0.6	0.5	0.5	0.5	0.5
1 40	----	1.0	1.0	0.9	0.9	0.8	0.8	0.7	0.7	0.7	0.6	0.6	0.6	0.6
2 00	----	----	1.0	1.0	0.9	0.9	0.9	0.8	0.8	0.7	0.7	0.7	0.7	0.6
2 20	----	----	----	1.0	1.0	1.0	0.9	0.9	0.8	0.8	0.8	0.7	0.7	0.7
2 40	----	----	----	----	1.0	1.0	1.0	0.9	0.9	0.9	0.8	0.8	0.8	0.7
3 00	----	----	----	----	----	1.0	1.0	1.0	0.9	0.9	0.9	0.9	0.8	0.8
3 20	----	----	----	----	----	----	1.0	1.0	1.0	1.0	0.9	0.9	0.9	0.8
3 40	----	----	----	----	----	----	----	1.0	1.0	1.0	1.0	0.9	0.9	0.9
4 00	----	----	----	----	----	----	----	----	1.0	1.0	1.0	1.0	0.9	0.9
4 20	----	----	----	----	----	----	----	----	----	1.0	1.0	1.0	1.0	0.9
4 40	----	----	----	----	----	----	----	----	----	----	1.0	1.0	1.0	1.0
5 00	----	----	----	----	----	----	----	----	----	----	----	1.0	1.0	1.0
5 20	----	----	----	----	----	----	----	----	----	----	----	----	1.0	1.0
5 40	----	----	----	----	----	----	----	----	----	----	----	----	----	1.0

Use Table A for all places except those listed below for Table B.
Use Table B for Deception Pass, Seymour Narrows, Sergius Narrows, Isanotski Strait, and all stations in Table 2 which are referred to them.

1. From predictions find the time of slack water and the time and velocity of maximum current (flood or ebb), one of which is immediately before and the other after the time for which the velocity is desired.
2. Find the interval of time between the above slack and maximum current, and enter the top of Table A or B with the interval which most nearly agrees with this value.
3. Find the interval of time between the above slack and the time desired, and enter the side of Table A or B with the interval which most nearly agrees with this value.
4. Find, in the table, the factor corresponding to the above two intervals, and multiply the maximum velocity by this factor. The result will be the approximate velocity at the time desired.

FIG. 7-6 Excerpt from current table to determine current at any time

Practice Problems •

1. Find the high and low tides for Kitimat (no. 1153 in "Table 2," Fig. 7–2) for June 7. Also, what will be the height of the tide at Kitimat at 1700?
2. Find the currents at Ripple Point (no. 615 in "Table 2," Fig. 7–5) on April 30.

Chapter 8
Piloting

Piloting is the art of conducting your ship safely in and out of harbors and through coastal waters, and it is indeed a fine art. With the enormous increase in boating and shipping of all kinds, the waterways are crowded, and unless each skipper knows what to do and can be depended on to do it, trouble is sure to develop. Never lose sight of that most important dictum: *Bring the ship back!* The art of piloting consists essentially of two parts: Stay out of trouble, and get to your destination safely. The first part is accomplished by everlasting alertness and never forgetting that basic principle: *Stay ahead of the ship!*

To accomplish this, the skipper must know his vessel inside out, the way she handles under all conditions of wind and wave and current, her limitations and peculiarities under specific conditions. He must know his rights and obligations in traffic and be able intelligently to appraise each situation as it occurs, and always be ready to stop his engines and drift or back up until a snarled-up traffic condition resolves itself. He must never blindly forge ahead into a situation from which he cannot extricate himself, and above all, he must *always have an avenue of escape.* If an intended maneuver does not work out, he must have a safe alternative planned *ahead of time,* and under the rule of good seamanship know when to take action, even in contravention of the Rules of the Road, to avoid collision.

In a study of avoidable ship losses, made by the U.S. Navy and reported in Bowditch, *The American Practical Navigator,* the following list of faults and errors were given as those most commonly responsible for collisions or strandings:

1. Failure to obtain or evaluate soundings
2. Failure to identify aids to navigation
3. Failure to use all navigational aids
4. Failure to correct charts from *Notices to Mariners*

5. Failure to adjust compass or keep an accurate deviation table
6. Failure to apply deviation, or to apply it correctly
7. Failure to apply variation or allow for changes in variation
8. Failure to keep a dead reckoning plot on the chart
9. Failure to check compass readings at frequent and regular intervals
10. Failure to plot information received
11. Failure to properly evaluate information received
12. Poor judgment
13. Failure to do own navigating (following another vessel)
14. Failure to obtain and use available information on charts
15. Poor ship organization
16. *Failure to keep ahead of the vessel*

Piloting in coastal waters calls for experience, judgment, and the ability to work rapidly and make instant decisions, to correctly interpret all available information, and to exercise common sense. A large order! The wise navigator is always observant of everything around him, even under the most favorable conditions—especially then! He makes sure he always knows where he is and never allows himself to become careless. He keeps an eye on the fog bank or the approaching squall and is ever ready to go to the chart and plot a safe course to shelter. Then, when visibility is poor and conditions difficult, the knowledge, experience, and ability developed at favorable times becomes invaluable.

I highly recommend reading chapter 23, "The Practice of Marine Navigation," in Bowditch. If you are going to sea at all, be a *sailor*. Observe the courtesies and traditions of the sea, have respect for the rights of others, and always be ready to assist anyone in trouble.

Aids to Navigation Every government provides certain aids to navigation in coastal waters. Lighthouses and radio beacons guide the navigator in his approach from the open ocean. Significant sea buoys indicate locations of harbors, waterways, and inlets. The safe channel into these are marked with channel buoys, obstruction buoys, turning buoys of various kinds and descriptions; and when the inner harbor is reached, there are anchorage buoys, quarantine buoys, and all sorts of special buoys marking special hazards to navigation. Many buoys are equipped with lights, whistles, bells, or horns to help the navigator identify them and their purpose. They have one thing in common: they are generally shown and described on your chart, so it becomes an absolute must for the skipper or navigator to study his chart carefully before entering any harbor or waterway, and to have his course of action carefully planned *ahead of time.*

Chart Symbols In this chapter there is a reprint of N.O. Chart #1, *Nautical Chart Symbols and Abbreviations,* which lists the types of symbols used on United States charts, including all kinds of aids to navigation as well as the symbols used to convey information regarding navigable waters, shorelines, structures on water as well as on land, soundings, etc. You must know Chart #1 forwards and backwards. Coming into a harbor on a dark night, it is too late to attempt looking up the meaning of that light you see flashing up ahead.

Lighted aids to navigation are distinguished by their *characteristic,* meaning the color or colors displayed and the sequence and duration of the periods of light and darkness; this description is always printed on the chart alongside the symbol for the particular light. The colors are usually white, red, or green. The light may be *fixed,* meaning that it burns steadily, or *flashing*—giving out a pattern of short or long flashes where the period of light is shorter than the period of darkness. If the duration of light is greater than that of darkness, the light is said to be *occulting.* Many different combinations of fixed, short or long flashing, and occulting lights are in use, but they all follow certain basic rules:

Fixed light—burns continuously
Flashing light—does not exceed 30 flashes per minute
Quick-flashing light—not less than 60 flashes per minute
Occulting light—period of light equal to or greater than period of darkness

Short flashes—period of light of about ½ second's duration
Long flash—period of light of about 2 seconds' duration
Alternating light—shows more than one color

In the case of lighthouses, the chart usually indicates the height of the light above sea level and the distance at which it can be seen out to sea by an observer at a height of 15 feet above the water. This can sometimes be used to approximate a vessel's distance off the light. When the light is first seen, the navigator may lower the height of his eye by squatting down. If the light disappears, he knows that he is at the limit of the range indicated on the chart. Like so many other time-honored devices from sailing ship days, this should be taken with a grain of salt. Wave action may raise or lower his eye level considerably, making the method quite inaccurate. Also, sometimes the luminous range of the light is less than the geographical range, so use caution and common sense.

Buoys In the American system, a cylindrical buoy with a flat top is called a *can*. It is always painted black and, if numbered, it has an *odd* number: 1, 3, 5, 7, etc. A cone-shaped buoy is called a *nun*. It is always painted red and, if numbered, it has an *even* number: 2, 4, 6, 8, etc. When we approach an American harbor or waterway from the sea, the outermost buoy is usually a lighted bell buoy, painted black and bearing the number 1. Such buoys are frequently larger than channel buoys and made of steel latticework construction. Further in, the channel will be marked on the port, or left, hand by black cans, numbered successively 3, 5, 7, etc., while the starboard, or right, side of the channel will be marked by red nuns marked 2, 4, 6, etc.

Lights on channel buoys, if they are lighted, are usually red or white on the starboard side and white or green on the port hand. In addition, certain special buoys are known by their colors, as follows:

Quarantine—yellow
Anchorage—white
Fishnets—black and white horizontal bands
Dredging—white with green tops

Seadromes—yellow and black vertical stripes
Mid-channel—black and white vertical stripes
Junction or obstruction—red and black horizontal stripes

Generally speaking, vertical stripes mean that you can pass close to the buoy, while horizontal stripes mean you should give the buoy a wide berth.

Various Buoyage Systems You would think that civilized countries could agree on a uniform system of buoys for everybody everywhere, but this is far from the case. Even within the United States, the system varies. In general, there are two main systems in effect, *lateral* and *cardinal.* The lateral system is used mostly where the coastline is fairly even, with definite entrances to bays and waterways. There you find the sea buoys previously mentioned at the outer entrance to the passage, and channel buoys mark the way into the harbor or waterway. The cardinal system is used where there is more of a rocky coast with many outlying hazards, such as rocks, reefs, shoals, etc. Under this system each hazard is marked separately by four buoys forming a square around the hazard. In many countries, you will find a combination of the two systems.

In 1889 an International Marine Conference was held in Washington at which it was recommended that in the lateral system buoys on the port side, entering from seaward, should be black and, if lighted, should use green or white lights, and starboard buoys should be painted red and use red or white lights. Many countries, including the U.S., adopted these recommendations.

In 1936 a League of Nations subcommittee recommended the exact opposite colors and lights, calling it the *uniform system.* In this method, port buoys are red and starboard buoys are black, again entering from seaward. Nations, like people, tend to be contrary, so as of this writing many European countries are using the new uniform system, while the U.S., Canada, and most other countries follow the 1889 system. The only way to be sure is to *consult your chart.*

United States System Since not all waterways necessarily lead landward at right angles to the coast, the U.S. has established the convention that from "seaward" means in a clockwise direction, i.e. southerly direction along the Atlantic coast, northerly and westerly along the Gulf coast, and northerly along the Pacific coast. The same system holds for the intracoastal waterway.

Uniform System Since this can be either uniform lateral or uniform cardinal, it is important that you consult your chart carefully where both are in use in the same waters. Special *topmarks* are used on various kinds of buoys, but the main thing to remember is that in the uniform lateral system the color of channel buoys are reversed. In the cardinal system, four buoys are used to mark a hazard and they are placed exactly north, east, south, and west of the danger. Different shapes are used, and the north and west buoys are black and white, while the south and east buoys are red and white. Suffice it to say: *You cannot be too careful!*

UNIFORM LATERAL SYSTEM

Fairways and Channels

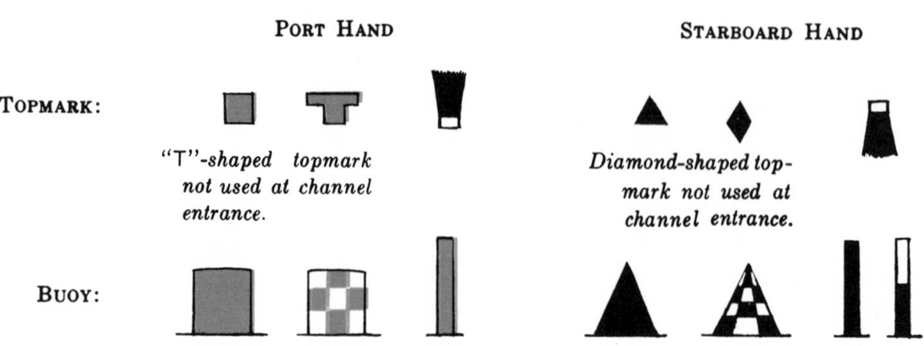

In secondary channels only, yellow *may be substituted for* white *in checkered buoys.*

	Port Hand	Starboard Hand
Marking:	Even numbers, commencing from seaward.	Odd numbers, commencing from seaward.
Light:	**Red, single flashing or occulting or group flashing or occulting, with a number of flashes or occultations up to four; or *white*, group flashing or occulting (2 or 4); both *red and white* with above characteristics.**	***White*, single flashing or occulting, or group flashing or occulting (3); or *green*, of a different character from wreck markings; or both *white and green* with the above characteristics.**

UNIFORM LATERAL SYSTEM

Middle Grounds

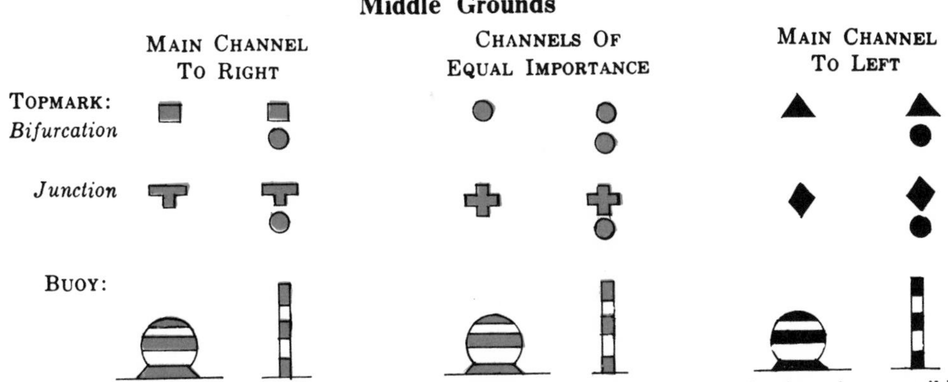

LIGHT: Distinctive where possible. Distinctive where possible. Distinctive where possible.

Mid Channel

TOPMARK: Shape optional, but not conical, cylindrical, or spherical.

BUOY: Shape optional, but not conical, cylindrical, or spherical.

COLOR: *Red-and-white* or *black-and-white* vertical stripes; topmark *red* or *black* to conform with buoy.

LIGHT: Different from neighboring lights.

UNIFORM CARDINAL SYSTEM

Danger Markings

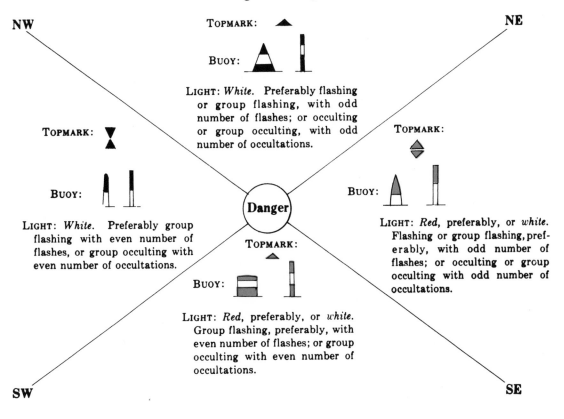

NW

NE

TOPMARK:

BUOY:

LIGHT: *White.* Preferably flashing or group flashing, with odd number of flashes; or occulting or group occulting, with odd number of occultations.

TOPMARK:

BUOY:

LIGHT: *White.* Preferably group flashing with even number of flashes, or group occulting with even number of occultations.

Danger

TOPMARK:

BUOY:

LIGHT: *Red*, preferably, or *white*. Flashing or group flashing, preferably, with odd number of flashes; or occulting or group occulting with odd number of occultations.

TOPMARK:

BUOY:

LIGHT: *Red*, preferably, or *white*. Group flashing, preferably, with even number of flashes; or group occulting with even number of occultations.

SW

SE

REVISED PRINTING, OCTOBER 1970

THIS PRINTING REFLECTS CORRECTIONS REPORTED IN NOTICE TO MARINERS 25, 1970

Chart No. 1

United States of America

NAUTICAL CHART SYMBOLS AND ABBREVIATIONS

U.S. DEPARTMENT OF COMMERCE
ENVIRONMENTAL SCIENCE SERVICES ADMINISTRATION
COAST AND GEODETIC SURVEY

GENERAL REMARKS

Chart No. 1 contains the standard symbols and abbreviations which have been approved for use on nautical charts published by the United States of America.

Symbols and abbreviations shown on Chart No. 1 apply to the regular nautical charts and may differ from those shown on certain reproductions and special charts. Symbols and abbreviations on certain reproductions and on foreign charts may be interpreted by reference to the Symbol Sheet or Chart No. 1 of the originating country.

Terms, symbols and abbreviations are numbered in accordance with a standard form approved by a Resolution of the Sixth International Hydrographic Conference, 1952.

Vertical figures indicate those items where the symbol and abbreviation are in accordance with the Resolutions of the International Hydrographic Conferences.

Slanting figures indicate no International Hydrographic Bureau symbol adopted.

Slanting figures underscored indicate U.S.A. and I.H.B. symbols do not agree.

Slanting figures asterisked indicate no U.S.A. symbol adopted.

An up-to-date compilation of symbols and abbreviations approved by resolutions of the International Hydrographic Conference is not currently available. Use of I.H.B. approved symbols and abbreviations by member nations is not mandatory.

Slanting letters in parentheses indicate that the items are in addition to those shown on the approved standard form.

Colors are optional for characterizing various features and areas on the charts.

Lettering styles and capitalization as used on Chart No. 1 are not always rigidly adhered to on the charts.

Longitudes are referred to the Meridian of Greenwich.

Scales are computed on the middle latitude of each chart, or on the middle latitude of a series of charts.

Buildings - A conspicuous feature on a building may be shown by a landmark symbol with descriptive note (See I-n & L-63). Prominent buildings that are of assistance to the mariner are crosshatched (See I-3a,5,47 & 66).

Shoreline is the line of Mean High Water, except in marsh or mangrove areas, where the outer edge of vegetation (berm line) is used. A heavy line (A-9) is used to represent a firm shoreline. A light line (A-7) represents a berm line.

Heights of land and conspicuous objects are given in feet above Mean High Water, unless otherwise stated in the title of the chart.

Depth Contours and Soundings may be shown in meters on charts of foreign waters.

Visibility of a light is in nautical miles for an observer's eye 15 feet above water level.

Buoys and Beacons - On entering a channel from seaward, buoys on starboard side are red with even numbers, on port side black with odd numbers. Lights on buoys on starboard side of channel are red or white, on port side white or green. Mid-channel buoys have black-and-white vertical stripes. Junction or obstruction buoys, which may be passed on either side, have red-and-black horizontal bands. This system does not always apply to foreign waters. The dot of the buoy symbol, the small circle of the light vessel and mooring buoy symbols, and the center of the beacon symbol indicate their positions.

Improved channels are shown by limiting dashed lines, the depth, month, and the year of latest examination being placed adjacent to the channel, except when tabulated.

U. S. Coast Pilots, Sailing Directions, Light Lists, Radio Aids, and related publications furnish information required by the navigator that cannot be shown conveniently on the nautical chart.

U. S. Nautical Chart Catalogs and Indexes list nautical charts, auxiliary maps, and related publications, and include general information (marginal notes, etc.) relative to the charts.

A glossary of foreign terms and abbreviations is generally given on the charts on which they are used, as well as in the Sailing Directions.

Charts already on issue will be brought into conformity as soon as opportunity affords.

All changes since the September 1963 edition of this publication are indicated by the symbol † in the margin immediately adjacent to the item affected.

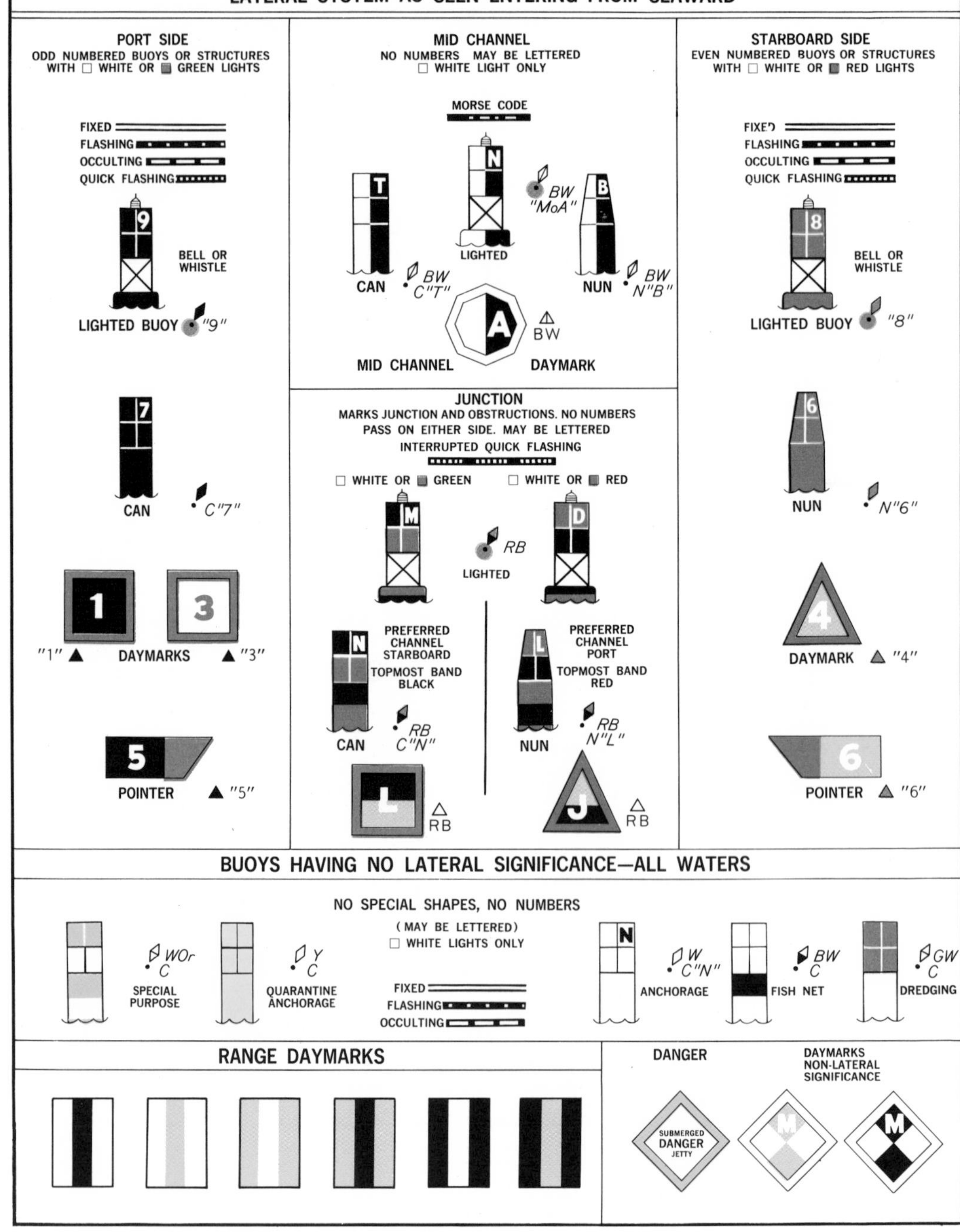
AIDS TO NAVIGATION ON NAVIGABLE WATERWAYS
except Western Rivers and Intracoastal Waterway
LATERAL SYSTEM AS SEEN ENTERING FROM SEAWARD
PORT SIDE
ODD NUMBERED BUOYS OR STRUCTURES
WITH WHITE OR GREEN LIGHTS
FIXED
FLASHING
OCCULTING
QUICK FLASHING
BELL OR WHISTLE
LIGHTED BUOY
"9"
CAN
C"7"
"1"
DAYMARKS
"3"
POINTER
"5"
MID CHANNEL
NO NUMBERS MAY BE LETTERED
WHITE LIGHT ONLY
MORSE CODE
BW
"MoA"
LIGHTED
CAN
BW
C"T"
NUN
BW
N"B"
BW
MID CHANNEL
DAYMARK
JUNCTION
MARKS JUNCTION AND OBSTRUCTIONS. NO NUMBERS
PASS ON EITHER SIDE. MAY BE LETTERED
INTERRUPTED QUICK FLASHING
WHITE OR GREEN
WHITE OR RED
RB
LIGHTED
PREFERRED CHANNEL STARBOARD
TOPMOST BAND BLACK
CAN
RB
C"N"
PREFERRED CHANNEL PORT
TOPMOST BAND RED
NUN
RB
N"L"
RB
RB
STARBOARD SIDE
EVEN NUMBERED BUOYS OR STRUCTURES
WITH WHITE OR RED LIGHTS
FIXED
FLASHING
OCCULTING
QUICK FLASHING
BELL OR WHISTLE
LIGHTED BUOY
"8"
NUN
N"6"
DAYMARK
"4"
POINTER
"6"
BUOYS HAVING NO LATERAL SIGNIFICANCE—ALL WATERS
NO SPECIAL SHAPES, NO NUMBERS
(MAY BE LETTERED)
WHITE LIGHTS ONLY
FIXED
FLASHING
OCCULTING
WOr
C
SPECIAL PURPOSE
Y
C
QUARANTINE ANCHORAGE
W
C"N"
ANCHORAGE
BW
C
FISH NET
GW
C
DREDGING
RANGE DAYMARKS
DANGER
SUBMERGED DANGER JETTY
DAYMARKS NON-LATERAL SIGNIFICANCE

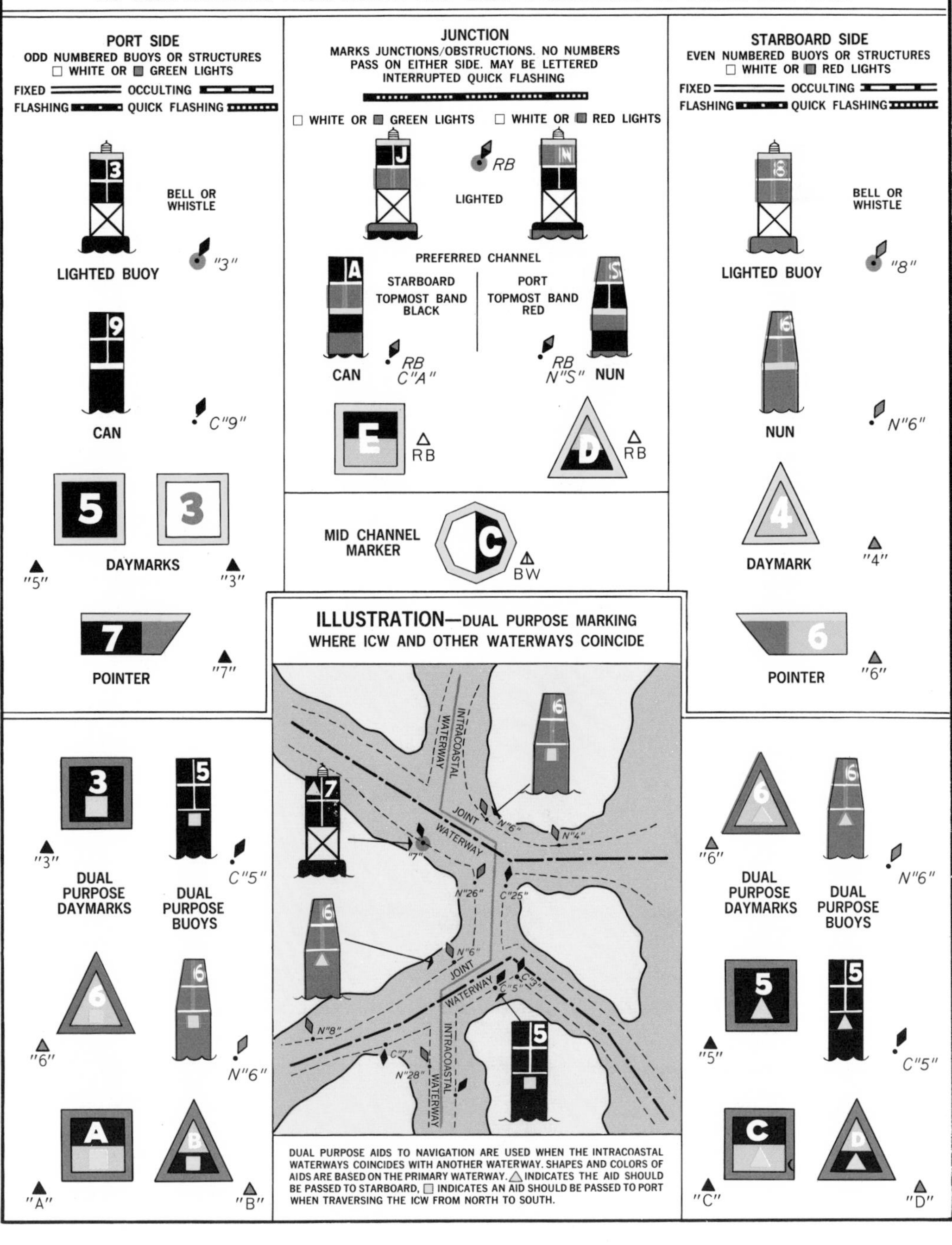
AIDS TO NAVIGATION ON THE INTRACOASTAL WATERWAY
AS SEEN ENTERING FROM NORTH AND EAST—PROCEEDING TO SOUTH AND WEST
PORT SIDE
ODD NUMBERED BUOYS OR STRUCTURES
WHITE OR GREEN LIGHTS
FIXED
OCCULTING
FLASHING
QUICK FLASHING
JUNCTION
MARKS JUNCTIONS/OBSTRUCTIONS. NO NUMBERS
PASS ON EITHER SIDE. MAY BE LETTERED
INTERRUPTED QUICK FLASHING
WHITE OR GREEN LIGHTS
WHITE OR RED LIGHTS
STARBOARD SIDE
EVEN NUMBERED BUOYS OR STRUCTURES
WHITE OR RED LIGHTS
BELL OR WHISTLE
LIGHTED BUOY
LIGHTED
PREFERRED CHANNEL
STARBOARD TOPMOST BAND BLACK
PORT TOPMOST BAND RED
CAN
NUN
DAYMARKS
DAYMARK
POINTER
MID CHANNEL MARKER
ILLUSTRATION—DUAL PURPOSE MARKING WHERE ICW AND OTHER WATERWAYS COINCIDE
INTRACOASTAL WATERWAY
JOINT WATERWAY
DUAL PURPOSE DAYMARKS
DUAL PURPOSE BUOYS
DUAL PURPOSE AIDS TO NAVIGATION ARE USED WHEN THE INTRACOASTAL WATERWAYS COINCIDES WITH ANOTHER WATERWAY. SHAPES AND COLORS OF AIDS ARE BASED ON THE PRIMARY WATERWAY. △ INDICATES THE AID SHOULD BE PASSED TO STARBOARD, □ INDICATES AN AID SHOULD BE PASSED TO PORT WHEN TRAVERSING THE ICW FROM NORTH TO SOUTH.

AIDS TO NAVIGATION ON WESTERN RIVERS

AS SEEN PROCEEDING IN THE DIRECTION (DESCENDING) OF RIVER FLOW

LEFT SIDE

☐ WHITE OR ■ RED LIGHTS
GROUP FLASHING (2)

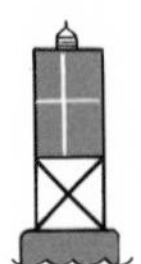

LIGHTED BUOY

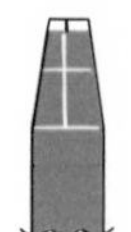

NUN

PASSING DAYMARK

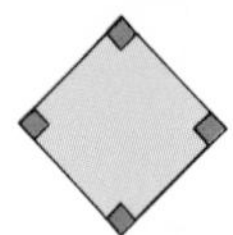

CROSSING DAYMARK

123.5

MILE BOARD

JUNCTION

MARKS JUNCTIONS AND OBSTRUCTIONS
PASS ON EITHER SIDE
INTERRUPTED QUICK FLASHING

☐ WHITE OR
■ RED LIGHTS

☐ WHITE OR
■ GREEN LIGHTS

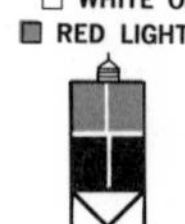

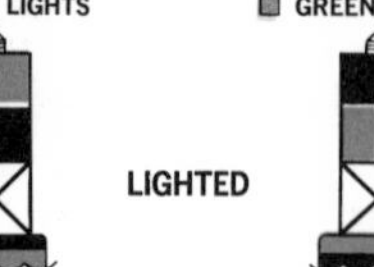

LIGHTED

NUN

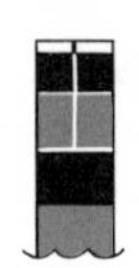

CAN

PREFERRED CHANNEL TO THE RIGHT
TOPMOST BAND RED
WHITE OR RED LIGHT

PREFERRED CHANNEL TO THE LEFT
TOPMOST BAND BLACK
WHITE OR GREEN LIGHT

RIGHT SIDE

☐ WHITE OR ■ GREEN LIGHTS
FLASHING

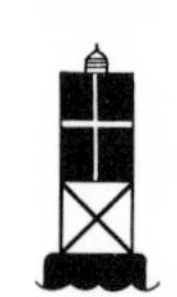

LIGHTED BUOY

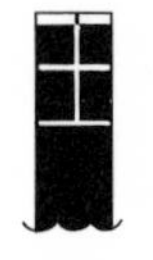

CAN

PASSING DAYMARK

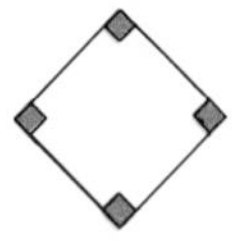

CROSSING DAYMARK

176.9

MILE BOARD

BUOYS HAVING NO LATERAL SIGNIFICANCE—ALL WATERS

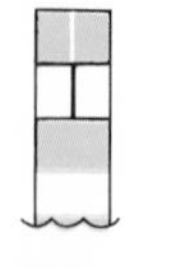

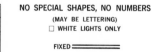

SPECIAL PURPOSE

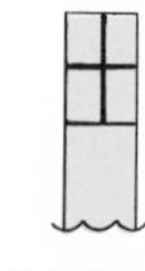

QUARANTINE ANCHORAGE

NO SPECIAL SHAPES, NO NUMBERS
(MAY BE LETTERING)
☐ WHITE LIGHTS ONLY

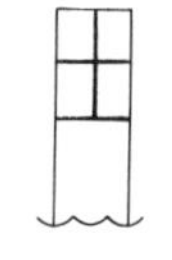

ANCHORAGE

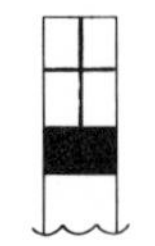

FISH NET

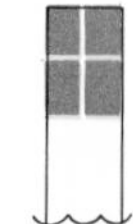

DREDGING

UNIFORM STATE WATERWAY MARKING SYSTEM

USED BY STATES IN STATE WATERS AND SOME NAVIGABLE WATERS

REGULATORY MARKERS (Information)

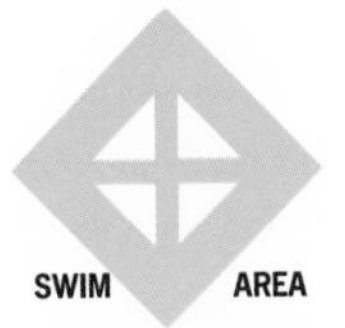

BOATS KEEP OUT

EXPLANATION MAY BE PLACED OUTSIDE THE CROSSED DIAMOND SHAPE, SUCH AS DAM, RAPIDS, SWIM AREA, ETC.

DANGER

THE NATURE OF DANGER MAY BE INDICATED INSIDE THE DIAMOND SHAPE, SUCH AS ROCK, WRECK, SHOAL, DAM, ETC.

CONTROLLED AREA

TYPE OF CONTROL IS INDICATED IN THE CIRCLE, SUCH AS 5 MPH, NO ANCHORING, ETC.

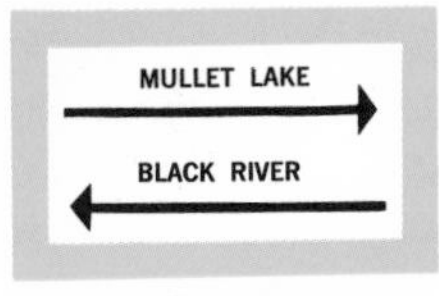

INFORMATION

FOR DISPLAYING INFORMATION SUCH AS DIRECTIONS, DISTANCES, LOCATIONS, ETC.

BUOY USED TO DISPLAY REGULATORY MARKERS

AIDS TO NAVIGATION

(ALL MAY SHOW WHITE REFLECTOR OR LIGHT)

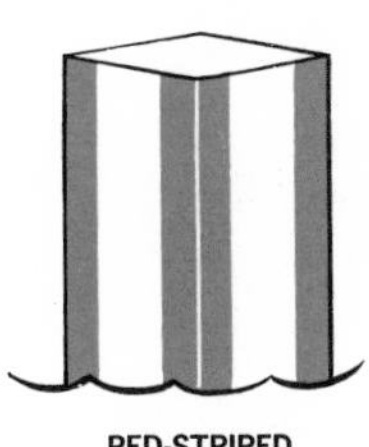

RED-STRIPED WHITE BUOY

INDICATES THAT BOAT SHOULD NOT PASS BETWEEN BUOY AND NEAREST SHORE

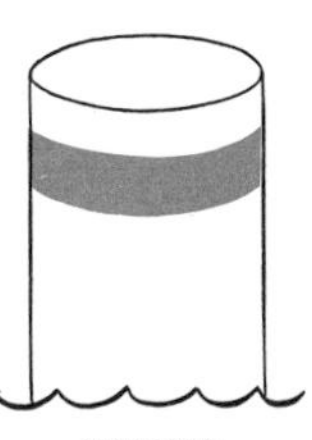

MOORING BUOY

WHITE WITH BLUE BAND

BLACK-TOPPED WHITE BUOY

BOAT SHOULD PASS TO NORTH OR EAST OF BUOY

RED-TOPPED WHITE BUOY

BOAT SHOULD PASS TO SOUTH OR WEST OF BUOY

CARDINAL SYSTEM

(MAY SHOW GREEN REFLECTOR OR LIGHT)

RED AND BLACK CAN BUOYS

ARE USUALLY FOUND IN PAIRS VESSELS SHOULD PASS BETWEEN THESE BUOYS

(MAY SHOW RED REFLECTOR OR LIGHT)

LEFT SIDE ——— (LOOKING UPSTREAM) ——— RIGHT SIDE

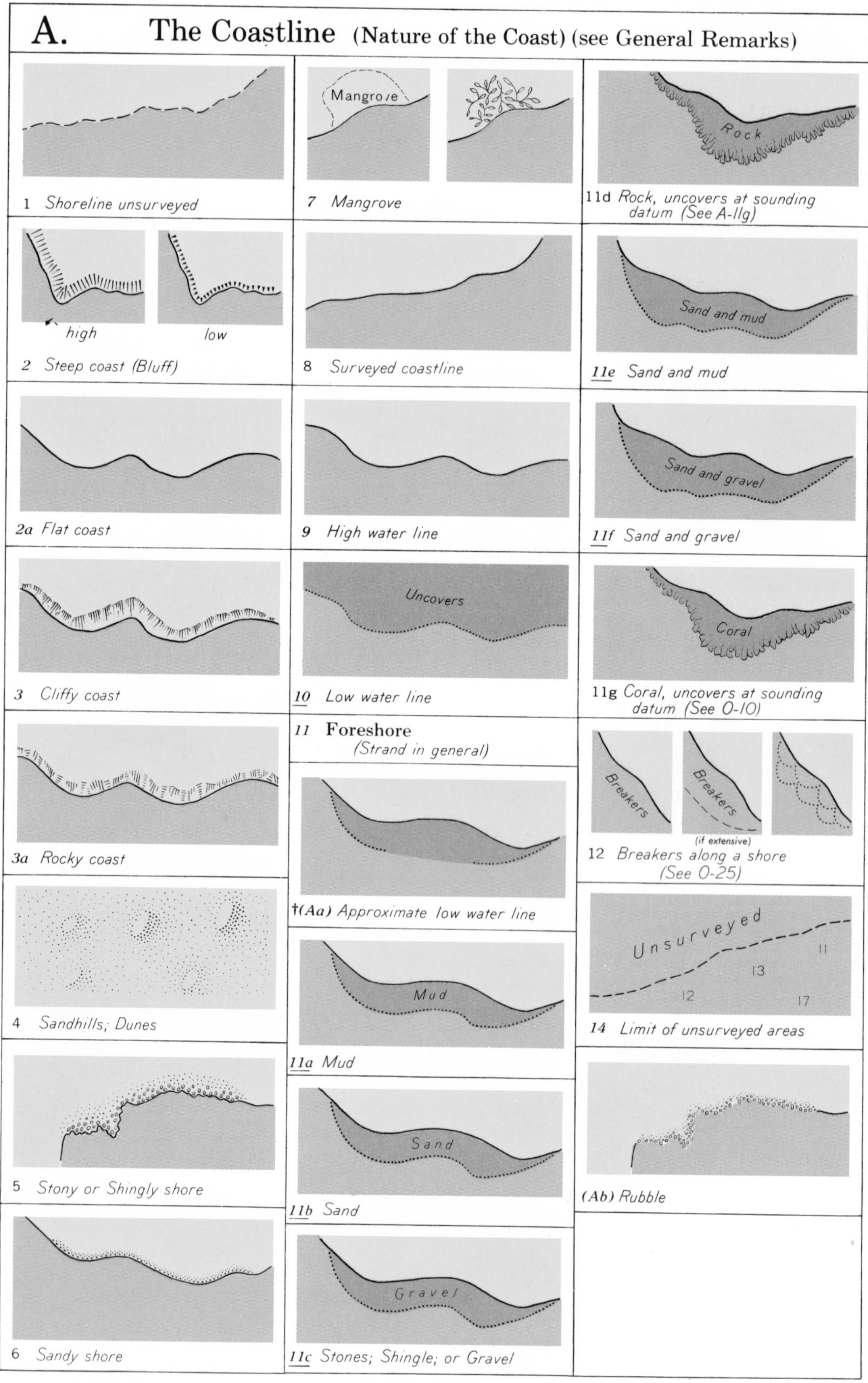
A. The Coastline (Nature of the Coast) (see General Remarks)
1 Shoreline unsurveyed
Mangrove
7 Mangrove
Rock
11d Rock, uncovers at sounding datum (See A-11g)
high
low
2 Steep coast (Bluff)
8 Surveyed coastline
Sand and mud
11e Sand and mud
2a Flat coast
9 High water line
Sand and gravel
11f Sand and gravel
3 Cliffy coast
Uncovers
10 Low water line
Coral
11g Coral, uncovers at sounding datum (See O-10)
3a Rocky coast
11 Foreshore
(Strand in general)
Breakers
Breakers
(if extensive)
12 Breakers along a shore (See O-25)
†(Aa) Approximate low water line
4 Sandhills; Dunes
Mud
11a Mud
Unsurveyed
11
13
12
17
14 Limit of unsurveyed areas
5 Stony or Shingly shore
Sand
11b Sand
(Ab) Rubble
6 Sandy shore
Gravel
11c Stones; Shingle; or Gravel

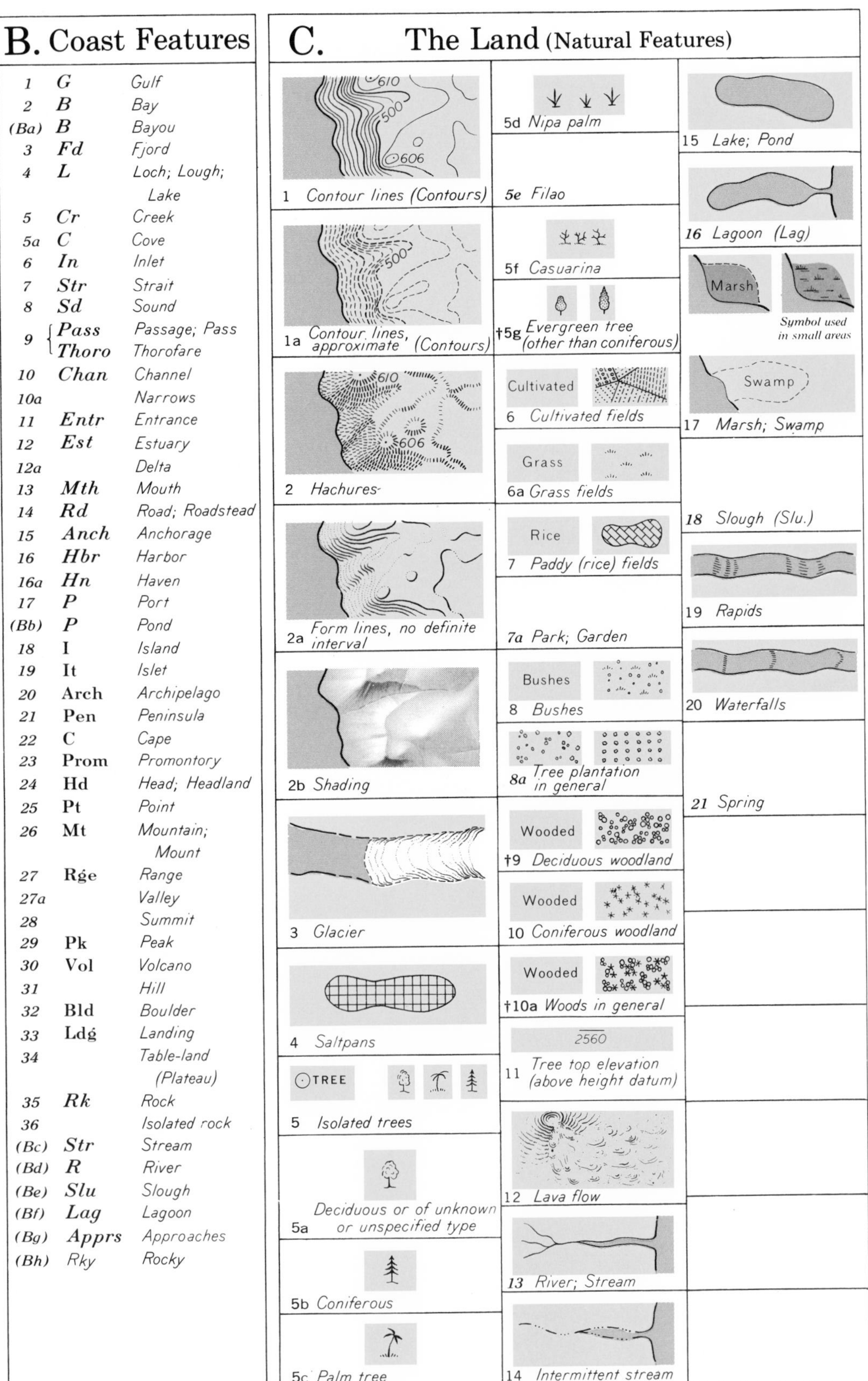
B. Coast Features
1 G Gulf
2 B Bay
(Ba) B Bayou
3 Fd Fjord
4 L Loch; Lough; Lake
5 Cr Creek
5a C Cove
6 In Inlet
7 Str Strait
8 Sd Sound
9 Pass Passage; Pass
Thoro Thorofare
10 Chan Channel
10a Narrows
11 Entr Entrance
12 Est Estuary
12a Delta
13 Mth Mouth
14 Rd Road; Roadstead
15 Anch Anchorage
16 Hbr Harbor
16a Hn Haven
17 P Port
(Bb) P Pond
18 I Island
19 It Islet
20 Arch Archipelago
21 Pen Peninsula
22 C Cape
23 Prom Promontory
24 Hd Head; Headland
25 Pt Point
26 Mt Mountain; Mount
27 Rge Range
27a Valley
28 Summit
29 Pk Peak
30 Vol Volcano
31 Hill
32 Bld Boulder
33 Ldg Landing
34 Table-land (Plateau)
35 Rk Rock
36 Isolated rock
(Bc) Str Stream
(Bd) R River
(Be) Slu Slough
(Bf) Lag Lagoon
(Bg) Apprs Approaches
(Bh) Rky Rocky
C. The Land (Natural Features)
610
500
606
1 Contour lines (Contours)
500
1a Contour lines, approximate (Contours)
610
606
2 Hachures
2a Form lines, no definite interval
2b Shading
3 Glacier
4 Saltpans
TREE
5 Isolated trees
5a Deciduous or of unknown or unspecified type
5b Coniferous
5c Palm tree
5d Nipa palm
5e Filao
5f Casuarina
†5g Evergreen tree (other than coniferous)
Cultivated
6 Cultivated fields
Grass
6a Grass fields
Rice
7 Paddy (rice) fields
7a Park; Garden
Bushes
8 Bushes
8a Tree plantation in general
Wooded
†9 Deciduous woodland
Wooded
10 Coniferous woodland
Wooded
†10a Woods in general
2560
11 Tree top elevation (above height datum)
12 Lava flow
13 River; Stream
14 Intermittent stream
15 Lake; Pond
16 Lagoon (Lag)
Marsh
Symbol used in small areas
Swamp
17 Marsh; Swamp
18 Slough (Slu.)
19 Rapids
20 Waterfalls
21 Spring

D. Control Points

	Symbol	Abbreviation	Description
1	△		*Triangulation point (station)*
†*1a*			*Astronomic Station*
2	⊙		*Fixed point (landmark) (See L-63)*
†*(Da)*	∘		*Fixed point (landmark, position approx.)*
3	· 256		*Summit of height (Peak) (when not a landmark)*
(Db)	256		*Peak, accentuated by contours*
(Dc)	256		*Peak, accentuated by hachures*
(Dd)			*Peak, elevation not determined*
(De)	⊙ 256		*Peak, when a landmark*
4	⊕	Obs Spot	*Observation spot*
**5*		BM	*Bench mark*
†6	View X		*View point*
7			*Datum point for grid of a plan*
8			*Graphical triangulation point*
9		Astro	*Astronomical*
10		Tri	*Triangulation*
(Df)		C of E	*Corps of Engineers*
12			*Great trigonometrical survey station*
13			*Traverse station*
14		Bdy Mon	*Boundary monument*
(Dg)	◇		*International boundary monument*

E. Units

1	hr	*Hour*	†*14a*		*Greenwich*
2	m; min	*Minute (of time)*	*15*	pub	*Publication*
3	sec	*Second (of time)*	*16*	Ed	*Edition*
4	m	*Meter*	*17*	corr	*Correction*
4a	dm	*Decimeter*	*18*	alt	*Altitude*
4b	cm	*Centimeter*	*19*	ht; elev	*Height; Elevation*
4c	mm	*Millimeter*	20	°	*Degree*
4d	m^2	*Square meter*	21	′	*Minute (of arc)*
4e	m^3	*Cubic meter*	22	″	*Second (of arc)*
5	km	*Kilometer*	23	No	*Number*
6	in	*Inch*	*(Ea)*	St M	*Statute mile*
7	ft	*Foot*	*(Eb)*	msec	*Microsecond*
8	yd	*Yard*	†*(Ec)*	Hz	*Hertz (cps)*
9	fm	*Fathom*	†*(Ed)*	kHz	*Kilohertz (kc)*
10	cbl	*Cable length*	†*(Ee)*	MHz	*Megahertz (Mc)*
11	M	*Nautical mile*	†*(Ef)*	cps	*Cycles/second(Hz)*
12	kn	*Knot*	†*(Eg)*	kc	*Kilocycle (kHz)*
12a	t	*Ton*	†*(Eh)*	Mc	*Megacycle (MHz)*
12b	cd	*Candela (new candle)*			
13	lat	*Latitude*			
14	long	*Longitude*			

F. Adjectives, Adverbs and other abbreviations

1	gt	*Great*
2	lit	*Little*
3	lrg	*Large*
4	sml	*Small*
5		*Outer*
6		*Inner*
7	mid	*Middle*
8		*Old*
9	anc	*Ancient*
10		*New*
11	St	*Saint*
12	conspic	*Conspicuous*
13		*Remarkable*
14	D . Destr	*Destroyed*
15		*Projected*
16	dist	*Distant*
17	abt	*About*
18		*See chart*
18a		*See plan*
19		*Lighted; Luminous*
20	sub	*Submarine*
21		*Eventual*
22	AERO	*Aeronautical*
23		*Higher*
†*23a*		*Lower*
24	exper	*Experimental*
25	discontd	*Discontinued*
26	prohib	*Prohibited*
27	explos	*Explosive*
28	estab	*Established*
29	elec	*Electric*
30	priv	*Private, Privately*
31	prom	*Prominent*
32	std	*Standard*
33	subm	*Submerged*
34	approx	*Approximate*
†*35*		*Maritime*
†*36*	maintd	*Maintained*
†*37*	aband	*Abandoned*
†*38*	temp	*Temporary*
†*39*	occas	*Occasional*
†*40*	extr	*Extreme*
†*41*		*Navigable*
†*42*	N M	*Notice to Mariners*
†*(Fa)*	L N M	*Local Notice to Mariners*
†*43*		*Sailing Directions*
†*44*		*List of Lights*
(Fb)	unverd	*Unverified*
(Fc)	AUTH	*Authorized*
(Fd)	CL	*Clearance*
(Fe)	cor	*Corner*
(Ff)	concr	*Concrete*
(Fg)	fl	*Flood*
(Fh)	mod	*Moderate*
(Fi)	bet	*Between*
(Fj)	1st	*First*
(Fk)	2nd	*Second*
(Fl)	3rd	*Third*
(Fm)	4th	*Fourth*

G. Ports and Harbors

No.	Symbol	Abbr.	Description
1		Anch	*Anchorage (large vessels)*
†2		Anch	*Anchorage (small vessels)*
3		Hbr	*Harbor*
4		Hn	*Haven*
5		P	*Port*
6		Bkw	*Breakwater*
•6a			*Dike*
7			*Mole*
8			*Jetty (partly below MHW)*
8a			*Submerged jetty*
(Ga)			*Jetty (small scale)*
9		Pier	*Pier*
10			*Spit*
11			*Groin (partly below MHW)*
12	ANCHORAGE PROHIBITED	ANCH PROHIB	*Anchorage prohibited (See P-25)*
†12a			*Anchorage reserved*
†12b	QUARANTINE ANCHORAGE	QUAR ANCH	*Quarantine anchorage*
13	Spoil Area		*Spoil ground*
(Gb)	Dumping Ground		*Dumping ground*
(Gc)	80 83 Disposal Area 85 Depths from survey of JUNE 1968 90 98		*Disposal area*
14		Fsh stks	*Fisheries; Fishing stakes*
14a			*Fish trap; Fish weirs (actual shape charted)*
14b			*Duck blind*
15			*Tunny nets (See G-14a)*
15a	Oys	Oys	*Oyster bed*
16		Ldg	*Landing place*
17			*Watering place*
18		Whf	*Wharf*
19			*Quay*

No.	Symbol	Abbr.	Description
20			*Berth*
20a	14		*Anchoring berth*
20b	3		*Berth number*
21		Dol	*Dolphin*
22			*Bollard*
23			*Mooring ring*
24			*Crane*
25			*Landing stage*
25a			*Landing stairs*
26		Quar	*Quarantine*
27			*Lazaret*
*28		Harbor Master	*Harbor master's office*
29		Cus Ho	*Customhouse*
30			*Fishing harbor*
31			*Winter harbor*
32			*Refuge harbor*
33		B Hbr	*Boat harbor*
34			*Stranding harbor (uncovers at LW)*
35			*Dock*
36			*Dry dock (actual shape on large-scale charts)*
37			*Floating dock (actual shape on large-scale charts)*
38			*Gridiron; Careening grid*
39			*Patent slip; Slipway; Marine railway*
39a		Ramp	*Ramp*
†40	Lock		*Lock (point upstream) (See H-13)*
41			*Wet dock*
42			*Shipyard*
43			*Lumber yard*
44		Health Office	*Health officer's office*
45		Hk	*Hulk (actual shape on lrg. scale charts) (See O-11)*
46	PROHIBITED AREA	PROHIB AREA	*Prohibited area*
†46a	10		*Calling-in point for vessel traffic control*
47			*Anchorage for seaplanes*
48			*Seaplane landing area*
49	Under construction		*Work in progress*
50			*Under construction*
† 51			*Work projected*
(Gd)	Subm ruins		*Submerged ruins*

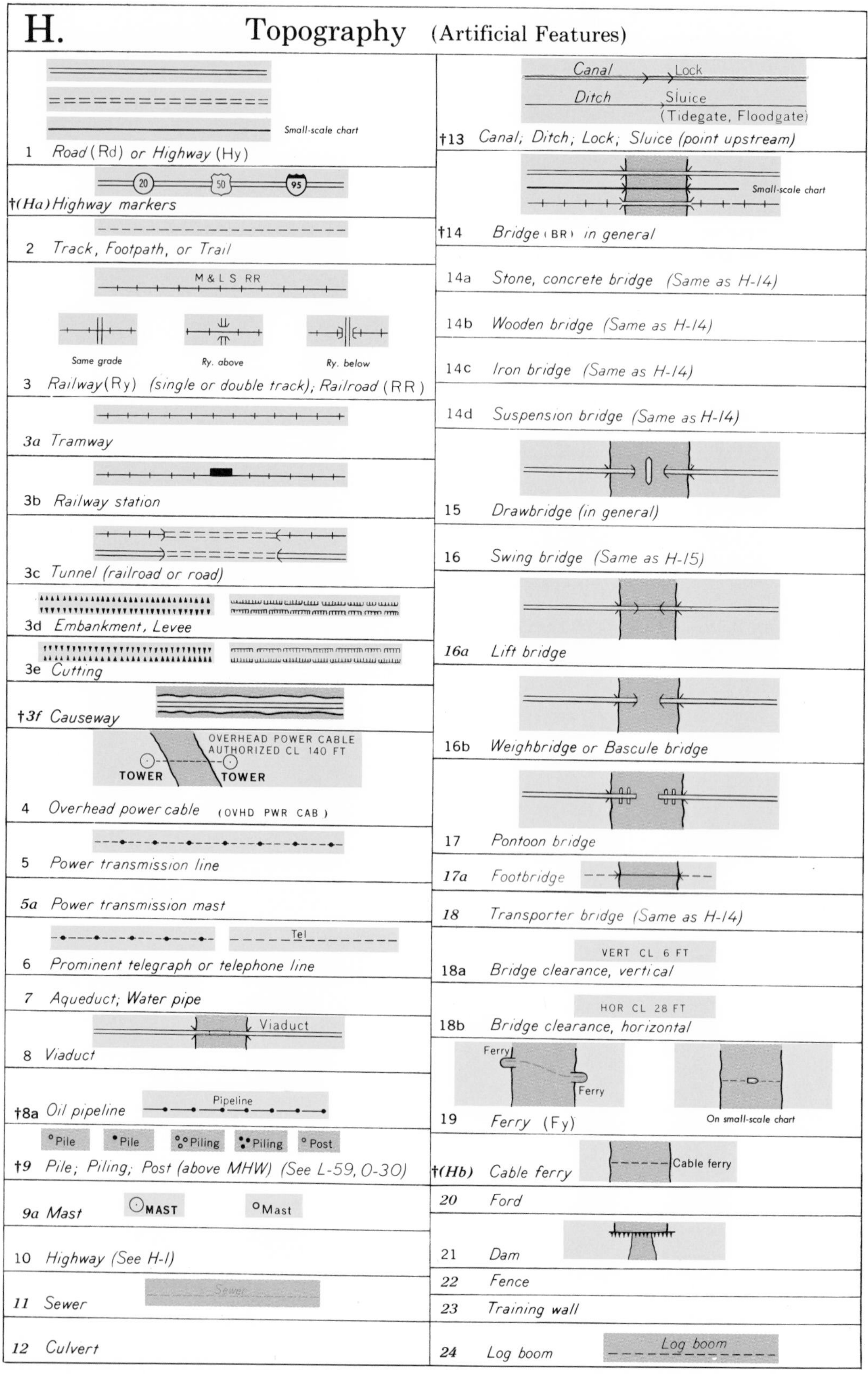
H. Topography (Artificial Features)
Small-scale chart
1 Road (Rd) or Highway (Hy)
20
50
95
†(Ha) Highway markers
2 Track, Footpath, or Trail
M & L S RR
Same grade
Ry. above
Ry. below
3 Railway (Ry) (single or double track); Railroad (RR)
3a Tramway
3b Railway station
3c Tunnel (railroad or road)
3d Embankment, Levee
3e Cutting
†3f Causeway
OVERHEAD POWER CABLE
AUTHORIZED CL 140 FT
TOWER
TOWER
4 Overhead power cable (OVHD PWR CAB)
5 Power transmission line
5a Power transmission mast
Tel
6 Prominent telegraph or telephone line
7 Aqueduct; Water pipe
Viaduct
8 Viaduct
Pipeline
†8a Oil pipeline
Pile
Pile
Piling
Piling
Post
†9 Pile; Piling; Post (above MHW) (See L-59, O-30)
MAST
Mast
9a Mast
10 Highway (See H-1)
Sewer
11 Sewer
12 Culvert
Canal
Lock
Ditch
Sluice
(Tidegate, Floodgate)
†13 Canal; Ditch; Lock; Sluice (point upstream)
Small-scale chart
†14 Bridge (BR) in general
14a Stone, concrete bridge (Same as H-14)
14b Wooden bridge (Same as H-14)
14c Iron bridge (Same as H-14)
14d Suspension bridge (Same as H-14)
15 Drawbridge (in general)
16 Swing bridge (Same as H-15)
16a Lift bridge
16b Weighbridge or Bascule bridge
17 Pontoon bridge
17a Footbridge
18 Transporter bridge (Same as H-14)
VERT CL 6 FT
18a Bridge clearance, vertical
HOR CL 28 FT
18b Bridge clearance, horizontal
Ferry
Ferry
On small-scale chart
19 Ferry (Fy)
Cable ferry
†(Hb) Cable ferry
20 Ford
21 Dam
22 Fence
23 Training wall
Log boom
24 Log boom

I. Buildings and Structures (see General Remarks)

No.	Symbol	Abbreviation	Meaning
1			*City or Town (large scale)*
(Ia)	# o		*City or Town (small scale)*
2			*Suburb*
3		Vil	*Village*
3a			*Buildings in general*
4		Cas	*Castle*
5			*House*
6			*Villa*
7			*Farm*
8		Ch	*Church*
8a		Cath	*Cathedral*
8b	⊙SPIRE	Spire	*Spire; Steeple*
9			*Roman Catholic Church*
†10			*Temple*
11			*Chapel*
†12			*Mosque*
†12a			*Minaret*
(Ib)			*Moslem Shrine*
†13			*Marabout*
†14		Pag	*Pagoda*
†15			*Buddhist Temple; Joss-House*
†15a			*Shinto Shrine*
16			*Monastery; Convent*
17			*Calvary; Cross*
17a	Cem		*Cemetery, Non-Christian*
18			*Cemetery, Christian*
18a			*Tomb*
19			*Fort (actual shape charted)*
†20			*Battery*
21			*Barracks*
22			*Powder magazine*
23	Airport		*Airplane landing field*
24			*Airport, large scale (See P-13)*
(Ic)			*Airport, military (small scale)*
†*(Id)*			*Airport, civil (small scale)*
25			*Mooring mast*
26	King St	St	*Street*

No.	Symbol	Abbreviation	Meaning
26a	Locust Ave	Ave	*Avenue*
†*26b*	Grand Blvd	Blvd	*Boulevard*
27		Tel	*Telegraph*
28		Tel Off	*Telegraph office*
29		P O	*Post office*
30		Govt Ho	*Government house*
31			*Town hall*
32		Hosp	*Hospital*
33			*Slaughterhouse*
34		Magz	*Magazine*
34a			*Warehouse; Storehouse*
35	⊙MON °Mon		*Monument*
36	⊙CUP °Cup		*Cupola*
37	⊙ELEV °Elev		*Elevator; Lift*
(Ie)		Elev	*Elevation; Elevated*
38			*Shed*
39			*Zinc roof*
40	Ruins °Ru		*Ruins*
41	⊙TR °Tr		*Tower*
†*(If)*	⊙ABAND LT HO		*Abandoned lighthouse*
42	⊙WINDMILL		*Windmill*
†43			*Watermill*
43a	⊙WINDMOTOR		*Windmotor*
44	⊙CHY °Chy		*Chimney; Stack*
45	⊙S'PIPE °S'pipe		*Water tower; Standpipe*
46			*Oil tank*
47		Facty	*Factory*
48			*Saw mill*
49			*Brick kiln*
50			*Mine; Quarry*
51	°Well		*Well*
52			*Cistern*
53	⊙TANK °Tk		*Tank*
54			*Noria*
55			*Fountain*

I. Buildings and Structures (continued)

No.	Symbol	Abbr.	Meaning
61		Inst	*Institute*
62			*Establishment*
63			*Bathing establishment*
64		Ct Ho	*Courthouse*
65		Sch	*School*
(Ig)		H S	*High school*
(Ih)		Univ	*University*
66		Bldg	*Building*
67		Pav	*Pavilion*
68			*Hut*
69			*Stadium*
70		T	*Telephone*
71			*Gas tank; Gasometer*
72	⊙GAB °Gab		*Gable*
73			*Wall*
†74			*Pyramid*
†75			*Pillar*
†76			*Oil derrick*
(Ii)		Ltd	*Limited*
(Ij)		Apt	*Apartment*
(Ik)		Cap	*Capitol*
(Il)		Co	*Company*
(Im)		Corp	*Corporation*
(In)	⊙		*Landmark (conspicuous object)*
(Io)	°		*Landmark (position approx.)*

J. Miscellaneous Stations

No.	Symbol	Abbr.	Meaning
1		Sta	*Any kind of station*
2		Sta	*Station*
3	 C G		*Coast Guard station (Similar to Lifesaving Sta.)*
(Ja)	 ⊙C G WALLIS SANDS		*Coast Guard station (when landmark)*
†4	⊙LOOK TR		*Lookout station; Watch tower*
5			*Lifeboat station*
6	 LS S		*Lifesaving station (See J-3)*
7		Rkt Sta	*Rocket station*
8	⊙PIL STA		*Pilot station*
9		Sig Sta	*Signal station*
10		Sem	*Semaphore*
11		S Sig Sta	*Storm signal station*
12			*Weather signal station*
(Jb)	⊙W B SIG STA		*Weather Bureau signal station*
13			*Tide signal station*
14			*Stream signal station*
15			*Ice signal station*
16			*Time signal station*
†16a			*Manned oceanographic station*
†16b			*Unmanned oceanographic station*
17			*Time ball*
18			*Signal mast*
19	⊙FS ⊙FP °FS °FP		*Flagstaff; Flagpole*
†19a	⊙F TR °F Tr		*Flag tower*
20			*Signal*
21		Obsy	*Observatory*
22		Off	*Office*
(Jc)	°BELL		*Bell (on land)*
(Jd)	°HECP		*Harbor entrance control post*

K. (! new optional symbol) Lights

No.	Symbol	Meaning	No.	Symbol	Meaning
†1		*Position of light*	29	F Fl	*Fixed and flashing light*
2	Lt	*Light*	30	F Gp Fl	*Fixed and group flashing light*
†(Ka)		*Riprap surrounding light*	†30a	Mo	*Morse code light*
3	Lt Ho	*Lighthouse*	31	Rot	*Revolving or Rotating light*
4	 AERO AERO	*Aeronautical light (See F-22)*			
4a		*Marine and air navigation light*	41		*Period*
5	Bn Bn	*Light beacon*	42		*Every*
6		*Light vessel; Lightship*	43		*With*
8		*Lantern*	44		*Visible (range)*
9		*Street lamp*	(Kb)	M	*Nautical mile (See E-11)*
10	REF	*Reflector*	(Kc)	m; min	*Minutes (See E-2)*
11	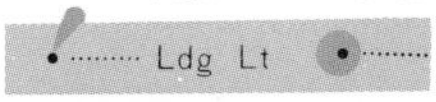 Ldg Lt Ldg Lt	*Leading light*	(Kd)	sec	*Seconds (See E-3)*
12	 RED RED	*Sector light*	45	Fl	*Flash*
13	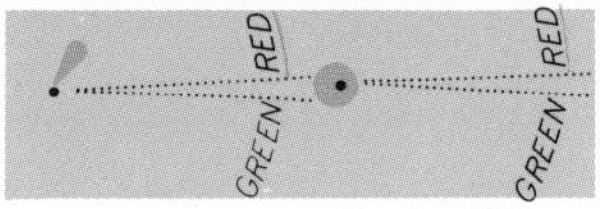 RED GREEN RED GREEN	*Directional light*	46	Occ	*Occultation*
			46a		*Eclipse*
14		*Harbor light*	47	Gp	*Group*
15		*Fishing light*			
16		*Tidal light*	48	Occ	*Intermittent light*
17	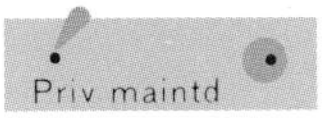 Priv maintd	*Private light (maintained by private interests; to be used with caution)*	49	SEC	*Sector*
21	F	*Fixed light*	50		*Color of sector*
22	Occ	*Occulting light*	51	Aux	*Auxiliary light*
23	Fl	*Flashing light*	52		*Varied*
†23a	E Int	*Isophase light (equal interval)*	61	Vi	*Violet*
24	Qk Fl	*Quick flashing (scintillating) light*	62		*Purple*
25	Int Qk Fl I Qk Fl	*Interrupted quick flashing light*	63	Bu	*Blue*
			64	G	*Green*
25a	S Fl	*Short flashing light*	65	Or	*Orange*
26	Alt	*Alternating light*	66	R	*Red*
27	Gp Occ	*Group occulting light*	67	W	*White*
28	Gp Fl	*Group flashing light*	67a	Am	*Amber*
28a	S-L Fl	*Short-long flashing light*	68	OBSC	*Obscured light*
28b		*Group short flashing light*	†68a	Fog Det Lt	*Fog detector light (See N-Nb)*

K. Lights (continued)

69		*Unwatched light*	79		*Front light*
70	Occas	*Occasional light*	80	Vert	*Vertical lights*
71	Irreg	*Irregular light*	81	Hor	*Horizontal lights*
72	Prov	*Provisional light*	(Kf)	VB	*Vertical beam*
73	Temp	*Temporary light*	(Kg)	RGE	*Range*
(Ke)	D; Destr	*Destroyed*	(Kh)	Exper	*Experimental light*
74	Exting	*Extinguished light*	(Ki)	TRLB	*Temporarily replaced by lighted buoy showing the same characteristics*
75		*Faint light*			
76		*Upper light*	(Kj)	TRUB	*Temporarily replaced by unlighted buoy*
77		*Lower light*	(Kk)	TLB	*Temporary lighted buoy*
78		*Rear light*	(Kl)	TUB	*Temporary unlighted buoy*

L. Buoys and Beacons (see General Remarks)

1	•	*Position of buoy*	17	RB RB	*Bifurcation buoy (RBHB)*
2		*Light buoy*	18	RB RB	*Junction buoy (RBHB)*
3	BELL	*Bell buoy*	19	RB RB	*Isolated danger buoy (RBHB)*
3a	GONG	*Gong buoy*	20	RB G	*Wreck buoy (RBHB or G)*
4	WHIS	*Whistle buoy*	20a	RB G	*Obstruction buoy (RBHB or G)*
5	C	*Can or Cylindrical buoy*	21	Tel	*Telegraph-cable buoy*
6	N	*Nun or Conical buoy*	22		*Mooring buoy (colors of mooring buoys never carried)*
7	SP	*Spherical buoy*	22a		*Mooring*
8	S	*Spar buoy*	22b	Tel	*Mooring buoy with telegraphic communications*
†8a	P	*Pillar or Spindle buoy*	22c	T	*Mooring buoy with telephonic communications*
9		*Buoy with topmark (ball) (see L-70)*	23		*Warping buoy*
10		*Barrel or Ton buoy*	24	Y	*Quarantine buoy*
(La)		*Color unknown*	†24a		*Practice area buoy*
(Lb)	FLOAT	*Float*	25	Explos Anch	*Explosive anchorage buoy*
12	FLOAT	*Lightfloat*	25a	AERO	*Aeronautical anchorage buoy*
13		*Outer or Landfall buoy*	26	Deviation	*Compass adjustment buoy*
14	BW	*Fairway buoy (BWVS)*	27	BW	*Fish trap (area) buoy (BWHB)*
14a	BW	*Mid-channel buoy (BWVS)*	27a		*Spoil ground buoy*
†15	R "2" R "2"	*Starboard-hand buoy (entering from seaward)*	†28	W	*Anchorage buoy (marks limits)*
16	"1"	*Port-hand buoy (entering from seaward)*	†29	Priv maintd	*Private aid to navigation (buoy) (maintained by private interests, use with caution)*

L. Buoys and Beacons (continued)

No.	Symbol	Abbr.	Description
30			Temporary buoy (See Ki,j,k,l)
30a			Winter buoy
31		HB	Horizontal stripes or bands
32		VS	Vertical stripes
33		Chec	Checkered
†33a		Diag	Diagonal bands
41		W	White
42		B	Black
43		R	Red
44		Y	Yellow
45		G	Green
46		Br	Brown
47		Gy	Gray
48		Bu	Blue
†48a		Am	Amber
†48b		Or	Orange
51			Floating beacon
52	RW Bn, W Bn, R Bn		Fixed beacon (unlighted or daybeacon)
	Bn		Black beacon
	Bn		Color unknown
†(Lc)	MARKER, Marker		Private aid to navigation
53		Bn	Beacon, in general (See L-52)
54			Tower beacon
55			Cardinal marking system
56	Deviation Bn		Compass adjustment beacon
57			Topmarks (See L-9, 70)
58			Telegraph-cable (landing) beacon
†59	Piles, Piles		Piles (See O-30, H-9)
			Stakes
	Stumps		Stumps (See O-30)
			Perches
61	CAIRN, Cairn		Cairn
62			Painted patches
63			Landmark (conspicuous object) (See D-2)
(Ld)			Landmark (position approximate)
64		REF	Reflector
65	MARKER		Range targets, markers
(Le)	W Or, W Or		Special-purpose buoys
†66			Oil installation buoy
†67			Drilling platform (See O-Ob, O-Oc)
70			Note: TOPMARKS on buoys and beacons may be shown on charts of foreign waters. The abbreviation for black is not shown adjacent to buoys or beacons.
(Lf)	Ra Ref		Radar reflector (See M-13)

M. Radio and Radar Stations

No.	Symbol	Description
1	° R Sta	*Radio telegraph station*
2	° R T	*Radio telephone station*
3	R Bn	*Radiobeacon*
4	R Bn	*Circular radiobeacon*
5	R D	*Directional radiobeacon; Radio range*
6		*Rotating loop radiobeacon*
7	R D F	*Radio direction finding station*
(Ma)	TELEM ANT	*Telemetry antenna*
†*(Mb)*	R RELAY MAST	*Radio relay mast*
†*(Mc)*	MICRO TR	*Microwave tower*
9	R MAST	*Radio mast*
	R TR	*Radio tower*
†*9a*	TV TR	*Television mast; Television tower*
10	R TR (WBAL) 1090 Kc	*Radio broadcasting station (commercial)*
10a	° R Sta	*Q.T.G. Radio station*
11	Ra	*Radar station*
12	Racon	*Radar responder beacon*
13	Ra Ref	*Radar reflector (See L-Lf)*
14	Ra (conspic)	*Radar conspicuous object*
14a		*Ramark*
15	D F S	*Distance finding station (synchronized signals)*
†16	AERO R Bn 302	*Aeronautical radiobeacon*
†17	° Decca Sta	*Decca station*
†18	° Loran Sta Venice	*Loran station (name)*
†*19*	CONSOL Bn 190 Kc MMF	*Consol (Consolan) station*
(Md)	AERO R Rge 342	*Aeronautical radio range*
(Me)	Ra Ref Calibration Bn	*Radar calibration beacon*
(Mf)	LORAN TR SPRING ISLAND	*Loran tower (name)*
†*(Mg)*	R TR F R Lt	*Obstruction light*

N. Fog Signals

No.	Symbol	Description
1	Fog Sig	*Fog-signal station*
2		*Radio fog-signal station*
3	*GUN*	*Explosive fog signal*
4		*Submarine fog signal*
5	*SUB-BELL*	*Submarine fog bell (action of waves)*
6	*SUB-BELL*	*Submarine fog bell (mechanical)*
7	*SUB-OSC*	*Submarine oscillator*
8	*NAUTO*	*Nautophone*
9	*DIA*	*Diaphone*
10	*GUN*	*Fog gun*
11	*SIREN*	*Fog siren*
12	*HORN*	*Fog trumpet*
13	*HORN*	*Fog horn*
†*13a*	*HORN*	*Electric fog horn*
14	*BELL*	*Fog bell*
15	*WHIS*	*Fog whistle*
16	*HORN*	*Reed horn*
17	*GONG*	*Fog gong*
†18		*Submarine sound signal not connected to the shore (See N-5,6,7)*
†18a		*Submarine sound signal connected to the shore (See N-5,6,7)*
(Na)	*HORN*	*Typhon*
(Nb)	*Fog Det Lt*	*Fog detector light (See K 68a)*

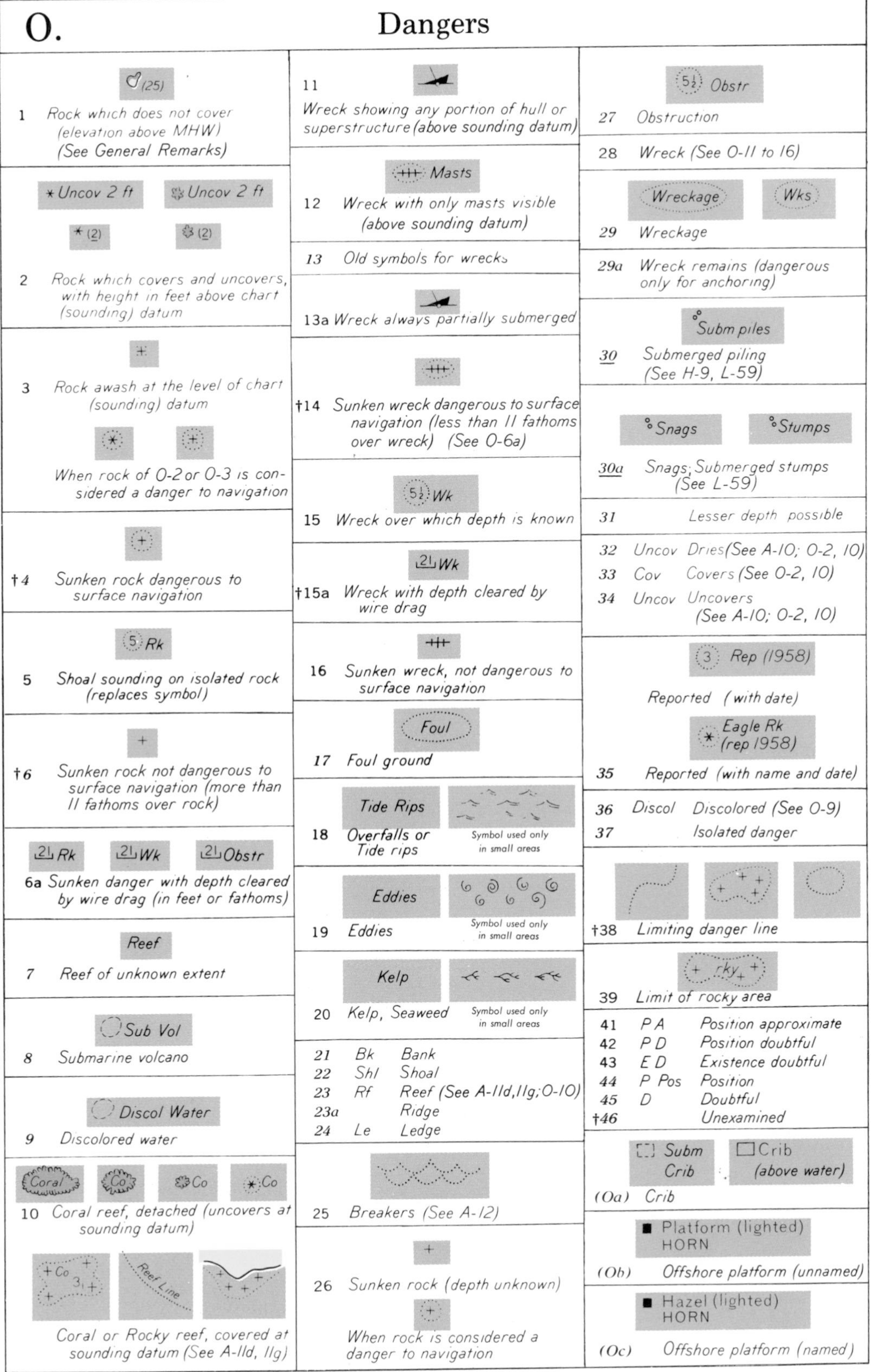
O.
Dangers
(25)
1 Rock which does not cover (elevation above MHW) (See General Remarks)
Uncov 2 ft
Uncov 2 ft
(2)
(2)
2 Rock which covers and uncovers, with height in feet above chart (sounding) datum
3 Rock awash at the level of chart (sounding) datum
When rock of O-2 or O-3 is considered a danger to navigation
†4 Sunken rock dangerous to surface navigation
5 Rk
5 Shoal sounding on isolated rock (replaces symbol)
†6 Sunken rock not dangerous to surface navigation (more than 11 fathoms over rock)
21 Rk
21 Wk
21 Obstr
6a Sunken danger with depth cleared by wire drag (in feet or fathoms)
Reef
7 Reef of unknown extent
Sub Vol
8 Submarine volcano
Discol Water
9 Discolored water
Coral
Co
Co
Co
10 Coral reef, detached (uncovers at sounding datum)
Co
3
Reef Line
Coral or Rocky reef, covered at sounding datum (See A-11d, 11g)
11
Wreck showing any portion of hull or superstructure (above sounding datum)
Masts
12 Wreck with only masts visible (above sounding datum)
13 Old symbols for wrecks
13a Wreck always partially submerged
†14 Sunken wreck dangerous to surface navigation (less than 11 fathoms over wreck) (See O-6a)
5½ Wk
15 Wreck over which depth is known
21 Wk
†15a Wreck with depth cleared by wire drag
16 Sunken wreck, not dangerous to surface navigation
Foul
17 Foul ground
Tide Rips
18 Overfalls or Tide rips
Symbol used only in small areas
Eddies
19 Eddies
Symbol used only in small areas
Kelp
20 Kelp, Seaweed
Symbol used only in small areas
21 Bk Bank
22 Shl Shoal
23 Rf Reef (See A-11d, 11g; O-10)
23a Ridge
24 Le Ledge
25 Breakers (See A-12)
26 Sunken rock (depth unknown)
When rock is considered a danger to navigation
5½ Obstr
27 Obstruction
28 Wreck (See O-11 to 16)
Wreckage
Wks
29 Wreckage
29a Wreck remains (dangerous only for anchoring)
Subm piles
30 Submerged piling (See H-9, L-59)
Snags
Stumps
30a Snags; Submerged stumps (See L-59)
31 Lesser depth possible
32 Uncov Dries (See A-10; O-2, 10)
33 Cov Covers (See O-2, 10)
34 Uncov Uncovers (See A-10; O-2, 10)
3 Rep (1958)
Reported (with date)
Eagle Rk (rep 1958)
35 Reported (with name and date)
36 Discol Discolored (See O-9)
37 Isolated danger
†38 Limiting danger line
rky
39 Limit of rocky area
41 PA Position approximate
42 PD Position doubtful
43 ED Existence doubtful
44 P Pos Position
45 D Doubtful
†46 Unexamined
Subm Crib
Crib (above water)
(Oa) Crib
Platform (lighted) HORN
(Ob) Offshore platform (unnamed)
Hazel (lighted) HORN
(Oc) Offshore platform (named)

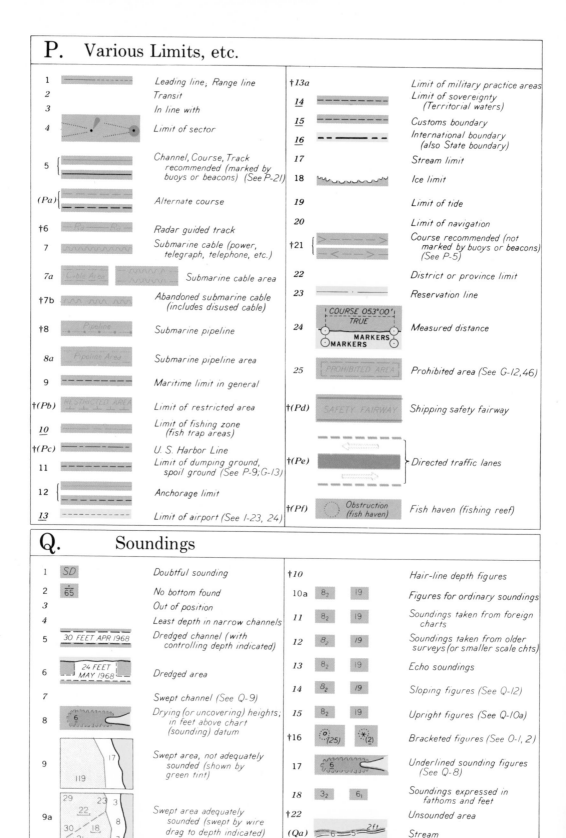

P. Various Limits, etc.

No.	Symbol	Description
1		Leading line; Range line
2		Transit
3		In line with
4		Limit of sector
5		Channel, Course, Track recommended (marked by buoys or beacons) (See P-21)
(Pa)		Alternate course
†6	Ra Ra	Radar guided track
7		Submarine cable (power, telegraph, telephone, etc.)
7a	Cable Area	Submarine cable area
†7b		Abandoned submarine cable (includes disused cable)
†8	Pipeline	Submarine pipeline
8a	Pipeline Area	Submarine pipeline area
9		Maritime limit in general
†(Pb)	RESTRICTED AREA	Limit of restricted area
10		Limit of fishing zone (fish trap areas)
†(Pc)		U. S. Harbor Line
11		Limit of dumping ground, spoil ground (See P-9; G-13)
12		Anchorage limit
13		Limit of airport (See I-23, 24)
†13a		Limit of military practice areas
14		Limit of sovereignty (Territorial waters)
15		Customs boundary
16		International boundary (also State boundary)
17		Stream limit
18		Ice limit
19		Limit of tide
20		Limit of navigation
†21		Course recommended (not marked by buoys or beacons) (See P-5)
22		District or province limit
23		Reservation line
24	COURSE 053°00' TRUE; MARKERS; MARKERS	Measured distance
25	PROHIBITED AREA	Prohibited area (See G-12, 46)
†(Pd)	SAFETY FAIRWAY	Shipping safety fairway
†(Pe)		Directed traffic lanes
†(Pf)	Obstruction (fish haven)	Fish haven (fishing reef)

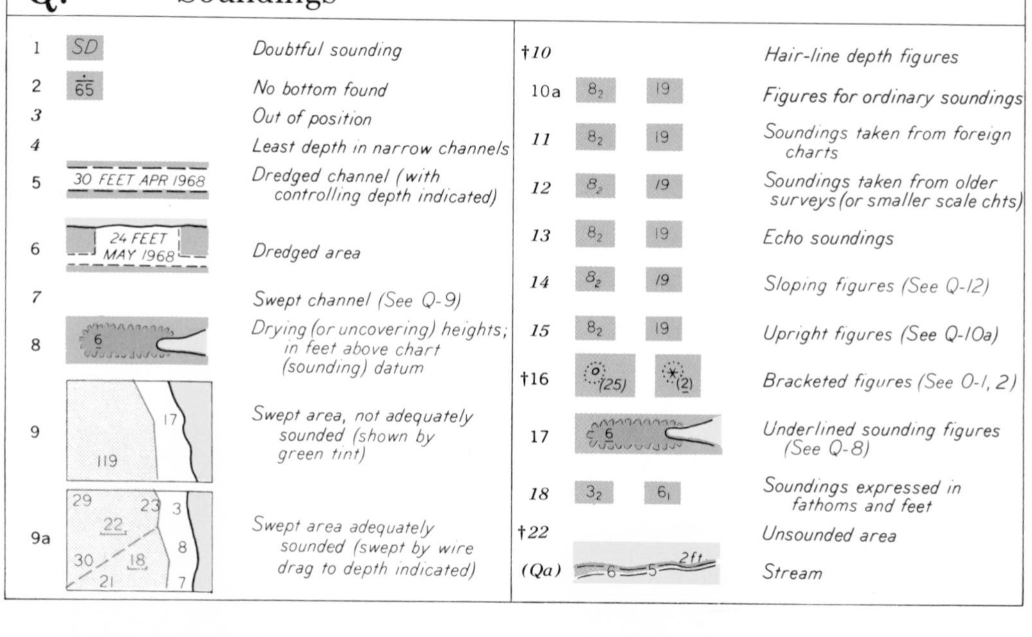

Q. Soundings

No.	Symbol	Description
1	SD	Doubtful sounding
2	65	No bottom found
3		Out of position
4		Least depth in narrow channels
5	30 FEET APR 1968	Dredged channel (with controlling depth indicated)
6	24 FEET MAY 1968	Dredged area
7		Swept channel (See Q-9)
8	6	Drying (or uncovering) heights; in feet above chart (sounding) datum
9	17, 119	Swept area, not adequately sounded (shown by green tint)
9a	29, 23, 3, 22, 8, 30, 18, 21, 7	Swept area adequately sounded (swept by wire drag to depth indicated)
†10		Hair-line depth figures
10a	8_2 19	Figures for ordinary soundings
11	8_2 19	Soundings taken from foreign charts
12	8_2 19	Soundings taken from older surveys (or smaller scale chts)
13	8_2 19	Echo soundings
14	8_2 19	Sloping figures (See Q-12)
15	8_2 19	Upright figures (See Q-10a)
†16	(25) (2)	Bracketed figures (See O-1, 2)
17	6	Underlined sounding figures (See Q-8)
18	3_2 6_1	Soundings expressed in fathoms and feet
†22		Unsounded area
(Qa)	6 5 2ft	Stream

R. Depth Contours and Tints (see General Remarks)

Feet	Fathoms		Feet	Fathoms	
0	0	···········	300	50	—·····—·····—
6	1	···········	600	100	------------
12	2	···········	1,200	200	-- -- -- --
18	3	···········	1,800	300	--- --- ---
24	4	···· ···· ····	2,400	400	---- ---- ----
30	5	····· ····· ·····	3,000	500	----- ----- -----
36	6	--- --- --- ---	6,000	1,000	-········-········-
60	10	–·–·–·–·–·–	12,000	2,000	--·········--········--
120	20	–··–··–··–··–	18,000	3,000	---·········---········
180	30	–···–···–···–	Or continuous lines, with values		——— 5 ——— (blue or black) ——— 100 ———
240	40	—····—····—····—			

S. Quality of the Bottom

†1	*Grd*	*Ground*	24	*Oys*	*Oysters*	50	*spk*	*Speckled*
2	*S*	*Sand*	25	*Ms*	*Mussels*	51	*gty*	*Gritty*
3	*M*	*Mud; Muddy*	26	*Spg*	*Sponge*	†52	*dec*	*Decayed*
4	*Oz*	*Ooze*	†27	*K*	*Kelp*	53	*fly*	*Flinty*
5	*Ml*	*Marl*	28	*Wd*	*Sea-weed*	54	*glac*	*Glacial*
6	*Cl*	*Clay*	28	*Grs*	*Grass*	†55	*ten*	*Tenacious*
7	*G*	*Gravel*	†29	*Stg*	*Sea-tangle*	56	*wh*	*White*
8	*Sn*	*Shingle*	†31	*Spi*	*Spicules*	57	*bk*	*Black*
9	*P*	*Pebbles*	32	*Fr*	*Foraminifera*	58	*vi*	*Violet*
10	*St*	*Stones*	33	*Gl*	*Globigerina*	59	*bu*	*Blue*
11	*Rk; rky*	*Rock; Rocky*	34	*Di*	*Diatoms*	60	*gn*	*Green*
11a	*Blds*	*Boulders*	35	*Rd*	*Radiolaria*	61	*yl*	*Yellow*
12	*Ck*	*Chalk*	36	*Pt*	*Pteropods*	62	*or*	*Orange*
12a	*Ca*	*Calcareous*	37	*Po*	*Polyzoa*	63	*rd*	*Red*
13	*Qz*	*Quartz*	†38	*Cir*	*Cirripeda*	64	*br*	*Brown*
†13a	*Sch*	*Schist*	†38a	*Fu*	*Fucus*	65	*ch*	*Chocolate*
14	*Co*	*Coral*	†38b	*Ma*	*Mattes*	66	*gy*	*Gray*
(Sa)	*Co Hd*	*Coral head*	39	*fne*	*Fine*	67	*lt*	*Light*
15	*Mds*	*Madrepores*	40	*crs*	*Coarse*	68	*dk*	*Dark*
16	*Vol*	*Volcanic*	41	*sft*	*Soft*			
(Sb)	*Vol Ash*	*Volcanic ash*	42	*hrd*	*Hard*	†70	*vard*	*Varied*
17	*La*	*Lava*	43	*stf*	*Stiff*	†71	*unev*	*Uneven*
18	*Pm*	*Pumice*	44	*sml*	*Small*	†*(Sc)*	*S/M*	*Surface layer and Under layer*
19	*T*	*Tufa*	45	*lrg*	*Large*			
20	*Sc*	*Scoriae*	46	*stk*	*Sticky*			
21	*Cn*	*Cinders*	47	*brk*	*Broken*			
†*21a*		*Ash*	47a	*grd*	*Ground (Shells)*	76		*Fresh water springs in sea-bed*
22	*Mn*	*Manganese*	†48	*rt*	*Rotten*			
23	*Sh*	*Shells*	†49	*str*	*Streaky*			

T. Tides and Currents

No.	Abbreviation	Meaning
1	*HW*	*High water*
1a	*HHW*	*Higher high water*
2	*LW*	*Low water*
(Ta)	*LWD*	*Low water datum*
2a	*LLW*	*Lower low water*
3	*MTL*	*Mean tide level*
4	*MSL*	*Mean sea level*
4a		*Elevation of mean sea level above chart (sounding) datum*
5		*Chart datum (datum for sounding reduction)*
6	*Sp*	*Spring tide*
7	*Np*	*Neap tide*
†7a	*MHW*	*Mean high water*
8	*MHWS*	*Mean high water springs*
8a	*MHWN*	*Mean high water neaps*
8b	*MHHW*	*Mean higher high water*
†8c	*MLW*	*Mean low water*
9	*MLWS*	*Mean low water springs*
9a	*MLWN*	*Mean low water neaps*
9b	*MLLW*	*Mean lower low water*
10	*ISLW*	*Indian spring low water*
11		*High water full and change (vulgar establishment of the port)*
12		*Low water full and change*
13		*Mean establishment of the port*
13a		*Establishment of the port*
14		*Unit of height*
15		*Equinoctial*
16		*Quarter; Quadrature*
17	*Str*	*Stream*
18	2 kn	*Current, general, with rate*
19	2 kn	*Flood stream (current) with rate*
20	2 kn	*Ebb stream (current) with rate*
21	Tide gauge	*Tide gauge; Tidepole; Automatic tide gauge*
23	*vel*	*Velocity; Rate*
24	*kn*	*Knots*
25	*ht*	*Height*
26		*Tide*
27		*New moon*
28		*Full moon*
29		*Ordinary*
30		*Syzygy*
31	*fl*	*Flood*
32		*Ebb*
33		*Tidal stream diagram*
34	A B	*Place for which tabulated tidal stream data are given*
35		*Range (of tide)*
36		*Phase lag*
(Tb)		*Current diagram, with explanatory note*

U. Compass

VAR 14° 45′ W (1968)
ANNUAL INCREASE 2′

Compass Rose

The outer circle is in degrees with zero at true north. The inner circles are in points and degrees with the arrow indicating magnetic north.

No.	Abbreviation	Meaning
1	N	*North*
2	E	*East*
3	S	*South*
4	W	*West*
5	NE	*Northeast*
6	SE	*Southeast*
7	SW	*Southwest*
8	NW	*Northwest*
9	N	*Northern*
10	E	*Eastern*
11	S	*Southern*
12	W	*Western*
21	brg	*Bearing*
†22	T	*True*
23	mag	*Magnetic*
24	var	*Variation*
25		*Annual change*
25a		*Annual change nil*
26		*Abnormal variation; Magnetic attraction*
27	deg	*Degrees (See E-20)*
28	dev	*Deviation*

Index of Abbreviations

A

Abbreviation	Meaning	Reference
aband.	Abandoned	F 37
ABAND LT HO	Abandoned lighthouse	If
abt.	About	F 17
AERO	Aeronautical	F 22; K 4
AERO R. Bn.	Aeronautical radiobeacon	M 16
AERO R. Rge.	Aeronautical radio range	Md
alt.	Altitude	E 18
Alt	Alternating (light)	K 26
Am	Amber	K 67a; L 48a
anc.	Ancient	F 9
Anch	Anchorage	B 15; G 1,2
Anch prohib	Anchorage prohibited	G 12
approx.	Approximate	F 34
Apprs.	Approaches	Bg
Apt.	Apartment	Ij
Arch.	Archipelago	B 20
Astro.	Astronomical	D 9
AUTH.	Authorized	Fc
Aux	Auxiliary (light)	K 51
Ave.	Avenue	I 26a

B

Abbreviation	Meaning	Reference
B	Bay	B 2
B	Bayou	Ba
B	Black	L 42
Bdy. Mon.	Boundary monument	D 14
BELL	Fog Bell	N 14
bet.	Between	Fi
B Hbr	Boat harbor	G 33
Bk	Bank	O 21
bk	Black	S 57
Bkw.	Breakwater	G 6
Bld	Boulder	B 32
Bldg.	Building	I 66
Blds	Boulders	S 11a
Blvd.	Boulevard	I 26b
B.M.	Bench mark	D 5
Bn	Beacon (in general)	L 52,53
BR.	Bridge	H 14
Br	Brown	L 46
br	Brown	S 64
brg.	Bearing	U 21
brk	Broken	S 47
Bu	Blue	K 63; L 48
bu	Blue	S 59
BWHB	Black and white horizontal bands	L 27
BWVS	Black and white vertical stripes	L 14,14a

C

Abbreviation	Meaning	Reference
C	Can; Cylindrical (buoy)	L 5
C	Cape	B 22
C	Cove	B 5a
Ca	Calcareous	S 12a
Cap.	Capitol	Ik
Cas.	Castle	I 4
Cath.	Cathedral	I 8a
cbl.	Cable length	E 10
C. G.	Coast Guard	J 3, Ja
ch	Chocolate	S 65
Ch.	Church	I 8
Chan	Channel	B 10
Chec	Checkered (buoy)	L 33
CHY.	Chimney	I 44
Cir	Cirripeda	S 38
Ck	Chalk	S 12
Cl	Clay	S 6
CL.	Clearance	Fd
cm.	Centimeter	E 4b
Cn	Cinders	S 21
Co.	Company	Il
Co	Coral	S 14
Co Hd	Coral head	Sa
concr.	Concrete	Ff
conspic.	Conspicuous	F 12
C. of E.	Corps of Engineers	Df
cor.	Corner	Fe
Corp.	Corporation	Im
Cov	Covers	O 33
corr.	Correction	E 17
cps	Cycles/second	Ef
Cr.	Creek	B 5
crs	Coarse	S 40
Cswy.	Causeway	H 3f
Ct. Ho.	Courthouse	I 64
CUP.	Cupola	I 36
Cus. Ho.	Customhouse	G 29

D

Abbreviation	Meaning	Reference
D	Doubtful	O 45
D.; Destr.	Destroyed	F 14; Ke
dec.	Decayed	S 52
deg.	Degrees	U 27
dev.	Deviation	U 28
Diag	Diagonal bands	L 33a
D. F. S.	Distance finding station	M 15
Di	Diatoms	S 34
DIA	Diaphone	N 9
Discol	Discolored	O 36
discontd.	Discontinued	F 25
dist.	Distant	F 16
dk	Dark	S 68
dm.	Decimeter	E 4a
Dol	Dolphin	G 21

E

Abbreviation	Meaning	Reference
E.	East, Eastern	U 2,10
Ed.	Edition	E 16
E.D.	Existence doubtful	O 43
elec.	Electric	F 29
elev.	Elevation	E 19
ELEV.	Elevator, Lift	I 37
Elev.	Elevation, Elevated	Ie
Entr	Entrance	B 11
E Int	Isophase lt.(equal interval)	K 23a
Est	Estuary	B 12
estab.	Established	F 28
Exper	Experimental (light)	Kh
exper.	Experimental	F 24
explos.	Explosive	F 27

Explos Anch	Explosive Anchorage (buoy)	L 25
Exting	Extinguished (light)	K 74
extr.	Extreme	F 40

F

F	Fixed (light)	K 21
Facty.	Factory	I 47
Fd	Fjord	B 3
F Fl	Fixed and flashing (light)	K 29
F Gp Fl	Fixed and group flashing (light)	K 30
Fl	Flash, Flashing (light)	K 23, 45
fl.	Flood	Fg; T 31
fly	Flinty	S 53
fm	Fathom	E 9
fne	Fine	S 39
Fog Det Lt	**Fog detector light**	**K 68a; Nb**
Fog Sig.	Fog signal station	N 1
FP.	Flagpole	J 19
Fr	Foraminifera	S 32
FS.	Flagstaff	J 19
Fsh stks	Fishing stakes	G 14
ft.	Foot	E 7
Ft.	Fort	I 19
F. TR.	Flag tower	J 19a
Fu	**Fucus**	**S 38a**
Fy.	Ferry	H 19

G

G	Gulf	B 1
G	Gravel	S 7
G	Green	K 64
G	Green	L 20, 20a, 45
GAB.	Gable	I 72
Gl	Globigerina	S 33
glac	Glacial	S 54
gn	Green	S 60
GONG	Fog gong	N 17
Govt. Ho.	Government House	I 30
Gp	Group	K 47
Gp Fl	Group flashing	K 28
Gp Occ	Group occulting	K 27
Grd, grd	Ground	S 1, 47a
Grs	Grass	S 28
gt.	Great	F 1
gty	Gritty	S 51
GUN	Explosive fog signal	N 3
GUN	Fog gun	N 10
Gy	Gray	L 47
gy	Gray	S 66

H

HB	Horizontal bands or stripes	L 31
Hbr	Harbor	B 16; G 3
Hd.	Head, Headland	B 24
HECP	Harbor entrance control post	Jd
Hk	Hulk	G 45
HHW	Higher high water	T 1a
Hn	Haven	B 16a; G 4
Hor	Horizontal lights	K 81
HOR. CL.	Horizontal clearance	H 18b
HORN	Fog trumpet; Fog horn; Reed horn; Typhon	N 12, 13, **13a**, 16, **Na**
Hosp.	Hospital	I 32
hr.	Hour	E 1
hrd	Hard	S 42
H. S.	High School	Ig
ht.	Height	E 19; T 25
HW	High water	T 1
Hy.	Highway	H 1
Hz	**Hertz**	**Ec**

I

I.	Island	B 18
I Qk; Int Qk	Interrupted quick	K 25
in.	Inch	E 6
In	Inlet	B 6
Inst.	Institute	I 61
Irreg	Irregular	K 71
ISLW	Indian spring low water	T 10
It.	Islet	B 19

K

K	Kelp	S 27
kc	**Kilocycle**	**Eg**
kHz	**Kilohertz**	**Ed**
km.	Kilometer	E 5
kn	Knots	E 12; T 24

L

L	Loch, Lough, Lake	B 4
La	Lava	S 17
Lag	Lagoon	Bf; C 16
lat.	Latitude	E 13
Ldg.	Landing; Landing place	B 33; G 16
Ldg. Lt.	Leading light	K 11
Le	Ledge	O 24
LLW	Lower low water	T 2a
L.N.M.	**Local Notice to Mariners**	**Fa**
long.	Longitude	E 14
LOOK. TR.	Lookout station; Watch tower	J 4
lrg	Large	F 3; S 45
LS. S.	Lifesaving station	J 6
Lt.	Light	K 2
lt	Light	S 67
Ltd.	Limited	Ii
Lt. Ho.	Lighthouse	K 3
LW	Low water	T 2
LWD	Low water datum	Ta

M

M	Nautical mile	E11; Kb
M	Mud, Muddy	S 3
m.	Meter	E 4, **d, e**
m. ; min.	Minute (of time)	E2; **Kc**
Ma	**Mattes**	**S 38b**
mag.	Magnetic	U 23
Magz.	Magazine	I 34
maintd.	Maintained	F 36

Mc	**Megacycle**	**Eh**
Mds	Madrepores	S 15
MHHW	Mean higher high water	T 8b
MHW	Mean high water	T 7a
MHWN	Mean high water neaps	T 8a
MHWS	Mean high water springs	T 8
MHz	**Megahertz**	**Ee**
MICRO. TR.	**Microwave tower**	**Mc**
mid.	Middle	F 7
Mkr	Marker	**Lc**
Ml	Marl	S 5
MLLW	Mean lower low water	T 9b
MLW	Mean low water	T 8c
MLWN	Mean low water neaps	T 9a
MLWS	Mean low water springs	T 9
mm.	Millimeter	E 4c
Mn	Manganese	S 22
Mo.	Morse **code light**	K 30a
mod.	Moderate	**Fh**
MON.	Monument	I 35
Ms	Mussels	S 25
M. Sec.	Microsecond	**Eb**
MSL	Mean sea level	T 4
Mt.	Mountain, Mount	B 26
Mth	Mouth	B 13
MTL	Mean tide level	T 3

N

N.	North; Northern	U 1, 9
N	Nun; Conical (buoy)	L 6
NAUTO	Nautophone	N 8
NE.	Northeast	U 5
N.M.	**Notice to Mariners**	**F 42**
No.	Number	E 23
Np	Neap tide	T 7
NW.	Northwest	U 8

O

OBSC	Obscured (light)	K 68
Obs. Spot	Observation spot	D 4
Obstr.	Obstruction	O 27
Obsy.	Observatory	J 21
Occ	Occulting (light); Occultation	K 22, 46
Occ	Intermittent (light)	K 48
Occas	Occasional (light)	F 39; K 70
Off.	Office	J 22
or	Orange	S 62
Or	Orange	K 65; L48b
OVHD. PWR. CAB.	Overhead power cable	H 4
Oys	Oysters; Oyster bed	S 24; G 15a
Oz	Ooze	S 4

P

P	Pebbles	S 9
P	Pillar (buoy)	L8a
P	Pond	Bb
P.	Port	B 17; G 5
P. A.	Position approximate	O 41
Pag.	Pagoda	I 14
Pass	Passage, Pass	B 9
Pav.	Pavilion	I 67
P. D.	Position doubtful	O 42
Pen.	Peninsula	B 21
PIL. STA.	Pilot station	J 8
Pk.	Peak	B 29
Pm	Pumice	S 18
Po	Polyzoa	S 37
P. O.	Post Office	I 29
P.; Pos.	Position	O 44
priv.	Private, Privately	F 30
Priv. maintd.	Privately maintained	K 17; L 29
Prohib.	Prohibited	F 26
prom.	Prominent	F 31
Prom.	Promontory	B 23
Prov	Provisional (light)	K 72
Pt.	Point	B 25
Pt	Pteropods	S 36
pub.	Publication	E 15
PWI	**Potable water intake**	

Q

Quar.	Quarantine	G 26
Qk Fl	Quick flashing (light)	K 24
Qz	Quartz	S 13

R

R	Red	K 66; L 15,43
R.	River	**Bd**
Ra	Radar station	M 11
Racon	Radar responder beacon	M 12
Ra (conspic)	Radar conspicuous object	M 14
Ra Ref	Radar reflector	Lf; M 13
RBHB	Red and black horizontal bands	L 17, 18, 19, 20, 20a
R Bn	Red beacon	L 52
R. Bn.	Radiobeacon	M 3, 4, 6
Rd	Radiolaria	S 35
rd	Red	S 63
Rd.	Road	H 1
Rd	Road, Roadstead	B 14
R.D.	Directional Radiobeacon; Radio range	M 5
R. D. F.	Radio direction finding station	M 7
REF	Reflector	K 10; L 64
Rep.	Reported	O 35
Rf	Reef	O 23
Rge.	Range	B 27
RGE	Range	**Kg**
Rk.	Rock	B 35
Rk, rky	Rock, Rocky	S 11
Rky.	Rocky	**Bh**
R. MAST	Radio mast	M 9
Rot	Revolving; Rotating (light)	K 31
RR.	Railroad	H 3
R.RELAY MAST	**Radio relay mast**	**Mb**
R. Sta.	Radio telegraph station; Q.T.G. Radio station	M 1, 10a
R. T.	Radio telephone station	M 2
rt	Rotten	S 48

R. TR.	Radio tower	M 9
Ru.	Ruins	I 40
RW Bn	Red and white beacon	L 52
Ry.	Railway	H 3

S

S	Sand	S 2
S	South; Southern	U 3, 11
S	Spar (buoy)	L 8
Sc	Scoriae	S 20
Sch.	Schist	S 13a
Sch.	School	I 65
Sd.	Sound	B 8
SD	Sounding doubtful	Q 1
SE.	Southeast	U 6
sec.	Second (of time)	E 3
sec	Seconds	Kd
SEC	Sector	K 49
Sem.	Semaphore	J 10
S Fl	Short flashing (light)	K 25a
sft	Soft	S 41
Sh	Shells	S 23
Shl	Shoal	O 22
Sig. Sta.	Signal station	J 9
SIREN	Fog siren	N 11
S-L Fl	Short-long flashing (light)	K 28a
Slu	Slough	Be; C 18
sml	Small	F 4 : S 44
Sn	Shingle	S 8
Sp	Spring tide	T 6
SP	Spherical (buoy)	L 7
Spg	Sponge	S 26
Spi	Spicules	S 31
S'PIPE	Standpipe	I 45
spk	Speckled	S 50
S. Sig. Sta.	Storm signal station	J 11
St.	Saint	F 11
St.	Street	I 26
St	Stones	S 10
Sta.	Station	J 1, 2
std.	Standard	F 32
stf	Stiff	S 43
Stg	Sea-tangle	S 29
stk	Sticky	S 46
St. M.	Statute mile	Ea
Str	Strait	B 7
Str	Stream	Bc; T 17
str	Streaky	S 49
sub	Submarine	F 20
SUB-BELL	Submarine fog bell	N 5,6
subm	Submerged	F 33
Subm	Submerged	Oa,30
Subm Ruins	Submerged ruins	Gd
SUB-OSC	Submarine oscillator	N 7
Sub Vol	Submarine volcano	O 8
SW.	Southwest	U 7

T

T.	Telephone	I 70; L 22c
T	True	U 22
T	Tufa	S 19
TB	Temporary buoy	L 30
Tel.	Telegraph	I 27; L 22b
Telem Ant	Telemetry antenna	Ma
Tel. Off.	Telegraph office	I 28
Temp	Temporary (light)	F 38; K 73
ten	Tenacious	S 55
Thoro	Thorofare	B 9
Tk.	Tank	I 53
TR.	Tower	I 41
TRLB, TRUB,	TLB, TUB	Ki, j, k, l
Tri.	Triangulation	D 10
TV TR.	Television tower (mast)	M 9a

U

Uncov	Uncovers	O 2
Uncov.	Uncovers; Dries	O 32, 34
Univ.	University	Ih
unverd.	Unverified	Fb
unev	Uneven	S 71

V

var.	Variation	U 24
vard	Varied	S 70
VB	Vertical beam	Kf
vel.	Velocity	T 23
Vert	Vertical (lights)	K 80
VERT. CL.	Vertical clearance	H 18a
Vi	Violet	K 61
vi	Violet	S 58
View X	View point	D 6
Vil.	Village	I 3
Vol.	Volcano	B 30
Vol	Volcanic	S 16
Vol Ash	Volcanic ash	Sb
VS	Vertical stripes	L 32

W

W.	West; Western	U 4, 12
W	White	K 67; L 41
wh	White	S 56
W Bn	White beacon	L 52
W.B. SIG.STA.	Weather Bureau signal station	Jb
Wd	Sea-weed	S 28
Whf.	Wharf	G 18
WHIS	Fog whistle	N 15
Wk	Wreck	O 15, 28
Wks	Wreckage	O 29
W Or	White and orange	Le

Y

Y	Yellow	L 24, 44
yl	Yellow	S 61
yd.	Yard	E 8

1st	First	Fj
2nd	Second	Fk
3rd	Third	Fl
4th	Fourth	Fm

°	Degree	E 20
′	Minute (of arc)	E 21
″	Second (of arc)	E 22

Chapter 9

The Rules of the Road

The International Rules of the Road is a set of conventions and traffic rules agreed to by most of the world's maritime nations and universally observed on the high seas. They are from time to time revised at international conventions in an attempt to bring them into line with the needs of modern shipping. However, to this day they remain an archaic set of rules, all but impossible to read intelligently, a patchwork of conflicting and ambiguous regulations, badly in need of complete overhaul—which at this writing is not in sight.

In addition, since the International Rules of the Road apply only on the high seas, each country has usually felt it necessary to devise a different set of rules of its own for exclusive use on its own inland waterways and harbors. In the United States we have no less than *five* such complete sets of rules, namely:

Inland Rules of the Road
Rules of the Road for the Great Lakes
Rules of the Road for western rivers
Pilot Rules for inland waters
Motorboat Act

These sets of rules are even more extreme than the international rules in their shortcomings, but it is unlikely that they are going to be revised in the foreseeable future, so we must live with them and obey them.

The primary purpose of the Rules of the Road is to prevent collision between vessels of all kinds, under all circumstances, in all waters. It has been said that if the rules were followed implicitly at all times by all vessels, no collision could ever occur. This is probably not true. What is true is that most collisions occur in broad daylight in perfect visibility and are due to misunderstanding and faulty judgment on the part of the men in command.

However, as navigators it is our duty to learn and know the rules and be ready to observe and practice them at all times—correctly. When emergency stares you in the face there will never be time to look up the applicable rule. You must so steep yourself in this knowledge that you instinctively do the right thing—and know why! The great Admiral Knight, who wrote the famous *Knight's Seamanship,* used to make all his officers read the entire Rules of Road every time they left for sea—even if they had read them the week before!

If you do not have a copy of the Rules of the Road, it is available free by writing the Commandant (CHS), U.S. Coast Guard Headquarters, Washington, D.C., or asking for it at any Coast Guard office. It can also be had from the Supt. of Documents, but that takes longer.

In this chapter we shall discuss mainly the International and Inland Rules of the Road, get the most important information across, make some comparisons, and note some differences. The rest of your knowledge will come from actually reading the rules as often as possible, and relating your reading to this chapter in case you become confused —as well you may. But don't feel discouraged—everybody has trouble reading the rules.

In this discussion, there will be no attempt to cover or enumerate every single item of information in the rules. The approach is from the standpoint of the amateur boat operator who wants to know all he *needs* to know to do the right thing on the water. The professional officer in the merchant marine or the Navy must learn everything in the rules to pass his examinations. The boat builder must know all the technical details pertaining to installation and performance of navigational equipment, and will likely get his information from a naval architect; these people will take a different approach to the rules.

What the amateur sailor wants to know is: What must I do to be correct and what is the meaning of that which I hear and see around me on the water?

Organization The International Rules of the Road consist of thirty-one main *rules,* and each rule may have several subdivisions. The Inland Rules have thirty-two main *articles,* and each article may have several subdivisions. In many places the two sets agree, and in many others they show differences. The rules and articles are divided into six parts, labeled A to F.

Where Rules Apply International Rules apply on the so-called high seas or international waters, for which each country sets its own limiting lines. In the U.S. the line of demarcation between inland waters and the high seas is determined by the Coast Guard and is specifically and precisely described in Part 82 of the Pilot Rules for all U.S. coasts. Generally speaking, the line passes through the outermost buoys or other aids to navigation and runs parallel to the coastline, but not always.

The Inland Rules apply to most harbors and inland waterways, with certain exceptions, mainly the Great Lakes and the large rivers. For example, in the Gulf of Mexico, International Rules prevail. And at the mouth of the Mississippi River, Inland Rules take over as far as the Huey P. Long Bridge, at which point the Rules of the Road for western rivers must be observed.

Penalties The International Rules provide no penalty for violations of the rules, presumably because it would be difficult to enforce. The Inland Rules specifically provide a penalty of up to $500 plus damages for any pilot, engineer, mate, or master who violates the rules. They also provide a fine of $500 for the *vessel* itself, if it is operated in violation of the rules, and—nasty idea—half of the fine goes to the informer.

In addition, although not a part of the rules as such, the Motorboat Act of 1940 provides for a penalty of up to $2,000 and/or up to one year in prison for negligent operation of a motorboat, and lesser fines, up to $200, for operating in violation of the regulations of that act.

Now let us examine the six main divisions, or parts, of the rules. Both International and Inland Rules follow the same system of division into parts.

Part A— Preliminary and Definitions

Here we find the ground rules and basic definitions that are the foundation for all the rules. We learn, for instance, that the International Rules apply to seaplanes in the water, whereas the Inland Rules ignore seaplanes. The following definitions and rules are important.

Required Lights on Vessels must be shown from sunset to sunrise and no lights may be shown which can be mistaken for prescribed lights. The International Rules allow you to show these lights between sunrise and sunset if visibility is restricted.

Power-Driven Vessel or Steam Vessel means any vessel propelled by machinery. A vessel under both sail *and* power is considered a power-driven vessel; but if a power vessel is operated under sail only, she is considered a sailing vessel.

Under Way is a term meaning that a vessel is not at anchor, not made fast to the shore, and not aground. This is important to remember, because different signals are given and different lights and shapes are displayed in each situation.

Visible When applied to lights shall mean visible on a dark night with a clear atmosphere.

In Sight Vessels are in sight *only* when one can be observed visually from the other. This can be an important distinction in fog, for example, where fog signals are given as long as passing vessels cannot see one another; but as soon as the other ship is sighted, regular traffic signals are given.

Short Blast a blast of sound of about 1 second's duration.

Prolonged Blast One that lasts from 4 to 6 seconds.

Whistle Any apparatus, operated by power, that can make loud blasts of sound. It can be a steam whistle, air whistle, or electrical horn.

Foghorn A device which makes a hornlike sound and is operated by either mechanical means or blown by mouth. Actually, there is no real definition of a foghorn anywhere in the rules.

Engaged in Fishing Means fishing with nets, lines, or trawls, but does not include fishing with trolling lines. (You will hear more about this later in the rules. Essentially, it means that the usual privileges of right of way given fishing vessels are not extended to vessels sailing along pulling trolling lines behind them.)

Section A would have been the logical place to give a *complete* set of basic definitions and basic ground rules, but this is not the case.

Part B—Lights and Shapes

Here the fun begins. There is no earthly reason for the difference in required lights in the two sets of rules, but they are there and we must reckon with them.

To begin with, under Inland Rules, all vessels under 65 feet, except tugboats, come under the Motorboat Act, which will be discussed separately. The following therefore applies in general to larger ships.

Running Lights •

All power-driven vessels under way must carry a green sidelight on the starboard side and a red sidelight on the port side, each to show from dead ahead to 2 points (22½°) abaft the beam. They must also have a white stern light with a sector of 12 points (135°), showing dead astern, 6 points either side the center line. (There are 32 points in a circle, each point equal to 11¼°.)

These vessels must also carry two white range lights, the after light being higher than the forward light. They are carried on the masts; but if a vessel has only one mast, then the forward light is carried in the forepart of the vessel. On the high seas, both lights are the same and both show in a sector of 20 points, 10 either side. Vessels under 150 feet in length need carry only one masthead light, but may carry both.

The Inland Rules provide a distinction: A vessel which *may* go on the high seas (called a seagoing vessel) can have the same 20-point range lights as called for under International Rules, described above; but if such vessel does not go on the high seas, she must have a 32-point (360°) *after* range light, instead of the 20-point light.

Under Inland Rules all ferryboats carry two white 360° range lights (visible all around the horizon) at an equal height above the deck.

Lights for Tugboats •

These are of special importance to the yachtsman or other small-boat operator, because they reveal the meaning of all those lights one may see up ahead on a dark night. It is entirely possible that two sets of lights may be connected by a steel hawser, and anyone trying to go between could come to serious grief.

On the high seas, a tugboat pulling behind her a tow that is over 600 feet long carries on the after mast two more white 20-point lights, or a total of three identical lights in a vertical line. If the tow is less than 600 feet, she carries only one more such light, or a total of two. The vessel being towed must carry red and green sidelights and a white stern light. In the daytime, both tug and tow display from the yardarm a black diamond-shaped object if tow is in excess of 600 feet.

In inland waters, a tugboat that has the tow alongside or is pushing it ahead shows two identical white lights on the after mast and, if she is pulling her tow astern, regardless of length, she carries three white lights in a vertical line. As always, the regular after range light is one of these. If this tug is headed for the high seas (seagoing vessel), the range and towing lights can all be 20 points; but if she is operating only in inland waters, these must be 32-point lights. Note that the forward range light is always a 20-point light so as not to interfere with visibility from the bridge. A bright light forward at night can prevent a person from seeing into the darkness.

If a tug in inland waters is pushing the tow ahead, she must show at the stern two amber lights similar in construction to the stern light, that is, showing in a sector of 12 points. This is important to remember when you are overtaking a tug pushing a tow ahead on some dark night.

Vessels towed in inland waters must also show the red and green sidelights, but do not show any white lights. This, however, does not apply to barges, canal boats, etc., which under an elaborate set of rules of their own do show white lights, but no colored lights.

Other Vessels •

In Section B, the International Rules list lights and shapes for vessels under certain circumstances, while the Inland Rules get around to this in the Pilot Rules. For the sake of clarity, we shall cover both sets here.

Vessel Not Under Command Only the International Rules cover this specifically. If a vessel is not under command she will show two red lights vertically, and in the daytime she will show two black balls at the yardarm, in a vertical line. However, any time in inland waters you see two red lights in a vertical line, you will know that the vessel is not free to maneuver, the signal being used often on work vessels of various descriptions.

On the high seas, any work boats—such as those that lay cable or perform service or salvage work—other than fishing boats, pilot boats, and minesweepers, while at work and therefore unable to maneuver freely, show at night three lights in a vertical line, the top and bottom lights red and the middle light white. In the daytime they show three shapes, two red balls with a white diamond shape in the middle.

The Pilot Rules provide a nightmare of different signals, different for each type of vessel and each condition of operation. For the amateur it is sufficient that you read over this part of the Pilot Rules once and then remember henceforth that every time you see vertically displayed red lights, usually two, and various shapes in various colors and stripes, you have some kind of working vessel that you should stay clear of. Whether it is a Coast Guard buoy tender or a National Ocean Survey vessel is probably of little importance. You know that you must give them a clear berth since they are not free to move, so evaluate each situation as it arrives. Watch, however, for a vessel towing submerged objects. She shows two red and two white towing lights in a vertical line, but obviously cannot show a light on the tow.

Minesweeper. The Inland Rules have nothing to say on this, but the International Rules state that a minesweeper must carry a green 360° light at the top of the foremast and a similar green light at the end(s) of the yardarm on the side(s) where danger exists. In the daytime she carries black balls instead of the green lights. When shown, these signals mean it is not safe to approach within half a mile astern or a quarter-mile on the side where danger exists.

Sailing Vessels Under both Inland and International Rules, sailing vessels carry the colored sidelights and the white stern lights, but not any other white lights. In addition, on the high seas a sailing vessel *may* carry two lights at the top of the foremast, red over green, both 20-point lights, visible for 2 miles.

It is further provided under both sets of rules that if the weather is bad, vessels under forty feet need not display the lights, but must keep them handy to flash on approach of other vessels. Rowboats or very small sailboats need only carry a flashlight to show when needed.

Remember • If a vessel is under both sail and power, she is considered a power boat.

Pilot Vessels Here there is little difference between the two sets of rules. A regular, power-driven pilot vessel cruising on her station will carry the regular sidelights, but in addition she will carry a white light at the masthead visible around the horizon and, vertically below, a red light. In addition, she will show a white flare-up light every 10 minutes or so.

A sailing vessel serving as a pilot vessel will not show the red light, but will show a white 360° light at the masthead, visible for 3 miles. She will also show the colored running lights when approaching other vessels.

Fishing Vessels The Inland Rules simply specify that a vessel trawling, dredging, or fishing with any kind of gear must show a red light over a white light somewhere in the rigging. In the daytime she shows a basket, hoisted in the rigging. Of course, in all these situations, if they are under way they must show the regular running lights; but if they are anchored or drifting they douse their running lights.

Under International Rules, vessels fishing (except those

trawling) show the same red over white lights as in inland waters. A vessel with its trawl out must show a green over a white light in the rigging. All such working lights are visible all around the horizon. In the daytime on the high seas, fishing vessels must display a black shape consisting of two cones, points together, vertically one above the other. If gear extends out more than 500 feet, a black cone, point upward, is displayed in the direction of the gear. At night, such vessels may flash lights on their gear to attract attention. However, remember that vessels with trolling lines are not considered fishing vessels. Vessels show running lights only if making way.

Anchor Lights and Shapes Under both sets of rules, vessels that are under 150 feet in length and at anchor must show a white 32-point light hoisted in the forepart of the vessel (usually on the bowstay). If they are over 150 feet, a similar second light is to be hoisted near the stern and lower than the forward light. In the daytime, any vessel at anchor must hoist a black ball in the forward rigging.

Under International Rules, a vessel aground at night must display the regular lights for a vessel at anchor, and must also show two red vertical lights (same as for a vessel not under command); in the daytime she shows three black balls hoisted vertically. The Inland Rules provide no instruction for a vessel aground, but the courts have ruled that a vessel aground in inland waters for purposes of lights is a vessel at anchor.

The government may designate certain inland areas as specific boat anchorages, and vessels under 65 feet when anchored there need not show any lights or shapes.

Finally, part B provides that a vessel under both sail and power on the high seas shall carry by day a black conical shape, point downward to convey this fact, and the Inland Rules finish off by stating that a steamer, with funnels up, proceeding under sail alone, *may* carry a black ball in the rigging! File and forget!

Part C—Sound Signals and Conduct in Restricted Visibility

This section begins with the statement that power-driven vessels give their fog signals on the whistle or siren, and sailing vessels give theirs on the foghorn. Power-driven vessels must have a foghorn, but they can only use it if they are being towed, in which case they may give the signal on the foghorn instead of the whistle.

When Signals Are Given In fog, mist, falling snow, or heavy rainstorms, whether by day or night. This is important. Fog signals are, however, never given when ships are in sight of one another.

Power-Driven Vessel Under Way—High Seas Gives a prolonged blast not more than 2 minutes apart. *Inland waters:* Gives prolonged blast not more than 1 minute apart.

Power-Driven Vessel Stopped and Making No Way—High Seas Gives two prolonged blasts every 2 minutes, with 1 second between them.

Sailing Vessel Under Way Some rules apply to high seas and inland waters. Signals are given every minute as follows:

Vessel on starboard tack (having the wind on the starboard side)—one blast

Vessel on port tack (having the wind on the port side)—two blasts in succession

Vessel with wind abaft the beam—three blasts in succession

The rules do not state whether they should be long or short blasts.

Vessel at Anchor Inland Rules simply state that you must ring the bell rapidly for 5 seconds every minute, except in designated anchorages, where no signal is required. International Rules also say to ring the bell rapidly for 5 seconds every minute; in addition, vessels over 350 feet in length must give a different signal, such as beating a gong, on the stern for 5 seconds every minute. Every vessel at anchor may also, if desired, give a warning signal of one short, one prolonged, and one short blast on the whistle.

Vessels Towing or Being Towed Under Inland Rules a tugboat with tow gives a prolonged blast every minute, followed by two short blasts, and her tow may give the same signal, presumably on a foghorn.

Under International Rules the same signal is given, not only by tugboats, but also by other boats that cannot maneuver freely, such as cable ships, etc.; but a fog signal can be given only by the last vessel in the tow, and consists of *four* blasts—*one prolonged* blast followed by *three short* blasts—which can be given on the whistle or foghorn, immediately after the signal given by the towing vessel. This is a great help to other vessels because it distinguishes between tug and tow.

Vessels Aground In international waters a vessel aground gives the same signal as a vessel at anchor: bell and, if over 350 feet, gong, and in addition three separate distinct strokes on the bell just before and after ringing the bell.

Inland Rules are silent on this, but courts have ruled a vessel aground must give *distress* signals, i.e., continuous sounding of the whistle.

There are various other miscellaneous provisions you will note as you read the rules. Small boats need not make these signals, but should make some other noise that can be heard. A pilot vessel cruising on her station in international waters must give the regular signals for vessels under way or stopped, but in addition she gives an identifying signal of *four short* blasts. This is helpful knowledge when you are trying to pick up a pilot in the fog. Don't confuse this with the danger signal of five short blasts in international waters and four short blasts in inland waters.

Now comes the really important part of this section: *speed in fog*. The rules say that you must go at *moderate speed* in fog, but they don't say what moderate speed is. The courts have held that "moderate speed" is such that you can come to a full stop in one-half the visible distance ahead. With that to go by, each skipper will decide what to do. However, there is another important rule: A power-driven vessel hearing, apparently forward of the beam, the fog signal of another vessel he cannot see must stop his engines and navigate with caution until danger of collision is past. The foregoing can be found in both Inland and

International Rules, but the latter adds an important provision:

If you detect another vessel forward of your beam, you *must* take *early* and *substantial* action to avoid collision. It is not enough to change the course slightly and slow down a little. If necessary, you must stop, reverse engines, and do anything else that will prevent danger.

Part D—Steering and Sailing Rules

The rules in this section apply only to vessels that are approaching and within sight of one another, and they begin by pointing out that risk of collision can be ascertained by carefully watching the compass bearing of the other vessel. If the bearing does not change materially, a risk of collision exists. This is very good advice and should be used in all crossing situations.

Sailing Vessels

First we are given the rules for sailing vessels. The International Rules are simple:

1. A vessel with the wind on the port side must keep out of the way of a vessel which has the wind on the starboard side.
2. When both have the wind on the same side, the vessel to windward shall keep out of the way of the vessel to leeward.

The Inland Rules are more specific:

1. A vessel running free keeps out of the way of a vessel close-hauled.
2. A vessel close-hauled on the port tack gives way to a vessel close-hauled on the starboard tack.
3. If both are running free with the wind on opposite sides, the vessel with wind on the port side gives way to the other.

4. If both are running free with wind on the same side, the vessel to windward keeps out of the way of the other.
5. A vessel that has the wind aft must stay clear of the other vessel.

Power Vessels

High seas If two vessels are meeting nearly head-on, each shall change his course to starboard so that they will pass port to port. As they change the course each shall give one blast on the whistle to indicate that she is *changing course.* Unless a vessel changes course, she does not give a signal on the high seas. In the head-on situation *neither* is the privileged vessel.

If two vessels are in a crossing situation, the vessel that has the other on her own starboard side in the sector from dead ahead to 2 points abaft the beam (same as the sector of her green sidelight), is the burdened vessel and must keep out of the way of the other vessel. She must, if necessary, stop, reverse her engines, change course to starboard, or do whatever is necessary to keep clear and under no circumstances attempt to pass ahead of the other vessel. The privileged vessel, i.e., the vessel that has the right of way, must keep course and speed, and if the burdened vessel does not keep clear, she must give the *danger signal*—five or more short blasts in rapid succession.

Inland Waters If two vessels are meeting head-on or nearly so, they shall pass port to port, changing course if necessary, and each shall signify her intent by one short and distinct blast on the whistle, which must instantly be answered by the other.

If the vessels are nearly head-on, but so far to starboard of one another that it makes better sense to pass starboard to starboard, then each shall signify that intent by giving two short blasts of the whistle. In inland waters, these signals must always be answered in kind by the other vessel.

If two vessels are in a crossing situation, the one having the other on her own starboard side in the sector from dead vessel and must give way to the other vessel, which is ahead to 2 points abaft the beam is considered the burdened considered to be the privileged vessel. The privileged vessel is required to hold course and speed; the burdened vessel must take whatever action needed to keep clear, and she must never pass ahead or turn left. To signify intent, either vessel gives one short blast on the whistle, which in this case means: "I am going to leave you on my port side." The other vessel answers with the same signal to indicate that she agrees.

The Pilot Rules expressly forbid the use of *cross signals* —answering one blast with two or vice versa. If the skipper does not agree to a signal or maneuver, he must give the *danger signal*—four or more short blasts in rapid succession—and both vessels must stop, and reverse if necessary, until a proper understanding is arrived at.

When one vessel wishes to overtake another in inland waters, she gives one blast if she intends to leave the vessel ahead on her own port side, and two blasts if she wishes to leave the other vessel to starboard. She must then wait until the vessel ahead answers with the same signal, indicating consent, after which she can proceed with caution. Unless the overtaking vessel gets this consent she may not proceed. If the vessel ahead deems the overtaking to be dangerous, she must give the danger signal. She cannot ignore the overtaking vessel.

When a vessel approaches a bend in a channel beyond which visibility is restricted, she must give one long blast on the whistle when she is half a mile from the bend. Another vessel around the bend and within a half mile of the bend must immediately answer with a long blast, after which the two vessels begin to exchange the regular passing signals.

A Vessel Leaving a Dock, where other ships are likely to pass, must give one long blast. If her engines are going astern or, with engines stopped, she is moving astern, she must also give three short blasts to indicate that fact. If she is backing out, for purposes of determining right of way her stern is considered to be her bow while she is making sternway, but the courts usually have ruled this to be a "special circumstance" where everyone must maneuver with caution until clear.

Comparison of International and Inland Signals •

Before going further into this subject, let us note the difference between traffic signals on the high seas and in inland waters. On the high seas a signal of one blast means: "I am directing my course to starboard." Two blasts mean: "I am directing my course to port." These signals are given only when an actual change of course takes place, and they are not answered. The privileged vessel must hold course and speed, and the burdened vessel must give way—i.e., slow up, stop, turn left or right, but not pass ahead. Three blasts mean: "My engines are going full speed astern." (Courts have ruled that the signal must be given even when the engines are not "full speed" astern. If the engines are going astern at all, or the vessel is making sternway, the signal must be given.)

In inland waters, the signals are *passing signals,* showing intent, whether accompanied by a change of course or not. The Pilot Rules require that signals be given by vessels within half a mile of one another, if they can see each other. One blast means: "I am leaving you on my port side." Two blasts mean: "I am leaving you on my starboard side." Three blasts mean: "My engines are going astern." One- and two-blast signals must always be answered in inland waters. In poor visibility, only fog signals are given.

The Danger Signal is not less than five short blasts on the high seas and not less than four in inland waters.

Sailing Vessels have the right of way over power-driven vessels, both on the high seas and in inland waters. However, this rule does not give a small sailing vessel the right to hamper, in a narrow channel, the safe passage of a power-driven vessel which can navigate only inside such a channel. The latter regulation was added in 1967, and at the same time the Inland Rules were amended to state: "In narrow channels a steam vessel [i.e., any power vessel] of less than 65 feet in length shall not hamper the safe passage of a vessel which can navigate only inside that channel." In other words, a big ship in a narrow channel has the right of way over smaller boats, including sailboats.

A burdened vessel must always take *early* and *positive*

action to stay clear of the privileged vessel. There is no room for brinksmanship here. An overtaking vessel is always a burdened vessel and must stay clear of the overtaken vessel. The rules provide that any vessel approaching another from more than 2 points abaft her beam is an overtaking vessel, and if she is in doubt, she should assume that she is an overtaking vessel.

All vessels under way shall keep clear of *fishing vessels* engaged in fishing, but a fishing vessel does not have the right to obstruct a fairway, such as a channel or other narrow passage. Finally, D provides what is perhaps the most important rule in the book, *the prudence rule:*

"In obeying and construing these Rules due regard shall be had to all dangers of navigation and collision and to any special circumstances, including the limitations of the craft involved, which may render a departure from the above rules necessary in order to avoid immediate danger."

This is the one rule you should study carefully and then *memorize!* It means you must try to avoid the collision whether you have the right of way or not.

Part E—Sound Signals for Vessels in Sight of One Another

This is really a recapitulation of Part D and should have been included in that section as we have done here. The only new thing added is, under International Rules, permission to use a visual signal that operates simultaneously with the sound signals given on the whistle. The signal is in the form of a bright white light, visible all around the horizon for 5 miles. This light goes on automatically when the whistle is sounded.

Part F—Miscellaneous

This part contains the all-important *rule of good seamanship,* Rule 29 of the International Rules and Article 29 of the Inland Rules, which says:

"Nothing in these rules shall exonerate any vessel or the

owner, master, or crew thereof, from the consequences of any neglect to carry lights or signals, or of any neglect to keep a proper look-out, or of the neglect of any precaution which may be required by the ordinary practice of seamen, or by the *special circumstances of the case*."

Whereas Rule 27 said you must be ready to depart from the rules if circumstances require it, Rule 29 says that you must use common sense where *special circumstances* occur for which specific action is not spelled out in the rules. What all this really means is that you are not privileged to have an accident! You must obey the rules to the last minute, but when disaster stares you in the face, you must be ready to throw the rules to the wind, break them if that will avoid a collision and exercise the seamanlike judgment that will avoid disaster. You *may* have had the right of way up to the point of collision, but if you don't do all you can to avoid it, you have no rights at all.

This part of the rules also lists eleven distress signals approved under International Rules, and three that are approved under Inland Rules.

Other Rules

If you are going to operate on the Great Lakes or on the western rivers of the U.S., it is imperative that you obtain copies of the rules for those waters and study them carefully. You will find, for example, that within the Great Lakes Rules there is an entirely separate set of rules for the St. Mary's River in Michigan. It is obviously impossible for one person to know all these rules perfectly, so concentrate on the rules for those waters in which you regularly operate and don't worry about the others until you have to go there.

The Motorboat Act

This U.S. Motorboat Act, dating back to 1940, has had a few revisions since it was first promulgated. Since most yachts and smaller pleasure boats come within the pro-

Lights Required on Boats Underway Between Sunset and Sunrise
For Power Boats Under 65 Feet and All Sailing Vessels

Vessels at anchor must display anchor lights except those under 65 feet in "special anchorage area"

MOTORBOAT ACT (Act of April 25, 1940).—

used where Inland, Western Rivers and Great Lakes Rules apply

POWER ALONE	SAIL and POWER	AUXILIARY: SAIL ALONE*	SAILBOATS
under 26′ in length 32 pts 2 mi white red green comb 20 pts 1 mi	32 pts 2 mi white red green comb 20 pts 1 mi	12 pts 2 mi white red green comb 20 pts 1 mi	12 pts 2 mi white red green 10 pts 2 mi – Sidelights
26′ to 65′ in length 32 pts 2 mi white 10 pts 1 mi red green white 10 pts 1 mi 20 pts 2 mi	32 pts 2 mi white 10 pts 1 mi red green white 10 pts 1 mi 20 pts 2 mi	12 pts 2 mi white 10 pts 1 mi red green 10 pts 1 mi	*Stern light not required for vessels under sail alone on Great Lakes Manually propelled vessels shall have a white light ready to be temporarily exhibited in time to prevent collision.

INTERNATIONAL RULES.—

required on high seas, may be used inland

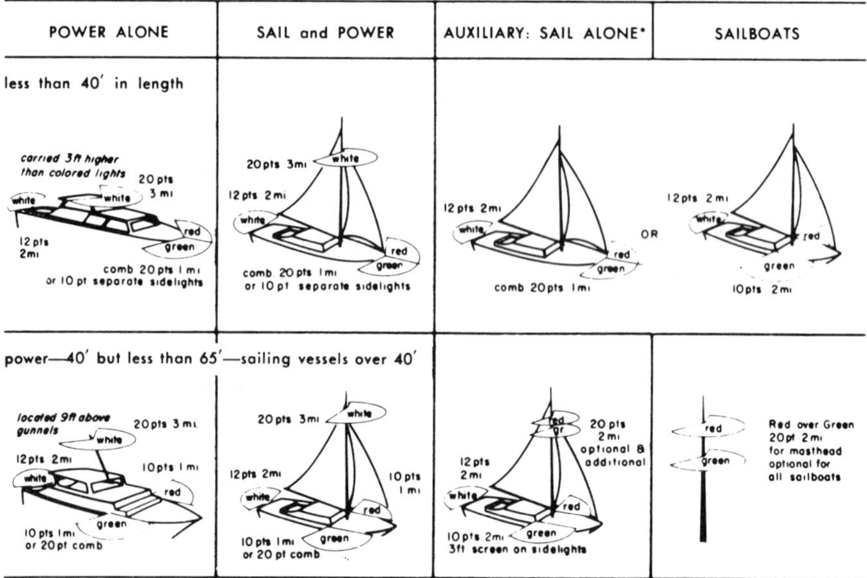

FIG. 9-1 Required lights on boats under 65 feet and all sailing vessels

visions of the act, it is essential that you know what it is all about.

To begin with, it defines a motorboat as a vessel less than 65 feet in length and driven by machinery, *except* tugboats driven by steam. Next, it divides all motorboats into four groups according to size:

Class A—less than 16 feet in length
Class 1—16 feet or over and less than 26 feet
Class 2—26 feet or over and less than 40 feet
Class 3—40 feet or over and not more than 65 feet

For these four classes—and, of course, included are sailing auxiliaries when operated under power—the act prescribes a variety of lights and equipment. These are best studied in the diagrams in Fig. 9–1, taken from the Coast Guard *Boating Guide,* C.G. 340. Note that motorboats in inland waters *may* carry the lights prescribed by the International Rules, but the opposite is not allowed. When in international waters you must obey International Rules.

If a boat is operated in violation of these regulations a fine of $100 can be levied, and if the boat is carrying passengers for hire the fine is $200. It can be imposed on the owner, the operator, or both. If a boat is operated in a *negligent* manner, the operator can be fined up to $2,000 and/or sentenced up to one year in jail. If a boat is in an accident where there is personal injury or death, or damage to property of more than $100, a report must be filed with the Coast Guard or with state authorities.

Practice Problems •

Following are typical lights you will see at night at sea. What kind of vessel is indicated in each case, and from what angle are you viewing it?

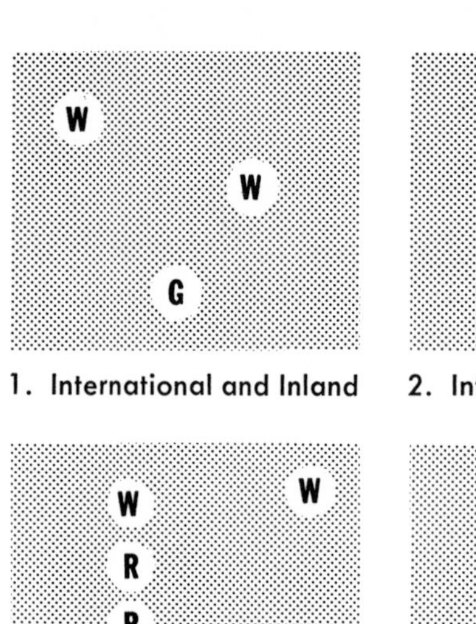

1. International and Inland

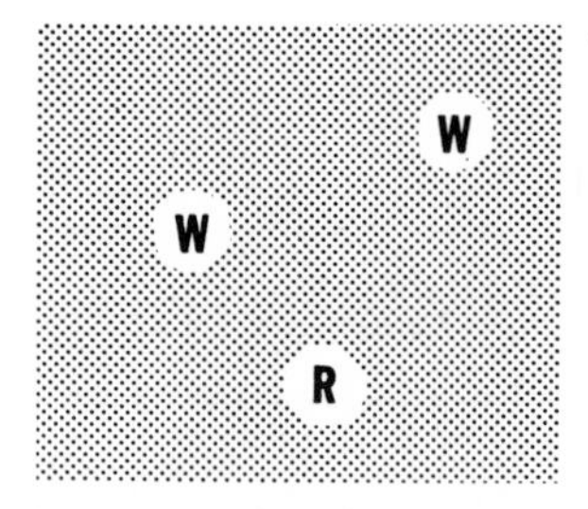

2. International and Inland

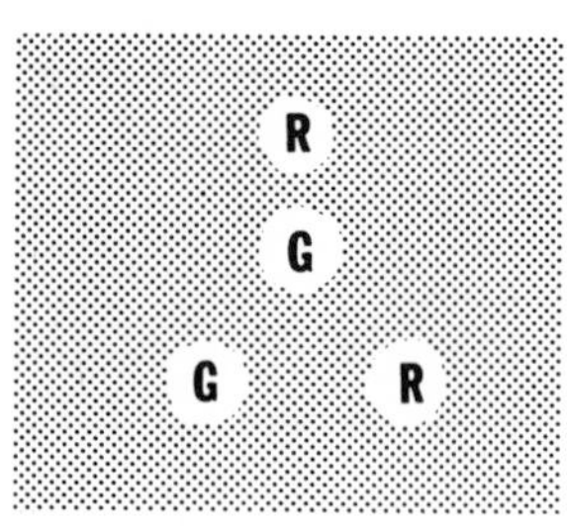

3. International

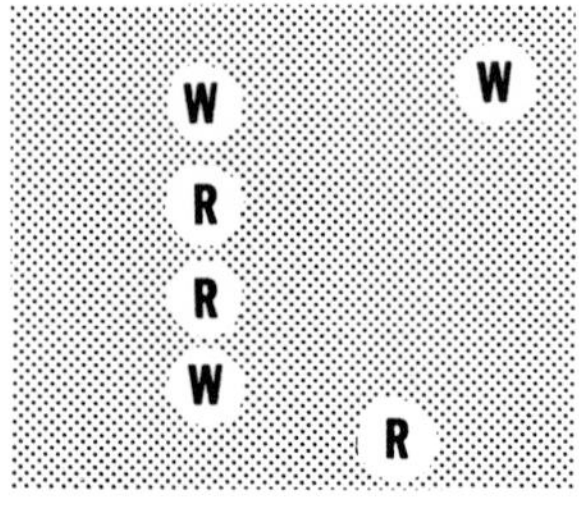

4. Inland

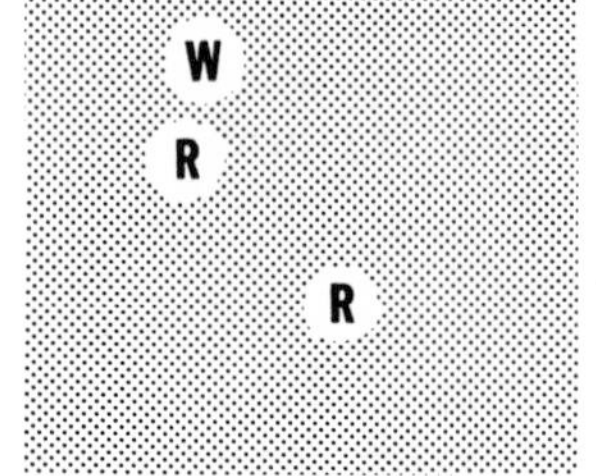

5. International and Inland

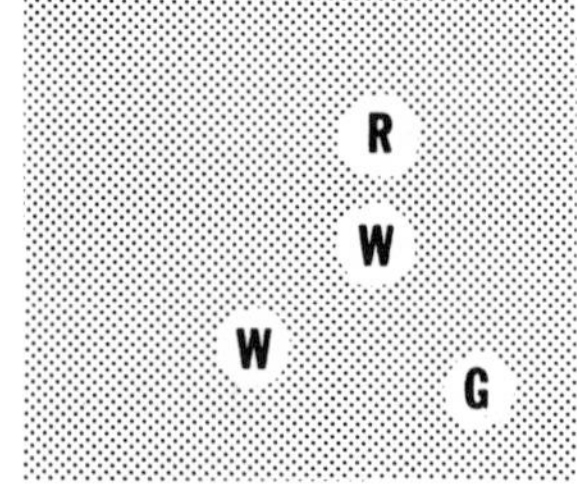

6. International

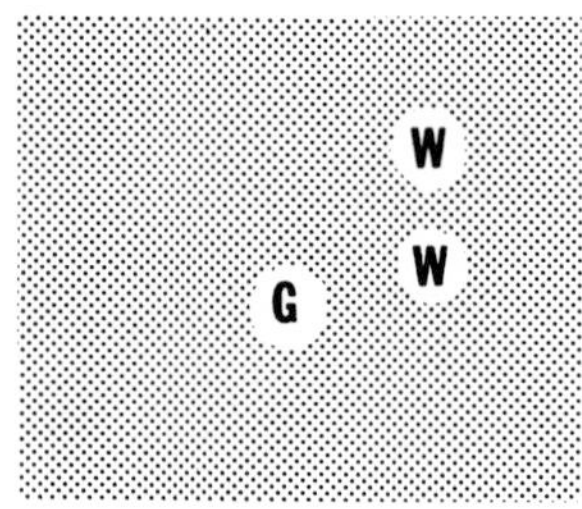

7. International

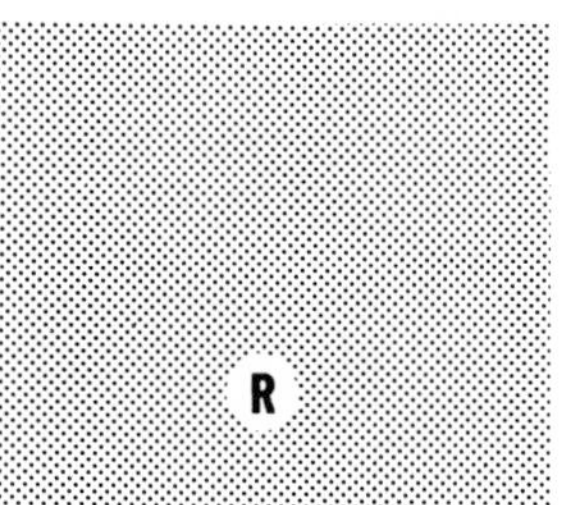

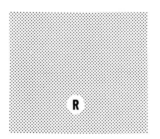

8. International and Inland

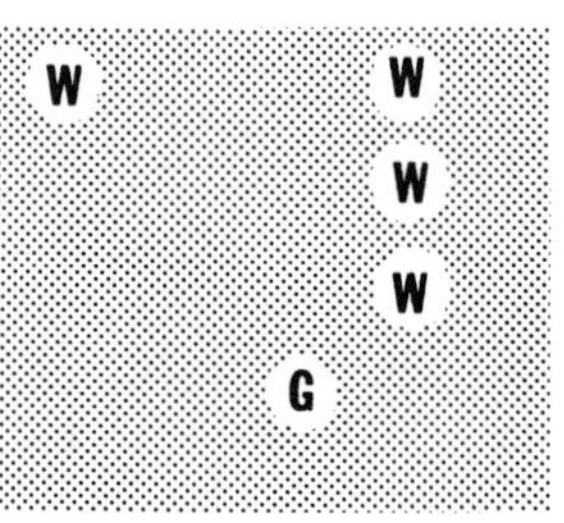

9. International and Inland

G – Green R – Red W – White

PART II

Electronic Navigation

Electronic science has taken enormous strides since the invention of wireless telegraphy, and it is natural that scientists have found many useful and practical applications in the field of navigation. The first was radio, the sending of the human voice over the airwaves, carrying messages, giving weather warnings, providing an easy means of communication from ship to ship and between ship and shore.

The second important step was the sending of time signals to ships at sea, enabling them to check their chronometers daily and thus improve their navigation. Later, various maritime countries established fixed shore stations to which ships could radio for a bearing of the ship from the station. Each bearing, of course, would be a line of position, and if two stations were available they would provide a fix. Next came the development of a ship-borne radio direction finder together with vast implementation of marine and aircraft radio beacons along our coastlines. Ultimately, distance-measuring equipment was incorporated in many such devices, particularly in the air, where omnirange navigation reached a high degree of development, so that a pilot could fix his position as so many miles in a given direction from a radio beacon on land, or perhaps on an ocean station ship.

During World War II American and British scientists independently developed radar, and shortly afterward loran (for *long-range navigation)* was perfected at the Massachusetts Institute of Technology. Both were extremely useful in both sea and air navigation. Loran is based on our ability to locate a position as the intersection of two or more hyperbolic lines of position on a special loran chart by measuring the difference in the time it takes synchronized radio pulses from two widely separated stations to reach the ship. The method has seen several refinements and new approaches, as in Decca navigation and the still newer Omega navigation system.

With the advent of our exploration of space, still more electronic research has enabled us to develop inertial navigation systems which make use of complex electronic sensors and acceleration-measuring devices. Once the initial latitude and longitude of point of departure (such as the end of a runway) is fed into the system, computers take over and account for every motion of an aircraft in altitude, distance, and azimuth, recording this motion as a trace on an actual chart as the aircraft travels over its path.

Satellite navigation makes use of equipment which measures a Doppler shift of an approaching or receding satellite. The navigator feeds an estimated position and the ship's speed and direction into a ship-borne computer and each satellite provides him with a fix four times a day (or night) in the form of a printed statement of his latitude and longitude, or as a direct trace on a chart.

Both inertial and satellite systems require the use of enormously expensive equipment and will be of theoretical interest only to the yachtsman or small-vessel operator. The navigator must always keep in mind that electronic equipment is subject to failure of many kinds, and he must at a moment's notice be prepared to fall back on the methods used by sailors for hundreds of years and rely on sextant, watch, pelorus, and compass.

Chapter 10

Direction-Distance Methods

Although there are still some shore-based radio direction finder stations around the world, which on request will give the bearing of a ship from the station, the most common method is to have a radio direction finder instrument, commonly known as RDF, aboard each vessel. There are many different models on the market, and, as always with such devices, it is important to study the instruction manual that comes with each set. However, they all work on the same basic principle, using a directional antenna to show the direction of the sending station from the ship.

Sources The stations are usually one of five kinds: (1) a marine transmitter located on the shore; (2) a radio beacon on a buoy in a fixed location at sea; (3) a radio beacon on an ocean station ship or lighthouse structure; (4) an aeronautical radio beacon; or (5) a commercial broadcasting station. Regular radio beacons usually operate in the medium-frequency range.

H.O. 117, *Radio Navigational Aids,* lists all the regular marine radio beacons, whether on land or sea, giving their operating frequency and recognition signal. The latter is usually a combination of dots and dashes that may or may not be the same as Morse code letters, but are not intended to be so. Some aeronautical beacons are indicated along coastlines on marine charts and they are of course shown completely on proper aeronautical charts. When regular radio beacons are used, the set is simply tuned to the proper frequency and the operator makes sure he can identify the recognition signal before he begins to take bearings.

When a commercial broadcasting station is used, it is important to know the exact antenna location, because it is frequently in some remote place in higher terrain, miles from the actual station. It should then be plotted on the chart. Because many such stations have frequencies that are close together and they announce their call letters infre-

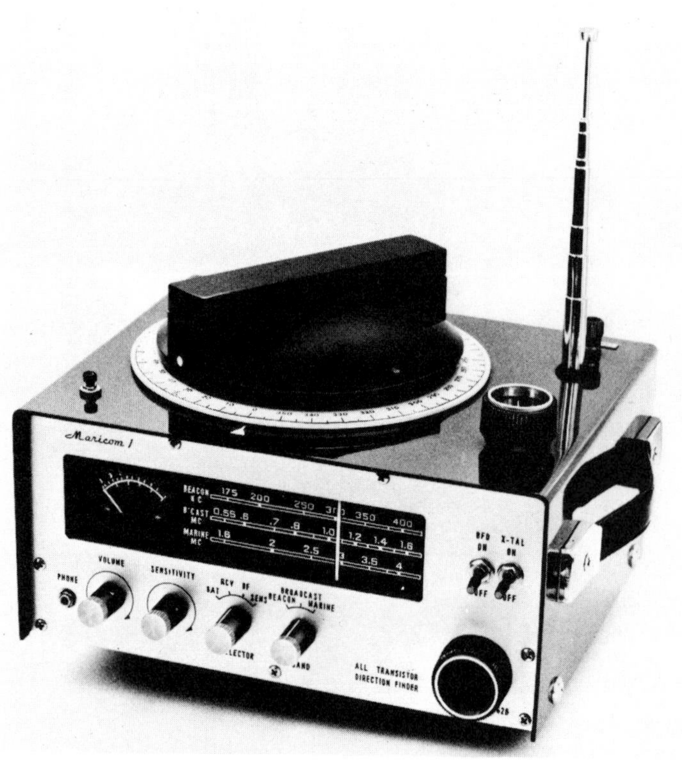

FIG. 10-1
Radio direction finders
Left: Portable RDF

(COURTESY MARITIME COMMUNICATIONS, INC.)

Below: Automatic RDF

(COURTESY RAYTHEON COMPANY)

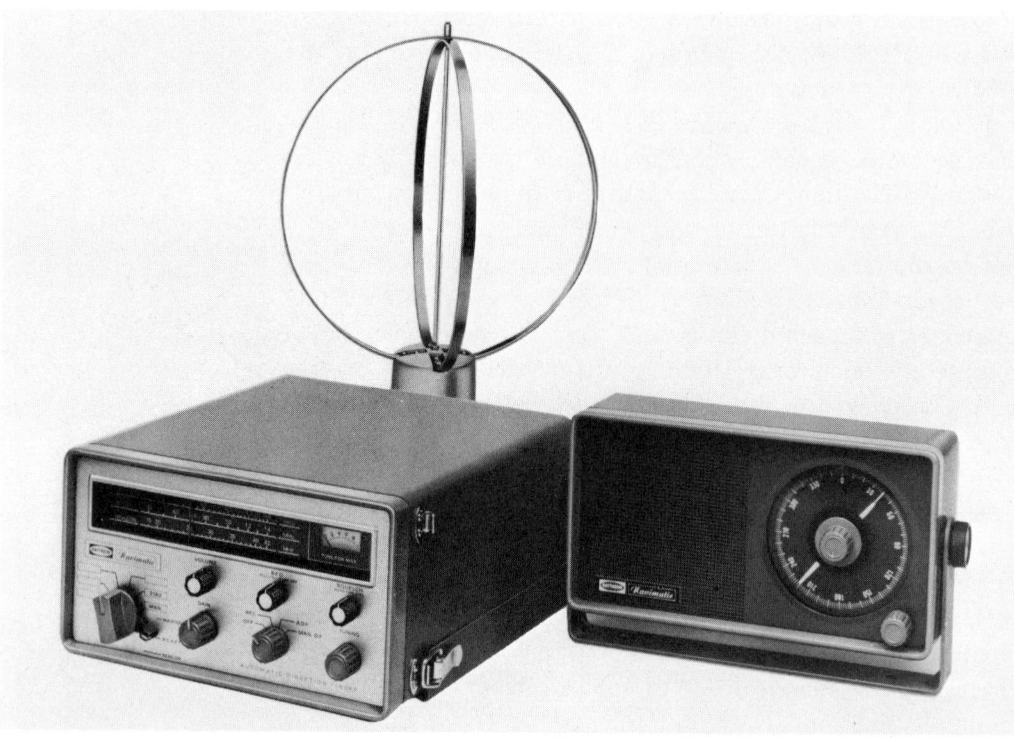

quently, it is sometimes necessary to listen to an entire program before you can be sure which station you are working. For this reason, regular radio beacons are preferred.

Antenna The antennae used in radio direction finders are often of a loop type. When the loop is turned so that it is in line with the straight line from the ship to the beacon, the loudest signal is heard from the station. When the antenna is turned so the loop is squarely across this direction, the minimum signal is heard. It is easier to get clear resolution of a minimum signal than a maximum signal and the set is therefore tuned so that the signal disappears entirely at the minimum, or *null,* antenna position. This direction is then read in relation to the ship's compass and a *compass bearing* is obtained.

Operation The directional antenna of the RDF is connected to a pointer that turns within a circle, comparable to a compass card. The graduations are usually in whole degrees, from 0° to 360°. The set has a lubber's line, similar to that of the compass, and the graduated circle is rotatable and can be clamped with 0° opposite the lubber's line for relative bearings, or with the compass, magnetic, or true course opposite the reference mark, for taking compass, magnetic, or true bearings, as will shortly be explained. When the set is installed aboard ship, or if a portable set is used, it is essential that the lubber's line be parallel to the keel.

Remember that aboard a vessel, our only sense of direction in the absence of familiar landmarks is given by the compass, and that radio bearings, like visual bearings, must be referred to the compass. It is therefore imperative that the helmsman watch his compass when bearings are taken.

In the usual procedure, the frequency and recognition signal of a beacon are obtained from the chart or H.O. 117, and the antenna is turned until a good clear null is obtained, at which moment the bearing is read from the card and the time is noted. There are two separate possibilities to be considered:

Card Clamped at 0° Opposite Lubber's Line This means that the 0° mark is in line with the bow and the bearing will be *relative* to the ship's bow. This is probably the easiest method for the single-handed skipper who has no helmsman. He steers with one hand and manipulates the RDF with the other, turning the antenna until he gets the best null while reasonably on his course. At this point he leaves the RDF alone, but swings slightly off course to either side until he gets a perfect null—in effect turning the antenna with the boat—and at the moment he has a sharp null he reads the compass course. It always pays to check the reading more than once. Note the time, then read the pointer on the RDF. (See Fig. 10–2.)

This is a *relative bearing*. It must be converted to a *magnetic* or *true bearing* before it can be plotted. I prefer to convert all bearings and courses to *true*. As mentioned before, you can plot from the magnetic compass rose, and so long as you are consistent, there is nothing wrong with this method. The bearing can be read clockwise from the bow through 360°, or it can be read to port or starboard

FIG. 10-2

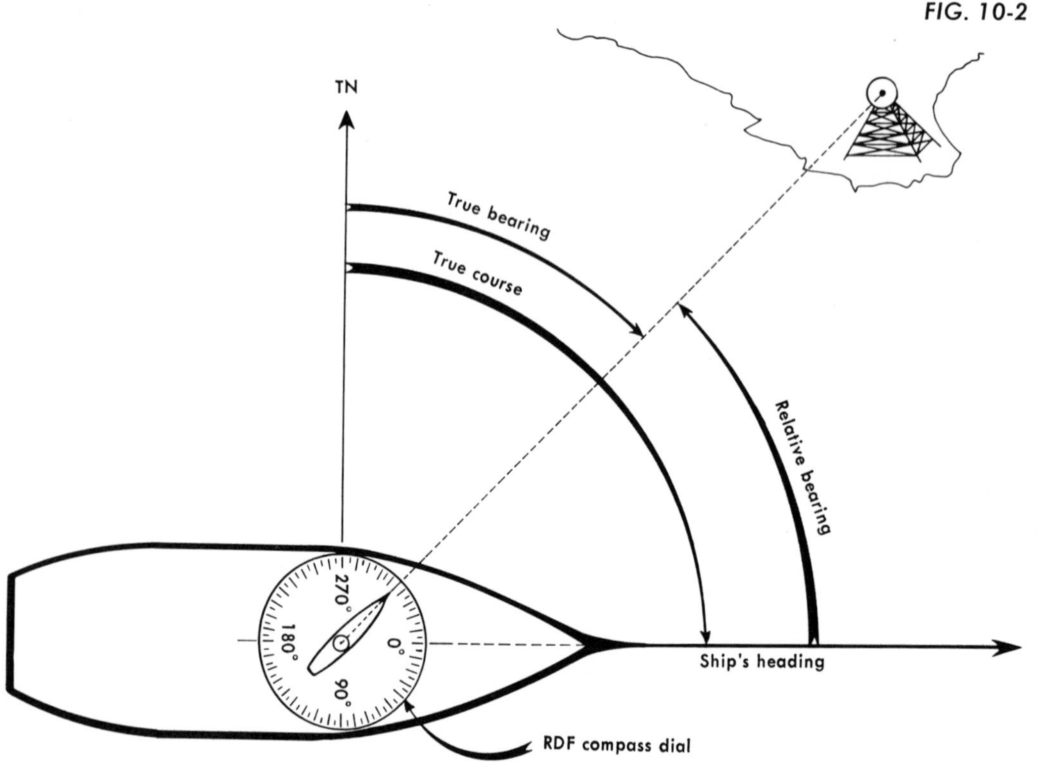

of the bow through 180°. Clockwise is the same as starboard, and such a bearing is converted according to this rule:

Compass bearing = Compass course + Relative bearing (Stbd.)

If the bearing is read as so many degrees on the port bow, in which case it can vary from 0° to 180°, the bearing is subtracted from the course. Rule:

Compass bearing = Compass course – Relative bearing (Port)

You apply *deviation* and *variation* to this compass bearing to get the true bearing, which is plotted *from the beacon to the ship*. Remember that you can always add or subtract 360° to your figures to allow subtraction or to bring them below 360° if they exceed that.

Card Clamped with Course Opposite Lubber's Line This is a more direct method and can be used when you have a helmsman. If you set the compass course opposite the lubber's line, the card is an exact replica of the compass card —*if you are exactly on course*—and you will now read a *compass bearing* on the RDF. This is then converted to a true course for plotting.

However, every compass course you steer corresponds to a true course (TC), usually the TC you have laid down on the chart. Therefore, you can also clamp the card with the *true course* opposite the lubber's line and read a *true bearing* straight from the RDF.

The trick here is that you must be *on course* at the moment of reading; small boats frequently yaw 10° either side of the intended course. You therefore instruct the helmsman to be doubly careful, and while you work the RDF, he sings out, "On—on—on—on—on. . . ," while he is exactly on course, changing to, "Off—off—off—off. . . ," when he falls off course. You wait and make sure you have your null while he is on course. If he is not able to hold a course, it is better to take relative bearings and have him read the course when you have a good null and shout "Mark!"

Errors The various types of error that may affect an RDF reading are calibration, land effect, night effect, great circle correction, quadrantal error, and reciprocal error.

Calibration Reception of the incoming signal can be distorted by metal or electric wiring in the vicinity of the antenna, just as metal and wiring can affect the compass. Whenever a new installation is made on a vessel, or if the superstructure is altered, it is advisable to check for such deviation and—if it is appreciable—to swing ship, as explained below, and set up an RDF deviation table, since the error will not be the same on all headings.

This is usually done by anchoring the vessel within sight of a radio beacon. The position of the anchorage is determined by bearings on landmarks, and the *true bearing* of the beacon from the vessel is ascertained by a visual bearing also. If the vessel is not too close to the beacon, this true bearing will not change materially as she swings to her anchor. The vessel is now placed on headings 30° apart and a radio bearing is taken on each heading and converted to a true bearing. By comparing the visual with the radio bearing, the error of the latter is determined as so many degrees east or west of the actual true bearing. These errors are listed in a table that is kept near the instrument and applied to all future readings.

Another method is to slowly cruise around a buoy, if there is one in a convenient spot, within sight of the beacon. The true bearing from buoy to beacon is established from the chart or by taking visual bearings. Radio bearings are obtained as the vessel passes the buoy on the different required headings, converted to true bearings, and then compared with the actual direction of the beacon to determine errors. If you do this with a portable RDF set, make sure it is placed in the same spot every time it is used.

Land Effect Radio waves are deflected when they pass over any considerable land area or cross islands or high peaks. This would make them unreliable, and since there is no way of determining the error, it is best to be cautious, and preferably use beacons or stations that are close to the water. Of course, at no time will a radio bearing be as accurate as a visual bearing, a fact which the navigator must constantly bear in mind.

Night Effect During the night, but particularly within half an hour of sunrise or sunset, radio waves are likely to show aberrations which make it difficult to get clear, sharp nulls, with a resulting loss of accuracy.

Great Circle Correction Since radio waves travel in great circles around the Earth and since most of our plotting is done on a Mercator chart, there can be a considerable difference between the direction of the great circle track followed by the signal, and the straight line from the station to the ship that we would draw on our chart. This applies particularly where considerable distances are involved. If the station is only 50 or 75 miles away, or if it is nearly due north or south of the vessel, no correction need be considered.

The RDF gives a great circle direction and we apply a correction to obtain a Mercator direction we can plot. Table 1 of Bowditch and H.O. 117, *Radio Navigational Aids,* both list these corrections. It is not difficult to reason out which way to apply the correction if you remember that a great circle route always curves away from the equator. This makes it possible to state these simple rules:

Ship in North Latitude—If station is *east* of your ship, add correction.
If station is *west* of your ship, subtract correction.
Ship in South Latitude—Reverse above rules.

Quadrantal Error Particularly on large ships with steel hulls, there can be another error induced in incoming radio signals. Because they are most noticeable 45° either side of the bow and stern, these are called quadrantal errors. They will show up in the deviation table if you have constructed one.

Reciprocal Error It is possible to mistake an incoming signal if the antenna is turned 180° and you read the reciprocal bearing. The navigator will always be alert to this possibility, but can avoid it by consulting the chart and noting the approximate bearing of the beacon from the ship. If he accidentally gets a reciprocal bearing, he will turn the antenna rather than apply 180° to the bearing, since this could be inaccurate.

Automatic Radio Direction Finder (ADF) New inventions and improvements in existing equipment take place constantly, and the RDF has experienced many changes since the first sets came out. New antenna designs and improved solid-state electronics provide simpler and better performance. The automatic RDF uses a fixed-loop antenna with one or two loops, mounted high in the vessel. When the set is tuned to a station, the direction is automatically recorded by an arrow on a dial built into the set. Depending on the particular instrument used, the bearings can be relative, compass, magnetic, or true. If they are not true or magnetic, they must be converted to be plotted as previously described. With these modern instruments, there is no possibility of getting a reciprocal bearing. Because the set can be left on and the arrow watched continuously, such sets lend themselves well to *homing* on a beacon.

Omnirange Navigation (VOR) Although designed mainly for aircraft use, omnirange—"omni" or VOR (very-high-frequency omnirange), as the system is called for short—is beginning to be used on many vessels, taking advantage of the large number of directional aircraft beacons that line our coasts. Special marine omni receivers, such as the one pictured in this chapter, have been designed and are working very well on small vessels, as they do not necessarily need a high antenna.

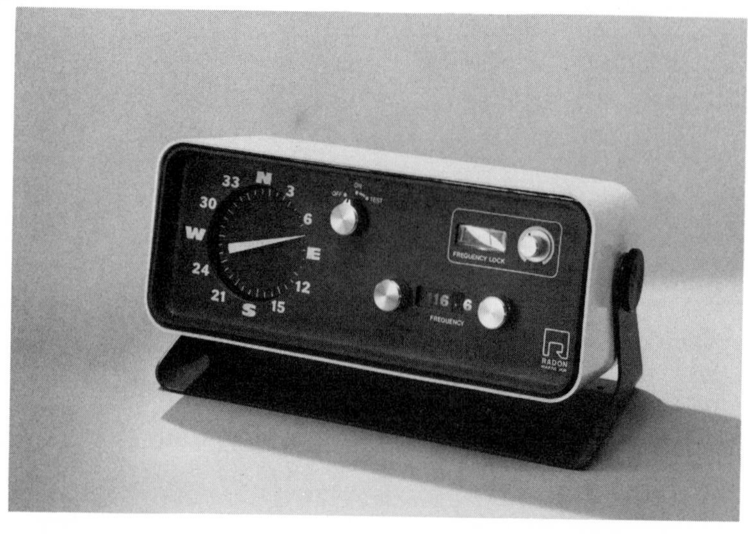

FIG. 10-3
Marine VOR omnirange receiver

(COURTESY RADON INCORPORATED)

VOR (omni) signals are radiated from many hundreds of land-based beacons operated by the Federal Aviation Administration (FAA). The signals use very-high-frequency (VHF) signals and are thus limited to line-of-sight reception. The accuracy is about twice as good as with conventional radio direction finders.

Each station sends out directional signals like the spokes of a wheel, each spoke 1 degree apart from the next. The signal pattern is oriented with the 0° beam, or *radial,* as each of these signals are called, pointed toward *magnetic north.* When the set is tuned to a particular station, it identifies the radial on which the vessel is located and displays the magnetic bearing *from* the station *to* the vessel on a simple 360° dial on the front panel of the receiver. If two or more stations are within reach, a fix is quickly plotted. Since these bearings are oriented to magnetic north, they can be plotted directly on the chart, using the magnetic compass rose. There is no need to apply corrections, and the system is independent of the ship's heading. This device lends itself particularly well to plotting and observing danger bearings in coastwise operations.

In aircraft, distance-measuring equipment (DME) has been developed in conjunction with VOR, in the form of an automatic device that constantly records the distance to the station. The military version of this kind of combination of omni and DME is known as tacan.

Consolan Until 1972 there were two consolan stations in the United States, at San Francisco and at Nantucket, but the latter was closed down and it is not known when or if it will be reactivated.

In Europe a slightly different system, called *consol,* is in operation with a total of six stations located in Spain, France, Ireland, Norway, and two in northern Russia. The American station operates on 192 kHz while those abroad range from 250 to 350 kHz. Essentially, they are all directional in operation, sending out a radial pattern of dots and dashes, the individual rays of which can be identified on a chart or determined from special tables. H.O. 117, *Radio Navigational Aids,* gives full details of operation of all the stations, as well as the required tables.

Equipment Signals can be received on any low-frequency

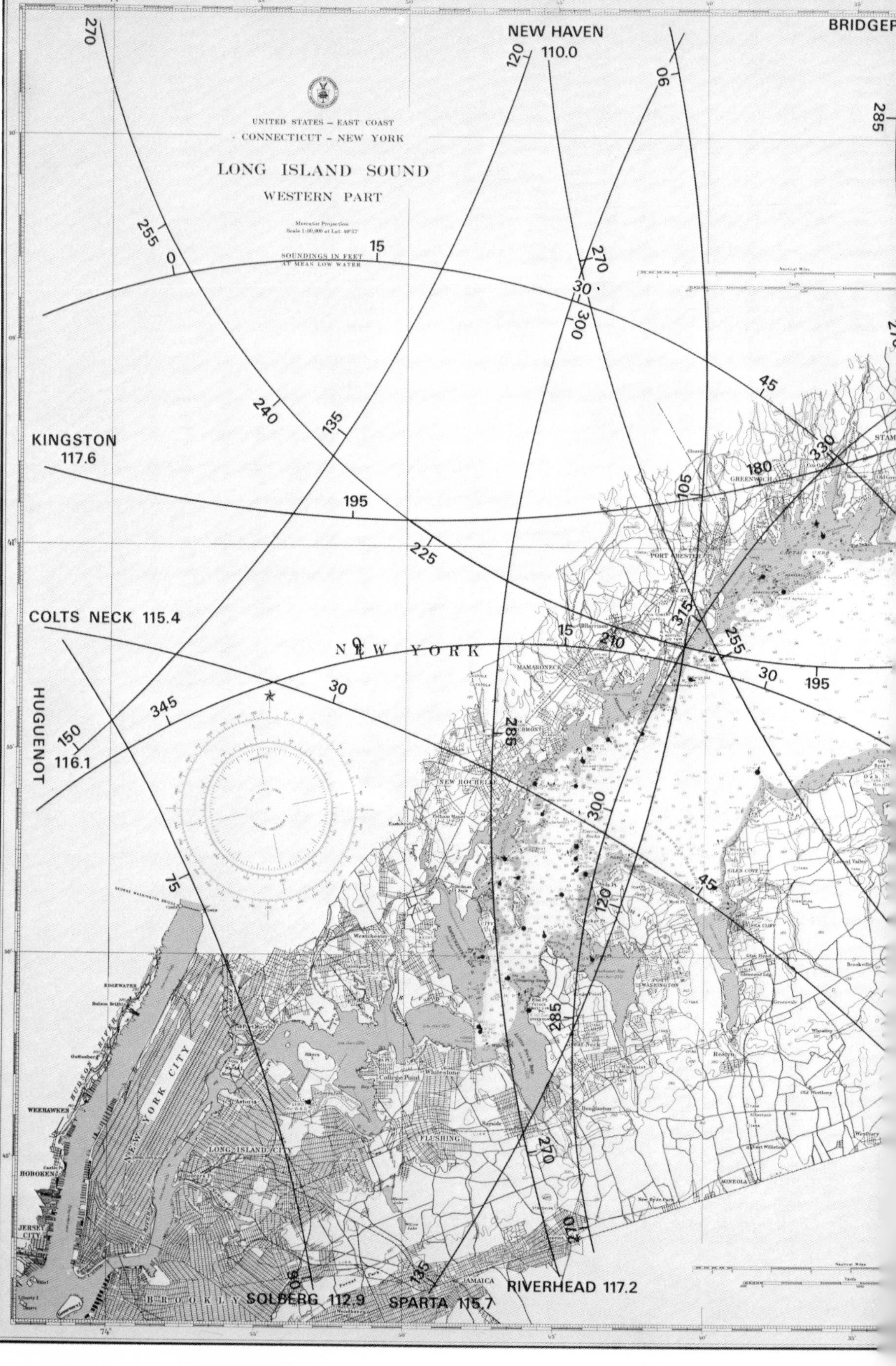

UNITED STATES – EAST COAST
CONNECTICUT – NEW YORK
LONG ISLAND SOUND
WESTERN PART
NEW HAVEN
110.0
BRIDGEPO
KINGSTON
117.6
COLTS NECK 115.4
HUGUENOT
116.1
SOLBERG 112.9
SPARTA 115.7
RIVERHEAD 117.2
NEW YORK
NEW YORK CITY
GREENWICH
PORT CHESTER
MAMARONECK
NEW ROCHELLE
GLEN COVE
SEA CLIFF
PORT WASHINGTON
FLUSHING
LONG ISLAND CITY
JAMAICA
BROOKLYN
HOBOKEN
WEEHAWKEN
EDGEWATER
HUDSON RIVER
College Point
Astoria
Roslyn
MINEOLA

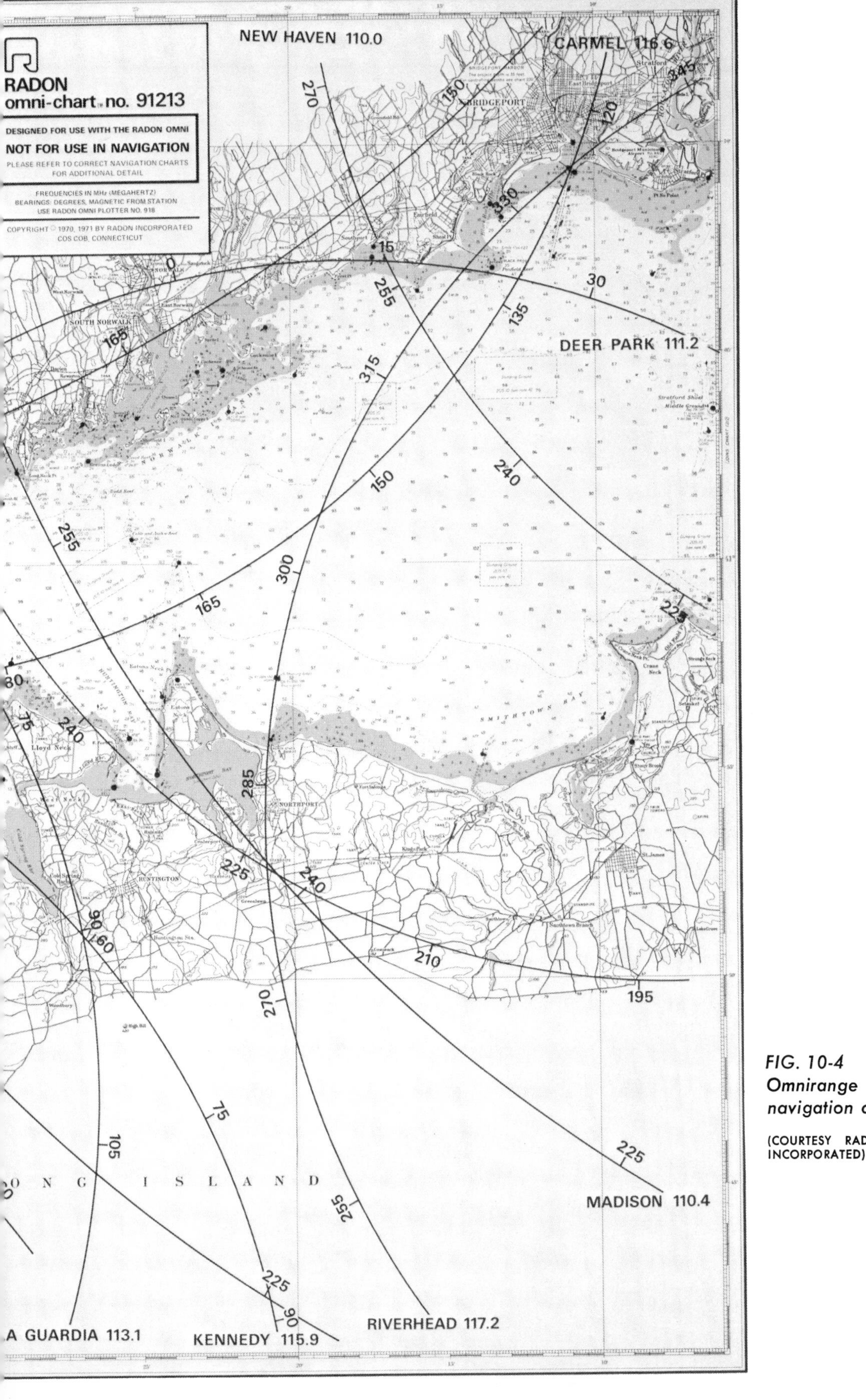

FIG. 10-4
Omnirange navigation chart

(COURTESY RADON INCORPORATED)

radio receiver, and most radio direction finders are satisfactory, using them with the loop antenna turned for maximum volume. If a communications receiver is used, it should have a beat frequency oscillator that can be cut in while the automatic volume control is cut out.

Principle A pair of towers at the station send out a pattern of alternate dot and dash sectors, each approximately 12° wide, like spokes of a wheel. The sectors are separated by an *equisignal.* By carefully counting the number of dots and dashes on either side of the equisignal during a transmission cycle, a ray is identified as being either a dot or a dash line of position, and the number of dots or dashes determine its position in the pattern to within a degree or so. The line can either be identified on a consolan chart, or the special table in H.O. 117 will convert the count to a true bearing from the station.

Operation The receiver is tuned to the proper frequency and the call letters of the station identified. The operator waits for a 2½-second silent interval, which signifies the beginning of a transmission cycle. He then carefully counts the number of dots or dashes heard during the first part of the transmission, stopping when the equisignal is heard. Depending on his location, the transmission might begin with either dots or dashes. If the first part, before the equisignal, is in dots, the second part, after the equisignal, will be in dashes. He counts the dots or dashes, as the case may be, *after* the equisignal as well. A complete cycle would comprise 60 signals of dots and dashes, but some of these are masked by the equisignal. Therefore, if the operator adds his counts of dots and dashes, the total is less than 60. The difference between the total and 60 is divided in two, and half is added to the count *first heard,* be it dots or dashes. This number identifies the ray, which is the ship's line of position, on the chart, or, if tables are used, it converts into a bearing from the station.

Example • After the silent period, the operator counts 20 dashes before the equisignal and 36 dots after the signal. Total is 56. This means that 4 signals were lost in the equisignal. Half of this differ-

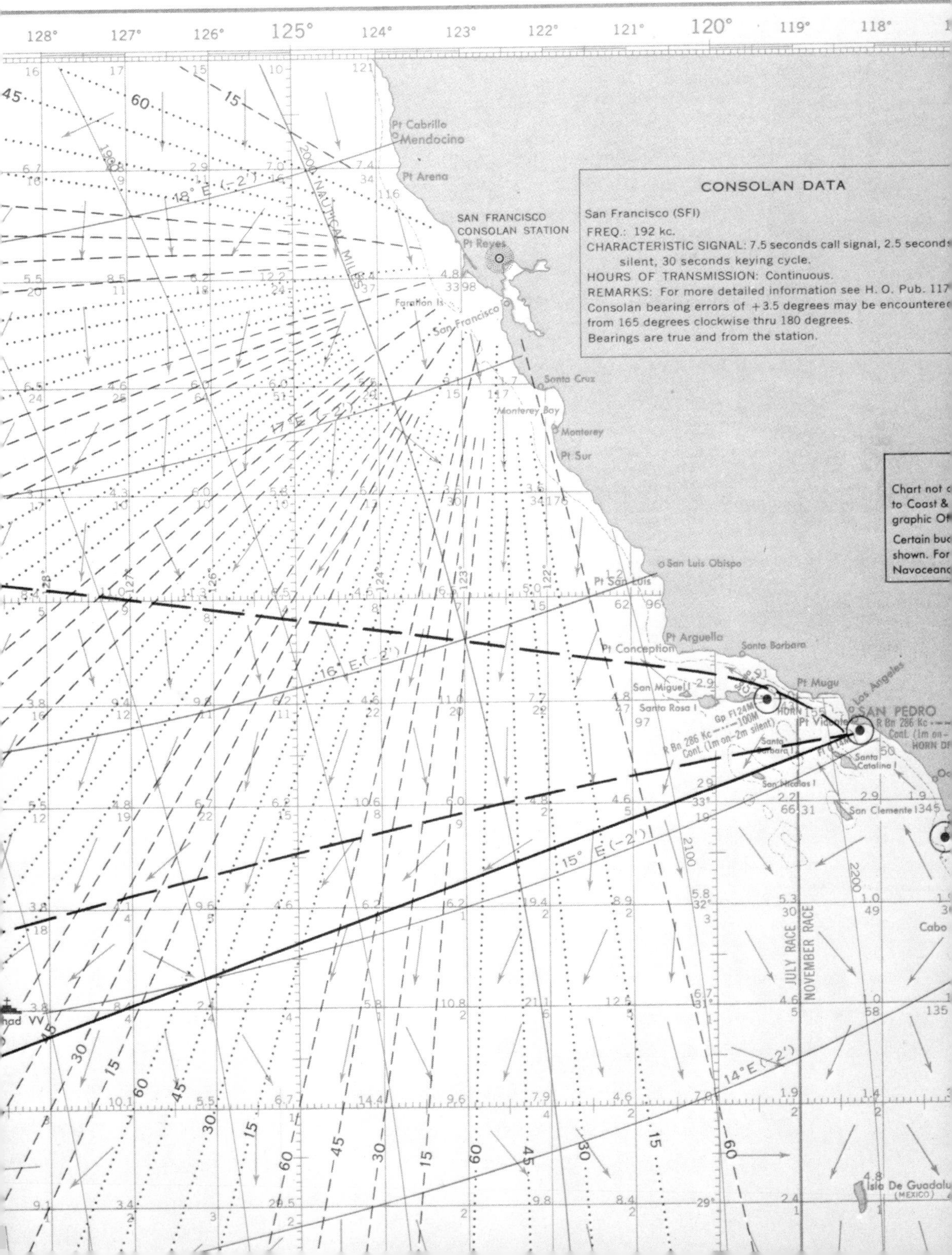

FIG. 10-5 *Consolan chart—Plotting Chart, Pacific Yacht Races, San Pedro to Honolulu including Acapulco and Mazatlán*

ence, or 2, is added *to the first count,* giving him 22 dashes. With this information, the position on the chart is readily located. (It is suggested that N.O. 117 be read carefully for information on fringe operation and the possibilities of error.)

Errors The incoming signal has followed a great circle track and for plotting on a Mercator chart must be corrected. The consolan tables give these corrections and the rules for applying them. If an error in counting is made, or if dots are confused with dashes, the result is usually an impossible position that is immediately recognized and discarded. As with other equipment, the experience of the operator is most important.

Limitations Consolan signals reach out 1,400 miles or more from the station. They are not usable in the two sectors at the ends of a base line through the two transmitting towers, and these sectors are so marked on the chart. Greatest accuracy is in a direction of 90° from the base line. There is a possibility of confusion in selecting the proper sector on the chart, but a consolan reading should always be used in conjunction with a DR position or RDF bearing that would serve to indicate the correct sector on the chart. During night operation, there might be interference between ground waves and sky waves, and a number of readings should be taken. If they conflict, the method should not be relied on. Consolan is intended as a long-range navigational aid. It should never be used within 50 miles of the station.

Chapter 11

Hyperbolic Systems of Position Finding

The basis for the theory used in hyperbolic navigation systems is the fact that we are able to identify and measure with great accuracy radio signals sent in synchronized pattern from two different shore-based stations.

A hyperbola is a curve constructed on the principle that the difference in distance of every point on the curve from two fixed points, or foci, is a constant value. For example, if the constant difference is 10 miles, every point on the hyperbolic curve would be 10 miles further away from one focus than from the other focus.

Since radio waves travel at a known constant speed, any distance traveled can be expressed in units of time, such as microseconds (millionths of a second), instead of linear units, such as miles. It is therefore possible to construct a hyperbola based on fixed time differences instead of fixed linear distances (See Fig. 11–1).

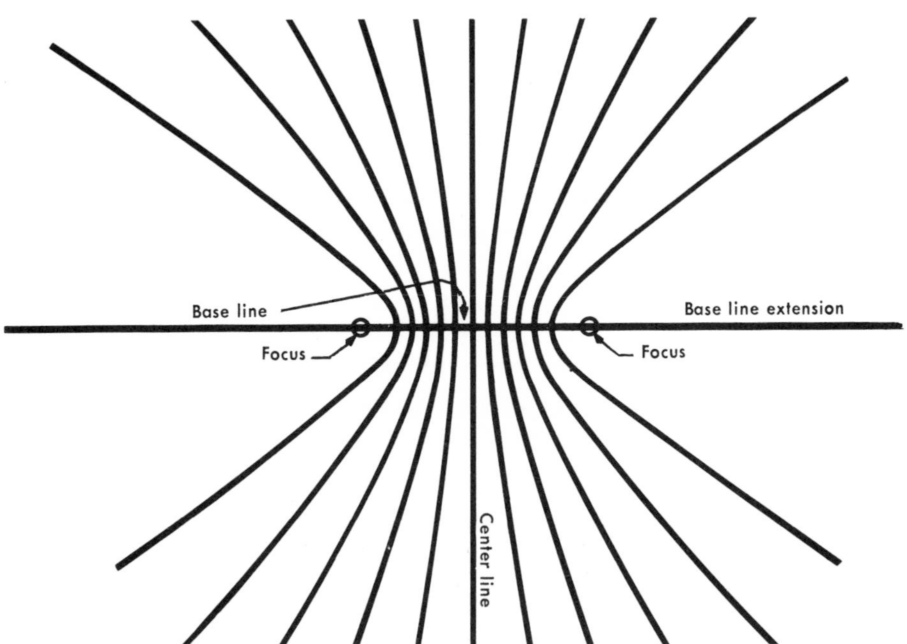

FIG. 11-1

In hyperbolic navigation systems, two basic approaches are used. Hyperbolic lines of position (LOPs) are identified by measuring the difference in arrival of time signals from two stations. This is the principle of loran navigation. A further refinement, used in Omega and Decca navigation, is to consider the space between two LOPs as a *lane,* and by phase difference measurements of continuous-wave radio signals establish the ship's position *within the lane.* An accuracy to within as little as 50 feet is theoretically possible using this system. The advantage is that by using predetermined time differences from transmitters of known location, families of hyperbolic curves based on these differences can be printed on any navigation chart.

Over the years, several different hyperbolic systems of navigation have been developed, beginning with loran during World War II. Decca is a British system, widely used in Europe and to some extent in the U.S. and other parts of the world; but neither loran nor Decca has achieved worldwide coverage. Omega, developed by research sponsored by the U.S. Navy, provides worldwide, all-weather, day and night coverage, using only eight stations around the world. The methods in current use and discussed in this chapter are (1) Omega; (2) loran A, loran C, loran D; (3) Decca; (4) shoran, lorac, Raydist.

Omega

Omega is a very long range system using VLF (very-low-frequency) radio waves. Propagation of such signals is stable and reliable under all conditions and affected only by the daily movements of the ionosphere. Since this interference is predictable, tables are available to provide applicable *sky-wave corrections.*

When in full operation, the Omega system will have eight stations around the world, spaced some 6,000 miles apart. Only six stations are needed for worldwide navigation coverage, leaving two extra stations for use in case of system failure or shutdowns. Any two stations may be used to set up a pattern of *lanes.* The average width of these lanes is 8 miles, but can reach 75 miles due to the spreading of the

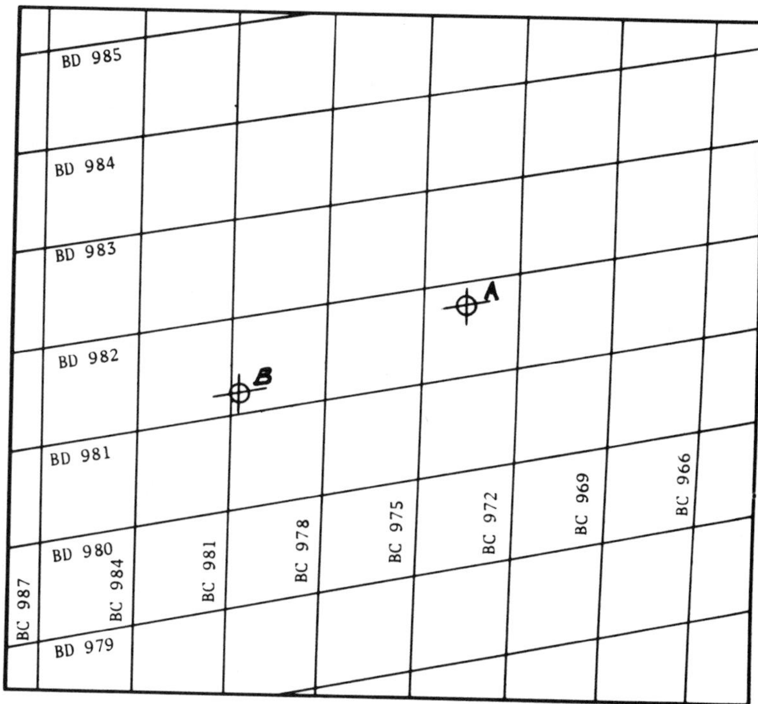

FIG. 11-2
Omega chart

hyperbolic LOPs at great distances from the foci. The LOPs are identified by two letters denoting the two stations used and a whole number; two LOPs enclose a lane. The receiver provides the navigator with the lower number of the LOP of a lane, and a two-digit decimal fraction denoting the *centilane,* or hundredth of a lane, at which the ship is actually located.

Fig. 11–2 shows a typical Omega chart. The lines are hyperbolic, but because of the great distances involved they appear as practically straight lines for a small area. From a digital readout on the receiver, corrected for sky-wave effect, the coordinates of point *A* are obtained as BD lane 981.80 and BC lane 973.60, and the point is plotted accordingly. When the ship has moved to point *B,* the corrected coordinates will read BD 981.20 and BC 980.90.

Principle The basic frequencies used are 10.2, 11.33, and 13.6 kHz. When the system is in complete operation, there will be eight stations transmitting a signal on each of these frequencies once every 10 seconds, following the pattern shown in Fig. 11–3.

The 10-second signal pattern is synchronized with Universal Time (GMT), and the operator can, if necessary, establish the time of beginning of the signal cycle by listen-

OMEGA SIGNAL FORMAT

START ← 10 SECONDS → START → ETC.

TRANSMISSION INTERVAL	0.9	1.0	1.1	1.2	1.1	0.9	1.2	1.0	0.9
STATION A	10.2	13.6	11 1/3	—f_1→					10.2
B	—f_2→	10.2	13.6	11 1/3	—f_2				
C		—f_3→	10.2	13.6	11 1/3	—f_3			
D			—f_4→	10.2	13.6	11 1/3	—f_4		
E				—f_5→	10.2	13.6	11 1/3	—f_5→	
F					—f_6→	10.2	13.6	11 1/3	—f_6
G	11 1/3					—f_7→	10.2	13.6	11 1/3
H	13.6	11 1/3					—f_8→	10.2	13.6

→| |← 0.2 SEC.

FIG. 11-3

ing simultaneously to a receiver tuned to station WWV. Operation on 10.2 kHz alone is possible; the other two frequencies are needed mainly to remove lane ambiguity when equipment is restarted after a system failure. The receiver measures the phase difference of a signal sent from two stations, related to a hyperbolic LOP plotted on the chart. The wavelength of the 10.2-kHz frequency is 16 miles, and since the phase is repeated twice in a wavelength, the resulting lane width is about 8 miles.

Operation The Omega system is designed for continuous operation, which is a drawback for small vessels with limited power supply. The receiver is set to the coordinates of the point of departure, and if all goes well it will continuously track the progress of the ship across or along the lanes as the voyage progresses. Position readings can be taken at any time and plotted on the chart in a matter of minutes. There are many different receivers on the market and each will differ slightly in operation, so it is necessary for the navigator to carefully read the instructions that come with the equipment he is to use.

A typical modern Omega receiver is shown in Fig. 11–4. Other sets may have different configurations, but essentially the same methods of operation are followed, as described in the steps listed.

The set illustrated has a *power* switch for turning the set on. It has a *frequency selector* switch which can be set to 10.2 or 13.6 kHz (this receiver does not use the third frequency). There is a jack for headphones and a volume control, to be used when the initial setting is made. In the upper right-hand corner are the *station selector* dials, each of which can be set to any of the eight stations, designated by the letters A through H. Any two stations will give a line of position (LOP), and the setting shown provides LOP #1 from stations A and B, and LOP #2 from stations C and D. The switches marked *display up–down* and *timing advance–retard* are used for the initial orientation of the receiver. The *display selector* switch is pushed for either LOP #1 or LOP #2. It also has an *off* setting to save electricity. When the LOP #2 switch is pushed in, the digital readout window just above will show the lane reading for the stations selected, in this case AB. The first digit of the lane number is left out, as there is never any doubt what it is. (A mistake in the first digit would give a lane a thousand miles away and this would be immediately apparent.) Given are the two significant whole numbers of the LOP, and after the decimal point are shown the centilanes, in this case 0.67 of the width of the lane indicated by the first two numbers. To get a corresponding reading for stations CD, LOP #2 switch is pushed.

FIG. 11-4
Omega receiver

(COURTESY MICRO INSTRUMENT CO.)

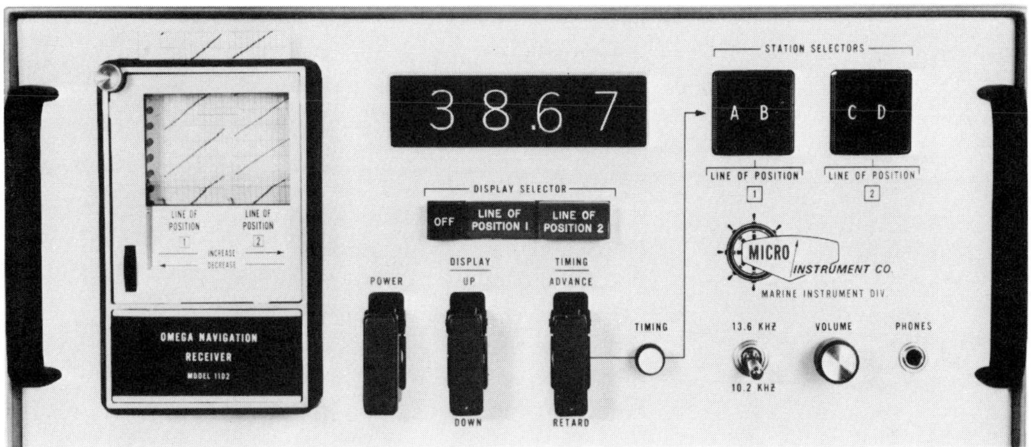

At the left is a moving paper strip which traces each LOP continuously as the vessel moves along or across the lanes. If the ship stays in a lane, a continuous vertical trace appears; but if the course lies across the lane, the trace cuts diagonally across the paper. When it reaches the edge of the graph, it is crossing into a new lane and the trace immediately appears on the other side of the strip. Each diagonal trace thus counts one lane; in this manner the set keeps a record of the total lanes crossed. The graphic recording is important, and is always inspected before a reading is taken to make sure that there has been a continuity in the traces. If a system failure occurs, either because a station is temporarily shut down, because of a power failure aboard ship, or because severe magnetic disturbances have interfered, the trace instantly shows the malfunction by moving in a random manner across the paper. Since the strip moves about 1 inch per hour, it is possible to determine the approximate time the interruption occurred and thus reestablish the lane count. Many navigators prefer to annotate the recorded strip, marking the lane numbers on the traces. If a failure has occurred, the receiver must be reset to new coordinates which must be within ±4 miles of the exact position for the following readings to be correct.

A step-by-step procedure for operating the type of receiver illustrated in Fig. 11–4 would go as follows:

Step 1. While still in port, prior to departure, plot ship's position at the dock as accurately as possible on the Omega chart. Determine from the chart the coordinates to be shown on the receiver for this position. Turn the set on.

Step 2. Synchronize the receiver with the Omega signal pattern. Plug in the headphone and adjust the volume. Listen for the loudest signal in the pattern. (In the U.S. it will be station D, located in North Dakota). Set the letter designation for the loudest station in the first (left-hand) space of the station selectors. Set the other three selectors to display the station pairs you wish to use, always keeping the loudest station in the left-hand position. Different makes of receivers will use different procedures for synchronization, but on the receiver illustrated, it is done by activating the timing light during the 1-second transmission of the first (left-hand) Omega station. The timing switch is used to advance or retard the light to match exactly the duration of the tone from the station as heard in the headphone.

Step 3. You are now ready to set the digital readout to the correct initial reading, but first an allowance must be made for the sky-wave correction (SWC). When navigating at sea, the position to be plotted is derived from the digital readout, with the SWC applied. A special set of tables is published by the Naval Oceanographic Office with sky-wave corrections for all situations, based on the following factors:

a. Frequency used, i.e., 10.2 or 13.6 kHz
b. Latitude and longitude of ship, each within 4°
c. Pairs of Omega stations used
d. First or second half of the month, i.e., 1–15 or 16–31
e. GMT of observation to the nearest hour

Corrections are labeled either plus or minus and for position fixing at sea are applied to the digital readout with sign as given. However, when first setting up the readout, using a known Omega LOP taken from the chart, the SWC is applied to this LOP with sign *reversed* to obtain initial readout. You actually set the dials to give the *uncorrected* reading, so that when the SWC is applied, the correct LOP is obtained.

Having determined what the uncorrected reading should be for the first pair of stations, push LOP #1 switch, just below the digital window, and move the *display up–down* thumbwheel until the two correct numbers appear to the left of the decimal point. The fraction to the right of the decimal point is not adjustable, but will settle at the correct reading shortly after the receiver is activated.

Step 4. The receiver is now ready to be used. After the ship is under way, and when a position is wanted, the navigator follows these simple steps:

a. Examine traces on the paper strip chart to make sure there has been continuous operation on both pairs of stations.
b. Push LOP #1 switch and record digital readout.
c. Push LOP #2 switch and record digital readout.
d. Look up SWC in tables for each reading and apply with sign as given to obtain corrected LOP.
e. Plot the corrected LOPs for a fix.

As time goes on, modern technology will no doubt simplify the system and the equipment so that a continuous digital readout of latitude and longitude will be available by inspection at all times. However, the navigator must never rely solely on a single mechanical or electronic system. He must always be ready to verify a position with his sextant. This is especially true in Omega navigation. If operation of the system is interrupted for any reason, the lane count is lost and must be reestablished by determining the ship's position by conventional means, be it dead reckoning, celestial observations, or other electronic methods.

Where Omega charts are not available for a given area, it is possible to use special Omega tables, published by the Naval Oceanographic Office, to plot the LOPs. These tables can in fact be used to prepare an Omega chart on an ordinary Mercator chart or plotting sheet.

The average accuracy of Omega LOPs is from less than 1 mile to 3 miles, depending on conditions. By using special additional equipment, greater accuracy can be attained, but for normal navigation this is not needed. Because Omega operates day and night, in all weather, and because only three of the eight stations are needed to create two pairs of stations, it is probably the ultimate electronic system that will be developed for marine navigation.

Loran

Loran is an acronym for *lo*ng-*ra*nge *n*avigation. The system was developed early in World War II and has played an important role in navigation ever since. With the advent of Omega, it is likely to become less important, except that for small-vessel navigation it has certain advantages. A loran receiver is turned on only when a position is needed and thus causes far less drain on electric power than Omega, which must be kept in continuous operation. Many thousands of loran sets are now in use aboard craft, large and small, and the new sets being produced are increasingly simple to operate. Loran, in general, has a daytime range limit of about a thousand miles from the station, increasing at night to about two thousand miles, depending on equipment and conditions. It is extremely reliable in operation

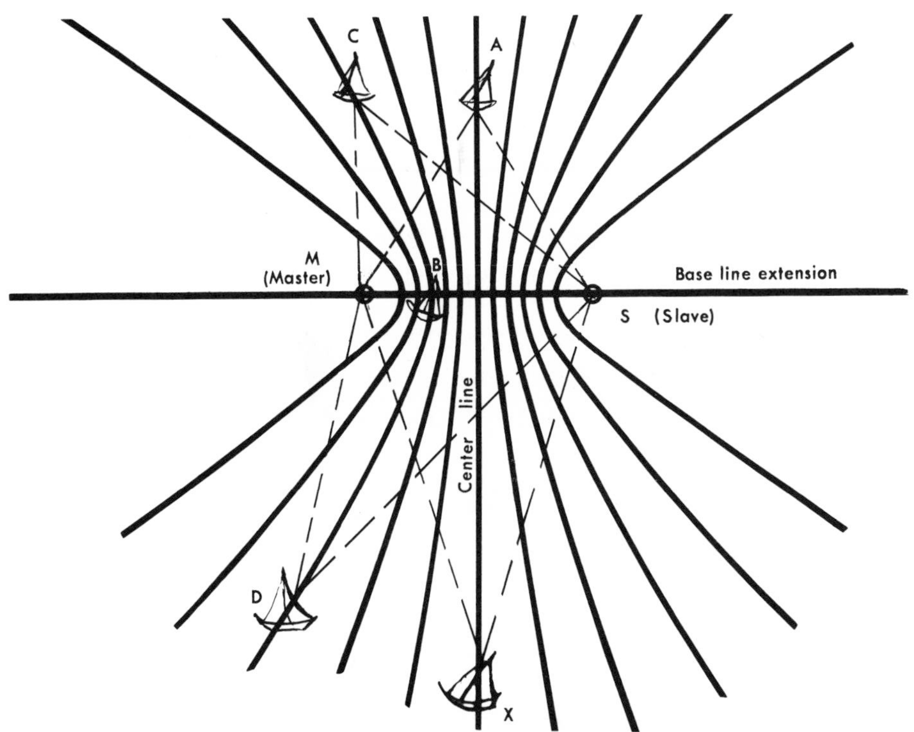

FIG. 11-5
Loran lines of position

and only temporarily affected by magnetic disturbances, such as lightning. Once understood, its operation is fairly simple, and accuracy down to within a fraction of a mile is obtainable.

Principle In Fig. 11–5 are shown two transmitters, *M* (for *master*) and *S* (for *slave*), located perhaps two hundred miles apart and accurately plotted on the chart in their geographic positions. The line connecting them is called the *base line*. Halfway between the stations is a line perpendicular to the base line and called the *center line*. Obviously, all points on this center line are equidistant from the stations.

Assuming that the two stations send out a radio pulse simultaneously, vessel *A* will receive both pulses at the same instant. Vessel *X* will also receive the two pulses simultaneously, but a little later than vessel *A*, being further from the stations. In fact, any vessel on this center line will receive the two pulses at the same time, and, conversely, if a vessel does receive the two pulses simultaneously, it must of necessity be located on this center line. This then becomes a line of position, and can be plotted on the chart as such.

Next look at vessel *B*. It is closer to *M* than to *S* and will therefore receive the signal from *M* first. The signal from *S* must travel farther and is therefore received a fraction of time later, the difference being actually the distance *B–S* — *B–M*, expressed in units of time, such as microseconds (millionths of seconds: μsec.). Let us call this difference *K*.

A hyperbola can now be constructed so that every point on the curve is the distance *K* further from *S* than from *M*. For example, ship *C* is the distance *M–C* from *M* and the distance *M–C* + *K* from *S*. Ship *D* is the distance *M–D* from *M* and *M–D* + *K* from *S*. It follows that if a ship receives a signal from *M*, and *K* microseconds later receives a simultaneously sent signal from *S*, the ship *must* be somewhere on the hyperbola through *C* and *D*, which now becomes a hyperbolic line of position, identified by the time difference *K*. A single pair of stations can give a single LOP only. A second pair of stations is needed to provide a cross fix with another LOP.

In the hyperbolic systems, curves are constructed with predetermined time difference constants that vary by equal increments, thus producing a family of curves around a station, and an identical, reversed set of curves can be constructed around the other station. Because the time differences are predetermined, the curves can be established and overprinted on any chart.

In actual practice, the shipboard receiver can readily identify the incoming signal and determine the correct LOP to be used, and a trained operator has no difficulty determining his position. To remove the possibility of ambiguity in signals, the master always transmits first. When this signal is received at the slave station, it triggers the transmitter there, establishing the synchronization.

Loran A Loran A is the basic loran system and the one most commonly used, covering large areas of the world, but not all areas. Transmitters are located strategically for best operation, and a single master station often operates with several slave stations, and within the system a single location may serve as both master and slave.

Because about a hundred stations and many sets of hyperbolic curves are in use and needed, it is necessary to establish differences in the transmissions that can be identified on the receiver. This is done in three ways: by using three different *channels* or *frequencies,* by having three different basic *pulse* (or *signal*) *recurrence rates,* and by having within each basic rate eight *specific repetition rates.*

The frequencies used are:

Channel 1—1,950 kHz
Channel 2—1,850 kHz
Channel 3—1,900 kHz
Channel 4—1,750 kHz (kept in reserve)

The three basic pulse repetition rates are:

S (for *special*)—using 20 pulses per second at 50,000-μsec. intervals
L (for *low*)—using 25 pulses per second at 40,000-μsec. intervals
H (for *high*)—using 33⅓ pulses per second at 30,000-μsec. intervals

The specific pulse recurrence rates are:

STATION NO.	H	L	S
0	30,000–μsec. interval	40,000–μsec. interval	50,000–μsec. interval
1	29,900	39,900	49,900
2	29,800	39,800	49,800
3	29,700	39,700	49,700
4	29,600	39,600	49,600
5	29,500	39,500	49,500
6	29,400	39,400	49,400
7	29,300	39,300	49,300

Stations are identified by a threefold designation based on channel, basic recurrence rate, and specific recurrence rate. Thus 3L6 is a family of curves so identified on the chart, representing a station that sends on 1,900 kHz, 25 pulses per second at 39,400-μsec. intervals. Each hyperbolic LOP within the family is further identified by its time difference constant. A line on the chart might thus be designated as 3L6 2700, meaning that the time difference between receiving the signals from master and slave is 2,700 μsec. everywhere along that curve.

In actual operation aboard ship, the receiver has dials for setting the three station designators. The incoming signals appear on an electronic scope in the form of a luminous trace. The upper trace is from the master and the lower trace is from the slave. The receiver has three function switches, labeled 1, 2, and 3. In function 1, the signals appear as vertical lines on square pedestals drifting across the screen. The motion is stopped with a drift-control switch and the operator makes certain that the (lower) slave pedestal is to the right of the master pedestal on the upper trace. The function switch is moved to position 2, where the signals appear enlarged, and with the proper control, the slave pulse is placed directly under the master pulse. In function 3, both pulses appear on the same line and a fine matching is made where one is exactly superimposed on the other. At this point the time difference in microseconds is read on a digital readout window. On older sets there might be no digital readout available, in which case a different measurement method is followed. In all

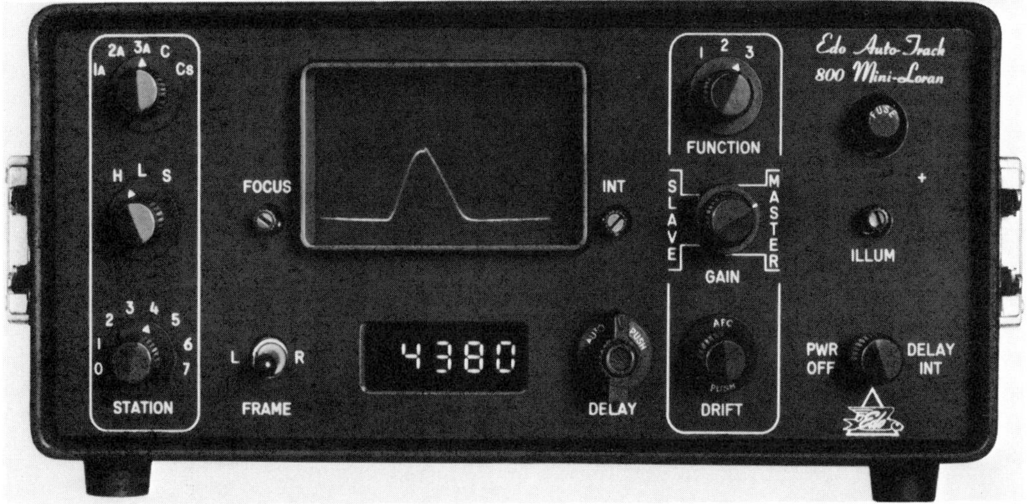

FIG. 11-6
Modern loran receiver for loran A and C

(COURTESY EDO COMMERCIAL CORPORATION)

cases, of course, the operator must follow the instructions that come with his particular receiver.

Fig. 11–6 shows a versatile portable receiver which is suitable for both boats and aircraft, and which operates on both loran A and C. In the upper left-hand corner is the *channel selector*. In this instrument three loran A frequencies are in use, labeled 1A, 2A, and 3A; *C* and *Cs* (for "C special") are channels for loran C. Below the channel selector is the *basic recurrence rate* switch, which is set to *high, low,* or *special*. Below that is the *specific pulse recurrence rate* switch, with positions numbered from 0 to 7. A station is tuned in by the setting of these three dials. The *frame* switch, marked L and R, is used to move the signals right or left on the display scope. The *function* switch has three settings as discussed before. There is a *gain* control which regulates the amplitude of the signals. The *drift* control is used to stop the signals from drifting off the screen. Once stopped, this control is pushed in and becomes automatic in its operation. The *delay* control is used to position the slave signal manually. A typical operation would involve the following steps:

1. From the loran A chart, determine which station is to be used.
2. Turn the set on with switch in lower right-hand corner.
3. Set *station* controls to desired settings. If the station selected from the loran chart is labeled 3H5, set switches 3A–H–5.

4. Set *function* switch to 1 and pull out *delay* and *drift* controls for manual operation. The pedestals will now appear on the screen.
5. Adjust the *gain* control until a stationary loran signal appears on each trace.
6. Use *frame* switch to position master signal near the center of the master pedestal.
7. Use *delay* control to place slave signal on slave pedestal.
8. Set *function* switch to 2. Use *frame* switch to position master signal on master strobe. Stop drift and push *drift* control in. The master signal will now remain on the strobe due to automatic frequency control.
9. Rotate *delay* control to position slave pulse on slave strobe. Push *delay* control back in to lock slave pulse in position.
10. Set *function* switch to 3.
11. Adjust *gain* controls until the two signals are of equal amplitude and appear as one signal.
12. Read the loran LOP on the digital readout.
13. Plot the LOP on the chart.

Note: When this receiver is properly adjusted and locked to a station, it will automatically track the changing LOPs, changing the numbers in the digital readout as the vessel moves along its track.

Fig. 11–7 shows the appearance of the signals in the three settings of the *function* switch. With minor variations, all loran receivers will function in a similar manner.

FIG. 11-7
Appearance of loran signals

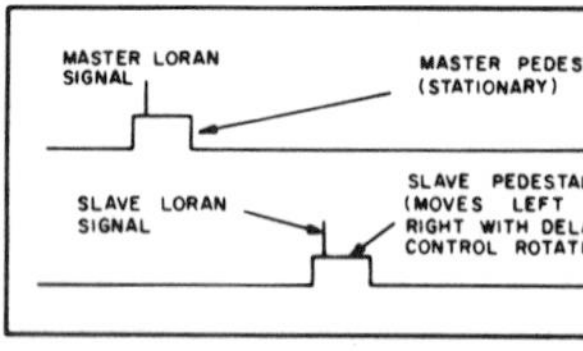

Function 1

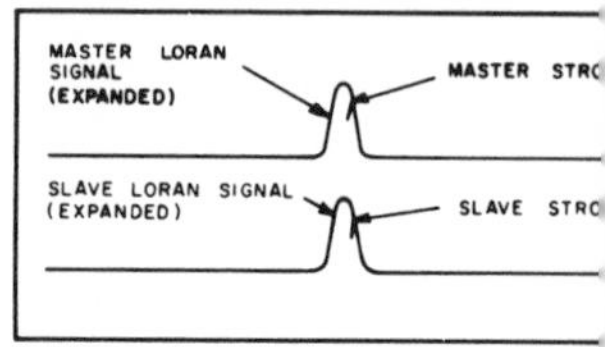

Function 2

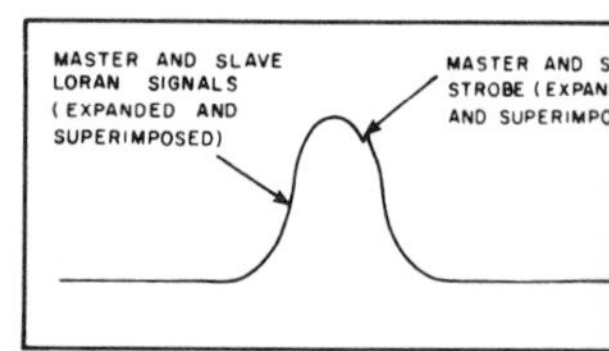

Function 3

Sky Waves Some of the radio signals from loran stations follow the curvature of the Earth from station to ship and are known as ground waves. Others travel skyward where they meet the ionosphere and are bounced back to Earth. They are known as *sky waves,* and since they travel further than the ground waves, they arrive a little later. Loran receivers often pick up both ground waves and sky waves from the same station. Both can be used, but if the sky waves are measured, a special correction must be applied to allow for the extra time of travel. Such corrections are available in tables published by the Naval Oceanographic Office and are also often printed on the charts.

Great care must be taken by the loran operator to distinguish between ground waves and sky waves. The first sky wave to arrive is called a one-hop, E-layer wave, but often a ground wave is followed by a whole train of sky waves. Most navigators prefer to use one-hop waves only, but experienced operators can successfully make use of two-hop waves when necessary, and sky waves extend the range of the stations, particularly at night.

An experienced loran operator has no real difficulty recognizing sky waves. For one thing, they are subject to fading and collapsing, often within as little as one minute, and they also tend to split, breaking into two or more humps that fade more or less independently. If there is a possibility of mistake, the operator will carefully watch a signal for several minutes to see if it begins to show the characteristics of a sky wave. If he is accustomed to taking frequent readings, he will have no difficulty in detecting the presence of sky waves. Usually, the greater the distance from the transmitter, the steadier the sky wave.

During the day, loran A reception reaches out about 700 to 1,000 miles. At night, using sky waves, signals can be

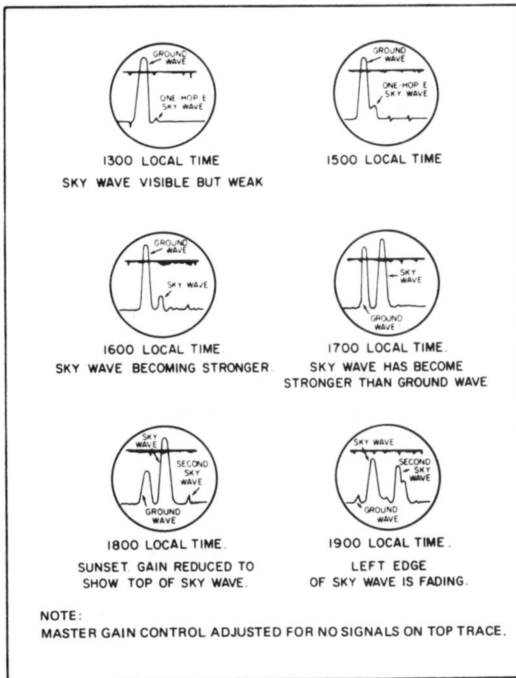

FIG. 11-8
Typical ground- and sky-wave presentation, loran A

used up to 2,000 miles away, but ground waves are rarely received beyond 450 miles at night. Fig. 11–8 shows typical conformations of sky waves.

Loran C The loran C system is similar to loran A, but in addition to time difference measurement makes use of a phase difference comparison, as in Omega. Loran C operates on a much lower frequency, around 100 kHz, and the stations have longer base lines than in loran A, with the result that signals travel farther and a greater accuracy is obtainable. Daytime reception by ground waves reaches out to twelve hundred miles and nighttime reception of sky waves is possible up to thirty-five hundred miles under good conditions. Special loran C charts and special sky-wave corrections are available. The system was developed after World War II and now covers large areas of the Earth.

In loran C a slightly different system of station identification is used. One master station will work with as many as four slave stations, designated on the chart by the letters W, X, Y, and Z. For the single frequency of 100 kHz there are six basic repetition rates as follows:

H	33⅓	pulses	per	second
L	25	"	"	"
S	20	"	"	"
SH	16⅔	"	"	"
SL	12½	"	"	"
SS	10	"	"	"

For each of these rates there are eight specific pulse repetition rates, as in loran A.

Various receivers have different arrangements for tuning, but on the EDO receiver illustrated in Fig. 11–6, there are two channel positions for loran C, the one marked *C* and the one marked *Cs* (for "C special"). The C setting is used with the H, L, and S basic repetition rates, and the Cs setting is used for SH, SL, and SS. A typical designation would be SL3-W, which would call for setting the top dial to Cs, the middle dial to L, and the bottom dial to 3. The W means that the master is paired with the slave station designated W. Again, it is always necessary to carefully study the instruction manual for each receiver.

With both loran A and loran C, appropriate charts are commonly used. However, the Naval Oceanographic Office also publishes special computation tables for both systems. At each entry, the latitude and longitude of two points on the charts are obtained, and the line connecting them is the resulting LOP. This can then be plotted on a regular chart or on a plotting sheet. Tables are used mostly where very great accuracy is desired.

Two difficulties that sometimes beset the beginning loran operator are *spillovers* and *ghost pulses*. Spillover occurs when the ship is close to a transmitter, but working with another transmitter, similar to the effect of having a powerful radio station next door when we are trying to hear a weaker station. If spillover is suspected, it can be detected by tuning to the frequency of the nearby station. The spillover signal becomes stronger, while the one of the correct frequency disappears. Ghost pulses will occur when an incorrect basic pulse recurrence rate is tuned in. They can be mistaken for ordinary loran signals, but the experienced operator will recognize a flickering in a ghost signal and the fact that the trace itself is continuously under the signal, whereas it should be interrupted under the pip. Whenever a loran LOP is obtained that does not make sense, the operator should suspect spillover or ghosts and reexamine his scope.

Loran stations are very reliable in their operation, but if they develop trouble or get out of synchronization, the signal begins to blink, as a warning to the operator that the station is having trouble.

Loran D Loran D is a low-frequency loran system, operating in the 90–110 kHz range, designed essentially for mobile military or surveying use. The range is limited to about five hundred miles and its main application has been where mobile transmitters have been temporarily set up in a special area of operations, whether for use by ships or aircraft. The system is of little concern to the marine navigator who is not in the military service.

Decca

Decca is a high-precision hyperbolic system developed in England and used widely in Europe and in waters where there is a great deal of British shipping. An accuracy of within 150 yards by day and 800 yards by night is possible at 250 miles from the stations.

The system uses phase comparison to determine the Lanes of Position established by a master and three slaves. The stations are usually less than one hundred miles from the master and arranged in a star pattern. No matching of signals is required, as in loran, and the shipboard receiver has three dials, known as Decometers, each giving a reading of a different slave station in relation to the master. Special Decca charts are used, where the lanes associated with the different slaves are printed in red, green, and purple for easy identification. The lane reading is taken directly from the Decometer, and any two slaves give a fix. The third station helps provide a three-way fix and serves as a check on the other slaves. The reading indicates only the location within the lane and does not identify the lane itself. This is done with a counter, or by keeping a DR plot.

FIG. 11-9
Decca navigator

COURTESY OF ITT DECCA MARINE INC.

Decca also provides automatic tracking equipment, mostly for aircraft, where a continuous trace on a rolling chart indicates the position of the craft at all times. The system is stable, reliable, accurate, but operates at shorter range than does either loran or Omega. The Decca Corporation leases the equipment to users and supplies operational instruction to all users. Because the system is easy to use, it has found favor with fishing boat captains who operate within the limited areas.

Shoran; Lorac; Raydist

These are three of several electronic methods used in short-range position finding, mostly for marine surveying, and therefore of relatively little interest to the marine navigator.

Shoran *Shoran* is an acronym for *sho*rt-*ra*nge *n*avigation. Two stations, or transponders, are set up on shore at a known distance apart. Using ultrahigh-frequency (UHF) wavelengths, a transmitter-receiver combination on the survey vessel can send electronic pulses to each transponder, and the receiver picks up the return pulses from each, measuring the time of travel and automatically converting it into miles and hundredths of miles to an accuracy of within 30–50 feet. Other variations of the same principle can produce even higher accuracy, but all are limited to line-of-sight operation because of the high frequency used.

Lorac *Lorac stands for lo*ng-range *ac*curacy, and is another hyperbolic system used for precise marine surveying. One master and two slave stations are used, producing two families of intersecting hyperbolic curves. The stations are only about 35 miles apart and the lanes between LOPs are so narrow that an accuracy as close as 3 feet has been obtained. Signals are usable up to 150 miles away, and special charts and special equipment are needed for use aboard the survey vessel. The system has no applications in general marine navigation.

Raydist Several different modes of operation of the Raydist system are available, and they are invariably used where high-precision marine surveys are required. Because very low frequencies are used, the system is not limited to line-of-sight observations but can be effective at distances up to 200 miles. For the general marine navigator these last three methods have no practical importance and for this reason are not discussed in detail here.

Chapter 12

Radar Navigation

The word *radar* comes from *ra*dio *d*etection *a*nd *r*anging, which exactly describes the function it performs. A radio beam from the ship "detects" an object when it strikes that object, and is reflected back to the ship, where the radar set indicates not only the direction of the object, but its distance as well, thus establishing its "range." The principle used in radar was discovered independently in America and in Britain before World War II. A great deal of research and development was done early in the war in both countries, and during the war radar became a valuable tool for detecting enemy vessels and planes.

Since World War II tremendous refinements have been made, resulting in highly sophisticated equipment used for many purposes in ships, aircraft, and shore installations. Navigation in fog, collision avoidance, and traffic control in the air and in harbors and rivers are only a few of the more important problems that have been solved by the use of radar. Even our hoary Rules of the Road have finally recognized the importance of radar by devoting an entire section to its use at sea.

FIG. 12-1
Small vessel radar

(COURTESY RAYTHEON COMPANY)

Principle A radar installation consists basically of a transmitter, a receiver, and a rotating antenna located as high as possible on the ship. The transmitter sends a series of sharp pulses through the directional antenna, the transmission being in the form of a narrow beam, less than 1° wide horizontally, but extending vertically perhaps 15° above and below the horizontal, depending on the purpose of the set, so that it may detect objects on the water as well as in the sky. This vertical beam is directed by the rotating antenna so that it continuously sweeps through 360° of the horizon. Radar is essentially a line-of-sight device. When the beam strikes a solid object, such as a ship, a buoy, or a coastline, it is reflected back to the ship's antenna, amplified in the receiver, and displayed as an illuminated "pip" on the radar screen.

This radar screen is actually a cathode-ray tube (CRT), like a television screen, but usually circular. The ship itself appears as a dot of light at the center of the screen, and the revolving radar beam appears as an illuminated line, or trace, radiating from the center of the screen to the edge, and sweeping around the screen in perfect synchronization with the motion of the antenna on the mast. When the beam strikes a solid object and is reflected back, a brightly illuminated pip appears on the trace; the distance from the center of the screen to the pip indicates the distance of the object from the ship. At the outer edge of the screen, a 360° compass rose, which can be adjusted to either true north or to show 0° dead ahead, enables the navigator to read either the true or the relative bearing of the pip, and hence of the object. The inside of the screen is coated with a special chemical that retains the illumination of the pip after the beam has swept past it and holds it until the beam comes around again and reactivates the image. Thus, the screen shows a continuous indication of all solid objects within the range of the beam.

In the language of radar, solid objects are called *targets.* The radarscope itself is called a *plan position indicator* (PPI) because it presents a plan view of the situation, with the ship in the center, surrounded by whatever targets exist, largely as it would be seen from an overhead aircraft. The electronic beam transmitted from the antenna is actually a very thin, pie-shaped segment, but it does get wider the further it travels, and when a signal is returned it shows the width of the beam at the point of impact and therefore tends to show a target wider than it actually is. For example, a buoy some distance away would show as a small arc instead of a point, and the actual bearing of that buoy would be taken through the center of that arc. Naturally, if the target is a continuous coastline, there is a continuous return of signals, and so the screen shows a continuous image of the coastline.

The higher the frequency of transmission, the shorter the pulses that are sent out, and the narrower the beam width. This is important where two separate targets may be fairly close together. Because the pip is wider than the width of the target warrants, the two targets may blend into one another on the scope and show as a single object. The ability of a radar set to separate targets that are close together is known as *bearing resolution.* However, the shorter the pulse, the better will also be the *range resolution,* the ability of the equipment to separate objects in depth along the same bearing. For example, if two ships or two small islands are on the same bearing, one close behind the other, they may show as a single target.

A radar receiver can be adjusted for operation at different ranges, such as 1 mile, 2 miles, 5 miles, 10 miles, 20 miles, etc. If the sweep trace travels from the center of the scope to the edge in the time it takes a transmitted pulse to travel from the antenna to a target 5 miles away and back to the antenna, then the set is tuned to the 5-mile range. On most radars, illuminated range rings can be projected on the scope to measure such distances, and the operator has a choice of ranges. Radar equipment is known according to the frequency, and hence the wavelength, it uses. High-frequency, short-wavelength sets are known as 3-centimeter radars and provide fine resolution in depth and bearing over short distances. For this reason they are popular for use on small craft that cannot provide enough antenna height for long-range work. In the medium range is the 5-centimeter radar, and for long-range work the 10 centimeter equipment is used, provided sufficient antenna height is possible. Large ships often carry both a 3-cm. and a 10-cm. radar, the first for piloting in close waters and the second for long-range work. However, the range depends not only on frequency, but also on power output, antenna height, and power of resolution.

Operation A skilled radio navigator must have a great deal of experience, knowledge of his equipment, and expert judgment. This is best acquired during the day in clear weather, when he can visually compare the actual targets around him with their appearance on the PPI scope. He then learns the typical pip for certain buoys (with or without radar reflectors), small and large vessels, and various types of coastlines. Above all he learns the limitations of his set in resolution of bearing and depth. For example, he may see that a ship close to shore does not show up as a separate target, or that an inlet is blotted out due to excessive beam width, or that the scope shows the hills back from the coastline instead of the beach, giving a false impression of the distance to shore. Having learned to become observant of these limitations, he is less likely to be fooled by target conformation during periods of heavy fog or other poor visibility. Eventually, he will learn to recognize a rainsquall, falling snow, the effect of waves to windward and leeward, and the results of rolling of the vessel. He develops confidence in his equipment and in his judgment.

There are many radar sets on the market for both large and small vessels, and it is of course necessary to study carefully the manual that comes with a particular set. However, since they all operate on the same principles, their method of operation is essentially the same, depending somewhat on the sophistication and number of controls available. A typical small-vessel radar is illustrated in Fig. 12–1.

The following step-by-step procedure covers most modern radars:

Step 1. Make sure that all control knobs are turned *off* or are turned counterclockwise all the way. Now turn the power switch to *standby,* or to *power on* if no heating-up period is required.

Step 2. From *standby,* after 3 or 4 minutes, turn to *operate*. Turn the *brilliance* or *intensity* control up until the sweep trace is barely visible.

Step 3. Some sets have a *focus* control. This

FIG. 12-2
Radar receiver

(COURTESY RAYTHEON COMPANY)

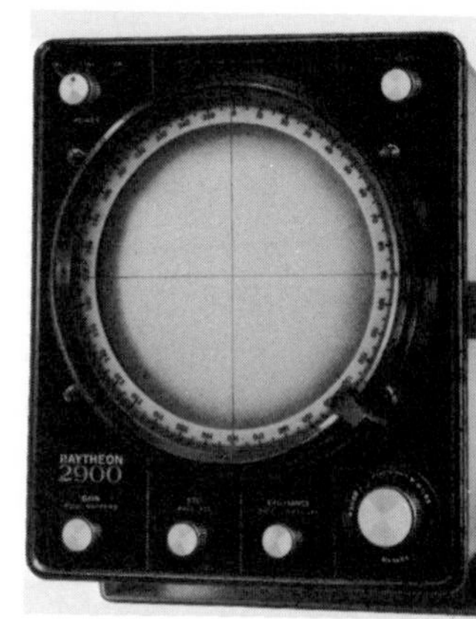

should now be turned until the trace is as thin and sharp as possible.

Step 4. Now adjust the *gain* control. This is perhaps the most important and sensitive part of good operation. Turn it up until you have a fairly bright, light-flecked background, at which time you should pick up small targets that normally might not reflect enough energy to stand out. If you have rain or snow, reduce the gain until the rain or snow disappears and only the targets are left. Reducing the gain tends to narrow the beam width and give finer resolution in bearing and depth both. Whenever you have a difficult situation, such as trying to pick up a buoy in rough water or to locate an inlet in the shoreline, try reducing the gain while you study the scope. However, it should be turned back to normal setting and kept there for routine operation.

Step 5. Frequently a rough sea reflects radar signals and creates a bright target area around the ship, usually called *clutter.* It is always worse on the windward side and it may well obscure close-by targets of little reflecting power. It is very difficult to pick up a small buoy in a high sea. To reduce clutter, most sets have a separate control, known as *sensitivity time control* (STC), *suppressor,* or *anticlutter.* This important control requires a light touch, because, if used to excess, it will also eliminate the targets themselves. Try operating it in conjunction with the gain control, reducing or increasing it in small amounts until the target is visible through the clutter.

Step 6. The radar will have a *cursor* for taking bearings on objects. Here it is important to remember that the pips on the scope are distorted by excessive beam width. For a bearing on a buoy, appearing as a small arc, it is best to bisect the arc. If you are taking bearings on a headland, remember that the edge of the land probably shows further seaward than is actually the case, because of beam width. However, study the chart to see if there is a flat shore in front of the headland showing on the scope, and take this into consideration when measuring the bearing. On newer sets, the cursor is not limited to operation from the center of the scope, but can be moved about the screen at will and used for measuring ranges or courses—especially if you are plotting on the screen, as explained later in the chapter.

Step 7. To measure distances, or *ranges,* a set will have either a *fixed-range-rings* control or a *variable-range-ring* control. This should be kept turned off except when actually used, so that the thickness of the lines does not obscure a target. Also, when in use, the lines should be kept as thin and clear as possible, for the same reason. The distances you measure with the range-ring devices will be very accurate and perhaps provide a greater degree of accuracy than any other information obtained from the radar.

Step 8. Occasionally an area of heavy rain or snow, or even very heavy fog, may obscure a target, such as a vessel, located in the middle of the area. Most sets are likely to have a *fast time constant* (FTC) control that can help distinguish the more solid target amid the surrounding reflections.

Step 9. This involves the use of the *range* control. When the set was first turned on, it could have been set to any of the several ranges available, from the 1-mile range for close work to the

50-mile range, or higher, if available. At sea, the most sensible setting is 20 miles, because that is roughly the distance to the horizon on a large vessel. On a smaller vessel an 8- or 10-mile range may be more suitable. When you change from one range to another, the entire picture on the scope becomes mixed up until the old markings have disappeared and the new images have become established, so it is best not to switch ranges if you are in the middle of a close-in maneuver with other vessels around.

Step 10. Some sets may have a *heading flasher* control to regulate the brightness of the heading indicator at the lubber's line. This line should be set to lowest usable visibility as a matter of practice. No unnecessary bright lines or markers are desirable, and continued use at high power can cause deterioration of the screen coating.

Newer radars provide a different type of scope presentation, where all stationary targets, such as shorelines and aids to navigation, remain in fixed positions on the scope while your vessel and others are shown to move along their respective tracks in relation to the stationary features. This gives a true presentation of vessel movement. An adjustable and completely movable electronic cursor can be used to determine courses of your own and other vessels as well as distances. Course projections can be made with crayon directly on the scope to indicate danger of collision. Such sets provide controls for adjusting the position of the ship to any convenient position by simply moving the total picture north, south, east, or west. In fact, some sets will do this automatically when your vessel reaches a certain limiting range on the scope.

Radar Plotting When another or perhaps several other vessels are spotted on the radarscope, it is desirable to determine ahead of time what is likely to happen: whether a danger of collision exists or will develop, at what range and time another ship will cross your course, and what will be the *closest point of approach* (CPA). This can be accomplished by any one of several different plotting methods, and the plotting may be done right on the radar screen, on a chart, on a radar plotting sheet, on the Navy maneuvering board, or on special radar plotting devices.

If you are the navigator on a large vessel, it is essential that you know all the methods of quick, accurate plotting, *and that you plot and retain the record of all situations that could become critical. You will never be blamed for plotting more than necessary, but the admiralty courts have held vessels at fault in collision cases because radar was available but either it was not used or the navigator failed to plot the movements—and to keep the plot—of the vessels involved.* A ship's navigation officer—and that is *any* officer on watch and in charge of the bridge, be he the chief, second, or third mate—who has failed to plot his radar observations and interpret them correctly, is likely, in case of collision, to lose his license and thus abruptly terminate his seafaring career. It is interesting that the law does not specify that a vessel must be equipped with radar; but *if it is,* the Rules of the Road provides an *Annex to the Rules* that states that the radar should be used to prevent collisions, and the courts have ruled that the radar *must* be so used. But the presence of, or use of, radar does not excuse the vessel from observing all the Rules of the Road, especially Rule 16 pertaining to proceeding at moderate speed during poor visibility and stopping when a signal is heard forward of the beam.

The easiest of all methods is to plot with crayon on the scope of a radar that keeps stationary targets in fixed positions and shows the movements of the vessels. If a permanent record of the plot is desired, a thin plastic sheet is placed over the scope and the plotting is done on that. Older radars had a screen protected by an outer glass covering, removed an inch or two from the cathode-ray tube. Such instruments did not lend themselves well to direct plotting on the screen, because of the parallax created in the distance between the two surfaces. Newer sets have a special *reflection plotter,* where the images from the cathode-ray tube are reflected to the outer glass covering without distortion, allowing the navigator to plot directly with soft crayon on this outer surface or on a clear plastic sheet placed over this surface. The main advantage of plotting directly on the screen or an overlay is that no time is lost transferring data from screen to plotting paper, and the possibility of making errors in the transferred data is eliminated. Also, the navigator can keep his eye on the scope, where the action is, rather than disturb his scope vision by stopping to look at white paper under electric light.

Regardless of where you plot, there are basically only two methods of doing it. The first is known as the *true* or *geographic plot* and the second is called the *relative-motion plot*. If you are a professional navigator, you must be thoroughly versed in both methods and attain perfect proficiency so that you can rapidly and accurately plot several moving targets at the same time. A large vessel cannot stop suddenly or change course abruptly, so the plotting must be done well in advance so that steps may be taken in time to avoid collision.

The best way to attain this proficiency, after the theory is learned, is to practice in the daytime whenever opportunity is afforded, so that you can visually confirm the accuracy of your plots and figures. This will give you the confidence you need to practice radar navigation in heavy fog and crowded waters.

On smaller vessels which can quickly stop, reverse, or change course, plotting is less essential, but a good small-boat navigator should know at least one method. The easier of the two, the geographic plot, is based on common-sense plotting of observed positions and is explained here. For the person who wishes to become proficient in relative-motion plotting there are several specialized texts available, including N.O. 1310, *Radar Navigation Manual;* N.O. 257, *Radar Plotting Manual;* and N.O. 217, *Maneuvering Board Manual.*

Geographical Plot This plot can be made on a chart, on the scope, or, as we have done here, on a polar coordinate plotting sheet, also known as a *radar plotting sheet.* (See Fig. 12–3.) Assume you are on a slow ship traveling at 6 knots, and you have the radar set with 0° at the lubber's line so that it will show relative bearings. At 1000 you pick up a

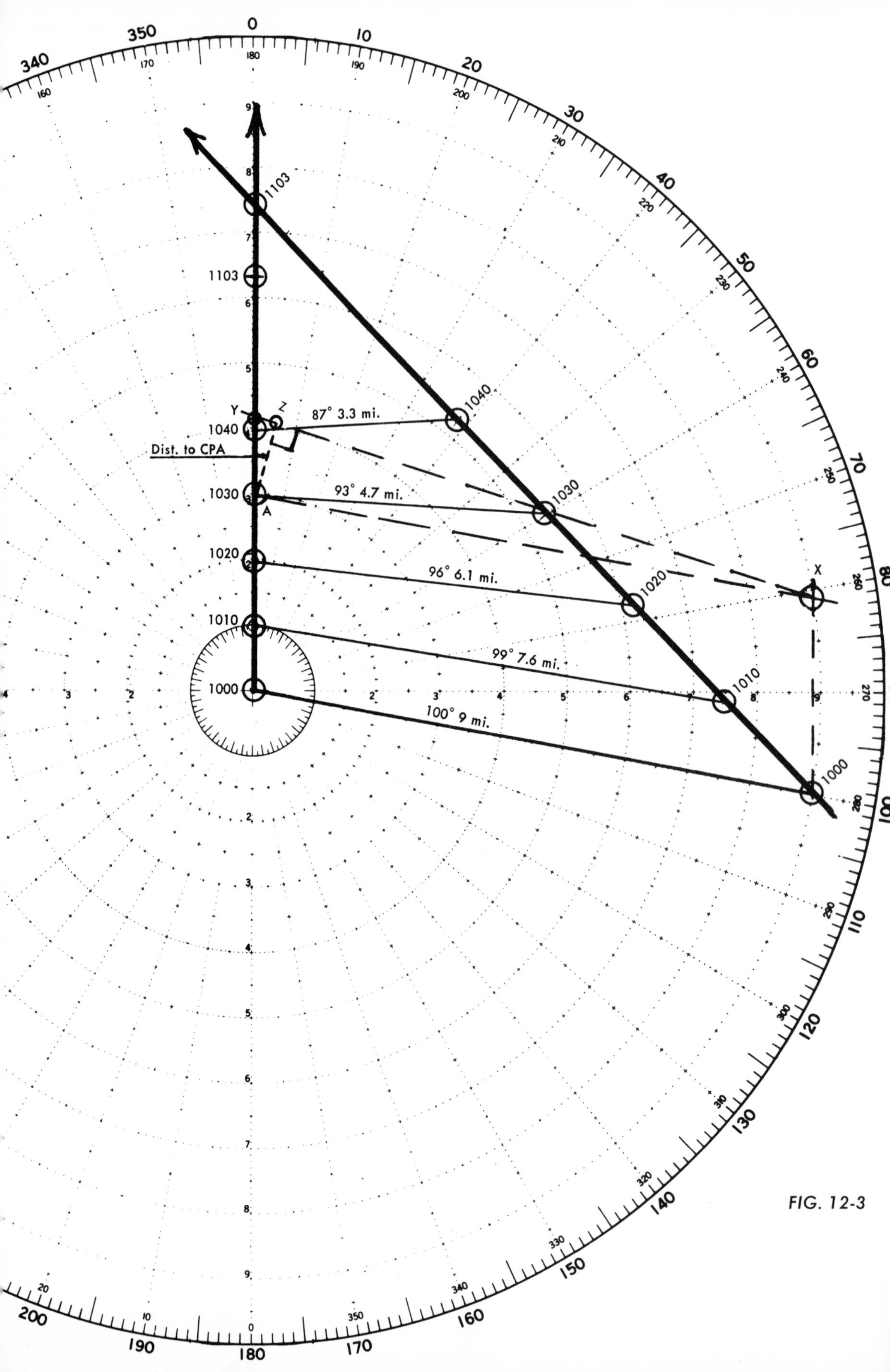
1103
1103
Y
Z
1040
87° 3.3 mi.
1040
Dist. to CPA
1030
93° 4.7 mi.
1030
A
1020
96° 6.1 mi.
1020
X
1010
99° 7.6 mi.
1010
1000
100° 9 mi.
1000

FIG. 12-3

ship coming from a little abaft your starboard beam and you begin to track it, taking bearings and ranges every 10 minutes. The following readings are obtained:

Time	*Bearing*	*Distance*
1000	100°	9.0 miles
1010	099°	7.6
1020	096°	6.1
1030	093°	4.7
1040	087°	3.3

Admittedly, you could have started your plot with only three of these readings, but you decided to take five to get a real good check.

On this kind of plot, your own ship is assumed to be at the center of the diagram at the time of the first reading, so you plot the initial position of the other vessel, bearing 100° and distant 9 miles from the center. Since the scope is set with 0° forward, your motion on this plotting sheet will be along the 0° line, or straight up. You now mark off the distances you have sailed in the 10-minute intervals between bearings. Since you are going at 6 knots, you travel 1 mile in 10 minutes, marking each position with the time as shown. You now plot the successive positions of the other vessel, according to bearing and distance, *not from the center of the diagram, but from your own position at the time the bearing was taken.* This produces a series of points along the course of the other vessel. A straight line through these points establishes his course line with respect to your own, and if you project it forward it will show where it will eventually cross your own course, provided neither of you changes course or speed. By measuring the intervals along his course line, you establish that he is making 12 knots.

Next you can determine the time when he will cross your course line. With dividers you measure the linear distance from his 1040 position to the intersection of the two course lines, determining it to be 4.6 miles. At a speed of 12 knots, this will take him 23 minutes, so he will cross your course at 1103. You can now determine where *you* will be at 1103. Since you travel at 6 knots, you will go 2.3 miles in 23 minutes, and you mark off that distance from your own

1040 position. This shows that at the moment he crosses your course line, he will be a little over a mile ahead, provided again that your observations have been accurate, that the speed of your own vessel is correctly estimated, and that he does not change his speed. If you wish to establish his true course, it can be done easily from this diagram. Transferring his course line to the center of the diagram, you see that his relative course is 315°, or 45° to the left of your own course. If your true course should be 115°, his course will thus be 115° − 45° = 070° true.

In radar plotting we are concerned with the critical *closest point of approach* (CPA). Large vessels cannot risk coming too close, especially in fog; thus, it is important to establish what the CPA will be in every instance. It is not necessarily the distance he will cross ahead of you, or you ahead of him, and in many cases it is much less, so it must be determined. On the geographic plot it can be done by trial and error with the help of dividers, but it can also be determined by a simple construction we borrow from the techniques used in relative-motion plotting.

Fig. 12–3 illustrates the method. Select any of the plotted positions on your own course line, such as your position at 1030, which we will call point *A*. Draw the line *A–X* parallel to the first bearing at 1000, and of the same length (9 miles in this case), in effect creating a parallelogram. Now draw a line through point *X* and the other vessel's position at 1030, and extend it until it crosses your own course line at point *Y*. The distance *A–Y* will be the distance the other vessel will cross ahead of you at 1103. To find the CPA, draw a line from *A* perpendicular to line *X–Y*. The length of this line *A–Z* will be the distance of the other vessel at the closest point of approach, in this case about 1.1 miles.

The geographic plot has given us the data we need to determine what our future action must be, depending on who has the right of way. If any change of course or speed is necessary, the law requires that it be done early and that it be substantial. The burdened ship cannot wait until the last moment to take action, nor is a series of small course changes acceptable. The change must be such that the other vessel is immediately cognizant thereof and can determine the change visually or on his own radarscope.

The drawback to the geographical plot is that it is a

relatively slow process. For this reason, professional navigators who do a great deal of radar plotting, often with several ships simultaneously, prefer the *relative-motion plot.* As mentioned before, several specialized publications are available for this purpose, so it is not discussed here.

In busy harbors in many parts of the world, ship traffic is controlled by radar installations ashore, and on certain river systems a chain of radar stations directs and controls the traffic, with enormous savings of time and money and a great increase in ship safety. In the United States a few experiments have been conducted by the Coast Guard at Long Beach, New York, and at San Francisco, but as yet no effective system of control has been established. With the advent of supertankers and their possible threat to the environment, it is inevitable that shortly coastal and harbor control of shipping, even for larger pleasure craft, will be established, in the same manner as airports control not only local traffic but cross-country routes as well.

Depth Sounders

The *depth sounder* is an instrument for measuring the depth of water between the ship's bottom and the ocean floor. It consists of a transmitter, a transducer, an amplifier, and a receiver. The transducer is secured to the bottom of a hull. When activated, it sends out sound waves that are usually directed vertically downward. Sound travels at approximately 4,800 feet per second, and as the signal proceeds from the transducer, the sound waves spread out in a cone-shaped pattern that, depending on the depth, may cover a considerable area of the ocean floor. After striking the bottom, the sound waves are echoed back to the transducer, which amplifies the return signal and transmits it to the receiver, where it is displayed as either a flash, a digital readout, or a continuous trace on a graph. Sometimes the graph system is combined with a flasher or a digital readout. The result is a measurement of the time interval it took the sound wave to reach bottom and travel back, converted in the receiver display to read in either feet or fathoms.

The distance measured is from the bottom of the vessel

FIG. 12-4
Flashing depth finder
Flashing and recording depth finder

(COURTESY RAYTHEON COMPANY)

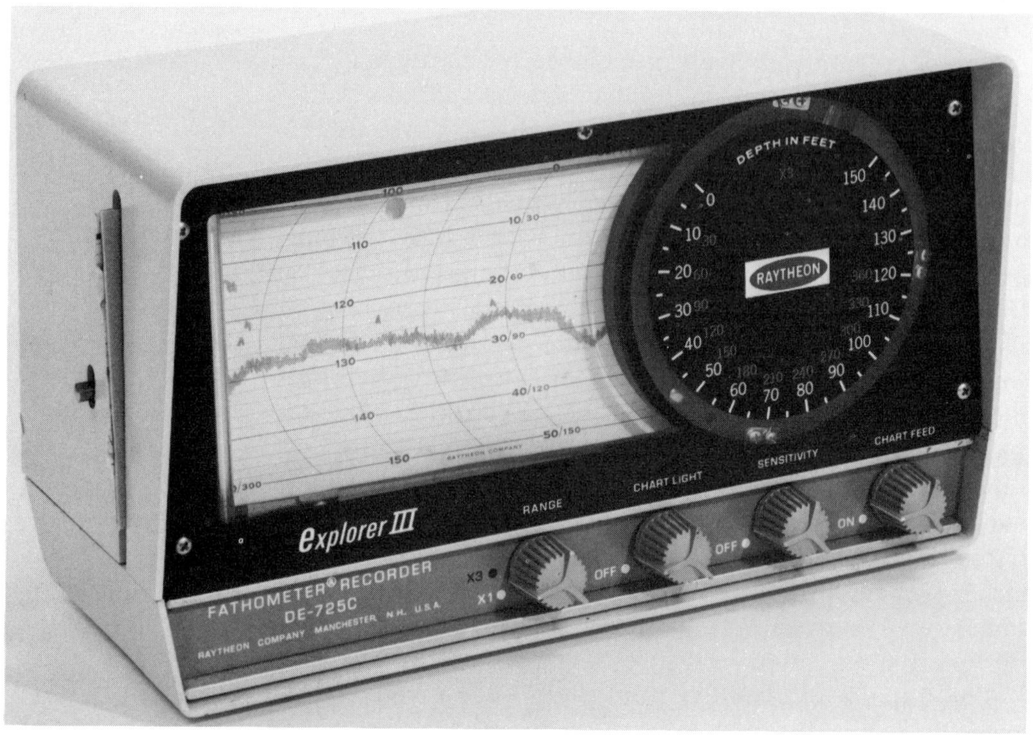

to the highest point within the base of the sound cone on the bottom. Some instruments can be adjusted for the ship's draft so that they record the actual distance from water surface to bottom. For purposes of marine surveying, the latter is the desired information, but for purposes of vessel operation, we are more interested in the depth of water beneath the hull. In all cases, the state of the tide may have to be considered. Most charts show soundings when the tide is at mean low water.

The depth sounder is a great improvement over the old hand lead line in terms of accuracy, convenience, and expenditure of effort. It serves many purposes, but in particular it warns a vessel of the danger of shallow water. Some instruments have an alarm bell that rings when recordings reach a preset minimum allowable depth.

In the actual operation of a depth sounder certain peculiarities may occur, usually in the form of double signals. For example, a large school of fish will create an echo that will show before the return from the bottom—a very convenient aid for fishermen—so a double return is shown. At greater depths in certain areas a *scattering layer* may be encountered. It varies in depth between day and night and is believed to be a dense mass of plankton that is able to return an echo, and in fact at times has been known to blanket the bottom signal.

Whenever multiple returns show up on the indicator, reducing the gain will usually eliminate all but the desired recordings.

When the depth sounder is used for navigation, as described in Chapter 5, it is essential that you consult the tide table and apply the height of tide to recordings before you make comparisons with the charted soundings. The depth sounder is a particularly useful instrument to have when you decide to approach a shore in fog and follow a certain depth contour to a harbor entrance.

For modern marine surveying purposes, where exact charting of the ocean-bottom contour is carried out, highly sophisticated equipment has been devised. With the increased need for underwater navigation by long-range submarines, exact knowledge in this area is, of course, essential.

Sonar

The word *sonar* comes from *so*und *na*vigation *r*anging and is the system developed for underwater detection by warships. Again, it makes use of the principle that sound waves travel through the water and are reflected back when they strike a solid object, such as a submarine. The sonar transducer, however, can direct the transmissions in a horizontal direction and usually rotates through the entire 360° horizontal circle. It is equipped to pick up not only its own echoes, but also the sound waves sent out by the machinery of other vessels. With the very sophisticated equipment developed by the U.S. Navy, it is often possible to determine not only the bearing and distance of a vessel, but also what type of vessel it is. The sounds emitted by certain vessels, referred to as a "signature," enable a skilled operator with modern equipment to tell many identifying facts about the vessel.

Sonar is also used in modern ocean-bottom survey work. Transponders, which are really small portable radio stations that emit signals on request, are located very accurately on the ocean bottom, enclosing the area to be surveyed. The survey vessel uses these transponders as reference points. When the request for transmission is made electronically, the transponder sends out sound waves, which are then measured in bearing and range at the survey ship to establish a very accurate position.

For the yachtsman, fisherman, or other small-vessel operator, the system is of general interest only, for which reason operational details are not discussed here.

Chapter 13

The Marine Radiotelephone System

The marine telephone is not a navigational instrument as such, but it is so important to the safety of everyone aboard ship that a separate chapter is devoted to it here. The importance of the radiotelephone was forcibly brought home to me on a dark night in the Pacific in 1943 when I spent hours trying to raise a shore station in New Guinea to tell them our small vessel was sinking. The shore operator had gone to sleep and never heard me.

On large vessels, trained radio operators keep watch around the clock, but on a small vessel the skipper is usually his own operator, and in emergency situations everything depends on how well he knows his equipment and proper procedure. When the dreaded "Mayday" is sent out, things happen fast, and if you are involved, either you can make a real contribution to the saving of life or you may interfere with those who know what to do and how to do it, and perhaps thwart their best efforts. With the enormous increase in the number of new people who take to the water and who are both inexperienced and untrained in proper boat handling, it is essential that they be made fully aware of their responsibilities in following established marine radio communications procedures, and learn how to handle the equipment skillfully, precisely, and with no waste of anybody's time.

Equipment Prior to January 1, 1972, vessels were mostly equipped with double-side-band (DSB) AM radiotelephones that, depending on power used, had considerable range. One difficulty with this system is that the transmission used up about 6 kHz of the frequency spectrum, with the result that the number of available frequencies is severely limited. Transmissions are also subject to severe interference from static and from other, far-off stations on the same frequency at the same time.

Because the system was unsatisfactory, and because the airwaves were becoming hopelessly crowded, the law was changed in favor of *single-side-band* (SSB) and *very-high-*

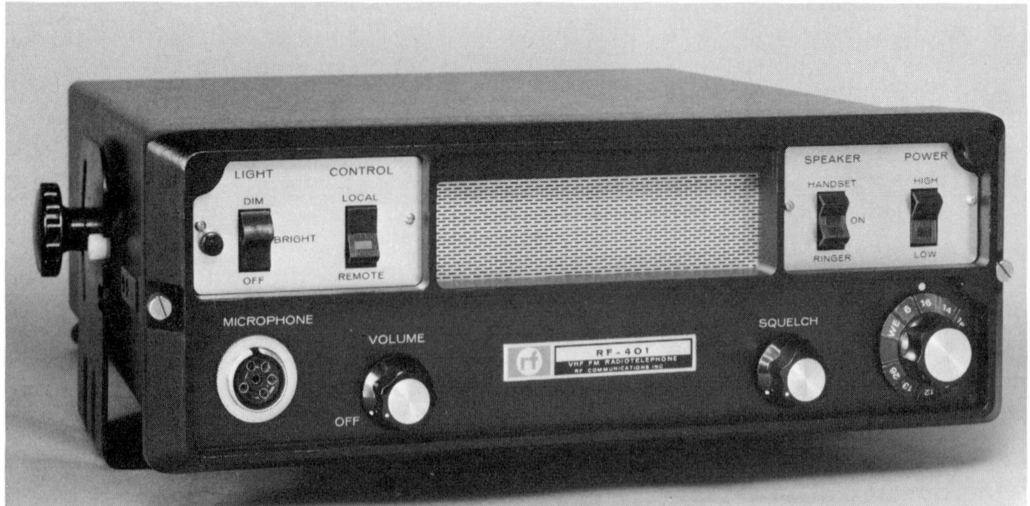

FIG. 13-1
Modern VHF FM radiotelephone for 12 channels

frequency (VHF) FM equipment. Boatowners who acquired DSB equipment prior to January 1, 1972, are allowed to use these sets until 1977 only. Meantime, all new installations require that a VHF FM radiotelephone be aboard before a license can be granted to install the SSB equipment.

VHF FM radiotelephones, because of the high frequencies used, are line-of-sight transmissions, and are therefore limited to about 50 miles, depending on the height of the sending and receiving antennae. A clear, sharp signal is provided, almost entirely free from static interference. The system affords thirty-eight different channels for various purposes. It is intended for use in all local short-range communications, such as ship-to-shore, shore-to-ship, ship-to-ship, local Coast Guard, and local National Weather Service reporting. Channel 16 is the national *distress, safety, and calling* channel and channel 6 is used exclusively for *intership safety*. Installation of both are mandatory and are monitored by the Coast Guard. The use of VHF equipment has contributed vastly toward relieving radio traffic congestion in many areas, but beyond 50 miles from shore it is of little value, except for nearby intership communications.

Single-side-band radiotelephones use only half the spectrum width of DSB transmitters and therefore allow many more frequencies to be used. In addition, the power input is much more efficiently used, with the result that for the same power input, an SSB telephone may be many times as powerful as the DSB installation. This is the radio that will be used for long-distance conversation, up to two or three thousand miles in range, with greater clarity and less interference than the older types.

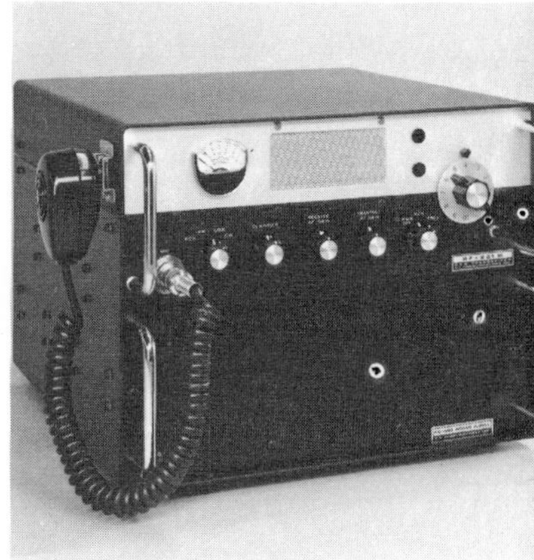

FIG. 13-2
Modern SSB radiotelephone for 10 channels

Operation and Procedure To operate a radiotelephone, you must obtain an operator's permit from the Federal Communications Commission, and they will also issue you a *station license.* When you use your radiotelephone, you must have aboard your station license, your operator's permit, and a radio logbook; you must also have a copy of the FCC regulations, either at home or on the boat.

On your equipment, certain frequencies are mandatory, such as channels 16 and 6 on your VHF set, and 2182 kHz on your DSB or SSB set. The frequency 2182 kHz is the international *calling and distress* frequency, and when your receiver is not used for other purposes, it should be left on 2182 so that you will be sure to hear a distress signal, should one be sent. The frequencies 2638 and 2738 kHz are set aside for ship-to-ship communication. Various vessels have a number of other channels and frequencies available for various purposes, such as talking to the local marine operator for a connection into the general telephone system. In each case, your local marine electronics people can supply specific information for your locality.

Using a marine telephone is like using a huge party line ashore: everybody can hear what you are saying and everybody wants to use the telephone at the same time you do. To make the system work, it is necessary to know the procedure perfectly, to use courtesy and common sense, to avoid unnecessary conversation, and always to be ready to give precedence to distress and other urgent calls. Certain established routines, conventions, and language must be strictly followed. Remember that you can be heard only when you push the button on the microphone you have in your hand, and you can hear only when the button is released.

To Make a Call. You can make a call on a specific working frequency if you know that an operator is listening, be it another ship or the shore marine operator. At times, by agreement, you will then shift to another working frequency for the actual conversation. If you are not using a specific frequency, you can make a general call on 2182 kHz on DSB or SSB or channel 16 on VHF, establish contact with the party you are calling, and then agree to change to another working frequency. You are not allowed to hold your conversation on the *calling frequency,* except in emergency. In any case, *before you talk, listen to make certain that no one else is talking.* In the examples that follow, you are the yacht *Polaris,* station WY2740.

Calling Another Vessel

Step. 1. Turn set on and listen to make sure no one is talking on 2182 kHz.

Step 2. Push Button and say: "WJ5510, this is WY2740, yacht *Polaris.* Over." If necessary, make your call three times, but do not exceed 30 seconds' total transmission. If there is no answer, wait at least 2 minutes before repeating call.

Step 3. When contact is made, the other vessel will answer: "WY2740, this is WJ5510, yacht *Aurora.* Over."

Step 4. You say: "WJ5510, this is WY2740. Please turn to 2,738 for message. Over."

Step 5. He says: "WY2740, this is WJ5510. Roger. Out."

Step 6. You switch to 2,738 and transmit: "WJ5510, yacht *Aurora,* this is WY2740, yacht *Polaris.* Do you hear me? Over."

Step 7. He says: "WY2740, this is WJ5510. Loud and clear. Over."

Step 8. You say: "WJ5510, this is WY2740. . . ." Now you give him the message. It may involve an exchange of conversation, but at each step the two stations must be identified. When finished, you say: "This is WY2740, yacht *Polaris.* Out."

This entire exchange must not exceed 3 minutes, and under the rules, you may not call the same vessel again for at least 10 minutes.

Calling Shore to Make a Regular Telephone Call To call shore for a regular call, since you will have previously made arrangements with the telephone company handling this traffic, you will have been given various frequencies on which you can call the operator, and they will have set up an account for you so that they can bill you at the end of each month.

Step 1. Turn to the proper frequency and make sure no one is talking. Then push the button and say: "San Francisco marine operator. This is WY2740, yacht *Polaris.* Over."

Step 2. If there is no answer, wait at least 2 minutes before placing the call again. When the answer comes, you will hear: "WY2740, yacht *Polaris,* this is San Francisco marine operator. Over."

Step 3. You say: "This is WY2740, yacht *Polaris,* calling [give the regular telephone number you wish to contact]. Over." When you get your call through, the other person must be made aware that you can either talk or listen, but not both.

Step 4. When your call is finished, you say: "This is WY2740, yacht *Polaris.* Out."

How to Receive Calls at Sea To make sure you will hear if anyone calls you, leave the receiver on at 2,182 kHz, or, if you have VHF, leave channel 16 on. When you hear your call letters and the name of your vessel, you simply pick up the microphone, push the button and say: "[station and name of caller], this is WY2740, yacht *Polaris.* Over." You will then arrange the proper frequency to talk on, if the caller is another vessel, and switch to that. If it is a call from shore, the marine operator will tell you which frequency to switch to. Then proceed as previously described. On the other hand, if you have made arrangements ahead of time to be called on a certain working frequency at a predetermined time, or if you have a standing arrangement with another station to use such frequency for frequent calls, then you may have a second receiver set to this frequency to avoid using the calling frequency. This is usually a great time-saver.

How to Send a Distress Call In a *real* emergency, where the loss of life and/or boat is imminent, perhaps by sinking or fire or being dead in the water and about to be sent crashing on a rocky shore, you send the international distress signal, "Mayday," on channel 16 (VHF) or 2,182 kHz. Now all ordinary radiotelephone traffic must stop. Your call will be answered by boats in the vicinity and/or the Coast Guard, and everybody will cooperate to get help to you as fast as possible. To save time, the correct procedure must be followed.

Step 1. Activate the radiotelephone alarm signal, if your set has one. It will be picked up as a wavering two-tone signal by radios tuned to this frequency, and in some cases will trigger an automatic device that will give an alarm. Pick up your microphone and say: "Mayday. Mayday. Mayday. This is WY2740, yacht *Polaris.* This is WY2740 yacht *Polaris.* This is WY2740, yacht *Polaris.*" Note that you make each statement three times.

Step 2. You do not wait for any acknowledgment, but proceed to give your distress message. Despite the urgency of the situation, try to speak calmly and clearly. Repeat the Mayday call and your identification, then say (for example): "Mayday. WY2740, yacht *Polaris.* I am 20 miles due west of Santa Barbara Island and sinking fast. Engine dead, shipping heavy waves. Need immediate assistance, six people aboard. *Polaris* is 30-foot cabin cruiser, white hull, blue deckhouse. Standing by on 2,182 kHz. This is WY2740, yacht *Polaris.*" Also repeat the distress message two times again, then listen for response.

How to Respond to a Distress Call If you hear a Mayday, stop all other activity and listen. You may be the nearest vessel, in which case you *must* go to his rescue; or there may be other vessels nearer, in which case you *must* keep off the air and let the others talk, nevertheless standing by to see if there is something you can do. Assume now that you are on another vessel and hear *Polaris's* Mayday. If there is no response for a minute or two, you get on 2,182 and say: "WY2740, *Polaris, Polaris, Polaris.* This is [give your call letters and vessel's name, stated three times]. Received Mayday."

At this point, you again wait for a minute or two to see if other vessels or perhaps a shore station answer. If not, you continue: "Mayday. WY2740, *Polaris.* This is [your call letters and name]. I am 15 miles west of Santa Barbara Island, 5 miles due east of your position. Can make 10 knots. Will reach you in 30 minutes. This is [your call letters and name]. Over."

Note that all distress traffic is preceded by the word Mayday, to let everybody know of the emergency so they won't interfere. If someone nevertheless interferes, the shore station, such as the Coast Guard, will tell him, "Seelonce Mayday," which means for him to get off the air. If you on your boat wish to silence such a person, you send "Seelonce, distress," then your own call letters and name. ("Seelonce" is the French *silence,* just as "Mayday" is taken from *m'aidez,* French for "help me.")

If you hear a Mayday and no one answers, but you realize you are too far away to effect a rescue in time, you must *relay* the information and try to reach a shore station or the Coast Guard. In that case you will transmit as follows:

1. The radiotelephone alarm, if you have the equipment.
2. "Mayday relay. Mayday relay. Mayday relay."
3. "This is [your call letters and vessel name]."
4. The name of the *station you are calling,* stated three times.

Calling Off the Emergency When the situation has resolved itself, hopefully with a successful rescue, the station in charge of the rescue coordination, be it a shore station or the rescue vessel itself, will transmit on the distress frequency:

1. "Mayday."
2. "To all stations. To all stations. To all stations."

3. Call letters and own name.
4. Time of day.
5. Call letters and name of *vessel in distress.*
6. "Seelonce feenee" ["silence finished"].

How to Send an Urgent Signal The *urgent signal* is used in situations that do not warrant a Mayday call but where urgent action is nevertheless required. You may be out of gas and drifting on a lee shore or have broken a mast and need a tow. The signal used is: "Pan. Pan. Pan," sent on the distress frequency. The radiotelephone alarm may *not* be used for a Pan signal, except where a shore station has an urgent storm warning, or where a person is lost overboard and other vessels are needed to effect rescue.

The sequence of the message is:

1. "Pan. Pan. Pan."
2. Vessel's call letters and name.
3. Position of vessel.
4. Nature of trouble, number of people aboard, description of vessel.
5. Call letters and name of vessel in trouble.

How to Send a Safety Signal The *safety signal* is the third in the order of priority of emergency signals, after the distress (Mayday) signal and the urgency (Pan) signal. The word used is "security," stated three times. This type of message is used to inform others of a danger to the safety of navigation or of important meteorological information.

The signal is initiated on the distress frequency, but the message is given on a working frequency, if possible. The sequence is:

1. "Security. Security. Security."
2. "This is [your call letters and name]. Shift to 2,638 kHz."
3. On 2,638 kHz: "Security. Security. Security. This is [your call letters and name]."
4. The message follows (could be a sunken barge adrift in a fairway, an important navigation light extinguished, etc.).
5. "This is [call letters and name]. Out."

Miscellaneous Procedures Formerly it was possible to call the Coast Guard and get a check on your radiotelephone equipment, but because these tests became too numerous the practice was discontinued, and the Coast Guard will no longer accept calls for tests.

The radiotelephone can also be used to obtain weather bureau marine forecasts, and the government is increasingly providing VHF coverage of our coastal areas with continuously updated weather reports. If you ever have to abandon ship, leave the transmitter locked on the air, if possible, so that a rescue vessel can take RDF bearings on your position. In the excitement of the emergency, remember to speak distinctly, using the phonetic alphabet for call letters.

PHONETIC ALPHABET

ALPHA	**FOXTROT**	**KILO**	**PAPA**	**UNIFORM**	**ZULU**
BRAVO	**GOLF**	**LIMA**	**QUEBEC**	**VICTOR**	
CHARLIE	**HOTEL**	**MILE**	**ROMEO**	**WHISKEY**	
DELTA	**INDIA**	**NOVEMBER**	**SIERRA**	**X RAY**	
ECHO	**JULIET**	**OSCAR**	**TANGO**	**YANKEE**	

Above all, remember that when the Mayday signal is heard, the chips are down and somebody is in trouble. This is no time to play games or fool around. If you are found guilty of interfering with *any* radio communications, let alone an emergency signal, or if you ever send out a false distress signal, you have probably had your last radio license, not to speak of the penalties you will pay—and they will never be high enough!

A final word for the person who does not have a radiotelephone aboard: If you suddenly see an aircraft circling you, opening and closing his throttle or changing his propeller pitch so you notice the difference in the sound, he is not playing games. He wants to direct you to a vessel in distress. You must by all means follow in the direction he

Channel Designator	Frequency (MHz) Ship	Coast	Points of Communication	Channel Usage
DISTRESS, SAFETY AND CALLING (MANDATORY)				Vessel & Coast Stations are required to maintain a listening watch during hours of service.
16	156.800	156.800	Intership & ship to coast	
INTERSHIP SAFETY (MANDATORY)				For intership safety only.
06	156.300	156.300	Intership	
PORT OPERATIONS				These channels may be used only in or near a port, in locks or waterways with traffic limited to movement of ships or safety of ships or persons. Channel 12 is recommended for non-distress communications with the Coast Guard or Harbormaster.
65	156.275	156.275	Intership & ship to coast	
66	156.325	156.325	Do	
12	156.600	156.600	Do	
73	156.675	156.675	Do	
14	156.700	156.700	Do	
74	156.725	156.725	Do	
20	157.000	161.600	Do	
NAVIGATIONAL				For safety in ship movements and is primarily ship-to-ship and secondarily ship-to-coast.
13	156.650	156.650	Intership & ship to coast	
ENVIRONMENTAL				Receive only channels, for the transmission of information pertaining to weather, hazards to navigation and notices to mariners.
15		156.750	Coast to ship	
WX		162.55	Do	
WX2		162.40	Do	
STATE CONTROL				State control channel for use by non-federal agencies and states.
17	156.850	158.850	Ship to coast	
COMMERCIAL				May be used only by commercial vessels for messages relating to ship business, except Channel 9 is shared by commercial and non-commercial vessels. Channel 88 is limited to use by ships engaged in commercial fishing, and ship to aircraft communications where the aircraft is associated with fishing operations.
07	156.350	156.350	Intership & ship to coast	
67	156.375	....	Intership	
08	156.400	....	Do	
09	156.450	156.450	Intership & ship to coast	
10	156.500	156.500	Do	
11	156.550	156.550	Do	
77	156.875	....	Intership	
18	156.900	156.900	Intership & ship to coast	
19	156.950	156.950	Do	
79	156.975	156.975	Do	
80	157.025	157.025	Do	
88	157.425	....	Intership	
NONCOMMERCIAL				For pleasure craft communications relating to needs of the vessel. Channels 69, 71 and 78 are available to marinas, yacht clubs and other organizations offering services or supplies to non-commercial vessels.
68	156.425	156.425	Intership & ship to coast	
09	156.450	156.450	Ship to coast	
69	156.475	156.475	Do	
70	156.525	....	Intership	
71	156.575	156.575	Ship to coast	
72	156.625	....	Intership	
78	156.925	156.925	Ship to coast	
PUBLIC CORRESPONDENCE				Marine-operator channels for use by any vessel in establishing communications with land-line telephones or reaching a vessel that is out of ship-to-ship range.
24	157.200	161.800	Ship to public coast	
84	157.225	161.825	Do	
25	157.250	161.850	Do	
85	157.275	161.875	Do	
26	157.300	161.900	Do	
86	157.325	161.925	Do	
27	157.350	161.950	Do	
87	157.375	161.975	Do	
28	157.400	162.000	Do	

Recommended Channelization

The FCC requires that all mobile maritime stations be equipped with Channel 06, 16, and at least one working channel.

Channel	Purpose	Comments
06	Ship-to Ship safety	Required on all ship stations.
16	Distress, safety and calling	Required on all ship and coast stations.
26	Marine Operator	Primary public coast channel.
28	Marine Operator	Secondary public coast channel.
12	Port Operations	Primary—for non-distress traffic with Coast Guard and Harbormasters.
14*	Port Operations	Secondary (as above)
68	Intership and Ship-to-Coast	Non-commercial traffic.
70	Intership only	Primary, non-commercial traffic.
72	Intership only	Secondary, non-commercial traffic.
69	Ship-to-Coast	Primary, Limited coast stations.
71	Ship-To-Coast	Secondary, limited coast stations.
WX1**	N.O.A.A. Weather	Primary weather channel.

Notes: *Substitute with channel 18A in San Francisco/Seattle area.
**Substitute with WX2 (162.40 MHz) in Santa Cruz/Monterey area.

Most of the 10 and 25-watt VHF sets now on the market offer a 12-channel capability and are sold with two to five channels already installed. Additional channels to fit the individual's requirements can then be added at additional cost. The average yachtsman could satisfy most of his requirements with six to nine channels. This list is a general guide. For local channel assignments to yacht clubs,

FIG. 13-3 Channels and frequencies for VHF FM radiotelephone operation

COURTESY INT
INCORPORATE

indicates. (Naturally, if you have a radiotelephone, you will attempt to contact the pilot). If your help should no longer be needed, he will cross your path several times, again giving sound signals by throttle or propeller pitch.

Whenever you have been involved in an emergency, notify the Coast Guard as soon as the emergency is over so that they can go about their other business.

The table, Fig. 13–3, lists the exact frequencies that correspond to the channel designations on the VHF FM radiotelephones and indicates how these channels are allotted for various purposes.

Chapter 14

Weather Reports and Time Signals

Weather Reports

Advance weather information is all-important to the navigator. It could spell the difference between a pleasant or an unpleasant voyage and sometimes between safety and disaster. If the navigator knows and understands the weather ahead, or if he is able to track the movements of a storm, he can take evasive action in ample time, save time, wear, and tear on vessel and personnel, and sometimes save lives.

Weather information in populated coastal areas is readily available from various sources. In the U.S. the National Weather Service, a branch of the National Oceanographic and Atmospheric Agency (NOAA) of the Department of Commerce, through its many divisions and agencies supplies weather information for the entire country and for the North Atlantic Ocean from the equator northward as far east as 35° W longitude, and for the North Pacific Ocean from the equator northward as far west as 170° E longitude. It is possible that at some future date, through international agreement, this coverage may be extended to the South Atlantic and the South Pacific as well, and possibly to other bodies of water if other countries agree.

Weather information is available in several ways, but of main interest to the mariner are the following:

1. Wireless transmission (W/T) of facsimile weather maps that are reproduced by a machine in the chart room of a ship at sea and interpreted by the navigation officer or the ship's master. A good knowledge of meteorology is required for this approach.
2. Wireless transmission in Morse code of coded weather reports, giving the data with which the navigator can construct his own weather map. This requires the navigator to be an ex-

perienced meteorologist who can not only draw, but interpret, the map. Amateurs in ocean races have been known to record transmissions on a tape recorder and then play them back at slow speed to enable them to read the Morse code. For details of stations, frequencies, times, and codes, you must consult N.O. 118, *Radio Weather Aids.*

3. Radiotelephone reports from U.S. Coast Guard stations, announced on 2,182 kHz and 156.8 MHz and usually given on 2,670 kHz and 156.6 MHz.
4. VHF FM continuous-voice weather reports from many National Weather Service stations around the country. These reports are updated at least every 6 hours, but more often as required. They are available on 166.55 MHz and can be heard up to about 40 miles from the station, depending on local conditions.
5. Marine forecasts and warnings directly from National Weather Service offices may be retransmitted by commercial stations, usually as part of a news program. For the time of such marine weather reports, the local newspaper should be consulted.
6. Weather broadcasts by air navigation radio stations, some continuous, others intermittent. They broadcast in the 200- to 400-kHz band. Exact frequencies should be obtained locally.
7. On July 1, 1971, the National Bureau of Standards in cooperation with the National Weather Service began broadcasting storm warnings for the North Atlantic—at the tenth minute of each hour, over WWV, Fort Collins, Colorado—and for the North Pacific—at the forty-sixth minute of each hour, over WWVH in Kauai, Hawaii. Both operate on 2.5, 5, 10, 15, and 20 MHz on a 24-hour basis, and WWV also transmits on 25 MHz. The broadcasts are brief and are confined to giving the latitude and longitude of the storm center, the direction and speed at which the storm is moving, and an estimate of the winds in the area. Because these stations are readily heard by small vessels at great

distances, the broadcasts enable small-boat navigators to plot a storm movement hourly and thus to take early evasive action. It is expected that this service will be expanded to other oceans at a later date.

There is thus a wealth of weather information available, and it is up to the navigator to make the best use of it. It has often been said, with great truth, that the long ocean races, which always involve top boats, top skippers, and top crews, are almost invariably won by the vessel with the best meteorologist aboard.

Marine Weather Services Charts These are special charts issued by the U.S. Department of Commerce for various areas of United States waters. They show the location of transmitting stations, give the telphone numbers of Weather Bureau Offices in that area, and then proceed to list the sources, frequencies, nature and time of transmission weather reports and storm warnings within that area. They are invaluable to the yachtsman. A listing of available charts follows:

Eastport, Me. to Montauk Point, N. Y.
Montauk Point, N. Y. to Manasquan, N. J.
Manasquan, N. J. to Cape Hatteras, N. C.
Cape Hatteras, N. C. to Savannah, Ga.
Savannah, Ga. to Apalachicola, Fla.
Apalachicola, Fla. to Morgan City, La.
Morgan City, La. to Brownsville, Tex.
Point Conception, Calif. to Mexican Border
Eureka, Calif. to Point Conception, Calif.
Canadian Border to Eureka, Calif.
Great Lakes: Michigan and Superior
Great Lakes: Erie, Huron, and Ontario
Hawaiian Waters
Puerto Rico and Virgin Islands
Alaskan Waters

Copies of these charts are available from the Superintendent of Documents, U.S. Government Printing Office, Washington, D.C. 20402, at 15 cents each.

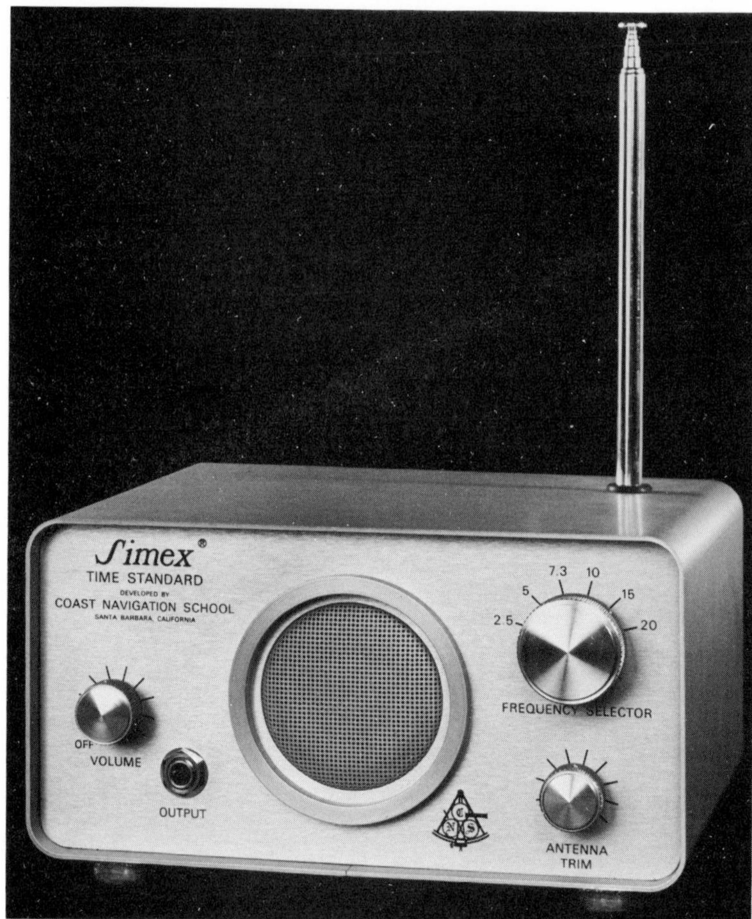

FIG. 14-1
WWV time signal receiver

Time Signals

The navigator needs to know exact time to the second. In former days he relied on one or more chronometers, accurate clocks that were set to Greenwich Mean Time (GMT) at the beginning of a voyage. These were checked against radio time signals every day if possible, and a log was kept of the loss or gain record of the chronometer. Thus, by applying a known chronometer error to the reading, a person would always have the exact GMT. The tendency on modern vessels is to omit the chronometer and simply use a watch with a good sweep second hand. The watch is checked against a time signal immediately before taking sights and the error noted or the watch set to the exact minute and second if possible.

Time signals are available in code from the U.S. Naval Observatory, but it is simpler to tune in to the National

FIG. 14-2 *World-Wide Time Signal Sources*

Call Sign	Location	Power kw	Period of Operation		Frequency mHz	Duration of Emission	Days and Hours of Operation
			Days per Week	Hours per Day		Minutes of Time Signals	
ATA	New Delhi, India	2	5	5	10	Continuous	0530-1030, Mon.-Fri.
CHU	Ottawa, Canada	5	7	24	3.3, 7.3, 14.6	Continuous	Continuous
FFH	Paris, France	5	5	$8^1/_2$	2.5	30 in each 60	0800-1630, Mon.-Fri.
HBN	Neuchatel, Switzerland	0.5	7	24	5	5 in each 10	Continuous
IAM	Rome, Italy	1	6	1	5	10 in each 15	0700-0800, Not Sunday
IBF	Torino, Italy	5	7	$2^3/_4$	5	Continuous for 15 min.	From 45 to 60 min. 0645 to 1745
JJY	Tokyo, Japan	2	7	24	2.5, 5, 10, 15	Continuous	Continuous, except 25th to 34th min. of each hr.
LOL	Buenos Aires, Argentina	2	7	5	5, 10, 15	60 min.	0500, 0800, 1100, 1400, 1700, 2000, GMT
MSF	Rugby, England	0.5	7	24	2.5, 5, 10	5 in each 10	Continuous
OMA	Prague, Czechoslovakia	1	7	24	2.5	15 in each 30	Continuous
WWV	Fort Collins, USA	2.5 to 10	7	24	2.5, 5, 10, 15, 20	Continuous	Continuous
WWVH	Kauai, Hawaii	1 to 2	7	24	2.5, 5, 10, 15, 20	Continuous	Continuous
RWM &	Moscow	20	7	19	5, 10, 15	6 in each 60	First 6 min. of each hr.
RES	Soviet Union		7	19	5, 10, 15	6 in each 60	First 6 min. of each hr.
ZUO	Olifantsfontein, South Africa	4	7	24	5	Continuous	Continuous
ZUO	Johannesburg, South Africa	0.25	7	24	10	Continuous	Continuous

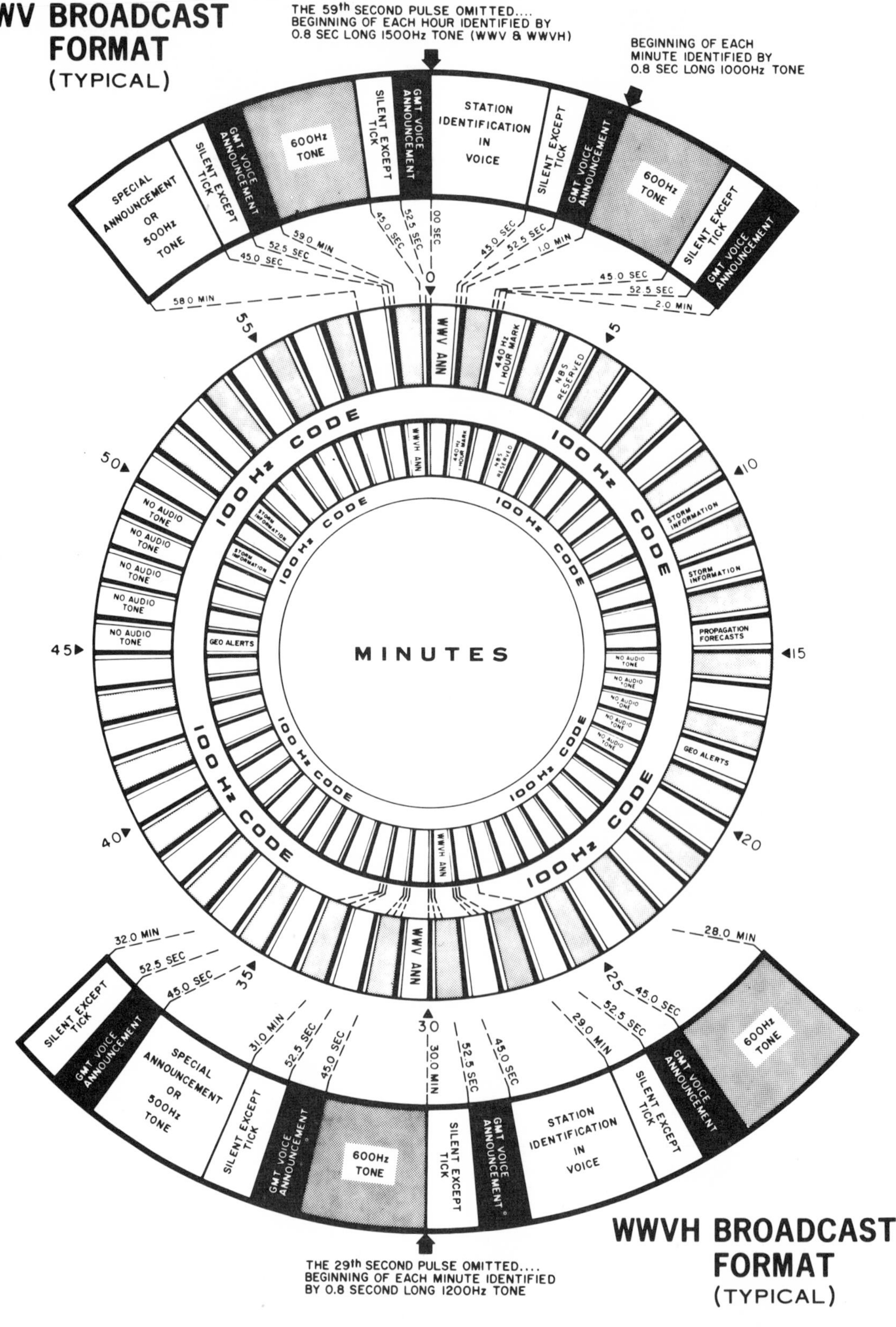

FIG. 14-3 WWV and WWVH broadcast format

(COURTESY U.S. DEPARTMENT OF COMMERCE, NBS SPECIAL PUBLICATION 236)

NBS FREQUENCY AND TIME BROADCAST SERVICES

Time Signals

Program

;ommon usage of the name Greenwich Mean Time MT) includes any of the astronomers Universal ne scales and rather coarse approximations to these les. This time (GMT) is basically just the local ar time at the Greenwich Meridian (longitude zero) ›ressed on a 24-hour clock starting at midnight, :enwich, England.

3ecause of the common usage of the name Green- :h Mean Time, the time announcements on WWV 1 WWVH are referred to by this name. More pre- ely, the actual reference time scale is the Coordi- :ed Universal Time Scale as maintained by the Na- nal Bureau of Standards, UTC(NBS).

The 0 to 24 hour system is used starting with 0000 midnight at longitude zero. The first two figures 'e the hour, and the last two figures give the num- ͬ of minutes past the hour when the tone returns. e time announcement refers to the end of an an- uncement interval, i.e., to the time when the audio ıe occurs.

At WWV a voice annoucement of Greenwich Mean me is given during the last 7.5 seconds of every nute. At 1035 GMT, for instance, the voice an- uncement given in English is: "At the tone—ten urs, thirty-five minutes Greenwich Mean Time."

At WWVH a voice announcement of Greenwich :an Time occurs during the period 45 seconds to .5 seconds after the minute. It should be noted that : voice announcement for WWVH precedes that of WV by 7.5 seconds. However, the tone markers ferred to in both announcements occur simultan- usly, though they may not be so received due to opagation effects.

Corrections

Commencing January 1, 1972, all the standard :quency time signal emissions from WWV, WWVH d WWVB will contain information and corrections the difference between UTC time signals and Astro- ›mical Time, UT1.

The method of coding the UT1 corrections after nuary 1, 1972 uses a system of double seconds lses. The first through the seventh seconds pulse, ıen marked by a double pulse, will indicate a "plus" rrection, and from the ninth through the fifteenth a ıinus" correction. The eighth seconds pulse is not ed. The amount of correction is determined by unting the number of seconds pulses that are ›ubled. For example, if the first, second, and third conds pulses are doubled, the UT1 correction is lus" 0.3 second. Or if the ninth, tenth, eleventh, elfth, thirteenth, and fourteenth seconds pulses are ›ubled, the UT1 correction is "minus" 0.6 second.

Official Announcements

Propagation Forecasts

A forecast of radio propagation conditions is broadcast in voice during part of every 15th minute of each hour from WWV. The announcements are short-term forecasts and refer to propagation along paths in the North Atlantic area, such as Washington, D. C. to London or New York to Berlin. These forecasts are also applicable to high latitudes provided the appropriate time correction is made for other latitudes. The forecasts are prepared by the Office of Telecommunications Services Center, OT, Boulder, Colorado.

Geophysical Alerts

Current geophysical alerts (Geoalerts) as declared by the World Warning Agency of the International Ursigram and World Days Service (IUWDS) are broadcast in voice during the 19th minute of each hour from WWV and during the 46th minute of each hour from WWVH. The messages are changed daily at 0400 UT with provisions to provide immediate alerts of outstanding occurring events. These are followed by summary information on selected solar and geophysical events in the past 24 hours and corresponding forecasts prepared by the Space Environment Services Center, NOAA, Boulder, Colorado.

Storm Warnings

A program is being implemented to broadcast storm and hurricane warnings over WWV and WWVH soon after July 1, 1971. Initially, the areas of coverage will be the waters of the North Atlantic and North Pacific. The storm warning broadcasts will be voice announcements and will be prepared by the National Weather Bureau.[8]

Station Identification

WWV and WWVH identify by voice (in English) every 30 minutes. The voice announcements are automatically synchronized recordings, not live broadcasts. The announcer for WWV is Mr. Don Elliott of Atlanta, Georgia; the announcer for WWVH is Mrs. Jane Barbe, also of Atlanta.

Radiated Power

Frequency, MHz	Radiated Power, kw			
	WWV	WWVH	WWVB	WWVL
2.5	2.5	2.5	—	—
5	10	10	—	—
10	10	10	—	—
15	10	10	—	—
20	2.5	2.5	—	—
25	2.5	—	—	—

FIG. 14-4

(EXCERPTS FROM NBS SPECIAL PUBLICATION 236, COURTESY NATIONAL BUREAU OF STANDARDS, U.S. DEPARTMENT OF COMMERCE)

Bureau of Standard stations, WWV in Fort Collins, Colorado, and WWVH in Kauai, Hawaii. Both operate on 2.5, 10, 15, and 20 MHz; in addition, WWV transmits on 25 MHz. The signals are given in voice every minute, with continuous time ticks every second in between.

At certain times the stations also give other information, mainly propagation forecasts, telling you what kind of receptions you can expect for the next several hours.

WWV and WWVH are heard almost all over the world. During the day you will get best results on 10, 15, and 20 MHz; at night the signals are usually heard best on 2.5, 5, and 10 MHz. If you are cruising in British waters, the BBC has an excellent system of time signals on ordinary broadcast frequencies. But if you have a radio that will pick up WWV, you can also make use of the foreign stations listed in Fig. 14–2.

Figure 14–3 gives the signal patterns of WWV and WWVH and other pertinent information about these signals. Eventually they will be transmitted via satellite, which will ensure even better reception.

PART III

Celestial Navigation

Chapter 15

Celestial Definitions and Coordinates

Celestial navigation is the practice of the knowledge by which we determine our position on the surface of the ocean by making observations of specific celestial bodies, namely the sun, the moon, the planets Venus, Jupiter, Saturn, and Mars, and fifty-seven selected stars that we call "navigation stars." In celestial navigation we usually use a precision instrument called a *sextant,* by which we measure the vertical angle between the celestial body observed and the point on our horizon directly below that body. By timing the observation carefully, usually to the nearest second of time, and referring to a special *almanac* and a volume of *navigational tables,* we can translate this observation into a *line of position* on our chart of the ocean and know that at the time of the observation we were somewhere on that line of position. The accuracy is usually within a mile or two. This is really all there is to celestial navigation and it is quite simple. To practice such navigation expertly, we must understand the basic principles of the procedure, learn the mechanics of the almanac and the navigation tables, and discipline ourselves to work our numbers methodically and accurately. Most calculations are made on prepared forms in order to eliminate memory work. If you understand what you are doing, it will all make good sense and you can reason your way to the correct answer. Reason is always superior to memory.

Line of Position Principle This is really getting ahead of ourselves, but it is usually better to know in advance where we are going. Fig. 15–1 shows a star in the sky: it could be the sun, the moon, or a planet. A line from the star to the center of the Earth pierces the surface of the Earth at a point called the *geographical position* (GP) of the star; this point is also called the substellar, subsolar, sublunar point, depending on the body observed. Navigators with sextants are stationed at points *A, B,* and *C,* where at any given instant they can measure the angle between the star and

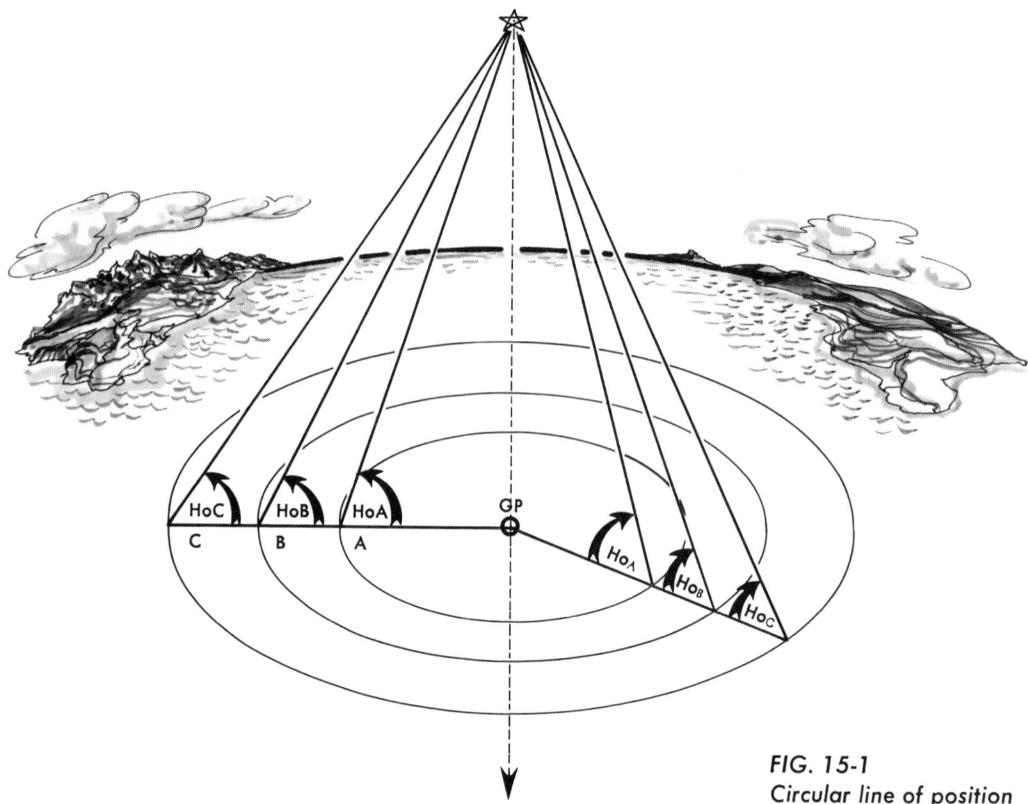

FIG. 15-1
Circular line of position principle

the horizon, called the (observed) *altitude,* H_o of the star. If we use the geographical position (GP) as a center and draw three circles on the surface of the Earth through the points *A, B,* and *C,* the following statements become obvious:

1. **Navigator at *A* observes a larger altitude than navigator at *B*. *B* observes a smaller altitude than *A*, but larger than *C*. *C*** observes a smaller altitude than either *B* or *A*. Or: $H_{oA} > H_{oB} > H_{oC}$, where ">" means "is greater than."
2. Any and all observers stationed anywhere on the circle through *A* will, at any given instant, observe the identical altitude, H_{oA}, of the star. Observers on the circle through *B* will all observe an identical altitude, and the same would hold true for observers on the circle through *C*.
3. Therefore, at any given moment, if an observer measures the identical altitude as the navigator at *A*, he *must* be located on the

circle through *A*. If he measures the same altitude as the man at *B,* he must be on the circle through *B*. And the same holds true for observers who get the same altitude as the man at *C:* they must be on the same circle as the observer at *C*.

4. The general statement can be made that if we observe a smaller altitude we are *further away* from the GP, and if we have a greater altitude we are *closer to* the GP.

By geometry we can show that the difference in H_o at points *A, B,* or *C,* measured in *minutes of arc,* is equal to the *difference* in the *radius* of the corresponding circle, *measured in nautical miles.* You have now learned the single most important basic principle used in modern navigation.

In actual navigation we know *approximately* where we are, and we try to find out *exactly* where we are. If we take point *C* to be our approximate position—we actually call it our *assumed position* (AP)—we are able for any instant of time to calculate what the altitude and direction of a given body would be if we were, in fact, at *C*. If we measure a smaller altitude with our sextant, we know that we must be on a circle outside *C,* or *away* from the assumed position. If our observation gives a greater altitude, we know we are on a new circle inside *C, toward* the GP. The *calculated* altitude for the assumed position AP is named H_c, and the actual observed altitude at any place is called H_o. The difference between H_c and H_o in minutes of arc is called the *intercept,* for which the symbol *a* is sometimes used. It is measured in nautical miles and always labeled *away* or *toward.*

Method of Obtaining a Line of Position (LOP) At a suitable time we observe the altitude of the celestial body and time it. We *assume* a position AP in the vicinity of our dead reckoning position, and for the time of the observation, with the help of the almanac and our navigation table, calculate what the altitude and bearing of the body would be if we were at the AP. Comparing this calculated altitude H_c with the observed altitude H_o gives us our *intercept* in nautical miles, which we can readily determine as *away* or *toward.* We now plot the assumed position AP on our chart, and through it draw a line in the direction of the celestial body. The intercept is measured from AP along this line, toward or away from the body observed. At the end of the intercept we draw a straight line at right angles to the direction of the star, and this is our *line of position* (LOP). Note that we do not need to know where the GP is located, nor do we plot it. Because it is usually many hundreds of miles away, the circle is very large and for a relatively short distance, say less than 50 miles, it can be considered as a straight line on our chart, which is the reason we can safely draw out LOP as a straight line.

***Example* •** True bearing of star, called the *azimuth (Zn)* is 225°; intercept is 5 miles *away*. Plot LOP. See Fig. 15–2.

Having obtained one LOP, we merely know that we are somewhere along that line. A second LOP is needed to determine a fix.

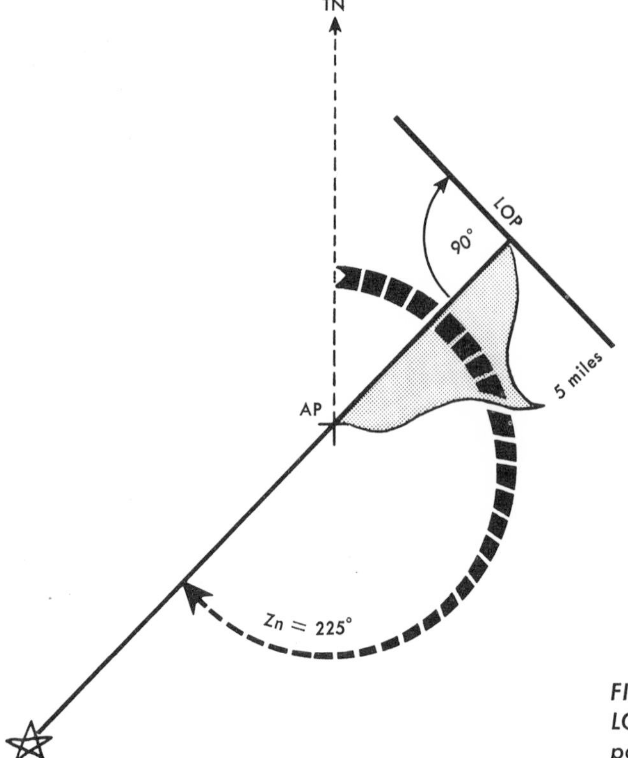

FIG. 15-2
LOP plotted from assumed position

This is the main method used in present-day sextant navigation. A couple of easy ways of obtaining a latitude line of position will be explained later, but they are less important. However, before we can begin to practice this simple line of position navigation, we must learn to orient ourselves with respect to a celestial body in the sky, to use time correctly, and to know how to use the *Nautical Almanac, Air Almanac,* and the various navigation tables. The first step is to get a concept of the celestial sphere.

The Celestial Sphere Imagine yourself standing in an open field on a clear night, watching the splendor of the sky. It appears that you are surrounded by a huge dome of enormous radius, on the inside of which the stars are tacked in place in regular patterns called *constellations.* We know it isn't that way, but it might as well be, since the nearest star is some 25 trillion miles away from us. For purposes of navigation it suits us to say that the Earth is surrounded by a hugh globe, called the *celestial sphere,* on which the stars are fixed. The center of the celestial sphere is at the center of the Earth. The sphere and the stars are fixed in space, but at the center the Earth rotates around its polar axis once every 24 hours, and this rotation causes the *apparent* rotation of the stars around our sky. The diameter of the celestial sphere is considered infinite, and we are not concerned with the *distance* of the stars as such, only the position of the star relative to our own geographical location on Earth.

The moon and the planets are members of the solar system, and because they have a separate motion in orbit in relation to the Earth, they are not fixed in the sky, but move a little in relation to the stars each night. The ancients called them the *wanderers of the sky*—a most appropriate name. However, the stars are practically permanent in their locations in the sky, and therefore we can assign them geographical position on the celestial sphere, comparable to the manner in which we locate a city on Earth by its latitude and longitude. It is quite simple.

Celestial Coordinates First visualize the Earth as a globe located at the center of a much larger globe, the celestial sphere. Now extend the Earth's polar axis until it reaches the

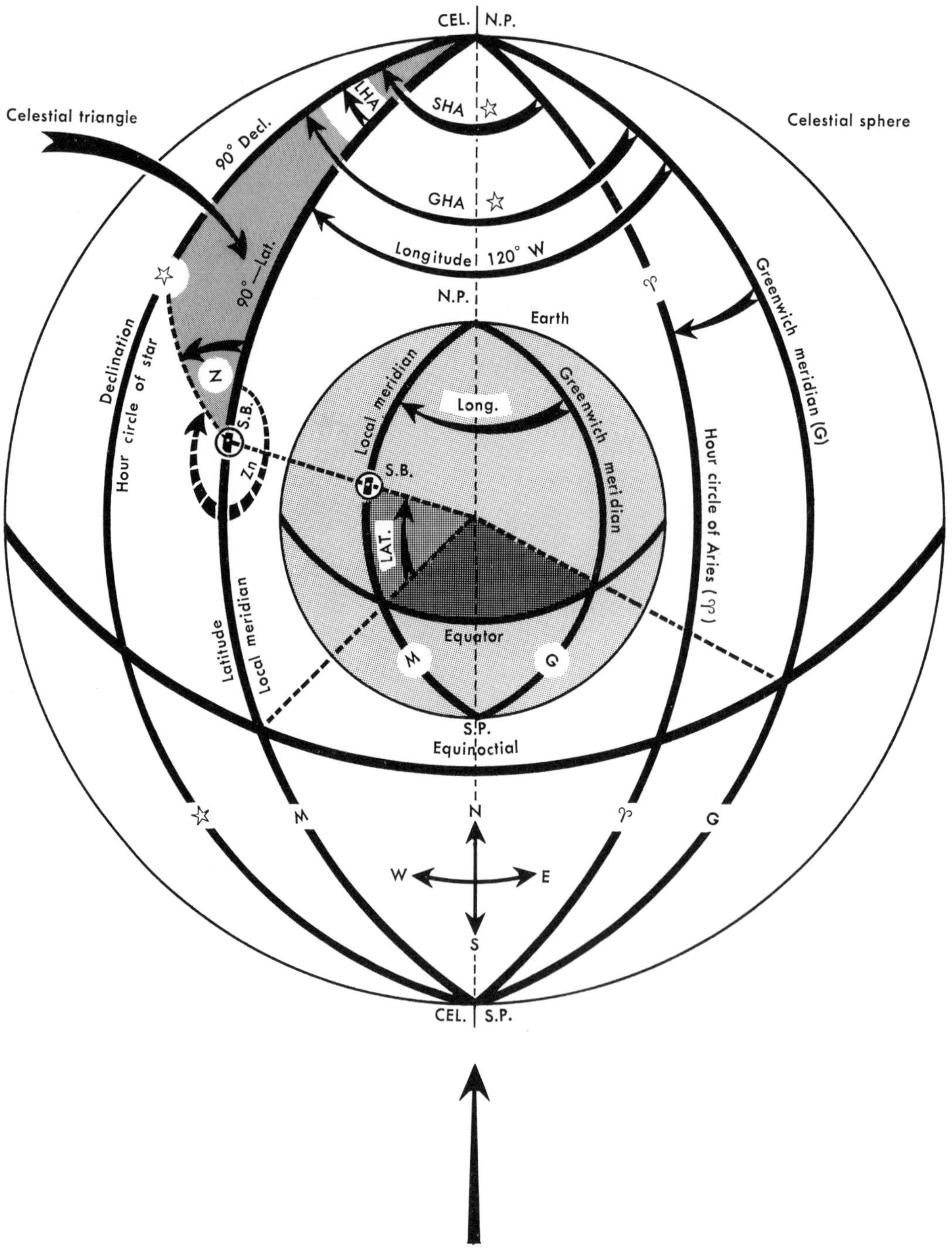

FIG. 15-3 The Earth and the celestial sphere

celestial sphere, where it establishes the *celestial north and south poles* (see Fig. 15–3).

Extend the *plane* of the Earth's equator until this plane intersects the celestial sphere and establishes the equator of that sphere also. However, to distinguish the two, we call the celestial equator the *equinoctial.* We now have a celestial sphere with an equator and poles, so we can establish location of celestial bodies by celestial latitude and longitude in the same manner we establish such things on Earth. Again to make a distinction, celestial latitude is called *declination,* which is measured north or south of the (celestial) equator just like latitude on Earth.

Celestial longitude in a sense can be reckoned in three different ways, so it requires a little explanation. The reference plane for both latitude and declination is simple: it is the plane of the equator and is the same for the Earth as for the celestial sphere. Longitude on Earth is measured east or west of Greenwich, England, an arbitrary starting place decided on by geographers many years ago. (They could just as well have decided on any other place.) In the sky we reckon celestial longitude from an imaginary meridian called the *hour circle of the first point of Aries.* It is so named because, when it was selected, it passed through the brightest star—or point—in the constellation of Aries. Since it shifts a little each year, due to the *precession of the equinoxes,* it is now some 30° away from Aries. It is actually determined as the celestial meridian through the center of the sun on March 21 when the sun crosses the celestial equator from south to north declination. If you could see it in the sky, it would pass through the celestial North and South poles, of course, and through the stars *Caph* and *Alpheratz.*

Meridians of longitude in the sky are called *hour circles.* Like meridians on Earth, they are great circles that pass through both poles. Celestial longitude is reckoned *from the hour circle of Aries to the hour circle that passes through the celestial body in question.*

If we measure eastward from the hour circle of Aries to the hour circle of the body, we call it not longitude but *right ascension,* really an astronomical term. Celestial longitude, unlike longitude on Earth, which is measured up to 180° east or west of Greenwich, is measured in one direction only and can therefore have a *maximum value* of 360°.

Right ascension is therefore celestial longitude, measured *eastward* from the hour circle of the first point of Aries, usually just called *Aries*. Right ascension is, as mentioned, an astronomical term, and it is usually expressed in *units of time*. The Earth turns once on its axis in 24 hours, and any place on Earth revolves through 360° in that period. It might also be said that the sun appears to move around us in a circle of 360° in 24 hours, which means that it moves 15° in 1 hour, 1° in 4 minutes, etc. (More about this in the next chapter.) We can therefore express the position of the sun at any given moment as being so many *degrees* east of us, or we can express it as so many *hours and minutes and seconds*. There is, in astronomy and in navigation, a definite relationship between arc and time. Astronomers like to work with time, so right ascension is expressed in time: hours, minutes, seconds. However, if we go the other way from Aries—*westward*—to the hour circle through the body, the measurement is called *sidereal hour angle,* and it is given in (angular) degrees and minutes. This is the more common method used in navigation. Let us therefore get in the habit of considering celestial longitude as *sidereal hour angle* (SHA), measured *westward* from Aries to the hour circle through the body, in degrees from 0° to 360°. The navigation almanacs give the *SHAs* and *declinations* of all celestial bodies used in navigation for every day in the year. For the stars there is little change from day to day, but for sun, moon, and planets there is a considerable daily change to reckon with. It follows that if right ascension (RA) is measured *east* from Aries and if sidereal hour angle (SHA) is measured *west* from Aries, then

$$\text{RA} + \text{SHA} = 360° \quad \text{or} \quad \text{RA} = 360° - \text{SHA}$$
$$\text{or} \quad \text{SHA} = 360° - \text{RA}$$

A geographical position for a celestial body on the celestial sphere can thus be given as so many degrees of declination, north or south, and so many degrees of sidereal hour angle, west of Aries. For example, in Fig. 15–3, we show a star with a declination of 45° north and SHA of 130°.

The Earth constantly spins on its axis from west to east inside the celestial sphere, making it appear as if the stars were moving from east to west, and it is awkward to consider our relationship to the stars because they are so far away. To make it easier to arrive at a working relationship with the celestial bodies, we imagine we can inflate the Earth like a balloon, equally in all directions, until it is the same size as the celestial sphere. Our equator is now the same as the equinoctial and our poles are the same as the celestial poles. In Fig. 15–3 we show the Earth in the center, with the Greenwich meridian and a meridian through Santa Barbara, California, at 120° W longitude. The city itself, "SB," is shown at latitude 34° N. When we pretend to inflate the Earth, SB is projected to a new position on the celestial sphere, along a straight line from the center of the Earth, but its latitude and longitude are unchanged. However, now we are on the same surface as the stars and it is easier to consider the relationship. Actually, our place on the celestial sphere is really the *zenith* of Santa Barbara, the point directly over our head in the sky.

The triangle formed by the *pole,* the *star,* and our *zenith* is called the *celestial triangle* and is the basis for our navigation.

In order to approach a solution to the celestial triangle, we project certain information onto the celestial sphere. The *Greenwich meridian* is shown in its proper place, as is our Santa Barbara meridian. The angle between them is obviously our longitude, 120° W. The hour circle of Aries is shown, and from it we can establish the hour circle of the star, in this case 130° west of Aries, since the SHA of this star is 130°. The distance from the equinoctial to the star is the declination of the star, in this case 45° N.

Now we proceed to tie it all together by relating the rotational effect to the *Greenwich meridian.* For the instant of time when the sextant observation is made, we stop the Earth in its rotation so we can observe the relationship between Earth and sky. The four hour circles with which we are concerned are shown in Fig. 15–3. The angles between hour circles are known as *hour angles.* The angle between the Greenwich meridian (*G*) and our local meridian (*M*) is the same on the celestial sphere as it was on Earth, and it is our *longitude,* as mentioned before.

The angle between the Greenwich meridian and the hour circle of Aries at the moment of observation is called the *Greenwich hour angle of Aries.* It is measured *westward* from Greenwich and has a maximum value of 360°. Its symbol is GHA ♈.

The angle between the hour circle of Aries and the hour circle of the star, measured *westward* from Aries, is the *sidereal hour angle* (SHA) of the star. The angle between the Greenwich meridian and the hour circle of the star is called the *Greenwich hour angle of the star* (GHA★), and is always measured *westward* from Greenwich and has a maximum value of 360°. From the drawing, it is obvious that GHA★ = GHA ♈ + SHA★.

The angle between our local meridian (*M*), extended to the celestial sphere, and the hour circle of the star is called the *local hour angle* (LHA) of the star. In this drawing it is equal to GHA minus the longitude because we are in west longitude. Later we shall show that when we are in east longitude, LHA = GHA plus the longitude. Local hour angle is always reckoned westward from the local meridian and has a maximum value of 360°.

Note that we now know three things about the celestial triangle if we have a certain location and a certain star at a certain instant of time (which is always the instant when you make your sextant observation): (1) one side equals 90° minus the latitude of the observer; (2) the other side equals 90° minus the declination of the star; and (3) the enclosed angle is the local hour angle. With this information we can obtain any other information that we want by simple mathematics.

Actually what we need is two items: the altitude of the star as observed by the navigator at SB, and the bearing of the star at SB. In former days this was worked out by trigonometry, but today we have several sets of tables that provide complete solutions to all possible forms of the celestial triangles, so all we have to do is to look up the information. Most tables will give us the angle *Z*, shown in the diagram at SB. This angle is called the *azimuth*, and it gives us the direction of the star from SB. However, for plotting purposes we like to have the direction given as a bearing from *true north*, so we convert *Z* into the angle Z_n, the bearing from true north, as shown in Fig. 15–3. This will be discussed in further detail later.

Actual Procedure As mentioned before, our aim is to

compare a calculated altitude H_c with an actual observed altitude H_o in order to obtain the intercept. We select a convenient *assumed position,* near our dead reckoning position (the method of selection will be explained later). We then obtain the data we need as follows:

Latitude—We use the latitude of the assumed position.
Longitude—We use the longitude of the assumed position.
Declination of star—We find it listed in the almanac.
Sidereal hour angle—We find it listed in the almanac.
Greenwich hour angle of Aries—We find it listed in the almanac.
Greenwich hour angle of the star—We calculate the sum of GHA ♈ and SHA★.
Local hour angle of the star—We calculate it from GHA★ and longitude.

We enter the navigation table with *latitude, declination,* and *local hour angle.* We can then extract H_c and the Azimuth Z. Sometimes this must be converted to Z_n by rules given in the table.

We have in this example talked about an observation on a star. The procedure is the same for the sun, moon, and planets, except that the almanac gives the Greenwich hour angle of these bodies directly, so it is even simpler. Actually, the GHA of a celestial body is a third indication of its celestial longitude, although it is not generally considered as such.

Finding LHA It is obviously not practical to draw a picture such as Fig. 15–3 every time we take a sight, so we use a simple device called an *hour angle diagram* to help us orient ourselves. Imagine that you are far outside the celestial sphere, below the celestial South Pole and in line with the polar axis. When you look toward the center of the Earth, you would see two concentric circles with the South Pole (Ps) of the Earth in the middle. The outer circle would be the outline of the *equinoctial* and the inner circle would be the Earth's *equator*. You see, radiating out from the center as straight lines, the various meridians and hour circles. Since we have inflated the Earth to the same size as the celestial

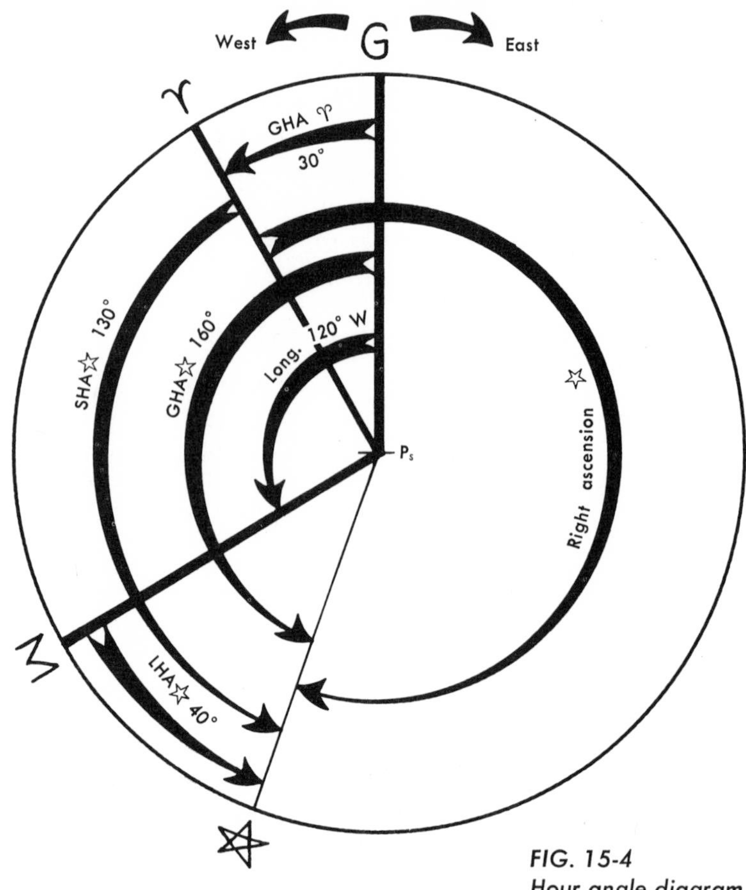

FIG. 15-4
Hour angle diagram

sphere, it is customary to omit the equator from the picture. Taking Fig. 15–3 as an example, if we turn the diagram so that the Greenwich meridian (*G*) is at the top (we *always* show *G* at the top in this and in similar diagrams called *time diagrams,* which you will learn about later), the result will be as shown in Fig 15–4.

Note that if you stand at the South Pole, all directions are *north,* and therefore *east is to your right and west is to your left.* Our meridian (*M*) is 120° west of Greenwich. All Greenwich hour angles and all local hour angles are always measured *westward.* Only a local meridian in *east* longitude would ever be indicated eastward from *G*. From the simple arrangement of these angles, it is easy to see what to add and subtract to find the LHA of the body observed. On the following page are a number of examples for both east and west longitudes. For convenience we have eliminated the hour circle of Aries where stars are shown and have just shown the GHA of the star. From a careful examination of

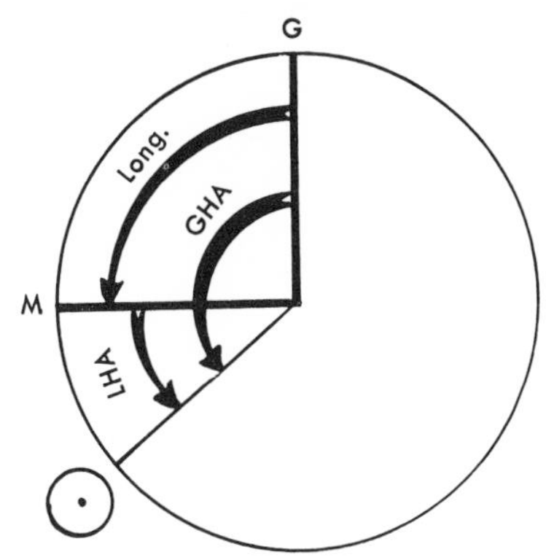

$LHA = GHA - long.$
$LHA = 130° - 90°$
$LHA = 40°$

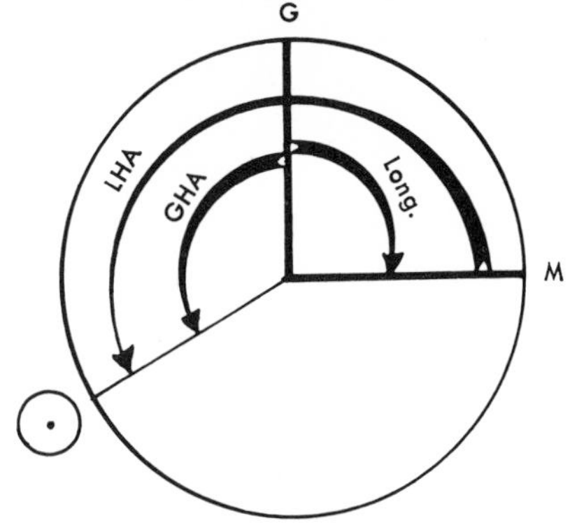

$LHA = GHA + long.$
$LHA = 120° + 90°$
$LHA = 210°$

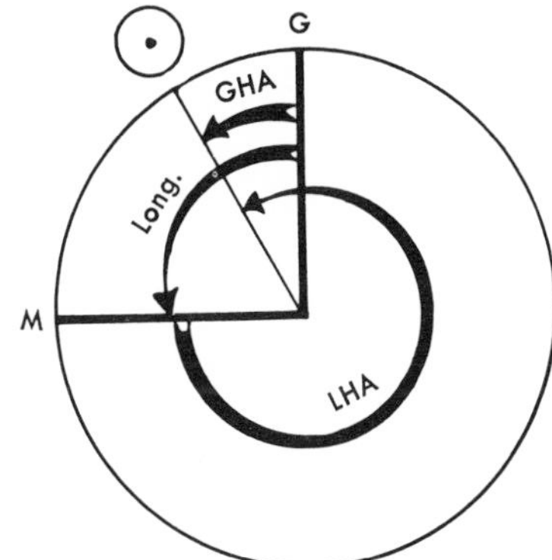

$LHA = 360° - (long. - GHA)$
$LHA = 360° - (90° - 30°)$
$LHA = 300°$
or, using rule, Pg. 212
$LHA = GHA - long.$
$LHA = (360° + 30°) - 90°$
$LHA = 300°$

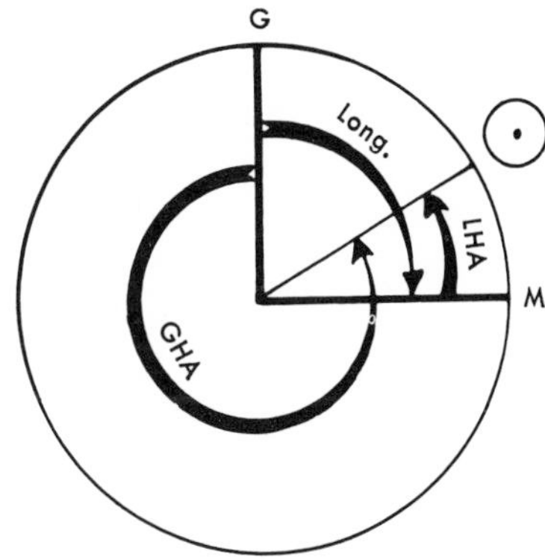

$LHA = GHA + long. - 360°$
$LHA = 300 + 90° - 360°$
$LHA = 30°$

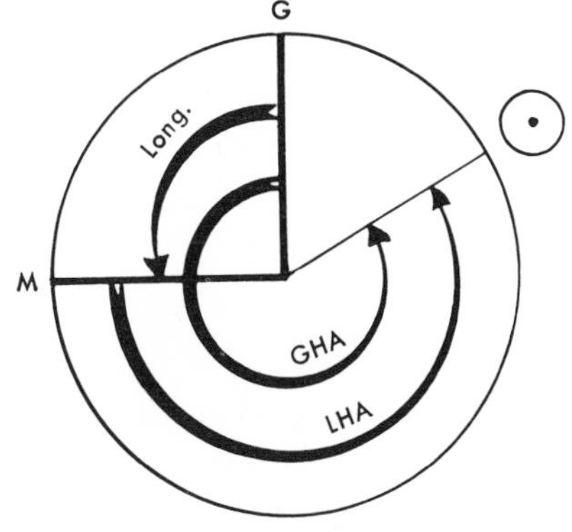

$LHA = GHA - long.$
$LHA = 300° - 90°$
$LHA = 210°$

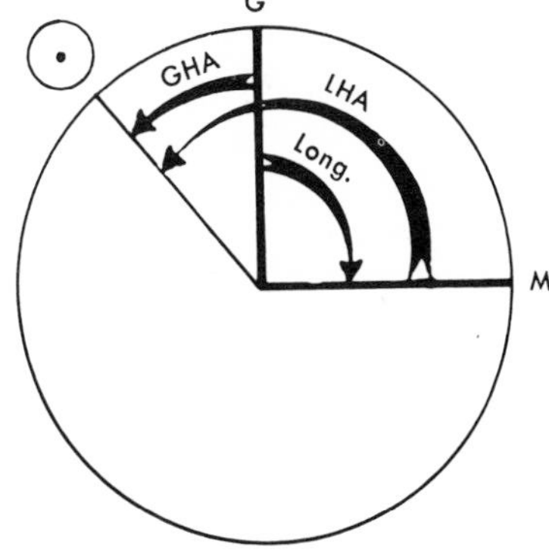

$LHA = GHA + long.$
$LHA = 40° + 90°$
$LHA = 130°$

FIG. 15-5

these examples, you will note that the following rules hold true:

LHA of (any) celestial body = GHA of body *minus* west longitude
LHA of (any) celestial body = GHA of body *plus* east longitude

When necessary you can add 360° or drop 360° to make addition or subtraction possible, without affecting the final result.

It is most essential that you carefully work through each of the examples that follow so you understand not only the diagram but the manner in which local hour angle is determined and the reason the two given rules apply in the various circumstances. In most of your celestial observations, you will need to determine the LHA of the body observed in exactly the manner shown in Fig. 15–5.

Meridian Angle *(angle t)* When you use Sight Reduction Tables N.O. 229 and N.O. 249, you enter the table with the LHA of the body, as described previously. However, if you use Sight Reduction Table H.O. 214, which for many years has been a favorite with marine navigators, but which is slated to be replaced by N.O. 229, you enter the table with the *meridian angle,* the symbol for which is *t*. The angle *t* is the angle between the local meridian and the hour circle of the celestial body, measured *east* or *west* of the local meridian *M,* whichever gives the smaller angle. (In a way this method is similar to the way in which we measure longitude on Earth—east or west of Greenwich.)

Thus, *t* can never exceed 180°, but we must always be careful to label it *east* (E) or *west* (W). Once you know how to find LHA, it is easy to find the angle *t* if you remember the following (see Fig. 15–6):

If LHA is less than 180°, *t* = LHA and *t* is labeled *west.*
If LHA is more than 180°, *t* = 360° − LHA, and *t* is labeled *east.*

FIG. 15-6
LHA less than 180°

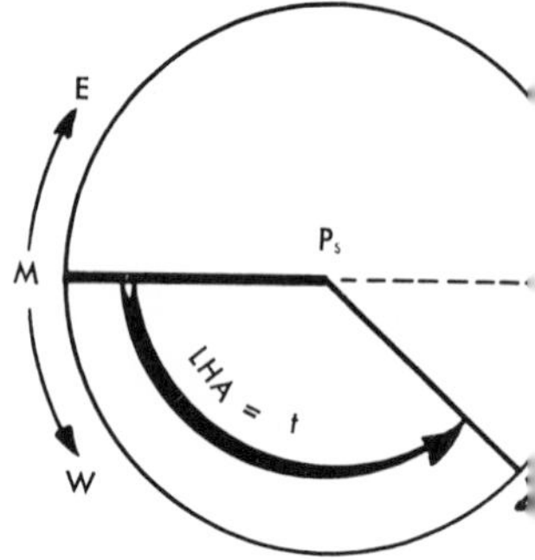

LHA greater than 180°

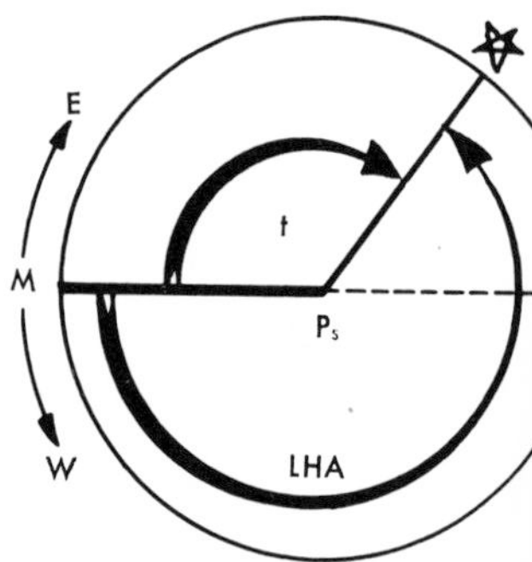

Practice Problems • In the following problems, find both LHA and the meridian angle, *t*.

1. GHA of Aries is 47°
   SHA of star is 93°
   Longitude is 120° W
2. GHA of Aries is 117°
   SHA of star is 242°
   Longitude is 45° W
3. GHA of Aries is 252°
   SHA of star is 120°
   Longitude is 97° W
4. GHA of Aries is 357°
   SHA of star is 243°
   Longitude is 117° E
5. GHA of sun is 275°
   Longitude is 45°
6. GHA of moon is 190°
   Longitude is 170° E
7. GHA of Venus is 37°
   Longitude is 145° W
8. GHA of Saturn is 333°
   Longitude is 117° E

Chapter 16

Time

Time is based on the motion of the Earth with respect to the sun and the stars. We know that the Earth turns on its axis once a day and at the same time revolves around the sun in a slightly elliptical pattern once a year, following a path inclined to our equator at about 23.5°. This makes it appear as if the sun rotates around the Earth once every day, and, with respect to the stars, as if the sun follows a path in the sky inclined at 23.5° to our equator. This apparent path of the sun in the sky is called the *ecliptic.*

In the period called a *solar year*—the time it takes the sun to return to the same place in our sky—the Earth makes 365¼ rotations about its polar axis, from west to east. During this time the Earth also makes a complete revolution around the sun, traveling in an easterly direction, with the result that it unwinds itself to the extent of one revolution with respect to the sun. As a result, we have 365¼ solar days in a solar year. Since our calendar is set up for a year of 365 days, we accumulate an extra day every four years, when February is given twenty-nine days.

The duration of daily rotation with respect to the sun is called a *solar day,* and for purposes of timekeeping we divide it up into 24 equal hours, and hours are divided into minutes and seconds. However, with respect to the stars, the Earth makes 366¼ revolutions in a solar year, and if days were based on the movement of the Earth with respect to stars, a star day, called a *sidereal day,* would have a duration of 23 hours, 56 minutes, and 4 seconds of solar time.

Since the Earth turns through 360° in a period of 24 hours, there is a distinct and fixed relationship between angular motion, called *hour angle,* and time, according to the following table:

Time		Angular Measurement	Angular Measurement		Time
24 hours	=	360°	1°	=	4 minutes
1 hour	=	15°	1′	=	4 seconds
1 minute	=	15′	15″	=	1 second
1 second	=	15″			

With this table, we can easily convert time to arc and arc to time, but it is more convenient to use the conversion table (Fig. 16–1) given in both the *Nautical Almanac* and *Air Almanac.*

Apparent Time If we measure our time by the sun as we see it, we call this *apparent time.* However, because the Earth moves in an elliptical path around the sun, the change of hour angle of the sun, which is the basis for measuring time, is slightly irregular. The sun appears to move faster at one time than at another, for the Earth moves faster in the wintertime than in the summertime. Astronomers prefer to measure time by the moon, which is a more accurate time-keeper for scientific purposes, but again not suitable for human activities. We therefore invent the *mean sun.*

Mean Time The *mean sun* is an imaginary sun that *revolves around the Earth* at a perfectly uniform rate, completing a revolution in exactly the same time it takes the Earth to revolve around the actual sun. Time based on this sun is called *mean time.* There are exactly 24 equal hours of mean time each day, and the mean sun moves through exactly 15° of *hour angle* during each hour. For this to be possible, the mean sun is sometimes ahead of the real sun and sometimes behind it. The difference is called *the equation of time.* It has a maximum value of 16 minutes. We are rarely concerned with this difference in modern navigation, but you should understand the significance. The almanacs give the equation of time for every day in the year. When the mean sun is on the exact opposite side of the Earth from us, 180° from our own meridian, our day begins, and in navigation we express that moment as 00-00-00, "zero hours." The mean sun then moves 15° per hour, and in 12 hours covers the 180° to our meridian, and we say that the time is 12-00-00, "twelve hours," or *noon.* As the sun continues, we use a 24-hour system to determine our time. Thus, 3 p.m. is 15-00-00, or "fifteen hours," and this continues until the sun again reaches the opposite side of the Earth at 24-00-00, "twenty-four hours," at which instant it is also 00-00-00 of the next day. If a time is given as 17-35-10, it means 35 minutes and 10 seconds past 5 p.m.

CONVERSION OF ARC TO TIME

0°–59°		60°–119°		120°–179°		180°–239°		240°–299°		300°–359°			0′·00	0′·25	0′·50	0′·75
°	h m	°	h m	°	h m	°	h m	°	h m	°	h m	′	m s	m s	m s	m s
0	0 00	60	4 00	120	8 00	180	12 00	240	16 00	300	20 00	0	0 00	0 01	0 02	0 03
1	0 04	61	4 04	121	8 04	181	12 04	241	16 04	301	20 04	1	0 04	0 05	0 06	0 07
2	0 08	62	4 08	122	8 08	182	12 08	242	16 08	302	20 08	2	0 08	0 09	0 10	0 11
3	0 12	63	4 12	123	8 12	183	12 12	243	16 12	303	20 12	3	0 12	0 13	0 14	0 15
4	0 16	64	4 16	124	8 16	184	12 16	244	16 16	304	20 16	4	0 16	0 17	0 18	0 19
5	0 20	65	4 20	125	8 20	185	12 20	245	16 20	305	20 20	5	0 20	0 21	0 22	0 23
6	0 24	66	4 24	126	8 24	186	12 24	246	16 24	306	20 24	6	0 24	0 25	0 26	0 27
7	0 28	67	4 28	127	8 28	187	12 28	247	16 28	307	20 28	7	0 28	0 29	0 30	0 31
8	0 32	68	4 32	128	8 32	188	12 32	248	16 32	308	20 32	8	0 32	0 33	0 34	0 35
9	0 36	69	4 36	129	8 36	189	12 36	249	16 36	309	20 36	9	0 36	0 37	0 38	0 39
10	0 40	70	4 40	130	8 40	190	12 40	250	16 40	310	20 40	10	0 40	0 41	0 42	0 43
11	0 44	71	4 44	131	8 44	191	12 44	251	16 44	311	20 44	11	0 44	0 45	0 46	0 47
12	0 48	72	4 48	132	8 48	192	12 48	252	16 48	312	20 48	12	0 48	0 49	0 50	0 51
13	0 52	73	4 52	133	8 52	193	12 52	253	16 52	313	20 52	13	0 52	0 53	0 54	0 55
14	0 56	74	4 56	134	8 56	194	12 56	254	16 56	314	20 56	14	0 56	0 57	0 58	0 59
15	1 00	75	5 00	135	9 00	195	13 00	255	17 00	315	21 00	15	1 00	1 01	1 02	1 03
16	1 04	76	5 04	136	9 04	196	13 04	256	17 04	316	21 04	16	1 04	1 05	1 06	1 07
17	1 08	77	5 08	137	9 08	197	13 08	257	17 08	317	21 08	17	1 08	1 09	1 10	1 11
18	1 12	78	5 12	138	9 12	198	13 12	258	17 12	318	21 12	18	1 12	1 13	1 14	1 15
19	1 16	79	5 16	139	9 16	199	13 16	259	17 16	319	21 16	19	1 16	1 17	1 18	1 19
20	1 20	80	5 20	140	9 20	200	13 20	260	17 20	320	21 20	20	1 20	1 21	1 22	1 23
21	1 24	81	5 24	141	9 24	201	13 24	261	17 24	321	21 24	21	1 24	1 25	1 26	1 27
22	1 28	82	5 28	142	9 28	202	13 28	262	17 28	322	21 28	22	1 28	1 29	1 30	1 31
23	1 32	83	5 32	143	9 32	203	13 32	263	17 32	323	21 32	23	1 32	1 33	1 34	1 35
24	1 36	84	5 36	144	9 36	204	13 36	264	17 36	324	21 36	24	1 36	1 37	1 38	1 39
25	1 40	85	5 40	145	9 40	205	13 40	265	17 40	325	21 40	25	1 40	1 41	1 42	1 43
26	1 44	86	5 44	146	9 44	206	13 44	266	17 44	326	21 44	26	1 44	1 45	1 46	1 47
27	1 48	87	5 48	147	9 48	207	13 48	267	17 48	327	21 48	27	1 48	1 49	1 50	1 51
28	1 52	88	5 52	148	9 52	208	13 52	268	17 52	328	21 52	28	1 52	1 53	1 54	1 55
29	1 56	89	5 56	149	9 56	209	13 56	269	17 56	329	21 56	29	1 56	1 57	1 58	1 59
30	2 00	90	6 00	150	10 00	210	14 00	270	18 00	330	22 00	30	2 00	2 01	2 02	2 03
31	2 04	91	6 04	151	10 04	211	14 04	271	18 04	331	22 04	31	2 04	2 05	2 06	2 07
32	2 08	92	6 08	152	10 08	212	14 08	272	18 08	332	22 08	32	2 08	2 09	2 10	2 11
33	2 12	93	6 12	153	10 12	213	14 12	273	18 12	333	22 12	33	2 12	2 13	2 14	2 15
34	2 16	94	6 16	154	10 16	214	14 16	274	18 16	334	22 16	34	2 16	2 17	2 18	2 19
35	2 20	95	6 20	155	10 20	215	14 20	275	18 20	335	22 20	35	2 20	2 21	2 22	2 23
36	2 24	96	6 24	156	10 24	216	14 24	276	18 24	336	22 24	36	2 24	2 25	2 26	2 27
37	2 28	97	6 28	157	10 28	217	14 28	277	18 28	337	22 28	37	2 28	2 29	2 30	2 31
38	2 32	98	6 32	158	10 32	218	14 32	278	18 32	338	22 32	38	2 32	2 33	2 34	2 35
39	2 36	99	6 36	159	10 36	219	14 36	279	18 36	339	22 36	39	2 36	2 37	2 38	2 39
40	2 40	100	6 40	160	10 40	220	14 40	280	18 40	340	22 40	40	2 40	2 41	2 42	2 43
41	2 44	101	6 44	161	10 44	221	14 44	281	18 44	341	22 44	41	2 44	2 45	2 46	2 47
42	2 48	102	6 48	162	10 48	222	14 48	282	18 48	342	22 48	42	2 48	2 49	2 50	2 51
43	2 52	103	6 52	163	10 52	223	14 52	283	18 52	343	22 52	43	2 52	2 53	2 54	2 55
44	2 56	104	6 56	164	10 56	224	14 56	284	18 56	344	22 56	44	2 56	2 57	2 58	2 59
45	3 00	105	7 00	165	11 00	225	15 00	285	19 00	345	23 00	45	3 00	3 01	3 02	3 03
46	3 04	106	7 04	166	11 04	226	15 04	286	19 04	346	23 04	46	3 04	3 05	3 06	3 07
47	3 08	107	7 08	167	11 08	227	15 08	287	19 08	347	23 08	47	3 08	3 09	3 10	3 11
48	3 12	108	7 12	168	11 12	228	15 12	288	19 12	348	23 12	48	3 12	3 13	3 14	3 15
49	3 16	109	7 16	169	11 16	229	15 16	289	19 16	349	23 16	49	3 16	3 17	3 18	3 19
50	3 20	110	7 20	170	11 20	230	15 20	290	19 20	350	23 20	50	3 20	3 21	3 22	3 23
51	3 24	111	7 24	171	11 24	231	15 24	291	19 24	351	23 24	51	3 24	3 25	3 26	3 27
52	3 28	112	7 28	172	11 28	232	15 28	292	19 28	352	23 28	52	3 28	3 29	3 30	3 31
53	3 32	113	7 32	173	11 32	233	15 32	293	19 32	353	23 32	53	3 32	3 33	3 34	3 35
54	3 36	114	7 36	174	11 36	234	15 36	294	19 36	354	23 36	54	3 36	3 37	3 38	3 39
55	3 40	115	7 40	175	11 40	235	15 40	295	19 40	355	23 40	55	3 40	3 41	3 42	3 43
56	3 44	116	7 44	176	11 44	236	15 44	296	19 44	356	23 44	56	3 44	3 45	3 46	3 47
57	3 48	117	7 48	177	11 48	237	15 48	297	19 48	357	23 48	57	3 48	3 49	3 50	3 51
58	3 52	118	7 52	178	11 52	238	15 52	298	19 52	358	23 52	58	3 52	3 53	3 54	3 55
59	3 56	119	7 56	179	11 56	239	15 56	299	19 56	359	23 56	59	3 56	3 57	3 58	3 59

FIG. 16-1

When Sun is at	Time at M is
1...........	0000 July 4
2...........	0600 " 4
3...........	1200 " 4
4...........	1600 " 4
5...........	2100 " 4
6...........	0300 " 5

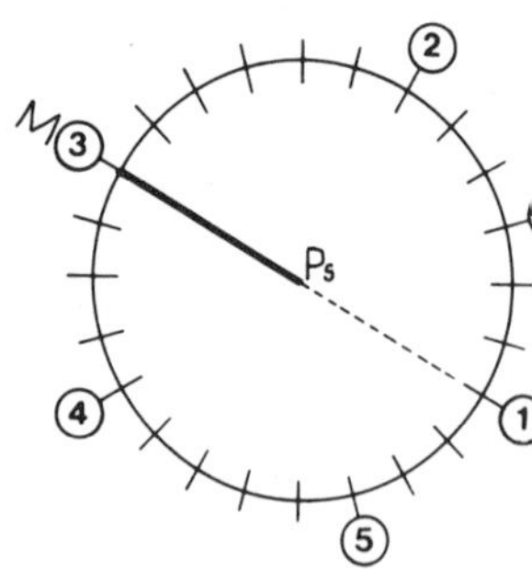

FIG. 16-2
Time diagram

In Fig. 16–2 we have introduced a drawing known as a *time diagram.* It resembles an hour angle diagram, but is used only with the sun to tell time. The diagram shows our meridian (M) radiating out from the South Pole; the dotted line is the part of the meridian circle that is on the other side of the Earth, and is labeled m. The solid line M is called the *upper branch* of the meridian, and the dotted line is the *lower branch.* Each numbered position of the sun shows how time progresses through a day at the rate of 15° per hour. Since everyone on the same meridian of longitude has the same time, latitude does not enter into this.

The apparent motion of the sun around the Earth causes the time to change constantly everywhere. Wherever the mean sun is in line with the observer's meridian, his *local mean time* (LMT) is 12-00-00, or noon. This also means that no two places in different longitudes can have the same mean time, because the mean sun can only be in one place at any one moment. This is best illustrated on a time diagram, where we can show any number of different meridians. However, we shall just show our local meridian M and the Greenwich meridian G together with the lower branches, m and g, of both meridians. This is a standard time diagram, and if you make it a habit to draw one in all problems, you will never be wrong on your calculations of time. We *always* place the Greenwich meridian straight up. Then east longitude is to the *right,* and west longitude is to the *left.* In Fig. 16–3 we are showing the observer's meridian M to be in 90° *west* longitude. Note that 90° is equal to an hour angle, or time difference, of 6 hours exactly.

	Time at M	Time at G
1	0000	0600
2	0600	1200
3	1200	1800
4	1800	0000 (next day)
5	2100	0300 (" ")

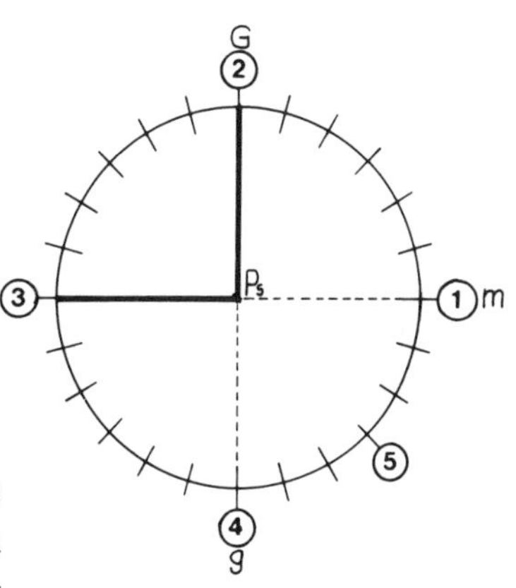

FIG. 16-3
Time diagram

When the sun is in position 1, at *m,* it is zero hours at our meridian. However, it is 6 hours since the sun passed *g* and started a new day at Greenwich, so the time at Greenwich is now 0600. When the sun reaches position 2, 6 hours later, our time at *M* will be 0600, and it is 1200 noon at Greenwich. At position 3, it is noon our time, and 1800, or 6 p.m., at Greenwich. At position 4, the time at Greenwich is midnight, 2400, or 0000 of the new day. So the new day has started at Greenwich, but our time at *M* is only 1800. With the sun at position 5, the Greenwich Mean Time (GMT) is 0300 of the new day, and our local time at *M* is 2100. Not until the sun again reaches position 1 does the next day begin for the observer at *M*. Note that the difference between LMT and GMT is always 6 hours, corresponding to a longitude of 90°. This enables us to make the following true statements:

The mean time of two places differs as their longitude, converted to time.
When the sun is between g and m, or between m and g, always using the smaller angle, there is a change of date between the two locations. There can be a change of date only when the sun is in this sector.
If the sun has crossed g before it crosses m, the Greenwich date will be one day higher than the local date while there is a different date in effect.
If the sun has crossed m before it crosses g, the local date will be one day higher than the Greenwich date while there is a different date in effect.

Note that these statements also relate to east and west longitude. If you are in *west* longitude, *m* will always be to the right of *g*, and *the sun must cross* g *before* m. If you are in *east* longitude, *m* will always be to the left of *g* and *the sun must cross* m *before* g. We can thus state further:

> *When there is a change of date in effect, the observer in west longitude will have a lower date than Greenwich and the observer in east longitude will have a higher date than Greenwich.*

Longitude 135° E, or 9 hours

	Time at M	*Time at G*
1	0900 July 4	0000 July 4
2	1200 " 4	0300 " 4
3	1700 " 4	0800 " 4
4	2100 " 4	1200 " 4
5	0000 " 5	1500 " 4
6	0500 " 5	2000 " 4

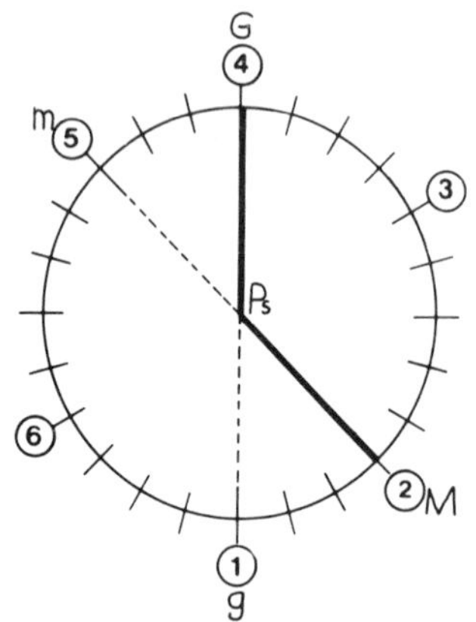

FIG. 16-4
Time diagram

In these examples we have used even numbers for time and for longitude, but the principles hold true for any longitude and any time. In the following examples we have converted longitude to time, using the conversion table (Fig. 16–1). Keep in mind that we are dealing strictly with *mean time* in this discussion, but the same rules for time differences also apply to *apparent time.* We rarely have occasion to consider apparent time, but again we have both *local apparent time* (LAT) and *Greenwich apparent time* (GAT). Apparent time of two places also differs as their exact longitude. When the actual sun we can see, the *apparent sun,* is directly over our meridian, our *local apparent time* is 1200, at which moment we often observe the sun for an especially easy calculation of latitude. As mentioned before, the difference between mean and apparent time is the equation of time.

Examples •

Rule: LMT + west long. = GMT and GMT − west long. = LMT
LMT − east long. = GMT GMT + east long. = LMT

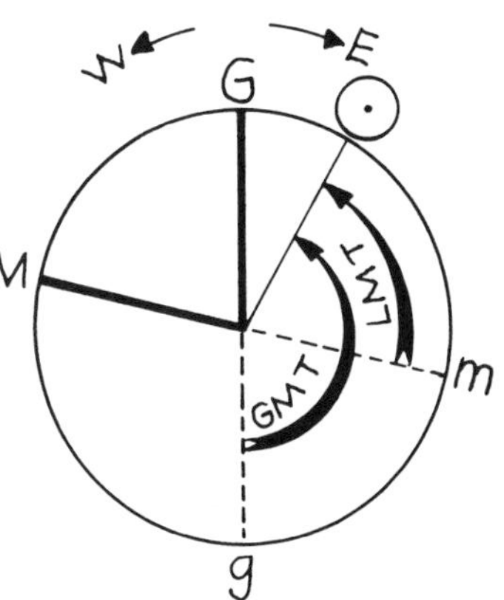

Long. 76°14′ W
LMT: 05-11-12, Feb.1
Long. (W) in time: +5-04-56
GMT: 10-16-08, Feb. 1

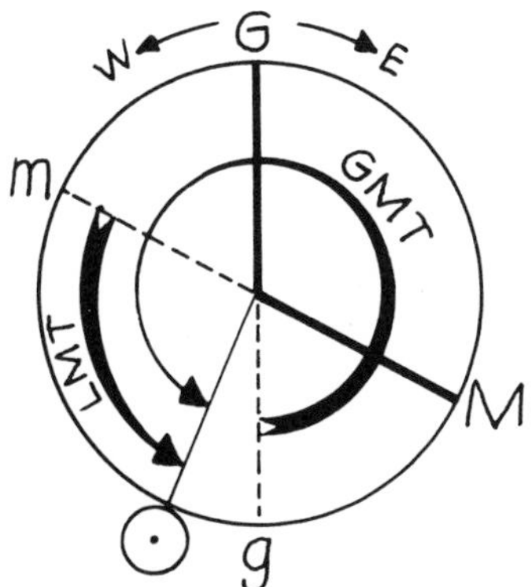

Long. 117°43′ E
LMT: 06-11-40, Feb. 1
Long. (E) in time: —7-50-52
GMT: 22-20-48, Jan. 31

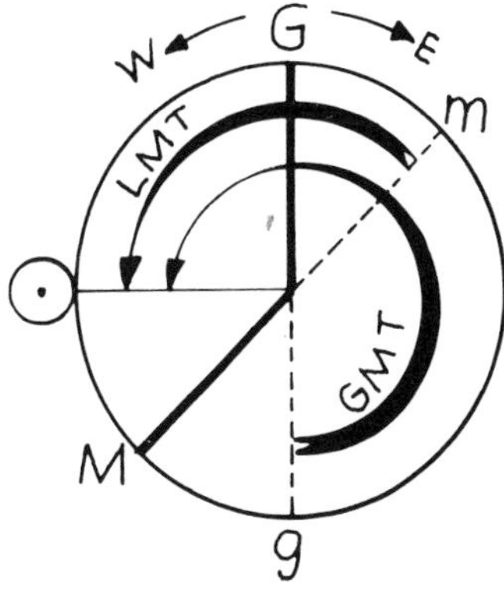

Long. 135° W, or 9 hours
LMT: 09-00-00, Jan. 5
Long. (W) in time: + 9 hours
GMT: 18-00-00, Jan. 5

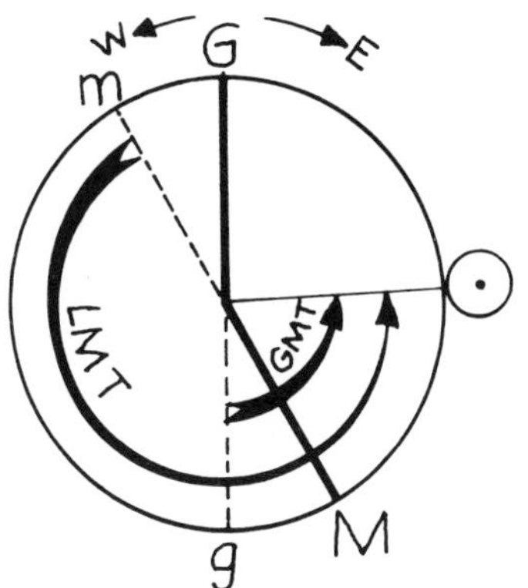

Long. 150° E, or 10 hours
LMT: 16-47-13, Feb. 5
Long. (E) in time: —10 hours
GMT: 06-47-13, Feb. 5

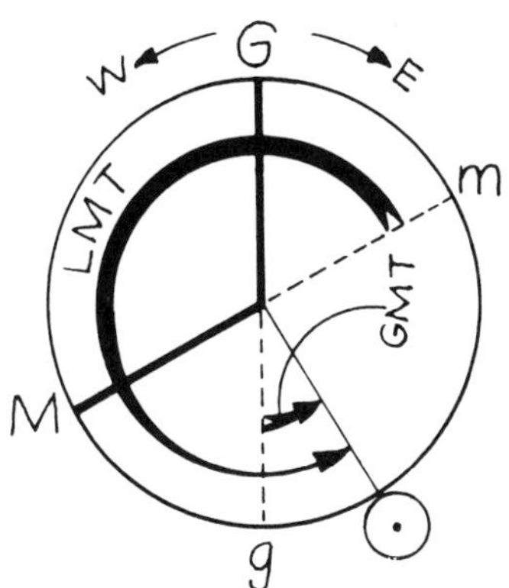

Long. 117°43′ W
LMT: 10-03-17, July 4
Long. (W) in time: +7-50-52
GMT: 26-54-09—or
02-54-09, July 5

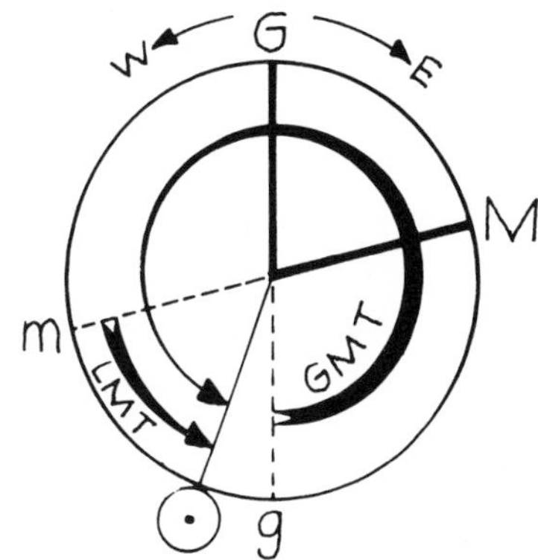

Long. 76°14′ E
GMT: 23-05-15, Sept. 4
Long. (E) in time: +5-04-56
LMT: 28-10-11—or
4-10-11, Sept. 5

FIG. 16-5

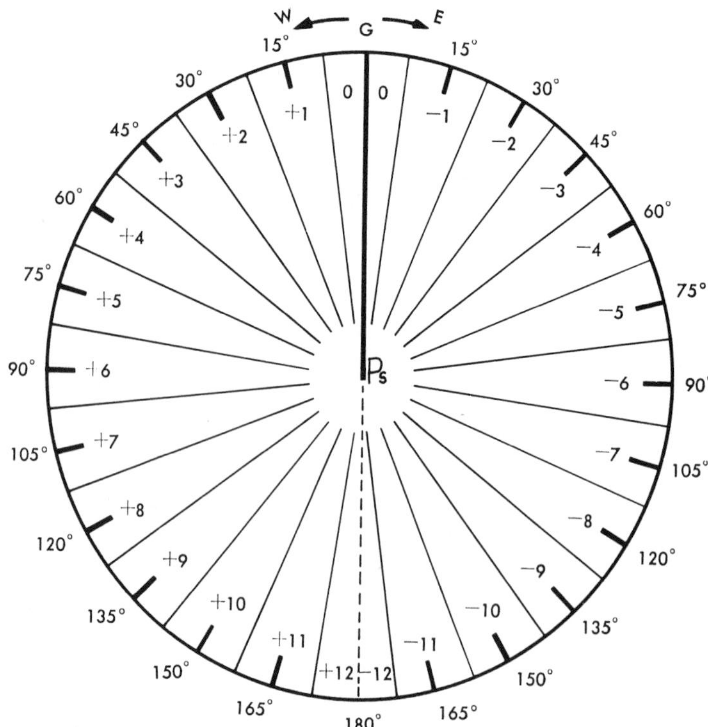

FIG. 16-6
Time zone diagram

Zone Time If we use apparent time or mean time, based on the apparent and the mean sun respectively, the time of day would depend on our exact longitude. A person standing 2 feet to the east or west of us would have a slightly different time. Obviously, this is not a very practical arrangement, so a system of *time zones* was established, and people living within each time zone agreed to keep the same time on their watches. This is called *zone time* and is the system of time we use universally around the world in our daily activities (see Fig. 16–6).

Each time zone is 15° of longitude in width. It is conveniently *centered* around a *central meridian,* and these in turn are spaced 15° apart. We begin with the 0° meridian at Greenwich, and the time zone extends 7.5° either side, from 7.5° W longitude to 7.5° E longitude. Everybody, regardless of latitude, who lives in this zone keeps the same time, zone time (ZT), which is the *mean time of the* 0°, or *Greenwich, meridian.** We also know this as GMT,

* Actually, England uses a "zone difference" of −1 hour in order to have the same zone time as most European countries; only western Africa uses a zone difference of zero hours (see text for explanation).

Greenwich Mean Time. *In each time zone, the time kept as zone time is the local mean time of the central meridian.* Since these central meridians are spaced 15° apart—at 0°, 15°, 30°, 45°, 60°, etc. up to 180°—it follows that the time differs exactly 1 hour from one zone to the next. Each zone is given a number, called the *zone description,* or *zone difference* (ZD), from 0 at Greenwich to 12 at the 180th meridian. Zone description numbers have a plus (+) or minus (—) prefix to indicate how they are applied to local time to obtain the corresponding Greenwich time: *a minus in east longitude and a plus in west longitude.*

Example • If your ZT is 15-13-41 and you live in New York, which is in time zone +5, the GMT at that instant is 20-13-41. If your ZT is 22-15-30 in Sydney, Australia, which is in time zone −10, the GMT is 12-15-30. Note that this can also give rise to a change of date. For example, if your ZT at Sydney is 0500 on July 4, the GMT is 1900, July 3 ($5^h + 24^h - 10^h = 19^h$). If the ZT in New York is 2200 on July 4, GMT is 0300, July 5 ($22^h + 5^h - 24^h = 3^h$).

The reason we are so concerned with Greenwich time is that all navigation is based on GMT and our almanacs are based on GMT, as will be explained later. Air navigators refer to GMT as *zulu time.*

To determine the ZD for any place on Earth you can either consider the actual longitude and figure it out, or you can consult a *zone chart of the world.* You will find that in some areas the time zone boundaries have been "bent" around certain smaller areas to avoid having a small country keep two different times within its borders.

Crossing the International Date Line When you cross the 180th meridian, also known as the International Date Line, you experience a change of date. The zone time is the same on either side of this meridian, but the ZD is —12 in the eastern hemisphere and +12 in the western hemisphere. When you cross from west to east longitude, you lose a day. Crossing from east to west longitude, you gain a day.

The best way to prove this to yourself is to draw a time diagram.

An instant of time is the same all over the world, no matter what we call the time or the date. Let us select the moment when GMT is 1600 on July 4. A vessel in 179°59′ W longitude is in time zone +12. A vessel in 179°59′ E longitude is in time zone —12. However, remember that when we go from GMT to ZT, we reverse the signs. Both vessels are about to cross the 180th meridian.

Vessel in west longitude
GMT = 1600 on July 4
ZD = −12
ZT = 0400 on July 4
This vessel will gain a day.

Vessel in east longitude
GMT = 1600 on July 4
ZD = +12
ZT = 0400 on July 5
This vessel will lose a day.

***Examples* •**

Long. 129° E
Local date: Jan. 10
ZT: 13-15-12
Find ZD, GMT, Greenwich date

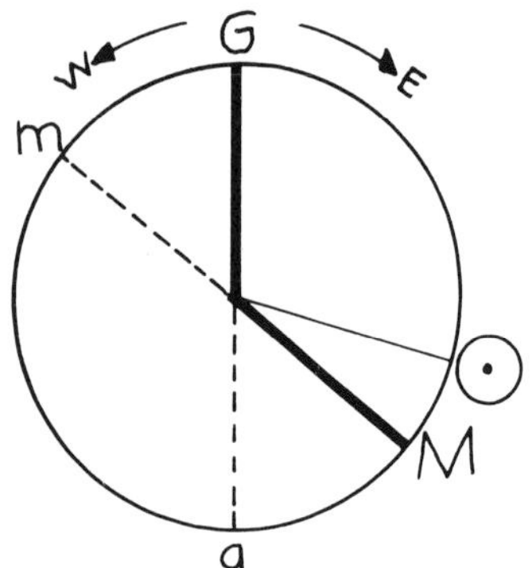

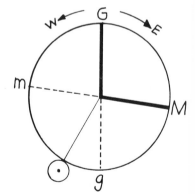

ZT: 13-15-12
ZD: −9
GMT: 4-15-12
Greenwich date: Jan. 10

Long. 70° W
WT: 16-23-22
Watch is 18 sec. slow
Local date: July 15
Find ZD, ZT, GMT, Greenwich date

WT: 16-23-22
WE: +18 sec.
ZT: 16-23-40
ZD: +5
GMT: 21-23-40
Greenwich date: July 15

Long. 98° E
Greenwich date: Sept. 1
GMT: 20-47-17
Find ZD, ZT, local date

GMT: 20-47-17
ZD: −7 (but add)
ZT: 3-47-17 (next day)
Local date: Sept. 2
(Note that we reversed the sign of the ZD because we are going from GMT to ZT.)

FIG. 16-7

Practice Problems •

July 9
WT of sight: $18^{h}12^{m}55^{s}$
Watch is 37 seconds slow
Long. 126° E
ZT of sight?
ZD?
GMT?
Greenwich date?

July 11
WT of sight: $05^{h}11^{m}27^{s}$
Watch is 19 seconds fast
Long. 126° E
ZT of sight?
ZD?
GMT?
Greenwich date?

May 15
WT of sight: $19^{h}42^{m}37^{s}$
Watch is 5 seconds slow
Long. 119° W
ZT of sight?
ZD?
GMT?
Greenwich date?

Chapter 17

The Nautical Almanac, The Air Almanac

The *Nautical Almanac* and the *Air Almanac* are prepared by the U.S. Naval Observatory and provide us with the data regarding celestial bodies that we need in order to calculate our sights and obtain the *computed altitude* H_c, the *bearing of the observed body, Z,* and occasionally other information. The U.S. Observatory works in cooperation with the British and other foreign governments to provide this information, and the almanacs are printed in several other languages, although the information is the same.

The *Nautical Almanac* covers 12 months of the year and figures are usually given to the nearest *tenth of a minute of arc.* The *Air Almanac* covers 4 months in each volume, so the user has to buy three volumes a year. Being designed for celestial air navigation, where more speed and less accuracy is required, the *Air Almanac* gives figures to the *nearest whole minute,* although it does have provisions for greater accuracy should it be needed. The reason we discuss the *Air Almanac* here is that many marine navigators like to use it because they find that it saves them time and that it is accurate enough for day-to-day navigation.

As mentioned earlier, we enter our navigation tables with latitude, declination, and hour angle, be it LHA (local hour angle) or meridian angle *t*. Hour angle and declination are obtained from the almanac, together with certain correction figures that are applied to sextant observations. Since it would be impossible to have an almanac that gave data for every possible place on Earth, all information is given for an observer at Greenwich and based on Greenwich Mean Time (GMT). By applying our own longitude to this information, we are able to adapt it to our own use.

Nautical Almanac The *Nautical Almanac* is organized so that each pair of facing pages covers three consecutive days. (See Figs. 17–1 and 17–2.) For each whole hour of each day there is given the Greenwich hour angle (GHA) and the declination (dec.) for the planets, the sun, and the

JANUARY 1, 2, 3 (THURS., FRI., SAT.)

G.M.T. d	h		ARIES G.H.A.	VENUS −3·5 G.H.A.	VENUS Dec.	MARS +1·0 G.H.A.	MARS Dec.	JUPITER −1·5 G.H.A.	JUPITER Dec.	SATURN +0·5 G.H.A.	SATURN Dec.
d	h		° ′	° ′	° ′	° ′	° ′	° ′	° ′	° ′	° ′
1	00		100 13·8	185 22·2	S23 37·9	116 17·9	S 7 43·3	249 40·2	S11 08·9	69 27·8	N 9 49·3
	01		115 16·3	200 21·2	37·9	131 18·6	42·6	264 42·3	09·0	84 30·2	49·3
	02		130 18·8	215 20·2	37·8	146 19·3	41·8	279 44·5	09·1	99 32·7	49·3
	03		145 21·2	230 19·3	· · 37·8	161 20·1	· · 41·0	294 46·6	· · 09·2	114 35·2	· · 49·4
	04		160 23·7	245 18·3	37·8	176 20·8	40·3	309 48·7	09·3	129 37·7	49·4
	05		175 26·2	260 17·3	37·8	191 21·6	39·5	324 50·9	09·4	144 40·2	49·4
	06		190 28·6	275 16·4	S23 37·8	206 22·3	S 7 38·8	339 53·0	S11 09·5	159 42·6	N 9 49·4
	07		205 31·1	290 15·4	37·8	221 23·1	38·0	354 55·1	09·7	174 45·1	49·4
	08	T	220 33·5	305 14·4	37·8	236 23·8	37·3	9 57·3	09·8	189 47·6	49·4
	09	H	235 36·0	320 13·4	· · 37·7	251 24·6	· · 36·5	24 59·4	· · 09·9	204 50·1	· · 49·4
	10	U	250 38·5	335 12·5	37·7	266 25·3	35·8	40 01·5	10·0	219 52·6	49·4
	11	R	265 40·9	350 11·5	37·7	281 26·0	35·0	55 03·7	10·1	234 55·0	49·4
	12	S	280 43·4	5 10·5	S23 37·7	296 26·8	S 7 34·2	70 05·8	S11 10·2	249 57·5	N 9 49·4
	13	D	295 45·9	20 09·6	37·7	311 27·5	33·5	85 07·9	10·3	265 00·0	49·4
	14	A	310 48·3	35 08·6	37·6	326 28·3	32·7	100 10·1	10·4	280 02·5	49·4
	15	Y	325 50·8	50 07·6	· · 37·6	341 29·0	· · 32·0	115 12·2	· · 10·5	295 05·0	· · 49·4
	16		340 53·3	65 06·6	37·6	356 29·8	31·2	130 14·4	10·6	310 07·4	49·4
	17		355 55·7	80 05·7	37·5	11 30·5	30·5	145 16·5	10·7	325 09·9	49·5
	18		10 58·2	95 04·7	S23 37·5	26 31·3	S 7 29·7	160 18·6	S11 10·9	340 12·4	N 9 49·5
	19		26 00·7	110 03·7	37·5	41 32·0	28·9	175 20·8	11·0	355 14·9	49·5
	20		41 03·1	125 02·8	37·5	56 32·7	28·2	190 22·9	11·1	10 17·3	49·5
	21		56 05·6	140 01·8	· · 37·4	71 33·5	· · 27·4	205 25·0	· · 11·2	25 19·8	· · 49·5
	22		71 08·0	155 00·8	37·4	86 34·2	26·7	220 27·2	11·3	40 22·3	49·5
	23		86 10·5	169 59·8	37·3	101 35·0	25·9	235 29·3	11·4	55 24·8	49·5
2	00		101 13·0	184 58·8	S23 37·3	116 35·7	S 7 25·2	250 31·5	S11 11·5	70 27·3	N 9 49·5
	01		116 15·4	199 57·9	37·3	131 36·5	24·4	265 33·6	11·6	85 29·7	49·5
	02		131 17·9	214 56·9	37·2	146 37·2	23·6	280 35·7	11·7	100 32·2	49·5
	03		146 20·4	229 55·9	· · 37·2	161 38·0	· · 22·9	295 37·9	· · 11·8	115 34·7	· · 49·5
	04		161 22·8	244 55·0	37·1	176 38·7	22·1	310 40·0	11·9	130 37·2	49·5
	05		176 25·3	259 54·0	37·1	191 39·4	21·4	325 42·2	12·0	145 39·6	49·6
	06		191 27·8	274 53·0	S23 37·1	206 40·2	S 7 20·6	340 44·3	S11 12·2	160 42·1	N 9 49·6
	07		206 30·2	289 52·0	37·0	221 40·9	19·8	355 46·4	12·3	175 44·6	49·6
	08		221 32·7	304 51·1	37·0	236 41·7	19·1	10 48·6	12·4	190 47·1	49·6
	09	F	236 35·1	319 50·1	· · 36·9	251 42·4	· · 18·3	25 50·7	· · 12·5	205 49·5	· · 49·6
	10	R	251 37·6	334 49·1	36·9	266 43·2	17·6	40 52·9	12·6	220 52·0	49·6
	11	I	266 40·1	349 48·2	36·8	281 43·9	16·8	55 55·0	12·7	235 54·5	49·6
	12	D	281 42·5	4 47·2	S23 36·8	296 44·7	S 7 16·1	70 57·1	S11 12·8	250 57·0	N 9 49·6
	13	A	296 45·0	19 46·2	36·7	311 45·4	15·3	85 59·3	12·9	265 59·4	49·6
	14	Y	311 47·5	34 45·2	36·7	326 46·2	14·5	101 01·4	13·0	281 01·9	49·6
	15		326 49·9	49 44·3	· · 36·6	341 46·9	· · 13·8	116 03·6	· · 13·1	296 04·4	· · 49·6
	16		341 52·4	64 43·3	36·5	356 47·7	13·0	131 05·7	13·2	311 06·9	49·7
	17		356 54·9	79 42·3	36·5	11 48·4	12·3	146 07·9	13·3	326 09·3	49·7
	18		11 57·3	94 41·4	S23 36·4	26 49·2	S 7 11·5	161 10·0	S11 13·4	341 11·8	N 9 49·7
	19		26 59·8	109 40·4	36·4	41 49·9	10·7	176 12·1	13·6	356 14·3	49·7
	20		42 02·3	124 39·4	36·3	56 50·7	10·0	191 14·3	13·7	11 16·8	49·7
	21		57 04·7	139 38·5	· · 36·2	71 51·4	· · 09·2	206 16·4	· · 13·8	26 19·2	· · 49·7
	22		72 07·2	154 37·5	36·2	86 52·1	08·5	221 18·6	13·9	41 21·7	49·7
	23		87 09·6	169 36·5	36·1	101 52·9	07·7	236 20·7	14·0	56 24·2	49·7
3	00		102 12·1	184 35·5	S23 36·0	116 53·6	S 7 06·9	251 22·9	S11 14·1	71 26·6	N 9 49·7
	01		117 14·6	199 34·6	36·0	131 54·4	06·2	266 25·0	14·2	86 29·1	49·7
	02		132 17·0	214 33·6	35·9	146 55·1	05·4	281 27·2	14·3	101 31·6	49·8
	03		147 19·5	229 32·6	· · 35·8	161 55·9	· · 04·7	296 29·3	· · 14·4	116 34·1	· · 49·8
	04		162 22·0	244 31·7	35·7	176 56·6	03·9	311 31·4	14·5	131 36·5	49·8
	05		177 24·4	259 30·7	35·7	191 57·4	03·2	326 33·6	14·6	146 39·0	49·8
	06		192 26·9	274 29·7	S23 35·6	206 58·1	S 7 02·4	341 35·7	S11 14·7	161 41·5	N 9 49·8
	07		207 29·4	289 28·8	35·5	221 58·9	01·6	356 37·9	14·8	176 43·9	49·8
	08	S	222 31·8	304 27·8	35·4	236 59·6	00·9	11 40·0	14·9	191 46·4	49·8
	09	A	237 34·3	319 26·8	· · 35·4	252 00·4	7 00·1	26 42·2	· · 15·0	206 48·9	· · 49·8
	10	T	252 36·8	334 25·9	35·3	267 01·1	6 59·4	41 44·3	15·1	221 51·4	49·8
	11	U	267 39·2	349 24·9	35·2	282 01·9	58·6	56 46·5	15·3	236 53·8	49·9
	12	R	282 41·7	4 23·9	S23 35·1	297 02·6	S 6 57·8	71 48·6	S11 15·4	251 56·3	N 9 49·9
	13	D	297 44·1	19 22·9	35·0	312 03·4	57·1	86 50·8	15·5	266 58·8	49·9
	14	A	312 46·6	34 22·0	34·9	327 04·1	56·3	101 52·9	15·6	282 01·2	49·9
	15	Y	327 49·1	49 21·0	· · 34·9	342 04·9	· · 55·5	116 55·1	· · 15·7	297 03·7	· · 49·9
	16		342 51·5	64 20·0	34·8	357 05·6	54·8	131 57·2	15·8	312 06·2	49·9
	17		357 54·0	79 19·1	34·7	12 06·4	54·0	146 59·3	15·9	327 08·6	49·9
	18		12 56·5	94 18·1	S23 34·6	27 07·1	S 6 53·3	162 01·5	S11 16·0	342 11·1	N 9 49·9
	19		27 58·9	109 17·1	34·5	42 07·9	52·5	177 03·6	16·1	357 13·6	49·9
	20		43 01·4	124 16·2	34·4	57 08·6	51·7	192 05·8	16·2	12 16·1	50·0
	21		58 03·9	139 15·2	· · 34·3	72 09·4	· · 51·0	207 07·9	· · 16·3	27 18·5	· · 50·0
	22		73 06·3	154 14·2	34·2	87 10·1	50·2	222 10·1	16·4	42 21·0	50·0
	23		88 08·8	169 13·3	34·1	102 10·9	49·5	237 12·2	16·5	57 23·5	50·0
Mer. Pass.			h m 17 12·3	v −1·0	d 0·1	v 0·7	d 0·8	v 2·1	d 0·1	v 2·5	d 0·0

STARS Name	S.H.A.	Dec.
	° ′	°
Acamar	315 42·8	S 40 25
Achernar	335 50·6	S 57 23
Acrux	173 46·3	S 62 55
Adhara	255 37·9	S 28 55
Aldebaran	291 26·7	N 16 27
Alioth	166 49·1	N 56 07
Alkaid	153 24·6	N 49 27
Al Na'ir	28 24·8	S 47 06
Alnilam	276 19·3	S 1 13
Alphard	218 28·0	S 8 31
Alphecca	126 38·9	N 26 48
Alpheratz	358 17·6	N 28 55
Altair	62 40·5	N 8 47
Ankaa	353 47·8	S 42 28
Antares	113 06·8	S 26 22
Arcturus	146 25·7	N 19 20
Atria	108 38·7	S 68 58
Avior	234 31·0	S 59 24
Bellatrix	279 06·8	N 6 19
Betelgeuse	271 36·4	N 7 24
Canopus	264 10·1	S 52 40
Capella	281 22·4	N 45 58
Deneb	49 54·4	N 45 10
Denebola	183 06·9	N 14 44
Diphda	349 28·6	S 18 09
Dubhe	194 31·0	N 61 54
Elnath	278 53·7	N 28 35
Eltanin	91 01·9	N 51 29
Enif	34 19·5	N 9 44
Fomalhaut	16 00·1	S 29 47
Gacrux	172 37·7	S 56 56
Gienah	176 26·0	S 17 22
Hadar	149 35·0	S 60 13
Hamal	328 37·7	N 23 19
Kaus Aust.	84 27·6	S 34 24
Kochab	137 18·7	N 74 16
Markab	14 11·2	N 15 02
Menkar	314 49·1	N 3 58
Menkent	148 46·5	S 36 13
Miaplacidus	221 46·3	S 69 35
Mirfak	309 27·1	N 49 45·7
Nunki	76 39·2	S 26 20·3
Peacock	54 11·1	S 56 50·2
Pollux	244 07·3	N 28 06·0
Procyon	245 33·6	N 5 18·3
Rasalhague	96 37·2	N 12 34·6
Regulus	208 18·0	N 12 06·8
Rigel	281 43·2	S 8 14·0
Rigil Kent.	140 37·1	S 60 42·6
Sabik	102 50·4	S 15 41·5
Schedar	350 18·2	N 56 22·7
Shaula	97 06·8	S 37 05·1
Sirius	259 02·2	S 16 40·3
Spica	159 05·9	S 11 00·4
Suhail	223 16·3	S 43 18·5
Vega	81 01·6	N 38 45·1
Zuben'ubi	137 41·9	S 15 55·1

	S.H.A.	Mer. Pass.
	° ′	h m
Venus	83 45·9	11 41
Mars	15 22·7	16 13
Jupiter	149 18·5	7 17
Saturn	329 14·3	19 15

FIG. 17-1 Excerpt from Nautical Almanac

JANUARY 1, 2, 3 (THURS., FRI., SAT.)

G.M.T.	SUN G.H.A.	SUN Dec.	MOON G.H.A.	v	MOON Dec.	d	H.P.
h	° ′	° ′	° ′	′	° ′	′	′
00	179 10·8	S 23 03·4	271 18·0	15·4	S 6 20·4	14·6	55·9
01	194 10·5	03·2	285 52·4	15·4	6 35·0	14·6	56·0
02	209 10·2	03·0	300 26·8	15·3	6 49·6	14·6	56·0
03	224 09·9	· · 02·8	315 01·1	15·2	7 04·2	14·6	56·0
04	239 09·6	02·6	329 35·3	15·2	7 18·8	14·6	56·1
05	254 09·3	02·4	344 09·5	15·1	7 33·4	14·5	56·1
06	269 09·0	S 23 02·2	358 43·6	15·1	S 7 47·9	14·6	56·1
07	284 08·7	02·0	13 17·7	14·9	8 02·5	14·5	56·2
08	299 08·4	01·8	27 51·6	14·9	8 17·0	14·5	56·2
09	314 08·1	· · 01·6	42 25·5	14·9	8 31·5	14·5	56·2
10	329 07·8	01·4	56 59·4	14·8	8 46·0	14·5	56·3
11	344 07·5	01·2	71 33·2	14·6	9 00·5	14·5	56·3
12	359 07·2	S 23 01·0	86 06·8	14·7	S 9 15·0	14·4	56·3
13	14 06·9	00·8	100 40·5	14·5	9 29·4	14·4	56·4
14	29 06·6	00·6	115 14·0	14·5	9 43·8	14·4	56·4
15	44 06·3	· · 00·4	129 47·5	14·4	9 58·2	14·4	56·4
16	59 06·0	00·2	144 20·9	14·3	10 12·6	14·4	56·5
17	74 05·7	23 00·0	158 54·2	14·2	10 27·0	14·3	56·5
18	89 05·5	S 22 59·8	173 27·4	14·1	S 10 41·3	14·3	56·5
19	104 05·2	59·6	188 00·5	14·1	10 55·6	14·3	56·6
20	119 04·9	59·4	202 33·6	13·9	11 09·9	14·2	56·6
21	134 04·6	· · 59·2	217 06·5	13·9	11 24·1	14·2	56·6
22	149 04·3	58·9	231 39·4	13·8	11 38·3	14·2	56·7
23	164 04·0	58·7	246 12·2	13·7	11 52·5	14·1	56·7
2 00	179 03·7	S 22 58·5	260 44·9	13·6	S 12 06·6	14·1	56·8
01	194 03·4	58·3	275 17·5	13·5	12 20·7	14·1	56·8
02	209 03·1	58·1	289 50·0	13·4	12 34·8	14·0	56·8
03	224 02·8	· · 57·9	304 22·4	13·3	12 48·8	14·0	56·9
04	239 02·5	57·7	318 54·7	13·3	13 02·8	14·0	56·9
05	254 02·2	57·4	333 27·0	13·1	13 16·8	13·9	56·9
06	269 01·9	S 22 57·2	347 59·1	13·0	S 13 30·7	13·9	57·0
07	284 01·6	57·0	2 31·1	12·9	13 44·6	13·8	57·0
08	299 01·3	56·8	17 03·0	12·8	13 58·4	13·8	57·1
F 09	314 01·0	· · 56·6	31 34·8	12·7	14 12·2	13·8	57·1
R 10	329 00·8	56·3	46 06·5	12·6	14 26·0	13·6	57·1
I 11	344 00·5	56·1	60 38·1	12·5	14 39·6	13·7	57·2
D 12	359 00·2	S 22 55·9	75 09·6	12·4	S 14 53·3	13·6	57·2
A 13	13 59·9	55·7	89 41·0	12·3	15 06·9	13·5	57·3
Y 14	28 59·6	55·4	104 12·3	12·2	15 20·4	13·5	57·3
15	43 59·3	· · 55·2	118 43·5	12·0	15 33·9	13·5	57·3
16	58 59·0	55·0	133 14·5	11·9	15 47·4	13·3	57·4
17	73 58·7	54·8	147 45·4	11·9	16 00·7	13·3	57·4
18	88 58·4	S 22 54·5	162 16·3	11·7	S 16 14·0	13·3	57·5
19	103 58·1	54·3	176 47·0	11·6	16 27·3	13·2	57·5
20	118 57·8	54·1	191 17·6	11·4	16 40·5	13·1	57·5
21	133 57·5	· · 53·9	205 48·0	11·4	16 53·6	13·1	57·6
22	148 57·3	53·6	220 18·4	11·2	17 06·7	13·0	57·6
23	163 57·0	53·4	234 48·6	11·1	17 19·7	13·0	57·6
3 00	178 56·7	S 22 53·2	249 18·7	11·0	S 17 32·7	12·8	57·7
01	193 56·4	52·9	263 48·7	10·8	17 45·5	12·8	57·7
02	208 56·1	52·7	278 18·5	10·7	17 58·3	12·8	57·8
03	223 55·8	· · 52·5	292 48·2	10·6	18 11·1	12·6	57·8
04	238 55·5	52·2	307 17·8	10·5	18 23·7	12·6	57·9
05	253 55·2	52·0	321 47·3	10·3	18 36·3	12·5	57·9
06	268 54·9	S 22 51·8	336 16·6	10·2	S 18 48·8	12·4	57·9
07	283 54·6	51·5	350 45·8	10·1	19 01·2	12·3	58·0
S 08	298 54·3	51·3	5 14·9	10·0	19 13·5	12·3	58·0
A 09	313 54·1	· · 51·0	19 43·9	9·8	19 25·8	12·1	58·1
T 10	328 53·8	50·8	34 12·7	9·7	19 37·9	12·1	58·1
U 11	343 53·5	50·6	48 41·4	9·5	19 50·0	12·0	58·1
R 12	358 53·2	S 22 50·3	63 09·9	9·4	S 20 02·0	11·9	58·2
D 13	13 52·9	50·1	77 38·3	9·3	20 13·9	11·8	58·2
A 14	28 52·6	49·8	92 06·6	9·1	20 25·7	11·7	58·3
Y 15	43 52·3	· · 49·6	106 34·7	9·0	20 37·4	11·7	58·3
16	58 52·0	49·3	121 02·7	8·8	20 49·1	11·5	58·3
17	73 51·7	49·1	135 30·5	8·7	21 00·6	11·4	58·4
18	88 51·5	S 22 48·9	149 58·2	8·6	S 21 12·0	11·3	58·4
19	103 51·2	48·6	164 25·8	8·4	21 23·3	11·2	58·5
20	118 50·9	48·4	178 53·2	8·3	21 34·5	11·1	58·5
21	133 50·6	· · 48·1	193 20·5	8·2	21 45·6	11·0	58·5
22	148 50·3	47·9	207 47·7	8·0	21 56·6	10·9	58·6
23	163 50·0	47·6	222 14·7	7·8	22 07·5	10·8	58·6
	S.D. 16·3	d 0·2	S.D. 15·3		15·6		15·9

Lat.	Twilight Naut.	Twilight Civil	Sunrise	Moonrise 1	Moonrise 2	Moonrise 3	Moonrise 4
°	h m	h m	h m	h m	h m	h m	h m
N 72	08 23	10 40	■	01 23	03 47	■	■
N 70	08 04	09 48	■	01 13	03 21	06 21	■
68	07 49	09 16	■	01 04	03 01	05 24	■
66	07 37	08 52	10 26	00 58	02 46	04 51	08 02
64	07 26	08 33	09 49	00 52	02 33	04 27	06 43
62	07 17	08 18	09 22	00 47	02 23	04 08	06 07
60	07 09	08 05	09 02	00 43	02 14	03 52	05 41
N 58	07 02	07 54	08 45	00 39	02 06	03 39	05 20
56	06 55	07 44	08 31	00 35	01 59	03 28	05 04
54	06 49	07 35	08 19	00 32	01 53	03 18	04 50
52	06 44	07 28	08 08	00 30	01 47	03 10	04 37
50	06 39	07 20	07 58	00 27	01 42	03 02	04 26
45	06 28	07 05	07 38	00 22	01 32	02 46	04 04
N 40	06 18	06 52	07 22	00 18	01 23	02 32	03 46
35	06 09	06 40	07 08	00 14	01 15	02 21	03 31
30	06 00	06 30	06 56	00 10	01 09	02 11	03 18
20	05 44	06 11	06 35	00 05	00 58	01 54	02 56
N 10	05 28	05 54	06 17	00 00	00 48	01 40	02 37
0	05 12	05 38	06 00	24 39	00 39	01 26	02 19
S 10	04 53	05 20	05 43	24 30	00 30	01 13	02 01
20	04 31	05 00	05 24	24 20	00 20	00 59	01 43
30	04 02	04 35	05 03	24 09	00 09	00 42	01 22
35	03 44	04 21	04 50	24 03	00 03	00 33	01 09
40	03 22	04 03	04 35	23 56	24 22	00 22	00 55
45	02 52	03 41	04 18	23 48	24 10	00 10	00 38
S 50	02 08	03 12	03 56	23 38	23 55	24 18	00 18
52	01 42	02 57	03 45	23 34	23 48	24 08	00 08
54	01 02	02 40	03 33	23 29	23 40	23 57	24 23
56	////	02 19	03 20	23 24	23 32	23 45	24 06
58	////	01 51	03 04	23 18	23 22	23 30	23 46
S 60	////	01 08	02 44	23 11	23 11	23 14	23 21

Lat.	Sunset	Twilight Civil	Twilight Naut.	Moonset 1	Moonset 2	Moonset 3	Moonset 4
°	h m	h m	h m	h m	h m	h m	h m
N 72	■	13 27	15 45	10 16	09 25	■	■
N 70	■	14 19	16 03	10 30	09 54	08 35	■
68	■	14 52	16 18	10 40	10 15	09 33	■
66	13 41	15 15	16 31	10 49	10 32	10 08	08 49
64	14 19	15 34	16 41	10 57	10 46	10 33	10 09
62	14 45	15 49	16 51	11 03	10 58	10 53	10 46
60	15 06	16 02	16 59	11 09	11 08	11 09	11 12
N 58	15 23	16 14	17 06	11 14	11 17	11 23	11 33
56	15 37	16 24	17 12	11 19	11 25	11 35	11 51
54	15 49	16 33	17 18	11 23	11 32	11 46	12 05
52	16 00	16 41	17 24	11 26	11 39	11 55	12 18
50	16 09	16 48	17 29	11 30	11 44	12 03	12 30
45	16 30	17 03	17 40	11 37	11 57	12 21	12 53
N 40	16 46	17 17	17 50	11 43	12 07	12 36	13 13
35	17 00	17 28	17 59	11 49	12 16	12 49	13 29
30	17 12	17 38	18 08	11 53	12 24	13 00	13 43
20	17 32	17 56	18 24	12 01	12 38	13 19	14 06
N 10	17 51	18 13	18 40	12 09	12 50	13 35	14 27
0	18 08	18 30	18 56	12 16	13 01	13 51	14 46
S 10	18 25	18 48	19 15	12 22	13 12	14 06	15 06
20	18 43	19 08	19 37	12 30	13 24	14 23	15 27
30	19 05	19 32	20 05	12 38	13 38	14 42	15 51
35	19 17	19 47	20 23	12 43	13 46	14 54	16 05
40	19 32	20 05	20 46	12 48	13 55	15 07	16 22
45	19 50	20 27	21 16	12 55	14 06	15 22	16 42
S 50	20 12	20 55	21 59	13 03	14 20	15 42	17 07
52	20 22	21 10	22 24	13 06	14 26	15 51	17 19
54	20 34	21 27	23 03	13 10	14 33	16 01	17 33
56	20 48	21 48	////	13 15	14 40	16 13	17 49
58	21 04	22 16	////	13 20	14 49	16 26	18 08
S 60	21 23	22 58	////	13 25	14 59	16 42	18 33

Day	SUN Eqn. of Time 00ʰ	SUN Eqn. of Time 12ʰ	SUN Mer. Pass.	MOON Mer. Pass. Upper	MOON Mer. Pass. Lower	Age	Phase
	m s	m s	h m	h m	h m	d	
1	03 16	03 30	12 04	06 05	18 27	23	☾
2	03 45	03 59	12 04	06 50	19 13	24	
3	04 13	04 27	12 04	07 38	20 05	25	

FIG. 17-2 Excerpt from Nautical Almanac

moon. The GHA of Aries is also given for each hour, but since it is purely an hour circle in the sky, it has no declination. Note that GHA *always* increases with time, but declination may increase or decrease with time. Fig. 17–1 has a column headed "stars," in which is given the sidereal hour angle (SHA) and declination of the fifty-seven stars we use in navigation. Just below that table is a listing of SHA for the planets and the LMT of their meridian passage. This information is theoretically for the middle of the three days, but close enough for all three. Across the bottom of each page are certain interpolation factors that will be discussed later.

Fig. 17–2 has columns for the sun and the moon, again giving GHA and declination. Note that declination must always be marked north (N) or south (S). Fig. 17–2 also has special tables for morning twilight, sunrise, and moonrise, and tables for evening twilight, sunset, and moonset. The times given are local mean time and are the same for all longitudes on a certain day, but vary with latitude.

Note that two kinds of twilight are given, civil and nautical. *Civil twilight* occurs when the sun is 6° below the horizon, at which time the stars begin to be visible and the horizon is clear enough for taking sextant observations. *Nautical twilight* occurs when the sun is 12° below the horizon, at which time it is usually too dark to take sights.

At the bottom of the twilight tables, the almanac lists the LMT of *meridian passage*—the moment when the body crosses our meridian extended out to the celestial sphere —for the sun and the moon. It also gives the age and phase of the moon, and the equation of time—the difference between the real and the mean sun for two instants of time each day, zero hours and 1200. From this table you can tell which sun is ahead and by how much. For example, for January 1 at 1200, the equation of time is given as $3^{m}30^{s}$ and the time of meridian passage *by the actual sun* is at LMT 1204. Since *local apparent time* of meridian passage is always 1200 LAT, the fact that the actual sun crosses the meridian at 1204 LMT means that the mean sun is ahead of the actual sun, as it crossed the meridian 3 minutes (and 30 seconds) before the actual sun got to the meridian. In present-day navigation, we would not ordinarily use equation of time, nautical twilight, sunrise, sunset, moonrise, and moonset, but the information is there in case anyone would like to know these things. However, the time of civil twilight is used daily for setting up predicted altitude and bearings of navigation stars from the star finder.

Interpolation These "daily pages" of the *Nautical Almanac* give us our basic data of GHA and declination for every hour, but since sights are taken at any time, we must be able to determine intermediate values for minutes and seconds. The mechanics vary slightly with each celestial body, because the rate of change in GHA and declination is not uniform. To provide us with a means of accurate interpolation, the *Nautical Almanac* contains a section known as "Tables of Increments and Corrections" (the yellow-page section of the almanac) in which we can find the change for any combination of minutes and seconds we wish. Each page covers a certain number of minutes and 60 seconds of that minute (see Fig. 17–3). There are three separate columns for sun and planets, Aries, and moon. On the right-hand side of each table are columns headed "*v* or *d*" and "Corr^{n}" ("correction"). To explain this, let us again examine the bottom line of Fig. 17–1.

On the bottom line is given meridian passage $17^{h}12.3^{m}$. This is for general information and would not be used in navigation. At the bottom of the four columns for planets we find the letters *v* and *d,* followed by a number. The *v* value is the *average change per hour* in GHA during the three days listed. The *d* value is the *average change per hour* in declination during those three days. The *v* and *d* values are used for interpolation in the increments and corrections (I&C) tables, as we shall shortly demonstrate.

At the bottom of the column headed "Sun" (Fig. 17–2) we find "SD 16.3" and "*d* 0.2." This means that the semidiameter of the sun during the three days is 16.3′ of arc and the hourly change in declination is 0.2′. Usually, we are not concerned with either of these figures in our practical work.

At the bottom of the column headed "Moon" we find the semidiameter (SD) given for each of the three days. Because of the moon's proximity to the Earth, its apparent rate of change of position is rapid. For this reason the almanac

20^m	SUN PLANETS	ARIES	MOON	v or d	Corr^n	v or d	Corr^n	v or d	Corr^n
s	° ′	° ′	° ′	′	′	′	′	′	′
00	5 00·0	5 00·8	4 46·3	0·0	0·0	6·0	2·1	12·0	4·1
01	5 00·3	5 01·1	4 46·6	0·1	0·0	6·1	2·1	12·1	4·1
02	5 00·5	5 01·3	4 46·8	0·2	0·1	6·2	2·1	12·2	4·2
03	5 00·8	5 01·6	4 47·0	0·3	0·1	6·3	2·2	12·3	4·2
04	5 01·0	5 01·8	4 47·3	0·4	0·1	6·4	2·2	12·4	4·2
05	5 01·3	5 02·1	4 47·5	0·5	0·2	6·5	2·2	12·5	4·3
06	5 01·5	5 02·3	4 47·8	0·6	0·2	6·6	2·3	12·6	4·3
07	5 01·8	5 02·6	4 48·0	0·7	0·2	6·7	2·3	12·7	4·3
08	5 02·0	5 02·8	4 48·2	0·8	0·3	6·8	2·3	12·8	4·4
09	5 02·3	5 03·1	4 48·5	0·9	0·3	6·9	2·4	12·9	4·4
10	5 02·5	5 03·3	4 48·7	1·0	0·3	7·0	2·4	13·0	4·4
11	5 02·8	5 03·6	4 49·0	1·1	0·4	7·1	2·4	13·1	4·5
12	5 03·0	5 03·8	4 49·2	1·2	0·4	7·2	2·5	13·2	4·5
13	5 03·3	5 04·1	4 49·4	1·3	0·4	7·3	2·5	13·3	4·5
14	5 03·5	5 04·3	4 49·7	1·4	0·5	7·4	2·5	13·4	4·6
15	5 03·8	5 04·6	4 49·9	1·5	0·5	7·5	2·6	13·5	4·6
16	5 04·0	5 04·8	4 50·2	1·6	0·5	7·6	2·6	13·6	4·6
17	5 04·3	5 05·1	4 50·4	1·7	0·6	7·7	2·6	13·7	4·7
18	5 04·5	5 05·3	4 50·6	1·8	0·6	7·8	2·7	13·8	4·7
19	5 04·8	5 05·6	4 50·9	1·9	0·6	7·9	2·7	13·9	4·7
20	5 05·0	5 05·8	4 51·1	2·0	0·7	8·0	2·7	14·0	4·8
21	5 05·3	5 06·1	4 51·3	2·1	0·7	8·1	2·8	14·1	4·8
22	5 05·5	5 06·3	4 51·6	2·2	0·8	8·2	2·8	14·2	4·9
23	5 05·8	5 06·6	4 51·8	2·3	0·8	8·3	2·8	14·3	4·9
24	5 06·0	5 06·8	4 52·1	2·4	0·8	8·4	2·9	14·4	4·9
25	5 06·3	5 07·1	4 52·3	2·5	0·9	8·5	2·9	14·5	5·0
26	5 06·5	5 07·3	4 52·5	2·6	0·9	8·6	2·9	14·6	5·0
27	5 06·8	5 07·6	4 52·8	2·7	0·9	8·7	3·0	14·7	5·0
28	5 07·0	5 07·8	4 53·0	2·8	1·0	8·8	3·0	14·8	5·1
29	5 07·3	5 08·1	4 53·3	2·9	1·0	8·9	3·0	14·9	5·1
30	5 07·5	5 08·3	4 53·5	3·0	1·0	9·0	3·1	15·0	5·1
31	5 07·8	5 08·6	4 53·7	3·1	1·1	9·1	3·1	15·1	5·2
32	5 08·0	5 08·8	4 54·0	3·2	1·1	9·2	3·1	15·2	5·2
33	5 08·3	5 09·1	4 54·2	3·3	1·1	9·3	3·2	15·3	5·2
34	5 08·5	5 09·3	4 54·4	3·4	1·2	9·4	3·2	15·4	5·3
35	5 08·8	5 09·6	4 54·7	3·5	1·2	9·5	3·2	15·5	5·3
36	5 09·0	5 09·8	4 54·9	3·6	1·2	9·6	3·3	15·6	5·3
37	5 09·3	5 10·1	4 55·2	3·7	1·3	9·7	3·3	15·7	5·4
38	5 09·5	5 10·3	4 55·4	3·8	1·3	9·8	3·3	15·8	5·4
39	5 09·8	5 10·6	4 55·6	3·9	1·3	9·9	3·4	15·9	5·4
40	5 10·0	5 10·8	4 55·9	4·0	1·4	10·0	3·4	16·0	5·5
41	5 10·3	5 11·1	4 56·1	4·1	1·4	10·1	3·5	16·1	5·5
42	5 10·5	5 11·4	4 56·4	4·2	1·4	10·2	3·5	16·2	5·5
43	5 10·8	5 11·6	4 56·6	4·3	1·5	10·3	3·5	16·3	5·6
44	5 11·0	5 11·9	4 56·8	4·4	1·5	10·4	3·6	16·4	5·6
45	5 11·3	5 12·1	4 57·1	4·5	1·5	10·5	3·6	16·5	5·6
46	5 11·5	5 12·4	4 57·3	4·6	1·6	10·6	3·6	16·6	5·7
47	5 11·8	5 12·6	4 57·5	4·7	1·6	10·7	3·7	16·7	5·7
48	5 12·0	5 12·9	4 57·8	4·8	1·6	10·8	3·7	16·8	5·7
49	5 12·3	5 13·1	4 58·0	4·9	1·7	10·9	3·7	16·9	5·8
50	5 12·5	5 13·4	4 58·3	5·0	1·7	11·0	3·8	17·0	5·8
51	5 12·8	5 13·6	4 58·5	5·1	1·7	11·1	3·8	17·1	5·8
52	5 13·0	5 13·9	4 58·7	5·2	1·8	11·2	3·8	17·2	5·9
53	5 13·3	5 14·1	4 59·0	5·3	1·8	11·3	3·9	17·3	5·9
54	5 13·5	5 14·4	4 59·2	5·4	1·8	11·4	3·9	17·4	5·9
55	5 13·8	5 14·6	4 59·5	5·5	1·9	11·5	3·9	17·5	6·0
56	5 14·0	5 14·9	4 59·7	5·6	1·9	11·6	4·0	17·6	6·0
57	5 14·3	5 15·1	4 59·9	5·7	1·9	11·7	4·0	17·7	6·0
58	5 14·5	5 15·4	5 00·2	5·8	2·0	11·8	4·0	17·8	6·1
59	5 14·8	5 15·6	5 00·4	5·9	2·0	11·9	4·1	17·9	6·1
60	5 15·0	5 15·9	5 00·7	6·0	2·1	12·0	4·1	18·0	6·2

21^m	SUN PLANETS	ARIES	MOON	v or d	Corr^n	v or d	Corr^n	v or d	Corr^n
s	° ′	° ′	° ′	′	′	′	′	′	
00	5 15·0	5 15·9	5 00·7	0·0	0·0	6·0	2·2	12·0	
01	5 15·3	5 16·1	5 00·9	0·1	0·0	6·1	2·2	12·1	
02	5 15·5	5 16·4	5 01·1	0·2	0·1	6·2	2·2	12·2	
03	5 15·8	5 16·6	5 01·4	0·3	0·1	6·3	2·3	12·3	
04	5 16·0	5 16·9	5 01·6	0·4	0·1	6·4	2·3	12·4	
05	5 16·3	5 17·1	5 01·8	0·5	0·2	6·5	2·3	12·5	
06	5 16·5	5 17·4	5 02·1	0·6	0·2	6·6	2·4	12·6	
07	5 16·8	5 17·6	5 02·3	0·7	0·3	6·7	2·4	12·7	
08	5 17·0	5 17·9	5 02·6	0·8	0·3	6·8	2·4	12·8	
09	5 17·3	5 18·1	5 02·8	0·9	0·3	6·9	2·5	12·9	
10	5 17·5	5 18·4	5 03·0	1·0	0·4	7·0	2·5	13·0	
11	5 17·8	5 18·6	5 03·3	1·1	0·4	7·1	2·5	13·1	
12	5 18·0	5 18·9	5 03·5	1·2	0·4	7·2	2·6	13·2	
13	5 18·3	5 19·1	5 03·8	1·3	0·5	7·3	2·6	13·3	
14	5 18·5	5 19·4	5 04·0	1·4	0·5	7·4	2·7	13·4	
15	5 18·8	5 19·6	5 04·2	1·5	0·5	7·5	2·7	13·5	
16	5 19·0	5 19·9	5 04·5	1·6	0·6	7·6	2·7	13·6	
17	5 19·3	5 20·1	5 04·7	1·7	0·6	7·7	2·8	13·7	
18	5 19·5	5 20·4	5 04·9	1·8	0·6	7·8	2·8	13·8	
19	5 19·8	5 20·6	5 05·2	1·9	0·7	7·9	2·8	13·9	
20	5 20·0	5 20·9	5 05·4	2·0	0·7	8·0	2·9	14·0	
21	5 20·3	5 21·1	5 05·7	2·1	0·8	8·1	2·9	14·1	
22	5 20·5	5 21·4	5 05·9	2·2	0·8	8·2	2·9	14·2	
23	5 20·8	5 21·6	5 06·1	2·3	0·8	8·3	3·0	14·3	
24	5 21·0	5 21·9	5 06·4	2·4	0·9	8·4	3·0	14·4	
25	5 21·3	5 22·1	5 06·6	2·5	0·9	8·5	3·0	14·5	
26	5 21·5	5 22·4	5 06·9	2·6	0·9	8·6	3·1	14·6	
27	5 21·8	5 22·6	5 07·1	2·7	1·0	8·7	3·1	14·7	
28	5 22·0	5 22·9	5 07·3	2·8	1·0	8·8	3·2	14·8	
29	5 22·3	5 23·1	5 07·6	2·9	1·0	8·9	3·2	14·9	
30	5 22·5	5 23·4	5 07·8	3·0	1·1	9·0	3·2	15·0	
31	5 22·8	5 23·6	5 08·0	3·1	1·1	9·1	3·3	15·1	
32	5 23·0	5 23·9	5 08·3	3·2	1·1	9·2	3·3	15·2	
33	5 23·3	5 24·1	5 08·5	3·3	1·2	9·3	3·3	15·3	
34	5 23·5	5 24·4	5 08·8	3·4	1·2	9·4	3·4	15·4	
35	5 23·8	5 24·6	5 09·0	3·5	1·3	9·5	3·4	15·5	
36	5 24·0	5 24·9	5 09·2	3·6	1·3	9·6	3·4	15·6	
37	5 24·3	5 25·1	5 09·5	3·7	1·3	9·7	3·5	15·7	
38	5 24·5	5 25·4	5 09·7	3·8	1·4	9·8	3·5	15·8	
39	5 24·8	5 25·6	5 10·0	3·9	1·4	9·9	3·5	15·9	
40	5 25·0	5 25·9	5 10·2	4·0	1·4	10·0	3·6	16·0	
41	5 25·3	5 26·1	5 10·4	4·1	1·5	10·1	3·6	16·1	
42	5 25·5	5 26·4	5 10·7	4·2	1·5	10·2	3·7	16·2	
43	5 25·8	5 26·6	5 10·9	4·3	1·5	10·3	3·7	16·3	
44	5 26·0	5 26·9	5 11·1	4·4	1·6	10·4	3·7	16·4	
45	5 26·3	5 27·1	5 11·4	4·5	1·6	10·5	3·8	16·5	
46	5 26·5	5 27·4	5 11·6	4·6	1·6	10·6	3·8	16·6	
47	5 26·8	5 27·6	5 11·9	4·7	1·7	10·7	3·8	16·7	
48	5 27·0	5 27·9	5 12·1	4·8	1·7	10·8	3·9	16·8	
49	5 27·3	5 28·1	5 12·3	4·9	1·8	10·9	3·9	16·9	
50	5 27·5	5 28·4	5 12·6	5·0	1·8	11·0	3·9	17·0	
51	5 27·8	5 28·6	5 12·8	5·1	1·8	11·1	4·0	17·1	
52	5 28·0	5 28·9	5 13·1	5·2	1·9	11·2	4·0	17·2	
53	5 28·3	5 29·1	5 13·3	5·3	1·9	11·3	4·0	17·3	
54	5 28·5	5 29·4	5 13·5	5·4	1·9	11·4	4·1	17·4	
55	5 28·8	5 29·7	5 13·8	5·5	2·0	11·5	4·1	17·5	
56	5 29·0	5 29·9	5 14·0	5·6	2·0	11·6	4·2	17·6	
57	5 29·3	5 30·2	5 14·3	5·7	2·0	11·7	4·2	17·7	
58	5 29·5	5 30·4	5 14·5	5·8	2·1	11·8	4·2	17·8	
59	5 29·8	5 30·7	5 14·7	5·9	2·1	11·9	4·3	17·9	
60	5 30·0	5 30·9	5 15·0	6·0	2·2	12·0	4·3	18·0	

FIG. 17-3 Interpolation table from Nautical Almanac

gives us the *v* and *d* values for every hour of the day, instead of once a day as for the planets. The final column under "Moon" is headed "HP" (for horizontal parallax), a figure we shall discuss when we come to sextant corrections. We are now ready to learn how to interpolate GHA and declination. Let us begin with the sun.

Example • *Sun*—We require the GHA and declination of the sun for January 1 at 13^{h}20^{m}33^s. We do this by finding the GHA for 13 hours from the daily page and for 20^{m}33^s from the I&C tables.

From the daily page for January 1, GHA for 13^h is	14° 06.9′
From the I&C table (Fig. 17–3), "Sun and planets," 20^{m}33^s, the GHA is	5° 08.3′
(There is no *v* correction.) Total GHA is	19° 15.2′

It is customary to obtain the declination of the sun by inspection and eye interpolation from the daily page. For 13^h the declination is *south* (S) 23°00.8′ and for 14^h it is S 23°00.6′. Since our time is 13^{h}20^{m}33^s, which is closer to 13½^h than to 13^h, we split the difference and use a declination of 23°00.7′. *Note that in this case the declination is decreasing with increase in time.* If we had wanted to, we could have used the interpolation figure at the bottom of the daily column, $d = 0.2'$. If we go to the I&C table we used before, for 20^m, and look in the first column headed "*v* or *d*," we find opposite 0.2′ a correction of 0.1′. Applying this to S 23°00.8′ (decreasing), we arrive at a declination of S 23°00.7′. With the sun and the planets we usually can interpolate by eye on the daily pages, but with the moon, we nearly always must use the *v* and *d* corrections.

Example • *Aries*—We require the GHA of Aries on January 2 at 23^{h}21^{m}27^s. From the daily page we find:

GHA of Aries for 23^h	87° 09.6′
From I&C tables, GHA of Aries for 21^{m}27^s	5° 22.6′
(There is no *v* correction for Aries.) Total GHA	92° 32.2′

As explained before, Aries is a reference meridian in the sky and is not a celestial body, so it has longitude only, and no declination. To find the GHA of any star, we simply add the GHA of Aries for the moment of observation to the SHA of the star, taken from the daily page.

***Example* •** *Planet*—We require the GHA and declination of Mars on January 3 at 05-20-51. Note that $v = 0.7'$ and $d = 0.8'$.

From daily page, GHA of Mars for 05^h is	191° 57.4′
From I&C tables, GHA for 20^m51^s is	5° 12.8′
For a v factor of 0.7′, the correction is	0.2′
Total GHA	197° 10.4′

Note: The v correction to GHA is always added, except for Venus at certain times of the year when v is marked with a minus sign, indicating that it is to be subtracted. (See next example.)

Declination of Mars for 05^h is	S 7° 03.2′	
Declination increases 0.8′ in the next hour, or 0.3′ in 20^m		
Using the I&C tables, the d correction for 0.8′ is		0.3′ (decreasing)
Declination for 05-20-51 is	S 7° 02.9′	

Note that we got the same correction by estimating 20^m to be one-third of an hour, as we did by using the I&C table. Also note that when you look for a v or d factor in these tables, there is no connection between the seconds column and the place where we find the v or d correction. We just make sure we are in the correct column for minutes.

***Example* •** *Planet*—We require the GHA and declination of Venus on January 1 at 17-21-43. Note that v is $-1.0'$, telling you to subtract, and that $d = 0.1'$, which means that you can ignore it, as we work no closer than 0.1′.

GHA of Venus for 17^h		80° 05.7′
GHA of planets for 21^m43^s		5° 25.8′
	Total	85° 31.5′
Less v correction for 1.0′		0.4′
	GHA of Venus	85° 31.1′

Declination by inspection is S 23° 37.5′.

Example • *Moon*—We require the GHA and declination of the moon for January 2 at 01-20-11. Note that $v = 13.5'$ and $d = 14.1'$. Declination is *decreasing*.

GHA of moon for 01^h		275° 17.5′
GHA of moon for 20^m11^s		4° 49.0′
v correction for 13.5′		4.6′
	Total GHA	280° 11.1′

Declination of moon for 01^h	S 12° 20.7′
Correction for d of 14.1′ is	−4.8′
	S 12° 15.9′

Example • *Star*—We require the GHA and declination of the star Canopus on January 1 at 10-21-23 GMT. Remember that GHA of star = GHA of Aries + SHA of star.

GHA of Aries for 10^h on January 1		250° 38.5′
GHA of Aries for 21^m23^s		5° 21.6′
	Total GHA of Aries	256° 00.1′
SHA of Canopus (from daily page)		264° 10.1′
	GHA of Canopus at 10-21-23	520° 10.2′
	Minus	360°
	GHA	160° 10.2′

The declination of Canopus is given on the daily page as S 52°40.6′. The manner in which the rest of the *Nautical Almanac* is used is best discussed when we come to the point where we need the information.

Air Almanac The *Air Almanac* is designed for air navigators, who are allowed greater tolerances in their work than marine navigators. Because of an airplane's much greater speed, air navigators need to work quickly to fix their positions, and accuracy is not quite so important, so long as it is within reason. Unlike the *Nautical Almanac,* which gives data to the nearest tenth of a minute and provides for close interpolation, the *Air Almanac* gives information to the nearest whole minute. (Only when certain astrotrackers are used do air navigators use tenths of minutes, and special tables in the *Air Almanac* provide the means for doing that.)

The first thing you will notice about the *Air Almanac* is that it is bound with a spiral binder, making it easy to tear out the current page at the end of the day and throw it away. Next, you will notice that each right-hand page (Fig. 17–4) covers the first 12 hours of a day and that the other side of the page (Fig. 17–5) covers the hours from 1200 to 2400. Information is given for every 10 minutes of GMT. Every page presents the GHA and declination of the sun, Aries, the *visible* planets (eliminating those that can be seen in the daytime only), and the moon. Each page also has separate columns for moonrise and for the moon's parallax (to be explained later), as well as the semidiameter (S.D.) of sun and moon for that day. Instead of the table of increments and corrections we used in the *Nautical Almanac,* there is given a simple interpolation table for the 10-minute intervals inside the front cover (Fig. 17–6). Here also is found the list of fifty-seven navigation stars with their SHA and declination. Other tables will be explained as we need to use them. The following examples will demonstrate the use of this almanac.

Example • *Sun*—We require the GHA and declination of the sun for January 1 at 13-20-33. (Note that this is the same example we used with the *Nautical Almanac.*)

GHA for 1320 (Fig. 17–5)	19° 07.0′
GHA for 33ˢ (Fig. 17–6)	0° 08′
Total GHA	19° 15′

(vs. 19° 15.2′ with *Nautical Almanac*)

Declination is S 23° 00.7′

(same as *Nautical Almanac*)

GREENWICH A. M. JANUARY 1 (THURSDAY)

GMT	☉ SUN GHA	SUN Dec.	ARIES GHA ♈	MARS 1.0 GHA	MARS Dec.	JUPITER −1.5 GHA	JUPITER Dec.	SATURN 0.5 GHA	SATURN Dec.	◑ MOON GHA	MOON Dec.
h m	° ′	° ′	° ′	° ′	° ′	° ′	° ′	° ′	° ′	° ′	° ′
00 00	179 10.9	S23 03.4	100 13.8	116 18	S 7 43	249 40	S11 09	69 28	N 9 49	271 18	S 6 22
10	181 40.9	03.4	102 44.2	118 48		252 11		71 58		273 44	24
20	184 10.8	03.3	105 14.7	121 18		254 41		74 29		276 10	26
30	186 40.8	· 03.3	107 45.1	123 48	· ·	257 11	· ·	76 59	· ·	278 36	· 29
40	189 10.7	03.3	110 15.5	126 18		259 42		79 29		281 01	31
50	191 40.7	03.2	112 45.9	128 48		262 12		82 00		283 27	34
01 00	194 10.6	S23 03.2	115 16.3	131 19	S 7 42	264 42	S11 09	84 30	N 9 49	285 53	S 6 36
10	196 40.6	03.2	117 46.7	133 49		267 13		87 01		288 19	39
20	199 10.5	03.1	120 17.1	136 19		269 43		89 31		290 44	41
30	201 40.5	· 03.1	122 47.5	138 49	· ·	272 13	· ·	92 01	· ·	293 10	· 44
40	204 10.4	03.1	125 17.9	141 19		274 44		94 32		295 36	46
50	206 40.4	03.0	127 48.4	143 49		277 14		97 02		298 02	48
02 00	209 10.3	S23 03.0	130 18.8	146 19	S 7 41	279 45	S11 09	99 33	N 9 49	300 27	S 6 51
10	211 40.3	03.0	132 49.2	148 49		282 15		102 03		302 53	53
20	214 10.2	03.0	135 19.6	151 20		284 45		104 34		305 19	56
30	216 40.2	· 02.9	137 50.0	153 50	· ·	287 16	· ·	107 04	· ·	307 44	6 58
40	219 10.1	02.9	140 20.4	156 20		289 46		109 34		310 10	7 01
50	221 40.1	02.9	142 50.8	158 50		292 16		112 05		312 36	03
03 00	224 10.0	S23 02.8	145 21.2	161 20	S 7 41	294 47	S11 09	114 35	N 9 49	315 02	S 7 05
10	226 40.0	02.8	147 51.6	163 50		297 17		117 06		317 27	08
20	229 09.9	02.8	150 22.0	166 20		299 47		119 36		319 53	10
30	231 39.9	· 02.7	152 52.5	168 50	· ·	302 18	· ·	122 06	· ·	322 19	· 13
40	234 09.8	02.7	155 22.9	171 21		304 48		124 37		324 44	15
50	236 39.8	02.7	157 53.3	173 51		307 18		127 07		327 10	18
04 00	239 09.7	S23 02.6	160 23.7	176 21	S 7 40	309 49	S11 09	129 38	N 9 49	329 36	S 7 20
10	241 39.7	02.6	162 54.1	178 51		312 19		132 08		332 01	22
20	244 09.6	02.6	165 24.5	181 21		314 49		134 39		334 27	25
30	246 39.6	· 02.5	167 54.9	183 51	· ·	317 20	· ·	137 09	· ·	336 53	· 27
40	249 09.5	02.5	170 25.3	186 21		319 50		139 39		339 19	30
50	251 39.5	02.5	172 55.7	188 51		322 21		142 10		341 44	32
05 00	254 09.5	S23 02.4	175 26.2	191 22	S 7 39	324 51	S11 09	144 40	N 9 49	344 10	S 7 35
10	256 39.4	02.4	177 56.6	193 52		327 21		147 11		346 36	37
20	259 09.4	02.4	180 27.0	196 22		329 52		149 41		349 01	39
30	261 39.3	· 02.3	182 57.4	198 52	· ·	332 22	· ·	152 11	· ·	351 27	· 42
40	264 09.3	02.3	185 27.8	201 22		334 52		154 42		353 53	44
50	266 39.2	02.3	187 58.2	203 52		337 23		157 12		356 18	47
06 00	269 09.2	S23 02.2	190 28.6	206 22	S 7 38	339 53	S11 10	159 43	N 9 49	358 44	S 7 49
10	271 39.1	02.2	192 59.0	208 52		342 23		162 13		1 10	52
20	274 09.1	02.2	195 29.4	211 23		344 54		164 43		3 35	54
30	276 39.0	· 02.1	197 59.9	213 53	· ·	347 24	· ·	167 14	· ·	6 01	· 56
40	279 09.0	02.1	200 30.3	216 23		349 54		169 44		8 27	7 59
50	281 38.9	02.1	203 00.7	218 53		352 25		172 15		10 52	8 01
07 00	284 08.9	S23 02.0	205 31.1	221 23	S 7 38	354 55	S11 10	174 45	N 9 49	13 18	S 8 04
10	286 38.8	02.0	208 01.5	223 53		357 25		177 16		15 44	06
20	289 08.8	02.0	210 31.9	226 23		359 56		179 46		18 09	09
30	291 38.7	· 01.9	213 02.3	228 53	· ·	2 26	· ·	182 16	· ·	20 35	· 11
40	294 08.7	01.9	215 32.7	231 24		4 57		184 47		23 01	13
50	296 38.6	01.9	218 03.1	233 54		7 27		187 17		25 26	16
08 00	299 08.6	S23 01.8	220 33.5	236 24	S 7 37	9 57	S11 10	189 48	N 9 49	27 52	S 8 18
10	301 38.5	01.8	223 04.0	238 54		12 28		192 18		30 18	21
20	304 08.5	01.8	225 34.4	241 24		14 58		194 48		32 43	23
30	306 38.4	· 01.7	228 04.8	243 54	· ·	17 28	· ·	197 19	· ·	35 09	· 25
40	309 08.4	01.7	230 35.2	246 24		19 59		199 49		37 35	28
50	311 38.3	01.7	233 05.6	248 54		22 29		202 20		40 00	30
09 00	314 08.3	S23 01.6	235 36.0	251 25	S 7 36	24 59	S11 10	204 50	N 9 49	42 26	S 8 33
10	316 38.2	01.6	238 06.4	253 55		27 30		207 21		44 52	35
20	319 08.2	01.6	240 36.8	256 25		30 00		209 51		47 17	38
30	321 38.1	· 01.5	243 07.2	258 55	· ·	32 30	· ·	212 21	· ·	49 43	· 40
40	324 08.1	01.5	245 37.7	261 25		35 01		214 52		52 09	42
50	326 38.0	01.5	248 08.1	263 55		37 31		217 22		54 34	45
10 00	329 08.0	S23 01.4	250 38.5	266 25	S 7 35	40 02	S11 10	219 53	N 9 49	57 00	S 8 47
10	331 37.9	01.4	253 08.9	268 55		42 32		222 23		59 25	50
20	334 07.9	01.4	255 39.3	271 26		45 02		224 53		61 51	52
30	336 37.8	· 01.3	258 09.7	273 56	· ·	47 33	· ·	227 24	· ·	64 17	· 54
40	339 07.8	01.3	260 40.1	276 26		50 03		229 54		66 42	57
50	341 37.7	01.3	263 10.5	278 56		52 33		232 25		69 08	8 59
11 00	344 07.7	S23 01.2	265 40.9	281 26	S 7 35	55 04	S11 10	234 55	N 9 49	71 34	S 9 02
10	346 37.6	01.2	268 11.4	283 56		57 34		237 25		73 59	04
20	349 07.6	01.2	270 41.8	286 26		60 04		239 56		76 25	07
30	351 37.5	· 01.1	273 12.2	288 56	· ·	62 35	· ·	242 26	· ·	78 50	· 09
40	354 07.5	01.1	275 42.6	291 27		65 05		244 57		81 16	11
50	356 37.4	01.1	278 13.0	293 57		67 35		247 27		83 42	14

Lat.	Moonrise	Diff.
N		
°	h m	m
72	01 23	67
70	01 13	61
68	01 04	56
66	00 58	52
64	00 52	49
62	00 47	47
60	00 43	44
58	00 39	43
56	00 35	41
54	00 32	39
52	00 30	38
50	00 27	37
45	00 22	34
40	00 18	32
35	00 14	30
30	00 10	29
20	00 05	26
10	00 00	24
0	24 39	23
10	24 30	21
20	24 20	18
30	24 09	16
35	24 03	14
40	23 56	12
45	23 48	10
50	23 38	08
52	23 34	06
54	23 29	05
56	23 24	04
58	23 18	02
60	23 11	00
S		

Moon's P. in A.

° Alt.	′ + Corr.	° Alt.	′ + Corr.
0		55	
	56		31
8		57	
	55		30
13		58	
	54		29
17		59	
	53		28
20		60	
	52		27
23		61	
	51		26
25		62	
	50		25
28		64	
	49		24
30		65	
	48		23
32		66	
	47		22
34		67	
	46		21
35		68	
	45		20
37		69	
	44		19
39		70	
	43		18
40		71	
	42		17
42		72	
	41		16
43		73	
	40		15
45		75	
	39		14
46		76	
	38		13
48		77	
	37		12
49		78	
	36		11
50		79	
	35		10
52		80	
	34		
53			
	33		
54			
	32		
55			
	31		
57			

Sun SD 16.3′
Moon SD 15′
Age 23d

FIG. 17-4 Excerpt from Air Almanac

GREENWICH P. M. JANUARY 1 (THURSDAY)

GMT h m	☉ SUN GHA ° ′	SUN Dec. ° ′	ARIES GHA ♈ ° ′	MARS 1.0 GHA ° ′	MARS Dec ° ′	JUPITER –1.5 GHA ° ′	JUPITER Dec. ° ′	SATURN 0.5 GHA ° ′	SATURN Dec. ° ′	◑ MOON GHA ° ′	MOON Dec. ° ′
12 00	359 07.4	S23 01.0	280 43.4	296 27	S 7 34	70 06	S11 10	249 58	N 9 49	86 07	S 9 16
10	1 37.3	01.0	283 13.8	298 57		72 36		252 28		88 33	19
20	4 07.3	01.0	285 44.2	301 27		75 07		254 58		90 58	21
30	6 37.2	· 00.9	288 14.6	303 57	· ·	77 37	· ·	257 29	· ·	93 24	· 23
40	9 07.2	00.9	290 45.0	306 27		80 07		259 59		95 50	26
50	11 37.1	00.8	293 15.5	308 57		82 38		262 30		98 15	28
13 00	14 07.1	S23 00.8	295 45.9	311 28	S 7 33	85 08	S11 10	265 00	N 9 49	100 41	S 9 31
10	16 37.0	00.8	298 16.3	313 58		87 38		267 30		103 06	33
20	19 07.0	00.7	300 46.7	316 28		90 09		270 01		105 32	35
30	21 36.9	· 00.7	303 17.1	318 58	· ·	92 39	· ·	272 31	· ·	107 58	· 38
40	24 06.9	00.7	305 47.5	321 28		95 09		275 02		110 23	40
50	26 36.8	00.6	308 17.9	323 58		97 40		277 32		112 49	43
14 00	29 06.8	S23 00.6	310 48.3	326 28	S 7 32	100 10	S11 10	280 03	N 9 49	115 14	S 9 45
10	31 36.7	00.6	313 18.7	328 58		102 40		282 33		117 40	47
20	34 06.7	00.5	315 49.2	331 29		105 11		285 03		120 06	50
30	36 36.6	· 00.5	318 19.6	333 59	· ·	107 41	· ·	287 34	· ·	122 31	· 52
40	39 06.6	00.5	320 50.0	336 29		110 12		290 04		124 57	55
50	41 36.5	00.4	323 20.4	338 59		112 42		292 35		127 22	57
15 00	44 06.5	S23 00.4	325 50.8	341 29	S 7 32	115 12	S11 11	295 05	N 9 49	129 48	S 9 59
10	46 36.4	00.4	328 21.2	343 59		117 43		297 35		132 13	10 02
20	49 06.4	00.3	330 51.6	346 29		120 13		300 06		134 39	04
30	51 36.3	· 00.3	333 22.0	348 59	· ·	122 43	· ·	302 36	· ·	137 05	· 07
40	54 06.3	00.3	335 52.4	351 30		125 14		305 07		139 30	09
50	56 36.2	00.2	338 22.8	354 00		127 44		307 37		141 56	11
16 00	59 06.2	S23 00.2	340 53.3	356 30	S 7 31	130 14	S11 11	310 07	N 9 49	144 21	S10 14
10	61 36.1	00.2	343 23.7	359 00		132 45		312 38		146 47	16
20	64 06.1	00.1	345 54.1	1 30		135 15		315 08		149 12	19
30	66 36.0	· 00.1	348 24.5	4 00	· ·	137 45	· ·	317 39	· ·	151 38	· 21
40	69 06.0	00.1	350 54.9	6 30		140 16		320 09		154 03	23
50	71 35.9	00.0	353 25.3	9 00		142 46		322 39		156 29	26
17 00	74 05.9	S23 00.0	355 55.7	11 31	S 7 30	145 17	S11 11	325 10	N 9 50	158 55	S10 28
10	76 35.9	23 00.0	358 26.1	14 01		147 47		327 40		161 20	31
20	79 05.8	22 59.9	0 56.5	16 31		150 17		330 11		163 46	33
30	81 35.8	· 59.9	3 27.0	19 01	· ·	152 48	· ·	332 41	· ·	166 11	· 35
40	84 05.7	59.9	5 57.4	21 31		155 18		335 12		168 37	38
50	86 35.7	59.8	8 27.8	24 01		157 48		337 42		171 02	40
18 00	89 05.6	S22 59.8	10 58.2	26 31	S 7 29	160 19	S11 11	340 12	N 9 50	173 28	S10 42
10	91 35.6	59.7	13 28.6	29 01		162 49		342 43		175 53	45
20	94 05.5	59.7	15 59.0	31 32		165 19		345 13		178 19	47
30	96 35.5	· 59.7	18 29.4	34 02	· ·	167 50	· ·	347 44	· ·	180 44	· 50
40	99 05.4	59.6	20 59.8	36 32		170 20		350 14		183 10	52
50	101 35.4	59.6	23 30.2	39 02		172 50		352 44		185 35	54
19 00	104 05.3	S22 59.6	26 00.7	41 32	S 7 29	175 21	S11 11	355 15	N 9 50	188 01	S10 57
10	106 35.3	59.5	28 31.1	44 02		177 51		357 45		190 26	10 59
20	109 05.2	59.5	31 01.5	46 32		180 22		0 16		192 52	11 02
30	111 35.2	· 59.5	33 31.9	49 02	· ·	182 52	· ·	2 46	· ·	195 17	· 04
40	114 05.1	59.4	36 02.3	51 32		185 22		5 17		197 43	06
50	116 35.1	59.4	38 32.7	54 03		187 53		7 47		200 08	09
20 00	119 05.0	S22 59.4	41 03.1	56 33	S 7 28	190 23	S11 11	10 17	N 9 50	202 34	S11 11
10	121 35.0	59.3	43 33.5	59 03		192 53		12 48		204 59	13
20	124 04.9	59.3	46 03.9	61 33		195 24		15 18		207 25	16
30	126 34.9	· 59.3	48 34.3	64 03	· ·	197 54	· ·	17 49	· ·	209 50	· 18
40	129 04.8	59.2	51 04.8	66 33		200 24		20 19		212 16	21
50	131 34.8	59.2	53 35.2	69 03		202 55		22 49		214 41	23
21 00	134 04.7	S22 59.2	56 05.6	71 34	S 7 27	205 25	S11 11	25 20	N 9 50	217 07	S11 25
10	136 34.7	59.1	58 36.0	74 04		207 55		27 50		219 32	28
20	139 04.6	59.1	61 06.4	76 34		210 26		30 21		221 58	30
30	141 34.6	· 59.0	63 36.8	79 04	· ·	212 56	· ·	32 51	· ·	224 23	· 32
40	144 04.5	59.0	66 07.2	81 34		215 26		35 21		226 49	35
50	146 34.5	59.0	68 37.6	84 04		217 57		37 52		229 14	37
22 00	149 04.4	S22 58.9	71 08.0	86 34	S 7 26	220 27	S11 11	40 22	N 9 50	231 40	S11 39
10	151 34.4	58.9	73 38.5	89 04		222 58		42 53		234 05	42
20	154 04.3	58.9	76 08.9	91 34		225 28		45 23		236 31	44
30	156 34.3	· 58.8	78 39.3	94 05	· ·	227 58	· ·	47 54	· ·	238 56	· 47
40	159 04.2	58.8	81 09.7	96 35		230 29		50 24		241 22	49
50	161 34.2	58.8	83 40.1	99 05		232 59		52 54		243 47	51
23 00	164 04.1	S22 58.7	86 10.5	101 35	S 7 26	235 29	S11 11	55 25	N 9 50	246 13	S11 54
10	166 34.1	58.7	88 40.9	104 05		238 00		57 55		248 38	56
20	169 04.0	58.7	91 11.3	106 35		240 30		60 26		251 03	11 58
30	171 34.0	· 58.6	93 41.7	109 05	· ·	243 00	· ·	62 56	· ·	253 29	12 01
40	174 03.9	58.6	96 12.2	111 35		245 31		65 26		255 54	03
50	176 33.9	58.6	98 42.6	114 06		248 01		67 57		258 20	05

Lat. °	Moon-set h m	Diff. m
N		
72	10 16	–22
70	10 30	–16
68	10 40	–11
66	10 49	–08
64	10 57	–05
62	11 03	–03
60	11 09	–01
58	11 14	+01
56	11 19	03
54	11 23	04
52	11 26	06
50	11 30	07
45	11 37	09
40	11 43	11
35	11 49	13
30	11 53	15
20	12 01	17
10	12 09	20
0	12 16	22
10	12 22	24
20	12 30	27
30	12 38	29
35	12 43	31
40	12 48	33
45	12 55	35
50	13 03	38
52	13 06	39
54	13 10	40
56	13 15	42
58	13 20	44
60	13 25	46
S		

Moon's P. in A.

Alt. °	Corr. + ′	Alt. °	Corr. + ′
0		54	
	57		32
2		56	
	56		31
11		57	
	55		30
15		58	
	54		29
18		59	
	53		28
21		60	
	52		27
24		62	
	51		26
26		63	
	50		25
28		64	
	49		24
30		65	
	48		23
32		66	
	47		22
34		67	
	46		21
36		68	
	45		20
38		69	
	44		19
39		70	
	43		18
41		71	
	42		17
42		73	
	41		16
44		74	
	40		15
45		75	
	39		14
47		76	
	38		13
48		77	
	37		12
49		78	
	36		11
51		79	
	35		10
52		80	
	34		
53			
	33		
54			
	32		
56			

Sun SD 16.3′
Moon SD 15′
Age 23d

FIG. 17-5 Excerpt from Air Almanac

STARS, JAN.—APR.

No.	Name	Mag.	S.H.A.	Dec.
			° ′	° ′
7*	*Acamar*	3·1	315 43	S.40 26
5*	*Achernar*	0·6	335 51	S.57 23
30*	*Acrux*	1·1	173 46	S.62 56
19	*Adhara* †	1·6	255 38	S.28 56
10*	*Aldebaran* †	1·1	291 27	N.16 27
32*	*Alioth*	1·7	166 49	N.56 07
34*	*Alkaid*	1·9	153 24	N.49 27
55	*Al Na'ir*	2·2	28 25	S.47 06
15	*Alnilam* †	1·8	276 19	S. 1 13
25*	*Alphard* †	2·2	218 28	S. 8 32
41*	*Alphecca* †	2·3	126 38	N.26 49
1*	*Alpheratz* †	2·2	358 18	N.28 56
51*	*Altair* †	0·9	62 40	N. 8 47
2	*Ankaa*	2·4	353 48	S.42 28
42*	*Antares* †	1·2	113 06	S.26 22
37*	*Arcturus* †	0·2	146 25	N.19 20
43	*Atria*	1·9	108 38	S.68 58
22	*Avior*	1·7	234 31	S.59 25
13	*Bellatrix* †	1·7	279 07	N. 6 19
16*	*Betelgeuse* †	0·1–1·2	271 36	N. 7 24
17*	*Canopus*	−0·9	264 10	S.52 41
12*	*Capella*	0·2	281 23	N.45 58
53*	*Deneb*	1·3	49 54	N.45 10
28*	*Denebola* †	2·2	183 07	N.14 44
4*	*Diphda* †	2·2	349 29	S.18 09
27*	*Dubhe*	2·0	194 31	N.61 55
14	*Elnath* †	1·8	278 54	N.28 35
47	*Eltanin*	2·4	91 01	N.51 29
54*	*Enif* †	2·5	34 19	N. 9 44
56*	*Fomalhaut* †	1·3	16 00	S.29 47
31	*Gacrux*	1·6	172 37	S.56 57
29*	*Gienah* †	2·8	176 26	S.17 23
35	*Hadar*	0·9	149 34	S.60 14
6*	*Hamal* †	2·2	328 38	N.23 19
48	*Kaus Aust.*	2·0	84 27	S.34 24
40*	*Kochab*	2·2	137 18	N.74 16
57	*Markab* †	2·6	14 11	N.15 03
8*	*Menkar* †	2·8	314 49	N. 3 58
36	*Menkent*	2·3	148 46	S.36 14
24*	*Miaplacidus*	1·8	221 46	S.69 36
9*	*Mirfak*	1·9	309 27	N.49 46
50*	*Nunki* †	2·1	76 39	S.26 20
52*	*Peacock*	2·1	54 11	S.56 50
21*	*Pollux* †	1·2	244 07	N.28 06
20*	*Procyon* †	0·5	245 34	N. 5 18
46*	*Rasalhague* †	2·1	96 37	N.12 35
26*	*Regulus* †	1·3	208 18	N.12 07
11*	*Rigel* †	0·3	281 43	S. 8 14
38*	*Rigil Kent.*	0·1	140 36	S.60 43
44	*Sabik* †	2·6	102 50	S.15 42
3*	*Schedar*	2·5	350 18	N.56 23
45*	*Shaula*	1·7	97 06	S.37 05
18*	*Sirius* †	−1·6	259 02	S.16 40
33*	*Spica* †	1·2	159 05	S.11 01
23*	*Suhail*	2·2	223 16	S.43 19
49*	*Vega*	0·1	81 01	N.38 45
39	*Zuben'ubi* †	2·9	137 41	S.15 55

INTERPOLATION OF G.H.A. F3

Increment to be added for intervals of G.M.T. to G.H.A. of: Sun, Aries (♈) and planets; Moon

SUN, etc.		MOON	SUN, etc.		MOON	SUN, etc.		MOON
m s		m s	m s		m s	m s		m s
00 00	° ′	00 00	03 17	° ′	03 25	06 37	° ′	06 52
01	0 00	00 02	21	0 50	03 29	41	1 40	06 56
05	0 01	00 06	25	0 51	03 33	45	1 41	07 00
09	0 02	00 10	29	0 52	03 37	49	1 42	07 04
13	0 03	00 14	33	0 53	03 41	53	1 43	07 08
17	0 04	00 18	37	0 54	03 45	06 57	1 44	07 13
21	0 05	00 22	41	0 55	03 49	07 01	1 45	07 17
25	0 06	00 26	45	0 56	03 54	05	1 46	07 21
29	0 07	00 31	49	0 57	03 58	09	1 47	07 25
33	0 08	00 35	53	0 58	04 02	13	1 48	07 29
37	0 09	00 39	03 57	0 59	04 06	17	1 49	07 33
41	0 10	00 43	04 01	1 00	04 10	21	1 50	07 37
45	0 11	00 47	05	1 01	04 14	25	1 51	07 42
49	0 12	00 51	09	1 02	04 19	29	1 52	07 46
53	0 13	00 55	13	1 03	04 23	33	1 53	07 50
00 57	0 14	01 00	17	1 04	04 27	37	1 54	07 54
01 01	0 15	01 04	21	1 05	04 31	41	1 55	07 58
05	0 16	01 08	25	1 06	04 35	45	1 56	08 02
09	0 17	01 12	29	1 07	04 39	49	1 57	08 06
13	0 18	01 16	33	1 08	04 43	53	1 58	08 11
17	0 19	01 20	37	1 09	04 48	07 57	1 59	08 15
21	0 20	01 24	41	1 10	04 52	08 01	2 00	08 19
25	0 21	01 29	45	1 11	04 56	05	2 01	08 23
29	0 22	01 33	49	1 12	05 00	09	2 02	08 27
33	0 23	01 37	53	1 13	05 04	13	2 03	08 31
37	0 24	01 41	04 57	1 14	05 08	17	2 04	08 35
41	0 25	01 45	05 01	1 15	05 12	21	2 05	08 40
45	0 26	01 49	05	1 16	05 17	25	2 06	08 44
49	0 27	01 53	09	1 17	05 21	29	2 07	08 48
53	0 28	01 58	13	1 18	05 25	33	2 08	08 52
01 57	0 29	02 02	17	1 19	05 29	37	2 09	08 56
02 01	0 30	02 06	21	1 20	05 33	41	2 10	09 00
05	0 31	02 10	25	1 21	05 37	45	2 11	09 04
09	0 32	02 14	29	1 22	05 41	49	2 12	09 09
13	0 33	02 18	33	1 23	05 46	53	2 13	09 13
17	0 34	02 22	37	1 24	05 50	08 57	2 14	09 17
21	0 35	02 27	41	1 25	05 54	09 01	2 15	09 21
25	0 36	02 31	45	1 26	05 58	05	2 16	09 25
29	0 37	02 35	49	1 27	06 02	09	2 17	09 29
33	0 38	02 39	53	1 28	06 06	13	2 18	09 33
37	0 39	02 43	05 57	1 29	06 10	17	2 19	09 38
41	0 40	02 47	06 01	1 30	06 15	21	2 20	09 42
45	0 41	02 51	05	1 31	06 19	25	2 21	09 46
49	0 42	02 56	09	1 32	06 23	29	2 22	09 50
53	0 43	03 00	13	1 33	06 27	33	2 23	09 54
02 57	0 44	03 04	17	1 34	06 31	37	2 24	09 58
03 01	0 45	03 08	21	1 35	06 35	41	2 25	10 00
05	0 46	03 12	25	1 36	06 39	45	2 26	
09	0 47	03 16	29	1 37	06 44	49	2 27	
13	0 48	03 20	33	1 38	06 48	53	2 28	
17	0 49	03 25	37	1 39	06 52	09 57	2 29	
03 21	0 50	03 29	06 41	1 40	06 56	10 00	2 30	

* Stars used in H.O. 249 (A.P. 3270) Vol. 1.

† Stars that may be used with Vols. 2 and 3.

FIG. 17-6 Excerpt from Air Almanac

Note that Fig. 17–6 is called a *Critical Table.* The time varies by 4-second steps, and we select the 4-second span that contains our exact time and use the indicated increment of GHA. When, as in this case, our time is indicated precisely (33^s), we always take the *upper* figure from the table—in this case, 0°08′ instead of 0°09′. *The same column is used for the sun, Aries, and the Planets. A separate column is provided for the moon.*

Example • *Star*—We require the GHA and declination of the star Canopus on January 1 at 10-21-23.

GHA of Aries at 1020	255° 39′	(Round off to nearest minute)
GHA of Aries for 1^m23^s	0° 21′	
Total GHA of Aries	256° 00′	
SHA of Canopus	264° 10′	
GHA of Canopus	520° 10′	
Minus	360°	
GHA	160° 10′	Dec. S 52°41′
(vs. 160°10.2′ with *Nautical Almanac*)		(vs. S 52°40.6′)

As you work with the *Air Almanac* you come to realize that there would rarely be a difference of as much as 1 minute—and since this is 1 mile on the surface of the ocean, the accuracy of the *Air Almanac* is perfectly adequate for ordinary marine navigation. We shall explain the full use of both almanacs in this book, but as stated in the Introduction, my personal preference is to use the *Air Almanac* in conjunction with the N.O. 249 navigation tables, which we shall discuss later.

Practice Problems • Using the *Nautical Almanac* excerpts in this chapter, find the Greenwich Hour Angle (GHA) and declination in the following observations:

1. Sun, January 1, 18-21-17 GMT
2. Moon, January 1, 04-20-47 GMT
3. Jupiter, January 1, 23-21-53 GMT
4. Capella, January 1, 11-20-40 GMT

(Remember to use the v and d corrections where applicable.)

Determine GHA and declination for the same observations, using the *Air Almanac* excerpts in chapter.

Chapter 18

The Sextant

The *sextant* is a precision instrument for measuring the vertical angle between a celestial body and the horizon directly below it. This angle, as read on the sextant, is called the *sextant altitude,* the symbol for which is H_s. To this reading we apply several corrections to obtain a final theoretically correct angle called the *observed altitude,* symbol H_o.

Construction The sextant itself consists basically of a triangular frame, to which is attached a handle for holding it in the right hand. The curved part of the frame is a graduated arc, called the *limb,* which is divided into whole degrees from 0° to 126°, with six degree marks below 0°. The geometric center of this arc is the center of the pivot at the apex of the frame.

An *index arm,* which pivots about the center of the arc, is mounted on the frame so that the lower assembly of the arm slides along the limb, guided by rollers in a groove of the limb. In the opening at the lower center of this arm,

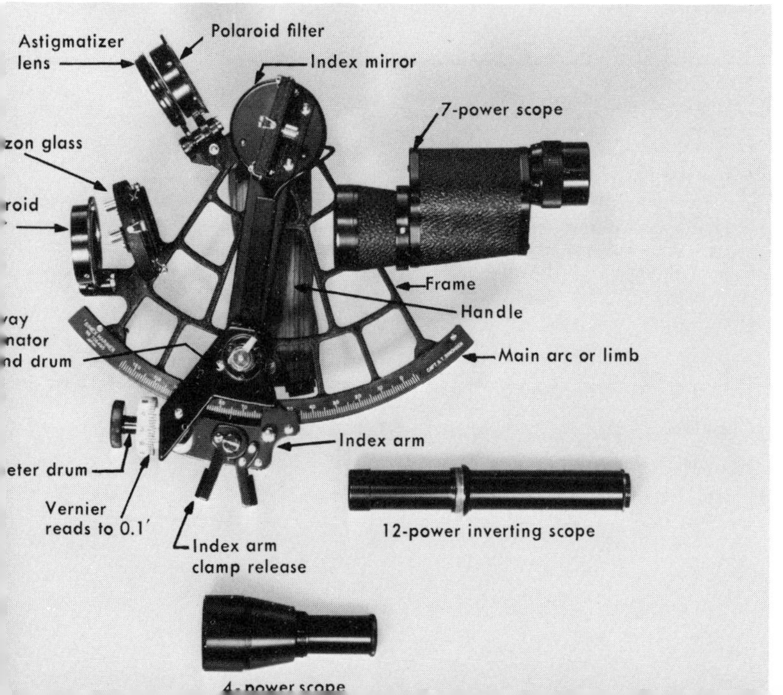

FIG. 18-1
Modern micrometer sextant

(COURTESY COAST NAVIGATION SCHOOL)

opposite the degree marks on the limb, is an *index mark* that is used for reading the whole degrees on the limb. Mounted on the lower end of the arm is a device, called the *micrometer drum,* for reading minutes and fractions of minutes. This drum reads exactly 60 minutes on the circumference, and one full turn of the drum moves the index arm 1° along the limb.

On some sextants there is a single index mark opposite the drum for reading minutes. We usually estimate the reading to the nearest tenth of a minute (0.1′), which is more than close enough.

Other models have a small *vernier scale* opposite the drum for reading fractions of minutes. The lower *whole* minute is read opposite the zero mark on the vernier. To find what additional fraction of a minute to read, look along the division marks on the vernier until you find a mark that lines up with a minute mark on the drum. The additional fraction of a minute is determined by the division of the vernier scale.

The vernier scale is equal to one full minute. If your vernier is divided into six parts, then each part is equal to ⅙ minute, or 10 seconds. If your vernier has ten divisions, then each division is equal to 0.1′. You count the divisions on the vernier scale to the point where the marks on the scale and the drum coincide, and thus determine the correct fraction of a minute. It is best to work with tenths of minutes, rather than with seconds. *If you prefer* (and many do) *not to use the vernier, just read the drum opposite the zero mark on the vernier and estimate to the nearest tenth of a minute.*

FIG. 18-2
Vernier reading to 0.1 minute of arc

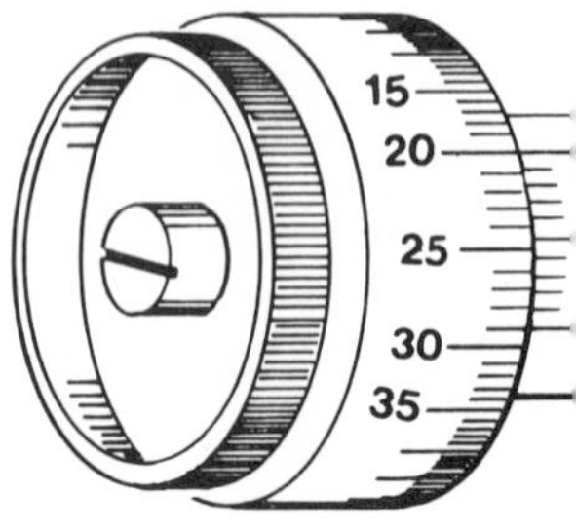

On the upper part of the index arm, perpendicular to the plane of the frame, is a rectangular *index mirror* that is permanently fastened to the arm and moves with the arm.

Vernier reading to 10 seconds of arc

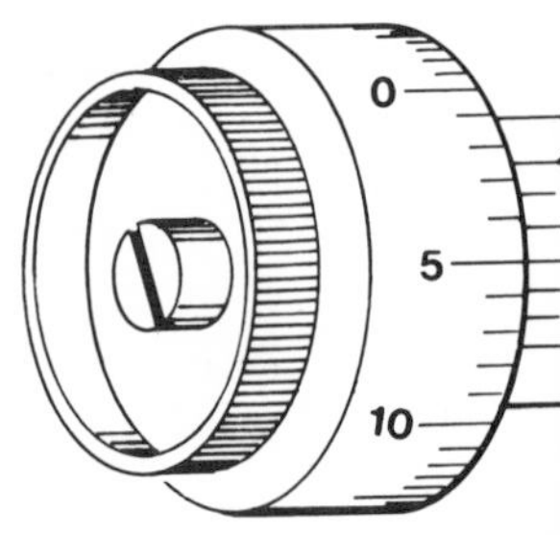

Mounted solidly on the forward part of the frame is a *horizon glass,* which is often circular. The right-hand part of this horizon glass is a silvered mirror, and the left-hand part is clear glass. On some models, the horizon glass is rectangular and consists of the mirror part only, the clear glass part having been left off as unnecessary. The horizon glass is also perpendicular to the plane of the frame. When you buy a sextant, insist on aluminized mirrors (rather than silvered mirrors), for they will not corrode.

On the after side of the frame, the *telescope* is held by a special bracket. The telescope is adjusted by turning the knurled eyepiece to obtain the clearest image. Sextant telescopes are usually 2.5×, 3×, 4×, 6×, or 7× power, and some sextants come with several scopes.

Mounted in front of both the index mirror and the horizon glass are devices for providing eye protection against the sun. On older sextants, there is a choice of shade glasses of varying darkness. You begin with the darkest glass, and if it is too dark, choose a lighter one. On newer instruments, the protection is a Polaroid filter, adjusted by turning the knurled ring. Again, you begin with the darkest setting and adjust to suit your own eyesight.

Mounted on the index arm is a small electric light for reading the degrees and minutes. It is operated by a button on the handle (the batteries are inside the handle). This eliminates having to handle a flashlight when taking sights at dusk or dawn. Always make sure the contacts are kept bright and clean, or the light may not work.

On some sextants there will be mounted, in front of the index mirror and on the same axle that holds the Polaroid filter or the shade glasses, a special clear lens called an *astigmatizer,* which transforms the image of the star into a streak of light and that of the sun or moon into a bar of light of the same diameter. When an astigmatizer is used, the streak of light is lined up with the edge of the sea horizon when the sight is taken. With this device it is not necessary to "roll" the sextant (as described later) to determine whether the star has been brought to the point on the horizon exactly below the star. Only when you are exactly below the star will the streak of light be parallel to the horizon.

At the moment we take a sight, the light from the celestial body is picked up in the index mirror, reflected to the horizon mirror, and then reflected through the telescope to the eye. Through the clear part of the horizon glass the navigator sees the actual sea horizon. The index arm is adjusted so that the image of the body, as seen in the horizon mirror, is exactly tangent to the horizon. The sextant angle H_s is then read on the limb in whole degrees opposite the index mark, and the minutes are read on the micrometer drum.

How to Use a Sextant Each person develops his own sextant techniques, but the following is probably the best method to follow.

Set the index arm to zero degrees (0°). Hold the sextant firmly in the right hand. Look at the horizon through the telescope and adjust the scope until the clearest focus is found. If the observation is to be on the sun, place a suitable shade glass in front of both mirrors. Experience will show the best shade to use in each case so that the outline of the sun will be clear and sharp without blinding the eye.

Now, through the sextant, look straight at the sun itself. You will see the actual sun through the clear part of the horizon glass, and alongside you will see the *image* of the sun in the horizon mirror, to the right of the actual sun. Move the index arm forward a slight amount. The actual sun remains stationary, but the image moves downward in the mirror. *Keeping the image in view in the mirror, holding the index arm stationary, tilt the SEXTANT forward.* The actual sun moves upward and out of sight. Move the sextant forward with a smooth, even motion, still keeping the image of the sun in the mirror, until you see the sea horizon through the clear part of the horizon glass. Adjust the index arm so that the lower edge of the sun touches the horizon. Rock the arc as you do so. Adjust the arm so that the sun just touches the horizon at the bottom of the swing. This insures the sextant being held vertically at the time of perfect adjustment. At the precise moment when you feel the adjustment to be perfect, mark the time and read the sextant angle H_s.

Always read the time first, then the angle. Write down the seconds, minutes, and hour of the sight, then read on the sextant the whole degrees, the minutes, and last of all the tenths of minutes.

When we observe the sun, we usually bring the lower edge in contact with the horizon. This is called a *lower-limb sight.* On rare occasions it may be advantageous to read the sun's upper limb, or edge. When you observe the moon, your sight may be either upper or lower limb, depending on the tilt of the moon. You must have a fully formed part of the circumference in contact with the horizon. With stars or planets, the image is a pinpoint of light that is simply brought down to the horizon. (See

Fig. 18–3.) You can learn to use a sextant in a few minutes of practice, and further practice will soon make it easy to bring the body down to the horizon in a smooth, even movement. Then gently roll the sextant from side to side a few times until your adjustment is perfect. Don't hesitate too long on this. Make up your mind and read the sextant. If you hold it too long, trying to get a better alignment, your arm becomes tired and your eye begins to water, and then you have trouble doing it at all. After all, as you will see later, we take more than one sight, and slight errors will average out in the end.

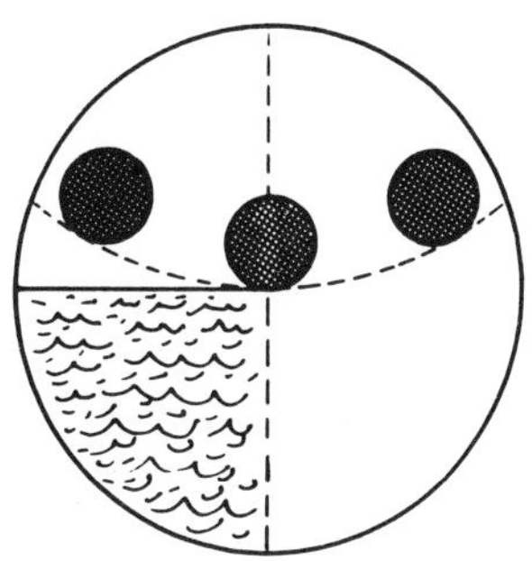

FIG. 18-3
Appearance of celestial bodies in horizon mirror: (A) Sun lower limb;

In the beginning, if you are not near water, simply bring the body down to the nearest housetop for practice. Later on we shall discuss the artificial horizon, which we use when not near the ocean.

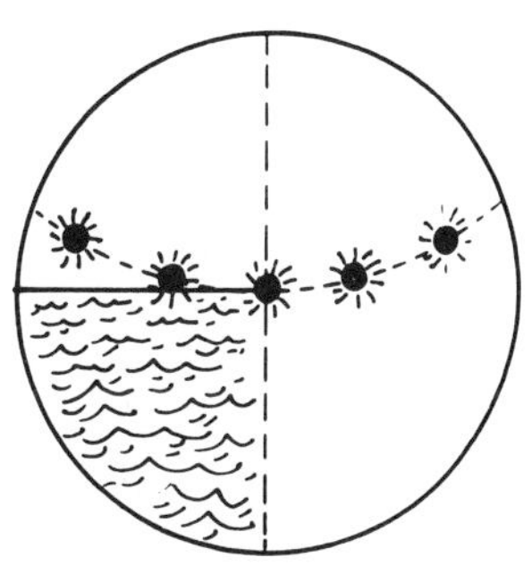

(B) Star or planet;

Sextant Errors The angle as read on the sextant, H_s, may contain errors due to inaccuracies in the instrument itself. These may be *constant errors* or *errors of adjustment.*

Constant errors are due to imperfect manufacture. They are usually negligible and can be ignored, but they are always indicated on the certificate mounted in the sextant box. They vary with altitude setting on the limb. Don't worry about it unless the error is large. In any case, it cannot be removed but, if large, can be allowed for. If less than 30″, ignore it for everyday work. Errors of adjustment are caused when the mirrors are out of adjustment, usually because they are not perpendicular to the plane of the frame, or not parallel when the sextant reads zero. They can be adjusted by small set screws, and you can easily do it yourself.

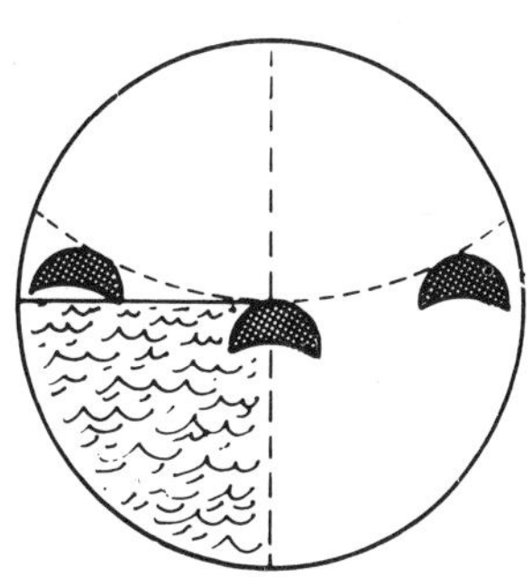

(C) Moon upper limb

Whatever the error of adjustment, it causes the sextant to read an angle that is either too large or too small. This error will be constant for all readings, and we call it the *index error.* Once we have determined how much it is, we apply this as a correction, called *index correction* (IC), which can be either plus (+) or minus (—).

Every time we use the sextant we check the index error in the following manner: Set the sextant to a zero-degree (0°) reading. Sight at the sea horizon or a star—a nearby object will not do. In the clear horizon glass you see the actual horizon, and the image of the horizon appears in the mirror part. Adjust the sextant arm so that the two form a continuous straight line—or, if you are using a star, adjust so that the image coincides exactly with the actual star. The instrument is now set for zero adjustment, and if there were no index error the sextant should read zero exactly. It rarely does. If there is a small, *positive* reading, say 5′, it means that the sextant will read 5′ more than the actual angle, so we have an index correction of —5′, which we must subtract from every reading we take thereafter. On the other hand, there are divisions below zero on the limb, and when we get a reading *off the arc,* say 7′ less than zero, we have a *negative* index error of 7′. In other words, the sextant is reading less than it should, and in every sight we must apply an index correction of +7′. Remember it this way: If it is on, take it off; if it is off, add it on.

Collimation Telescope Some sextants are equipped with a *collimation telescope,* which is a long, thin tube, usually of 12×-power magnification, but with a field of only 3°. It is also known as an inverting telescope, since it shows the images upside down.

At one time this was the only kind of scope available with a sextant. It is rather difficult to use because of the inversion and the small field, and nearly all sights should be taken with your regular 3×, 4×, or 7× scope.

When taking star sights with an inverting telescope, it is almost impossible to bring the star down to the horizon without losing sight of it. Old-time mariners therefore used the following procedure.

Set the sextant at zero reading. Turn the sextant upside down and look directly at the star. Keeping the star in view constantly, move the arm of the sextant and bring the horizon up to the star. Now turn the sextant right side up and complete the sight. The star will be on the horizon and there is no danger of your looking at the wrong star.

The cross hairs in the collimation telescope are used for lining up the axis of the telescope parallel to the plane of the frame of the sextant. There is a complete discussion of this process in Bowditch. However, with the advent of modern telescopes, the navigator need not bother with a collimation scope. Some sextants have eliminated it altogether, while others keep it as a concession to old-time navigators.

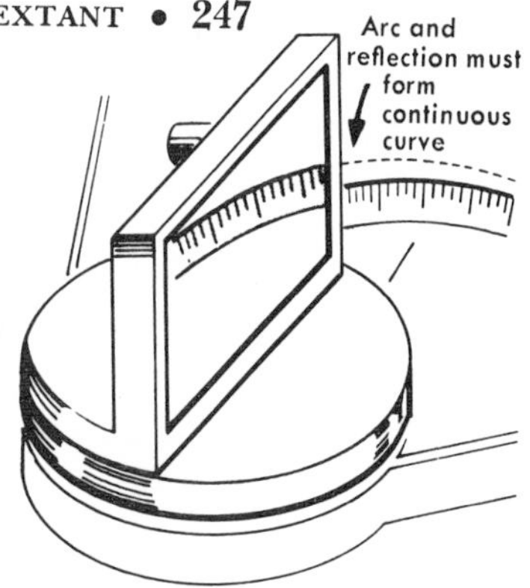

FIG. 18-4
Setting index mirror perpendicular to the frame

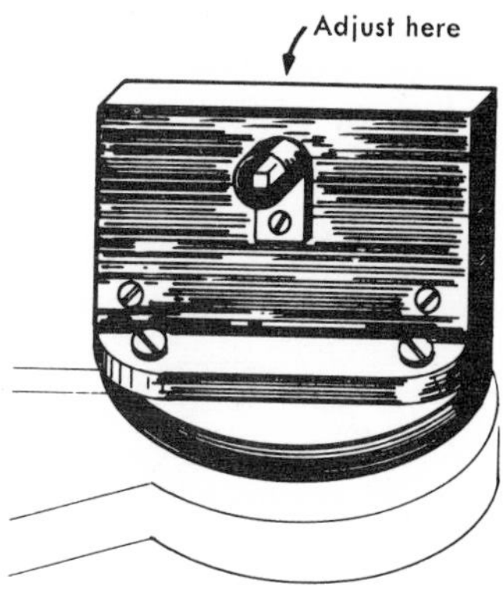

Adjusting the Sextant Due to shaking up in shipping, or perhaps due to the normal use you give it, a sextant may get out of adjustment which results in an index error. Each time you use the sextant, you must check the index error. If the index error is too large, or if you want no index error at all, you can adjust the sextant as follows. (Make sure to follow the sequence exactly.)

Adjustment #1 *Make the index mirror perpendicular to the plane of the sextant.* To do this, set the index arm to about 35°. Hold the sextant in your right hand, but turn it around so that you are looking into the index mirror (see Fig. 18–4). Hold the sextant so that you can see the reflection of the arc in the mirror, and also the actual arc just past the edge of the mirror. They must form a continuous curve, without a break. If they do not, the mirror is not perpendicular. Take the little wrench that came with the sextant and insert it on the set screw at the top of the mirror. Turn this screw until you see the arc and its image come together in a continuous line. When the adjustment is perfect, the index mirror is perpendicular to the plane of the sextant.

Adjustment #2 *Make the horizon mirror perpendicular to the plane of the sextant.* Here you are correcting for what is sometimes called "side error." It is determined by looking at a distant vertical line, such as a flagpole or a mast, or at night by looking at a star. The sextant must be set at zero reading. Move the sextant slightly from side to side, and you will see two flagpoles, a slight distance apart, or you may see two stars side by side. They should coincide. With the wrench inserted in the set screw at the *top* of the *horizon mirror,* turn this screw until you have brought the actual flagpole and the image into coincidence, or until the star and its image are superimposed. (With the star you may have to turn the micrometer drum slightly, if the image is a little higher than the star, or vice versa, in order to bring them side by side.) When the image and the actual object coincide, you have removed the side error. It is a delicate operation, so double-check your work. Gently does it. (See Fig. 18–5.)

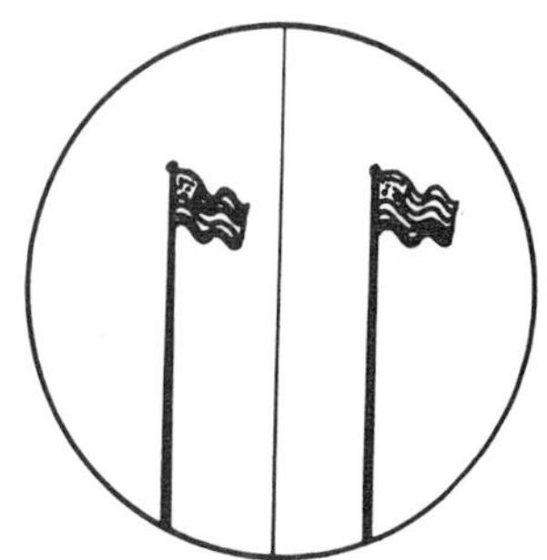

FIG. 18-5
(A) Showing side error
(B) Side error removed

Adjustment #3 *Remove the index error.* Set the index arm and the micrometer drum exactly at zero and look at the horizon. The actual horizon and the image must form a continuous straight line. You can also look at a star, and again the star and its image must coincide. Turn the set screw at the *base* of the horizon mirror until the horizon makes a straight line or until you get coincidence of the star with its image. You now should have no index error. (See Fig. 18–6.)

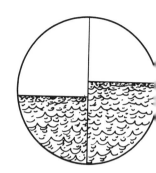

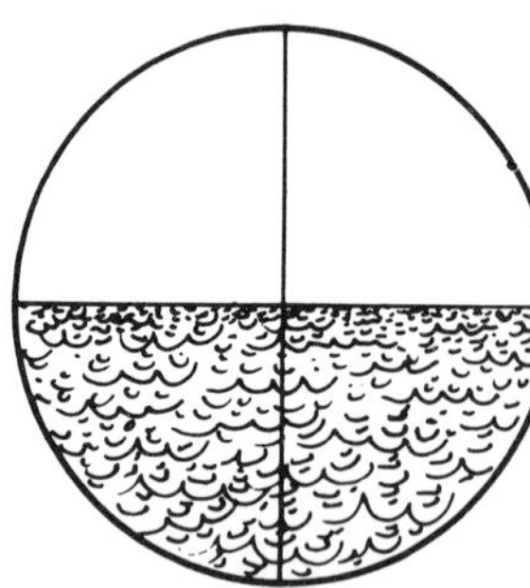

FIG. 18-6
(A) Showing index error

(B) Index error removed

Repeat Because one adjustment may cause a slight change in the other adjustments, it is wise when you have finished the three adjustments described to check your sextant all over again, beginning with #1, then #2, and finally #3. Slight additional adjustments may be necessary to get a perfect result. *However,* you must still check the index error *each time before you use the sextant.*

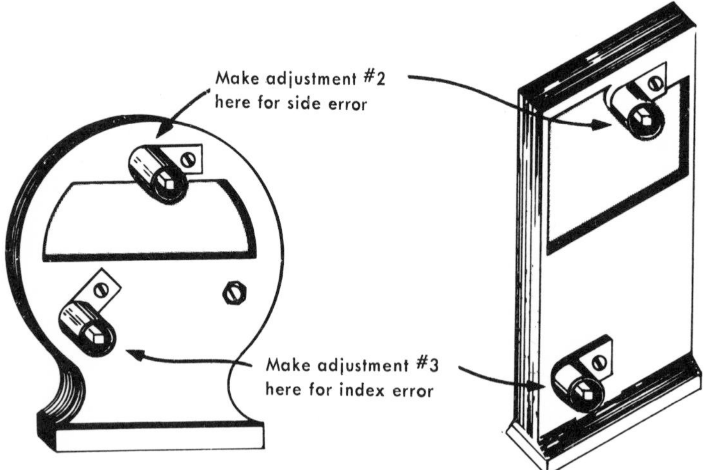

FIG. 18-7
(A) Circular horizon glass
(B) Rectangular Horizon glass

Repairing the Light Occasionally the light on a sextant ceases to work for one reason or another. Jarring during shipping, exposure to salt air, etc. can cause malfunction. Usually it is easily remedied if you follow the instructions below:

1. Make sure the batteries still have power in them.
2. Check the bulb; make sure it works, and that it is screwed in tightly.
3. Salt air corrodes. Make sure all contacts are metal bright, including bottom and top of batteries.

4. If light still does not work, remove batteries from handle and with a knife or file scrape all metal contacts.
5. If necessary, remove switch in handle. Turn sextant upside down and shake. Sometimes the factory has left sawdust in the handle, which interferes with the contacts.
6. Make sure switch plunger reaches brass contact when depressed.

If you have done everything so far and the light still does not work, the remaining possibility is that there is no ground connection from the base of the light assembly through the frame of the sextant to the switch. Turn the sextant upside down and locate on the back of the index arm the screws that hold the light assembly to the index arm. Remove *one* of these screws. With the point of a sharp knife, gently scrape the paint away under the screw head, so that when the screw is replaced there is metal-to-metal contact with the index arm. This completes the circuit and the light should work; if you still have trouble, take the sextant to an instrument shop, where they can locate the trouble in no time.

Care of Your Sextant Your sextant is a delicate instrument and deserves the best of care. It is easily put out of adjustment if roughly handled or dropped. If you will follow the rules given here, you should have no trouble.

1. Always handle the sextant box as if it were made of glass.
2. When the sextant is in its box, keep the box securely locked.
3. When you set the sextant box down on a rolling vessel, make sure it is wedged in, so that it cannot be dislodged and fall.
4. When you open the box, take the sextant out with your left hand, lifting it by the frame, then shift to the right hand, holding the sextant by the handle. Never lift it by the index arm.
5. When holding the sextant, be careful not to knock it against anything.

6. After taking a sight, if it is necessary to set down the sextant while you are writing your data, place it only where it cannot fall, and always resting on its legs. The preferable method is to hold the sextant in the left hand while writing with the right hand, so that you won't have to set it down or let go of it.
7. If mirrors or lenses get wet, dry them immediately with a soft cloth.
8. A black arc is kept clean by gently wiping it with a soft cloth. A brass arc can safely be polished gently with silver polish. (If you have an old-type vernier sextant with inlaid silver arc and very fine divisions, you must clean it *only* with a little oil and a soft cloth, or the markings will wear out.)
9. Very rarely will you need to oil moving parts, and then sparingly.
10. Use only soft lens paper or a very soft cloth on the mirrors and lenses.
11. If the sextant has not been used for some time, the batteries in the handle may corrode from exposure to sea air. When the sextant is not to be used for some time, it is best to remove the batteries. In any case, make sure the contacts and the metal surface on the bottom of the batteries are bright.
12. On a small vessel—as on a big one—build a safe, fitted compartment that will just hold the sextant box when it is not in use, so that no matter how much you roll and pitch, the box will not fall out.
13. Remember, a sextant is not a toy. It is an expensive precision instrument and must be treated as such. Don't let anybody handle your sextant unless you are sure that he is an expert and knows what he is doing. All you need is to drop a sextant on a hard surface—and you don't have a sextant any more. Beware, if you buy a second-hand sextant, that it has not been dropped and had the arc bent. If so, it is worthless.

Corrections to Sextant Readings There are a total of five corrections that are applied to the sextant altitude H_s to get the correct value we want, called the *observed altitude* H_o. They are: (1) index correction, (2) dip of the horizon, (3) refraction, (4) semidiameter, and (5) horizontal parallax. In extreme situations, a temperature correction is provided in the *Nautical Almanac,* but usually this can be ignored. It is important that you understand each type of correction. In this chapter we shall use the *Nautical Almanac* only.

Index Correction Index correction is necessitated by a combination of errors in the manufacture and errors of adjustment, as previously described. Index-correction is determined by the navigator whenever he starts using his sextant, usually by sighting on the horizon. It is either plus or minus, and it varies with the individual sextant.

Dip of the Horizon Using a sextant we seek the angle between a line of sight to the celestial body and a horizon that is tangent to the circle of the Earth at the place where we are standing (see Fig. 18–8). Since we cannot hold the sextant at water level, and since the horizon recedes the higher up we are, we always read a larger value than we should, depending on the *height of eye* above the water at the time of the observation.

The difference, due to a receding horizon, is called the *angle of dip.* It causes a larger sextant reading, and the correction is therefore always subtracted. It is determined entirely by our *height of eye* above sea level, and is listed inside the front and back covers of the almanac.

FIG. 18-8
Dip of the horizon

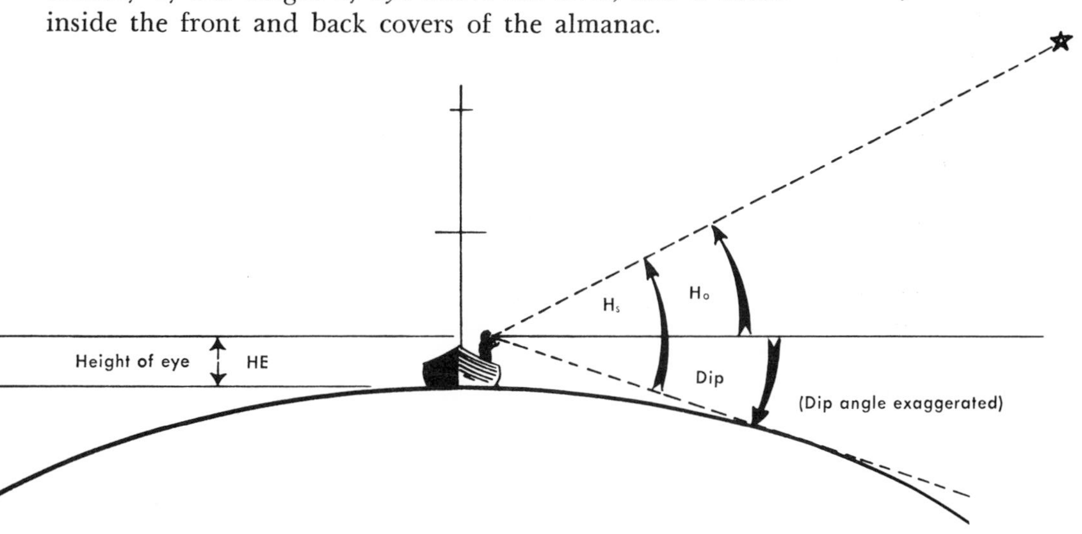

Example • If your height of eye is 15 feet, the correction for dip is −3.8′.

Refraction Refraction error is caused by the fact that the light from a celestial body travels through a medium of changing density, namely our atmosphere. The density of the atmosphere increases as we approach the Earth's surface, and as the light rays pass from lighter to heavier density they are bent, or refracted, toward the center of the Earth, or downward.

The more atmosphere the light passes through, the greater the refraction (see Fig. 18–9). A body low on the horizon would thus have maximum refraction, while a body directly overhead at our zenith has no refraction.

FIG. 18-9
Effect of refraction

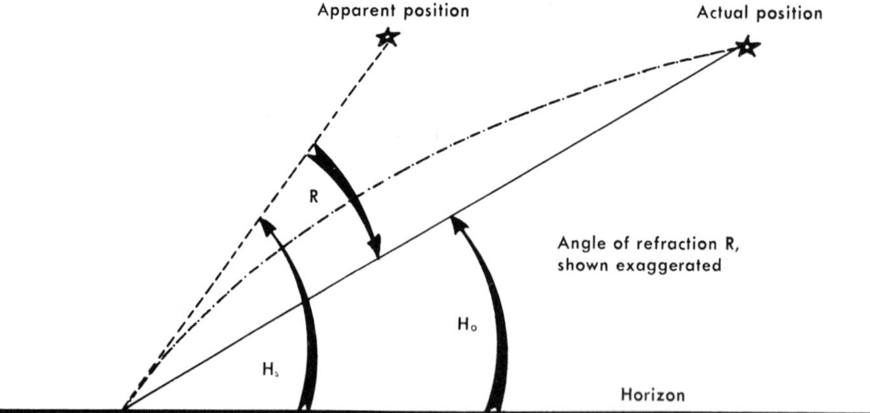

Refraction causes the body to be seen as if it were at a higher altitude in the sky. The correction must therefore be subtracted. It varies with the altitude of the body and is given in the *Nautical Almanac* as follows:

Stars and Planets The center table, inside the front cover (Figs. 18–14 and 18–15), gives the value of refraction correction for various altitudes. Note that it becomes zero at 90° altitude, when the body is directly overhead and in line with the center of the Earth. For Venus and Mars, small seasonal corrections are indicated in the same table.

The Sun Refraction is combined with semidiameter in the first table (Figs. 18–14 and 18–15). (We shall discuss semidiameter shortly.) Note that this table is a double table, the left half covering October to March, the right half April to September. Also, corrections are given for lower-limb and upper-limb observations of the sun. In both the sun and the star tables we enter with "App. Alt." (apparent altitude). At the bottom of the page this is explained as being the sextant reading, corrected for index error and dip. In ordinary, practical navigation, we omit this refinement, except for the moon, and we simply enter with the sextant altitude, or reading.

The Moon The *Nautical Almanac* gives a composite altitude-correction table inside the back cover of the book (Figs. 18–16 and 18–17), combining refraction, semidiameter, and horizontal parallax (discussed below). Examples at the end of this lesson will explain how you use this table.

Semidiameter This correction applies to the sun and the moon. Stars and planets appear as pinpoints of light and are placed directly on the horizon in our sextant sight. The sun and the moon are, of course, too large for this, and we therefore bring either the lower or the upper edge, or limb, into contact with the horizon. But since we need the altitude of the center of the body, we make a correction by adding half of the diameter of the body to a lower-limb sight, and subtracting it from an upper-limb sight. For the sun, this is taken care of in the table, Figs. 18–14 and 18–15, where it is combined with refraction.

FIG. 18-10
Correction for semidiameter

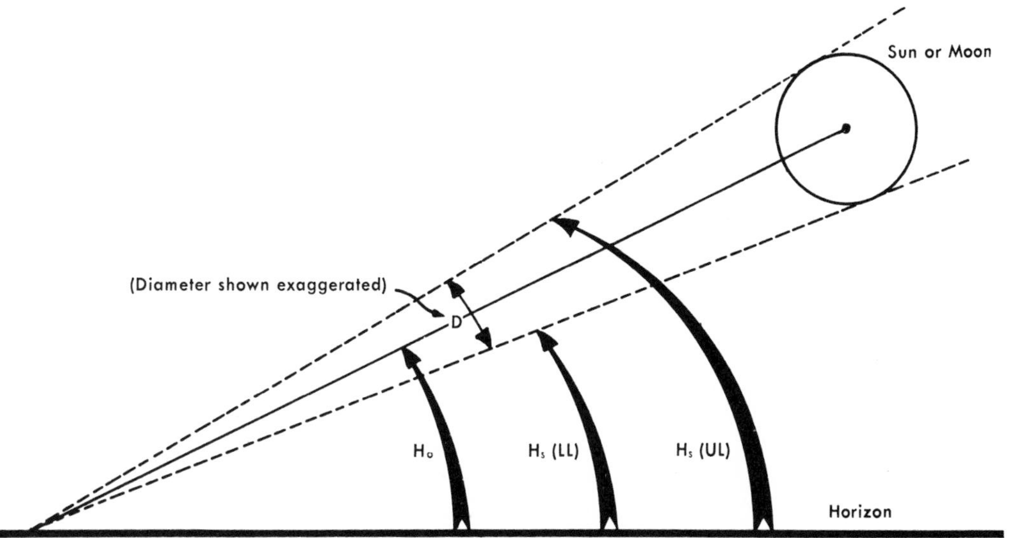

In the case of the moon, the arrangement is a little different, and whereas the correction for semidiameter is included in the combined table, Figs. 18–16 and 18–17, for a lower-limb (LL) observation, the table is so constructed that we must deduct 30′ from any upper-limb (UL) sight. The actual semidiameters for the sun and the moon are given in the daily pages, but we have no occasion to use them, as they are incorporated in the tables. (See Fig. 18–10.)

Horizontal Parallax In celestial navigation, our computations assume the observer to be at the center of the Earth. Since the stars are at such immense distances, it makes no difference to our altitude that we are not at the center. However, because the sun and (especially) the moon are so much closer, this difference, called *parallax,* must be reckoned with. (See Fig. 18–11.)

FIG. 18-11
Effect of parallax

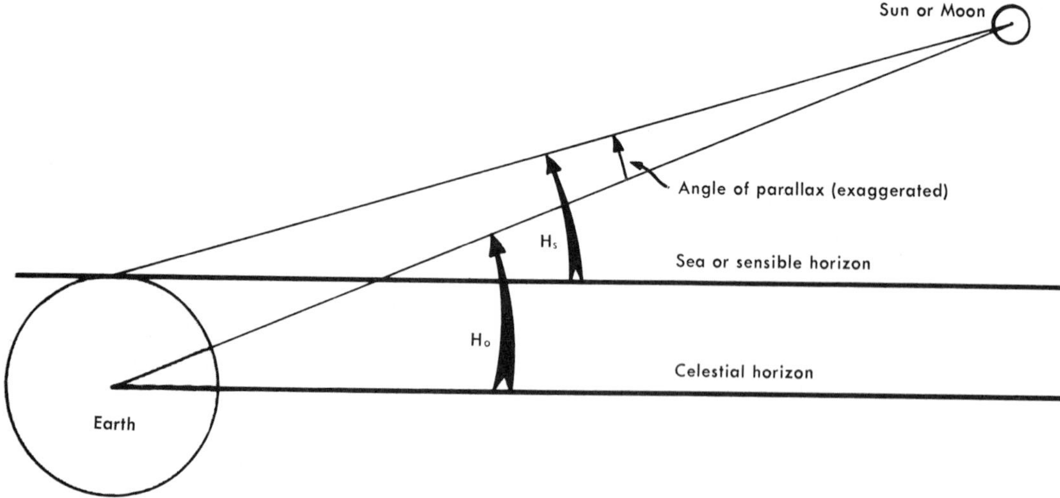

The observer can only measure the angle between the body and his so-called *sensible horizon,* a plane tangent to the surface of the Earth at this position. We wish, however, to measure the angle from the body to the *celestial horizon,* which is a plane passing through the center of the Earth parallel to the sensible horizon. The difference in the two angles, as shown in Fig. 18–11, is the *angle of parallax,* which we must add to the sextant altitude H_s to get the observed altitude H_o. There is a small amount of parallax for the sun included in the combined table, Figs. 18–14 and

18–15, but for the moon there is a larger, variable correction. The *Nautical Almanac* gives the horizontal parallax (HP) of the moon for every hour of the day, and we use this as a further key in looking up altitude corrections for the moon, Figs. 18–16 and 18–17.

How to Use Altitude Correction Tables

It is essential that you work through all the examples yourself, using the tables reproduced in Figs. 18–14, 18–15, 18–16, and 18–17.

On January 1, the sun, lower limb (LL), is observed. H_s is 45°35.2′. Index error is 7′ on the arc, height of eye 12 feet. Find H_o.

In all our altitude calculations we set up a standard table, listing the plus and minus values:

	+	−		
Index correction (IC)		7.0′ (*minus,* because it is on the arc)		
Dip for 12 ft.		3.4′ (*always minus*)		
App. alt. correction	15.3′			
Totals	15.3′	10.4′	H_s =	45° 35.2′
	−10.4′		Corr.	+4.9′
Net correction	+ 4.9′		H_o =	45° 40.1′

August 8; sun, upper limb (UL); H_s = 17°33.7′; IE 5′ off the arc; height of eye (HE) 30 ft. Find H_o.

	+	−		
IC	5′			
Dip		5.3′	H_s =	27° 33.7′
Alt. corr.		18.8′	Corr.	−19.1′
Totals	5′	24.1′	H_o =	27° 14.6′
		5.0′		
Net correction		−19.1′		

Feb. 1; star Procyon; $H_s = 45°17.4'$; IE 6′ on arc; HE 23 ft. Find H_o.

	+	−		
IC		6.0′		
Dip		4.7′	H_s =	45° 17.4′
Alt. corr.		1.0′	Corr.	−11.7′
Net correction		−11.7′	H_o =	45° 05.7′

Oct. 30; planet Venus; $H_s = 20°44.9'$; IE 7′ off arc; HE 40 ft. Find H_o.

	+	−		
IC	7.0′			
Dip		6.1′	H_s =	20° 44.9′
Alt. corr.		2.5′	Corr.	−0.8′
Season corr.	0.8′		H_o =	20° 44.1′
Totals	7.8′	8.6′		
		−7.8′		
Net correction		−0.8′		

Moon, LL; Jan. 1, 14-35-11 GMT; $H_s = 35°44.2'$; IE 5′ on arc; HE 28 ft. First we find the *apparent altitude.* IC is −5′ and dip is −5.1′, a total of −10.1′ subtracted from H_s to give app. alt. of 35°34.1′. Next we find the *horizontal parallax* (HP) for January 1 at 14-35-11 GMT from the almanac. It is 56.4′. (Sometimes we interpolate by eye for an intermediate value, but not this time.) Use Fig. 18–16 for altitudes to 35°, Fig 18–17 for values above 35°. We use Fig. 18–17. Apparent altitudes are given for every 10′, so we look up 35°30′, the nearest value to our app. alt. The correction is indicated as 56.2′. This is the first part of our correction.

Now continue vertically downward in the same column to the lower half of the table. On Figs. 18–16 and 18–17 are shown various values for HP, and the double columns give separate corrections for lower-limb ("L") and upper-limb ("U") sights. *Entire with the value of HP you obtained from the daily page,* in this case 56.4′.

In the "L" column we find a correction of 3.6′ for an HP of 56.4′. Now set up your table as follows (both corrections are always +):

	+	−		
IC		5.0′		
Dip		5.1′	H_s =	35° 44.2′
1st corr.	56.2′		Corr.	+49.7′
2nd corr.	3.6′		H_o =	36° 33.9′
	59.8′	10.1′		
	−10.1′			
Net correction	+49.7′			

Moon, UL; January 2, 16-10-40 GMT; H_s 29°42′; IE 10′ on arc; HE 17 ft. Find H_o.

Apparent altitude comes to 29°28′. HP for date and hour is 57.4′. Using left-hand page of tables, we find the first correction to be 59.1′ and the second correction in the lower table, same column, for HP 57.4′ to be 3.4′ (interpolate by eye). *Remember: You must subtract 30′* for the upper limb. Now set up the table:

		+	−		
IC			10′		
Dip			4′	H_s =	29° 42′
1st corr.		59.1′		Corr.	+18.5′
2nd corr.		3.4′		H_o =	30° 00.5′
UL corr.			30′		
	Totals	62.5′	44′		
		−44.0′			
Net correction		18.5′			

In your eye interpolations, you estimate values to the nearest tenth of a minute. This will correspond to a tenth of a mile in the final plotting of your position. In practical navigation we can come to within a mile or two of our actual position, so if you are off a tenth of a mile it does not make too much difference. However, we try to come as close as we can in our computations.

In this chapter we have discussed altitude corrections

taken from the *Nautical Almanac*. In Chapters 19 and 20 we will discuss the use of the *air almanac* for obtaining such corrections when we come to work the complete problems.

Using the Artificial Horizon If you are unable to practice sights on the actual sea horizon, you can take sights right in your own backyard using a so-called artificial horizon.

An *artificial horizon* consists of a small pool of liquid which has a good reflecting surface. Mercury is perfect, but we usually use a heavy motor oil of dark color. A flat pie tin, or even a paper plate, about 10 inches in diameter, is filled with about ½ inch of oil. The liquid will always be level and parallel to the plane of the natural horizon, and this is the principle that makes it possible to use it instead of the sea horizon.

When you use an artificial horizon, you may wish to remove the telescope from the sextant and learn to keep both eyes open when you take sights. It is a little more difficult than working on the actual horizon, but fifteen minutes of practice will enable you to master the technique, and sights can be taken with great accuracy.

The following procedure is used. Place the container of oil on a table or other support, a little above waist height. Stir the oil slowly to remove air bubbles. Keep it out of the wind or make a windbreak alongside. If the wind is troublesome, place a flat piece of windowglass over the plate. (There will be a double refraction that will cancel out and thus not affect the sight.) Stand back two or three feet, facing the sun, until the reflection of the sun is seen in the oil when you are standing upright in a relaxed position. You can even do this inside the house if window arrangement permits.

Set the sextant to zero reading, adjust shade glasses, and sight directly at the sun. Now bring the image of the sun in the mirror down into the pool, near the reflection as seen by the left eye directly and in the clear part of the horizon glass by the right eye. This requires a little patient practice. Use a smooth, even movement in bringing the sun down, and don't lose sight of the image in the mirror. Keep both eyes open and use the left eye to locate the reflection in the pool. If the sextant becomes heavy or your eyes tired, take a rest—then try again.

When you have the image in the pool, near the reflection, bring them together carefully by turning the tangent screw for fine adjustment. If the lower limb of the sun (or moon) is to be observed, place the *image above the reflection* so that the lower edge of the image just touches the upper edge of the reflection. Roll the sextant gently and adjust for perfect tangency at the bottom of the swing. Mark the time and read the sextant. (See Fig. 18–12.)

If the upper limb of the sun or moon is observed, bring the image *below* the reflection so that the upper edge of the image is tangent to the lower edge of the reflection as the sextant is rolled.

Using colored shade glasses will help you know which is the image and which is the reflection, in case you are in doubt. But remember this: the image moves as the sextant is rolled, while the reflection remains still.

You will probably not be able to do this with stars—except perhaps Sirius and Canopus, which are bright enough—but you can do it with Venus and Jupiter. In this case both image and reflection are pinpoints of light, and you simply make them coincide at the bottom of the swing when the sextant is rolled. You must always remember to stand so that you, the pool, and the point on the horizon directly below the body are in a straight line.

When you use an artificial horizon, there is no dip of the horizon, so no correction is needed for height of eye. The sextant angle you read is *twice* the actual altitude, because we are measuring both the angle of incidence and the equal angle of reflection from the pool to the eye. We therefore first apply the index error to the total angle read, then divide the result by 2 to obtain H_s, the angle we would have read if the sight had been taken on the sea horizon. This H_s needs no correction for index error (already done), nor for height of eye, but all other usual corrections are applied.

Keep the surface of the oil free from lint or dust and keep it out of the wind. Begin with the sun, which is easiest, although there will be no difficulty with the moon or the two brighter planets. Since most sextants have a maximum reading of 126°, when you use the artificial horizon, where

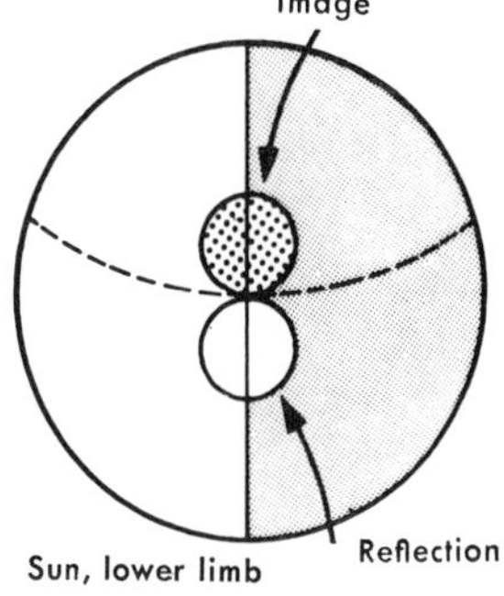

FIG. 18-12
Using the artificial horizon

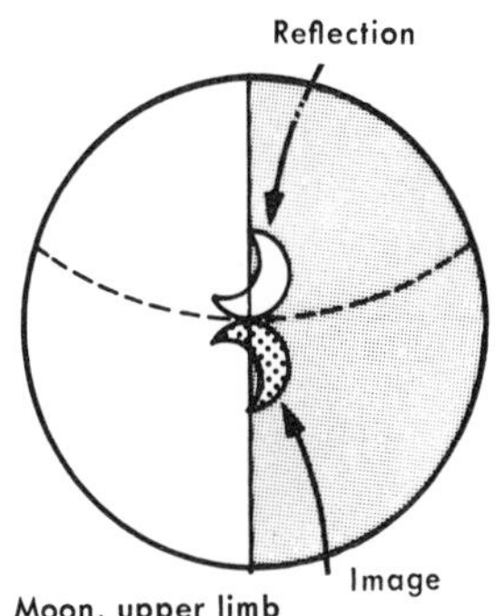

FIG. 18-13
Using the artificial horizon

the double angle is measured, you cannot take sights on bodies with altitudes greater than 63°.

Sights are free. You should take all the sights you can, and work out all you can find time for. With an artificial horizon you are in a known position and with practice and patience you will soon be rewarded by sights which accurately confirm this position within a mile or two. Speed and accuracy will follow if you practice enough.

***Example* •** Sun, LL, observed January 1 on artificial horizon. Total angle is 84°22′. IE is 5′ on the arc. Find H_o.

Total angle	=	84° 22′
Subtract IC		5′
Net angle		84° 17′
Divide by 2		42° 08.5′
Alt. corr.		+15.2′
H_o	=	42° 23.7′

***Practice Problems* •**

1. Sun, LL; Aug. 8; H_s = 15°42.3′; IE 3′ on arc; HE 23 ft. Find H_o.
2. Sun, UL; Jan. 1; H_s = 23°55.7′; IE 7′ off arc; HE 17 ft. Find H_o.
3. Star Sirius; H_s =44°45.9′; IE 3′ on arc; HE 12 ft. Find H_o.
4. Planet Venus; Aug. 9; H_s = 27°42′; IE 1′ off arc; HE 21 ft. Find H_o.
5. Moon, LL; Jan. 2, GMT 10-20-30; IE 10′ on arc; HE 30 ft.; H_s = 20°15′. Find H_o.
6. Moon, UL; Jan. 3, GMT 1-01-20; IE 2′ off arc; HE 42 ft.; H_s = 35°02.8′. Find H_o.

A2 ALTITUDE CORRECTION TABLES 10°-90°—SUN, STARS, PLANETS

SUN

OCT.—MAR. App. Alt.	Lower Limb	Upper Limb	APR.—SEPT. App. Alt.	Lower Limb	Upper Limb
° ′	′	′	° ′	′	′
9 34			9 39		
	+10·8	−21·5		+10·6	−21·2
9 45			9 51		
	+10·9	−21·4		+10·7	−21·1
9 56			10 03		
	+11·0	−21·3		+10·8	−21·0
10 08			10 15		
	+11·1	−21·2		+10·9	−20·9
10 21			10 27		
	+11·2	−21·1		+11·0	−20·8
10 34			10 40		
	+11·3	−21·0		+11·1	−20·7
10 47			10 54		
	+11·4	−20·9		+11·2	−20·6
11 01			11 08		
	+11·5	−20·8		+11·3	−20·5
11 15			11 23		
	+11·6	−20·7		+11·4	−20·4
11 30			11 38		
	+11·7	−20·6		+11·5	−20·3
11 46			11 54		
	+11·8	−20·5		+11·6	−20·2
12 02			12 10		
	+11·9	−20·4		+11·7	−20·1
12 19			12 28		
	+12·0	−20·3		+11·8	−20·0
12 37			12 46		
	+12·1	−20·2		+11·9	−19·9
12 55			13 05		
	+12·2	−20·1		+12·0	−19·8
13 14			13 24		
	+12·3	−20·0		+12·1	−19·7
13 35			13 45		
	+12·4	−19·9		+12·2	−19·6
13 56			14 07		
	+12·5	−19·8		+12·3	−19·5
14 18			14 30		
	+12·6	−19·7		+12·4	−19·4
14 42			14 54		
	+12·7	−19·6		+12·5	−19·3
15 06			15 19		
	+12·8	−19·5		+12·6	−19·2
15 32			15 46		
	+12·9	−19·4		+12·7	−19·1
15 59			16 14		
	+13·0	−19·3		+12·8	−19·0
16 28			16 44		
	+13·1	−19·2		+12·9	−18·9
16 59			17 15		
	+13·2	−19·1		+13·0	−18·8
17 32			17 48		
	+13·3	−19·0		+13·1	−18·7
18 06			18 24		
	+13·4	−18·9		+13·2	−18·6
18 42			19 01		
	+13·5	−18·8		+13·3	−18·5
19 21			19 42		
	+13·6	−18·7		+13·4	−18·4
20 03			20 25		
	+13·7	−18·6		+13·5	−18·3
20 48			21 11		
	+13·8	−18·5		+13·6	−18·2
21 35			22 00		
	+13·9	−18·4		+13·7	−18·1
22 26			22 54		
	+14·0	−18·3		+13·8	−18·0
23 22			23 51		
	+14·1	−18·2		+13·9	−17·9
24 21			24 53		
	+14·2	−18·1		+14·0	−17·8
25 26			26 00		
	+14·3	−18·0		+14·1	−17·7
26 36			27 13		
	+14·4	−17·9		+14·2	−17·6
27 52			28 33		
	+14·5	−17·8		+14·3	−17·5
29 15			30 00		
	+14·6	−17·7		+14·4	−17·4
30 46			31 35		
	+14·7	−17·6		+14·5	−17·3
32 26			33 20		
	+14·8	−17·5		+14·6	−17·2
34 17			35 17		
	+14·9	−17·4		+14·7	−17·1
36 20			37 26		
	+15·0	−17·3		+14·8	−17·0
38 36			39 50		
	+15·1	−17·2		+14·9	−16·9
41 08			42 31		
	+15·2	−17·1		+15·0	−16·8
43 59			45 31		
	+15·3	−17·0		+15·1	−16·7
47 10			48 55		
	+15·4	−16·9		+15·2	−16·6
50 46			52 44		
	+15·5	−16·8		+15·3	−16·5
54 49			57 02		
	+15·6	−16·7		+15·4	−16·4
59 23			61 51		
	+15·7	−16·6		+15·5	−16·3
64 30			67 17		
	+15·8	−16·5		+15·6	−16·2
70 12			73 16		
	+15·9	−16·4		+15·7	−16·1
76 26			79 43		
	+16·0	−16·3		+15·8	−16·0
83 05			86 32		
	+16·1	−16·2		+15·9	−15·9
90 00			90 00		

STARS AND PLANETS

App. Alt.	Corrn
° ′	′
9 56	
	−5·3
10 08	
	−5·2
10 20	
	−5·1
10 33	
	−5·0
10 46	
	−4·9
11 00	
	−4·8
11 14	
	−4·7
11 29	
	−4·6
11 45	
	−4·5
12 01	
	−4·4
12 18	
	−4·3
12 35	
	−4·2
12 54	
	−4·1
13 13	
	−4·0
13 33	
	−3·9
13 54	
	−3·8
14 16	
	−3·7
14 40	
	−3·6
15 04	
	−3·5
15 30	
	−3·4
15 57	
	−3·3
16 26	
	−3·2
16 56	
	−3·1
17 28	
	−3·0
18 02	
	−2·9
18 38	
	−2·8
19 17	
	−2·7
19 58	
	−2·6
20 42	
	−2·5
21 28	
	−2·4
22 19	
	−2·3
23 13	
	−2·2
24 11	
	−2·1
25 14	
	−2·0
26 22	
	−1·9
27 36	
	−1·8
28 56	
	−1·7
30 24	
	−1·6
32 00	
	−1·5
33 45	
	−1·4
35 40	
	−1·3
37 48	
	−1·2
40 08	
	−1·1
42 44	
	−1·0
45 36	
	−0·9
48 47	
	−0·8
52 18	
	−0·7
56 11	
	−0·6
60 28	
	−0·5
65 08	
	−0·4
70 11	
	−0·3
75 34	
	−0·2
81 13	
	−0·1
87 03	
	0·0
90 00	

App. Alt.	Additional Corrn
VENUS	
Jan. 1-July 22	
°	′
0	
	+ 0·1
42	
July 23-Sept. 5	
°	′
0	
	+ 0·2
47	
Sept. 6-Oct. 1	
°	′
0	
	+ 0·3
46	
Oct. 2-Oct. 16	
°	′
0	
	+ 0·4
11	
	+ 0·5
41	
Oct. 17-Oct. 24	
°	′
0	
	+ 0·5
6	
	+ 0·6
20	
	+ 0·7
31	
Oct. 25-Nov. 28	
°	′
0	
	+ 0·6
4	
	+ 0·7
12	
	+ 0·8
22	
Nov. 29-Dec. 6	
°	′
0	
	+ 0·5
6	
	+ 0·6
20	
	+ 0·7
31	
Dec. 7-Dec. 21	
°	′
0	
	+ 0·4
11	
	+ 0·5
41	
Dec. 22-Dec. 31	
°	′
0	
	+ 0·3
46	
MARS	
Jan. 1-Dec. 31	
°	′
0	
	+ 0·1
60	

DIP

Ht. of Eye	Corrn	Ht. of Eye	Corrn
ft.	′	ft.	′
1·1		44	
	−1·1		−6·5
1·4		45	
	−1·2		−6·6
1·6		47	
	−1·3		−6·7
1·9		48	
	−1·4		−6·8
2·2		49	
	−1·5		−6·9
2·5		51	
	−1·6		−7·0
2·8		52	
	−1·7		−7·1
3·2		54	
	−1·8		−7·2
3·6		55	
	−1·9		−7·3
4·0		57	
	−2·0		−7·4
4·4		58	
	−2·1		−7·5
4·9		60	
	−2·2		−7·6
5·3		62	
	−2·3		−7·7
5·8		63	
	−2·4		−7·8
6·3		65	
	−2·5		−7·9
6·9		67	
	−2·6		−8·0
7·4		68	
	−2·7		−8·1
8·0		70	
	−2·8		−8·2
8·6		72	
	−2·9		−8·3
9·2		74	
	−3·0		−8·4
9·8		75	
	−3·1		−8·5
10·5		77	
	−3·2		−8·6
11·2		79	
	−3·3		−8·7
11·9		81	
	−3·4		−8·8
12·6		83	
	−3·5		−8·9
13·3		85	
	−3·6		−9·0
14·1		87	
	−3·7		−9·1
14·9		88	
	−3·8		−9·2
15·7		90	
	−3·9		−9·3
16·5		92	
	−4·0		−9·4
17·4		94	
	−4·1		−9·5
18·3		96	
	−4·2		−9·6
19·1		98	
	−4·3		−9·7
20·1		101	
	−4·4		−9·8
21·0		103	
	−4·5		−9·9
22·0		105	
	−4·6		−10·0
22·9		107	
	−4·7		−10·1
23·9		109	
	−4·8		−10·2
24·9		111	
	−4·9		−10·3
26·0		113	
	−5·0		−10·4
27·1		116	
	−5·1		−10·5
28·1		118	
	−5·2		−10·6
29·2		120	
	−5·3		−10·7
30·4		122	
	−5·4		−10·8
31·5		125	
	−5·5		−10·9
32·7		127	
	−5·6		−11·0
33·9		129	
	−5·7		−11·1
35·1		132	
	−5·8		−11·2
36·3		134	
	−5·9		−11·3
37·6		136	
	−6·0		−11·4
38·9		139	
	−6·1		−11·5
40·1		141	
	−6·2		−11·6
41·5		144	
	−6·3		−11·7
42·8		146	
	−6·4		−11·8
44·2		149	

App. Alt. = Apparent altitude = Sextant altitude corrected for index error and dip.

FIG. 18-14 Excerpt from Nautical Almanac

ALTITUDE CORRECTION TABLES 0°–10°—SUN, STARS, PLANETS A3

App. Alt.	OCT.–MAR. SUN Lower Limb	OCT.–MAR. SUN Upper Limb	APR.–SEPT. SUN Lower Limb	APR.–SEPT. SUN Upper Limb	STARS PLANETS
° ′	′	′	′	′	′
0 00	−18·2	−50·5	−18·4	−50·2	−34·5
03	17·5	49·8	17·8	49·6	33·8
06	16·9	49·2	17·1	48·9	33·2
09	16·3	48·6	16·5	48·3	32·6
12	15·7	48·0	15·9	47·7	32·0
15	15·1	47·4	15·3	47·1	31·4
0 18	−14·5	−46·8	−14·8	−46·6	−30·8
21	14·0	46·3	14·2	46·0	30·3
24	13·5	45·8	13·7	45·5	29·8
27	12·9	45·2	13·2	45·0	29·2
30	12·4	44·7	12·7	44·5	28·7
33	11·9	44·2	12·2	44·0	28·2
0 36	−11·5	−43·8	−11·7	−43·5	−27·8
39	11·0	43·3	11·2	43·0	27·3
42	10·5	42·8	10·8	42·6	26·8
45	10·1	42·4	10·3	42·1	26·4
48	9·6	41·9	9·9	41·7	25·9
51	9·2	41·5	9·5	41·3	25·5
0 54	− 8·8	−41·1	− 9·1	−40·9	−25·1
0 57	8·4	40·7	8·7	40·5	24·7
1 00	8·0	40·3	8·3	40·1	24·3
03	7·7	40·0	7·9	39·7	24·0
06	7·3	39·6	7·5	39·3	23·6
09	6·9	39·2	7·2	39·0	23·2
1 12	− 6·6	−38·9	− 6·8	−38·6	−22·9
15	6·2	38·5	6·5	38·3	22·5
18	5·9	38·2	6·2	38·0	22·2
21	5·6	37·9	5·8	37·6	21·9
24	5·3	37·6	5·5	37·3	21·6
27	4·9	37·2	5·2	37·0	21·2
1 30	− 4·6	−36·9	− 4·9	−36·7	−20·9
35	4·2	36·5	4·4	36·2	20·5
40	3·7	36·0	4·0	35·8	20·0
45	3·2	35·5	3·5	35·3	19·5
50	2·8	35·1	3·1	34·9	19·1
1 55	2·4	34·7	2·6	34·4	18·7
2 00	− 2·0	−34·3	− 2·2	−34·0	−18·3
05	1·6	33·9	1·8	33·6	17·9
10	1·2	33·5	1·5	33·3	17·5
15	0·9	33·2	1·1	32·9	17·2
20	0·5	32·8	0·8	32·6	16·8
25	− 0·2	32·5	0·4	32·2	16·5
2 30	+ 0·2	−32·1	− 0·1	−31·9	−16·1
35	0·5	31·8	+ 0·2	31·6	15·8
40	0·8	31·5	0·5	31·3	15·5
45	1·1	31·2	0·8	31·0	15·2
50	1·4	30·9	1·1	30·7	14·9
2 55	1·6	30·7	1·4	30·4	14·7
3 00	+ 1·9	−30·4	+ 1·7	−30·1	−14·4
05	2·2	30·1	1·9	29·9	14·1
10	2·4	29·9	2·1	29·7	13·9
15	2·6	29·7	2·4	29·4	13·7
20	2·9	29·4	2·6	29·2	13·4
25	3·1	29·2	2·9	28·9	13·2
3 30	+ 3·3	−29·0	+ 3·1	−28·7	−13·0

App. Alt.	OCT.–MAR. SUN Lower Limb	OCT.–MAR. SUN Upper Limb	APR.–SEPT. SUN Lower Limb	APR.–SEPT. SUN Upper Limb	STARS PLANETS
° ′	′	′	′	′	′
3 30	+ 3·3	−29·0	+ 3·1	−28·7	−13·0
35	3·6	28·7	3·3	28·5	12·7
40	3·8	28·5	3·5	28·3	12·5
45	4·0	28·3	3·7	28·1	12·3
50	4·2	28·1	3·9	27·9	12·1
3 55	4·4	27·9	4·1	27·7	11·9
4 00	+ 4·5	−27·8	+ 4·3	−27·5	−11·8
05	4·7	27·6	4·5	27·3	11·6
10	4·9	27·4	4·6	27·2	11·4
15	5·1	27·2	4·8	27·0	11·2
20	5·2	27·1	5·0	26·8	11·1
25	5·4	26·9	5·1	26·7	10·9
4 30	+ 5·6	−26·7	+ 5·3	−26·5	−10·7
35	5·7	26·6	5·5	26·3	10·6
40	5·9	26·4	5·6	26·2	10·4
45	6·0	26·3	5·8	26·0	10·3
50	6·2	26·1	5·9	25·9	10·1
4 55	6·3	26·0	6·0	25·8	10·0
5 00	+ 6·4	−25·9	+ 6·2	−25·6	− 9·9
05	6·6	25·7	6·3	25·5	9·7
10	6·7	25·6	6·4	25·4	9·6
15	6·8	25·5	6·6	25·2	9·5
20	6·9	25·4	6·7	25·1	9·4
25	7·1	25·2	6·8	25·0	9·2
5 30	+ 7·2	−25·1	+ 6·9	−24·9	− 9·1
35	7·3	25·0	7·0	24·8	9·0
40	7·4	24·9	7·2	24·6	8·9
45	7·5	24·8	7·3	24·5	8·8
50	7·6	24·7	7·4	24·4	8·7
5 55	7·7	24·6	7·5	24·3	8·6
6 00	+ 7·8	−24·5	+ 7·6	−24·2	− 8·5
10	8·0	24·3	7·8	24·0	8·3
20	8·2	24·1	8·0	23·8	8·1
30	8·4	23·9	8·1	23·7	7·9
40	8·6	23·7	8·3	23·5	7·7
6 50	8·7	23·6	8·5	23·3	7·6
7 00	+ 8·9	−23·4	+ 8·6	−23·2	− 7·4
10	9·1	23·2	8·8	23·0	7·2
20	9·2	23·1	9·0	22·8	7·1
30	9·3	23·0	9·1	22·7	7·0
40	9·5	22·8	9·2	22·6	6·8
7 50	9·6	22·7	9·4	22·4	6·7
8 00	+ 9·7	−22·6	+ 9·5	−22·3	− 6·6
10	9·9	22·4	9·6	22·2	6·4
20	10·0	22·3	9·7	22·1	6·3
30	10·1	22·2	9·8	22·0	6·2
40	10·2	22·1	10·0	21·8	6·1
8 50	10·3	22·0	10·1	21·7	6·0
9 00	+10·4	−21·9	+10·2	−21·6	− 5·9
10	10·5	21·8	10·3	21·5	5·8
20	10·6	21·7	10·4	21·4	5·7
30	10·7	21·6	10·5	21·3	5·6
40	10·8	21·5	10·6	21·2	5·5
9 50	10·9	21·4	10·6	21·2	5·4
10 00	+11·0	−21·3	+10·7	−21·1	− 5·3

For bubble sextant observations ignore dip and use the star corrections for Sun, planets, and stars.

FIG. 18-15 Excerpt from Nautical Almanac

ALTITUDE CORRECTION TABLES 0°–35°—MOON

App. Alt.	0°–4° Corrⁿ	5°–9° Corrⁿ	10°–14° Corrⁿ	15°–19° Corrⁿ	20°–24° Corrⁿ	25°–29° Corrⁿ	30°–34° Corrⁿ	App. Alt.
′	° ′	° ′	° ′	° ′	° ′	° ′	° ′	′
00	0 33·8	5 58·2	10 62·1	15 62·8	20 62·2	25 60·8	30 58·9	00
10	35·9	58·5	62·2	62·8	62·1	60·8	58·8	10
20	37·8	58·7	62·2	62·8	62·1	60·7	58·8	20
30	39·6	58·9	62·3	62·8	62·1	60·7	58·7	30
40	41·2	59·1	62·3	62·8	62·0	60·6	58·6	40
50	42·6	59·3	62·4	62·7	62·0	60·6	58·5	50
00	1 44·0	6 59·5	11 62·4	16 62·7	21 62·0	26 60·5	31 58·5	00
10	45·2	59·7	62·4	62·7	61·9	60·4	58·4	10
20	46·3	59·9	62·5	62·7	61·9	60·4	58·3	20
30	47·3	60·0	62·5	62·7	61·9	60·3	58·2	30
40	48·3	60·2	62·5	62·7	61·8	60·3	58·2	40
50	49·2	60·3	62·6	62·7	61·8	60·2	58·1	50
00	2 50·0	7 60·5	12 62·6	17 62·7	22 61·7	27 60·1	32 58·0	00
10	50·8	60·6	62·6	62·6	61·7	60·1	57·9	10
20	51·4	60·7	62·6	62·6	61·6	60·0	57·8	20
30	52·1	60·9	62·7	62·6	61·6	59·9	57·8	30
40	52·7	61·0	62·7	62·6	61·5	59·9	57·7	40
50	53·3	61·1	62·7	62·6	61·5	59·8	57·6	50
00	3 53·8	8 61·2	13 62·7	18 62·5	23 61·5	28 59·7	33 57·5	00
10	54·3	61·3	62·7	62·5	61·4	59·7	57·4	10
20	54·8	61·4	62·7	62·5	61·4	59·6	57·4	20
30	55·2	61·5	62·8	62·5	61·3	59·6	57·3	30
40	55·6	61·6	62·8	62·4	61·3	59·5	57·2	40
50	56·0	61·6	62·8	62·4	61·2	59·4	57·1	50
00	4 56·4	9 61·7	14 62·8	19 62·4	24 61·2	29 59·3	34 57·0	00
10	56·7	61·8	62·8	62·3	61·1	59·3	56·9	10
20	57·1	61·9	62·8	62·3	61·1	59·2	56·9	20
30	57·4	61·9	62·8	62·3	61·0	59·1	56·8	30
40	57·7	62·0	62·8	62·2	60·9	59·1	56·7	40
50	57·9	62·1	62·8	62·2	60·9	59·0	56·6	50

H.P.	L	U	L	U	L	U	L	U	L	U	L	U	L	U	H.P.
′	′	′	′	′	′	′	′	′	′	′	′	′	′	′	′
54·0	0·3	0·9	0·3	0·9	0·4	1·0	0·5	1·1	0·6	1·2	0·7	1·3	0·9	1·5	54·0
54·3	0·7	1·1	0·7	1·2	0·7	1·2	0·8	1·3	0·9	1·4	1·1	1·5	1·2	1·7	54·3
54·6	1·1	1·4	1·1	1·4	1·1	1·4	1·2	1·5	1·3	1·6	1·4	1·7	1·5	1·8	54·6
54·9	1·4	1·6	1·5	1·6	1·5	1·6	1·6	1·7	1·6	1·8	1·8	1·9	1·9	2·0	54·9
55·2	1·8	1·8	1·8	1·8	1·9	1·9	1·9	1·9	2·0	2·0	2·1	2·1	2·2	2·2	55·2
55·5	2·2	2·0	2·2	2·0	2·3	2·1	2·3	2·1	2·4	2·2	2·4	2·3	2·5	2·4	55·5
55·8	2·6	2·2	2·6	2·2	2·6	2·3	2·7	2·3	2·7	2·4	2·8	2·4	2·9	2·5	55·8
56·1	3·0	2·4	3·0	2·5	3·0	2·5	3·0	2·5	3·1	2·6	3·1	2·6	3·2	2·7	56·1
56·4	3·4	2·7	3·4	2·7	3·4	2·7	3·4	2·7	3·4	2·8	3·5	2·8	3·5	2·9	56·4
56·7	3·7	2·9	3·7	2·9	3·8	2·9	3·8	2·9	3·8	3·0	3·8	3·0	3·9	3·0	56·7
57·0	4·1	3·1	4·1	3·1	4·1	3·1	4·1	3·1	4·2	3·1	4·2	3·2	4·2	3·2	57·0
57·3	4·5	3·3	4·5	3·3	4·5	3·3	4·5	3·3	4·5	3·3	4·5	3·4	4·6	3·4	57·3
57·6	4·9	3·5	4·9	3·5	4·9	3·5	4·9	3·5	4·9	3·5	4·9	3·5	4·9	3·6	57·6
57·9	5·3	3·8	5·3	3·8	5·2	3·8	5·2	3·7	5·2	3·7	5·2	3·7	5·2	3·7	57·9
58·2	5·6	4·0	5·6	4·0	5·6	4·0	5·6	4·0	5·6	3·9	5·6	3·9	5·6	3·9	58·2
58·5	6·0	4·2	6·0	4·2	6·0	4·2	6·0	4·2	6·0	4·1	5·9	4·1	5·9	4·1	58·5
58·8	6·4	4·4	6·4	4·4	6·4	4·4	6·3	4·4	6·3	4·3	6·3	4·3	6·2	4·2	58·8
59·1	6·8	4·6	6·8	4·6	6·7	4·6	6·7	4·6	6·7	4·5	6·6	4·5	6·6	4·4	59·1
59·4	7·2	4·8	7·1	4·8	7·1	4·8	7·1	4·8	7·0	4·7	7·0	4·7	6·9	4·6	59·4
59·7	7·5	5·1	7·5	5·0	7·5	5·0	7·5	5·0	7·4	4·9	7·3	4·8	7·2	4·7	59·7
60·0	7·9	5·3	7·9	5·3	7·9	5·2	7·8	5·2	7·8	5·1	7·7	5·0	7·6	4·9	60·0
60·3	8·3	5·5	8·3	5·5	8·2	5·4	8·2	5·4	8·1	5·3	8·0	5·2	7·9	5·1	60·3
60·6	8·7	5·7	8·7	5·7	8·6	5·7	8·6	5·6	8·5	5·5	8·4	5·4	8·2	5·3	60·6
60·9	9·1	5·9	9·0	5·9	9·0	5·9	8·9	5·8	8·8	5·7	8·7	5·6	8·6	5·4	60·9
61·2	9·5	6·2	9·4	6·1	9·4	6·1	9·3	6·0	9·2	5·9	9·1	5·8	8·9	5·6	61·2
61·5	9·8	6·4	9·8	6·3	9·7	6·3	9·7	6·2	9·5	6·1	9·4	5·9	9·2	5·8	61·5

DIP

Ht. of Eye	Corrⁿ	Ht. of Eye	Corrⁿ	Ht. of Eye	Corrⁿ
ft.	′	ft.	′	ft.	′
4·0		24		63	
	−2·0		−4·9		−7·8
4·4		26		65	
	−2·1		−5·0		−7·9
4·9		27		67	
	−2·2		−5·1		−8·0
5·3		28		68	
	−2·3		−5·2		−8·1
5·8		29		70	
	−2·4		−5·3		−8·2
6·3		30		72	
	−2·5		−5·4		−8·3
6·9		31		74	
	−2·6		−5·5		−8·4
7·4		32		75	
	−2·7		−5·6		−8·5
8·0		33		77	
	−2·8		−5·7		−8·6
8·6		35		79	
	−2·9		−5·8		−8·7
9·2		36		81	
	−3·0		−5·9		−8·8
9·8		37		83	
	−3·1		−6·0		−8·9
10·5		38		85	
	−3·2		−6·1		−9·0
11·2		40		87	
	−3·3		−6·2		−9·1
11·9		41		88	
	−3·4		−6·3		−9·2
12·6		42		90	
	−3·5		−6·4		−9·3
13·3		44		92	
	−3·6		−6·5		−9·4
14·1		45		94	
	−3·7		−6·6		−9·5
14·9		47		96	
	−3·8		−6·7		−9·6
15·7		48		98	
	−3·9		−6·8		−9·7
16·5		49		101	
	−4·0		−6·9		−9·8
17·4		51		103	
	−4·1		−7·0		−9·9
18·3		52		105	
	−4·2		−7·1		−10·0
19·1		54		107	
	−4·3		−7·2		−10·1
20·1		55		109	
	−4·4		−7·3		−10·2
21·0		57		111	
	−4·5		−7·4		−10·3
22·0		58		113	
	−4·6		−7·5		−10·4
22·9		60		116	
	−4·7		−7·6		−10·5
23·9		62		118	
	−4·8		−7·7		−10·6
24·9		63		120	

MOON CORRECTION TABLE

The correction is in two parts; the first correction is taken from the upper part of the table with argument apparent altitude, and the second from the lower part, with argument H.P., in the same column as that from which the first correction was taken. Separate corrections are given in the lower part for lower (L) and upper (U) limbs. All corrections are to be **added** to apparent altitude, *but 30′ is to be subtracted from the altitude of the upper limb.*

For bubble sextant observations ignore dip, take the mean of upper and lower limb corrections and subtract 15′ from the altitude.

App. Alt. = Apparent altitude = Sextant altitude corrected for index error and dip.

FIG. 18-16 Excerpt from Nautical Almanac

ALTITUDE CORRECTION TABLES 35°-90°—MOON

App. Alt.	35°–39° Corr^n	40°–44° Corr^n	45°–49° Corr^n	50°–54° Corr^n	55°–59° Corr^n	60°–64° Corr^n	65°–69° Corr^n	70°–74° Corr^n	75°–79° Corr^n	80°–84° Corr^n	85°–89° Corr^n	App. Alt.
00	35 56.5	40 53.7	45 50.5	50 46.9	55 43.1	60 38.9	65 34.6	70 30.1	75 25.3	80 20.5	85 15.6	00
10	56.4	53.6	50.4	46.8	42.9	38.8	34.4	29.9	25.2	20.4	15.5	10
20	56.3	53.5	50.2	46.7	42.8	38.7	34.3	29.7	25.0	20.2	15.3	20
30	56.2	53.4	50.1	46.5	42.7	38.5	34.1	29.6	24.9	20.0	15.1	30
40	56.2	53.3	50.0	46.4	42.5	38.4	34.0	29.4	24.7	19.9	15.0	40
50	56.1	53.2	49.9	46.3	42.4	38.2	33.8	29.3	24.5	19.7	14.8	50
00	36 56.0	41 53.1	46 49.8	51 46.2	56 42.3	61 38.1	66 33.7	71 29.1	76 24.4	81 19.6	86 14.6	00
10	55.9	53.0	49.7	46.0	42.1	37.9	33.5	29.0	24.2	19.4	14.5	10
20	55.8	52.8	49.5	45.9	42.0	37.8	33.4	28.8	24.1	19.2	14.3	20
30	55.7	52.7	49.4	45.8	41.8	37.7	33.2	28.7	23.9	19.1	14.1	30
40	55.6	52.6	49.3	45.7	41.7	37.5	33.1	28.5	23.8	18.9	14.0	40
50	55.5	52.5	49.2	45.5	41.6	37.4	32.9	28.3	23.6	18.7	13.8	50
00	37 55.4	42 52.4	47 49.1	52 45.4	57 41.4	62 37.2	67 32.8	72 28.2	77 23.4	82 18.6	87 13.7	00
10	55.3	52.3	49.0	45.3	41.3	37.1	32.6	28.0	23.3	18.4	13.5	10
20	55.2	52.2	48.8	45.2	41.2	36.9	32.5	27.9	23.1	18.2	13.3	20
30	55.1	52.1	48.7	45.0	41.0	36.8	32.3	27.7	22.9	18.1	13.2	30
40	55.0	52.0	48.6	44.9	40.9	36.6	32.2	27.6	22.8	17.9	13.0	40
50	55.0	51.9	48.5	44.8	40.8	36.5	32.0	27.4	22.6	17.8	12.8	50
00	38 54.9	43 51.8	48 48.4	53 44.6	58 40.6	63 36.4	68 31.9	73 27.2	78 22.5	83 17.6	88 12.7	00
10	54.8	51.7	48.2	44.5	40.5	36.2	31.7	27.1	22.3	17.4	12.5	10
20	54.7	51.6	48.1	44.4	40.3	36.1	31.6	26.9	22.1	17.3	12.3	20
30	54.6	51.5	48.0	44.2	40.2	35.9	31.4	26.8	22.0	17.1	12.2	30
40	54.5	51.4	47.9	44.1	40.1	35.8	31.3	26.6	21.8	16.9	12.0	40
50	54.4	51.2	47.8	44.0	39.9	35.6	31.1	26.5	21.7	16.8	11.8	50
00	39 54.3	44 51.1	49 47.6	54 43.9	59 39.8	64 35.5	69 31.0	74 26.3	79 21.5	84 16.6	89 11.7	00
10	54.2	51.0	47.5	43.7	39.6	35.3	30.8	26.1	21.3	16.5	11.5	10
20	54.1	50.9	47.4	43.6	39.5	35.2	30.7	26.0	21.2	16.3	11.4	20
30	54.0	50.8	47.3	43.5	39.4	35.0	30.5	25.8	21.0	16.1	11.2	30
40	53.9	50.7	47.2	43.3	39.2	34.9	30.4	25.7	20.9	16.0	11.0	40
50	53.8	50.6	47.0	43.2	39.1	34.7	30.2	25.5	20.7	15.8	10.9	50

H.P.	L	U	L	U	L	U	L	U	L	U	L	U	L	U	L	U	L	U	L	U	L	U	H.P.
54.0	1.1	1.7	1.3	1.9	1.5	2.1	1.7	2.4	2.0	2.6	2.3	2.9	2.6	3.2	2.9	3.5	3.2	3.8	3.5	4.1	3.8	4.5	54.0
54.3	1.4	1.8	1.6	2.0	1.8	2.2	2.0	2.5	2.3	2.7	2.5	3.0	2.8	3.2	3.0	3.5	3.3	3.8	3.6	4.1	3.9	4.4	54.3
54.6	1.7	2.0	1.9	2.2	2.1	2.4	2.3	2.6	2.5	2.8	2.7	3.0	3.0	3.3	3.2	3.5	3.5	3.8	3.7	4.1	4.0	4.3	54.6
54.9	2.0	2.2	2.2	2.3	2.3	2.5	2.5	2.7	2.7	2.9	2.9	3.1	3.2	3.3	3.4	3.5	3.6	3.8	3.9	4.0	4.1	4.3	54.9
55.2	2.3	2.3	2.5	2.4	2.6	2.6	2.8	2.8	3.0	2.9	3.2	3.1	3.4	3.3	3.6	3.5	3.8	3.7	4.0	4.0	4.2	4.2	55.2
55.5	2.7	2.5	2.8	2.6	2.9	2.7	3.1	2.9	3.2	3.0	3.4	3.2	3.6	3.4	3.7	3.5	3.9	3.7	4.1	3.9	4.3	4.1	55.5
55.8	3.0	2.6	3.1	2.7	3.2	2.8	3.3	3.0	3.5	3.1	3.6	3.3	3.8	3.4	3.9	3.6	4.1	3.7	4.2	3.9	4.4	4.0	55.8
56.1	3.3	2.8	3.4	2.9	3.5	3.0	3.6	3.1	3.7	3.2	3.8	3.3	4.0	3.4	4.1	3.6	4.2	3.7	4.4	3.8	4.5	4.0	56.1
56.4	3.6	2.9	3.7	3.0	3.8	3.1	3.9	3.2	3.9	3.3	4.0	3.4	4.1	3.5	4.3	3.6	4.4	3.7	4.5	3.8	4.6	3.9	56.4
56.7	3.9	3.1	4.0	3.1	4.1	3.2	4.1	3.3	4.2	3.3	4.3	3.4	4.3	3.5	4.4	3.6	4.5	3.7	4.6	3.8	4.7	3.8	56.7
57.0	4.3	3.2	4.3	3.3	4.3	3.3	4.4	3.4	4.4	3.4	4.5	3.5	4.5	3.5	4.6	3.6	4.7	3.6	4.7	3.7	4.8	3.8	57.0
57.3	4.6	3.4	4.6	3.4	4.6	3.4	4.6	3.5	4.7	3.5	4.7	3.5	4.7	3.6	4.8	3.6	4.8	3.6	4.8	3.7	4.9	3.7	57.3
57.6	4.9	3.6	4.9	3.6	4.9	3.6	4.9	3.6	4.9	3.6	4.9	3.6	4.9	3.6	4.9	3.6	5.0	3.6	5.0	3.6	5.0	3.6	57.6
57.9	5.2	3.7	5.2	3.7	5.2	3.7	5.2	3.7	5.2	3.7	5.1	3.6	5.1	3.6	5.1	3.6	5.1	3.6	5.1	3.6	5.1	3.6	57.9
58.2	5.5	3.9	5.5	3.8	5.5	3.8	5.4	3.8	5.4	3.7	5.4	3.7	5.3	3.7	5.3	3.6	5.2	3.6	5.2	3.5	5.2	3.5	58.2
58.5	5.9	4.0	5.8	4.0	5.8	3.9	5.7	3.9	5.6	3.8	5.6	3.8	5.5	3.7	5.5	3.6	5.4	3.6	5.3	3.5	5.3	3.4	58.5
58.8	6.2	4.2	6.1	4.1	6.0	4.1	6.0	4.0	5.9	3.9	5.8	3.8	5.7	3.7	5.6	3.6	5.5	3.5	5.4	3.5	5.3	3.4	58.8
59.1	6.5	4.3	6.4	4.3	6.3	4.2	6.2	4.1	6.1	4.0	6.0	3.9	5.9	3.8	5.8	3.6	5.7	3.5	5.6	3.4	5.4	3.3	59.1
59.4	6.8	4.5	6.7	4.4	6.6	4.3	6.5	4.2	6.4	4.1	6.2	3.9	6.1	3.8	6.0	3.7	5.8	3.5	5.7	3.4	5.5	3.2	59.4
59.7	7.1	4.6	7.0	4.5	6.9	4.4	6.8	4.3	6.6	4.1	6.5	4.0	6.3	3.8	6.2	3.7	6.0	3.5	5.8	3.3	5.6	3.2	59.7
60.0	7.5	4.8	7.3	4.7	7.2	4.5	7.0	4.4	6.9	4.2	6.7	4.0	6.5	3.9	6.3	3.7	6.1	3.5	5.9	3.3	5.7	3.1	60.0
60.3	7.8	5.0	7.6	4.8	7.5	4.7	7.3	4.5	7.1	4.3	6.9	4.1	6.7	3.9	6.5	3.7	6.3	3.5	6.0	3.2	5.8	3.0	60.3
60.6	8.1	5.1	7.9	5.0	7.7	4.8	7.6	4.6	7.3	4.4	7.1	4.2	6.9	3.9	6.7	3.7	6.4	3.4	6.2	3.2	5.9	2.9	60.6
60.9	8.4	5.3	8.2	5.1	8.0	4.9	7.8	4.7	7.6	4.5	7.3	4.2	7.1	4.0	6.8	3.7	6.6	3.4	6.3	3.2	6.0	2.9	60.9
61.2	8.7	5.4	8.5	5.2	8.3	5.0	8.1	4.8	7.8	4.5	7.6	4.3	7.3	4.0	7.0	3.7	6.7	3.4	6.4	3.1	6.1	2.8	61.2
61.5	9.1	5.6	8.8	5.4	8.6	5.1	8.3	4.9	8.1	4.6	7.8	4.3	7.5	4.0	7.2	3.7	6.9	3.4	6.5	3.1	6.2	2.7	61.5

FIG. 18-17 Excerpt from Nautical Almanac

Chapter 19

Celestial Navigation with N.O. 249, Vol. I for Stars

At this point we are ready to begin the complete process by which we determine our position on the open ocean. We shall begin with star sights and work them by N.O. 249 because that is the easiest process of all. In later chapters we shall show the manner in which sights on the sun, the planets, and the moon work out, not only with N.O. 249, but with H.O. 214 and N.O. 229. In this chapter we shall use the *Air Almanac,* because it permits us to use the simplest and quickest method; before we are finished, however, you will be equally at home with the *Nautical Almanac.* We have purposely relegated the finding of latitude at noon and by Polaris to later chapters. They are special methods —holdovers from sailing ship days when other sights were much more complicated—of questionable importance in our day.

Up to this point, we have learned how to use the sextant, how to apply corrections to the sextant reading, how to time our sights, how to use the almanacs, and how to obtain the local hour angle (LHA) or the angle t of the body we observe. Our procedure will be the complete process of planning, taking, working, and plotting three star sights at morning twilight on January 1. Our vessel is at DR position 33°15′ N, 119°15′ W. For almanac information, see the *Air Almanac* excerpts in Chapter 17 and this chapter.

***Example* •** The procedure is to first find out which are the best stars available for observation at morning twilight, to observe those stars, to obtain the exact watch time and the sextant altitude H_s, and then to obtain H_c (the computed altitude) and the bearing Z_n. We compare H_o and H_c to find the intercept, toward or away, and with this data we are able to plot our fix. Let us assume that our watch is 15 seconds fast, that height of eye is 12 feet, and that the index error on our sextant is 5′ off the arc. The complete operation, including plotting, is shown on the following pages, where the use of a work form and plotting sheet is shown. Because such work forms greatly simplify navigation, most navigators use them. They are available for all sets of tables.

Step 1. Determine the time of beginning of morning twilight on January 1 and the most suitable stars for observation. On page A63 of the *Air Almanac,* Fig. 19–1, we find that morning civil twilight at latitude 35° N on January 2, which represent the nearest degree of latitude and the nearest date, begins at 0640 LMT.

LMT of twilight	0640	Jan. 1
Longitude 119°15′ W	757	(in time to nearest minute)
Greenwich Mean Time	1437	Jan. 1
For 1437 GMT we find the GHA of Aries:		
GHA of Aries for 1430	318° 20′	
GHA of Aries for 7 min.	1° 45′	
GHA of Aries for 1437	320° 05′	
Subtract west longitude	119° 15′	
LHA of Aries	200° 50′	or 201°

For purposes of determining which stars are visible, we only need to know the LHA of Aries to the nearest whole degree. Therefore, at this point we shall introduce a shortcut which we shall also find useful on other occasions.

Shortcut In the calculations just shown, we applied the longitude twice: once when we added it in the form of time, 7^h57^m, and the second time when we subtracted the longitude from the GHA of Aries to find the LHA of Aries. Our shortcut consists of eliminating those two steps. We use our local time as Greenwich time, but the GHA of Aries we find in the table we call the LHA of Aries. It is as simple as that. In this case we use 0640 as GMT and find that the GHA of Aries to the nearest whole degree is 201°, and this is, in fact, our LHA as found above. There was only a difference of 20′, which is of no significance in this type of rough calculation.

Lat.	Dec. 30	January ↓ 2	5	8	11	14	17	20	23	26	29	February 1	4	7	10	Lat.
°	h m	h m	h m	h m	h m	h m	h m	h m	h m	h m	h m	h m	h m	h m	h m	°
N 72	10 49	10 40	10 31	10 20	10 09	09 57	09 45	09 32	09 20	09 07	08 54	08 40	08 27	08 13	08 00	N 72
70	09 52	09 48	09 43	09 37	09 30	09 22	09 13	09 03	08 54	08 43	33	21	08 10	07 59	07 47	70
68	09 19	09 16	09 12	09 08	09 02	08 56	08 49	08 42	34	25	16	08 07	07 57	47	36	68
66	08 54	08 52	08 50	08 46	08 42	37	31	25	18	08 10	08 03	07 54	46	37	27	66
64	35	33	31	29	25	21	16	08 11	08 05	07 58	07 51	44	36	28	20	64
62	19	18	16	14	08 11	08 08	08 03	07 59	07 54	48	42	35	28	21	13	62
N 60	08 06	08 05	08 04	08 02	07 59	07 56	07 53	07 49	07 44	07 39	07 33	07 27	07 21	07 15	07 08	N 60
58	07 55	07 54	07 53	07 51	49	46	43	40	36	31	26	21	15	09	07 03	58
56	44	44	43	42	40	38	35	32	28	24	19	15	09	07 04	06 58	56
54	36	35	35	34	32	30	28	25	21	18	14	09	07 04	06 59	54	54
52	27	28	27	26	25	23	21	18	15	12	08	07 04	06 59	55	50	52
N 50	07 20	07 20	07 20	07 19	07 18	07 17	07 15	07 12	07 10	07 07	07 03	06 59	06 55	06 51	06 46	N 50
45	07 04	07 05	07 05	07 04	07 04	07 03	07 01	06 59	06 57	06 55	06 52	49	46	42	38	45
40	06 51	06 52	06 52	06 52	06 51	06 51	06 50	48	47	45	43	40	38	35	32	40
→35	39	40	41	41	41	40	40	39	38	36	35	33	30	28	25	35
30	29	30	30	31	31	31	31	30	29	28	27	25	24	22	20	30
N 20	06 10	06 11	06 12	06 13	06 14	06 14	06 14	06 14	06 14	06 14	06 13	06 13	06 12	06 11	06 09	N 20
N 10	05 53	05 54	05 55	05 57	05 57	05 58	05 59	06 00	06 00	06 01	06 01	06 01	06 00	06 00	06 00	N 10
0	36	38	39	40	42	43	44	05 45	05 46	05 47	05 48	05 48	05 49	05 49	05 49	0
S 10	05 18	20	22	23	25	27	28	30	31	33	34	35	37	38	39	S 10
20	04 58	05 00	05 02	05 04	05 06	05 08	05 10	05 12	05 14	05 17	19	20	22	24	26	20
S 30	04 33	04 35	04 38	04 40	04 43	04 45	04 48	04 51	04 54	04 57	05 00	05 02	05 05	05 08	05 11	S 30
35	18	21	23	26	29	32	35	38	41	45	04 48	04 51	04 55	04 58	05 01	35
40	04 00	04 03	04 06	04 09	04 12	04 15	19	23	27	30	34	38	42	46	04 50	40
45	03 38	03 41	03 44	03 47	03 51	03 55	04 00	04 04	04 09	04 13	04 18	23	28	32	37	45
50	03 09	03 12	16	20	24	29	03 34	03 40	03 45	03 51	03 57	04 03	09	15	20	50
S 52	02 54	02 57	03 01	03 06	03 11	03 16	03 22	03 28	03 34	03 40	03 47	03 53	04 00	04 06	04 12	S 52
54	36	40	02 45	02 50	02 55	03 01	03 08	03 14	21	28	35	42	03 49	03 56	04 03	54
56	02 14	02 19	02 24	30	36	02 43	02 50	02 58	03 06	03 14	22	29	37	45	03 53	56
58	01 46	01 51	01 57	02 04	02 12	02 21	29	38	02 47	02 56	03 05	03 15	24	33	41	58
S 60	00 59	01 08	01 17	01 27	01 39	01 50	02 01	02 13	02 24	02 35	02 46	02 57	03 07	03 18	03 28	S 60

FIG. 19-1
Excerpt from Air Almanac

Step 2. Determine altitude and bearing of available stars at 0640, using volume I of N.O. 249. Latitude is 33° N, LHA is 201°. On page 95 of volume I we find seven stars listed for LHA of 201°. Those printed in *capital letters* are first-magnitude stars, and therefore preferable, but the three with an *asterisk* (*) are so marked because they will give the best crossing angle of the lines of position. We therefore select *Kochab, Antares,* and *Regulus* as the three stars we would like to observe, but just in case we have a cloudy sky, we write the others down to keep in reserve. We take out the following information (see Fig. 19–2):

Star	Kochab	Antares	Regulus
H_c	47°21′	16°20′	40°28′
Z_n	009°	138°	257°

With this information we are ready to take sights as soon

LAT 33°N

LHA ♈	Hc Zn	Hc Zn	Hc Zn	Hc Zn	Hc Zn	Hc Zn	Hc Zn
	*VEGA	Alphecca	ARCTURUS	*SPICA	REGULUS	*POLLUX	Dubhe
180	13 49 052	43 49 083	57 06 106	41 41 152	56 45 238	35 24 283	59 37 346
181	14 29 053	44 39 083	57 55 107	42 05 153	56 02 239	34 35 284	59 25 346
182	15 09 053	45 29 084	58 43 108	42 27 154	55 19 240	33 46 284	59 13 345
183	15 50 054	46 19 084	59 30 109	42 48 156	54 35 241	32 58 284	58 59 344
184	16 31 054	47 10 085	60 18 110	43 08 157	53 50 242	32 09 285	58 45 343
185	17 11 055	48 00 085	61 05 111	43 27 158	53 06 243	31 20 285	58 30 342
186	17 52 055	48 50 086	61 52 112	43 45 160	52 20 244	30 32 286	58 15 342
187	18 34 055	49 40 086	62 38 113	44 02 161	51 35 245	29 43 286	57 58 341
188	19 15 056	50 30 087	63 24 115	44 18 162	50 49 246	28 55 286	57 42 340
189	19 57 056	51 20 087	64 10 116	44 33 163	50 03 247	28 07 287	57 24 340
190	20 39 056	52 11 088	64 55 117	44 47 165	49 16 248	27 19 287	57 07 339
191	21 21 057	53 01 088	65 39 119	45 00 166	48 29 249	26 31 288	56 48 338
192	22 03 057	53 51 089	66 23 120	45 11 168	47 42 250	25 43 288	56 29 338
193	22 45 058	54 42 089	67 06 122	45 21 169	46 55 251	24 55 289	56 10 337
194	23 28 058	55 32 090	67 49 123	45 30 170	46 07 252	24 07 289	55 50 336
	*Kochab	VEGA	Rasalhague	*ANTARES	SPICA	*REGULUS	Dubhe
195	46 31 011	24 10 058	24 51 091	12 49 134	45 38 172	45 19 252	55 30 336
196	46 40 010	24 53 059	25 41 091	13 25 134	45 45 173	44 31 253	55 09 335
197	46 48 010	25 36 059	26 31 092	14 01 135	45 50 174	43 43 254	54 48 335
198	46 57 010	26 20 059	27 22 092	14 36 136	45 54 176	42 54 255	54 26 334
199	47 05 009	27 03 060	28 12 093	15 11 136	45 57 177	42 06 256	54 04 334
200	47 13 009	27 46 060	29 02 094	15 46 137	45 59 179	41 17 256	53 41 333
201	47 21 009	28 30 060	29 52 094	16 20 138	46 00 180	40 28 257	53 18 333
202	47 28 008	29 14 061	30 42 095	16 53 139	45 59 182	39 39 258	52 55 332
203	47 35 008	29 58 061	31 33 095	17 26 139	45 57 183	38 49 258	52 32 332
204	47 41 007	30 42 061	32 23 096	17 59 140	45 54 184	38 00 259	52 08 331
205	47 48 007	31 26 061	33 13 097	18 31 141	45 49 186	37 11 260	51 44 331
206	47 54 007	32 10 062	34 03 097	19 02 142	45 44 187	36 21 260	51 19 331
207	47 59 006	32 54 062	34 52 098	19 33 142	45 37 189	35 31 261	50 54 330
208	48 05 006	33 39 062	35 42 098	20 04 143	45 29 190	34 42 262	50 29 330
209	48 10 006	34 23 063	36 32 099	20 33 144	45 19 191	33 52 262	50 04 330
	*Kochab	VEGA	Rasalhague	*ANTARES	SPICA	*REGULUS	Dubhe
210	48 15 005	35 08 063	37 22 100	21 03 145	45 09	3 02 263	49 38 329
211	48 19 005	5 53 063	38 11 1	21 31 146	44 57	2 263	49 13 329
212	48 23 004	38 063	39 01	59 146	44	264	48 47 329
213	48 26 00	064	39 50	147	44	5	48 20 329
214	48 30 0	64	40 3				
			41				

FIG. 19-2
Excerpt from N.O. 249, Vol. I

as the horizon becomes visible. Since we know the approximate altitude, we can set the sextant to that angle, look in the indicated direction, and see our star, if we want to figure the exact watch time of the beginning of twilight, we can easily do so:

LMT of twilight	0640
Longitude in time	757
Greenwich Mean Time	1437
Zone description	−8
Zone time of twilight	0637

Actually, there can be a difference of up to 30 minutes between local mean time and zone time. But in practice we do not figure ZT for morning and evening sights because we are on deck as twilight approaches and can see when conditions are right for taking sights—meaning that we can see both the stars and the sea horizon.

Step 3. We take the actual sights and time them carefully with the following results:

	Kochab	Antares	Regulus
Watch time	06-41-33	06-43-15	06-45-27
Altitude H_s	47°12′	16°50′	39°00.5′

Step 4. We convert this information to a line of position (LOP) by determining an *intercept* and Z_n. This process is called "reducing" the sight, and the navigation tables are often referred to as *sight reduction tables.* It is preferable to use a work form on which you make the following initial entries: local date; Greenwich date; dead reckoning latitude and longitude; height of eye; index error on sextant; watch error; name of star; sextant altitude H_s; and watch time of sight. See Fig. 19–8.

Usually we first correct the sextant angle by applying index correction, dip of the horizon (based on height of eye), and refraction. Since we are using the *Air Almanac,* we find the dip of the horizon on the *outside of the back cover* (Fig. 19–3) and refraction on the *inside of the back cover* (Fig. 19–4). Refraction varies somewhat with an aircraft's altitude above sea level, but for marine navigation we assume we are at sea level and must therefore use the first column, which is headed "0." Refraction is found in the column headed "R_o."

For ordinary marine navigation it is not necessary to consider the temperature correction *f,* also shown inside the back cover. In this example, we know that the index error is 5′ *off* the arc, so the correction is +5′. Dip of the horizon for a height of eye of 12 feet is 3′, and this is always subtracted. Having determined the *total correction* for each of the three stars, we enter it in the main column and figure the value of H_o, the *observed altitude.* As mentioned before, when we work with the *Air Almanac* and the tables in N.O. 249, we omit tenths of minutes.

The refraction table (Fig. 19–4) is taken from the inside back cover of the *Air Almanac.* For ordinary marine naviga-

CORRECTIONS TO BE APPLIED TO MARINE SEXTANT ALTITUDES

MARINE SEXTANT ERROR

Sextant Number

Index Error ′

CORRECTIONS

In addition to sextant error and dip, corrections are to be applied for:

Refraction

Semi-diameter (for the Sun and Moon)

Parallax (for the Moon)

Dome refraction (if applicable)

CORRECTION FOR DIP OF THE HORIZON

To be subtracted from sextant altitude

Ht.	Dip	Ht.	Dip	Ht.	Dip	Ht.	Dip	Ht.	Dip
Ft.	′	Ft.	′	Ft.	′	Ft.	′	Ft.	′
0		114		437		968		1 707	
	1		11		21		31		41
2		137		481		1 033		1 792	
	2		12		22		32		42
6		162		527		1 099		1 880	
	3		13		23		33		43
12		189		575		1 168		1 970	
	4		14		24		34		44
21		218		625		1 239		2 061	
	5		15		25		35		45
31		250		677		1 311		2 155	
	6		16		26		36		46
43		283		731		1 386		2 251	
	7		17		27		37		47
58		318		787		1 463		2 349	
	8		18		28		38		48
75		356		845		1 543		2 449	
	9		19		29		39		49
93		395		906		1 624		2 551	
	10		20		30		40		50
114		437		968		1 707		2 655	

FIG. 19-3 Excerpt from Air Almanac

CORRECTIONS TO BE APPLIED TO SEXTANT ALTITUDE

REFRACTION

To be subtracted from sextant altitude (referred to as observed altitude in A.P. 3270)

R_o	Height above sea level in units of 1 000 ft. — Sextant Altitude: 0	5	10	15	20	25	30	35	40	45	50	55	R_o
′	° ′	° ′	° ′	° ′	° ′	° ′	° ′	° ′	° ′	° ′	° ′	° ′	′
	90	90	90	90	90	90	90	90	90	90	90	90	
0													0
	63	59	55	51	46	41	36	31	26	20	17	13	
1													1
	33	29	26	22	19	16	14	11	9	7	6	4	
2													2
	21	19	16	14	12	10	8	7	5	4	2 40	1 40	
3													3
	16	14	12	10	8	7	6	5	3 10	2 20	1 30	0 40	
4													4
	12	11	9	8	7	5	4 00	3 10	2 10	1 30	0 39	+0 05	
5													5
	10	9	7	5 50	4 50	3 50	3 10	2 20	1 30	0 49	+0 11	−0 19	
6													6
	8 10	6 50	5 50	4 50	4 00	3 00	2 20	1 50	1 10	0 24	−0 11	−0 38	
7													7
	6 50	5 50	5 00	4 00	3 10	2 30	1 50	1 20	0 38	+0 04	−0 28	−0 54	
8													8
	6 00	5 10	4 10	3 20	2 40	2 00	1 30	1 00	0 19	−0 13	−0 42	−1 08	
9													9
	5 20	4 30	3 40	2 50	2 10	1 40	1 10	0 35	+0 03	−0 27	−0 53	−1 18	
10													10
	4 30	3 40	2 50	2 20	1 40	1 10	0 37	+0 11	−0 16	−0 43	−1 08	−1 31	
12													12
	3 30	2 50	2 10	1 40	1 10	0 34	+0 09	−0 14	−0 37	−1 00	−1 23	−1 44	
14													14
	2 50	2 10	1 40	1 10	0 37	+0 10	−0 13	−0 34	−0 53	−1 14	−1 35	−1 56	
16													16
	2 20	1 40	1 20	0 43	+0 15	−0 08	−0 31	−0 52	−1 08	−1 27	−1 46	−2 05	
18													18
	1 50	1 20	0 49	+0 23	−0 02	−0 26	−0 46	−1 06	−1 22	−1 39	−1 57	−2 14	
20													20
	1 12	0 44	+0 19	−0 06	−0 28	−0 48	−1 09	−1 27	−1 42	−1 58	−2 14	−2 30	
25													25
	0 34	+0 10	−0 13	−0 36	−0 55	−1 14	−1 32	−1 51	−2 06	−2 21	−2 34	−2 49	
30													30
	+0 06	−0 16	−0 37	−0 59	−1 17	−1 33	−1 51	−2 07	−2 23	−2 37	−2 51	−3 04	
35													35
	−0 18	−0 37	−0 58	−1 16	−1 34	−1 49	−2 06	−2 22	−2 35	−2 49	−3 03	−3 16	
40													40
		−0 53	−1 14	−1 31	−1 47	−2 03	−2 18	−2 33	−2 47	−2 59	−3 13	−3 25	
45													45
		−1 10	−1 28	−1 44	−1 59	−2 15	−2 28	−2 43	−2 56	−3 08	−3 22	−3 33	
50													50
			−1 40	−1 53	−2 09	−2 24	−2 38	−2 52	−3 04	−3 17	−3 29	−3 41	
55													55
				−2 03	−2 18	−2 33	−2 46	−3 01	−3 12	−3 25	−3 37	−3 48	
60													60
							−2 53	−3 07	−3 19	−3 31	−3 42	−3 53	

f	Temperature in °C.: 0	5	10	15	20	25	30	35	40	45	50	55	f
	+47	+36	+27	+18	+10	+ 3	− 5	−13					
0·9													0·9
	+26	+16	+ 6	− 4	−13	−22	−31	−40					
1·0													1·0
	+ 5	− 5	−15	−25	−36	−46	−57	−68					
1·1													1·1
	−16	−25	−36	−46	−58	−71	−83	−95					
1·2													1·2
	−37	−45	−56	−67	−81	−95							

For these heights no temperature correction is necessary, so use $R = R_o$

$R = R_o \times f$

R_o	f = 0·9	1·0	1·1	1·2
′	′	′	′	′
0	0	0	0	0
1	1	1	1	1
2	2	2	2	2
3	3	3	3	4
4	4	4	4	5
5	5	5	5	6
6	5	6	7	7
7	6	7	8	8
8	7	8	9	10
9	8	9	10	11
10	9	10	11	12
12	11	12	13	14
14	13	14	15	17
16	14	16	18	19
18	16	18	20	22
20	18	20	22	24
25	22	25	28	30
30	27	30	33	36
35	31	35	38	42
40	36	40	44	48
45	40	45	50	54
50	45	50	55	60
55	49	55	60	66
60	54	60	66	72
f	0·9	1·0	1·1	1·2

Where R_o is less than 10′ or the height greater than 35 000 ft. use $R = R_o$

Choose the column appropriate to height, in units of 1 000 ft., and find the range of altitude in which the sextant altitude lies; the corresponding value of R_o is the refraction, to be subtracted from sextant altitude, unless conditions are extreme. In that case find f from the lower table, with critical argument temperature. Use the table on the right to form the refraction, $R = R_o \times f$.

FIG. 19-4 Excerpt from Air Almanac

tion, you might find it simpler to use the table below (Fig. 19–5), which is found inside the back cover of N.O. 249, Vol. I.

We now proceed to convert the *watch time* (WT) to *Greenwich Mean Time* (GMT). First we apply the *watch error.* Since the watch is 15 seconds fast, it is ahead of the real time, so we deduct 15 seconds from WT to obtain *zone time* (ZT), the time the watch would show if it had no error. To the ZT we apply *zone difference* (ZD), which in this case is 8 hours; and because we are in west longitude, Greenwich time is greater than local time, and so we add the ZD to the ZT to find GMT. An examination of the *time diagram* shows that there is no change of date.

For the GMT found, we now determine the GHA of Aries (♈) from the almanac. Whereas the *Nautical Almanac* gives the value for every whole hour, the *Air Almanac* gives it for 10-minute intervals. This saves time because we obtain the GHA ♈ for 14^h40^m for all three sights. Next we turn to the table Fig. 17–6, where we obtain the GHA of Aries for the remaining minutes and seconds in our GMT. Adding the two together, we have the total GHA ♈.

Next we determine the *assumed longitude.* This will be

TABLE 8.—Refraction

To be ***subtracted*** from sextant altitude

FIG. 19-5
From N.O. 249, Vol. I

R	Height in Thousands of Feet												R
	0	5	10	15	20	25	30	35	40	45	50	55	
	Sextant Altitude												
′	°	°	°	°	°	°	°	°	°	°	°	°	′
	90	90	90	90	90	90	90	90	90	90	90	90	
0													0
	63	59	55	51	46	41	36	31	26	20	17	13	
1													1
	33	29	26	22	19	16	14	11	9	7	6	4	
2													2
	21	19	16	14	12	10	8	7					
3													3
	16	14	12	10	8								
4													4
	12	11	9										
5													5
	10	9											

a longitude preferably within 30′ of the DR longitude, but so contrived that when we apply it to the GHA ♈, the LHA ♈ comes out a whole degree. In west longitude this obviously means that the minutes in the assumed longitude must be the same as the minutes in the GHA ♈. If you will stop for a moment to remember that when we are in east longitude we *add* the longitude to GHA ♈ to find the LHA ♈, then you can see that the minutes in the assumed longitude must be such that when they are added to the minutes of the GHA a whole degree results. (Therefore, minutes of assumed longitude = 60′ minus minutes of GHA.) You will observe this in future examples. For Kochab, for example, we select an assumed longitude of 119°10′ W, so that when we subtract it from the GHA we get an LHA of 202°.

Whenever we work three sights simultaneously, we always try to arrange the assumed longitudes so as to get the same LHA for all three sights. In this case we did not do this for Regulus, because the assumed longitude would have to be 120°08′ W, which is more than 30′ from the DR longitude. However, in actual practice you will find that the result will not be materially different. Later on when we discuss *multiple sights,* you will find that we *always* use the *same* LHA or *angle t* when we have taken three sights in succession on the same celestial body.

The next step is to enter volume I of N.O. 249 with latitude 33°, our *assumed latitude,* which is the whole degree of latitude nearest our DR latitude, and an LHA ♈ as indicated for each star. We immediately take out the *computed altitude* H_c and the true azimuth Z_n and enter them on our form. There is no interpolation and no correction. By comparing H_c with H_o, subtracting the smaller from the larger, we find the *intercept.* We mark this as *away* or *toward,* depending on which is the greater. If you don't navigate every day, you may have trouble remembering which is which, so the following may help you:

COAST	GUARD	ACADEMY
COMPUTED	GREATER	AWAY

We find it convenient to assign each sight a plotting symbol—usually a circle, a square, a triangle, or some other simple designation—to prevent possible confusion.

Step 5. Having obtained the assumed position, the true Azimuth Z_n, and the intercept, we are now ready to plot our line of position (LOP). This can be done right on an actual chart, but it is usually done on a separate *plotting sheet.* Plotting sheets take many forms, but essentially they cover a small area, one or two degrees of latitude and longitude of the part of the ocean where we are located. The Naval Oceanographic Office has special printed plotting sheets for specific latitudes, using several different sizes and scales, and they also sell pads of *universal plotting sheets,* which can be adapted for any latitude and longitude by using a variable scale printed on each page. It is common for navigators to construct their own so-called *small-area plotting sheet* similar to the one on which we have plotted the three star sights in this example. The method is simple.

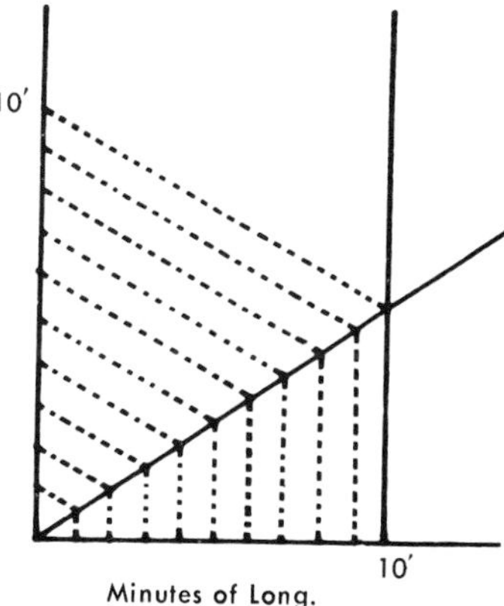

FIG. 19-6A
Methods for constructing longitude scale on plotting sheet

How to Construct a Plotting Sheet On a suitable size sheet of paper draw a vertical line on the left to represent a meridian of longitude on which you can construct a *latitude scale.* At 90° to this, draw a base line across the bottom of the page to represent a parallel of latitude, on which you can construct a *longitude scale.* First you establish the latitude scale by marking off a suitable number of sections, each representing 10′ of latitude—usually six or nine, so that the range is from 1–1½° in latitude. Divide one of these sections into ten equal parts, each of which will then be equal to 1′ of latitude, or *one nautical mile.* This scale will be used as your mileage scale. *Never use the longitude scale for measuring miles.*

Method of Constructing Longitude Scale What we are really doing is constructing a small portion of a Mercator chart. To get the correct relationship between the latitude and longitude scales we proceed as in Fig. 19–6A. At the lower left-hand corner we lay off *from* the base line an angle equal to our assumed latitude (in this example 33°). With dividers we measure off 10′ of latitude along the upper leg of this angle by swinging an arc as shown. Through the intersection, we drop a vertical line to the base line, and the distance on this base line to the corner is now equal to 10′ of longitude on a Mercator chart at the indicated latitude.

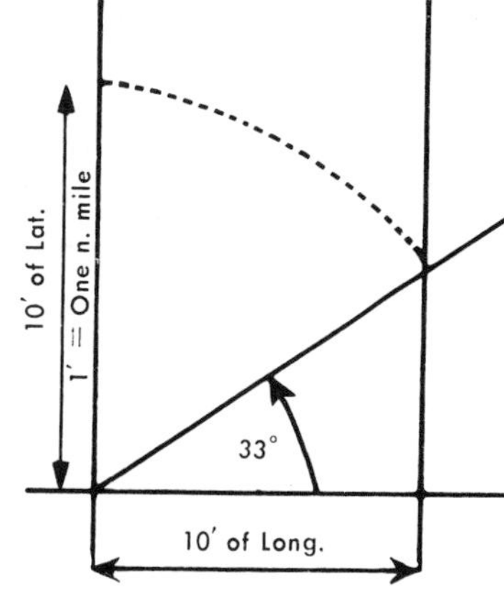

FIG. 19-6B

Fig. 19–6B shows the manner in which we can divide 10′ of longitude into ten equal parts. We established the units on the latitude scale when we set it up, so now we draw parallel lines from each minute of latitude to the leg of the base angle, and at the intersections we drop a perpendicular to the base. This divides the 10′ of longitude into ten equal parts, which we can now use for plotting our assumed longitudes.

It is customary to have the small-area plotting sheet cover about 2° of longitude, so we construct the divisions 10′ apart on the base line and draw our grid. Next we assign the desired numbers of latitude and longitude to our divisions, usually so that our DR position will fall in the middle of the plotting area. Here you must remember the following four cardinal rules:

1. In north latitude, latitude values increase *upward.*
2. In south latitude, latitude values increase *downward.*
3. In east longitude, longitude values increase to the *right.*
4. In west longitude, longitude values increase to the *left.*

At Coast Navigation School in Santa Barbara, California, we use printed forms on which the latitude scale is established, and we can thus easily construct the longitude scale for our assumed latitude, as shown in the plot at the end of this chapter.

All LOPs are plotted from the assumed position, using assumed latitude and assumed longitude—*never the dead reckoning position.* Note that all three sights will have the same assumed latitude, but each will have a different assumed longitude, taken from the work form, and indicated by the various plotting symbols. In the case of Kochab, we plot the assumed longitude as 119°10′ W, and through this point mark off 8° from true north, the Z_n, to indicate the direction of the geographical position (GP) of the star. Along this line we mark off the intercept of 9 miles (taken from the latitude scale at the left) in the direction of the star, since the intercept was marked *toward* ("T"). At the

TABLE 5.—Precession and Nutation Correction

LHA ♈	Latitude															LHA ♈
	N89°	N80°	N70°	N60°	N50°	N40°	N20°	0°	S20°	S40°	S50°	S60°	S70°	S80°	S89°	
	mi. °	mi. °	mi. °	mi. °	mi. °	mi. °	mi. °	mi. °	mi. °	mi. °	mi. °	mi. °	mi. °	mi. °	mi. °	
								1972								
°																°
0	1 000	1 020	1 040	1 050	2 050	2 060	2 070	2 070	2 070	2 060	2 060	1 050	1 040	1 030	1 010	0
30	1 030	1 040	1 050	2 060	2 060	2 070	2 070	2 070	2 070	2 060	1 050	1 040	1 020	1 000	1 340	30
60	1 060	1 070	2 070	2 070	2 080	2 080	2 080	2 080	2 070	1 070	1 060	1 040	1 000	1 320	1 310	60
90	1 090	1 090	2 090	2 090	2 090	2 090	2 090	2 090	2 090	1 090	1 080	0 —	0 —	1 280	1 270	90
120	1 120	1 110	2 110	2 100	2 100	2 100	2 100	2 100	2 100	1 110	1 120	1 140	0 —	1 230	1 240	120
150	1 140	1 130	1 120	2 120	2 110	2 110	2 110	2 110	2 110	2 120	1 130	1 140	1 160	1 190	1 210	150
180	1 170	1 150	1 140	1 130	2 120	2 120	2 110	2 110	2 110	2 120	1 130	1 130	1 140	1 160	1 180	180
210	1 200	1 180	1 160	1 140	1 130	2 120	2 110	2 110	2 110	2 110	2 120	2 120	1 130	1 140	1 150	210
240	1 230	1 220	1 180	1 140	1 120	1 110	2 110	2 100	2 100	2 100	2 100	2 110	2 110	1 110	1 120	240
270	1 270	1 260	0 —	0 —	1 100	1 090	2 090	2 090	2 090	2 090	2 090	2 090	2 090	1 090	1 090	270
300	1 300	1 310	0 —	1 040	1 060	1 070	2 080	2 080	2 080	2 080	2 080	2 080	2 070	1 070	1 060	300
330	1 330	1 350	1 020	1 040	1 050	2 060	2 070	2 070	2 070	2 070	2 070	2 060	1 060	1 050	1 040	330
360	1 000	1 020	1 040	1 050	2 050	2 060	2 070	2 070	2 070	2 060	2 060	1 050	1 040	1 030	1 010	360
								1973								
0	1 000	1 0[illegible]	2 040	2 050	2 060	3 0[illegible]	3 070	3 070	3 070	3 060	2 06[illegible]	2 050	2 040	1 020	1 000	0
30	1 030		2 060	2 060	3 070	[illegible]	3 070	3 070	3 070	2 060	[illegible]	1 040	1 020	1 350	1 330	30
60	1 [illegible]		070	3 080	3 080		080	3 080	2 080	2 07[illegible]		40	1 000	1 320	1 300	60
90			[illegible]	3 090	3 [illegible]		[illegible]	3 090	2 090	[illegible]			0 —	1 270	1 270	[illegible]
1[illegible]				3 100				3 100	2 10[illegible]				[illegible] 180	1 220	1 [illegible]	
				[illegible] 12[illegible]				110	[illegible]				160	1		

FIG. 19-7
Excerpt from N.O. 249, Vol. I

end of the intercept we draw a heavy straight line at 90° to the bearing, representing the LOP of Kochab. Proceeding in a similar manner with the other two stars, we obtain an intersection of the three LOPs. We call this point the *fix* and so label it, along with the time, usually that of the middle sight. Very often the three LOPs do not meet in a point, but form a small triangle. It is accepted practice to take the center of this triangle as our fix.

This plot is read as lat. 33°11′ N, long. 119°26.5′ W. Any LOP or fix obtained through the use of N.O. 249, Vol. I, is subject to a single correction for *precession* and *nutation,* taken from Table 5 at the back of N.O. 249 (Fig. 19–7). Precession of the equinox is the annual shift of the first point of Aries, also called the vernal equinox, but more precisely the position occupied by the sun each spring when it crosses the equinoctial and changes from south to north declination. Nutation is the error caused by the fact that the Earth wobbles slightly on its axis. Both precession and nutation affect the SHA of celestial bodies and their declination, and therefore affect the results of our observations. The correction varies from year to year and is always given as a number of miles in a given direction. We enter the

Coast Navigation School

SANTA BARBARA, CALIFORNIA

MULTIPLE SIGHT FORM FOR STARS, N.O. 249

WITH NAUTICAL ALMANAC

Name Simonsen

Local Date Jan. 1 Greenwich Date Jan. 1 DR Lat N 33° 15' DR Long W 119° 15'

Body	Kochab	Antares	Regulus
Hs	47° 12'	16° 50'	39° 00.5
Total Corr.	+1	−1	+1
Ho	47° 13'	16° 49'	39° 01.5
Watch Time	06-41-33	06-43-15	06-45-27
Watch Error	−15	−15	−15
Zone Time	06-41-18	06-43-00	06-45-12
Zone Descr. +	8	+8	+8
GMT	14-41-18	14-43-00	14-45-12
GHA ♈ Hrs. (14-40)	320° 50'	320° 50'	320° 50'
GHA ♈ Min. & Sec.	20'	45'	1° 18'
GHA ♈ Total	321° 10'	321° 35'	322° 08'
Assumed Long. −W, +E	119° 10'	119° 35'	119° 08
Apply 360° if necessary			
LHA ♈	202°	202°	203°
Assumed Lat. N/S	—	N 33°	—
From N.O. 249, Vol 1			
Hc	47° 28'	16° 53'	38° 49'
Ho	47° 37'	16° 49'	39° 01.5'
Intercept (T/A)	T 9 mi.	A 4 mi	T 12.5 mi
Zn	008°	139°	258°
Plotting Symbol	○	□	△

IE 5' off arc

WE 15 Sec. fast

HE 12 Ft.

Sextant Corrections

	+	−	+	−	+	−
IC	5		5		5	
Dip		3		3		
Refr.		1		3		
	5	4	5	6	5	
	4			5	4	
Total C	+1			−1	+1	

G

M

m

g

Time Diagram

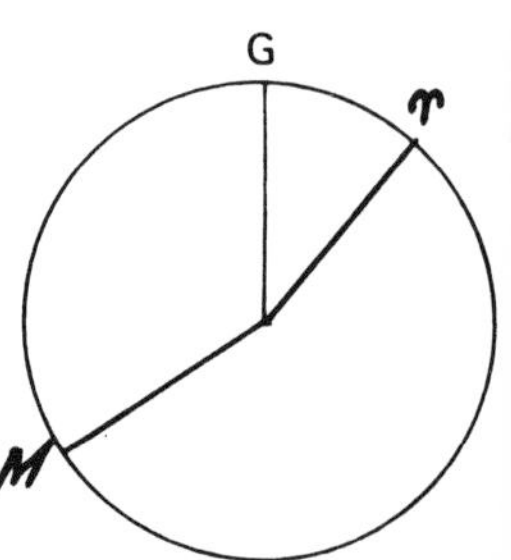

Hour Angle Diagram

TABLE 5 Correction 2 Mi 120° (1972)

(In this example, the Air Almanac is used)

FIG. 19-8

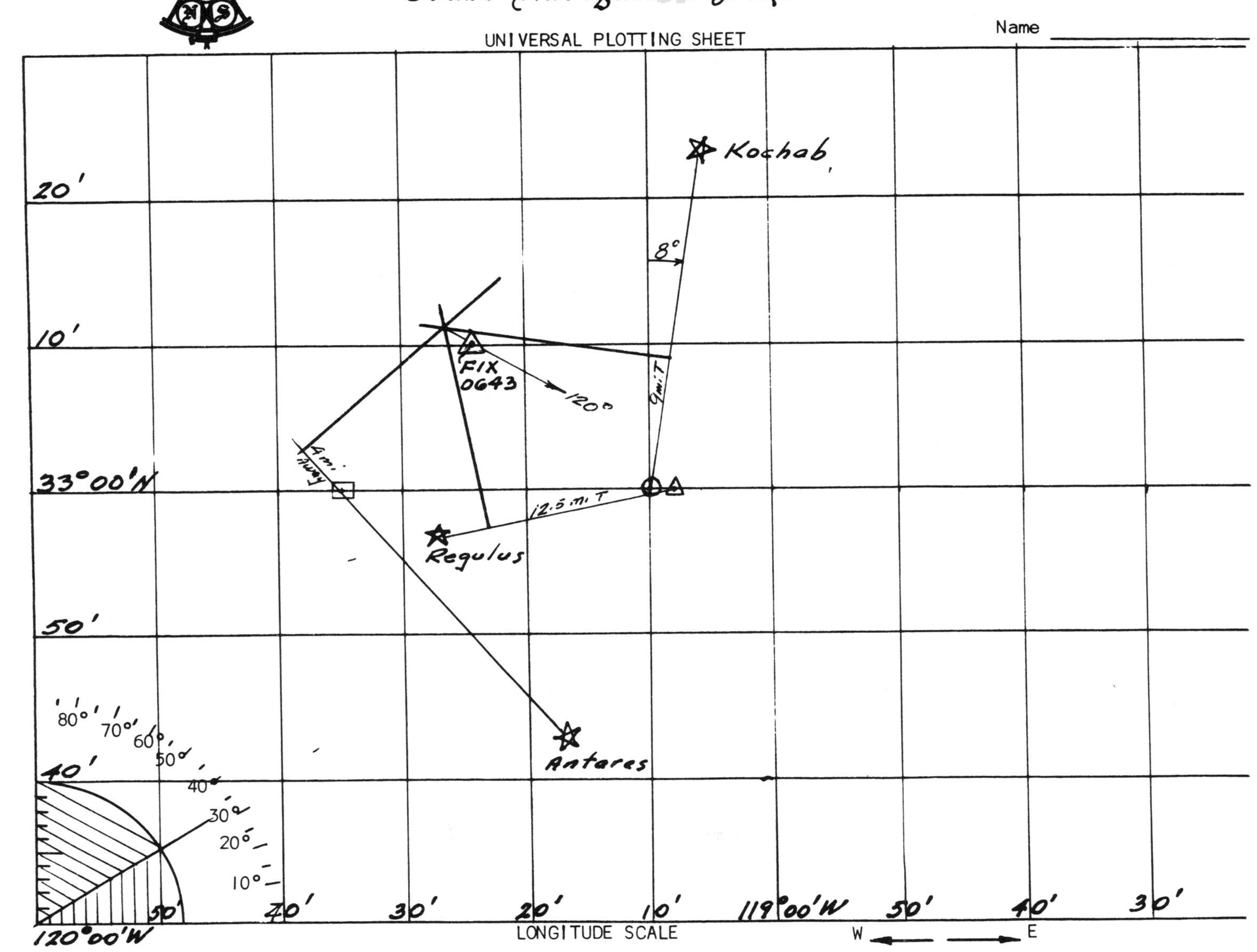

Name
UNIVERSAL PLOTTING SHEET
N
S
LATITUDE
20′
10′
33°00′N
50′
40′
Kochab
8°
9 mi T
FIX
0643
120°
4 mi
Away
12.5 mi T
Regulus
Antares
80°
70°
60°
50°
40°
30°
20°
10°
120°00′W
50′
40′
30′
20′
10′
119°00′W
50′
40′
30′
LONGITUDE SCALE
W
E

FIG. 19-9

table with approximate latitude and LHA of Aries. For lat. 33° N and LHA ♈ of 202°, the nearest values are lat. 40° N and LHA ♈ of 210°. For 1972 the correction is 2 miles in a direction of 120° true. Our final fix is thus lat. 33°10′ N, long. 119°24.5′ W. Depending on the conditions under which the sights were taken, the quality of equipment, and experience of the navigator, we can expect such a fix to be within a mile or two of our true position, but we must always be alert to the fact that we *might* be as much as four or five miles away. Certain errors are inherent in the figures we use, our judgment in observing the body on the horizon, and so on. Only practice taking many sights from a known position will indicate to you how accurate your procedures are.

This, then, is the manner in which sights are planned, executed, and plotted. It only remains to show the manner in which celestial bodies other than stars are observed and reduced, using other tables and either the *Air Almanac* or the *Nautical Almanac*.

Chapter 20

Celestial Navigation with N.O. 249, Vols. II and III for the Sun, Moon and Planets

Whereas N.O. 249, Vol. I, is set up for use with specific stars located at relatively fixed positions in the sky, volumes II and III are designed for use with the sun, moon, and planets, none of which are fixed in our sky but change their celestial coordinates constantly. They have one thing in common: they all move in a broad band within 30° of the equinoctial. Therefore, these two volumes cover declinations up to 30° North or South. Latitudes are covered from 0–39° in volume II and 40–89° in volume III. The tables are entered with assumed latitude, declination, and LHA of the body observed. They yield H_c and the azimuth angle Z. A single correction is applied to H_c and a formula is given for converting Z to Z_n. Values are to the nearest minute of arc.

Sun Observations

Example • Your vessel is at anchor on January 1 in DR position lat. 10°05′ S, long. 47°35′ E. You wish to determine the position accurately, so you take a sight on the sun in the morning and one in the afternoon and cross the two LOPs for a fix. The data is as follows: index error 7′ on the arc; watch error 13 seconds slow; height of eye 18 feet. At 09-15-33 you observe the sun, LL, at H_s 50°10.8′ and at 15-22-25 the H_s is 38°28.7′. Plot a fix, using the *Air Almanac* and N.O. 249. (See Figs. 20–1, 20–2, and 20–3.)

Again, the first step is to set down all known information on the work form. The complete solution and plot are shown on the following pages. The important new procedure to note is the manner in which the minutes of the assumed longitude are determined so that the LHA of the sun will come out in a whole degree. As previously mentioned, in east longitude, to find LHA we must make the minutes of the GHA and the minutes of the assumed longitude *add up to 60′*. Also note the construction of the plotting sheet. South latitude increases downward and east longitude increases to the right. When you correct sextant angles of the sun and the moon with the *Air Almanac,* you must apply the semidiameter separately. Once we determine the LHA of the sun, take the declination from the almanac, and decide on the assumed latitude, we are then ready to enter N.O. 249, Vol. II. We find the right combination of latitude 10° and declination 23°, *"same name"* (both south) on page 63 of volume II. For LHA of 321° we find $H_c = 50°34'$, d is —14′ and Z is 66°. The correction factor d is used to correct the tabular H_c for the difference in the even degree of declination used and the actual minutes in the declination. Table 5 at the back of volume II (Fig. 20–7) gives the corrections for all possible combinations of d and declination difference. We find that for d of —14′ and a declination difference of only 2′, the correction is 0′. The final H_c is thus unchanged at 50°34′. The azimuth angle Z is converted to Z_n, the bearing from true north, according to the four rules printed on each page and also on the work form. Since LHA is greater than 180°, $Z_n = 180° - Z = 180° - 66° = 114°$.

The second sight is worked in exactly the same manner, with the results shown. When plotted, the fix reads lat. 10°05′ S, long. 47°30′ E. Note that there is no correction for precession and nutation. This correction applies to stars only.

Planet Observations Planet observations are worked in an identical manner with the sun if you use the *Air Almanac,* except, of course, that there is no semidiameter to apply. The procedure is a little different with the *Nautical Almanac,* and to show the variations, the next sights are worked with that almanac. Use excerpts in Chapter 17.

Example • On the evening of January 2 you are in DR lat. 33°20′ S, long. 156°30′ E, off Australia's east coast. You observe Mars at 19-42-17 for an H_s of

Coast Navigation School

SANTA BARBARA, CALIFORNIA

MULTIPLE SIGHT FORM FOR SUN, N.O. 249

WITH ~~NAUTICAL~~ AIR ALMANAC

Name Simonsen

cal Date Jan. 1 Greenwich Date Jan. 1 DR Lat. S10°05' DR Long E47°35'

Body ☉	~~UL~~ LL	~~UL~~ LL	UL LL
Hs	50° 10.8'	38° 28.7'	
Total Corr.	+4'	+4'	
Ho	50° 14.8'	38° 32.7'	
Watch Time	09-15-33	15-22-25	
Watch Error	+13	+13	
Zone Time	09-15-46	15-22-38	
Zone Descr.	−3	−3	
GMT	06-15-46	12-22-38	
GHA of Sun Hrs	271° 39'	4° 07'	
GHA Min. & Sec.	1° 27'	0° 39'	
TOTAL GHA	273° 06'	4° 46'	
Assumed Long. (-W, +E)	47° 54	47° 14'	
Apply 360° if necessary			
LHA of Sun	321°	52°	
Declination N/S	S 23° 02'	S 23° 01'	
Assumed Lat. N/S	S 10°	S 10°	
From N.O. 249, Vol II or III			
d factor (+ / -)	−14	−6	
Hc (Tabular)	50° 34'	38° 45'	
Corr. for d(+ / -) Tab 5	0	0	
Hc	50° 34'	38° 45'	
Ho	50° 14.8'	38° 32.7'	
Intercept (T/A)	A 19.2	A 12.3	
Z	66°	69°	
Apply 360° or 180°	180°	180°	
Zn	114°	249°	
Plotting Symbol	○	□	

IE 7' on arc

WE 13 sec. slow

HE 18 Ft.

Sextant Corrections

	+	−
IC		7
Dip		4
~~Alt.~~ Ref. / S.D.	16	1
Totals	16	12
	12	
Total C.	+4'	

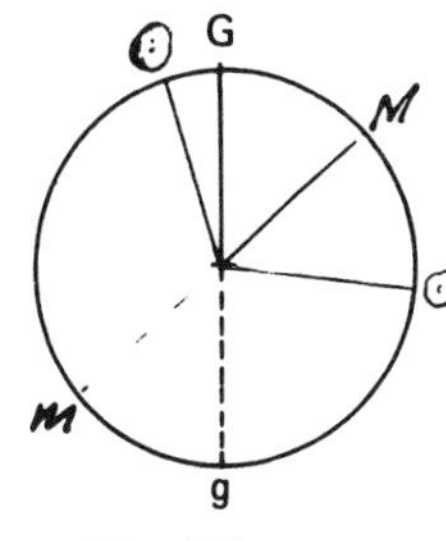

Time Diagram

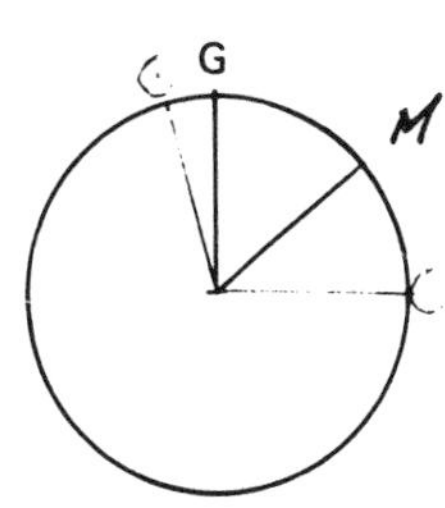

Hour Angle Diagram

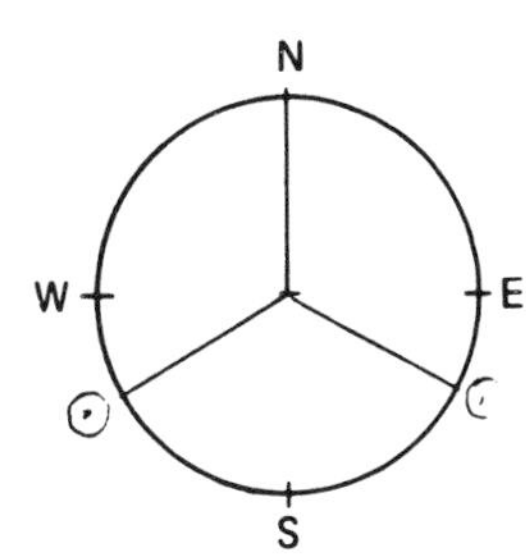

True Bearing Diagram

RULES:

NORTH LATITUDE		✓ SOUTH LATITUDE	
LHA GREATER THAN 180°	ZN = Z	LHA GREATER THAN 180°	ZN = 180° - Z
LHA LESS THAN 180°	ZN = 360° - Z	LHA LESS THAN 180°	ZN = 180° + Z

FIG. 20-1

DECLINATION (15°-29°) SAME NAME AS LATITUDE

LHA	19° Hc	d	Z	20° Hc	d	Z	21° Hc	d	Z	22° Hc	d	Z	23° Hc	d	Z	24° Hc	d	Z	25° Hc	d	Z	LHA
	° ′	′	°	° ′	′	°	° ′	′	°	° ′	′	°	° ′	′	°	° ′	′	°	° ′	′	°	
0	81 00	-60	0	80 00	-60	0	79 00	-60	0	78 00	-60	0	77 00	-60	0	76 00	-60	0	75 00	-60	0	360
1	80 57	60	6	79 57	59	5	78 58	60	5	77 58	60	4	76 58	60	4	75 58	60	4	74 58	60	4	359
2	80 48	59	12	79 49	59	11	78 50	59	10	77 51	59	9	76 52	60	8	75 52	59	8	74 53	60	7	358
3	80 33	58	18	79 35	57	16	78 38	58	14	77 40	59	13	76 41	58	12	75 43	59	11	74 44	59	10	357
4	80 12	55	23	79 17	56	21	78 21	57	19	77 24	57	17	76 27	58	16	75 29	57	15	74 32	58	14	356
5	79 47	-53	28	78 54	-54	25	78 00	-55	23	77 05	-56	21	76 09	-56	20	75 13	-57	18	74 16	-57	17	355
6	79 18	51	32	78 27	52	29	77 35	53	27	76 42	55	25	75 47	54	23	74 53	56	22	73 57	56	20	354
7	78 44	48	36	77 56	50	33	77 06	51	31	76 15	52	28	75 23	53	26	74 30	54	25	73 36	55	23	353
8	78 08	46	40	77 22	47	37	76 35	50	34	75 45	50	32	74 55	51	30	74 04	53	28	73 11	53	26	352
9	77 29	43	43	76 46	46	40	76 00	47	37	75 13	48	35	74 25	50	32	73 35	51	30	72 44	52	29	351
10	76 47	-40	46	76 07	-44	43	75 23	-45	40	74 38	-46	37	73 52	-48	35	73 04	-49	33	72 15	-50	31	350
11	76 04	39	49	75 25	41	45	74 44	43	43	74 01	44	40	73 17	46	38	72 31	48	35	71 43	48	34	349
12	75 19	37	51	74 42	39	48	74 03	40	45	73 23	43	42	72 40	45	40	71 55	45	38	71 10	47	36	348
13	74 33	35	53	73 58	37	50	73 21	39	47	72 42	41	45	72 01	43	42	71 18	44	40	70 34	45	38	347
14	73 45	33	55	73 12	35	52	72 37	37	49	72 00	39	47	71 21	41	44	70 40	43	42	69 57	44	40	346
15	72 56	-31	57	72 25	-33	54	71 52	-36	51	71 16	-37	48	70 39	-39	46	70 00	-41	44	69 19	-43	42	345
16	72 06	29	58	71 37	32	55	71 05	34	53	70 31	35	50	69 56	38	48	69 18	39	45	68 39	41	43	344
17	71 16	28	59	70 48	30	57	70 18	32	54	69 46	35	52	69 11	36	49	68 35	37	47	67 58	40	45	343
18	70 25	27	61	69 58	28	58	69 30	31	55	68 59	33	53	68 26	34	51	67 52	37	49	67 15	37	46	342
19	69 33	25	62	69 08	27	59	68 41	30	57	68 11	31	54	67 40	33	52	67 07	35	50	66 32	36	48	341
20	68 41	-24	63	68 17	-26	60	67 51	-28	58	67 23	-30	56	66 53	-32	53	66 21	-33	51	65 48	-35	49	340
21	67 48	23	64	67 25	24	61	67 01	27	59	66 34	29	57	66 05	30	55	65 35	32	52	65 03	34	50	339
22	66 55	22	65	66 33	23	62	66 10	26	60	65 44	27	58	65 17	29	56	64 48	31	54	64 17	32	52	338
23	66 01	20	65	65 41	23	63	65 18	24	61	64 54	26	59	64 28	28	57	64 00	30	55	63 30	31	53	337
24	65 07	19	66	64 48	21	64	64 27	24	62	64 03	25	60	63 38	26	58	63 12	29	56	62 43	30	54	336
25	64 13	-18	67	63 55	-21	65	63 34	-22	62	63 12	-24	60	62 48	-25	58	62 23	-28	56	61 55	-28	55	335
26	63 19	18	67	63 01	19	65	62 42	21	63	62 21	23	61	61 58	25	59	61 33	26	57	61 07	28	55	334
27	62 24	17	68	62 07	18	66	61 49	20	64	61 29	22	62	61 07	24	60	60 43	25	58	60 18	26	56	333
28	61 29	16	68	61 13	17	66	60 56	20	64	60 36	21	63	60 15	22	61	59 53	24	59	59 29	26	57	332
29	60 34	15	69	60 19	17	67	60 02	18	65	59 44	20	63	59 24	22	61	59 02	23	59	58 39	24	58	331
30	59 39	-14	69	59 25	-16	67	59 09	-18	66	58 51	-19	64	58 32	-21	62	58 11	-22	60	57 49	-24	58	330
31	58 44	14	70	58 30	15	68	58 15	17	66	57 58	18	64	57 40	20	62	57 20	21	61	56 59	23	59	329
32	57 48	13	70	57 35	14	68	57 21	16	67	57 05	18	65	56 47	19	63	56 28	20	61	56 08	22	60	328
33	56 52	12	70	56 40	14	69	56 26	15	67	56 11	17	65	55 54	18	63	55 36	19	62	55 17	21	60	327
34	55 57	12	71	55 45	13	69	55 32	15	67	55 17	16	66	55 01	17	64	54 44	19	62	54 25	20	61	326
35	55 01	-11	71	54 50	-13	69	54 37	-13	68	54 24	-16	66	54 08	-16	64	53 52	-18	63	53 34	-19	61	325
36	54 05	10	71	53 55	12	70	53 43	14	68	53 29	14	66	53 15	16	65	52 59	17	63	52 42	18	62	324
37	53 09	10	72	52 59	11	70	52 48	13	68	52 35	14	67	52 21	15	65	52 06	16	64	51 50	18	62	323
38	52 13	9	72	52 04	11	70	51 53	12	69	51 41	13	67	51 28	15	66	51 13	15	64	50 58	17	62	322
39	51 17	9	72	51 08	10	70	50 58	11	69	50 47	13	67	50 34	14	66	50 20	15	64	50 05	16	63	321
40	50 20	-8	72	50 12	-9	71	50 03	-11	69	49 52	-12	68	49 40	-13	66	49 27	-14	65	49 13	-16	63	320
41	49 24	8	72	49 16	9	71	49 07	10	69	48 57	11	68	48 46	13	66	48 33	13	65	48 20	15	63	319
42	48 28	8	73	48 20	8	71	48 12	10	70	48 02	10	68	47 52	12	67	47 40	13	65	47 27	14	64	318
43	47 31	6	73	47 25	8	71	47 17	9	70	47 08	11	68	46 57	11	67	46 46	12	66	46 34	13	64	317
44	46 35	6	73	46 29	8	71	46 21	8	70	46 13	10	69	46 03	11	67	45 52	11	66	45 41	13	64	316
45	45 38	-5	73	45 33	-7	72	45 26	-8	70	45 18	-9	69	45 09	-10	67	44 59	-12	66	44 47	-12	65	315
46	44 42	6	73	44 36	6	72	44 30	8	70	44 22	8	69	44 14	9	68	44 05	11	66	43 54	11	65	314
47	43 45	5	73	43 40	6	72	43 34	7	71	43 27	8	69	43 19	9	68	43 10	9	66	43 01	11	65	313
48	42 49	5	73	42 44	5	72	42 39	7	71	42 32	7	69	42 25	9	68	42 16	9	67	42 07	10	65	312
49	41 52	4	73	41 48	5	72	41 43	6	71	41 37	7	69	41 30	8	68	41 22	9	67	41 13	9	65	311
50	40 56	-4	74	40 52	-5	72	40 47	-5	71	40 42	-7	70	40 35	-7	68	40 28	-9	67	40 19	-9	66	310
51	39 59	3	74	39 56	5	72	39 51	5	71	39 46	6	70	39 40	7	68	39 33	7	67	39 26	9	66	309
52	39 02	3	74	38 59	4	72	38 55	4	71	38 51	6	70	38 45	6	69	38 39	7	67	38 32	8	66	308
53	38 06	3	74	38 03	3	72	38 00	5	71	37 55	5	70	37 50	6	69	37 44	6	67	37 38	8	66	307
54	37 09	2	74	37 07	3	72	37 04	4	71	37 00	5	70	36 55	5	69	36 50	6	67	36 44	7	66	306

FIG. 20-2

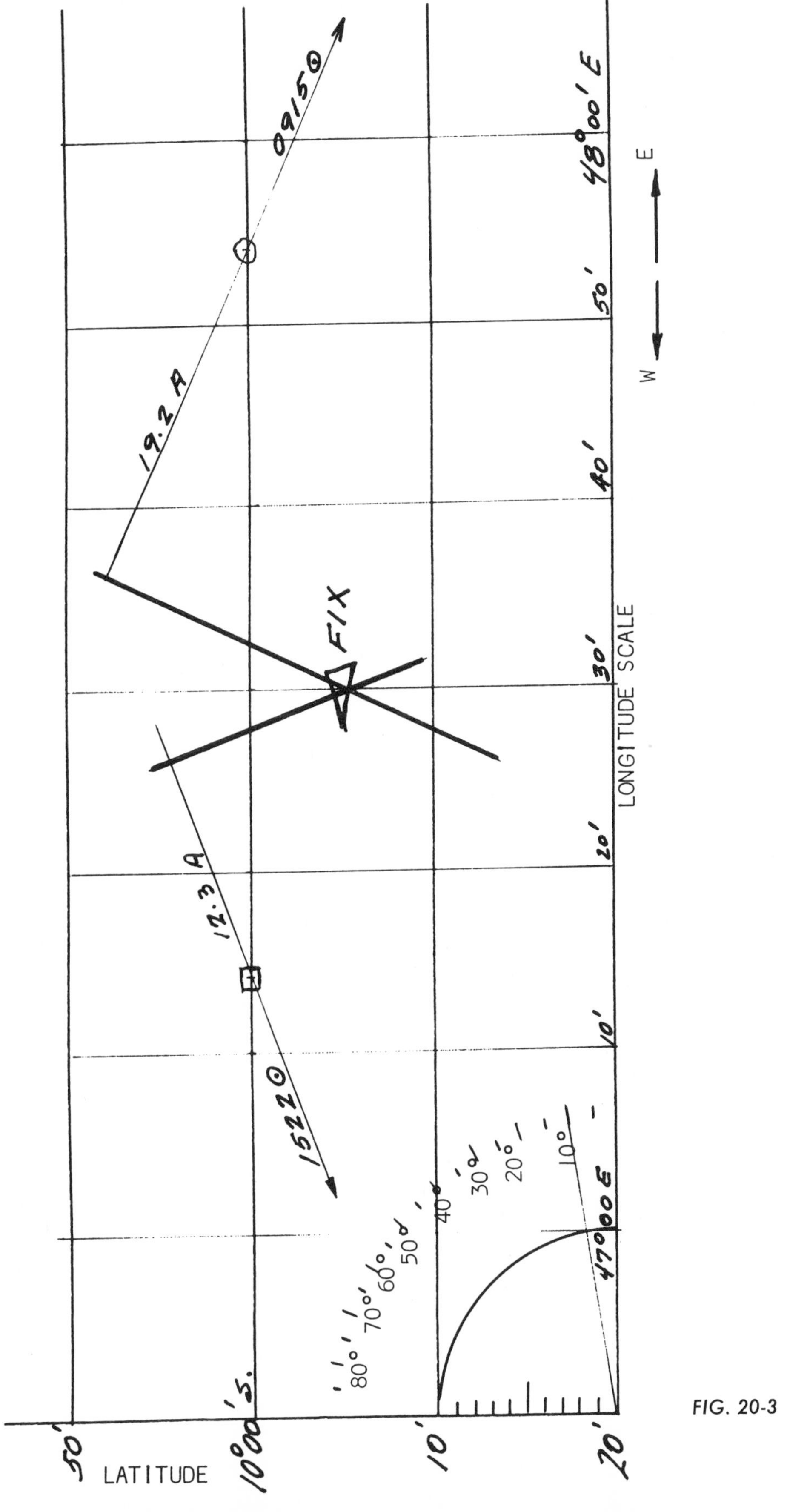

0915
19.2 A
48°00' E
50'
40'
FIX
30'
LONGITUDE SCALE
20'
12.3 A
10'
1522
47°00' E
W
E
10°
20°
30°
40°
50°
60°
70°
80°
50'
10°00'
5'
10'
20'
LATITUDE

FIG. 20-3

29°58.4′ and Saturn at 19-44-42, H_s of 45°02.8′. Index error is 3′ off the arc, watch is 10 seconds fast, and height of eye is 15 feet.

Step 1. Enter all known information on the work form. See Fig. 20–4.

Step 2. Correct sextant angles, using *Nautical Almanac.* Note that there is a small seasonal correction of 0.1′ for Mars. Determine H_o.

Step 3. Convert watch time to GMT and take out GHA of each planet for the whole hours of GMT. Note v factor. Take out declination for each planet for whole hours of GMT and note d factor.

Step 4. Go to tables of increments and corrections (I&C tables, Fig. 20–8) and take out the added GHA for the minutes and seconds of GMT, *and*—while you are on the same page—take out the v and d corrections and enter them on the work form also. The v corrections are always added, but the d correction may be plus or minus, depending on whether the declination of the planet is increasing or decreasing with an increase of time. In the case of Saturn there is no change, because $d = 0.0'$; but for Mars there is a small decrease of 0.6′.

Step 5. Determine assumed longitude and LHA in the same manner as before.

Step 6. Enter N.O. 249, Vol II, with latitude 33°. The data for Mars is found on page 198 and that for Saturn on page 200. Take out H_c, *d,* and *Z.* From Table 5, at the back of the volume, Fig. 20–7, find the d correction to H_c. Note that the correction for Mars is positive because d is +33, that for Saturn negative because d is −58.

Step 7. Determine H_c and Z_n as in previous examples.

Step 8. Construct a small-area plotting sheet, using 33° as the base angle and remem-

Coast Navigation School

SANTA BARBARA, CALIFORNIA

MULTIPLE SIGHT FORM FOR PLANETS
N.O. 249 WITH NAUTICAL ALMANAC

Name *Simonsen*

al Date *Jan. 2* Greenwich Date *Jan. 2* DR Lat. *S 33° 20'* DR Long *E 156° 30'*

ody	Mars	Saturn	
s	29° 58.4'	45° 02.8'	
otal Corr.	−2.4'	−1.8'	
o	29° 56'	45° 01'	
atch Time	19-42-17	19-44-42	
atch Error	−10	−10	
one Time	19-42-07	19-44-32	
one Descr. −	10	−10	
MT	09-42-07	09-44-32	
HA – Hours	251° 42.4'	205° 49.5'	
HA – M & S	10° 31.8	11° 08.0	
Corr. To GHA v=	0.7 0.5	2.5 1.9	
otal GHA	262° 14.7'	216° 59.4	
ssumed Long. +E -W	156° 45.3	156° 00.6	
60° *Subtract*	419° 360°	373° 360°	
HA	59°	13°	
ecl.	S 7° 18.3	N 9° 49.6	
orr. for d(+ / -) d=	−d=0.8 −0.6	d=0 0	
et Decl.	S 7° 17.7'	N 9° 49.6'	
ssumed Lat. N/S	S 33°	S 33°	
From N.O. 249, Vol II or III	Pg. 198	Pg. 200	
factor (+ / -)	+33	−58	
c (Tabular)	29° 41'	46° 13'	
Correction (+ / -)	+10'	−48'	
c	29° 51'	45° 25'	
o	29° 56'	45° 01'	
ntercept T/A	T 5mi	A 24mi	
	102°	161°	
Apply 360° or 180°	+180°	+180°	
n	282°	341°	
lotting Symbol	O	□	

IE *3' off*

WE *10sec. fast*

HE *15 Ft.*

Sextant Corrections

	M +	M −	S +	S −	+	−
IC	3		3			
Dip		3.8		3.8		
Alt.		1.7		1.0		
Venus or Mars Corr.	0.1					
	3.1	5.5	3	4.8		
		3.1		3		
Total C		−2.4		−1.8		

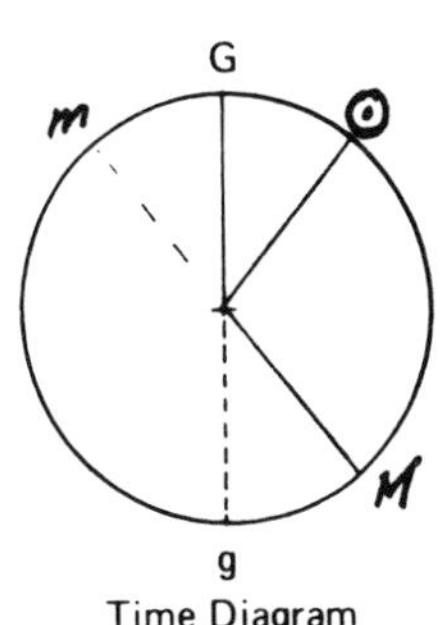

Time Diagram

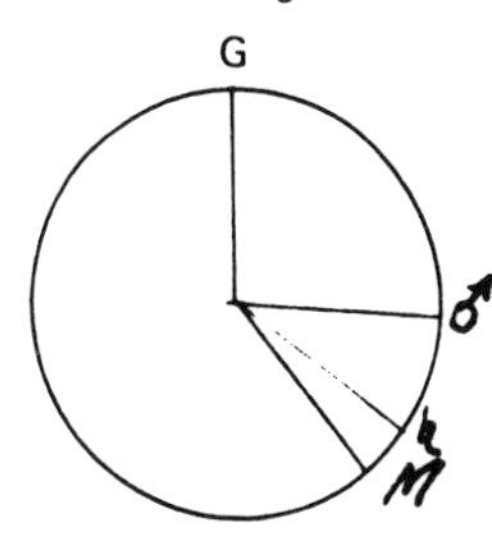

Hour Angle Diagram

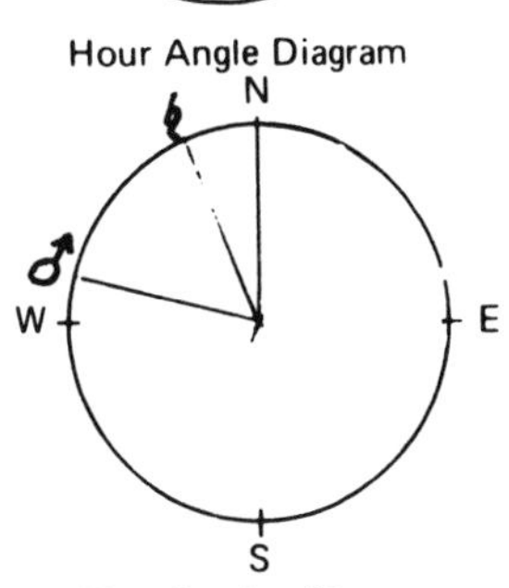

True Bearing Diagram

LES: NORTH LATITUDE
LHA GREATER THAN 180°, ZN = Z
LHA LESS THAN 180°, ZN = 360°-Z

✓ SOUTH LATITUDE
LHA GREATER THAN 180°, ZN = 180°-Z
LHA LESS THAN 180°, ZN = 180°+Z

FIG. 20-4

LAT 33°

LHA	0° Hc	d	Z	1° Hc	d	Z	2° Hc	d	Z	3° Hc	d	Z	4° Hc	d	Z	5° Hc	d	Z
16	53 44	56	152	52 48	55	153	51 53	56	154	50 57	56	154	50 01	56	155	49 05	56	155
15	54 06	-55	154	53 11	-56	154	52 15	-57	155	51 18	-56	156	50 22	-57	156	49 25	-56	157
14	54 28	56	155	53 32	57	156	52 35	56	157	51 39	57	157	50 42	57	158	49 45	57	158
13	54 48	57	157	53 51	56	158	52 55	58	158	51 57	57	159	51 00	57	159	50 03	57	160
12	55 07	57	159	54 10	57	159	53 13	58	160	52 15	57	160	51 18	58	161	50 20	58	161
11	55 25	58	160	54 27	58	161	53 29	57	161	52 32	58	162	51 34	58	162	50 36	58	163
10	55 41	-58	162	54 43	-58	163	53 45	-58	163	52 47	-59	163	51 48	-58	164	50 50	-58	164
9	55 56	59	164	54 57	58	164	53 59	59	165	53 00	58	165	52 02	59	165	51 03	58	166
8	56 09	59	166	55 10	58	166	54 12	59	166	53 13	59	167	52 14	59	167	51 15	59	167
7	56 21	59	167	55 22	59	168	54 23	59	168	53 24	59	168	52 25	60	169	51 25	59	169
6	56 31	59	169	55 32	59	169	54 33	60	170	53 33	59	170	52 34	59	170	51 35	60	170
5	56 40	-59	171	55 41	-60	171	54 41	-60	171	53 41	-59	172	52 42	-60	172	51 42	-59	172
4	56 47	59	173	55 48	60	173	54 48	60	173	53 48	60	173	52 48	59	173	51 49	60	174
3	56 53	60	175	55 53	60	175	54 53	60	175	53 53	59	175	52 54	60	175	51 54	60	175
2	56 57	60	176	55 57	60	176	54 57	60	177	53 57	60	177	52 57	60	177	51 57	60	177
1	56 59	60	178	55 59	60	178	54 59	60	178	53 59	60	178	52 59	60	178	51 59	60	178
0	57 00	-60	180	56 00	-60	180	55 00	-60	180	54 00	-60	180	53 00	-60	180	52 00	-60	180

LHA	6° Hc	d	Z	7° Hc	d	Z	8° Hc	d	Z	9° Hc	d	Z	10° Hc	d	Z
16	48 09	57	156	47 12	56	156	46 16	57	157	45 19	56	157	44 23	57	158
15	48 29	-57	157	47 32	-57	158	46 35	-57	158	45 38	-57	159	44 41	-57	159
14	48 48	57	159	47 51	58	159	46 53	57	160	45 56	57	160	44 59	58	160
13	49 06	58	160	48 08	57	161	47 11	58	161	46 13	58	161	45 15	58	162
12	49 22	58	162	48 24	58	162	47 26	58	162	46 28	58	163	45 30	58	163
11	49 38	59	163	48 39	58	163	47 41	58	164	46 43	59	164	45 44	58	164
10	49 52	-59	165	48 53	-58	165	47 55	-59	165	46 56	-59	166	45 57	-58	166
9	50 05	59	166	49 06	59	166	48 07	59	167	47 08	59	167	46 09	59	167
8	50 16	59	168	49 17	59	168	48 18	59	168	47 19	59	168	46 20	59	169
7	50 26	59	169	49 27	59	169	48 28	60	170	47 28	59	170	46 29	59	170
6	50 35	59	171	49 36	60	171	48 36	59	171	47 37	60	171	46 37	59	171
5	50 43	-60	172	49 43	-59	172	48 44	-60	173	47 44	-60	173	46 44	-59	173
4	50 49	60	174	49 49	60	174	48 49	59	174	47 50	60	174	46 50	60	174
3	50 54	60	175	49 54	60	175	48 54	60	176	47 54	60	176	46 54	60	176
2	50 57	60	177	49 57	60	177	48 57	60	177	47 57	59	177	46 58	60	177
1	50 59	60	178	49 59	60	179	48 59	60	179	47 59	60	179	46 59	60	179
0	51 00	-60	180	50 00	-60	180	49 00	-60	180	48 00	-60	180	47 00	-60	180

S. Lat. {LHA greater than 180°.......Zn=180−Z; LHA less than 180°...........Zn=180+Z}

DECLINATION (0°-14°) **CONTRARY** NAME TO LATITUDE

LAT 33°

LHA	0° Hc	d	Z	1° Hc	d	Z	2° Hc	d	Z	3° Hc	d	Z	4° Hc	d	Z	5° Hc	d	Z
53	30 19	38	112	30 57	37	111	31 34	37	111	32 11	36	110	32 47	36	109	33 23	36	108
54	29 32	38	112	30 10	37	111	30 47	36	110	31 23	36	109	31 59	36	108	32 35	36	107
55	28 45	+37	111	29 22	+37	110	29 59	+36	109	30 35	+36	108	31 11	+36	107	31 47	+35	106
56	27 58	37	110	28 35	36	109	29 11	37	108	29 48	35	108	30 23	36	107	30 59	34	106
57	27 11	36	110	27 47	37	109	28 24	35	108	28 59	36	107	29 35	35	106	30 10	35	105
58	26 23	37	109	27 00	36	108	27 36	35	107	28 11	35	106	28 46	35	105	29 21	35	104
59	25 36	36	108	26 12	35	107	26 47	36	106	27 23	35	105	27 58	34	105	28 32	35	104
60	24 48	+35	108	25 23	+36	107	25 59	+35	106	26 34	+35	105	27 09	+34	104	27 43	+35	103
61	24 00	35	107	24 35	35	106	25 10	35	105	25 45	35	104	26 20	34	103	26 54	34	102
62	23 11	36	106	23 47	35	105	24 22	35	104	24 57	34	104	25 31	34	103	26 05	34	102
63	22 23	35	106	22 58	35	105	23 33	35	104	24 08	34	103	24 42	34	102	25 16	33	101
64	21 34	35	105	22 09	35	104	22 44	34	103	23 18	35	102	23 53	33	101	24 26	34	100
65	20 46	+34	104	21 20	+35	103	21 55	+34	103	22 29	+34	102	23 03	+34	101	23 37	+33	100
66	19 57	34	104	20 31	35	103	21 06	34	102	21 40	34	101	22 14	33	100	22 47	33	99
67	19 08	34	103	19 42	34	102	20 16	34	101	20 50	34	100	21 24	33	100	21 57	34	99
68	18 19	34	102	18 53	34	102	19 27	34	101	20 01	33	100	20 34	34	99	21 08	33	98
69	17 29	35	102	18 04	34	101	18 38	33	100	19 11	34	99	19 45	33	98	20 18	33	97

LHA	6° Hc	d	Z	7° Hc	d	Z	8° Hc	d	Z	9° Hc	d	Z	10° Hc	d	Z
53	33 59	35	107	34 34	35	106	35 09	34	105	35 43	33	104	36 16	34	103
54	33 11	34	106	33 45	35	105	34 20	34	104	34 54	33	103	35 27	33	102
55	32 22	+35	105	32 57	+34	104	33 31	+34	103	34 05	+33	102	34 38	+33	101
56	31 33	35	105	32 08	34	104	32 42	34	103	33 16	33	102	33 49	32	101
57	30 45	34	104	31 19	34	103	31 53	33	102	32 26	33	101	32 59	33	100
58	29 56	34	103	30 30	34	102	31 04	33	101	31 37	33	100	32 10	32	99
59	29 07	34	103	29 41	33	102	30 14	33	101	30 47	33	100	31 20	32	99
60	28 18	+33	102	28 51	+34	101	29 25	+33	100	29 58	+32	99	30 30	+32	98
61	27 28	34	101	28 02	33	100	28 35	33	100	29 08	32	99	29 40	32	98
62	26 39	33	101	27 12	33	100	27 45	33	99	28 18	32	98	28 50	32	97
63	25 49	34	100	26 23	33	99	26 56	32	98	27 28	32	97	28 00	32	96
64	25 00	33	100	25 33	33	99	26 06	32	98	26 38	32	97	27 10	32	96
65	24 10	+33	99	24 43	+33	98	25 16	+32	97	25 48	+32	96	26 20	+32	95
66	23 20	33	98	23 53	33	97	24 26	32	97	24 58	32	96	25 30	32	95
67	22 31	32	98	23 03	33	97	23 36	32	96	24 08	32	95	24 40	31	94
68	21 41	32	97	22 13	33	96	22 46	32	95	23 18	32	94	23 50	31	94
69	20 51	32	97	21 23	33	96	21 56	32	95	22 28	31	94	22 59	32	93

S. Lat. {LHA greater than 180°.......Zn=180−Z; LHA less than 180°...........Zn=180+Z}

DECLINATION (0°-14°) **SAME** NAME AS LATITUDE

FIG. 20-5

Excerpts from N.O. 249, Vol. II

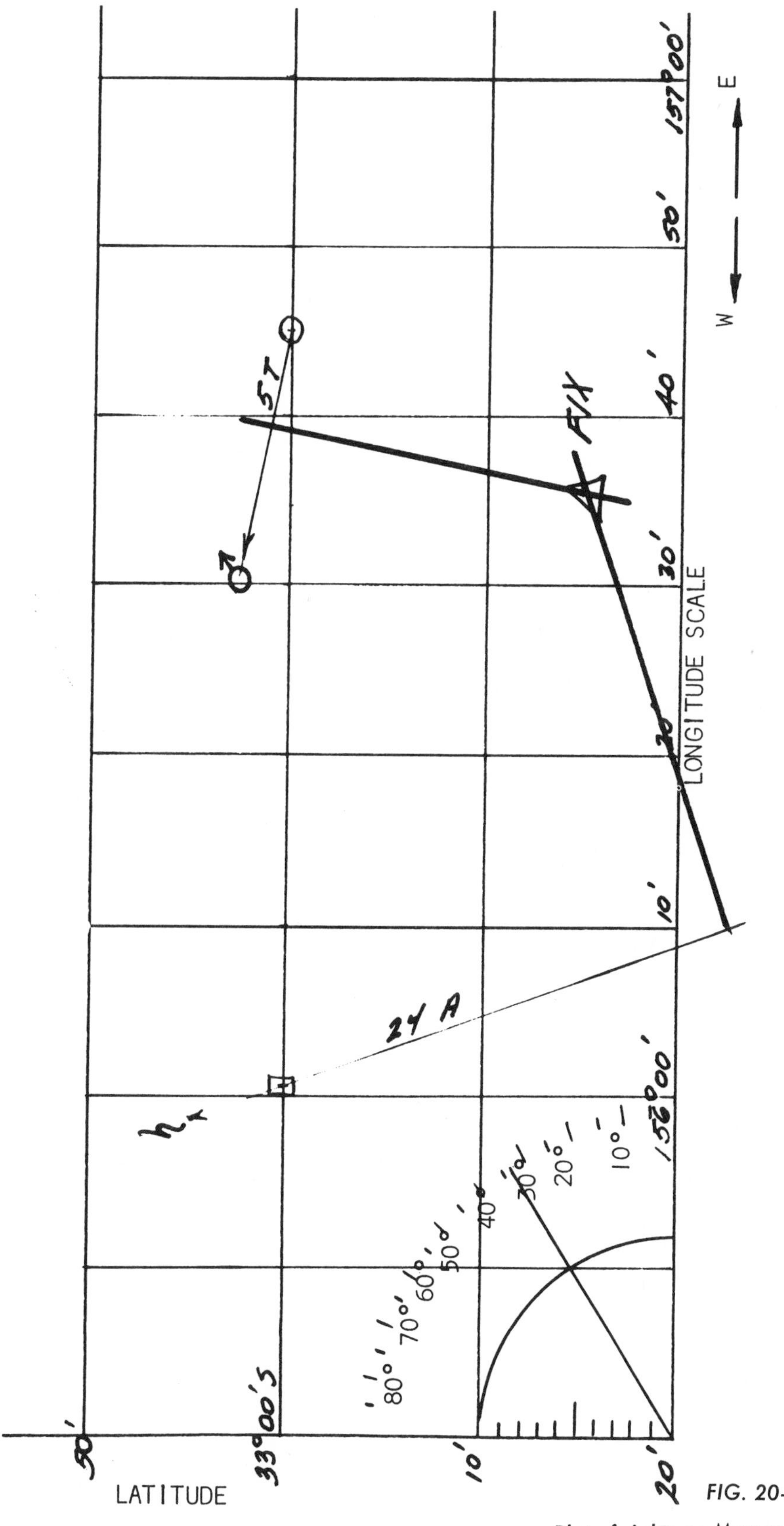

FIG. 20-6

Plot of sights on Mars and Saturn

TABLE 5.—Correction to Tabulated Altitude for Minutes of Declination

d / ′	1	2	3	4	5	6	7	8	9	10	11	12	13	14	15	16	17	18	19	20	21	22	23	24	25	26	27	28	29	30	31	32	33	34	35	36	37	38	39	40	41	42	43	44	45	46	47	48	49	50	51	52	53	54	55	56	57	58	59	60	d / ′
0	0	0	0	0	0	0	0	0	0	0	0	0	0	0	0	0	0	0	0	0	0	0	0	0	0	0	0	0	0	0	0	0	0	0	0	0	0	0	0	0	0	0	0	0	0	0	0	0	0	0	0	0	0	0	0	0	0	0	0	0	0
1	0	0	0	0	0	0	0	0	0	0	0	0	0	0	0	0	0	0	0	0	0	0	0	0	0	0	0	0	0	0	1	1	1	1	1	1	1	1	1	1	1	1	1	1	1	1	1	1	1	1	1	1	1	1	1	1	1	1	1	1	1
2	0	0	0	0	0	0	0	0	0	0	0	0	0	0	0	1	1	1	1	1	1	1	1	1	1	1	1	1	1	1	1	1	1	1	1	1	1	1	1	1	1	1	1	1	2	2	2	2	2	2	2	2	2	2	2	2	2	2	2	2	2
3	0	0	0	0	0	0	0	0	0	0	1	1	1	1	1	1	1	1	1	1	1	1	1	1	1	1	1	1	1	2	2	2	2	2	2	2	2	2	2	2	2	2	2	2	2	2	2	2	2	2	3	3	3	3	3	3	3	3	3	3	3
4	0	0	0	0	0	0	0	1	1	1	1	1	1	1	1	1	1	1	1	1	1	1	2	2	2	2	2	2	2	2	2	2	2	2	2	2	2	3	3	3	3	3	3	3	3	3	3	3	3	3	3	3	4	4	4	4	4	4	4	4	4
5	0	0	0	0	0	0	1	1	1	1	1	1	1	1	1	1	1	2	2	2	2	2	2	2	2	2	2	2	2	2	3	3	3	3	3	3	3	3	3	3	3	4	4	4	4	4	4	4	4	4	4	4	4	4	5	5	5	5	5	5	5
6	0	0	0	0	0	1	1	1	1	1	1	1	1	1	2	2	2	2	2	2	2	2	2	2	2	3	3	3	3	3	3	3	3	3	4	4	4	4	4	4	4	4	4	4	4	5	5	5	5	5	5	5	5	5	6	6	6	6	6	6	6
7	0	0	0	0	1	1	1	1	1	1	1	1	2	2	2	2	2	2	2	2	2	3	3	3	3	3	3	3	3	4	4	4	4	4	4	4	4	4	5	5	5	5	5	5	5	5	5	6	6	6	6	6	6	6	6	7	7	7	7	7	7
8	0	0	0	1	1	1	1	1	1	1	1	2	2	2	2	2	2	2	3	3	3	3	3	3	3	3	4	4	4	4	4	4	4	5	5	5	5	5	5	5	5	6	6	6	6	6	6	6	7	7	7	7	7	7	7	7	8	8	8	8	8
9	0	0	0	1	1	1	1	1	1	2	2	2	2	2	2	2	3	3	3	3	3	3	3	4	4	4	4	4	4	4	5	5	5	5	5	5	6	6	6	6	6	6	6	7	7	7	7	7	7	8	8	8	8	8	8	8	9	9	9	9	9
10	0	0	0	1	1	1	1	1	2	2	2	2	2	2	2	3	3	3	3	3	4	4	4	4	4	4	4	5	5	5	5	5	6	6	6	6	6	6	6	7	7	7	7	7	8	8	8	8	8	8	8	9	9	9	9	9	10	10	10	10	10
11	0	0	1	1	1	1	1	1	2	2	2	2	2	3	3	3	3	3	3	4	4	4	4	4	5	5	5	5	5	6	6	6	6	6	6	7	7	7	7	7	8	8	8	8	8	8	9	9	9	9	9	10	10	10	10	10	10	11	11	11	11
12	0	0	1	1	1	1	1	2	2	2	2	2	3	3	3	3	3	4	4	4	4	4	5	5	5	5	5	6	6	6	6	6	7	7	7	7	7	8	8	8	8	8	9	9	9	9	9	10	10	10	10	10	11	11	11	11	11	12	12	12	12
13	0	0	1	1	1	1	2	2	2	2	2	3	3	3	3	3	4	4	4	4	5	5	5	5	5	6	6	6	6	6	7	7	7	7	8	8	8	8	8	9	9	9	9	10	10	10	10	10	11	11	11	11	11	12	12	12	12	13	13	13	13
14	0	0	1	1	1	1	2	2	2	2	3	3	3	3	4	4	4	4	4	5	5	5	5	6	6	6	6	7	7	7	7	7	8	8	8	8	9	9	9	9	10	10	10	10	10	11	11	11	11	12	12	12	12	13	13	13	13	14	14	14	14
15	0	0	1	1	1	2	2	2	2	2	3	3	3	4	4	4	4	4	5	5	5	6	6	6	6	6	7	7	7	8	8	8	8	8	9	9	9	10	10	10	10	10	11	11	11	12	12	12	12	12	13	13	13	14	14	14	14	14	15	15	15
16	0	1	1	1	1	2	2	2	2	3	3	3	3	4	4	4	5	5	5	5	6	6	6	6	7	7	7	7	8	8	8	9	9	9	9	10	10	10	10	11	11	11	11	12	12	12	13	13	13	13	14	14	14	14	15	15	15	15	16	16	16
17	0	1	1	1	1	2	2	2	3	3	3	3	4	4	4	5	5	5	5	6	6	6	7	7	7	7	8	8	8	8	9	9	9	10	10	10	10	11	11	11	12	12	12	12	13	13	13	14	14	14	14	15	15	15	16	16	16	16	17	17	17
18	0	1	1	1	2	2	2	2	3	3	3	4	4	4	4	5	5	5	6	6	6	7	7	7	8	8	8	8	9	9	9	10	10	10	10	11	11	11	12	12	12	13	13	13	14	14	14	14	15	15	15	16	16	16	16	17	17	17	18	18	18
19	0	1	1	1	2	2	2	3	3	3	3	4	4	4	5	5	5	6	6	6	7	7	7	8	8	8	9	9	9	10	10	10	10	11	11	11	12	12	12	13	13	13	14	14	14	15	15	15	16	16	16	16	17	17	17	18	18	18	19	19	19
20	0	1	1	1	2	2	2	3	3	3	4	4	4	5	5	5	6	6	6	7	7	7	8	8	8	9	9	9	10	10	10	11	11	11	12	12	12	13	13	13	14	14	14	15	15	15	16	16	16	17	17	17	18	18	18	19	19	19	20	20	20
21	0	1	1	1	2	2	2	3	3	4	4	4	5	5	5	6	6	6	7	7	7	8	8	8	9	9	9	10	10	10	11	11	12	12	12	13	13	13	14	14	14	15	15	15	16	16	16	17	17	18	18	18	19	19	19	20	20	20	21	21	21
22	0	1	1	1	2	2	3	3	3	4	4	4	5	5	6	6	6	7	7	7	8	8	8	9	9	10	10	10	11	11	11	12	12	12	13	13	14	14	14	15	15	15	16	16	16	17	17	18	18	18	19	19	19	20	20	21	21	21	22	22	22
23	0	1	1	2	2	2	3	3	3	4	4	5	5	5	6	6	7	7	7	8	8	8	9	9	10	10	10	11	11	12	12	12	13	13	13	14	14	15	15	15	16	16	16	17	17	18	18	18	19	19	20	20	20	21	21	21	22	22	23	23	23
24	0	1	1	2	2	2	3	3	4	4	4	5	5	6	6	6	7	7	8	8	8	9	9	10	10	10	11	11	12	12	12	13	13	14	14	14	15	15	16	16	16	17	17	18	18	18	19	19	20	20	20	21	21	22	22	22	23	23	24	24	24
25	0	1	1	2	2	2	3	3	4	4	5	5	5	6	6	7	7	8	8	8	9	9	10	10	10	11	11	12	12	12	13	13	14	14	15	15	15	16	16	17	17	18	18	18	19	19	20	20	20	21	21	22	22	22	23	23	24	24	25	25	25
26	0	1	1	2	2	3	3	3	4	4	5	5	6	6	6	7	7	8	8	9	9	10	10	10	11	11	12	12	13	13	13	14	14	15	15	16	16	16	17	17	18	18	19	19	20	20	20	21	21	22	22	23	23	23	24	24	25	25	26	26	26
27	0	1	1	2	2	3	3	4	4	4	5	5	6	6	7	7	8	8	9	9	9	10	10	11	11	12	12	13	13	14	14	14	15	15	16	16	17	17	18	18	18	19	19	20	20	21	21	22	22	22	23	23	24	24	25	25	26	26	27	27	27
28	0	1	1	2	2	3	3	4	4	5	5	6	6	7	7	7	8	8	9	9	10	10	11	11	12	12	13	13	14	14	14	15	15	16	16	17	17	18	18	19	19	20	20	21	21	21	22	22	23	23	24	24	25	25	26	26	27	27	28	28	28
29	0	1	1	2	2	3	3	4	4	5	5	6	6	7	7	8	8	9	9	10	10	11	11	12	12	13	13	14	14	14	15	15	16	16	17	17	18	18	19	19	20	20	21	21	22	22	23	23	24	24	25	25	26	26	27	27	28	28	29	29	29
30	0	1	2	2	2	3	4	4	4	5	6	6	6	7	8	8	8	9	10	10	10	11	12	12	12	13	14	14	14	15	16	16	16	17	18	18	18	19	20	20	20	21	22	22	22	23	24	24	24	25	26	26	26	27	28	28	28	29	30	30	30
31	1	1	2	2	3	3	4	4	5	5	6	6	7	7	8	8	9	9	10	10	11	11	12	12	13	13	14	14	15	16	16	17	17	18	18	19	19	20	20	21	21	22	22	23	23	24	24	25	25	26	26	27	27	28	28	29	29	30	30	31	31
32	1	1	2	2	3	3	4	4	5	5	6	6	7	7	8	9	9	10	10	11	11	12	12	13	13	14	14	15	15	16	17	17	18	18	19	19	20	20	21	21	22	22	23	23	24	25	25	26	26	27	27	28	28	29	29	30	30	31	31	32	32
33	1	1	2	2	3	3	4	4	5	6	6	7	7	8	8	9	9	10	10	11	12	12	13	13	14	14	15	15	16	16	17	18	18	19	19	20	20	21	21	22	23	23	24	24	25	25	26	26	27	28	28	29	29	30	30	31	31	32	32	33	33
34	1	1	2	2	3	3	4	5	5	6	6	7	7	8	8	9	10	10	11	11	12	12	13	14	14	15	15	16	16	17	18	18	19	19	20	20	21	22	22	23	23	24	24	25	26	26	27	27	28	28	29	29	30	31	31	32	32	33	33	34	34
35	1	1	2	2	3	4	4	5	5	6	6	7	8	8	9	9	10	10	11	12	12	13	13	14	15	15	16	16	17	18	18	19	19	20	20	21	22	22	23	23	24	24	25	26	26	27	27	28	29	29	30	30	31	32	32	33	33	34	34	35	35
36	1	1	2	2	3	4	4	5	5	6	7	7	8	8	9	10	10	11	11	12	13	13	14	14	15	16	16	17	17	18	19	19	20	20	21	22	22	23	23	24	25	25	26	26	27	28	28	29	29	30	31	31	32	32	33	34	34	35	35	36	36
37	1	1	2	2	3	4	4	5	6	6	7	7	8	9	9	10	10	11	12	12	13	14	14	15	15	16	17	17	18	18	19	20	20	21	22	22	23	23	24	25	25	26	27	27	28	28	29	30	30	31	31	32	33	33	34	35	35	36	36	37	37
38	1	1	2	3	3	4	4	5	6	6	7	8	8	9	10	10	11	11	12	13	13	14	15	15	16	16	17	18	18	19	20	20	21	22	22	23	23	24	25	25	26	27	27	28	28	29	30	30	31	32	32	33	34	34	35	35	36	37	37	38	38
39	1	1	2	3	3	4	5	5	6	6	7	8	8	9	10	10	11	12	12	13	14	14	15	16	16	17	18	18	19	20	20	21	21	22	23	23	24	25	25	26	27	27	28	29	29	30	31	31	32	32	33	34	34	35	36	36	37	38	38	39	39
40	1	1	2	3	3	4	5	5	6	7	7	8	9	9	10	11	11	12	13	13	14	15	15	16	17	17	18	19	19	20	21	21	22	23	23	24	25	25	26	27	27	28	29	29	30	31	31	32	33	33	34	35	35	36	37	37	38	39	39	40	40
41	1	1	2	3	3	4	5	5	6	7	8	8	9	10	10	11	12	12	13	14	14	15	16	16	17	18	18	19	20	20	21	22	23	23	24	25	25	26	27	27	28	29	29	30	31	31	32	33	33	34	35	36	36	37	38	38	39	40	40	41	41
42	1	1	2	3	4	4	5	6	6	7	8	8	9	10	10	11	12	13	13	14	15	15	16	17	18	18	19	20	20	21	22	22	23	24	24	25	26	27	27	28	29	29	30	31	32	32	33	34	34	35	36	36	37	38	38	39	40	41	41	42	42
43	1	1	2	3	4	4	5	6	6	7	8	9	9	10	11	11	12	13	14	14	15	16	16	17	18	19	19	20	21	22	22	23	24	24	25	26	27	27	28	29	29	30	31	32	32	33	34	34	35	36	37	37	38	39	39	40	41	42	42	43	43
44	1	1	2	3	4	4	5	6	7	7	8	9	10	10	11	12	12	13	14	15	15	16	17	18	18	19	20	21	21	22	23	23	24	25	26	26	27	28	29	29	30	31	32	32	33	34	34	35	36	37	37	38	39	40	40	41	42	43	43	44	44
45	1	2	2	3	4	4	5	6	7	8	8	9	10	10	11	12	13	14	14	15	16	16	17	18	19	20	20	21	22	22	23	24	25	26	26	27	28	28	29	30	31	32	32	33	34	34	35	36	37	38	38	39	40	40	41	42	43	44	44	45	45
46	1	2	2	3	4	5	5	6	7	8	8	9	10	11	12	12	13	14	15	15	16	17	18	18	19	20	21	21	22	23	24	25	25	26	27	28	28	29	30	31	31	32	33	34	34	35	36	37	38	38	39	40	41	41	42	43	44	44	45	46	46
47	1	2	2	3	4	5	5	6	7	8	9	9	10	11	12	13	13	14	15	16	16	17	18	19	20	20	21	22	23	24	24	25	26	27	27	28	29	30	31	31	32	33	34	34	35	36	37	38	38	39	40	41	42	42	43	44	45	45	46	47	47
48	1	2	2	3	4	5	6	6	7	8	9	10	10	11	12	13	14	14	15	16	17	18	18	19	20	21	22	22	23	24	25	26	26	27	28	29	30	30	31	32	33	34	34	35	36	37	38	38	39	40	41	42	42	43	44	45	46	46	47	48	48
49	1	2	2	3	4	5	6	7	7	8	9	10	11	11	12	13	14	15	16	16	17	18	19	20	20	21	22	23	24	24	25	26	27	28	29	29	30	31	32	33	33	34	35	36	37	38	38	39	40	41	42	42	43	44	45	46	47	47	48	49	49
50	1	2	2	3	4	5	6	7	8	8	9	10	11	12	12	13	14	15	16	17	18	18	19	20	21	22	22	23	24	25	26	27	28	28	29	30	31	32	32	33	34	35	36	37	38	38	39	40	41	42	42	43	44	45	46	47	48	48	49	50	50
51	1	2	3	3	4	5	6	7	8	8	9	10	11	12	13	14	14	15	16	17	18	19	20	20	21	22	23	24	25	26	26	27	28	29	30	31	31	32	33	34	35	36	37	37	38	39	40	41	42	42	43	44	45	46	47	48	48	49	50	51	51
52	1	2	3	3	4	5	6	7	8	9	10	10	11	12	13	14	15	16	16	17	18	19	20	21	22	23	23	24	25	26	27	28	29	29	30	31	32	33	34	35	36	36	37	38	39	40	41	42	42	43	44	45	46	47	48	49	49	50	51	52	52
53	1	2	3	4	4	5	6	7	8	9	10	11	11	12	13	14	15	16	17	18	19	19	20	21	22	23	24	25	26	26	27	28	29	30	31	32	33	34	34	35	36	37	38	39	40	41	42	42	43	44	45	46	47	48	49	49	50	51	52	53	53
54	1	2	3	4	4	5	6	7	8	9	10	11	12	13	14	14	15	16	17	18	19	20	21	22	22	23	24	25	26	27	28	29	30	31	32	32	33	34	35	36	37	38	39	40	40	41	42	43	44	45	46	47	48	49	50	50	51	52	53	54	54
55	1	2	3	4	5	6	6	7	8	9	10	11	12	13	14	15	16	16	17	18	19	20	21	22	23	24	25	26	27	28	28	29	30	31	32	33	34	35	36	37	38	38	39	40	41	42	43	44	45	46	47	48	49	50	50	51	52	53	54	55	55
56	1	2	3	4	5	6	7	7	8	9	10	11	12	13	14	15	16	17	18	19	20	21	21	22	23	24	25	26	27	28	29	30	31	32	33	34	35	35	36	37	38	39	40	41	42	43	44	45	46	47	48	49	49	50	51	52	53	54	55	56	56
57	1	2	3	4	5	6	7	8	9	10	10	11	12	13	14	15	16	17	18	19	20	21	22	23	24	25	26	27	28	28	29	30	31	32	33	34	35	36	37	38	39	40	41	42	43	44	45	46	47	48	48	49	50	51	52	53	54	55	56	57	57

FIG. 20-7

bering that east longitude increases to the right. The sights are plotted, giving a fix at lat. 33°15′ S, long. 156°35′ E.

Moon Observations There is considerable difference in procedure for moon observations, depending on whether you use the *Air Almanac* or the *Nautical Almanac.* The following example is worked with both, so you can compare procedure and accuracy of results.

Example • The moon's *upper limb* (UL) is observed on January 1 at 06-58-31. H_s is 45°40′. Your DR position is 33°15′ N, 120°05′W. Index error is 7′ off the arc, watch is 27 seconds slow, height of eye is 24 feet.

With the *Air Almanac,* the procedure is straightforward, as for the other bodies, except that the sextant corrections include semidiameter and moon's parallax in altitude, both taken from the daily page. With the *Nautical Almanac,* however, we use the v and d corrections to modify the GHA and the declination. We note the nearest hourly figure for horizontal parallax (HP), which is 56.4′. Next we apply index correction and dip to the sextant reading H_s to obtain what is known as *apparent altitude,* the figure we must use when we enter the altitude-correction for the moon from Figs. 18–16 and 18–17. In this case we have apparent altitude = 45°42′. The nearest entry is 45°40′, for which the altitude correction is 50.0′. Going to the lower half of this table, *but staying in the same vertical column,* we find an additional correction opposite HP 56.4′, in the part of the column headed UL (for upper limb) of 3.1′. All corrections on this page are added, but we *must subtract 30′ for an upper-limb observation.*

The final altitude correction from the *Nautical Almanac* is 25.3′, as compared with 25′ from the *Air Almanac.* There is a 1.2′ difference in declinations obtained from the two almanacs, but the final difference in intercept is only 0.7 mile. We can afford to ignore this small difference in practical marine navigation. The results for Z_n are identical.

42m

42m	SUN PLANETS	ARIES	MOON	v or d	Corrn	v or d	Corrn	v or d	Corrn
s	° ′	° ′	° ′	′	′	′	′	′	′
00	10 30·0	10 31·7	10 01·3	0·0	0·0	6·0	4·3	12·0	8·5
01	10 30·3	10 32·0	10 01·5	0·1	0·1	6·1	4·3	12·1	8·6
02	10 30·5	10 32·2	10 01·8	0·2	0·1	6·2	4·4	12·2	8·6
03	10 30·8	10 32·5	10 02·0	0·3	0·2	6·3	4·5	12·3	8·7
04	10 31·0	10 32·7	10 02·3	0·4	0·3	6·4	4·5	12·4	8·8
05	10 31·3	10 33·0	10 02·5	0·5	0·4	6·5	4·6	12·5	8·9
06	10 31·5	10 33·2	10 02·7	0·6	0·4	6·6	4·7	12·6	8·9
07	10 31·8	10 33·5	10 03·0	0·7	0·5	6·7	4·7	12·7	9·0
08	10 32·0	10 33·7	10 03·2	0·8	0·6	6·8	4·8	12·8	9·1
09	10 32·3	10 34·0	10 03·4	0·9	0·6	6·9	4·9	12·9	9·1

44m

44m	SUN PLANETS	ARIES	MOON	v or d	Corrn	v or d	Corrn	v or d	Cor
s	° ′	° ′	° ′	′	′	′	′	′	
00	11 00·0	11 01·8	10 29·9	0·0	0·0	6·0	4·5	12·0	[illegible]
01	11 00·3	11 02·1	10 30·2	0·1	0·1	6·1	4·5	12·1	9
02	11 00·5	11 02·3	10 30·4	0·2	0·1	6·2	4·6	12·2	9
03	11 00·8	11 02·6	10 30·6	0·3	0·2	6·3	4·7	12·3	9
04	11 01·0	11 02·8	10 30·9	0·4	0·3	6·4	4·7	12·4	9
05	11 01·3	11 03·1	10 31·1	0·5	0·4	6·5	4·8	12·5	9
06	11 01·5	11 03·3	10 31·4	0·6	0·4	6·6	4·9	12·6	9
07	11 01·8	11 03·6	10 31·6	0·7	0·5	6·7	5·0	12·7	9
08	11 02·0	11 03·8	10 31·8	0·8	0·6	6·8	5·0	12·8	9
09	11 02·3	11 04·1	10 32·1	0·9	0·7	6·9	5·1	12·9	9
10	11 02·5	11 04·3	10 32·3	1·0	0·7	7·0	5·2	13·0	9
11	11 02·8	11 04·6	10 32·6	1·1	0·8	7·1	5·3	13·1	9
12	11 03·0	11 04·8	10 32·8	1·2	0·9	7·2	5·3	13·2	9
13	11 03·3	11 05·1	10 33·0	1·3	1·0	7·3	5·4	13·3	9
14	11 03·5	11 05·3	10 33·3	1·4	1·0	7·4	5·5	13·4	9
15	11 03·8	11 05·6	10 33·5	1·5	1·1	7·5	5·6	13·5	10
16	11 04·0	11 05·8	10 33·8	1·6	1·2	7·6	5·6	13·6	10
17	11 04·3	11 06·1	10 34·0	1·7	1·3	7·7	5·7	13·7	10
18	11 04·5	11 06·3	10 34·2	1·8	1·3	7·8	5·8	13·8	10
19	11 04·8	11 06·6	10 34·5	1·9	1·4	7·9	5·9	13·9	10
20	11 05·0	11 06·8	10 34·7	2·0	1·5	8·0	5·9	14·0	10
21	11 05·3	11 07·1	10 34·9	2·1	1·6	8·1	6·0	14·1	10
22	11 05·5	11 07·3	10 35·2	2·2	1·6	8·2	6·1	14·2	10
23	11 05·8	11 07·6	10 35·4	2·3	1·7	8·3	6·2	14·3	10
24	11 06·0	11 07·8	10 35·7	2·4	1·8	8·4	6·2	14·4	10
25	11 06·3	11 08·1	10 35·9	2·5	1·9	8·5	6·3	14·5	10
26	11 06·5	11 08·3	10 36·1	2·6	1·9	8·6	6·4	14·6	10
27	11 06·8	11 08·6	10 36·4	2·7	2·0	8·7	6·5	14·7	10
28	11 07·0	11 08·8	10 36·6	2·8	2·1	8·8	6·5	14·8	11
29	11 07·3	11 09·1	10 36·9	2·9	2·2	8·9	6·6	14·9	11
30	11 07·5	11 09·3	10 37·1	3·0	2·2	9·0	6·7	15·0	11
31	11 07·8	11 09·6	10 37·3	3·1	2·3	9·1	6·7	15·1	11
32	11 08·0	11 09·8	10 37·6	3·2	2·4	9·2	6·8	15·2	11
33	11 08·3	11 10·1	10 37·8	3·3	2·4	9·3	6·9	15·3	11
34	11 08·5	11 10·3	10 38·0	3·4	2·5	9·4	7·0	15·4	11

58m

50	14 42·5	14 44·9	14 02·3	5·0	4·9	11·0	10·7	17·0	16·6
51	14 42·8	14 45·2	14 02·5	5·1	5·0	11·1	10·8	17·1	16·7
52	14 43·0	14 45·4	14 02·8	5·2	5·1	11·2	10·9	17·2	16·8
53	14 43·3	14 45·7	14 03·0	5·3	5·2	11·3	11·0	17·3	16·9
54	14 43·5	14 45·9	14 03·3	5·4	5·3	11·4	11·1	17·4	17·0
55	14 43·8	14 46·2	14 03·5	5·5	5·4	11·5	11·2	17·5	17·1
56	14 44·0	14 46·4	14 03·7	5·6	5·5	11·6	11·3	17·6	17·2
57	14 44·3	14 46·7	14 04·0	5·7	5·6	11·7	11·4	17·7	17·3
58	14 44·5	14 46·9	14 04·2	5·8	5·7	11·8	11·5	17·8	17·4
59	14 44·8	14 47·2	14 04·4	5·9	5·8	11·9	11·6	17·9	17·5
60	14 45·0	14 47·4	14 04·7	6·0	5·9	12·0	11·7	18·0	17·6

FIG. 20-8

Coast Navigation School

SANTA BARBARA, CALIFORNIA

MULTIPLE SIGHT FORM FOR MOON, N.O. 249

WITH NAUTICAL ALMANAC

Name Simonsen

Local Date Jan. 1 Greenwich Date Jan. 1 DR Lat. N 33° 15' DR Long W 120° 05'

	Nautical Alm.		Air Alm.
Body	☽ UL ~~LL~~	☽ UL LL	☽ UL ~~LL~~
Hs	45° 40'		45° 40'
Total Corr.	+ 25.3		+ 25
Ho	46° 05.3		46° 05'
Watch Time	06-58-31		06-58-31
Watch Error	+27		+27
Zone Time	06-58-58		06-58-58
Zone Desc.	+8		+8
GMT	14-58-58	14-50	14-58-58
GHA of Moon Hrs.	115° 14'		127° 22'
GHA Min. & Sec.	14° 04.2'		2° 10'
GHA v Corr.	v= 14.5 14.1	v=	v=
TOTAL GHA	129° 32.3		129° 32'
Assumed Long. (-W,+E)	120° 32.3		120° 32'
Apply 360° if necessary			
LHA of Moon	9°		9°
Declination N/S	S 9° 43.8		S 9° 59'
Corr. for d(+ / -)	d= +14.4 +14'	d=	d=
Net Decl.	S 9° 57.8		
Assumed Lat. N/S	N 33°		N 33°
	From N. O. 249, Vol II or III		
d factor (+ / -)	−59		−59
Hc (Tabular)	47° 08'		47° 08'
d Correction (+ / -)	−57'		−58
Hc	46° 11'		46° 10'
Ho	46° 05.3'		46° 05'
Intercept (T/A)	A 5.7 mi		A 5 mi
Z	167°		167°
Apply 360° or 180°	360°		360°
Zn	193°		193°
Plotting Symbol			

IE 7' off arc

WE 27 sec. slow

HE 24 Ft.

HP 56.4'

Sextant Corrections (Naut. A.)

	+	−
IC	7	
Dip		4.8
Alt. Corr.	50	
H.P.	3.1	
UL (-30')		30
Totals	60.1	34.8
	34.8	
Total C.	25.3	

Sextant Corrections (Air A.)

	+	−
IC	7'	
Dip		5'
Alt. Corr.		1'
H.P.	39'	
~~UL (-30')~~ S.D.		15'
Totals	46'	21'
	21'	
Total C.	25'	

Time Diagram

Hour Angle Diagram

RULES:

NORTH LATITUDE		SOUTH LATITUDE	
LHA GREATER THAN 180°,	ZN = Z	LHA GREATER THAN 180°,	ZN = 180°-Z
LHA LESS THAN 180°,	ZN = 360°-Z	LHA LESS THAN 180°,	ZN = 180°+Z

FIG. 20-9

Chapter 21

How to Use H.O. 214

This set of tables evolved during World War II, quickly found favor with marine navigators, and has been popular ever since. It provides an accuracy of within 0.1 minute in computed altitude, and within 0.1 degree in azimuth, as compared to N.O. 249, which provides information to the nearest minute only. The Naval Oceanographic Office is planning to phase out H.O. 214 by about 1975 in favor of a new set of tables, N.O. 229, but it is certain that many navigators will continue to favor H.O. 214. Since the tables are usable indefinitely without revision, the method will remain popular for a long time to come.

The main difference between H.O. 214 and the other two sets of tables is that we enter with the *meridian angle*, or the *angle t*, which we discussed in earlier chapters. As shown in Fig. 1, when the LHA is less than 180°, LHA $= t$, and when LHA is more than 180°, $t = 360° -$ LHA. That is all there is to it. The angle t is always marked either east (E) or west (W), and t obviously cannot exceed 180°.

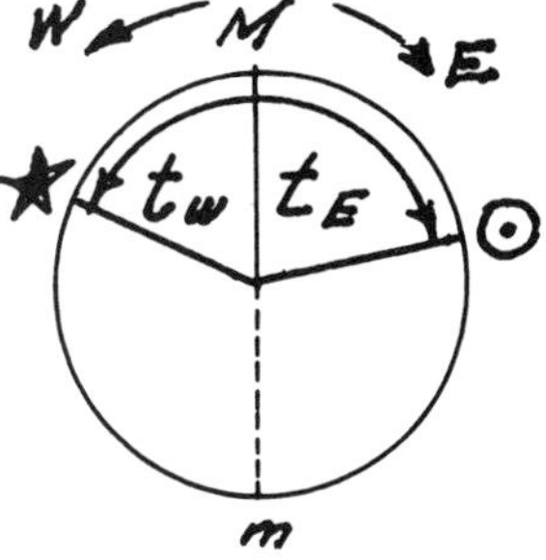

FIG. 21-1

A simple way to visualize the angle t, and whether it is east or west, is this: when the sun or a star is rising in the east, and before it reaches its highest altitude at the moment it transits our meridian, t is east; once the body has crossed the meridian and begins to sink lower in the sky, the angle t is west.

One advantage of H.O. 214 is that most declinations are given for every half-degree, instead of for every degree, as in the other two tables. This means less interpolation. You will notice in using H.O. 214 that there are a number of gaps in listed declinations. The reason is that the tables leave out those areas of the sky where there are no navigational stars, thus saving space and bulk. The set consists of nine volumes, each covering 10° of latitude. Most small vessels need only the first six volumes, unless they are going beyond 60° north or south.

Procedure

Because each volume covers 10° of latitude, for a given observation we first determine the volume to be used. A separate section is set aside for each whole degree of assumed latitude. Within this section, declinations are listed by every half-degree from 0° to the highest declination, north or south, that a star can have and still be visible at this latitude. Facing pages give data for latitude and declination *same name* and latitude and declination *contrary name*—and as mentioned before, it does not matter which is north and which is south, so long as they are either the same or opposite and we recognize the fact.

On every page, the extreme right- and left-hand columns are headed "HA," for *hour angle.* In these tables, HA means the *angle t, not* LHA. We enter the page with the correct *lower* half-degree of declination found in the line across the top of the page, and cross it with the value for *t.* In each column we find four values:

H_c Δd Δt Az.

We do not use Δt ("delta-tee") in our standard method of sight reduction. The instructions at the beginning of the table will explain what Δt is used for, if you are concerned. The value H_c is the *tabulated computed altitude for the assumed latitude and assumed longitude and the initial value of declination used.* However, H_c is affected by a change in declination, so we make an interpolation for the difference between the lower half-degree of declination with which we entered the tables and the *actual declination.* The value Δd ("delta-dee") is a percentage factor that indicates the change in altitude, *up* or *down,* during the next-higher 30′ of declination. When we first take out our data, we write down H_c, Δd, and Az. Next we look in the adjoining column to the right, for the next-higher value of declination, and determine whether the H_c listed there is larger or smaller than the one we wrote down. If it is larger, it means that

H_c increases with an increase in declination, and we place a plus (+) sign in front of Δd to remind us that the correction must be *added* to H_c. However, if the H_c in the adjoining column on the right is smaller, it means that the altitude decreases with an increase in declination, and we place a minus (−) sign in front of Δd, to remind us to *subtract* the correction.

Next, we determine the amount of the correction. This depends on Δd and on the difference between the *actual declination* and the lower declination with which we entered the table. For example, if actual declination is 30°47′ N, we enter the table with declination of 30°30′ and make a correction for 17′. This correction is found in a "Multiplication Table" inside the back cover (Fig. 21–3). Across the top of the page is found the declination difference in minutes, 1–15 on the left-hand side and 16–30 on the right-hand side. In the vertical column at each side of the page we find Δd from 01 at the top to 1.00 at the bottom. Corrections for fractions of minutes in the declination are taken from the separate table at the right-hand side of each page.

Note: The correction to H_c is found as a percentage of the declination difference. The value Δd is a percentage figure. At Δd of 01 is 1%, a Δd of 55 is 55%, and when you find a Δd of 1.0, it means a 100% correction. It is found at the bottom of the page, but it really need not be looked up, because the correction is exactly equal to the entire declination difference. The purpose of the multiplication table is simply to have the percentages precomputed for us to save time.

The *azimuth Z,* as taken from the table, must be converted to Z_n, as in the other tables, but the method is slightly different. The value Z is really the bearing of the celestial body at our assumed position, measured *east* or *west* of our *visible pole,* i.e., east or west of true north in north latitude and east or west of true south in south latitude. The rules are exactly the same as those given for N.O. 249 and N.O. 229, but since those rules are based on LHA, and we do not use LHA with H.O. 214, it is simpler to base the rules on

DECLINATION **SAME** NAME AS LATITUDE

Lat. 10°

0′ Az.	23° 00′ Alt.	Δd Δt	Az.	23° 30′ Alt.	Δd Δt	Az.	H.A.
°	° ′		°	° ′		°	°
00.0	**77 00.0**	1.0 04	00.0	**76 30.0**	1.0 03	00.0	**00**
04.3	**76 57.9**	1.0 10	04.1	**76 28.0**	1.0 10	03.9	1
08.5	**76 51.6**	99 17	08.1	**76 21.9**	99 17	07.8	2
12.6	**76 41.2**	97 24	12.1	**76 12.0**	98 23	11.6	3
16.6	**76 26.9**	96 30	15.9	**75 58.2**	96 29	15.3	4
20.4	**76 08.9**	93 36	19.6	**75 40.9**	94 35	18.9	**05**
24.0	**75 47.4**	91 41	23.1	**75 20.1**	91 40	22.2	6
27.4	**75 22.7**	88 46	26.4	**74 56.2**	89 45	25.5	7
30.5	**74 55.0**	85 51	29.5	**74 29.4**	86 49	28.5	8
33.5	**74 24.6**	82 55	32.4	**73 59.9**	83 53	31.4	9
36.2	**73 51.8**	79 58	35.1	**73 27.9**	80 57	34.0	**10**
38.8	**73 16.7**	76 62	37.6	**72 53.8**	77 60	36.5	1
41.1	**72 39.7**	73 65	40.0	**72 17.7**	74 63	38.8	2
43.3	**72 00.9**	70 67	42.1	**71 39.8**	71 66	41.0	3
45.3	**71 20.5**	67 70	44.1	**71 00.3**	68 68	43.0	4
47.1	**70 38.7**	64 72	46.0	**70 19.3**	65 70	44.8	**15**
48.8	**69 55.6**	61 74	47.7	**69 37.0**	63 72	46.5	6
50.4	**69 11.4**	59 76	49.2	**68 53.6**	60 74	48.1	7
51.8	**68 26.1**	56 77	50.7	**68 09.1**	58 76	49.6	8
53.2	**67 39.9**	54 78	52.1	**67 23.6**	55 77	51.0	9
54.4	**66 52.9**	51 80	53.3	**66 37.3**	53 78	52.2	**20**
55.6	**66 05.2**	49 81	54.5	**65 50.2**	51 80	53.4	1
56.6	**65 16.8**	47 82	55.5	**65 02.4**	49 81	54.5	2
57.6	**64 27.8**	45 83	56.5	**64 14.0**	47 82	55.5	3
58.5	**63 38.2**	43 84	57.5	**63 25.0**	45 83	56.5	4
59.3	**62 48.1**	41 84	58.3	**62 35.5**	43 83	57.3	**25**
60.1	**61 57.6**	40 85	59.1	**61 45.6**	41 84	58.2	6
60.9	**61 06.7**	38 86	59.9	**60 55.2**	39 85	58.9	7
61.5	**60 15.4**	36 86	60.6	**60 04.3**	38 85	59.6	8
62.2	**59 23.8**	35 86	61.2	**59 13.2**	36 86	60.3	9
62.7	**58 31.8**	33 87	61.8	**58 21.7**	34 86	60.9	**30**
63.3	**57 39.6**	32 88	62.4	**57 29.9**	33 87	61.5	1
63.8	**56 47.1**	30 88	62.9	**56 37.8**	32 87	62.1	2
64.3	**55 54.4**	29 88	63.4	**55 45.5**	30 88	62.6	3
64.7	**55 01.4**	28 89	63.9	**54 52.9**	29 88	63.1	4
65.1	**54 08.3**	27 89	64.3	**54 00.1**	28 88	63.5	**35**
65.5	**53 14.9**	25 89	64.7	**53 07.2**	26 89	63.9	6
65.9	**52 21.4**	24 90	65.1	**52 14.0**	25 89	64.3	7
66.2	**51 27.7**	23 90	65.5	**51 20.7**	24 89	64.7	8
66.6	**50 33.9**	22 90	65.8	**50 27.2**	23 89	65.0	9
66.8	**49 40.0**	21 90	66.1	**49 33.6**	22 90	65.3	**40**
67.1	**48 45.9**	20 90	66.4	**48 39.8**	21 90	65.6	1
67.4	**47 51.7**	19 90	66.6	**47 45.9**	20 90	65.9	2
67.6	**46 57.4**	18 91	66.9	**46 51.9**	19 90	66.2	3
67.8	**46 03.0**	17 91	67.1	**45 57.8**	18 90	66.4	4
68.0	**45 08.5**	16 91	67.3	**45 03.6**	17 90	66.6	**45**
68.2	**44 14.0**	15 91	67.5	**44 09.3**	16 91	66.8	6
68.4	**43 19.3**	14 91	67.7	**43 15.0**	15 91	67.0	7
68.6	**42 24.6**	13 91	67.9	**42 20.5**	14 91	67.2	8
68.7	**41 29.8**	12 91	68.1	**41 26.0**	13 91	67.4	9
68.9	**40 35.0**	12 92	68.2	**40 31.4**	12 91	67.5	**50**
69.0	**39 40.1**	11 92	68.3	**39 36.8**	11 91	67.7	1
69.1	**38 45.2**	10 92	68.5	**38 42.1**	11 91	67.8	2
69.2	**37 50.2**	09 92	68.6	**37 47.4**	10 91	67.9	3
69.3	**36 55.2**	08 92	68.7	**36 52.6**	09 91	68.0	4

DECLINATION **SAME** NAME AS LATITUDE

Lat. 33°

6° 30′ Alt.	Δd Δt	Az.	7° 00′ Alt.	Δd Δt	Az.	7° 30′ Alt.	Δd Δt	Az.	H.A.
° ′		°	° ′		°	° ′		°	°
63 30.0	1.0 02	180.0	**64 00.0**	1.0 02	180.0	**64 30.0**	1.0 02	180.0	**00**
63 29.0	1.0 05	177.8	**63 59.0**	1.0 05	177.7	**64 29.0**	1.0 05	177.7	1
63 26.1	1.0 08	175.6	**63 56.0**	1.0 08	175.5	**64 26.0**	1.0 08	175.4	2
63 21.2	1.0 11	173.3	**63 51.1**	1.0 12	173.2	**64 20.9**	99 12	173.1	3
63 14.4	99 14	171.1	**63 44.2**	99 15	171.0	**64 13.9**	99 15	170.8	4
63 05.7	99 18	169.0	**63 35.3**	99 18	168.8	**64 04.9**	99 18	168.6	**05**
62 55.2	98 21	166.8	**63 24.6**	98 21	166.6	**63 54.0**	98 21	166.4	6
62 42.8	97 24	164.7	**63 12.0**	97 24	164.4	**63 41.2**	97 24	164.2	7
62 28.6	97 27	162.6	**62 [illegible]**	97 27	162.3	**63 26[illegible]**	[illegible] 27	162.0	8
62 1[illegible]	[illegible]29	160.5	[illegible]	[illegible]	160.2	[illegible]	[illegible]	[illegible]	9
[illegible]			**[illegible] 10.4**	58 [illegible]	[illegible]	**[illegible].1**	59 80	[illegible]	
[illegible] 04.6	59 80	[illegible].9	**35 22.2**	59 81	10[illegible]	**35 39.7**	58 81	105.9	
34 16.4	59 81	106.2	**34 33.9**	58 81	105.7	**34 51.3**	58 81	105.2	3
33 28.0	58 81	105.5	**33 45.4**	58 81	105.0	**34 02.6**	57 81	104.5	4
32 39.4	58 81	104.8	**32 56.7**	57 81	104.3	**33 13.9**	57 82	103.9	**55**
31 50.7	57 81	104.2	**32 07.9**	57 82	103.7	**32 24.9**	57 82	103.2	6
31 01.8	57 82	103.5	**31 18.9**	57 82	103.0	**31 35.9**	56 82	102.5	7
30 12.8	57 82	102.8	**30 29.8**	56 82	102.3	**30 46.7**	56 82	101.9	8
29 23.7	56 82	102.2	**29 40.6**	56 82	101.7	**29 57.4**	56 82	101.2	9
28 34.4	56 82	101.5	**28 51.3**	56 82	101.1	**29 08.0**	56 83	100.6	**60**
27 45.1	56 82	100.9	**28 01.8**	56 83	100.4	**28 18.5**	55 83	100.0	1
26 55.6	56 83	100.3	**27 12.3**	55 83	99.8	**27 28.9**	55 83	99.3	2
26 06.1	[illegible]	99.7	**26 22.7**	[illegible]	99.2	**26 39.2**	[illegible]	98.7	3

FIG. 21-2
Excerpts from H.O. 214

DECLINATION **CONTRARY** NAME TO LATITUDE

9° 00′ Alt.	Δd Δt	Az.	9° 30′ Alt.	Δd Δt	Az.	10° 00′ Alt.	Δd Δt	Az.	10° 30′ Alt.	Δd Δt	Az.	11° 00′ Alt.	Δd Δt	Az.	11° 30′ Alt.	Δd Δt	Az.	H.A.
° ′		°	° ′		°	° ′		°	° ′		°	° ′		°	° ′		°	°
48 00.0	1.0 01	180.0	**47 30.0**	1.0 01	180.0	**47 00.0**	1.0 01	180.0	**46 30.0**	1.0 01	180.0	**46 00.0**	1.0 01	180.0	**45 30.0**	1.0 01	180.0	*00*
47 59.4	1.0 03	178.5	**47 29.4**	1.0 03	178.5	**46 59.4**	1.0 03	178.6	**46 29.4**	1.0 03	178.6	**45 59.4**	1.0 03	178.6	**45 29.4**	1.0 03	178.6	*1*
47 57.4	1.0 05	177.0	**47 27.4**	1.0 05	177.1	**46 57.5**	1.0 05	177.1	**46 27.5**	1.0 05	177.1	**45 57.5**	1.0 05	177.2	**45 27.5**	1.0 05	177.2	*2*
47 54.2	1.0 08	175.6	**47 24.2**	1.0 07	175.6	**46 54.3**	1.0 07	175.7	**46 24.4**	1.0 07	175.7	**45 54.4**	1.0 07	175.8	**45 24.5**	1.0 07	175.8	*3*
47 49.6	1.0 10	174.1	**47 19.8**	1.0 10	174.2	**46 49.9**	1.0 09	174.2	**46 20.0**	1.0 09	174.3	**45 50.1**	1.0 09	174.4	**45 20.2**	1.0 09	174.4	*4*
47 43.8	99 12	172.6	**47 14.0**	99 12	172.7	**46 44.2**	99 12	172.8	**46 14.4**	99 11	172.9	**45 44.5**	99 11	173.0	**45 14.7**	99 11	173.0	*05*
47 36.8	99 14	171.2	**47 07.0**	99 14	171.3	**46 37.3**	99 14	171.4	**46 07.5**	99 13	171.5	**45 37.8**	99 13	171.6	**45 08.0**	99 13	171.7	*6*
47 28.4	99 16	169.7	**46 58.8**	99 16	169.9	**46 29.1**	99 16	170.0	**45 59.4**	99 15	170.1	**45 29.8**	99 15	170.2	**45 00.1**	99 15	170.3	*7*
47 18.9	99 18	168.3	**46 49.3**	99 18	168.4	**46 19.7**	99 18	168.6	**45 50.2**	99 17	168.7	**45 20.6**	99 17	168.8	**44 51.0**	99 17	168.9	*8*
47 08.0	98 20	166.9	**46 38.6**	98 20	167.0	**46 09.1**	98 20	167.2	**45 39.7**	98 19	167.3	**45 10.2**	98 19	167.4	**44 40.7**	98 19	167.6	*9*
46 56.0	98 22	165.5	**46 26.7**	98 22	165.6	**45 57.4**	98 22	165.8	**45 28.0**	98 21	165.9	**44 58.7**	98 21	166.1	**44 29.3**	98 21	166.2	*10*
46 42.8	97 24	164.0	**46 13.6**	97 24	164.2	**45 44.4**	97 24	164.4	**45 15.2**	97 23	164.5	**44 46.0**	97 23	164.7	**44 16.7**	97 23	164.9	*1*
46 28.3	97 26	162.7	**45 59.3**	97 26	162.8	**45 30.3**	97 25	163.0	**45 01.2**	97 25	163.2	**44 32.1**	97 25	163.4	**44 03.0**	97 25	163.5	*2*
46 12.8	96 28	161.3	**45 43.9**	96 28	161.5	**45 15.0**	96 27	161.7	**44 46.1**	96 27	161.8	**44 17.2**	96 27	162.0	**43 48.2**	97 26	162.2	*3*
[illegible]56.0	96 30	159.9	**45 27.3**	96 29	160.1	**44 58.6**	96 29	160.3	**44 29.9**	96 29	160.5	**44 01.1**	96 29	160.7	**43 32.3**	96 28	160.9	*4*

whether the angle t is east or west of the meridian, as follows:

$$\text{North latitude} \begin{cases} \text{if } t \text{ is east, } Z_n = Z \\ \text{if } t \text{ is west, } Z_n = 360° - Z \end{cases}$$

$$\text{South latitude} \begin{cases} \text{if } t \text{ is east, } Z_n = 180° - Z \\ \text{if } t \text{ is west, } Z_n = 180° + Z \end{cases}$$

Example • We shall work all the examples in the previous chapter by H.O. 214 and show that the azimuths and intercepts are virtually identical. Since all the work down to the entry into the reduction tables is the same, except that we find t instead of LHA, we have shown only the part of the computation for altitude and azimuth. The necessary excerpts from the tables in H.O. 214 are shown (Fig. 21–2), and it is important that you work through the figures and see the manner in which they were obtained. The first sun sight is explained step by step:

Step 1. Determine the angle t, assumed latitude, and declination of body observed—i.e., 39° E, S 10°, S 23°02′.

Step 2. Enter proper volume (Volume II, lat. 10°–19°), proper latitude (10°), and locate declination to be used (23°00′ same name).

Step 3. Enter with HA = t (39°) and take out H_c, Δd, and az. (50°33.9′, −22, 65.8°). (Note that H_c for 23°30′ dec. is smaller, so mark Δd minus.)

Step 4. From multiplication table find correction for Δd and declination difference (22 and 02′). (Correction is 0.4′.) Apply to tabulated altitude and find H_c.

Step 5. Determine intercept. Convert azimuth to Z_n (18.7 miles away, Z_n = 180° − 65.8° = 114.2).

Step 6. With assumed position, intercept, and Z_n, plot LOP.

MULTIPLICATION TABLE

Δ	1′	2′	3′	4′	5′	6′	7′	8′	9′	10′	11′	12′	13′	14′	15′	Δ	0.1′	0.2′	0.3′	0.4′	0.5′	0.6′	0.7′	0.8′	0.9′
	DEC. DIFF. OR H. A. DIFF. (minutes of arc)																DEC. DIFF. OR H. A. DIFF. (tenths of minute								
01	0.0	0.0	0.0	0.0	0.1	0.1	0.1	0.1	0.1	0.1	0.1	0.1	0.1	0.1	0.2	01	0.0	0.0	0.0	0.0	0.0	0.0	0.0	0.0	0.
2	.0	.0	.1	.1	.1	.1	.1	.2	.2	.2	.2	.2	.3	.3	.3	2									
3	.0	.1	.1	.1	.2	.2	.2	.2	.3	.3	.3	.4	.4	.4	.5	3									
4	.0	.1	.1	.2	.2	.2	.3	.3	.4	.4	.4	.5	.5	.6	.6	4									
05	0.1	0.1	0.2	0.2	0.3	0.3	0.4	0.4	0.5	0.5	0.6	0.6	0.7	0.7	0.8	05	0.0	0.0	0.0	0.0	0.0	0.0	0.0	0.0	0.
6	.1	.1	.2	.2	.3	.4	.4	.5	.5	.6	.7	.7	.8	.8	.9	6								0.0	0.
7	.1	.1	.2	.3	.4	.4	.5	.6	.6	.7	.8	.8	.9	1.0	1.1	7							0.0	0.1	
8	.1	.2	.2	.3	.4	.5	.6	.6	.7	.8	.9	1.0	1.0	1.1	1.2	8						0.0	0.1		
9	.1	.2	.3	.4	.5	.5	.6	.7	.8	.9	1.0	1.1	1.2	1.3	1.4	9					0.0	0.1			
10	0.1	0.2	0.3	0.4	0.5	0.6	0.7	0.8	0.9	1.0	1.1	1.2	1.3	1.4	1.5	10	0.0	0.0	0.0	0.0	0.1	0.1	0.1	0.1	0.
1	.1	.2	.3	.4	.6	.7	.8	.9	1.0	1.1	1.2	1.3	1.4	1.5	1.7	1									
2	.1	.2	.4	.5	.6	.7	.8	1.0	1.1	1.2	1.3	1.4	1.6	1.7	1.8	2				0.0					
3	.1	.3	.4	.5	.7	.8	.9	1.0	1.2	1.3	1.4	1.6	1.7	1.8	2.0	3				0.1					
4	.1	.3	.4	.6	.7	.8	1.0	1.1	1.3	1.4	1.5	1.7	1.8	2.0	2.1	4									
15	0.2	0.3	0.5	0.6	0.8	0.9	1.1	1.2	1.4	1.5	1.7	1.8	2.0	2.1	2.3	15	0.0	0.0	0.0	0.1	0.1	0.1	0.1	0.1	0.
6	.2	.3	.5	.6	.8	1.0	1.1	1.3	1.4	1.6	1.8	1.9	2.1	2.2	2.4	6			0.0						0.
7	.2	.3	.5	.7	.9	1.0	1.2	1.4	1.5	1.7	1.9	2.0	2.2	2.4	2.6	7			0.1						0.
8	.2	.4	.5	.7	.9	1.1	1.3	1.4	1.6	1.8	2.0	2.2	2.3	2.5	2.7	8								0.1	
9	.2	.4	.6	.8	1.0	1.1	1.3	1.5	1.7	1.9	2.1	2.3	2.5	2.7	2.9	9								0.2	
20	0.2	0.4	0.6	0.8	1.0	1.2	1.4	1.6	1.8	2.0	2.2	2.4	2.6	2.8	3.0	20	0.0	0.0	0.1	0.1	0.1	0.1	0.1	0.2	0.
1	.2	.4	.6	.8	1.1	1.3	1.5	1.7	1.9	2.1	2.3	2.5	2.7	2.9	3.2	1							0.1		
2	.2	.4	.7	.9	1.1	1.3	1.5	1.8	2.0	2.2	2.4	2.6	2.9	3.1	3.3	2							0.2		
3	.2	.5	.7	.9	1.2	1.4	1.6	1.8	2.1	2.3	2.5	2.8	3.0	3.2	3.5	3									
4	.2	.5	.7	1.0	1.2	1.4	1.7	1.9	2.2	2.4	2.6	2.9	3.1	3.4	3.6	4		0.0				0.1			
25	0.3	0.5	0.8	1.0	1.3	1.5	1.8	2.0	2.3	2.5	2.8	3.0	3.3	3.5	3.8	25	0.0	0.1	0.1	0.1	0.1	0.2	0.2	0.2	0.

MULTIPLICATION TABLE

Δ	16′	17′	18′	19′	20′	21′	22′	23′	24′	25′	26′	27′	28′	29′	30′	Δ	0.1′	0.2′	0.3′	0.4′	0.5′	0.6′	0.7′	0.8′	0.9′
	DEC. DIFF. OR H. A. DIFF. (minutes of arc)																DEC. DIFF. OR H. A. DIFF. (tenths of minut								
01	0.2	0.2	0.2	0.2	0.2	0.2	0.2	0.2	0.2	0.3	0.3	0.3	0.3	0.3	0.3	01	0.0	0.0	0.0	0.0	0.0	0.0	0.0	0.0	0.
2	.3	.3	.4	.4	.4	.4	.4	.5	.5	.5	.5	.5	.6	.6	.6	2									
3	.5	.5	.5	.6	.6	.6	.7	.7	.7	.8	.8	.8	.8	.9	.9	3									
4	.6	.7	.7	.8	.8	.8	.9	.9	1.0	1.0	1.0	1.1	1.1	1.2	1.2	4									
05	0.8	0.9	0.9	1.0	[illegible]	[illegible]	1.1	1.2	1.2	[illegible]	1.3	1.4	1.4	1.5	1.5		[illegible]	0.0	0.0	0.0			[illegible]	0.0	0.
	1.0	1.0	1.1	[illegible]			1.3	1.4	1.4		[illegible]	1.6	1.7	1.7										0.0	0.
	[illegible]	1.2	1.3				[illegible]	1.6	1.7			1.9	2.0	2.0										0.1	
		1.4	[illegible]				[illegible]	1.8	[illegible]			[illegible]	2.2	[illegible]											
		[illegible]						2.1	[illegible]			[illegible]	2.5												
								[illegible]					[illegible]			45	[illegible]				0.2	0.3	[illegible]		[illegible]
6					[illegible]	[illegible]				[illegible]	[illegible]				[illegible]	6									
7					9.4	[illegible]				[illegible]	12.2				14.1	7									
8	[illegible]			[illegible]	9.6	10.1	[illegible]			12.0	12.5	[illegible]		[illegible]	14.4	8									
9	7.8			9.3	9.8	10.3	[illegible]		[illegible]	12.3	12.7	13.2	[illegible]	14.2	14.7	9			[illegible]		0.2				
50	8.0	[illegible]	[illegible]	9.5	10.0	10.5	11.0	[illegible]	[illegible]	12.5	13.0	13.5	14.0	14.5	15.0	50	0.1	0.1	0.2	0.2	0.3	0.3	0.4	0.4	[illegible]
1	8.2	8.7	9.2	9.7	10.2	10.7	11.2	[illegible]	12.2	12.8	13.3	13.8	14.3	14.8	15.3	1									
2	8.3	8.8	9.4	9.9	10.4	10.9	11.4	12.0	12.5	13.0	13.5	14.0	14.6	15.1	15.6	2									
3	8.5	9.0	9.5	10.1	10.6	11.1	11.7	12.2	12.7	13.3	13.8	14.3	14.8	15.4	15.9	3									
4	8.6	9.2	9.7	10.3	10.8	11.3	11.9	12.4	13.0	13.5	14.0	14.6	15.1	15.7	16.2	4									
55	8.8	9.4	9.9	10.5	11.0	11.6	12.1	12.7	13.2	13.8	14.3	14.9	15.4	16.0	16.5	55	0.1	0.1	0.2	0.2	0.3	0.3	0.4	0.4	0.
6	9.0	9.5	10.1	10.6	11.2	11.8	12.3	12.9	13.4	14.0	14.6	15.1	15.7	16.2	16.8	6								0.4	
7	9.1	9.7	10.3	10.8	11.4	12.0	12.5	13.1	13.7	14.3	14.8	15.4	16.0	16.5	17.1	7								0.5	
8	9.3	9.9	10.4	11.0	11.6	12.2	12.8	13.3	13.9	14.5	15.1	15.7	16.2	16.8	17.4	8						0.3			
9	9.4	10.0	10.6	11.2	11.8	12.4	13.0	13.6	14.2	14.8	15.3	15.9	16.5	17.1	17.7	9						0.4			
60	9.6	10.2	10.8	11.4	12.0	12.6	13.2	13.8	14.4	15.0	15.6	16.2	16.8	17.4	18.0	60	0.1	0.1	0.2	0.2	0.3	0.4	0.4	0.5	0.
1	9.8	10.4	11.0	11.6	12.2	12.8	13.4	14.0	14.6	15.3	15.9	16.5	17.1	17.7	18.3	1									0.
2	9.9	10.5	11.2	11.8	12.4	13.0	13.6	14.3	14.9	15.5	16.1	16.7	17.4	18.0	18.6	2				0.2					0.
3	10.1	10.7	11.3	12.0	12.6	13.2	13.9	14.5	15.1	15.8	16.4	17.0	17.6	18.3	18.9	3				0.3					
4	10.2	10.9	11.5	12.2	12.8	13.4	14.1	14.7	15.4	16.0	16.6	17.3	17.9	18.6	19.2	4							0.4		
65	10.4	11.1	11.7	12.4	13.0	13.7	14.3	15.0	15.6	16.3	16.9	17.6	18.2	18.9	19.5	65	0.1	0.1	0.2	0.3	0.3	0.4	0.5	0.5	0.
6	10.6	11.2	11.9	12.5	13.2	13.9	14.5	15.2	15.8	16.5	17.2	17.8	18.5	19.1	19.8	6									
7	10.7	11.4	12.1	12.7	13.4	14.1	14.7	15.4	16.1	16.8	17.4	18.1	18.8	19.4	20.1	7									
8	10.9	11.6	12.2	12.9	13.6	14.3	15.0	15.6	16.3	17.0	17.7	18.4	19.0	19.7	20.4	8								0.5	
9	11.0	11.7	12.4	13.1	13.8	14.5	15.2	15.9	16.6	17.3	17.9	18.6	19.3	20.0	20.7	9					0.3			0.6	
70	11.2	11.9	12.6	13.3	14.0	14.7	15.4	16.1	16.8	17.5	18.2	18.9	19.6	20.3	21.0	70	0.1	0.1	0.2	0.3	0.4	0.4	0.5	0.6	0.
1	11.4	12.1	12.8	13.5	14.2	14.9	15.6	16.3	17.0	17.8	18.5	19.2	19.9	20.6	21.3	1									
2	11.5	12.2	13.0	13.7	14.4	15.1	15.8	16.6	17.3	18.0	18.7	19.4	20.2	20.9	21.6	2									0.
3	11.7	12.4	13.1	13.9	14.6	15.3	16.1	16.8	17.5	18.3	19.0	19.7	20.4	21.2	21.9	3									0.
4	11.8	12.6	13.3	14.1	14.8	15.5	16.3	17.0	17.8	18.5	19.2	20.0	20.7	21.5	22.2	4		0.1				0.4			
75	12.0	12.8	13.5	14.3	15.0	15.8	16.5	17.3	18.0	18.8	19.5	20.3	21.0	21.8	22.5	75	0.1	0.2	0.2	0.3	0.4	0.5	0.5	0.6	0.
6	12.2	12.9	13.7	14.4	15.2	16.0	16.7	17.5	18.2	19.0	19.8	20.5	21.3	22.0	22.8	6									
7	12.3	13.1	13.9	14.6	15.4	16.2	16.9	17.7	18.5	19.3	20.0	20.8	21.6	22.3	23.1	7									
8	12.5	13.3	14.0	14.8	15.6	16.4	17.2	17.9	18.7	19.5	20.3	21.1	21.8	22.6	23.4	8							0.5		
9	12.6	13.4	14.2	15.0	15.8	16.6	17.4	18.2	19.0	19.8	20.5	21.3	22.1	22.9	23.7	9							0.6		
80	12.8	13.6	14.4	15.2	16.0	16.8	17.6	18.4	19.2	20.0	20.8	21.6	22.4	23.2	24.0	80	0.1	0.2	0.2	0.3	0.4	0.5	0.6	0.6	0.
1	13.0	13.8	14.6	15.4	16.2	17.0	17.8	18.6	19.4	20.3	21.1	21.9	22.7	23.5	24.3	1								0.6	
2	13.1	13.9	14.8	15.6	16.4	17.2	18.0	18.9	19.7	20.5	21.3	22.1	23.0	23.8	24.6	2								0.7	
3	13.3	14.1	14.9	15.8	16.6	17.4	18.3	19.1	19.9	20.8	21.6	22.4	23.2	24.1	24.9	3			0.2						0.
4	13.4	14.3	15.1	16.0	16.8	17.6	18.5	19.3	20.2	21.0	21.8	22.7	23.5	24.4	25.2	4			0.3						0.
85	13.6	14.5	15.3	16.2	17.0	17.9	18.7	19.6	20.4	21.3	22.1	23.0	23.8	24.7	25.5	85	0.1	0.2	0.3	0.3	0.4	0.5	0.6	0.7	0.
6	13.8	14.6	15.5	16.3	17.2	18.1	18.9	19.8	20.6	21.5	22.4	23.2	24.1	24.9	25.8	6									
7	13.9	14.8	15.7	16.5	17.4	18.3	19.1	20.0	20.9	21.8	22.6	23.5	24.4	25.2	26.1	7				0.3					
8	14.1	15.0	15.8	16.7	17.6	18.5	19.4	20.2	21.1	22.0	22.9	23.8	24.6	25.5	26.4	8				0.4					
9	14.2	15.1	16.0	16.9	17.8	18.7	19.6	20.5	21.4	22.3	23.1	24.0	24.9	25.8	26.7	9					0.4				
90	14.4	15.3	16.2	17.1	18.0	18.9	19.8	20.7	21.6	22.5	23.4	24.3	25.2	26.1	27.0	90	0.1	0.2	0.3	0.4	0.5	0.5	0.6	0.7	0.
1	14.6	15.5	16.4	17.3	18.2	19.1	20.0	20.9	21.8	22.8	23.7	24.6	25.5	26.4	27.3	1						0.5			
2	14.7	15.6	16.6	17.5	18.4	19.3	20.2	21.2	22.1	23.0	23.9	24.8	25.8	26.7	27.6	2						0.6	0.6		
3	14.9	15.8	16.7	17.7	18.6	19.5	20.5	21.4	22.3	23.3	24.2	25.1	26.0	27.0	27.9	3							0.7	0.7	
4	15.0	16.0	16.9	17.9	18.8	19.7	20.7	21.6	22.6	23.5	24.4	25.4	26.3	27.3	28.2	4								0.8	0.8
95	15.2	16.2	17.1	18.1	19.0	20.0	20.9	21.9	22.8	23.8	24.7	25.7	26.6	27.6	28.5	95	0.1	0.2	0.3	0.4	0.5	0.6	0.7	0.8	0.9
6	15.4	16.3	17.3	18.2	19.2	20.2	21.1	22.1	23.0	24.0	25.0	25.9	26.9	27.8	28.8	6									
7	15.5	16.5	17.5	18.4	19.4	20.4	21.3	22.3	23.3	24.3	25.2	26.2	27.2	28.1	29.1	7									
8	15.7	16.7	17.6	18.6	19.6	20.6	21.6	22.5	23.5	24.5	25.5	26.5	27.4	28.4	29.4	8									
9	15.8	16.8	17.8	18.8	19.8	20.8	21.8	22.8	23.8	24.8	25.7	26.7	27.7	28.7	29.7	9									
1.0	16.0	17.0	18.0	19.0	20.0	21.0	22.0	23.0	24.0	25.0	26.0	27.0	28.0	29.0	30.0	1.0	0.1	0.2	0.3	0.4	0.5	0.6	0.7	0.8	0.9
Δ	16′	17′	18′	19′	20′	21′	22′	23′	24′	25′	26′	27′	28′	29′	30′	Δ	0.1′	0.2′	0.3′	0.4′	0.5′	0.6′	0.7′	0.8′	0.9′

FIG. 21-3

	Sun, L.L.	Sun, L.L.
	From	Ch. 20
Ho	50° 14.8'	38° 32.7'
LHA	321°	52°
t = 360° − LHA 360°	360°	LHA = t_w
t (Mark E or W)	39° E	52° W
Ass. Latitude	S 10°	S 10°
Decl. N or S	S 23° 02'	S 23° 01'
Azimuth N/S Z E/W	S 65.8° E Zn = 180° − Z	From H.O. 214 S 68.5° W Zn = 180° + Z
Zn	114.2°	248.5°
△d (+ or −)	−22	−10
Altitude	50° 33.9'	38° 45.2
Corr. for △d	−0.4	−0.1
Hc	50° 33.5'	38° 45.1'
Ho	50° 14.8'	38° 32.7'
Intercept, T or A	A 18.7	A 12.4

	From Ch. 20	
	MARS	SATURN
Ho	29° 20'	45° 14'
t (Mark E or W) = LHA	59° W	13° W
Ass. Latitude	S 33°	S 33°
Decl. (N or S)		
Corr. for d (+ or −)		
Net Decl.	S 7° 17.7'	N 9° 49.6'
Azimuth N/S Z E/W	S 101.7° W Zn = 180° + Z	From H.O. 214 S 161.5° W Zn = 180° + Z
Zn	281.7°	341.5°
△d (+ or −)	+56	−96
Altitude	29° 40.6'	45° 43.9'
Corr. for △d	+9.9	−18.8
Hc	29° 50.5'	45° 25.1'
Ho	29° 20'	45° 14'
Intercept (T or A)	A 30.5 mi	A 11.1

	From Ch. 20	
	MOON UL	
Ho	46° 05.3'	
t (E or W) = LHA	9° W	
Ass. Latitude	33° N	
Decl. (N or S)		
Corr. for d (+ or −)	d =	d =
Net. Decl.	S 9° 57.8	
Azimuth N/S Z E/W	N 167° W Zn = 360° − Z	From H.O. 214
Zn	193°	
△d (+ or −)	−98	
Altitude	46° 38.6'	
Corr. for △d	−27.3	
Hc	46° 11.3'	
Ho	46° 05.3	
Intercept (T or A)	A 6 mi	

FIG. 21-4
Examples from Chapter 20, worked by H.O. 214

Although we have not shown an example here, star sights are worked with H.O. 214 in exactly the same manner as with the other bodies. After we have discussed the tables in N.O. 229 in the next chapter, you will realize that all sights depend on assumed latitude, declination, and either LHA or the angle *t*—with the exception that N.O. 249, Vol. I, uses the identity of specific stars, by name, instead of giving their declinations, thus saving a step in the computation, besides making it possible to use that volume as a star finder. The increased accuracy supposedly available with H.O. 214 and N.O. 229 is of doubtful importance in practical small-vessel navigation, because the other parameters are not of equal accuracy. Aside from possible error of a second or two in timing, the taking of a sextant sight from a heaving deck in a rough sea can be somewhat of an uncertain process, with room for errors of a minute or more. The art of navigation is to evaluate what you have intelligently, and be prepared to accept the fact that your fix is probably not the pinpoint position it appears to be on your chart.

Chapter 22

How to Use N.O. 229

The set of tables that comprise N.O. 229 were published in 1971, and are intended eventually to replace the tables of H.O. 214, which are slated to be phased out by about 1975. Like H.O. 214, these tables contain solutions to the celestial triangle and provide the same end results, namely computed altitude, H_c, and azimuth Z of any celestial body observed. Whereas H.O. 214 omitted data that could not be used in marine navigation, N.O. 229 contains complete coverage for every possible shape of the celestial triangle, whether a marine navigator needs it or not. The reason is that these tables are designed for uses other than marine celestial navigation. It is unlikely that this new set of tables will find favor with most marine navigators.

The set consists of six volumes, each covering 16° of latitude—e.g., 30–45°, inclusive. The arrangement of the data is very much like N.O. 249, which is used mainly for air navigation, but the interpolation arrangement is different and, unfortunately, in some situations quite involved. The tables are entered with assumed latitude, LHA, and declination, all in whole degrees.

The *opening entry* is made with *assumed latitude,* which is the whole degree of latitude nearest the *dead reckoning latitude.* Each volume covers 16° of latitude. The first half of each volume covers the first 8° (e.g. 30–37°) and the second half covers the rest (e.g., 38–45°). These latitudes are shown on horizontal lines across the *top* and *bottom* of each page. The first step is to locate the proper volume for desired *latitude,* and then to decide which *half* of the volume to use.

The *second step* is to locate the proper *local hour angle.* Please note that in H.O. 214 we work with the *meridian angle t,* but that in N.O. 229, as in N.O. 249, we use *local hour angle.* (The LHA is found on the work form by adding east longitude to or subtracting west longitude from the

GHA of the body observed.) Here we must observe a division of the left- and right-hand pages.

Left-hand pages are marked: *"Latitude same name" (as declination), both at the top AND bottom of the page.* The *top* and *bottom* of this page will list LHAs 0–90° and 270–360°.

Right-hand pages are marked: *"Latitude CONTRARY name" (to declination), at the top—BUT—the bottom of the page is marked "latitude SAME name" (as declination).* So here is where you must watch your step. The *upper* corner shows the same LHAs as the left-hand page, 0–90° and 270–360°, but the *lower* corner gives LHAs 90–180° and 180–270°.

Latitude *same name as* declination means that latitude and declination are *both* north or *both* south, and latitude *contrary name* to declination means that one is north and one is south—*and it does not matter which one is north and which south.*

Having determined (1) the volume to use, (2) whether to use the front or back half, (3) whether to use the left- or right-hand page, and (4) the page on which the correct LHA is to be found—you are now ready to look up your data, using the declination to the nearest *lower whole degree.*

Declination is given in a vertical column at either side of the page, and it is a simple matter to cross-reference latitude with declination on the page. Three figures are given: H_c, d, and Z. The value d is a *correction factor* used to adjust H_c up or down for the *minutes of declination*—because we entered with a whole degree of declination. It is marked plus (+) or minus (—).

Note that the value for d is sometimes printed in italics with a raised dot after it, which means that a special interpolation process called a "double second difference" must be used. Although Z is not so marked, it is a fact that you will often need to interpolate for the exact value of Z also, as explained in the following section. After interpolation, Z is then converted to Z_n according to the rules printed on every page. The *Simex work forms* provide the proper spaces for each of these operations and serve as your memory if you have trouble remembering what to do next. Inside the *front* cover is an *interpolation table for declination difference* (the exact number of *minutes* in the declination) for 0–32′, and inside the *back* cover the table continues for differences from 28′ to 59′, so there is a small overlap.

In this interpolation table we enter with the exact declination difference, in minutes and tenths of minutes, in the *vertical left-hand column,* and *correction factor* $\pm d$ across the top of the page. Note that d is broken up first in tens (10–20–30–40–50) on the left and then in units on the right, and that the units have a further vertical column for tenths.

***Example* •** Your *assumed latitude* is 50° N, LHA is 338°, and declination is 61°55.1′ N. Find H_c and Z_n.

This latitude is obviously found in volume IV, in the first half of the book. Since latitude and declination are *same name* (both north), we turn the pages until we find LHA 338° on the *left-hand* side, on page 46. We cross latitude 50° with declination 61° and take out the following:

$H_c = 73°31.4'$ $d = 32.9•$ $Z = 39.8°$

The dot after "32.9" means that a dsd (double second difference) is needed, so we take it out immediately. It is the difference between d for 60° of declination and d for 62° of declination (1 degree either side of the declination we used); in this case it is $35.3' - 30.4' = 4.9'$. Enter this on the work form. By looking at Z for declination 62°, you note a change of 2.9° that must also be interpolated if you want to be accurate. Because it is decreasing, enter —2.9° in the space for azimuth difference on the work form. You are now ready to turn to the interpolation table inside the back cover.

There are three figures you must obtain from the interpolation table for a declination difference of 55.1′, using a d of —32.9′:

Decrease in H_c for declination difference of 55.1′ and d of 30′	=	−27.5′
Decrease in H_c for declination difference of 55.1′ and d of 2.9′	=	−2.7′
Double second difference for 4.9′	=	+0.1′
Total correction to H_c	=	−30.1′
Tabular H_c	=	73° 31.4′
Net correction	=	−30.1′
Corrected H_c	=	73° 01.3′

22°, 338° L.H.A.

LATITUDE SAME NAME

Dec.	49° Hc	49° d	49° Z	50° Hc	50° d	50° Z	51° Hc	51° d	51° Z
°	° ′	′	°	° ′	′	°	° ′	′	°
55	75 16.0	−17.2·	57.7	75 46.6	−13.8·	61.0	76 14.1	−10.2·	64.6
56	74 58.8	20.8·	53.9	75 32.8	17.7·	57.1	76 03.9	14.2·	60.4
57	74 38.0	24.0·	50.3	75 15.1	21.2·	53.3	75 49.7	18.1·	56.4
58	74 14.0	27.1·	46.9	74 53.9	24.5·	49.6	75 31.6	21.7·	52.6
59	73 46.9	29.9·	43.7	74 29.4	27.6·	46.2	75 09.9	25.0·	48.9
60	73 17.0	−32.4·	40.6	74 01.8	−30.4·	42.9	74 44.9	−28.2·	45.4
→ 61	72 44.6	34.7·	37.8	73 31.4	32.9·	39.8	74 16.7	30.9·	42.1
62	72 09.9	36.8·	35.0	72 58.5	35.3·	36.9	73 45.8	33.5·	39.0
63	71 33.1	38.7	32.5	72 23.2	37.3·	34.2	73 12.3	35.8·	36.1
64	70 54.4	40.5	30.1	71 45.9	39.3	31.7	72 36.5	37.9·	33.3
65	70 13.9	−41.9	27.9	71 06.6	−40.9	29.3	71 58.6	−39.8	30.8
66	69 32.0	43.4	25.8	70 25.7	42.4	27.1	71 18.8	41.4	28.4
67	68 48.6	44.6	23.9	69 43.3	43.9	25.0	70 37.4	43.0	26.2
68	68 04.0	45.7	22.1	68 59.4	45.0	23.0	69 54.4	44.3	24.1
69	67 18.3	46.7	20.4	68 14.4	46.2	21.2	69 10.1	45.5	22.2

Data from Page 46

INTERPOLATION TABLE

Dec. Inc.	Tens 10′	20′	30′	40′	50′	Decimals	Units 0′	1′	2′	3′	4′	5′	6′	7′	8′	9′	Do Sec D a C
′	′	′	′	′	′	′	′	′	′	′	′	′	′	′	′	′	′
55.0	9.1	18.3	27.5	36.6	45.8	.0	0.0	0.9	1.8	2.8	3.7	4.6	5.5	6.5	7.4	8.3	
→ 55.1	9.2	18.3	[27.5]	36.7	45.9	.1	0.1	1.0	1.9	2.9	3.8	4.7	5.6	6.6	7.5	8.4	
55.2	9.2	18.4	27.6	36.8	46.0	.2	0.2	1.1	2.0	3.0	3.9	4.8	5.7	6.7	7.6	8.5	2.
55.3	9.2	18.4	27.6	36.9	46.1	.3	0.3	1.2	2.1	3.1	4.0	4.9	5.8	6.8	7.7	8.6	8.
55.4	9.2	18.5	27.7	36.9	46.2	.4	0.4	1.3	2.2	3.1	4.1	5.0	5.9	6.8	7.8	8.7	14.
																	20.
55.5	9.3	18.5	27.8	37.0	46.3	.5	0.5	1.4	2.3	3.2	4.2	5.1	6.0	6.9	7.9	8.8	25.
55.6	9.3	18.5	27.8	37.1	46.3	.6	0.6	1.5	2.4	3.3	4.3	5.2	6.1	7.0	8.0	8.9	31.
55.7	9.3	18.6	27.9	37.2	46.4	.7	0.6	1.6	2.5	3.4	4.3	5.3	6.2	7.1	8.0	9.0	37.
55.8	9.3	18.6	27.9	37.2	46.5	.8	0.7	1.7	2.6	3.5	4.4	5.4	6.3	7.2	8.1	9.1	
55.9	9.4	18.7	28.0	37.3	46.6 →	.9	0.8	1.8	[2.7]	3.6	4.5	5.5	6.4	7.3	8.2	9.2	
56.0	9.3	18.6	28.0	37.3	46.6	.0	0.0	0.9	1.9	2.8	3.8	4.7	5.6	6.6	7.5	8.5	
56.1	9.3	18.7	28.0	37.4	46.7	.1	0.1	1.0	2.0	2.9	3.9	4.8	5.7	6.7	7.6	8.6	

Data from Interpolation Table

Net GHA of Star			
Assumed Long. +E -W	SOLUTION	FOR Hc	AND Zn
360°			
LHA	338°	by	N.O. 229
Assumed Latitude	50° N		
Decl. (N or S)	61° 55.1 N		
From N.O. 229 – ENTER WITH ASS. LAT., LHA, NEXT LOWER WHOLE DEGREE OF DECL.			
INTERPOLATION FACTORS	± d = −32.9 dsd = + 4.9 ± Azimuth Dif. 2.9°	±d = ___ dsd = + ___ ±Azimuth Dif. ___	±d = ___ dsd = + ___ ±Azimuth Dif. ___
TABULAR Hc	73° 31.4		
Corr. for Tens ± Corr. for Units ± Corr. for dsd + TOTAL CORR.	− 27.5 − 2.7 + 0.1 − 30.1 30.1		
CORRECTED Hc	73° 01.3		
Ho			
INTERCEPT T/A			
TABULAR Z	39.8°		
Corr. for Az. Diff. ±	−2.7°		
CORRECTED Z	37.1°		
Apply 360° or 180°			
Zn	37.1°		
Plotting Symbol			

NORTH LATITUDE
LHA GREATER THAN 180°, ZN = Z
LHA LESS THAN 180°, ZN = 360° - Z

SOUTH LATITUDE
LHA GREATER THAN 180°, ZN = 180° - Z
LHA LESS THAN 180°, ZN = 180° + Z

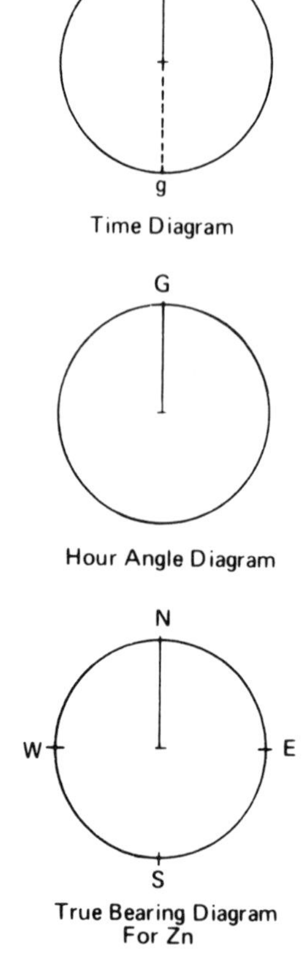

FIG. 22-1 Example of sight reduction by N.O. 229

Note how we found the double second difference correction. Opposite the declination increase, in this case 55.1′, but in the extreme *right-hand* column, marked "Double Second Diff. and Corr.," you locate 4.9′ as being between "2.9′" and "8.6′" and find the correction to be 0.1′. It is important that you use the block of figures in the vicinity, or opposite the declination increase. Remember: *dsd correction is always added.*

Next we interpolate the azimuth Z using the azimuth difference of —2.9° we previously noted. There is no specially indicated table for this, but we use the *units* block of figures opposite the declination difference and simply treat the units as whole degrees. Thus, for 2.9 units we find a correction of 2.7°. Therefore, $Z = 39.8° - 2.7° = 37.1°$.

Because 338° is greater than 180° and we are in north latitude, $Z_n = Z = 37.1°$, which you naturally plot as 037°.

Because this set of tables is intended for purposes other than marine navigation, there are a number of other approaches and explanations given at the beginning of each volume. They are of no concern to the yachtsman or ship's navigation officer and are needed only where scientific operations are involved. In cases where there is no dot after the *d* correction factor, it is safe to ignore the dsd correction; but you should always examine the azimuth difference to see if an interpolation is needed, remembering that we plot azimuths to the nearest whole degree only.

Like all the volumes of H.O. 214, and N.O. 249, Vols. II and III, the six volumes of N.O. 229 are also good for all time and never need to be revised or changed. N.O. 249, Vol. I, should be replaced every 5 years.

Chapter 23

Multiple Sight Procedures

You will from time to time hear marine navigators talk about taking several sights and "averaging" them, but don't you believe them! The only place where sights are averaged is in an airplane when a bubble sextant with an averaging device is used. Because it is is difficult to hold the bubble still on the body observed, the navigator holds it the best he can while he pushes a button that allows the sextant to take and record up to 120 readings during a 2-minute interval. This is carefully timed and the average of the readings is taken as the altitude for the middle of the 2-minute interval. This gives an adequate accuracy for aircraft work. However, it is hopeless to try to use a bubble sextant on a ship, as anyone who has done so will readily tell you.

At Coast Navigation School we teach a system that I have used for years at sea and that provides a very high degree of accuracy—along with a certain peace of mind. It is called the *multiple-sights system,* which simply means that you always take three sights in close succession on the same celestial body—never just one! It takes very little longer to take the three observations, but you then have the advantage that three times you judged the tangency on the horizon, three times you read the watch, and three times you read the altitude on the sextant. It is unlikely that you would be wrong three times, but you have had a chance to check yourself, and if you were wrong on any of the three sights, it would soon stand out like the proverbial sore finger—provided you *don't average the figures!* If you average figures and there is a big error in one of the sights, you have simply averaged a big error into the final result and fooled yourself.

Correct Method Take three sights in quick succession on the same body. First write down the time in seconds, minutes, and hours, and next the sextant angle, after each sight. With a little experience you will find that you are taking sights about a minute-and-a-half apart. Enter all three sights on a *mutiple-sight work form,* such as those we have used in this book. Work the three simultaneously. It takes little longer than doing a single computation since most of the figures are duplicates, *except* the minutes and seconds of time, the minutes of H_s, the final addition to the GHA, the assumed longitude, and the intercept. All altitude correction figures, declination, etc. are the same. You adjust the assumed longitude so that *you get the same LHA or angle t in all three sights.* This means that you make only a single entry into the navigation table and calculate only one H_c and one Z_n for all three sights. For plotting you have the *same assumed latitude and same* Z_n, *but three different assumed longitudes and three different intercepts.*

You now plot the three longitudes on the same assumed-latitude line, plot Z_n, and repeat it at all three points. Now mark off the three intercepts, giving you three points through which you could draw an LOP. However, you draw only a *single line of position through the three points,* judging by eye what you consider an average of the three points. This LOP must be at 90° to Z_n, as all LOPs are, *and it need not pass through any of the three intercept points.* It will, however, be an amazingly accurate line of position. Usually, if you are careful and conditions are favorable, you will find that the three points are very close together, and if you did draw three separate LOPs, one would practically be on top of the other. Under other conditions, this may not be so, but in that case your average LOP is likely to be closer to the actual position than any of the single lines would be. *If you had made a mistake,* it would stand out clearly, because one of the points would be far away from the other two. You can then either disregard that point, or go back and try to find where the error might lie—remembering that most of the errors made by navigators are in simple addition and subtraction!

If you observe three stars and take three sights on each, you will get an unbelievable accuracy and the whole process will take 45 minutes, once you get used to working the system. Surely that is not too much time to spend to make sure you know where you are before you set the course for the night. It makes for easy sleeping and no nasty surprises.

Coast Navigation School

SANTA BARBARA, CALIFORNIA

MULTIPLE SIGHT FORM FOR STARS, N.O. 249

WITH NAUTICAL ALMANAC

Name *Simonsen*

l Date *Jan. 1* Greenwich Date *Jan. 1* DR Lat. *N 34° 40'* DR Long *W 155° 10'*

ody	—	*Antares*	—
s	*12° 02'*	*12° 14'*	*12° 26'*
otal Corr.	*−5'*	*−5'*	*−5'*
o	*11° 57'*	*12° 09'*	*12° 21'*
/atch Time	*06-40-20*	*06-41-50*	*06-43-30*
/atch Error	*−10*	*−10*	*−10*
one Time	*06-40-10*	*06-41-40*	*06-43-20*
one Descr.	*+10*	*10*	*10*
MT	*16-40-10*	*16-41-40*	*16-43-20*
HA ♈ Hrs.	*350° 55'*	*350° 55'*	*350° 55'*
HA ♈ Min. & Sec.	*03*	*25*	*50*
HA ♈ Total	*350° 58'*	*351° 20'*	*351° 45'*
ssumed Long. −W, +E	*154° 58'*	*155° 20'*	*155° 45*
pply 360° necessary			
.HA ♈		*196°*	
ssumed Lat. N/S		*35° N*	
	From N.O. 249, Vol 1		
Hc	*12° 01'*	*12° 01'*	*12° 01'*
Ho	*11° 57'*	*12° 09'*	*12° 21'*
ntercept (T/A)	*A 4*	*T 8*	*T 20*
Zn		*135°*	
lotting Symbol	*A1*	*A2*	*A3*

IE *3' off*

WE *10s fast*

HE *15 Ft.*

Sextant Corrections

	+	−	+	−	+	−
IC			*3*			
Dip				*4*		
Refr.				*4*		
			3	*8*		
				3		
Total C				*−5'*		

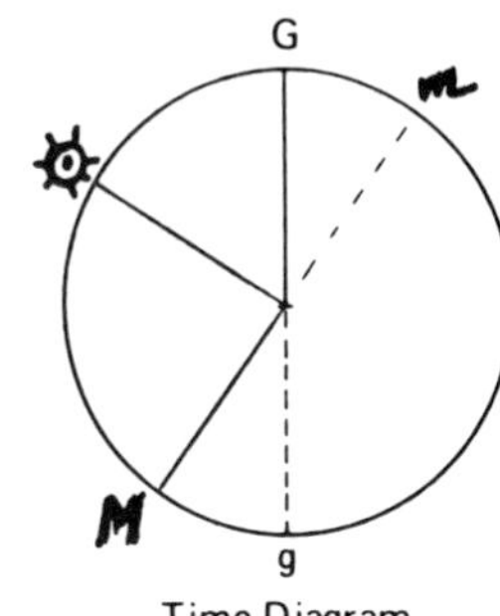

Time Diagram

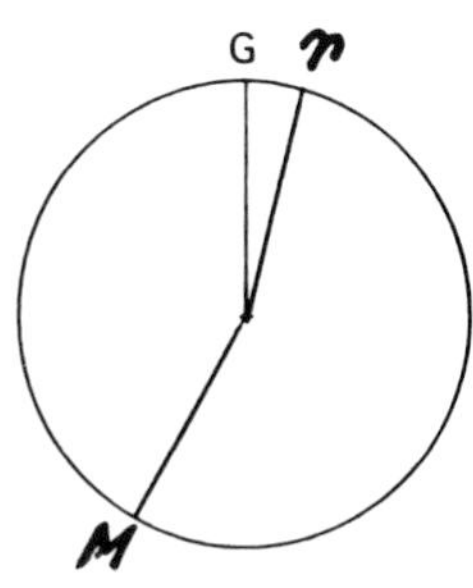

Hour Angle Diagram

BLE 5 Correction *3* Mi *120° (1973)*

FIG. 23-1

Coast Navigation School

SANTA BARBARA, CALIFORNIA

MULTIPLE SIGHT FORM FOR STARS, N.O. 249
WITH NAUTICAL ALMANAC

Name Jimonsen

Local Date Jan. 1 Greenwich Date Jan. 1 DR Lat. N34°40' DR Long W155° 1

Body	—	Regulus	—
Hs	43° 20'	43° 02'	42° 59'
Total Corr.	−2	−2	−2
Ho	43° 18'	43° 00'	42° 57'
Watch Time	06-45-05	06-46-40	06-47-10
Watch Error	−10	−10	−10
Zone Time	06-44-55	06-46-30	06-47-00
Zone Descr.	+10	10	10
GMT	16-44-55	16-46-30	16-47-00
GHA ♈ Hrs.	350° 55'	350° 55'	350° 55'
GHA ♈ Min. & Sec.	1° 14'	1° 38'	1° 45'
GHA ♈ Total	352° 09'	352° 33'	352° 40'
Assumed Long. −W, +E	155° 09'	155° 33'	155° 40'
Apply 360° if necessary			
LHA ♈		197°	
Assumed Lat. N/S		35° N	
From N.O. 249, Vol 1			
Hc	43° 08'	43° 08'	43° 08'
Ho	43° 18'	43° 00'	42° 57'
Intercept (T/A)	T 10	A 8	A 11
Zn		252°	
Plotting Symbol	R1	R2	R3

IE 3' off
WE 10ˢ fast
HE 15 Ft.

Sextant Corrections

	+	−	+	−	+	−
IC			3			
Dip				4		
Refr.				1		
			3	5		
				3		
Total C				−2'		

G
m
M
g

Time Diagram

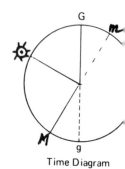

TABLE 5 Correction 3 Mi 120° (1973)

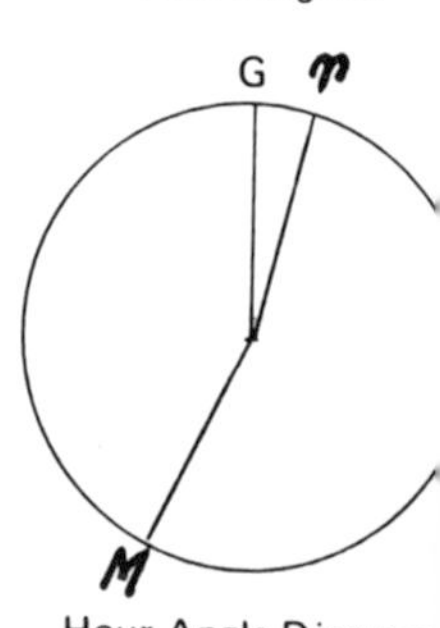

Hour Angle Diagram

FIG. 23-2

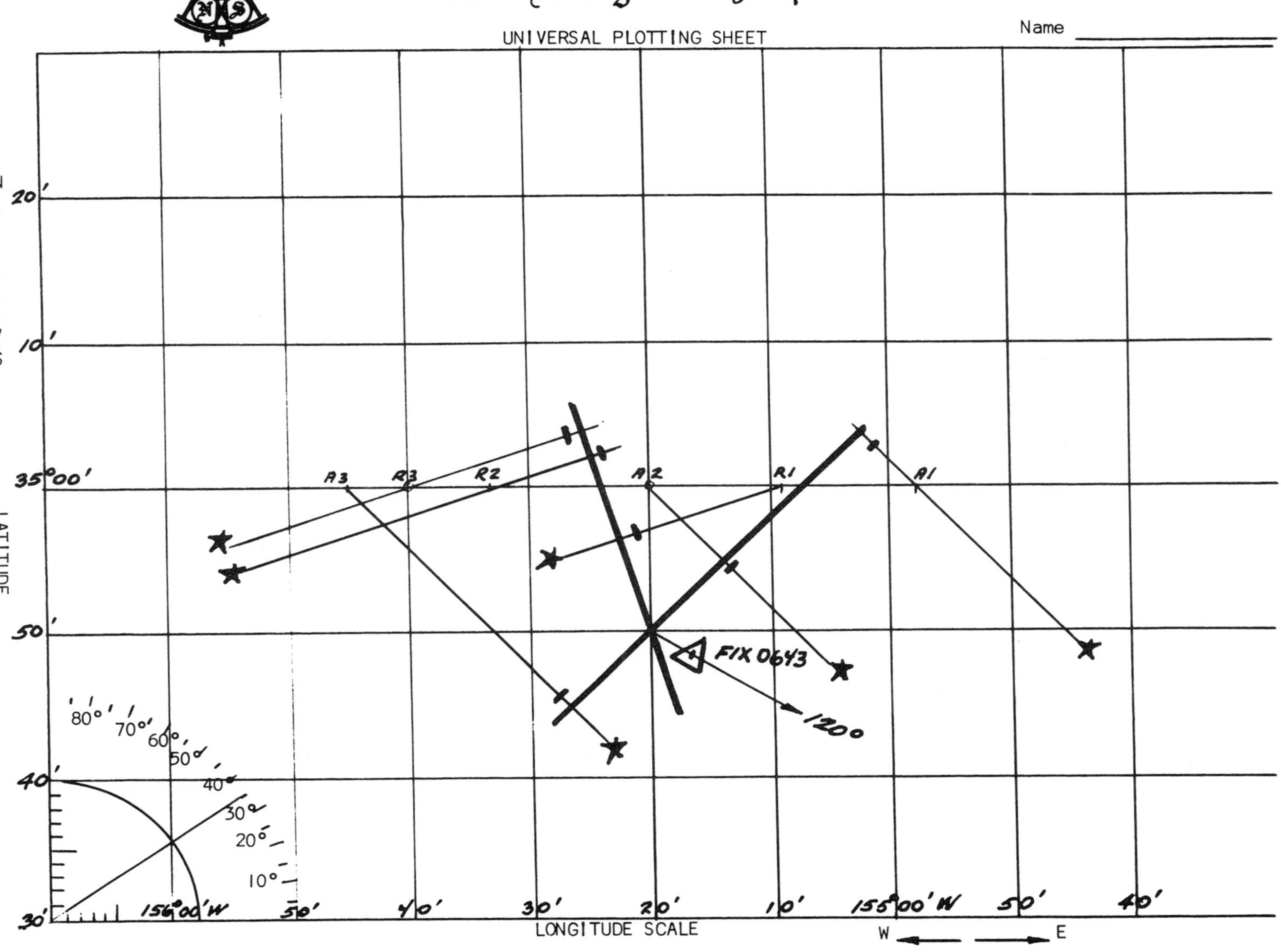
UNIVERSAL PLOTTING SHEET
Name
N
S
20'
10'
35°00'
LATITUDE
50'
40'
30'
A3
R3
R2
A2
R1
A1
FIX 0643
1200
80°
70°
60°
50°
40°
30°
20°
10°
156°00'W
50'
40'
30'
20'
10'
155°00'W
50'
40'
LONGITUDE SCALE
W
E

FIG. 23-3

This method, of course, is used where very precise navigation is required, such as in racing, making landfalls, or sailing through islands or shoals at night, where one mistake might be your last. There comes to mind a certain Bermuda race where the navigator of the leading vessel was a great sailor—but just a little rusty on his navigation. Approaching Bermuda, he got a shot at the sun—one sight. He could have taken more, but he took one sight. Shortly afterward the sun disappeared for the day. According to dead reckoning, and previous navigation, the island should be sighted soon. He went below and figured his sun sight, which also told him that Bermuda should be in sight—only it wasn't! The next hour or two were pure agony for him, the cold sweat pouring off his nose as he worked and reworked his single sight, trying to find where the error was, while his shipmates were beginning to give him increasingly dirty looks. Had he made a mistake in the time? . . . in the sextant reading? . . . in the calculations? No one will ever know—but it is for sure that it was the last time he took a *single* sight. Had he taken several, there would have been no doubt where he was.

The following pages illustrate multiple sights. For the sake of simplicity, only two observations are plotted. Note that neither LOP passes through any of the intercept points.

Chapter 24

The Noon Sight

The *noon sight* is the time-honored observation of the sun that navigators since Columbus have faithfully made every day the sun is visible. As the sun reaches the highest point in the sky for the day, at the precise moment when it is in line with and transits our meridian, the navigator observes the altitude. By combining altitude, declination, and his distance of 90° to the zenith, he obtains an easy solution for his latitude. To make sure he does not miss this important event of the day, the navigator stations himself on the bridge, sextant in hand, well before the sun reaches the meridian. He takes a number of sights, noting that the sun is still rising in the sky, and notes when it begins to level off. At transit the sun seems to hang for a moment at the same altitude, and then it begins to drop quite rapidly in its afternoon descent. The navigator has carefully recorded the maximum altitude, and it then only takes a minute to determine what his latitude is. If he is also able to time accurately the moment of transit, he can obtain a fairly good longitude as well.

In the early days of navigation, when timepieces were somewhat uncertain and could not be checked daily against a radio time signal, the noon sight was all-important, and prior to the invention of the chronometer it was almost the only method of celestial navigation available to the mariner. Even when chronometers became available, the computations for longitude involved considerable mathematics, sometimes beyond the capability of a simple sailing man, so many early mariners devised the ingenious system of heading north or south to the latitude of their destination, and when they reached that latitude, as revealed by the noon sight, they would turn east or west and stay on the same latitude day after day until they got where they were going. This procedure was called "running down the latitudes."

In modern navigation, the traditional noon sight is not important any more, having been made obsolete by availability of accurate time and easy navigation tables. There are certain drawbacks involved also:

1. You have to calculate in advance the predicted watch time of transit, based on your DR longitude, unless you are prepared to spend a lot of time waiting for the sun to get to the meridian.
2. The latitude obtained is not a real *noon* latitude in terms of ship's time. When the sun is on the meridian, it is 1200 *local apparent time* (LAT), which differs from local mean time (LMT) by the equation of time (Eq.T.). LMT differs from zone time (ZT) by as much as a half-hour. Eq.T. has a maximum of 16 minutes, so it is possible to have a difference of 46 minutes between transit and 1200 ZT. In modern navigation, the main significance of the noon position on a commercial ship is that it is the position wired daily to the home office of the owners, and it should therefore be given for 1200 ZT. Invariably, the noon latitude must be converted to that time.
3. If you have pinned your hopes on a noon observation and clouds cover the sun at that time, you have no position at all.
4. The noon sight simply gives a latitude, which is a line of position running due east or west. It is not necessarily any more accurate than any other line of position. If you are at nearly the same latitude as the sun's declination, it will be almost directly overhead at noon, and the sextant observation will be of doubtful accuracy.

For these reasons, the modern navigator prefers to observe the sun at 1200 ZT, if possible, and work the sight by his regular tables for a line of position. This line will run nearly east or west and must be crossed with another LOP for a fix at 1200 ZT. It takes less time to do this than to predict the watch time of noon, stand around for five or ten minutes before, then have to adjust the latitude to 1200 ZT. Of course, if he is a young officer sailing with a tyrannical and cantankerous skipper of the old school, he will dutifully take his noon observation the traditional way.

A yachtsman has no such problems, so he can navigate as he likes best. However, whether you ever use it or not, as a competent navigator you should know how to plan, take, and calculate a noon observation.

The Theory The best way to understand the procedure involved is to take a globe and locate your present position on it. Let us say you are in New York City, where the latitude is about 41° N. To make it easier, stick a pin in the globe at the location of New York City. Now turn the globe so that the North Pole points up to the left and the meridian of New York is right on the upper outline or edge of the globe. The pin is seen sticking out full length from the globe. In effect, you are out in space looking at Earth, and you have stopped it in its rotation at this precise moment when the meridian coincides with the outline of the Earth. The equator will be seen as a straight line sloping up to the right, and if you could see the polar axis, it would be a line at right angles to the equator, pointing up to the left.

FIG. 24-1 Principle of meridian altitude observation for latitude

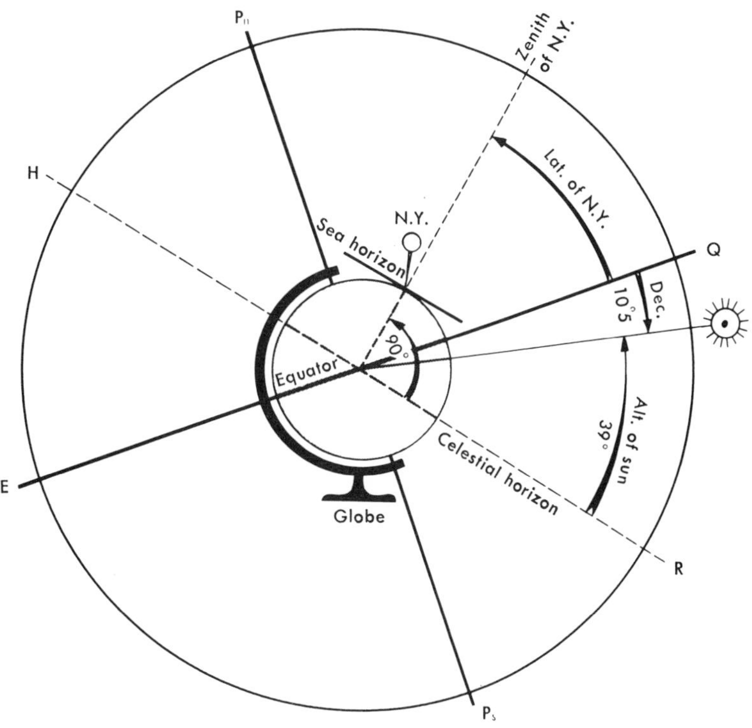

The latitude of New York City is obviously the angle between the equator and the pin that indicates the city.

Now imagine that you can also see the celestial sphere around the Earth, represented by the larger circle in Fig. 24–1. By extending the lines, we can show the celestial poles and the equinoctial. At the precise moment of meridian transit of the sun, it has just come up from behind the globe, and for the purpose of illustration we show it on the celestial sphere, *in the plane of our meridian.* Suppose that at the time of transit the sun has a declination of 10° S, which means that it is 10° south of the equinoctial. At this time we observe the sun with a sextant and get a corrected reading of 39°. This is the angle between the sun and our sensible or natural horizon; as you will recall from Chapter 18, however, it is also the angle between the sun and our *celestial horizon,* which is parallel to the natural horizon but passes through the center of the Earth. We can thus, in this single diagram, show the sun in its relation to the horizon and the equinoctial. From the diagram it is immediately apparent that we can find the latitude of New York City by adding the altitude and the declination and subtracting the sum from 90°.

This is the basic principle of the noon sight. As declination and latitude vary from north to south, we use other combinations of declination and altitude to find latitude. It is confusing to try to remember formulas and much better to draw a diagram for each situation. To simplify such a diagram, we eliminate the inside sphere representing the Earth, and turn the diagram around so that *zenith* is always straight up. Since we don't need the lower half of the diagram, we eliminate that also, using the *horizon* as our base line. (See Fig. 24–2), which shows a working diagram for the situation in Fig. 24–1.

FIG. 24-2
Latitude diagram

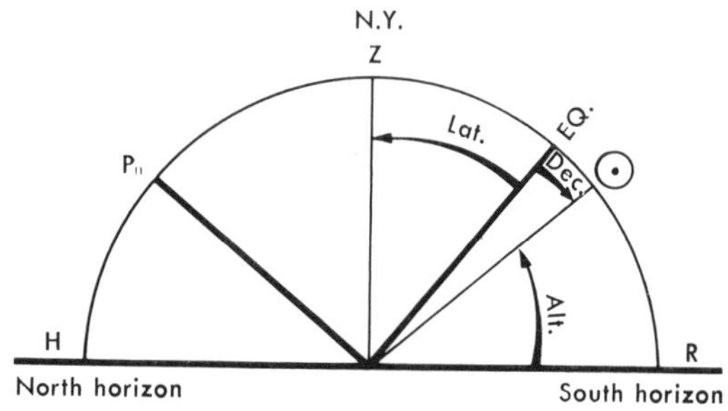

You can readily see that if the altitude is 39° and the declination is 10° S, then the latitude of New York City is 90° − (Altitude + Declination) = 90° − (39° + 10°) = 41° N. Point *Z* represents the observer's location in these diagrams, the point directly over his head on the celestial sphere. He is in north latitude because *Z* is located between the equator and the North Pole. *Because we are viewing the meridian from the west, the left side of this diagram always represents the north horizon and the right side the south horizon.*

There are three possible basic combinations that can occur in these diagrams, but in each case the picture will show you what to add and what to subtract to obtain the latitude. The three situations are as follows:

1. When latitude and declination are of *opposite names*—one north and one south. *Example:* You are in south latitude, alt. 35°, dec. 15° N.

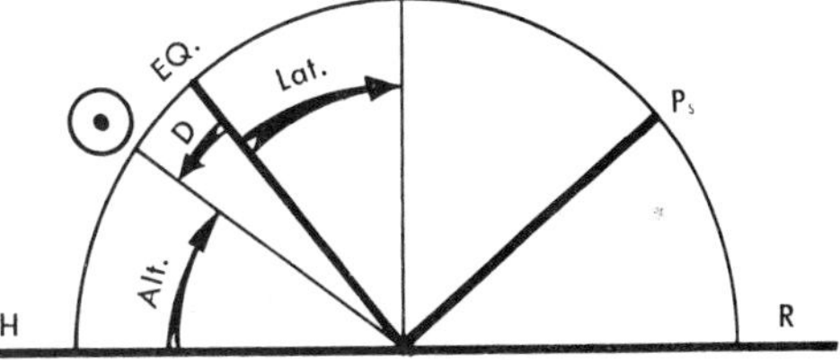

FIG. 24-3

2. When latitude and declination have the *same name*—both north or both south—but *latitude is greater than declination. Example:* You are in north latitude, alt. 45°, dec. 10° N.

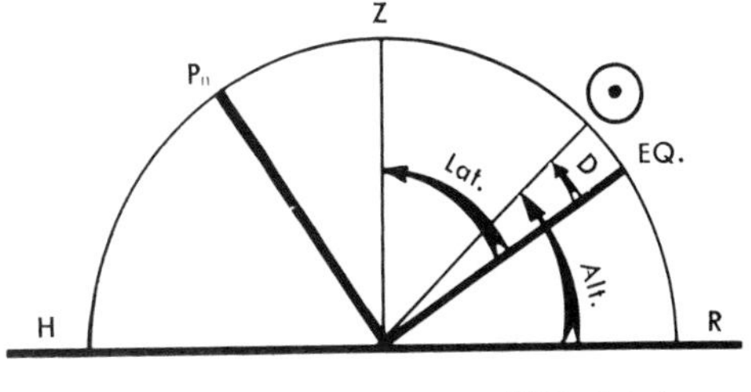

FIG. 24-4

3. When latitude and declination have the *same name,* but *declination is greater than latitude.* (Since the sun's maximum declination is 23° north or south, this can only happen when you are within 23° of the equator.) *Example:* You are in south latitude, alt. 80°, dec. 20° S.

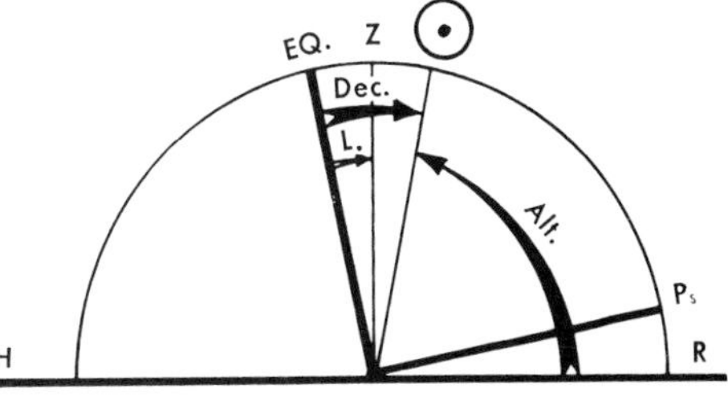

FIG. 24-5

Determining Longitude at Noon Determining longitude at noon is a relatively simple procedure that gives fairly good results. It is based on the principle that when the sun reaches our meridian at the moment of transit, its Greenwich hour angle is exactly equal to the longitude of an observer in *west* longitude, and equal to 360° minus the longitude of the observer who is in *east* longitude. The hour angle diagram (Fig. 24–6) shows this principle.

If we know the precise moment of GMT when the sun transits the meridian, we can take the GHA of the sun from the almanac and determine the longitude immediately. The difficulty lies in determining the exact moment of transit. The sun rises to the meridian fairly rapidly, then seems to hang at the same altitude for a minute or two before it begins to drop rapidly in altitude. There are two special methods for determining the time of transit:

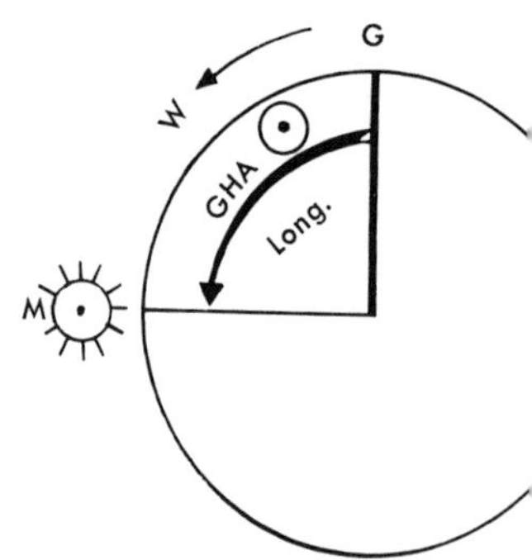

FIG. 24-6
Finding longitude at meridian transit

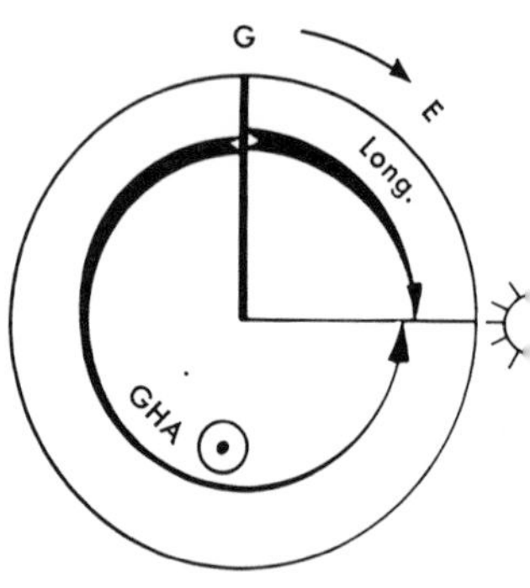

Method 1 • Take a sight about ten minutes before transit and note the time and altitude. Follow the sun to transit and observe maximum altitude for latitude determination. Now set the sextant to the same altitude you obtained in the first sight and wait for the sun to descend to that altitude on the other side of the meridian. You must be very precise in this observation and time the second reading carefully. Add the two times together and divide by 2 to find time of transit. You may have to adjust for the distance east or west a fast ship has moved between the two sights.

Example • On January 1, in DR longitude 168°10′ E, you observe the sun prior to transit at ZT 11-43-19. H_s is 35°17′. Around 1149 transit occurs and the H_s is 35°47′. You now set the sextant back to 35°17′ and wait for the sun to come down to exactly this reading again. You clock it at 11-54-57. Add this time to 11-43-19 and divide by 2. The result is 11-49-08, which is the zone time of transit. Convert this to GMT, find GHA of sun, and determine longitude. You are in time zone −11.

ZT	11-49-08
ZD	−11
GMT	00-49-08 Jan. 1
At 0040, GHA of sun is	189° 10.7′ (*Air Almanac*)
For 9^m08^s, GHA of sun is	2° 17′
At transit, GHA of sun is	191° 27.7′

East longitude = 360° − GHA

360°	=	359° 60′
GHA	=	191° 27.7′
Longitude	=	168° 32.3′ E

Method 2 • The second method involves a little more work, but is likely to be more accurate. Take from five to ten sights before transit, noting the sextant altitude and the time of each sight; observe the maximum altitude for transit; and then take another five or ten sights after transit. Plot these sights on graph paper, sextant altitude vs. watch time, and draw a fair curve through the plotted points. You will have a curve looking like a haystack. Divide it vertically into two equal halves. The midpoint will indicate the watch time of transit, which is converted to GMT. Taking the GHA of the sun (or other celestial body) for this GMT, a reasonably correct longitude is easily obtained.

For the best method of determining the midpoint of the graph, proceed as follows. Having plotted the points and drawn the curve, use your dividers to locate a series of midpoints *between the two branches of the curve* at several horizontal levels. Judging by eye, draw a vertical average line through these points to indicate the watch time of transit. In Fig. 24–7 we have indicated a midpoint for every minute of altitude. The accuracy provided with this kind of plot is within about 5′ of longitude, perhaps an average of 3 or 4 miles in most cases. Many yachtsmen have navigated around the world with just the knowledge of procedures discussed in this chapter, and one we know of managed to win first in class and third overall in the race from Victoria, B.C., to Maui, Hawaii, using these methods, having forgotten to bring both charts and navigation tables.

Predicting Watch Time of Transit The previous paragraph showed that time of transit depends on longitude. If we have a close estimate of our DR longitude at transit, it is easy to predict when transit occurs, but remember that the ship, the Earth, and the sun are moving constantly. The

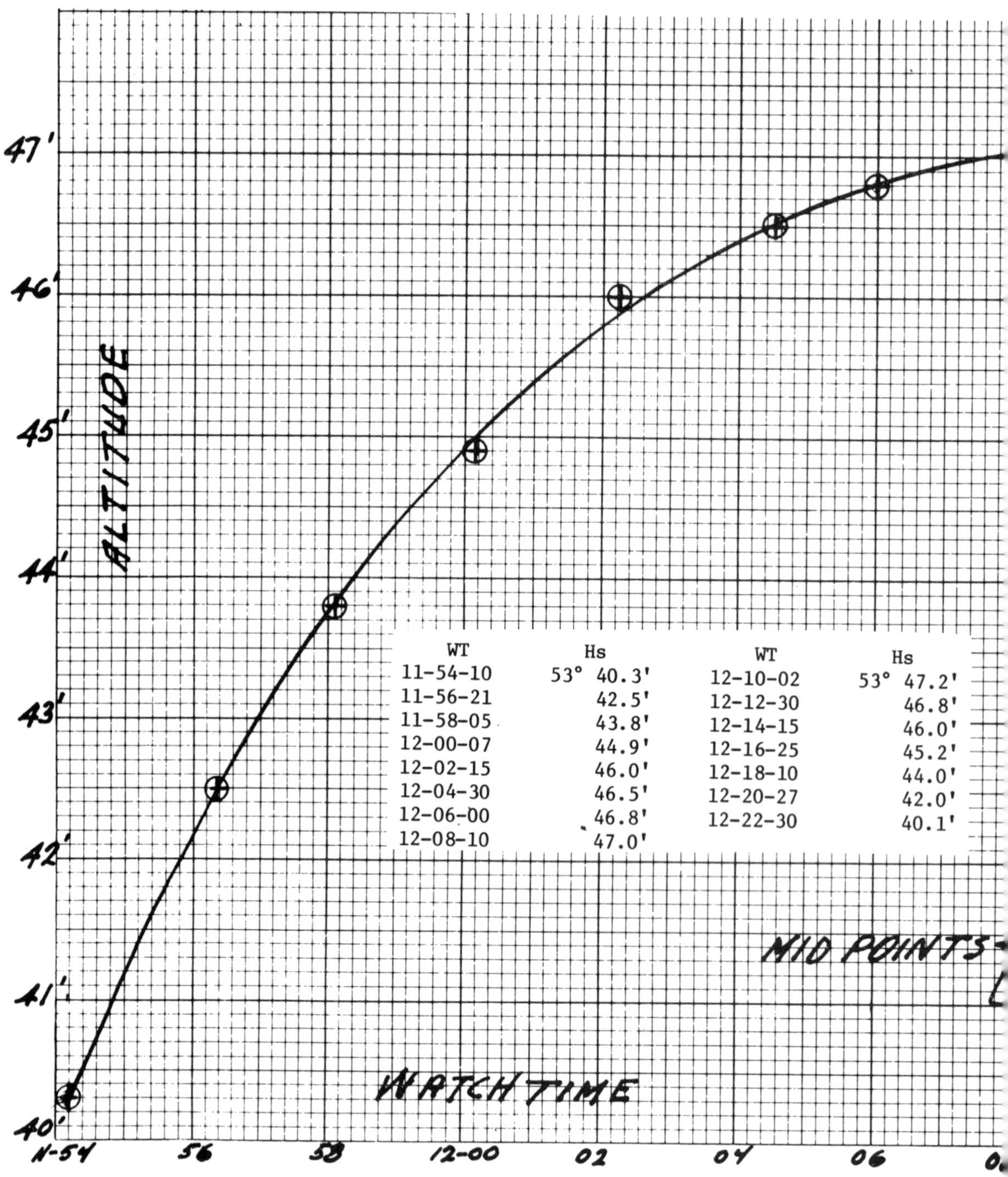

WT	Hs	WT	Hs
11-54-10	53° 40.3'	12-10-02	53° 47.2'
11-56-21	42.5'	12-12-30	46.8'
11-58-05	43.8'	12-14-15	46.0'
12-00-07	44.9'	12-16-25	45.2'
12-02-15	46.0'	12-18-10	44.0'
12-04-30	46.5'	12-20-27	42.0'
12-06-00	46.8'	12-22-30	40.1'
12-08-10	47.0'		

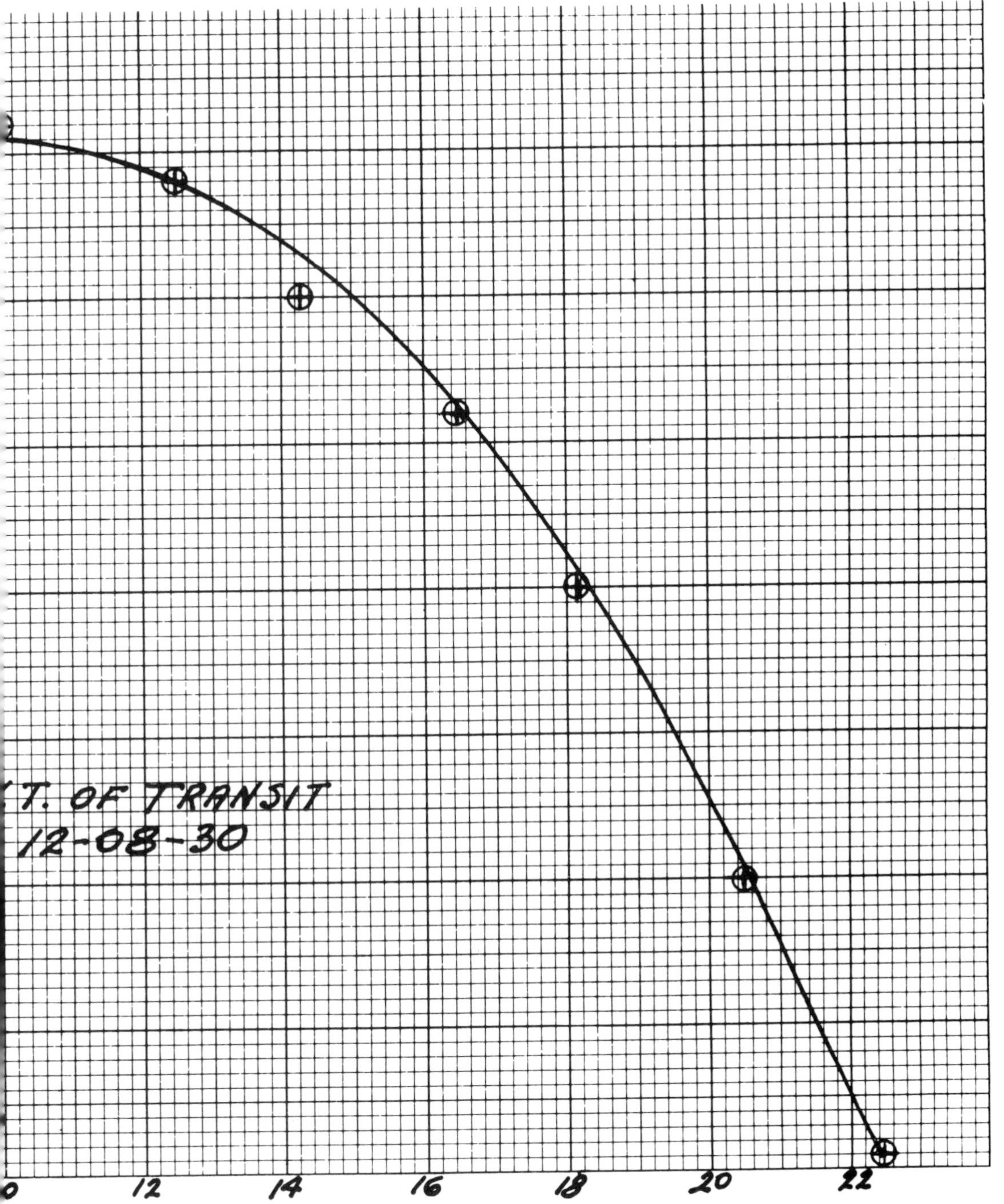

FIG. 24-7
Graph for determining longitude at noon

local mean time (LMT) of transit for any and all longitudes on any given day is the same, and is given daily in the almanac. Remembering that zone time in any time zone is the LMT of the central meridian of the zone, we thus know at what time transit occurs at the central meridian, in terms of zone time. If you then make a close estimate of your DR longitude at that time, you can determine the difference between it and the central meridian. This difference, converted to time, applied to the zone time of transit at the central meridian will give you your own zone time of transit. If you are east of the central meridian, your transit occurs earlier, so you subtract the time difference. If you are west, your transit occurs later, so you add the time difference.

Example • On January 1 you are sailing due west at 6 knots in latitude 35°50′ N, just off the west coast of Spain. Morning fix at ZT 0554 gave a longitude of 11°12′, but you have had no forenoon sights. The almanac gives LMT of transit of the sun as 1204 for this day. The central time meridian of your time zone is 15° W, so you know that transit at 15° W will occur at ZT 1204, same as the LMT.

Next determine the DR position on the chart for ZT 1204. Since the morning fix, you have sailed for 1204 — 0554 = 6^h10^m, or about 37 miles. Plotted on the chart, this gives a DR longitude at 1204 of 11°57′ W, or 15° — 11°57′ = 3°03′ east of the central time meridian. This is the arc the sun must travel from your DR position to transit at 15° W. Converted to time, 3°03′ is about 12 minutes. Transit at 11°57′ W will thus occur 12 minutes earlier, or at ZT 1204 — 12 = 1152.

If you wish to be very precise, or wish to check your work, you can now make a second estimate by plotting the DR longitude for ZT 1152, but it is not necessary. At that time you have sailed 1152 – 0554 = 5^h58^m, or about 35.8 miles. Your DR longitude will plot at 11°56′ W. This is 3°04′ east of 15° W, or again about 12 minutes. Thus, 1152 + 12^m = 1204, the ZT of transit at 15° W, which proves that a first estimate is usually all that is required, since we work to the nearest minute only. We would begin to take sights 10 minutes earlier, to allow for possible error in estimated speed, effect of current, etc.

A second method, preferred by many navigators, is to determine the LMT of the earlier fix and then advance this fix to LMT of transit. This gives a good DR position for time of transit and enables us to make use of the principle that, at transit, GHA of sun = west longitude and 360°− GHA of sun = east longitude. This is the method indicated on the Simex work form for noon sights.

In the example we have been discussing, our morning fix was obtained at 0554.

Zone time of fix	0554
ZD	+1
GMT of fix	0654
Longitude in time	45^m $(11°12' = 44^m48^s)$
LMT of fix	0609

According to the almanac, transit will occur everywhere at LMT 1204, so we will sail 1204 − 0609 = 5^h55^m, or about 35 miles until transit. If we advance the morning fix 35 miles along the course line, our DR longitude at transit will be 11°55′ W. We can now determine the exact GMT when the sun's GHA is the same as the longitude, 11°55′, using the *Air Almanac* as follows:

DR longitude at transit is	11° 55′
At GMT 1250, the GHA of the sun is	11° 37′
Additional GHA until transit is	18′

Using the table of conversion of arc to time, we find that it takes the sun 1^m12^s, to cover 18′ of arc. Therefore, the sun will be on the meridian at 1250 + 1^m12^s, or 1251 GMT (using nearest minute). Since the ZD is 1 hour, the zone time of transit will be 1151—close enough for our purposes. We shall probably be on deck with a sextant at 1140.

Although the sun is the body we most often observe at transit, it is entirely possible to make the same calculation with any celestial body and obtain a latitude line, although this is rarely done. The most desirable feature of the meridian transit sight is its accuracy, because the body remains practically stationary for a minute or two right at transit.

Chapter 25

Latitude by Polaris

If you study the geometry of the diagrams used in Chapter 24, you will see that *the altitude of the visible pole equals the observer's latitude.* By "visible pole," we mean the North Pole for an observer in north latitude, and the South Pole for observers in the southern hemisphere. Since Polaris, the North Star, is located almost exactly at the celestial North Pole, it becomes a simple matter to observe it in a sextant and obtain a quick latitude. Because Polaris is not *exactly* at the pole, a small correction is necessary. Actually, Polaris is located 52′ from the pole and thus circles the pole at that distance. When Polaris is directly above the pole, we must subtract 52′ from the corrected sextant reading; when it is exactly east or west of the pole, there is no correction; and when just below the pole, we add 52′ to H_o. The two almanacs give different tables (Figs. 25–1 and 25–2) for finding the correction, but both are entered with the LHA of Aries.

Using the *Air Almanac* The method using the *Air Almanac* is the simplest approach and yields a single correction *Q*, which can be plus or minus. The table of corrections is found at the end of the almanac and is actually good for 5 years, for an accuracy to within 1 minute.

Example • On January 1, Polaris is observed from DR latitude 33°10′ N. Longitude is 119°30′ W at 0640. Corrected sextant altitude H_o is 32°20′. Find latitude.

ZT of sight	06-40-00
ZD	+8
GMT of sight	14-40-00

GHA of Aries for 1440 is	320° 50′
Longitude	119° 30′
LHA of Aries is	201° 20′

POLARIS (POLE STAR) TABLE

FOR DETERMINING THE LATITUDE FROM A SEXTANT ALTITUDE

L.H.A.♈	Q	L.H.A.♈	Q	L.H.A.♈	Q	L.H.A.♈	Q	L.H.A.♈	Q	L.H.A.♈	Q	L.H.A.♈	Q	L.H.A.♈	Q
° ′	′	° ′	′	° ′	′	° ′	′	° ′	′	° ′	′	° ′	′	° ′	′
359 11	−45	82 09	−32	114 21	− 5	144 39	+22	188 25	+49	268 14	+28	299 37	+ 1	330 20	−26
1 18	−46	83 31	−31	115 27	− 4	145 52	+23	191 32	+50	269 32	+27	300 42	0	331 35	−27
3 35	−47	84 52	−30	116 33	− 3	147 05	+24	195 14	+51	270 49	+26	301 49	− 1	332 51	−28
6 02	−48	86 12	−29	117 39	− 2	148 19	+25	200 07	+52	272 05	+25	302 55	− 2	334 09	−29
8 45	−49	87 30	−28	118 44	− 1	149 34	+26	221 32	+51	273 20	+24	304 00	− 3	335 27	−30
11 49	−50	88 48	−27	119 50	0	150 50	+27	226 25	+50	274 34	+23	305 06	− 4	336 47	−31
15 28	−51	90 04	−26	120 57	+ 1	152 07	+28	230 07	+49	275 47	+22	306 12	− 5	338 08	−32
20 16	−52	91 19	−25	122 02	+ 2	153 25	+29	233 14	+48	277 00	+21	307 18	− 6	339 30	−33
41 23	−51	92 33	−24	123 08	+ 3	154 44	+30	235 59	+47	278 12	+20	308 24	− 7	340 54	−34
46 11	−50	93 47	−23	124 14	+ 4	156 04	+31	238 28	+46	279 23	+19	309 30	− 8	342 20	−35
49 50	−49	95 00	−22	125 19	+ 5	157 26	+32	240 46	+45	280 33	+18	310 36	− 9	343 48	−36
52 54	−48	96 12	−21	126 25	+ 6	158 49	+33	242 55	+44	281 43	+17	311 43	−10	345 17	−37
55 37	−47	97 24	−20	127 32	+ 7	160 14	+34	244 57	+43	282 53	+16	312 49	−11	346 50	−38
58 04	−46	98 34	−19	128 38	+ 8	161 41	+35	246 52	+42	284 02	+15	313 56	−12	348 24	−39
60 21	−45	99 44	−18	129 44	+ 9	163 09	+36	248 43	+41	285 10	+14	315 03	−13	350 02	−40
62 28	−44	100 54	−17	130 51	+10	164 40	+37	250 29	+40	286 19	+13	316 11	−14	351 43	−41
64 28	−43	102 03	−16	131 58	+11	166 13	+38	252 11	+39	287 26	+12	317 19	−15	353 28	−42
66 22	−42	103 12	−15	133 05	+12	167 49	+39	253 50	+38	288 34	+11	318 27	−16	355 17	−43
68 11	−41	104 20	−14	134 13	+13	169 28	+40	255 26	+37	289 41	+10	319 36	−17	357 11	−44
69 56	−40	105 28	−13	135 20	+14	171 10	+41	256 59	+36	290 48	+ 9	320 45	−18	359 11	−45
71 37	−39	106 36	−12	136 29	+15	172 56	+42	258 30	+35	291 55	+ 8	321 55	−19	1 18	−46
73 15	−38	107 43	−11	137 37	+16	174 47	+43	259 58	+34	293 01	+ 7	323 05	−20	3 35	−47
74 49	−37	108 50	−10	138 46	+17	176 42	+44	261 25	+33	294 07	+ 6	324 15	−21	6 02	−48
76 22	−36	109 56	− 9	139 56	+18	178 44	+45	262 50	+32	295 14	+ 5	325 27	−22	8 45	−49
77 51	−35	111 03	− 8	141 06	+19	180 53	+46	264 13	+31	296 20	+ 4	326 39	−23	11 49	−50
79 19	−34	112 09	− 7	142 16	+20	183 11	+47	265 35	+30	297 25	+ 3	327 52	−24	15 28	−51
80 45	−33	113 15	− 6	143 27	+21	185 40	+48	266 55	+29	298 31	+ 2	329 06	−25	20 16	−52
82 09		114 21		144 39		188 25		268 14		299 37		330 20		41 23	

Q, which does *not* include refraction, is to be applied to the corrected sextant altitude of *Polaris*.
Polaris: Mag. 2·1, S.H.A. 329° 10′, Dec. N. 89° 07′·6

FIG. 25-1
Polaris table from Air Almanac (for actual navigation, use current almanac)

From the Polaris table in the *Air Almanac* we find the correction to be applied for LHA of 201°:

$$\begin{aligned} Q &= +52' \\ H_o &= 32°\ 20' \\ \hline \text{Latitude} &= 33°\ 12'\ \text{N} \end{aligned}$$

Using the *Nautical Almanac* To obtain an accuracy to within 0.1′ in the correction to be applied to the altitude of Polaris, the *Nautical Almanac* uses three separate corrections, based on the LHA of Aries, the latitude of the observer, and the month of the year. The corrections are respectively labeled a_0, a_1, and a_2, and the corrections are so contrived that latitude $= H_o - 1° + a_0 + a_1 + a_2$.

POLARIS (POLE STAR) TABLES

FOR DETERMINING LATITUDE FROM SEXTANT ALTITUDE AND FOR AZIMUTH

L.H.A. ARIES	120°–129°	130°–139°	140°–149°	150°–159°	160°–169°	170°–179°	180°–189°	190°–199°	200°–209°	210°–219°	220°–229°	230°–239°
	a_0	a_0	a_0	a_0	a_0	a_0	a_0	a_0	a_0	a_0	a_0	a_0
°	° ′	° ′	° ′	° ′	° ′	° ′	° ′	° ′	° ′	° ′	° ′	° ′
0	0 58·5	1 07·6	1 16·3	1 24·5	1 32·0	1 38·4	1 43·7	1 47·6	1 50·0	1 50·9	1 50·2	1 48·1
1	0 59·4	08·5	17·2	25·3	32·7	39·0	44·1	47·9	50·1	50·9	50·1	47·8
2	1 00·3	09·3	18·0	26·1	33·4	39·6	44·6	48·2	50·3	50·9	49·9	47·4
3	01·2	10·2	18·9	26·9	34·0	40·1	45·0	48·4	50·4	50·9	49·8	47·1
4	02·1	11·1	19·7	27·6	34·7	40·7	45·4	48·7	50·5	50·8	49·6	46·8
5	1 03·1	1 12·0	1 20·5	1 28·4	1 35·3	1 41·2	1 45·8	1 49·0	1 50·6	1 50·8	1 49·3	1 46·4
6	04·0	12·9	21·3	29·1	36·0	41·7	46·2	49·2	50·7	50·7	49·1	46·0
7	04·9	13·7	22·2	29·9	36·6	42·2	46·5	49·4	50·8	50·6	48·9	45·7
8	05·8	14·6	23·0	30·6	37·2	42·7	46·9	49·6	50·8	50·5	48·6	45·3
9	06·7	15·5	23·8	31·3	37·8	43·2	47·2	49·8	50·9	50·4	48·3	44·8
10	1 07·6	1 16·3	1 24·5	1 32·0	1 38·4	1 43·7	1 47·6	1 50·0	1 50·9	1 50·2	1 48·1	1 44·4
Lat.	a_1	a_1	a_1	a_1	a_1	a_1	a_1	a_1	a_1	a_1	a_1	a_1
°	′	′	′	′	′	′	′	′	′	′	′	′
0	0·1	0·2	0·2	0·3	0·4	0·4	0·5	0·6	0·6	0·6	0·6	0·5
10	·2	·2	·3	·3	·4	·5	·5	·6	·6	·6	·6	·5
20	·3	·3	·3	·4	·4	·5	·5	·6	·6	·6	·6	·5
30	·4	·4	·4	·4	·5	·5	·6	·6	·6	·6	·6	·6
40	0·5	0·5	0·5	0·5	0·5	0·6	0·6	0·6	0·6	0·6	0·6	0·6
45	·5	·5	·5	·5	·6	·6	·6	·6	·6	·6	·6	·6
50	·6	·6	·6	·6	·6	·6	·6	·6	·6	·6	·6	·6
55	·7	·7	·7	·7	·6	·6	·6	·6	·6	·6	·6	·6
60	·8	·8	·8	·7	·7	·7	·6	·6	·6	·6	·6	·6
62	0·9	0·9	0·8	0·8	0·7	0·7	0·7	0·6	0·6	0·6	0·6	0·6
64	0·9	0·9	·9	·8	·8	·7	·7	·6	·6	·6	·6	·7
66	1·0	1·0	0·9	·9	·8	·7	·7	·6	·6	·6	·6	·7
68	1·1	1·1	1·0	0·9	0·9	0·8	0·7	0·6	0·6	0·6	0·6	0·7
Month	a_2	a_2	a_2	a_2	a_2	a_2	a_2	a_2	a_2	a_2	a_2	a_2
	′	′	′	′	′	′	′	′	′	′	′	′
Jan.	0·7	0·6	0·6	0·6	0·6	0·6	0·5	0·5	0·5	0·5	0·5	0·5
Feb.	·8	·8	·7	·7	·7	·6	·6	·6	·5	·5	·5	·4
Mar.	0·9	0·9	0·9	0·9	0·8	·8	·7	·7	·6	·6	·5	·5
Apr.	1·0	1·0	1·0	1·0	1·0	0·9	0·9	0·8	0·8	0·7	0·6	0·6
May	0·9	1·0	1·0	1·0	1·0	1·0	1·0	0·9	0·9	·8	·8	·7
June	·8	0·9	0·9	1·0	1·0	1·0	1·0	1·0	1·0	0·9	0·9	·8
July	0·7	0·7	0·8	0·8	0·9	0·9	1·0	1·0	1·0	1·0	1·0	0·9
Aug.	·5	·6	·6	·7	·7	·8	0·8	0·9	0·9	0·9	0·9	·9
Sept.	·3	·4	·4	·5	·5	·6	·7	·7	·8	·8	·9	·9
Oct.	0·2	0·3	0·3	0·3	0·4	0·4	0·5	0·5	0·6	0·6	0·7	0·8
Nov.	·2	·2	·2	·2	·2	·2	·3	·3	·4	·5	·5	·6
Dec.	0·3	0·2	0·2	0·2	0·2	0·2	0·2	0·2	0·2	0·3	0·4	0·4
Lat.	AZIMUTH											
°	°	°	°	°	°	°	°	°	°	°	°	°
0	359·1	359·2	359·2	359·3	359·4	359·5	359·6	359·8	359·9	0·1	0·2	0·4
20	359·1	359·1	359·2	359·2	359·3	359·5	359·6	359·7	359·9	0·1	0·2	0·4
40	358·9	358·9	359·0	359·1	359·2	359·3	359·5	359·7	359·9	0·1	0·3	0·5
50	358·7	358·7	358·8	358·9	359·0	359·2	359·4	359·6	359·9	0·1	0·3	0·5
55	358·5	358·5	358·6	358·8	358·9	359·1	359·4	359·6	359·8	0·1	0·4	0·6
60	358·3	358·3	358·4	358·6	358·8	359·0	359·3	359·5	359·8	0·1	0·4	0·7
65	358·0	358·0	358·2	358·3	358·6	358·8	359·1	359·5	359·8	0·1	0·5	0·8

FIG. 25-2
Excerpts from Polaris table in Nautical Almanac *(for actual navigation always use current almanac)*

Example • Using the same data as before, determine latitude by using the *Nautical Almanac.* We locate LHA of Aries at the top of the page as being between 200° and 209°, and all corrections are taken from this same vertical column. The correction a_0 for 201° is found in the second line as 1°50.1′. In the next lower section, same column, for latitude of 30° we find a_1 to be 0.6′. Still further down, opposite the month of January, we find a_2 as 0.5′. Thus, latitude = 32°20′ − 1° + 1°50.1′ + 0.6′ + 0.5′ = 33°11.2 N. This is 0.8 mile lower than the latitude found by using the *Q* correction in the *Air Almanac.* The *Nautical Almanac* is of course used where greater accuracy is required.

Azimuth by Polaris Both the *Air Almanac* and *Nautical Almanac* have tables for finding the azimuth of Polaris at the time of the observation, and there is little difference in the two tables. Both are entered with the LHA of Aries and the latitude of the observer, and the azimuth is given to the nearest tenth of a *degree.* Polaris can be as much as 2.5° east or west of the pole in azimuth. It thus affords a good compass check for deviation. Unfortunately, Polaris is a rather weak star and not always easy to observe.

FIG. 25-3
Checking compass error by Polaris

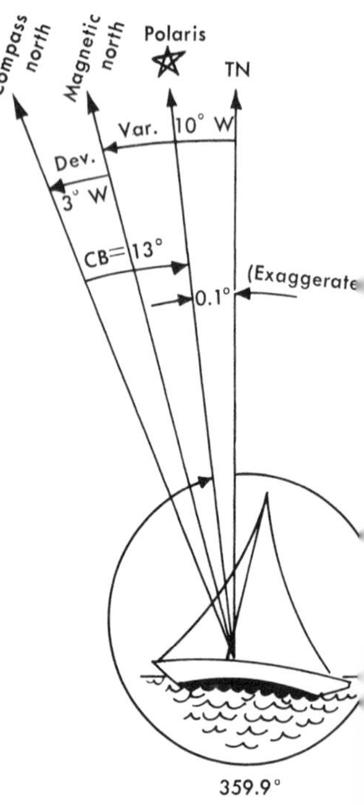

Example • The navigator in the previous example obtained a compass bearing of 013° on Polaris at the time of his observation. If variation is 10° W, what is deviation on this heading?

For latitude 30° and LHA of Aries of 201°, the true bearing of Polaris is 359.9°, or 0.1° west of true north. Compass north thus lies 13.1° west of true north, and if variation is 10° W, the deviation is 3.1° W on this heading. Since no one can take bearings that accurately, we call the deviation 3° W. (See Fig. 25–3.)

Chapter 26

Great Circle Sailing

By definition, a *great circle* on the surface of the Earth is any circle that has its center at the center of the Earth. Thus, for instance, all meridians are great circles, as is the equator; parallels of latitude (other than the equator) are not, however, since their centers are at points on the polar axis other than the center of the Earth. It is possible to draw an infinite number of great circles, and therefore possible to connect any two points on the globe by a great circle. Since a great circle is the shortest distance between two points on a globe, ships frequently plot and follow a great circle course across the ocean.

Great Circle Charts Nearly all great circle courses are determined by plotting on a chart using either a Mercator or gnomonic projection. The latter are often known as *great circle charts*. The Lambert conformal chart, used widely in aviation, is an example of such a chart. Meridians radiate as straight lines from the pole, and parallels of latitude appear as lines curving away from the pole. A straight line drawn on such a chart is very nearly a great circle. Since this line would not cross all meridians at the same angle, a single course for the track is not provided, but a series of courses can be measured with a protractor at various points along the track. To navigate along a great circle route, the course would have to be changed constantly. Since this is impossible, the navigator follows a series of small legs—either chords or tangents to the great circle track—that closely approximate the desired path. Some marine charts are beginning to be available on this kind of projection, and no doubt many more will be published in the future.

Great Circle Track on a Mercator Chart On a Mercator chart, all meridians are parallel and a straight course line intersects all meridians at the same angle. A straight line between two points on a Mercator chart is called a *rhumb* *line,* and this is the kind of course line we use for shorter distances. It is slightly longer than a great circle route between the same two points.

A great circle track can be constructed on a Mercator chart and will always be found to curve away from the equator. It can be plotted by first drawing a straight line between the two points involved on a gnomonic chart and then transferring a series of positions at small intervals along the track to the Mercator chart, plotting each point by its latitude and longitude taken from the gnomonic chart. The result is a series of straight segments that closely follow the great circle track. The distance between points should vary with the speed of the vessel. On a slow-sailing vessel it is sufficient to change course slightly once a day. On a fast cargo ship, a new course might be set every 6 or even every 4 hours. In aircraft it is customary to change every 5° of longitude or so. Each day the navigator determines how close to the desired track he is and makes his course changes accordingly.

Great Circle Track Charts The Naval Oceanographic Office publishes great circle track charts of the world and for specific main ports. These are Mercator charts on which the great circle track has been printed; usually distances are also indicated along each track. The navigator can plot his position on these charts, or he can transfer the tracks to another Mercator chart or plotting sheet.

For short distances, it does not pay to go to the trouble of using a great circle route. Likewise, when sailing due east or due west near the equator, or when sailing nearly due north or south, there is no advantage in great circle sailing. At times navigators will find that their great circle tracks take them too far north or too far south, so that ice becomes a problem, or the track may cross land or get too close to reefs or other dangers. In such cases only partial great circle sailing is used across clear water, and then where the distance warrants it.

Initial Course and Distance by Computation A great circle track can also be worked out by trigonometric computation, but no navigator in his right mind would spend the time doing it. The process is very complicated and gives no better results than the methods previously described.

Furthermore, the method gives only an initial course at the point of departure and distance to the point of destination. Each time a course change is desired, a new computation must be made.

The Sailings In sailing ship days, when good charts were not always plentiful, navigators were required to know a whole series of mathematical methods, called *the sailings,* for determining courses and distances between two points, using logarithmic functions, trigonometry, and a number of tables from Bowditch. There was *plane sailing, parallel sailing, mid-latitude sailing, Mercator sailing, composite sailing, and traverse sailing,* in addition, of course, to *great circle sailing*. Only the last has survived as being still useful, provided it does not have to be done by trigonometric computation. However, there are still examinations given in this country that require a knowledge of Mercator and mid-latitude sailings, although nobody at sea has been using them for many years. They are best relegated to oblivion along with such antiquities as the ancient lunar distances method and the time sight for longitude.

Initial Course and Distance by Tables Great circle courses are best determined by the use of the proper charts, but where these are not available, initial course and distance from the point of departure—or from any other point along the track—can readily be ascertained by using navigation tables, such as those in N.O. 229, 214, or 249. N.O. 214 is probably the best in this regard because decliniations are listed for every half-degree instead of every whole degree, as in N.O. 229 and 249. However, N.O. 229 is a more complete set of tables, having solutions for nearly every possible form the celestial triangle may take. N.O. 249 can only be used where the destination has a latitude, north or south, of less than 30°. The procedure is nearly the same with every set of tables, and it is fully explained in the introduction to each volume.

Remember that when you are figuring a great circle track, it is possible to go in opposite directions along the circle. Needless to say, we are concerned only with the shortest distance between the two points involved, point of departure and point of destination. To orient yourself, it sometimes helps to place a string on a globe between these two points to confirm what the initial course should be, especially where long distances are concerned. If you have to compute course and distance by table, you can simplify your work immensely by working from the nearest whole degree of latitude of both departure point and destination. On a long voyage, the difference in the initial course will be a fraction of a degree, and you cannot steer that close in any case; in addition, you will change course and figure many new courses along the track, so fractional values are of theoretical importance only. Of course, if you have to pass an examination, you will be asked to work from very exact positions, in which case you must interpolate in the tables for exact values. Such interpolations are fully explained in the introductions to the tables and are therefore not repeated here.

The rules for finding initial course and distance by table are the same no matter which set of tables you use, so we shall first give the rules and their variations, and then examples of their applications.

Rules •

1. Select the nearest whole degree of latitude for both point of departure and point of destination. (*Exception:* With N.O. 214 you can use nearest half-degree for latitude of destination.)
2. Substitute *latitude of departure for assumed latitude.*
3. Substitute *latitude of destination for declination.*
4. *Use difference of longitude between point of departure and destination as local hour angle* (LHA). Always use the *smaller* of the two possible values. LHA is always less than 180°.
5. *Enter table and extract* H_c and *azimuth Z.*
6. *Great circle distance in nautical miles is found by subtracting* H_c *from 90° and converting difference to minutes of arc.*
7. *Initial great circle course is determined from azimuth angle Z. Designate Z north or south according to latitude of departure, and name it east or west according to your direction of travel. Draw a longitude diagram to determine whether you travel east or west.* Thus, if you start out in north latitude and travel east, and Z is 37°, you will write *"course N 37° E."*

This means that the initial course is 037° true. "Course N 75° W" means that true course is 360° − 75° = 285°. "Course S 50° E" means that the true course is 180° − 50° = 130°. "Course C 115° W" means that the true course is 180° + 115° = 295°.

8. *When the latitudes of departure and destination lie in the same hemisphere, enter tables with declination same name as latitude. When the latitudes of departure and destination lie in different hemispheres (when you are crossing the equator), enter tables with declination opposite name to latitude.*
9. *When the difference of longitude (LHA) is too large for entry into the tables, subtract LHA from 180° and enter the table with the difference. Also:*

    a. *Reverse the designation of the latitude of destination (from north to south or vice versa).*
    b. *Add 90° to H_c to find distance.*
    c. *Subtract the azimuth Z from 180° to find a new, or corrected, value for Z. Label this new angle Z for latitude and direction of travel, as described in rule 7.*

Limitations When the situation is such that you cannot find suitable entering arguments for the tables you have, this method cannot be used. When you use the tables in N.O. 249, Vols. II and III (volume I is not used for great circle computations), the latitude of the destination cannot exceed 30° north or south, as this is the maximum declination tabulated in these tables.

Example 1 • Find the initial course and great circle distance from Montevideo, Uruguay (34°54′ S, 56°13′ W) to Capetown, South Africa (33°54′ S, 18°26′ E). First decide on the values you will use when you enter the tables.

FIG. 26-1

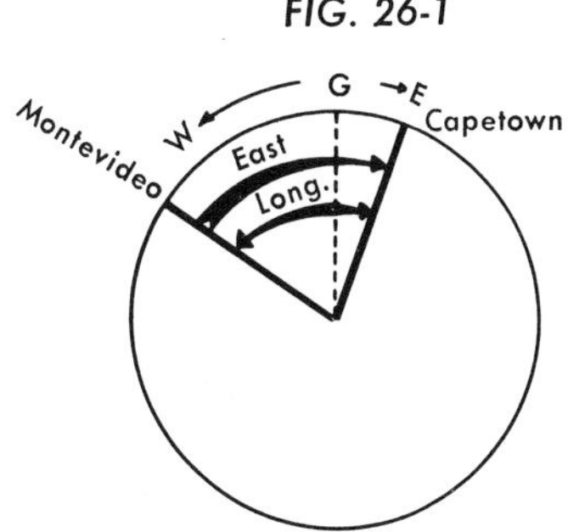

Step 1. Use 35° for assumed latitude.
Use 34° for declination—*same name.*
LHA = 56°13′ + 18°26′ = 74°39′; use 75°.
Direction of travel is *east* (see diagram).

Step 2. Since declination is 34°, you cannot use N.O. 249, so you use either N.O. 214 or N.O. 229, where you find the following:

H_c = 29°46.1′ | Z = 67.3°
90° − 29°46′ = 60°14′ | Initial course = S 67° E
60 × 60 = 3,600 miles | 180° − 67° = 113°
+ 14 | Initial course = 113°
Distance = 3,614 nautical miles

Example 2 • Find the initial course (IC) and great circle distance from San Francisco (37°49′ N, 122°25′ W) to Papeete, Tahiti (17°32′ S, 149°34′ W). Note that you are crossing the equator, so you must use latitude and declination *opposite name.*

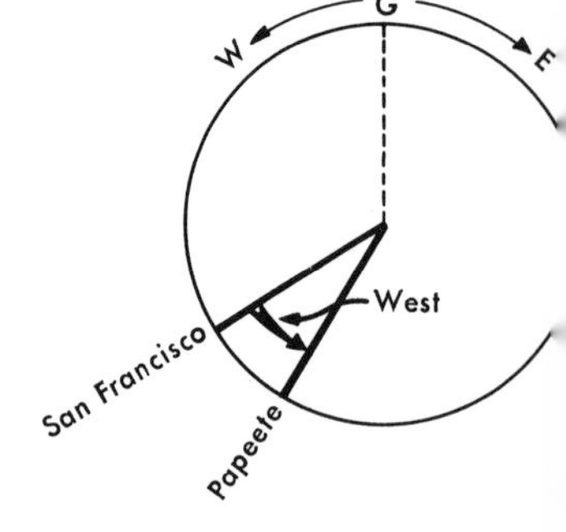

FIG. 26-2

Step 1. Use 38° for assumed latitude.
Use 17°30′ for declination (in N.O. 214).
Use 18° for declination in N.O. 249 or N.O. 229.
LHA = 149°34′ − 122°25′ = 27°09′: use 27°.
Direction of travel is *west* (see diagram).

Step 2. From the tables you extract the following values:

H_c = 28°58.8′ | Z = 150.3°
90° − 28°58.8′ = 61°01′ | IC = N 150° W
Distance = (61 × 60) + 1 = 3,661 nautical miles | Initial course = 210°

The figures were obtained from N.O. 214. If N.O. 229 or N.O. 249 were used, without interpolation, using a declination of 18°, the distance would be 3,689 miles and the initial course would be 151°. For a voyage of that length, where positions will be fixed and new courses computed many times, such small differences do not matter. However, if you must get precise figures, such as on an examination, you can interpolate accurately in the tables.

Example 3 • Find the great circle course and distance from Panama (7°28′ N, 80°00′ W) to Singapore (1°17′ N, 103°51′ E). Because of the great difference in longitude, the LHA will be too large for the tables and rule 9 must be followed.

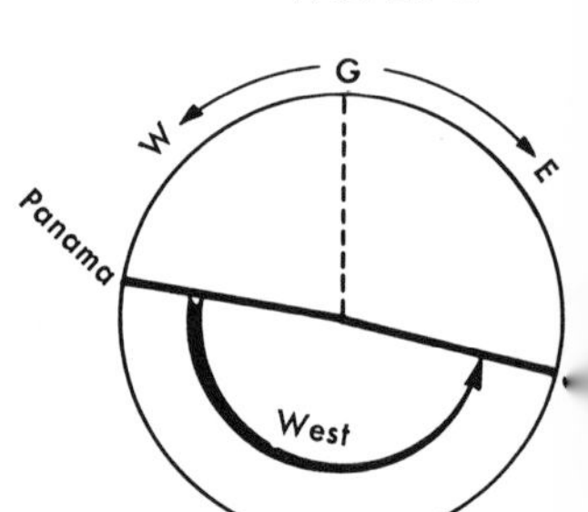

FIG. 26-3

Step 1. Use 7° for assumed latitude.
Use 1°30′ for declination (N.O. 214).
LHA = 360° − (80° + 104°) = 176°.
Direction of travel is *west.*
Since LHA of 176° is not to be found in the tables, we

use LHA = 180° − 176° = 4°. We also *Reverse the latitude of destination,* and therefore use latitude and declination *contrary name.*

Step 2. From N.O. 214, you obtain the following data:

H_c = 80° 36.6′
+90° (rule 9)
170° 36.6′

170 × 60 = 10,200
+ 37
Distance = 10,237 nautical miles

Z = 154.7°
Rule 9: Subtract from 180°
180° − 154.7° = 25.3°
IC = N 25.3′ W
IC = 360° − 25° = 335°

Chapter 27

Star Identification

The best way to become familiar with the stars and planets is to locate them in the sky and memorize their names and the constellations in which they are found. The student should follow the instructions given here, use any good star chart, or ask a navigator friend to teach him. Then he should make it a habit, whenever he has a moment under a starlit sky, to run his eye over all the visible navigation stars and planets and mentally name them, study their position in relation to other stars, and note their size and color. Stargazing is a fascinating hobby and naming the stars will soon become second nature.

A visit to one of the large planetariums will prove very interesting and informative. The Hayden Planetarium in New York City, for example, gives an excellent course in star identification for navigators.

It is best to begin by learning the stars in the more prominent constellations, concentrating on the brightest stars. Although there are fifty-seven stars listed in the *Nautical Almanac,* one can get by with knowing about forty of them, the others being so dim that they are difficult to observe in a sextant.

Remember that the stars are fixed in space. Because the Earth rotates from west to east, the stars appear to move in large circles around the Earth, appearing over our eastern horizon and setting in the west. The stars near the visible celestial pole appear simply to rotate around the pole, never sinking below the horizon. Those farther away from the pole dip below the horizon on part of their paths. Since the relative positions of the stars change very little, they can very readily be identified by their locations with respect to certain other stars.

Each star usually has a name of its own, such as Polaris, but it is also known by a Greek letter denoting, as a rule, its relative brightness in the constellation, followed by the Latin name of the constellation. Polaris is thus

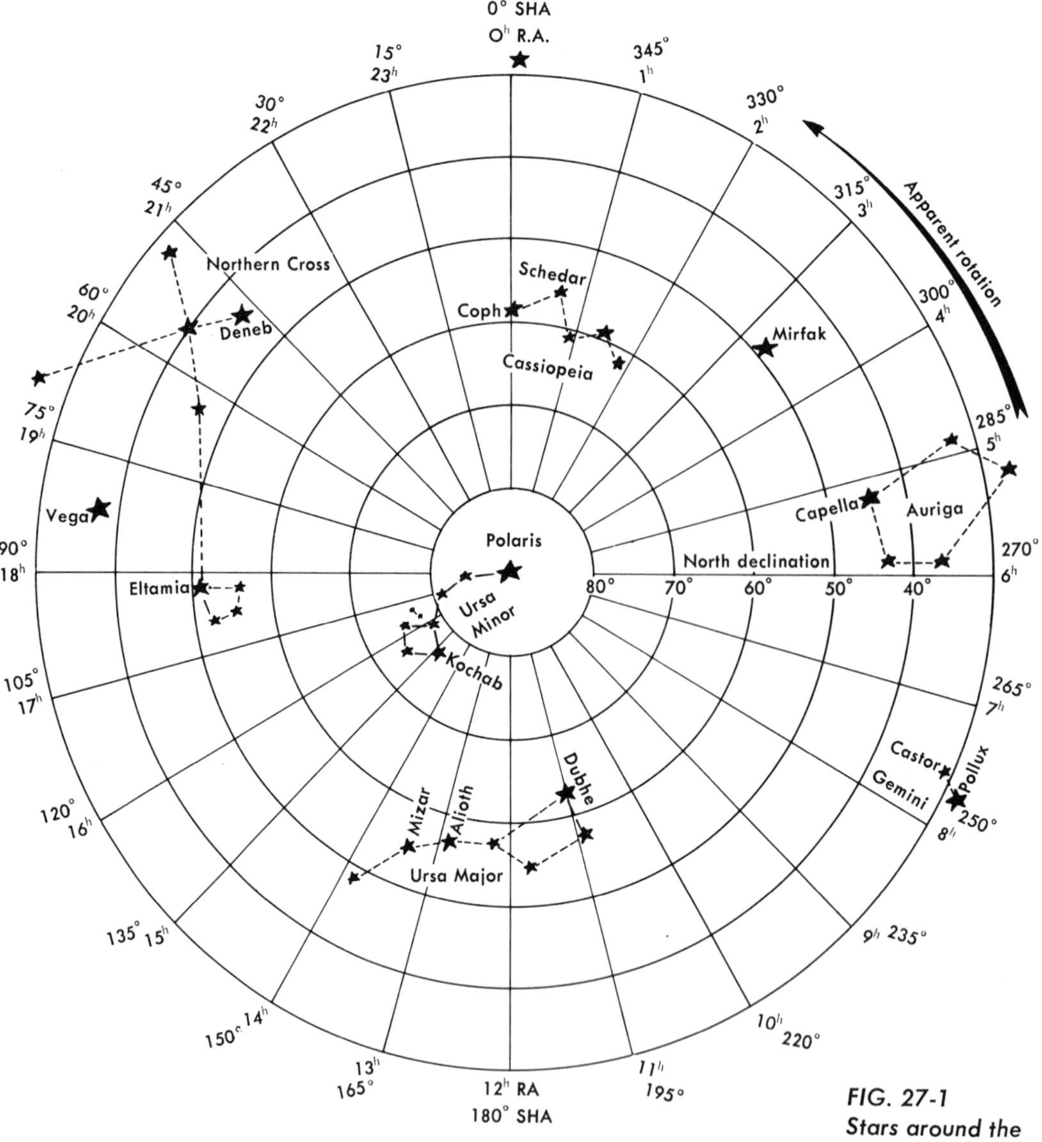

FIG. 27-1
Stars around the North Pole

known also as Alpha Ursae Minoris, meaning it is the first and, usually, the brightest star in the constellation of Ursa Minor, the Little Bear or Little Dipper. The name of the second-brightest star begins with Beta, the third with Gamma, the fourth with Delta, etc.

Stars Around the North Pole

If an observer were to stand at the North Pole, Polaris would be directly overhead. The other stars would appear to rotate counterclockwise around Polaris, but would never change their relative positions. As one moves away from the pole, Polaris would appear to move toward the horizon, and at the equator Polaris would be barely visible on the horizon.

Fig. 27–1 shows the main constellations seen when you look toward the North Pole. Only the navigation stars are named. Find each of these groups in the sky, identify the constellation, and name the navigation stars. Do this often enough until each one can be named. If in doubt, merely consult the chart and try again.

The following pointers may help in learning the circumpolar stars:

1. Note that Polaris is the last star in the handle of the Little Dipper. Polaris is about 1° away from the North Pole.
2. The two front stars in the Big Dipper point toward Polaris.
3. Whichever dipper is on top is always pouring its contents into the other.
4. Cassiopeia is almost directly opposite the Big Dipper across the pole and looks like an irregular W.
5. Capella, a very bright star, is in a pentagon of five stars, and it lines up with the top edge of the bowl in the Big Dipper.
6. Eltanin lines up with the cross arm in the Northern Cross, or Cygnus.

Intermediate Stars

The stars other than those always visible near the poles rise from the east horizon in a broad band, go overhead, and set in the west horizon. If the observer were able to stand directly on the equator and look due east, and if the stars were visible through a full 24-hour period, he would see this band of stars rise vertically from the horizon in the rotation, and with the relationship, shown in Figure 2. The equinoctial would be a vertical straight line rising out of the east point of the horizon. The stars in north declination would be on his left hand, and those

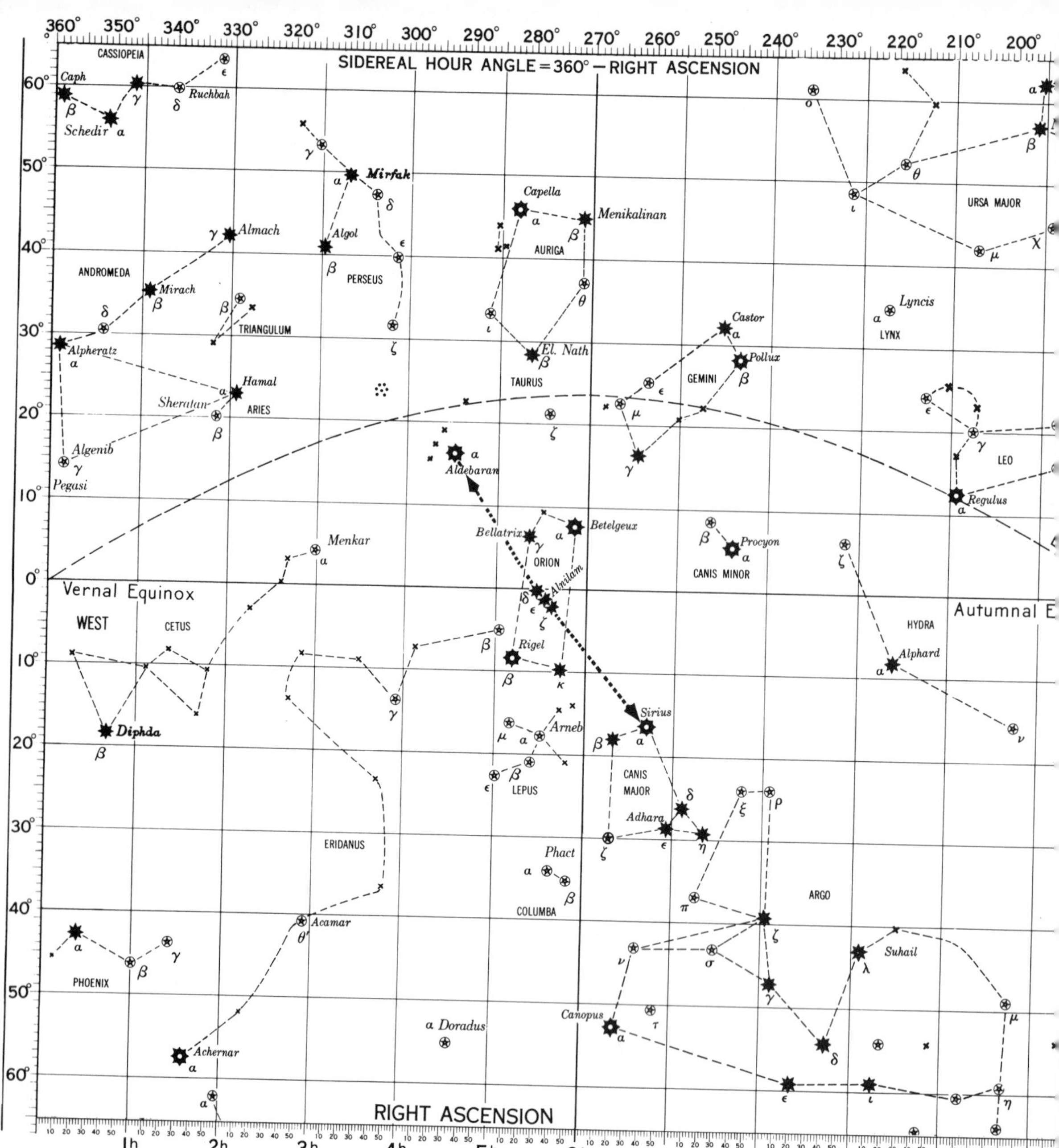

in south declination on his right. A ruler placed across the diagram at right angles to the equinoctial approximately represents his horizon at the equator. If the observer is in 30° N latitude, the horizon will be represented by the ruler tilted down 30° from the horizontal to the left. If he is in 45° S latitude, the horizon, as represented by the ruler, will be tilted 45° down to the right. In either case, the stars will no longer rise vertically, but at the angle indicated between the horizon and the vertical lines of the

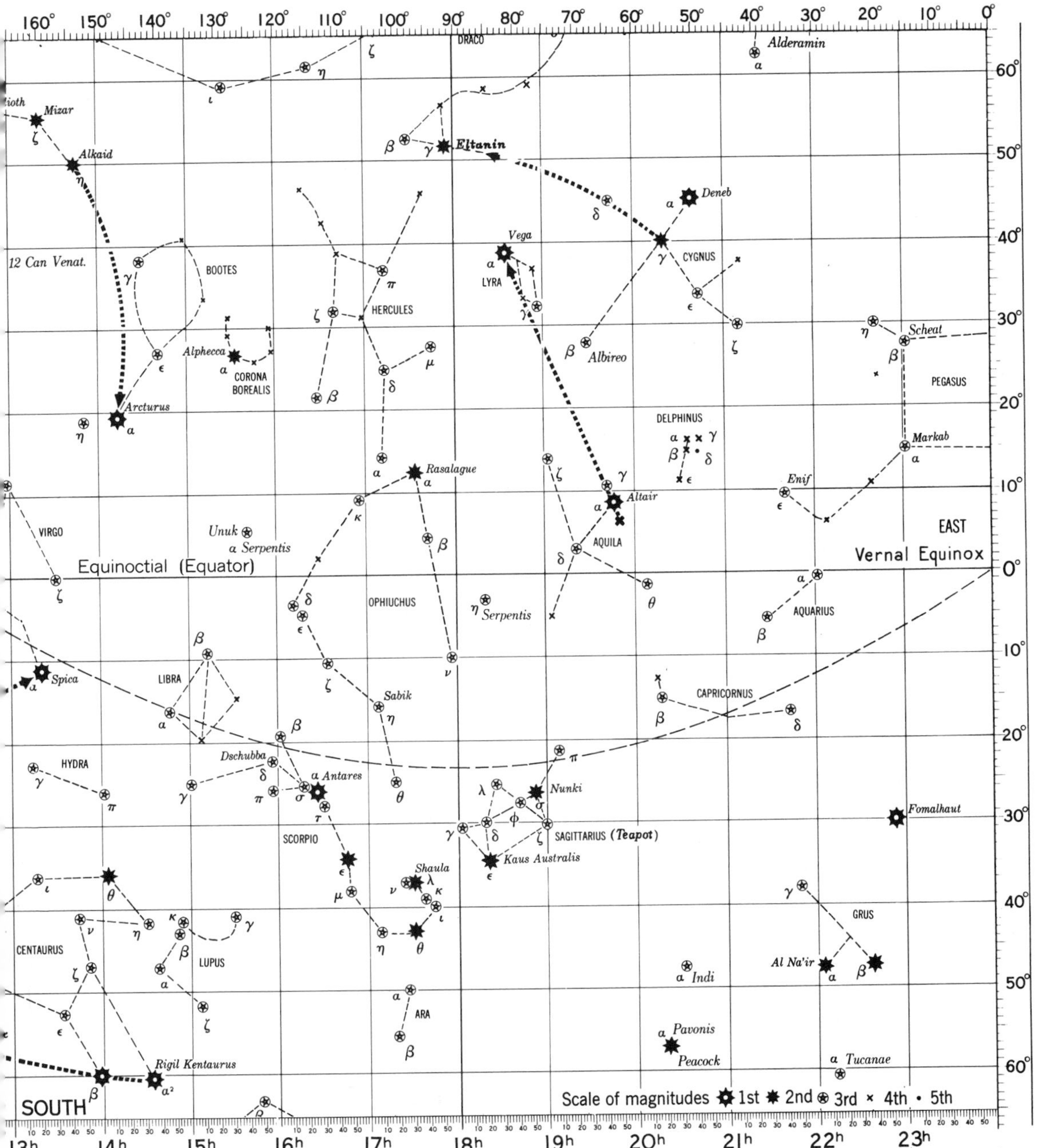

FIG. 27-2

diagram. These vertical lines actually represent the diurnal circles straightened out.

Fig. 27–2 shows the central band of stars—that is, those which are not normally considered circumpolar stars. They are plotted according to their declinations, north or south of the equinoctial, and also according to their right ascensions and their sidereal hour angles. Declination and latitude are measured in degrees, but right ascension is measured in hours, beginning from a celestial meridian known as the *hour circle of the vernal equinox*. This hour circle has zero hours right ascension. It can be located in the sky because it passes close to the stars Caph and Alpheratz, and, of course, through the poles.

An hour of right ascension is equal to 15° of arc, and the same star will cross the observer's meridian once every 24 hours. The top star in the belt of Orion has a right ascension (RA) of about 5½ hours. That means that it will cross the meridian, or appear above the horizon, 5½ hours later than the star Alpheratz. Also note that this top star in the belt of Orion is practically on the equinoctial, having almost zero declination.

The brightest star in the sky, Sirius, has an RA of about 7 hours, Regulus one of about 10 hours, Arcturus one of slightly over 14 hours, and Vega one of about 18½ hours. These bright stars make good reference points in the sky for estimating the right ascension and declination of unknown stars and planets.

To estimate declination, if it should ever be necessary, the navigator can follow this simple procedure. If he faces directly east, points his left hand at the celestial North Pole, and lets his right arm be a continuation of his left arm, his right hand will point to the celestial South Pole. If he lets his right arm swing up to make a right angle with his left arm, his right hand will then point directly to the equinoctial. If he lets his right arm describe a circle from east to west, maintaining the same angle, the right hand will sweep across the sky along the path of the equinoctial.

Any celestial body to the right of this path will have south declination, and any body to the left of this path will have north declination. The amount of declination can be estimated approximately by judging the angle between the equinoctial and the body, using as a yardstick the fact that the angle between the zenith and the horizon is 90°.

The right ascension of an unknown body can also be estimated from a visible star whose right ascension is known. Let one hand make a sweep from the North Pole, through the known star, to the South Pole. It will describe the hour circle of that star in the sky. Then let the other hand sweep from pole to pole through the unknown body, describing the hour circle of that body. Estimate the angle between these two hour circles approximately where they cross the equinoctial, and convert the degrees of angle into hours of right ascension by dividing by 15. If the unknown body is east of the known star, add the RA to that of the known star. If the unknown body is ahead, or west, of the known star, subtract the RA from that of the known star. Knowing the right ascension, and having estimated the declination as previously explained, the identity of the unknown body can be found from the star charts in the almanacs. Another bright star is not likely to be in that vicinity. However, if the unknown body cannot be identified on the star chart, it is probably a planet. Turn to the Almanacs and look at the declination and right ascension of the four navigational planets listed there, and instantly it will be seen which one has similar coordinates for that date.

Example • A fairly bright star is observed in the sky and the navigator wishes to know its identity. He knows, and can see, the constellation of Orion. He remembers that the upper star in the belt has zero declination and an RA of about 5½ hours. He then faces east and points one arm at the visible celestial pole, and with the other arm forms an angle of 90°. Sweeping this arm across the sky from east to west, through Orion's belt, he establishes the equinoctial line across the celestial sphere. Leaving one arm pointing to the equinoctial, he points with the other to the unknown body, and the estimated angle between them is the declination of that body. In this case he estimates that the star is about 15° north of the equinoctial. Next, he faces north and lets his right arm sweep from pole to pole and through Orion's belt, and his left arm from pole to pole through the unknown star. His arms have followed the track of the hour circles of the two bodies, and he estimates the angle between them, measured near the equinoctial, to be about 75°, or 5 hours of right ascension. Since the unknown star is east of, or following, Orion, it must have an RA of about 10½ hours. Consulting the star chart in the almanac, he finds that Regulus has an RA of slightly over 10 hours and a north declination of about 12°. Since there is no other bright star nearby, the unknown star must be Regulus.

Planets are not shown on star charts because they are members of the solar system and change their position in the sky throughout the year. Planets can usually be distinguished from stars because they glow with a steady light, whereas most stars twinkle. Jupiter and Venus are brighter than other planets or stars. Mars is usually quite reddish. Saturn can easily be mistaken for a star. However, when a bright body is seen in a position where no bright star should be, its right ascension and declination should be estimated and the planets for that day looked up to see which has similar coordinates.

When on watch at sea, looking at the sky night after night, one soon becomes thoroughly familiar with the positions of the stars. Because there are 366 "star days," but only 365 solar days, on a given night each star will appear over the horizon 4 minutes earlier than the night before. Thus, in the course of a year, all the stars become visible at one time or another.

It pays to note some of the more obvious relationships in the positions of the stars. Beginning with the Great Square of Pegasus, note that the most southerly star in the leading side is Markab. The most northerly star in the trailing side is Alpheratz. This side also forms the base of a triangle with Hamal at the apex. The leading side points to Fomalhaut, and the trailing side indicates the direction of Diphda.

The constellation of Orion serves to locate several stars. First note that Orion can be imagined to outline the figure of a man. There is a faintly indicated head, two shoulders consisting of Bellatrix and Betelgeuse, and a three-buttoned belt in which the center star is Alnilam. A dagger hangs down from the belt. Below the dagger is a bright star, Rigel, which is the left knee, and the right knee is indicated by a less bright star that is not a navigation star. The legs are not clearly outlined.

Follow the line of the belt downward to Orion's right, to Sirius, the Big Dog Star, the brightest star in the sky. Past Sirius comes the right-angled triangle which contains Adhara. Also on Orion's right, and roughly in line with the two shoulder stars, is Procyon, the Little Dog Star.

Follow the line of the belt upward, to Orion's left, and the constellation Taurus, the Bull, is visible as a V with a bright reddish star at the top of one branch. This star is Aldebaran. Past Aldebaran comes a pretty little constellation, looking somewhat like a dipper, known as the Pleiades or the Seven Little Sisters. They are not used in navigation.

If the observer sweeps his arm from Rigel, left knee, through Betelgeuse, right shoulder, he comes to a pair of stars known as Gemini, or the Heavenly Twins, Pollux and Castor. Although Castor is Alpha Geminorum and Pollux is Beta Geminorum, Pollux is the brighter of the two and is a navigation star. It is easy to tell which is which, because Castor is further north and slightly ahead of Pollux.

Next above the horizon will come the constellation of Leo, the Lion, which looks essentially like a sickle with a bright star, Regulus, at the end of the handle. Regulus and a fairly bright star in the curve of the sickle, together with two following stars, form an irregular rectangle. The two following stars form the base of a triangle, the apex of which is Denebola, the Tail of the Lion.

After Leo, but over in the southeast part of the horizon, comes a constellation of four stars that looks like a gaff mainsail. The constellation is Corvus, the Crow. The peak of the gaff points to a bright star, Spica, which will appear about an hour later.

The next bright star to appear over the horizon in north declination is Arcturus, a brilliant and beautiful star which is not readily mistaken for anything else. When the Big Dipper is visible, follow along the curve of the handle to come to Arcturus. If you continue further along the curve, you will be led to Spica. Shortly after Arcturus comes the Corona Borealis, a pretty crescent of stars with a single bright star, Alphecca, which is a navigation star.

Later, and still in north declination, comes the brilliant white star Vega, followed by the Northern Cross, slightly crooked, which is also called Cygnus, the Swan. The bright star at the top of the cross is called Deneb. In line with the cross arm of this constellation is Eltanin in Draco, the Dragon.

Vega is roughly in line with three stars in south declination, the center one of which, called Altair, is the brightest.

Low in the southeast horizon will now have appeared Scorpio, the constellation which really looks like a scorpion. There are several feelers, or stingers, radiating from a central bright star, Antares. The body of the scorpion curves away from Antares somewhat like a question mark, and the bright white star near the end of the tail is named Shaula.

Just below Scorpio comes a geometrical figure of stars, called Sagittarius, the Archer, but looking exactly like a teapot. It has a triangular lid, a handle, and a triangular spout. The star in the top of the handle is Nunki, and the star at the intersection of the base with the forward edge of the spout is called Kaus Australis. The teapot is constantly pouring hot tea on the tail of the scorpion, making it curl.

Below the teapot, but 4 hours later, comes a bright navigation star, Fomalhaut. This completes the main navigation stars in the central band as seen through a 24-hour period. Of course, you may have to wait several months before you will be able to see all of them. But learn what you can now, and later when you have developed the hobby you can locate all the navigation stars, including some of the weaker ones that have been omitted here. Because of your location in latitude, you may never be able to see the stars near the pole in the opposite latitude.

Stars Around the South Pole

The outstanding constellation near the celestial South Pole is the Southern Cross, which looks more like a kite. The cross revolves about the pole in such a manner that the stem of the cross always points in the direction of the celestial South Pole. There are no stars near the pole itself, and the foot of the cross, as marked by the star Acrux, is about 27° from the pole.

The Southern Cross is always readily identified by two very bright pointer stars, Alpha Centauri and Beta Centauri, which point directly to the top of the cross. The one farther away from the cross is Alpha Centauri, also known as Rigil Kentaurus, a favorite navigation star.

Following a line through the stem of the cross to the South Pole, an equal distance on the other side of the pole

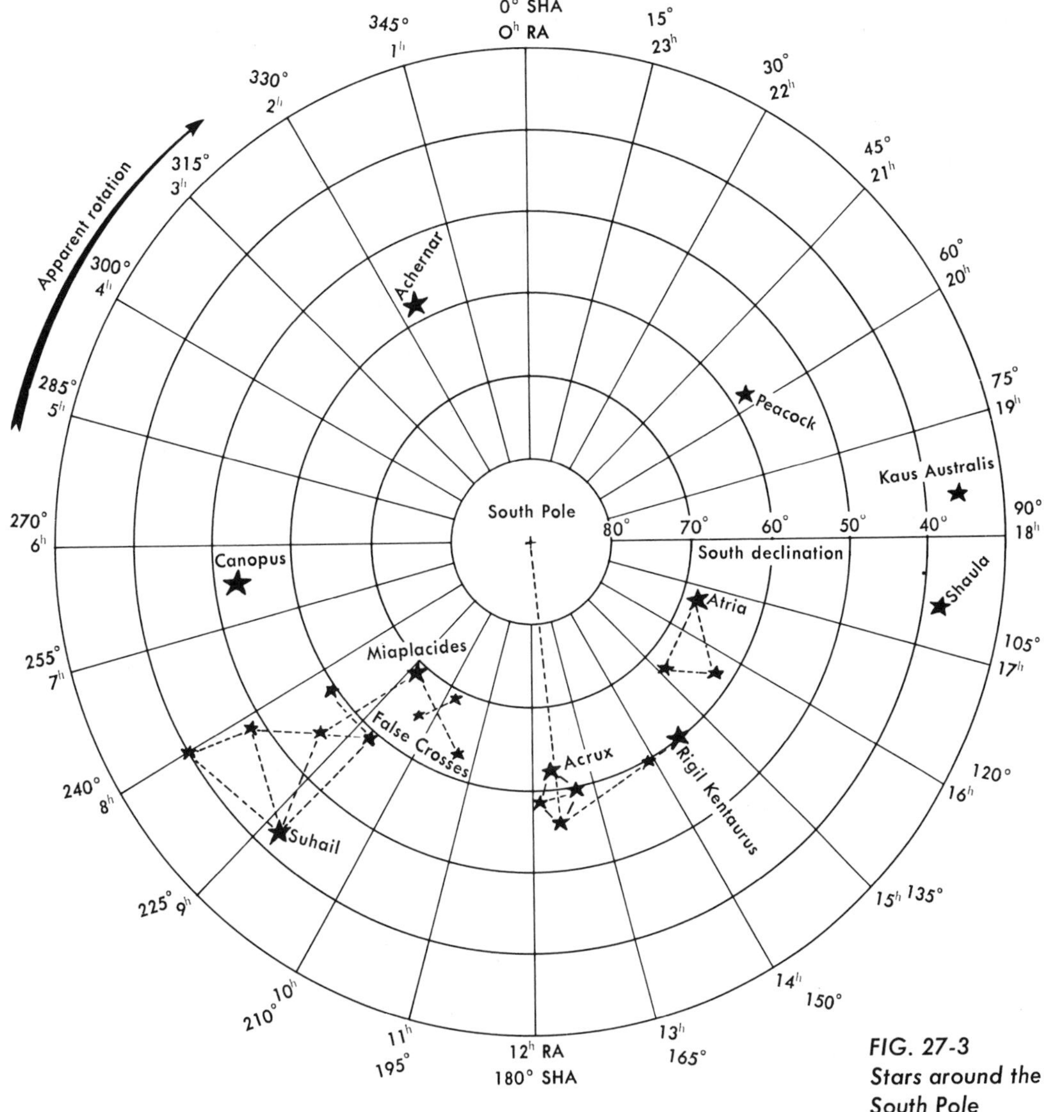

FIG. 27-3
Stars around the South Pole

is a bright star, Achernar, also used in navigation.

Approximately halfway between the cross and Achernar, going clockwise around the South Pole, is the second brightest star in the sky, Canopus.

There are several very weak navigation stars around the South Pole, but they are seldom used. There are also two "false" crosses, but a navigator familiar with the southern sky is not likely to make the mistake of using them. Whereas the stars around the celestial North Pole rotate counterclockwise, those around the South Pole rotate in a clockwise direction.

The Simex Star Finder

The Simex Star Finder was formerly marketed by the U.S. Navy as H.O. 2102-D, but since 1970 has been privately manufactured. It is a device that will predict the altitude and true bearing of a navigation star or planet, for any instant of time, anywhere in the world. The navigator uses it to determine beforehand which stars will be available for observation at twilight. With this information, he is able to begin taking sights before the stars are visible to the naked eye. He simply sets the sextant to the predicted altitude and sights at the horizon in the predicted direction. The star is quite easily picked up as a small white dot at or near the horizon, and in this manner much time is saved and many sights can be taken while the horizon is still clear, resulting in more accurate observations.

The Star Finder consists essentially of a white base plate with a circular diagram on each side, one for the northern hemisphere and one for the southern hemisphere, respectively identified by a large "N" or "S" in the center. The celestial pole is at the center of the diagram, and halfway from the pole to the edge of the plate is a circle denoting the celestial equator, the equinoctial. Around the outer edge of the plate is a circular scale marked in degrees and half-degrees, from 0° at the *hour circle of Aries* ♈ through 360°, denoting the right ascension of stars in degrees. On the plate itself, the navigation stars are plotted according to their RA and *declination.* On the side marked "N" for north, the stars between the pole and the equinoctial have north declination, and those outside the circle of the equinoctial are in south declination. On the side marked "S," the stars between the pole and the equinoctial are in south declination, those outside in north declination.

A series of transparent celluloid sheets, or platens, are provided for latitudes 10° apart—for 5°, 15°, 25°, 35°, etc. One side is marked "North Latitude" and the other side "South Latitude." Printed on these sheets in *blue* lines is an oval diagram with curved lines radiating from the center. One of these lines is straight and is extended from the center to the edge of the platen, terminating in a small arrow. The center of the oval diagram is the observer's

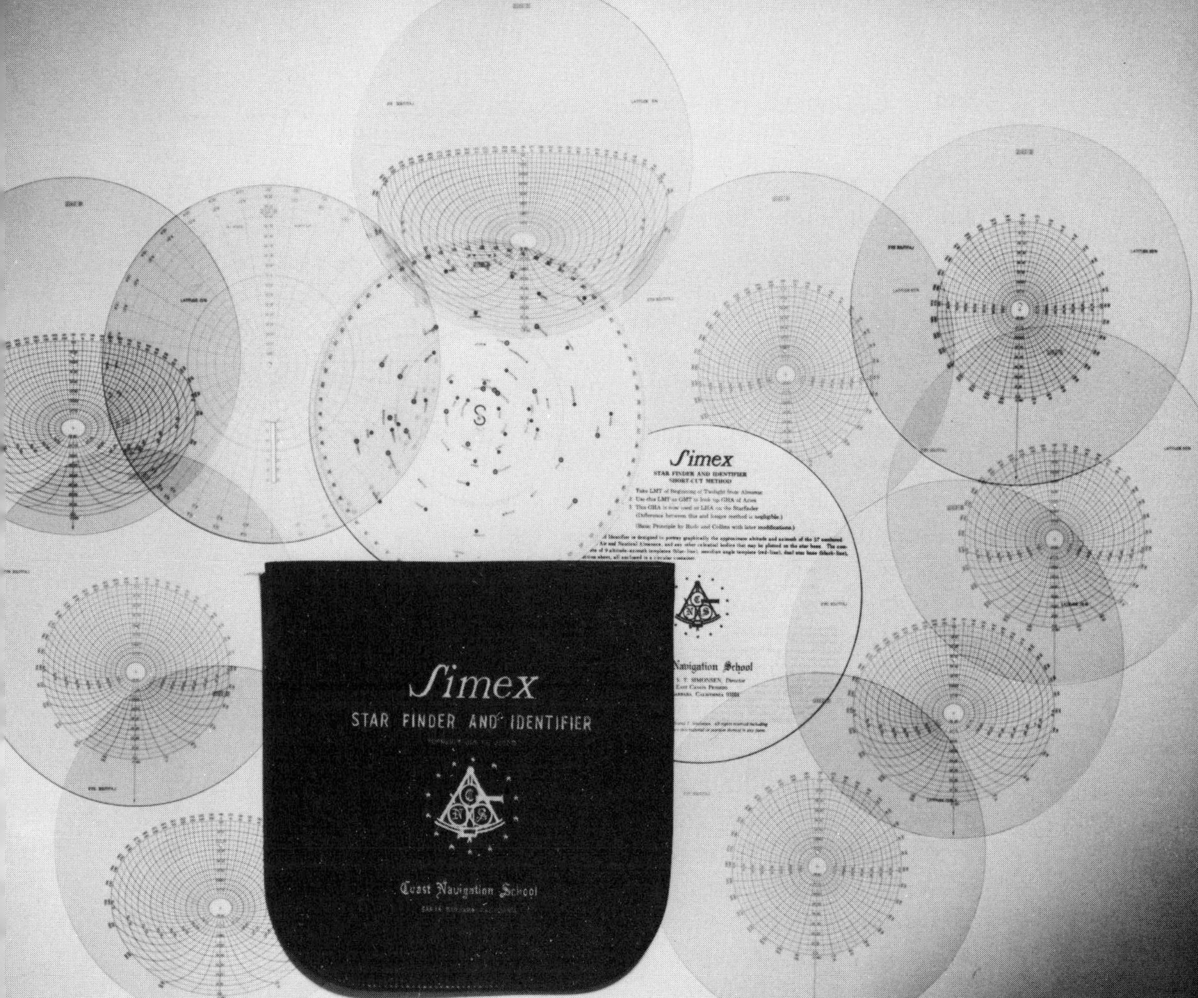

FIG. 27-4
Components of star finder

zenith point. The outer contour represents his horizon. Concentric ovals in blue lines are printed between the horizon and the zenith, every 5° apart, and labeled at every 10°. They measure altitude from the horizon, which is 0° altitude, to the zenith, which would be 90° altitude.

The curved lines radiating from the center indicate bearing, from 0° at the straight line to 180° on the opposite side of the diagram; intermediate bearings are labeled every 10°. At the center of this platen there is a small hole that enables us to mount it on a small peg at the center of the base plate. To use it in north latitude, the platen for the observer's approximate latitude (to the nearest 5°) is mounted on the base plate in such a manner that the *north side of both the base and the blue-line platen are up.* When used in south latitude, the south side of both base and platen must be used. This is important and must be checked carefully each time, as it is easy to make an error.

Printing of altitude and bearings on the transparent blue-line platen show through the plastic; so if the north side is up, the figures for the south side show in reverse and, of course, must not be used. A little practice will soon make it second nature for the navigator to select the correct arrangement. The straight line terminating in the arrow represents the observer's *meridian of longitude* as it would be projected on the celestial sphere, the familiar "*M*" of the hour circle diagram.

To use the Star Finder we orient our meridian, as represented by the straight blue line, with respect to the *hour circle of Aries,* "♈," on the base plate, according to the *local hour angle of Aries* at the instant of time for which the device is set up, usually the beginning of twilight. This means that we must first find the LHA of Aries.

The LMT of the beginning of *civil twilight* is listed in both almanacs daily for various deegrees of latitude. Remember that you do not use *nautical* twilight, which is also listed in the almanac. Knowing the time of the beginning of twilight, it is a simple matter to determine the LHA of Aries for that instant, in the same manner that we found it in Chapter 25, where we used it for determining latitude by Polaris. There is a shortcut which most navigators use, but first we shall present the steps of the theoretically correct method:

Step 1. Determine the LMT of the beginning of twilight from the almanac.

Step 2. Apply the DR longitude to LMT to find corresponding GMT.

Step 3. For this GMT, take the GHA of Aries from almanac.

Step 4. Apply DR longitude to the GHA of Aries to find the LHA of Aries (subtract west longitude, add east longitude).

Step 5. Apply zone description to GMT to determine zone time of beginning of twilight, so that you will know the time by your watch when you should begin to take sights. This is really not necessary, as you can judge when the time is right, but it does help you plan your activities.

The shortcut method, which gives results that are close enough for practical navigation, proceeds as follows:

Step 1. Find the LMT of beginning of twilight from almanac. Call it GMT.

Step 2. Use this GMT to determine the GHA of Aries from the almanac. Call this the LHA of Aries. Use this LHA ♈ to set up the Star Finder.

Note that in this method we simply omitted applying the longitude twice, once in time and once in degrees. You can prove the accuracy of this shortcut to yourself by working a problem both ways.

Having found the LHA of Aries, select the proper base plate, whether N or S, and the correct blue-line platen that is nearest to your latitude. Mount it on the peg on the base plate so that both sides show north or both show south. Set the arrow on the platen to the value for the LHA of Aries, using the outer degree scale on the base plate. On the base plate the hour circle of Aries is indicated at the 0° mark, so when you set the blue arrow to the value for LHA ♈, you have in effect placed your own meridian in the celestial sky for the instant of time concerned. You are now able to read the altitude and the bearing of visible navigation stars that show within the oval area that represents your visible sky. The altitudes of stars are determined by their location in relation to the concentric oval lines, and the bearings of stars can be read along the curved lines that radiate out from zenith and pass through or near the stars we are interested in. A certain amount of estimating is necessary, but if you come within one or two degrees of the actual position, you are close enough for practical purposes. Just make sure you do not read the reversed numbers on the platen—those which are to be used for the opposite side.

It is customary to list a larger number of stars than we intend to use, in case there is a cloudy sky and some may not be visible. Select the brighter stars, marked with a larger symbol on the base plate, and try to get good crossing angles and altitudes between 15° and 70°. Avoid stars at the zenith and those too close to the horizon.

Altitude and Bearings of Planets

Unlike stars, the planets change their position in the sky night after night, so they cannot be permanently shown on the base plate of the Star Finder. We must plot them each time we want to predict their positions at twilight. For this, the Star Finder provides a special transparent platen printed in *red.* There are various ways of using this platen, but the method that follows is the simplest. The only part of this platen that we are concerned with is the line with the arrow and the circle that represents the equinoctial. A slot is cut along this line, extending a small distance either side of the equinoctial for marking declinations on the base plate. The line itself represents the hour circle of the planet to be plotted.

Step 1. Determine the *right ascension and declination of each of the four planets.* The almanac gives daily the sidereal hour angle (SHA) of each planet in degrees close enough for the entire day. Remember that RA = 360° − SHA, so you simply subtract the SHA from 360° to find the right ascension in degrees, which is what we want. (Astronomers usually figure right ascension in time, but in this case we need it in degrees.) The declination is readily taken from the daily page for an approximately estimated GMT. The nearest hour is sufficiently accurate.

Step 2. Mount the *red-line platen* on the proper base plate, so that both read north or both read south. Now plot each planet in pencil on the base plate by setting the arrow to the *right ascension* on the outer degree scale of the base plate and by determining the proper declination north or south in the open slot. Marking to the nearest degree or two is close enough. Place a small symbol in pencil next to the mark, so that you will remember which planet is plotted at this point.

Step 3. Remove the red-line platen and replace it with the proper blue-line platen, the same you would have used for stars. By the same procedure you used to obtain the altitude and bearing of the stars, you now obtain the correct positions of the planets that are visible. If you have plotted all four, you will, of course, find that one or more is outside your horizon diagram, because it is not visible at this twilight. You can safely leave it plotted on the base plate for the next twilight, however, as the daily change is not that great.

When you come to take sights before the stars or planets are visible to the naked eye but clearly visible in a good sextant telescope, you may find that you have to do a little searching to locate the body. Assuming that you are looking in the right direction—and here you should swing your sextant across a 10° or so azimuth—try moving the micrometer drum a full turn in both directions and look again. With a little practice you will soon pick it up, but the nature of the Star Finder is such that it is only accurate within a degree or two.

The Star Finder is also used to plot Venus for a daytime sight, proceeding exactly as before, plotting its position first on the base plate, figuring the LHA ♈ for the time of intended observation, and determining predicted altitude and bearing.

There are other star finders on the market, but most are difficult to use, whereas over many years the instrument described has been found to be simplest to use.

Example • This example is given so that you make sure you have correctly set up your own Star Finder and have correctly read the data. Assuming that you are in DR latitude 32° S and that the LHA ♈ is 56°, list the main available navigation stars.

Set up the Star Finder, using the *south base plate* and the *south side* of the blue-line platen for 35° S latitude. Set the blue arrow to 56°. Now take out the altitude and bearings of the brighter stars, setting up a table as follows:

STAR	*ALTITUDE*	*BEARING*
Aldebaran	38°	015°
Rigel	57°	044°
Procyon	22°	067°
Sirius	46°	088°
Canopus	57°	136°
Acrux	15°	189°
Achernar	58°	214°
Fomalhaut	30°	253°
Diphda	46°	280°
Hamal	28°	334°

Chapter 28

Compass Error and Compass Adjusting

The deviation in a ship's compass is caused by magnetic metallic objects, electrical wiring, and the proximity of electronic equipment that has been installed near the compass. If the vessel is built of wood or fiberglass, the hull itself will not create a magnetic field, and deviation can then be traced to the sources mentioned. However, if the vessel has a steel hull and a steel superstructure, there is an inherent and more or less constant deviation due to this mass of steel and iron. The effect of deviation is to cause the compass needle to swing a certain amount east or west of magnetic north. In most cases deviation can be compensated for by the placement or adjustment of magnets either inside or around the compass, but if this does not remove all of the deviation, or if no compensation of the compass has taken place, it is customary to set up a deviation table for various headings of the vessel, usually 15° apart. This table is consulted and a new deviation is applied to the magnetic course every time the vessel changes to a new course.

However, deviation is subject to change from time to time, and is readily affected if magnetic objects are placed near the compass. Thus, to make sure there is no new or unknown error, it is customary on large vessels to check the compass error at least once a day and always when the course is changed. On smaller vessels, during long voyages the compass error should be checked at least once a day. This is usually done by taking a compass bearing on a celestial object at the same time that a regular sextant observation is made. The compass bearing is compared to the computed azimuth Z_n, and the difference is the total compass error. To this the variation for the locality is applied, and the amount due to deviation is thus determined. Whenever a compass has been adjusted, either by a professional compass adjuster or by the navigator himself, the last step is to "swing ship," which means placing the vessel on successive headings 30° apart in order to determine the residual deviation, if any, on each of these headings. These are then listed in a new deviation table.

Determining Compass Error On large vessels there are usually adequate facilities for taking bearings on a celestial body. Since most larger vessels have a gyrocompass, indicating true north, with repeaters on the wings of the bridge and on the upper bridge, the bearing is taken using an *azimuth ring* mounted on the repeater. At the time the bearing is taken, the compass course on the magnetic compass is read, as well as the gyro course. First the error of the gyro, if any, is determined. When applied to the gyro course it will give a corrected gyro, or *true,* course. The difference between this true course and the compass course is the total compass error, from which the deviation for this heading is determined. Although a vessel may have an elaborate gyrocompass, it is affected by power failure and other difficulties, and the navigator must at all times be prepared to rely on his magnetic compass.

Example 1 • A vessel is steering 110° by gyro. When exactly on 110° gyro, the compass course reads 125°. Variation is 15° W in this locality. A bearing is taken by gyro repeater on the sun, bearing 145°. When the sight is computed, using any navigation table, the Z_n of the sun is 148° for the instant of the observation. This means that the gyro has an error of 3° E. Therefore, when the magnetic compass course read 125°, the true course, or corrected gyro course, was actually 113°. The total compass error on the magnetic compass is therefore 125° − 113° = 12° W. Since the variation in the locale is 15° W, the magnetic compass has a deviation of 3° *east* when on compass course 125°. (See Fig. 28–1.)

Smaller vessels do not have gyros, and the magnetic compass is often placed in a position where it is impossible to take bearings directly over the compass. In that case, a *pelorus,* or "dumb compass," can be used to good advantage. It has an adjustable compass card over which is

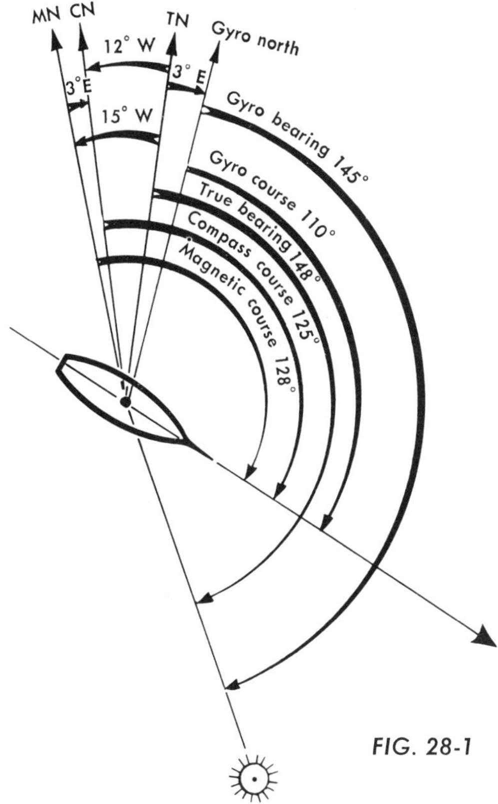

FIG. 28-1

mounted a pair of sighting vanes for taking bearings on either landmarks or celestial objects. It can be mounted in some convenient place on the vessel, such as the top of the wheelhouse or cabin, where visibility is good in all directions. Most peloruses are portable so they can be stowed when not in use. However, a pelorus has a lubber's line so that it can readily be aligned with the ship's keel. It is customary to set the card on the pelorus to the compass course being steered. When the ship is exactly on course, the pelorus is then a duplicate of the compass and a bearing taken will be a compass bearing. Since the compass points in the direction of magnetic north, this would be the magnetic bearing, if there were no deviation. For the instant of the observation, Z_n is computed, and by applying the variation to Z_n, the magnetic bearing of the celestial body is found. Comparing this with the actual compass bearing, the difference is the deviation for that heading.

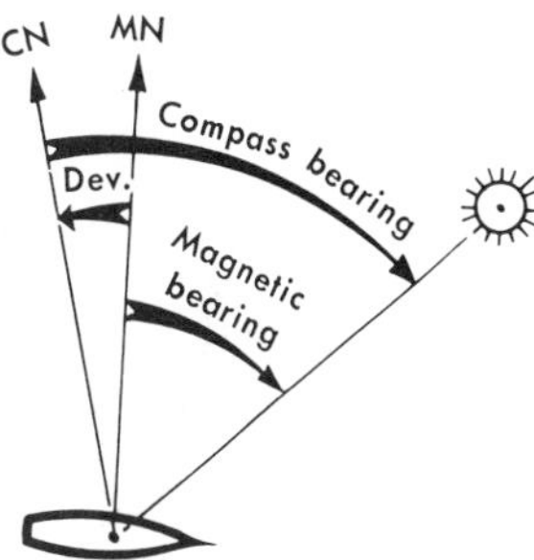

FIG. 28-2

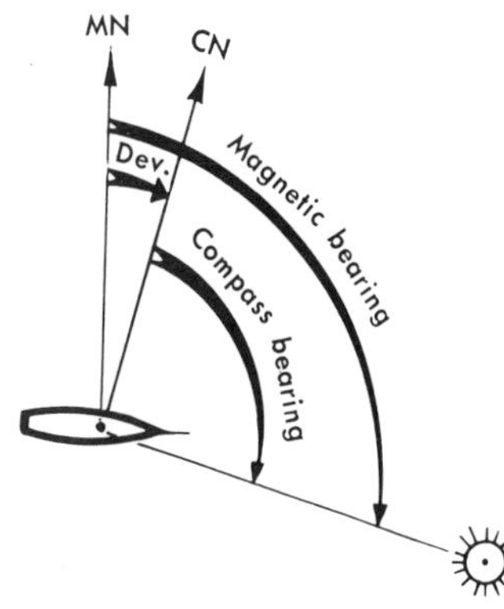

Remember • If the compass bearing is greater than the magnetic bearing, the *deviation is west.* If the compass bearing is less than the magnetic bearing, the *deviation is east.*

Example 2 • The vessel is on a course of 250° by compass. The variation (always available on the chart of the locality) is 10° E. The pelorus is set to 250°. When exactly on course, a bearing is taken on Venus, reading 140° by compass. A quick computation is made to find that Z_n is 154°. With 10° E variation, the magnetic bearing of Venus is 144°. Since the bearing by compass was 140°, it means that the deviation is 4° E.

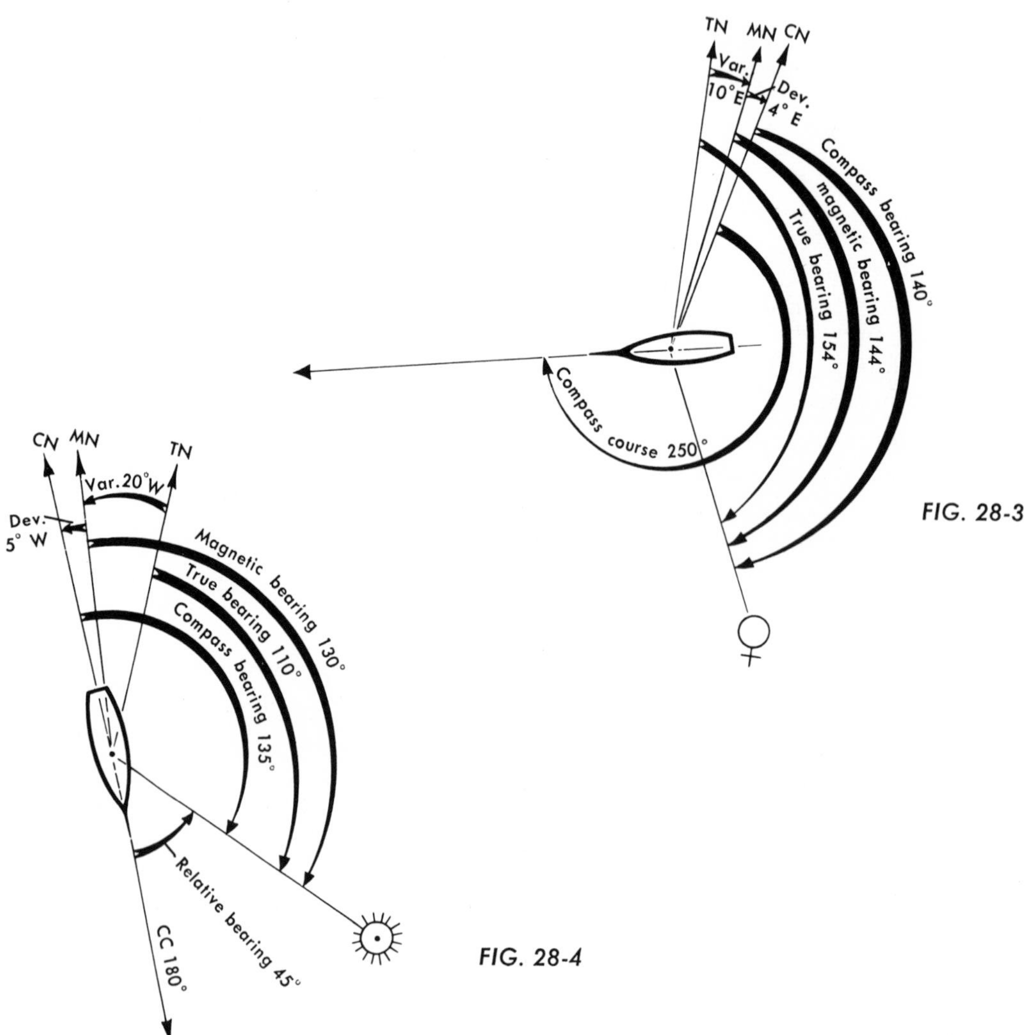

FIG. 28-3

FIG. 28-4

Sometimes it is more convenient to set the pelorus with 0° at the lubber's line and read relative bearings—usually when the going is rough and it is difficult to hold the vessel on a steady course. In that case, the relative bearing is applied to the compass course to find the corresponding compass bearing.

Example 3 • Vessel is on heading 180° by compass. Pelorus is set with 0° at the lubber's line, and a bearing on the sun is taken reading 45° on the port bow. Compass bearing is thus 180° − 45° = 135°. Variation for the area is 20° W. Z_n of the sun figures out to be 110°. Magnetic bearing is thus 130°. Deviation is 135° − 130° = 5° *west.* (See Fig. 28–4.)

Many navigators check for deviation by taking bearings at the same time they take regular sights, such as morning or afternoon sun sights. Since it is not possible to take a bearing exactly at the same time the sextant observation is made, there is room for a small error if the interval between the bearing and the sextant sight is more than a minute or two. The sun moves about 1° in azimuth every 4 minutes. The advantage of this method is that the navigator does not have to make a separate calculation for Z_n, but can use the same azimuth for plotting the LOP and for comparing bearings. However, for careful work, it is well worth taking the time and trouble to get a really good bearing and computing the Z_n for the exact time of the bearing.

Swinging Ship

Whenever anything has been done to a vessel that could change the deviation—such as alterations to the superstructure or installation of new equipment—it is customary to swing ship to determine what the new deviation is on various headings. Likewise, after a compass has been compensated, the adjuster swings ship to determine what deviation may still be left on certain headings.

The procedure generally used is to determine in advance the time and place for the operation. It is necessary to have sufficient room to maneuver on various headings, and the time should be chosen when the sun is not too high in the sky. For the time interval deemed necessary for the operation, a table of *azimuths of the sun* is prepared in advance, giving the Z_n of the sun for every 4 minutes. By applying the variation of the locality, the navigator then sets up a parallel column of *magnetic bearings of the sun* for the same instants of time. As the ship is placed on various headings 30° apart, actual compass bearings are taken on the sun and carefully timed. Deviation is then determined by comparing compass bearings with magnetic bearings for the same moment of time. For this work, bearings can be taken with an ordinary pelorus, but compass adjusters prefer to use the shadow-pin device, called a *compass corrector,* which they use while compensating the compass. (See Fig. 28–5.)

The following example will demonstrate the entire process. A compass corrector will be used. Remember that the reading of the shadow pin indicates the reciprocal of the sun's bearing and must be corrected by 180° to obtain the true direction of the sun.

FIG. 28-5
Compass corrector
(COURTESY AQUA METER)

Example 4 • Before beginning a long voyage, you decide to swing ship and make up a new deviation table. You are on San Francisco Bay, lat. 37°49′ N, long. 122°25′ W, and you decide to swing ship on January 4 between 1000 and 1100 zone time. Proceed as follows:

Step 1. Set up table of azimuths of the sun for 4-minute intervals from 1000 to 1100. You can use either almanac and any set of navigation tables you wish. We shall use the *Nautical Almanac* and N.O. 214. Remember that the meridian angle *t* must come out in whole degrees and that it diminishes 1° every 4 minutes up to noon, at which time it reaches zero and begins to increase again. The variation at San Francisco is taken at 15° E. (See *Nautical Almanac* and H.O. 214 excerpts in Fig. 28–6.)

Step 2. Time zone is +8, so ZT of 1000 is GMT of 1800. To make *t* come out in whole degrees, we must make the minutes in the GHA equal the minutes in the longitude.

Longitude	122° 25′
GHA of Sun at 1800 on January 4	88° 44.6′
Difference	33° 40.4′

From the I&C tables in the yellow pages, we find that it takes the sun 2^m42^s to travel 40.4′ of arc.

GHA of sun at 1800	88° 44.6′
GHA of sun for 2^m42^s	40.4′
GHA for 18-02-42 (1803)	89° 25′
Longitude	122° 25′
At GMT 1803, WT 1003, *t* is	33° *east*

Step 3. We can now set up the following table from N.O. 214, using latitude 38°N, dec. S 22°30′.

WT	t	$Z = Z_n$	− Var. 15° E	Magnetic Bearing
1003	33°	147.1°		132.1°
07	32	148.0		133.0
11	31	148.9		133.9
15	30	149.8		134.8
19	29	150.7		135.7
23	28	151.6		136.6
27	27	152.6		137.6
31	26	153.5		138.5
35	25	154.5		139.5
39	24	155.4		140.4
43	23	156.4		141.4
47	22	157.3		142.3
51	21	158.3		143.3
55	20	159.3		144.3
59	19	160.3		145.3
1103	18	161.3		146.3

Step 4. You are now ready to swing ship. On each course the movable compass card on the compass corrector is set to the compass course. You begin taking bearings at about 1000, note the time of each shadow pin reading carefully, and record the readings as shown in the following table. For the watch time of each reading, select, by interpolation where necessary, the correct magnetic bearing to the *nearest whole degree* from the table previously set up, and write these values alongside the corresponding compass bearings in the second table. Work out the deviation for each compass heading, using the following *rule:*

1. *When compass bearing is greater than magnetic bearing, deviation is west.*
2. *When compass bearing is less than magnetic bearing, deviation is east.*

		Shadow-pin			DEVIATION	
CH	WT	Reading	CB	MB	West	East
000°	1003	313°	133°	132°	1°	
030°	08	315	135	133	2°	
060°	13	318	138	134	4°	
090°	19	321	141	136	5°	
120°	24	320	140	137	3°	
150°	28	319	139	138	1°	
180°	34	319	139	139	0°	0°
210°	39	318	138	140		2°
240°	44	319	139	142		3°
170°	50	318	138	143		5°
300°	55	321	141	144		3°
330°	1100	324	144	145		1°
360°	1104	327	147	146	1°	

We can read the compass corrector to the nearest degree only, so we use whole degrees for compass bearings and for magnetic bearings. Deviation is always worked out in whole degrees, since you cannot steer any closer than that. Having worked out the second table, you are now ready to set up the actual deviation table. As shown below, we have set it up for compass headings 30° apart, but many navigators like to have a deviation table for every 15°, and therefore interpolate deviation for intermediate headings.

DEVIATION TABLE

COMPASS	DEVIATION		MAGNETIC
HEADING	WEST	EAST	HEADING
000°	1°		359°
030°	2°		028°
060°	4°		056°
090°	5°		085°
120°	3°		117°
150°	1°		149°
180°	—	—	180°
210°		2°	212°
240°		3°	243°
270°		5°	275°
300°		3°	303°
330°		1°	331°
360°	1°		359°

JANUARY 4,

G.M.T. d h	SUN G.H.A. ° ′	Dec. ° ′
4 00	178 49·7	S 22 47·4
01	193 49·5	47·1
02	208 49·2	46·9
03	223 48·9	. . 46·6
04	238 48·6	46·3
05	253 48·3	46·1
06	268 48·0	S 22 45·8
07	283 47·7	45·6
08	298 47·4	45·3
S 09	313 47·2	. . 45·1
U 10	328 46·9	44·8
N 11	343 46·6	44·5
D 12	358 46·3	S 22 44·3
A 13	13 46·0	44·0
Y 14	28 45·7	43·8
15	43 45·5	. . 43·5
16	58 45·2	43·2
17	73 44·9	43·0
18	88 44·6	S 22 42·7
19	103 44·3	42·4
20	118 44·0	42·2
21	133 43·7	. . 41·9
22	148 43·5	41·6
23	163 43·2	41·4

DECLINATION **CONTRARY** NAME TO LATITUDE

Lat. 38°

22° 00′ Alt. ° ′	Δd	Δt	Az. °	22° 30′ Alt. ° ′	Δd	Δt	Az. °	23° 00′ Alt. ° ′	Δd	Δt	Az. °	H.A. °
30 00.0	1.0	01	180.0	**29 30.0**	1.0	01	180.0	**29 00.0**	1.0	01	180.0	**00**
29 59.6	1.0	02	178.9	**29 29.6**	1.0	02	178.9	**28 59.6**	1.0	02	178.9	1
29 58.2	1.0	04	177.9	**29 28.2**	1.0	04	177.9	**28 58.3**	1.0	04	177.9	2
29 56.0	1.0	05	176.8	**29 26.1**	1.0	05	176.8	**28 56.1**	1.0	05	176.8	3
29 52.9	1.0	07	175.7	**29 23.0**	1.0	07	175.8	**28 53.1**	1.0	06	175.8	4
29 49.0	1.0	08	174.7	**29 19.1**	1.0	08	174.7	**28 49.2**	1.0	08	174.7	**05**
29 44.1	1.0	10	173.6	**29 14.3**	1.0	09	173.6	**28 44.4**	1.0	09	173.7	6
29 38.4	99	11	172.5	**29 08.6**	99	11	172.6	**28 38.8**	99	11	172.7	7
29 31.8	99	12	171.5	**29 02.1**	99	12	171.5	**28 32.3**	99	12	171.6	8
29 24.4	99	14	170.4	**28 54.7**	99	14	170.5	**28 25.0**	99	14	170.6	9
29 16.1	99	15	169.4	**28 46.5**	99	15	169.5	**28 16.8**	99	15	169.5	**10**
29 06.9	99	17	168.3	**28 37.4**	99	17	168.4	**28 07.8**	99	16	168.5	1
28 57.0	98	18	167.3	**28 27.5**	98	18	167.4	**27 58.0**	98	18	167.5	2
28 46.1	98	19	166.2	**28 16.7**	98	19	166.4	**27 47.3**	98	19	166.5	3
28 34.5	98	21	165.2	**28 05.2**	98	21	165.3	**27 35.9**	98	20	165.4	4
28 22.0	97	22	164.2	**27 52.8**	97	22	164.3	**27 23.6**	97	22	164.4	**15**
28 08.7	97	24	163.2	**27 39.6**	97	23	163.3	**27 10.5**	97	23	163.4	6
27 54.6	97	25	162.1	**27 25.6**	97	25	162.3	**26 56.6**	97	24	162.4	7
27 39.7	96	26	161.1	**27 10.8**	96	26	161.3	**26 42.0**	96	26	161.4	8
27 24.0	96	27	160.1	**26 55.3**	96	27	160.3	**26 26.5**	96	27	160.4	9
27 07.5	95	29	159.1	**26 38.9**	95	28	159.3	**26 10.3**	95	28	159.5	**20**
26 50.3	95	30	158.1	**26 21.8**	95	30	158.3	**25 53.3**	95	30	158.5	1
26 32.3	94	31	157.2	**26 04.0**	94	31	157.3	**25 35.6**	94	31	157.5	2
26 13.6	94	32	156.2	**25 45.4**	94	32	156.4	**25 17.2**	94	32	156.6	3
25 54.1	93	34	155.2	**25 26.1**	93	33	155.4	**24 58.0**	94	33	155.6	4
25 33.9	93	35	154.3	**25 06.1**	93	35	154.5	**24 38.1**	93	34	154.7	**25**
25 13.1	92	36	153.3	**24 45.3**	92	36	153.5	**24 17.6**	93	35	153.7	6
24 51.5	92	37	152.4	**24 23.9**	92	37	152.6	**23 56.3**	92	37	152.8	7
24 29.2	91	38	151.4	**24 01.8**	91	38	151.6	**23 34.3**	91	38	151.9	8
24 06.2	91	39	150.5	**23 39.0**	91	39	150.7	**23 11.7**	91	39	151.0	9
23 42.6	90	40	149.6	**23 15.5**	90	40	149.8	**22 48.4**	90	40	150.0	**30**
23 18.4	90	42	148.7	**22 51.4**	90	41	148.9	**22 24.5**	90	41	149.1	1
22 53.5	89	43	147.8	**22 26.7**	89	42	148.0	**21 59.9**	89	42	148.3	2
22 27.9	89	44	146.9	**22 01.4**	89	43	147.1	**21 34.7**	89	43	147.4	3
22 01.8	88	45	146.0	**21 35.4**	88	44	146.2	**21 09.0**	88	44	146.5	4
21 35.0	87	46	145.1	**21 08.8**	87	45	145.4	**20 42.6**	88	45	145.6	**35**

FIG. 28-6
Excerpts from Nautical Almanac *and* H.O. 214

Compass Adjusting

Many boatmen consider compass adjusting as a kind of black art practiced by a breed of specialists who commune with the sun, but certainly not with ordinary mortals. Actually, compass adjusting *is* a very fine art where large steel vessels and complicated magnetic fields are involved, but on yachts and smaller vessels the process is quite simple, and any skipper worth his salt should be able to compensate his own compass.

On a typical yacht of wood- or plastic-hull construction, it is usually possible to remove all deviation, unless there exists some unusual condition. With a steel hull, the situation can become a little more involved, and it may not always be possible to remove all the deviation. In that case, you remove as much as you can and make up a deviation table for the rest.

The magnetic compass is influenced by metal, wiring, or equipment in the boat, setting up the deviation. If the vessel has a steel hull, the hull itself has a strong magnetic field that gives you deviation. Let us talk first about boats with wood, plastic, or aluminum hulls. Deviation here is due entirely to magnetic influences in the vicinity of the compass, and we overcome or eliminate it with magnets by setting up a countermagnetic field. These magnets are usually built into newer compasses, but if your compass is not of this type, small deck magnets are placed around the compass at proper distances to eliminate deviation.

This type of deviation is at maximum on north-south and east-west headings. If we eliminate the error on these headings, we usually don't have to worry about anything in between. On a north-south heading, the error is removed with a deck magnet placed athwartship, centered across a fore-and-aft line through the center of the compass—or it is adjusted with built-in magnets by turning the adjusting screw on the right- or left-hand side of the compass (using a nonmagnetic screwdriver).

On an east-west heading (and it does not matter whether you are headed east or west), the error is removed with a deck magnet placed fore and aft, alongside the compass, and centered across an athwartship line through the center of the compass. If you have built-in magnets, you adjust this error with the adjusting screw found usually on the front of the compass (but sometimes on the back). On most modern compasses these adjusting screws are actually marked "N-S" or "E-W." In any case, if you are on a north-south heading, turning the "E-W" screw will not affect the compass, and vice versa.

Before adjusting the compass, make sure that all normal gear is in its proper place in the vicinity of the compass. Remember, if you place a camera with a built-in light-meter, a portable radio, steel tools, or even a steel beer can close to the compass, you induce error while it remains there. All wires near the compass should be twisted, and you should avoid using magnetic doorlatches in this area.

When ready to begin, place the ship first on a north or

south heading by compass, whichever is away from shore. Now, by means we shall discuss later, turn the vessel around and double back on the same track. If you first headed north, your compass should now read south. If it does not—and it rarely does—the difference is twice the deviation on that heading. Have your helmsman remain on that reverse track, usually by steering for a landmark (which is the reason you headed away from shore initially). Turn the adjusting screw on the side of the compass until you have removed half the error, or place a deck magnet athwartship on the fore-and-aft line of the compass, moving it away from or toward the compass, until half of the error is removed. Now place a piece of Scotch tape over the magnet to hold it in place for the time being. Repeat this process and make further refinements in the magnets, until you get an exact north or south reading on the return trip.

Example • You head north by compass, then double back on the same track. The compass should read 180° but it reads 160°. This means 10° deviation. Keep the vessel on the same track and adjust the magnets so that the compass reads 170°. You will probably have to make several runs before you get a perfect reading on the return trip—so be prepared to be patient.

Next, do the same thing on an east-west heading, this time using the adjusting screw located on the front of the compass, or placing a deck magnet fore and aft alongside and on the center line of the compass. It is necessary to have a good helmsman, and unless the water is fairly calm, don't bother with it. Wait for a calm day.

When all error is removed on the cardinal headings, you will probably find no deviation on any other heading. However, we always swing ship to make sure.

All of this is really quite easy if you do not have any abnormal deviation. If you do, and you cannot overcome it, call in the professional adjuster. However, the real difficulty usually lies in getting on the proper headings and staying there. There are several ways of doing this, one of which is quite good and very simple.

Select an area where there is enough room around a buoy, half a mile or so in all directions. Passing close to the buoy on the north compass heading, make a run of half a mile or so. Now drop overboard a paper marker (I have found that almost anything will do), quickly spin around, sail down the marker, and head back for the buoy. In this way you are on the same track and have time to make your adjustment before you reach the buoy. Do the same thing on an east-west run.

In some harbors there are ranges running magnetic north-south or east-west, but this is rather rare. If you are lucky enough to have this, simply put the boat on a north magnetic course on the range and adjust the magnets until the compass reads north. Do the same thing on an east heading, and you are finished. However, it is always necessary to check this on a reverse run, and should there be any error when the course is reversed, it is best to halve it with the magnets.

Now let us discuss the best way of doing it, the way the professional adjuster usually works. We use a sun pelorus. The following is a step-by-step procedure:

Step 1. Head the vessel north or south by compass, away from shore. Have the helmsman continuously say "On—on—on—on" while he is on course, and "Off—off—off—off" while he is off course. When he is on course, set the pelorus (with compass card screwed down tight) so that the sun's shadow is exactly 180°. Here you are not concerned whether the instrument is in line with the keel. It does not matter, but it should be set on a surface or held by hand so that it does not move with vibration.

Step 2. Tell the helmsman to come about and head on the reverse course by compass—north or south, as the case may be. If there is no deviation, the shadow will fall on 0° or N, but since there probably is error, it won't. The difference again is twice the deviation. Say that the shadow is on 350°. Now tell the helmsman to come to port 5°, until the shadow is on 355°. At that point, tell him to pick a landmark and hold a steady course. You remain at the pelorus long enough for him to get settled on his landmark and to make sure the shadow is still on 355°. Now adjust your magnets so that the compass reads north or south, whichever the case may be. You have now removed the error—you hope.

Step 3. Repeat this performance until you get the shadow exactly at 0° every time you make the reverse run. Here again, it takes patience, but it pays off.

Remember • Because the sun moves about 1° in azimuth every 4 minutes, you cannot wait too long between readings. Usually, however, we can set the pelorus to 180°, turn about, and make the adjustment in less than 2 minutes.

Step 4. Repeat this entire procedure on the east-west heading. When you have the error out on the cardinal headings, you must swing ship. Line up the lubber's line of the pelorus with the keel of the boat and set the compass card to read 0° on the lubber's line. Have the helmsman steer 0° by compass. Have him continuously say "On—on—on—on" while he is on course, and when he is on course read the shadow pin and the time and write both down. Now change the course to 30° and move the pelorus card to read 30° on the lubber's line also. It must always read the same as the compass. Again read the shadow and the time. Continue this way all around the compass.

If there is no residual deviation, the reading of the shadow pin should be the same on all headings, since it is set to the compass and since the sun does not move, except for the 1° every 4 minutes. If you do the work well, you will usually find that there is no deviation left in the compass readings. In all this, we must be reasonable and practical. The helmsman cannot always be within 1° of the course, and there is always the sluggishness of the compass to consider. The shadow of the pin is nearly 1° wide. However, neither can you steer within 1° when you are under way; so if you can get the deviation down to 1°, you can write it off as *no deviation.*

However, it is possible that, due to an unusual situation in your boat, there is still deviation left. In that case you can set up a table and calculate the deviation on each heading. You will then have to consult this deviation table each time you change course.

Always check to see if your compass is affected when you turn on such electrical equipment as radar, radios, electric windshield wipers, automatic pilot, radio direction finder, and fathometer. If so, this must be reckoned with, although you cannot adjust for such error. Simply get the vessel on the right course with the equipment turned off. Hold the course and switch it on. Whatever the new compass reading is, that is the course you must continue to steer.

Finally, let us consider the steel hull. It has a complex magnetic field, and on large vessels we must use heeling magnets and Flinders bars to overcome some of it, but in the smaller steel vessels such elaborate facilities are not available in the compass. However, the larger part of the deviation is still removed from the compass by magnets placed as described before, while the vessel is on the cardinal headings. In addition, a steel vessel will have what is called *quadrantal deviation,* introduced on intercardinal headings only. This can be compensated for by placing a hollow, soft-iron sphere, known as a *quadrantal sphere,* on each side of the compass.

The first step is to turn each sphere through 180° to see if that affects the compass. If either one does—and it must not—then it has somehow become invested with permanent magnetism and has to be demagnetized before it can be used. This will seldom happen, but should it occur, take the sphere to a TV repair shop. They will have a degaussing coil to do the job.

Assuming that the two spheres are all right, then simply place them in a midway position on their adjusting arms. Adjust the compass as before on the N-S and E-W headings. These spheres are of soft iron, and will not affect the compass on cardinal headings. When you are finished with the work previously described, place the vessel on a north heading and set the pelorus so that the shadow falls on north also.

Now swing the vessel to a course of 45° and settle on the new course. The shadow should now be on an intercardinal mark also. If it is not, change the course slightly until it is on the mark, and have the helmsman steer for a landmark on this new course. Now move the spheres in or out, keeping them symmetrically aligned at equal distances from the compass, until the compass reads 45° again. Having done this, there should be no deviation on any other intercardinal heading. However, we always swing ship to check, and if there is still deviation and we cannot get rid of it, then we must prepare a deviation table.

Once the error has been removed from the compass it will stay that way, unless and until you make some change that affects the compass magnets. Therefore, after you have had work done in the vicinity of the compass, always check it. On all long voyages, where you have plenty of time on your hands anyway, you should check your deviation by bearings on the sun regularly. For example, in ocean racing, where inches may count, you cannot afford to be going in the wrong direction because your compass is off.

Appendix

A.

NAUTICAL PUBLICATIONS

The mariner has available to him an enormous amount of valuable information in the form of charts and special publications, all designed to help him get where he is going safely and directly. This chapter outlines the main sources of such information and lists the more important and interesting publications. Because prices are subject to change, they have been omitted in most instances, but in each situation the latest appropriate catalog should be consulted for prices and ordering or purchasing addresses.

In the United States, the main agencies that furnish maritime charts and publications are as follows:

National Ocean Survey (formerly the U.S. Coast and Geodetic Survey)

a. Charts of American coastal waters
b. U.S. coast pilots, for American coastal waters only
c. Tide tables, covering most of the world
d. Tidal current tables, for American and foreign coasts
e. Tidal current charts, for American ports only
f. Charts of Great Lakes and connecting waters

U.S. Naval Observatory

All publications are sold through the Superintendent of Documents, U.S. Government Printing Office, Washington, D.C.

a. *Nautical Almanac*
b. *Air Almanac*

U.S. Coast Guard

All publications are sold through the Superintendent of Documents, U.S. Government Printing Office, Washington, D.C.

a. Light lists for U.S. coastal waters
b. Miscellaneous books and booklets pertaining to the regulation of vessels and their personnel

U.S. Army Corps of Engineers

a. Charts of U.S. navigable rivers

Naval Oceanographic Office (formerly the U.S. Hydrographic Office)

a. Charts of foreign waters
b. Miscellaneous charts and publications, navigation tables, etc.
c. Special charts and publications for official Navy use only

The National Ocean Survey and the Naval Oceanographic Office sell their publications directly to the public and through a network of agents across the country and abroad. Nearly every foreign country has a hydrographic office of its own that publishes charts and current tables for local waters. A complete listing of such offices is found at the end of the chapter. The Hydrographic Office of the British Admiralty also publishes charts for the entire world, as well as a number of valuable nautical publications. The sections that follow do not list *all* the publications of these organizations, but list in detail those that are most important to the navigator of large and small vessels.

National Ocean Survey

Catalogs

Nautical Chart Catalog 1: U.S. Atlantic and Gulf Coasts, including Puerto Rico and the Virgin Islands (Free)
Nautical Chart Catalog 2: Pacific Coast, including Hawaii, Guam, and Samoa Islands (Free)
Nautical Chart Catalog 3: Alaska (Free)
Index to Bathymetric Maps of various areas of the Continental Shelf (Free)

Special Publications

United States Coast Pilots as follows ($2.50 each):
No. 1 Eastport to Cape Cod
No. 2 Cape Cod to Sandy Hook
No. 3 Sandy Hook to Cape Henry
No. 4 Cape Henry to Key West

No. 5 Gulf of Mexico, Puerto Rico, and Virgin Islands
No. 7 California, Oregon, Washington, and Hawaii
No. 8 Alaska, Dixon Entrance to Cape Spencer
No. 9 Alaska, Cape Spencer to Beaufort Sea

Tide Tables as follows ($2.00 each):
East Coast, North and South America
West Coast, North and South America
Europe and West Coast of Africa
Central and Western Pacific and Indian Oceans

Tidal Current Tables as follows ($2.00 each):
Atlantic Coast of North America
Pacific Coast of North America and Asia

Tidal Current Charts (sets of twelve) as follows ($1.00 per set):
Boston Harbor
Narragansett Bay to Nantucket Sound
Narragansett Bay
Long Island Sound and Block Island Sound
New York Harbor
Delaware Bay and River
Upper Chesapeake Bay
Charleston Harbor, S.C.
San Francisco Bay
Puget Sound, Northern Part
Puget Sound, Southern Part
Chart #1, Nautical Chart Symbols and Abbreviations $0.50

U.S. Naval Observatory

The American Nautical Almanac (also published abroad by several foreign governments and in different languages) Annual $4.00 each
The Air Almanac (also published abroad) Covers 4 months $3.75 each
The American Ephemeris and Nautical Almanac (for astronomers and surveyors) Annual $6.25

U.S. Coast Guard

Light Lists of U.S. Coastal Waters:
Vol. I Atlantic Coast from St. Croix River, Maine, to Little River, South Carolina $4.25

Vol. II Atlantic and Gulf Coasts from Little River, S.C., to Rio Grande, Texas $4.75
Vol. III Pacific Coast and Pacific Islands $2.75
Vol. IV Great Lakes $2.00
Vol. V Mississippi River System $2.75

Miscellaneous Publications:
(order by number, i.e., CG-101)

C.G. no.	Title
101	*Specimen Examination for Merchant Marine Deck Officers*
108	*Rules and Regulations for Military Explosives and Hazardous Munitions*
115	*Marine Engineering Regulations*
123	*Rules and Regulations for Tank Vessels*
129	*Proceedings of the Marine Safety Council* (Monthly)
169	*Rules of the Road: International, Inland*
172	*Rules of the Road: Great Lakes*
174	*A Manual for the Safe Handling of Inflammable and Combustible Liquids*
175	*Manual for Lifeboatmen, Able Seamen, and Qualified Members of Engine Department*
176	*Load Line Regulations*
182	*Specimen Examinations for Merchant Marine Engineer Licenses*
184	*Rules of the Road: Western Rivers*
190	*Equipment Lists*
191	*Rules and Regulations for Licensing and Certificating of Merchant Marine Personnel*
200	*Marine Investigation Regulations and Suspension and Revocation Proceedings*
220	*Specimen Examination Questions for Licenses as Master, Mate, and Pilot of Central Western Rivers Vessels*
227	*Laws Governing Marine Inspection*
239	*Security of Vessels and Waterfront Facilities*
249	*Marine Safety Council Public Hearing Agenda* (Annual)
256	*Rules and Regulations for Passenger Vessels*
257	*Rules and Regulations for Cargo and Miscellaneous Vessels*
258	*Rules and Regulations for Uninspected Vessels*
259	*Electrical Engineering Regulations*
266	*Rules and Regulations for Bulk Grain Cargoes*
268	*Rules and Regulations for Manning of Vessels*
293	*Miscellaneous Electrical Equipment List*
320	*Rules and Regulations for Artificial Islands and Fixed Structures on the Outer Continental Shelf*

323 *Rules and Regulations for Small Passenger Vessels* (Under 100 Gross Tons)
329 *Fire Fighting Manual for Tank Vessels*

U.S. Army Corps of Engineers

Catalogs

Charts of the Great Lakes and Outflow Rivers, Lake Champlain, New York State Barge Canal System, Minnesota-Ontario Border Lakes (Free from Lake Survey District, Detroit, Mich.)
Illinois Waterway: Lake Michigan to Mississippi River (Free from Chicago District, Corps of Engineers, Chicago, Ill.)
Mississippi River: Cairo, Ill., to Minneapolis, Minn. (Free from Chicago District)
Mississippi River: Cairo, Ill., to Gulf of Mexico. (Free from Vicksburg District, Corps of Engineers, Vicksburg, Miss.)
Ohio River and Tributaries (Free from Corps of Engineers, Cincinnati, Ohio.
TVA Reservoirs, Tennessee River, and Tributaries (Free from Tennessee Valley Authority, Knoxville, Tenn.)
Black Warrior River, Alabama River, Tombigbee River, Apalachicola River and Pearl River (Free from Corps of Engineers, Mobile, Ala.)
Missouri River and Tributaries (Free from Corps of Engineers, Omaha, Neb.)
Gulf Intracoastal Waterway, Sabine River to the Rio Grande, Texas, Including Connecting Waterways and Ship Channels (Free from Corps of Engineers, Galveston, Texas)

Naval Oceanographic Office

Catalogs

N.O. Pub. No. 1-N-A, Special Purpose Navigational Charts and Publications (Free)
N.O. Pub. No. 1-N-B, Miscellaneous Charts and Sheets (Free)
N.O. Pub. No. 1-N-S, Catalog of Classified Charts (Not available to the public)
There are nine regional catalogs, covering various

areas of the world, each identified as "N.O. Pub. No. 1-N-[Region No.]"

Region no.

1. United States and Canada
2. Central and South America and Antarctica
3. Western Europe, Iceland, Greenland, and the Arctic
4. Scandinavia, Baltic, and USSR
5. Western Africa and the Mediterranean
6. Indian Ocean
7. Australia, Indonesia, and New Zealand
8. Oceania
9. East Asia

(There is a small charge for the regional catalogs.)

Special Publications

From the very large number of special charts and publications, the following are of general interest to many mariners, but the appropriate catalog should be consulted for the complete list. All should be ordered with the prefix "N.O." and the appropriate number.

Miscellaneous

N.O. no.	
5	*National Flags and Ensigns* of 45 Countries in color, 26″ × 38″ $0.50
6	*International Flags and Pennants with Morse Symbols* $0.10
102	*International Code of Signals* $4.00
65	*Track Chart of the World* $1.00
220	*Navigation Dictionary* $3.00
5025–38	A series of twelve sheets with borders, to be joined together on a wall to make a beautiful chart of the world in full color, 8′ high × 12′ long. At $18.00 it is a real bargain, almost cheaper than wall paper.
76	*Standard Time Zone Chart of the World* $1.00
5018	*Whale Chart, 1851,* by Lt. M. F. Maury, USN $0.50
5160	*Plotting Chart: Pacific Yacht Races,* San Pedro to Honolulu, including Acapulco and Mazatlan $2.00
16	*Pilot Chart* of the North Atlantic (Monthly) Per month $0.50
55	*Pilot Chart* of the North Pacific (Monthly) Per month $0.50

5091 *Maneuvering Board:* pad of 50 sheets $3.00

5093 *Radar Plotting Sheet:* pad of 50 sheets $2.00

Sailing Directions—Various numbers, seventy volumes covering various areas of the world, arranged in nine groups corresponding to the chart regions. Selling at $5.50 per volume but in process of being rewritten in somewhat different form, revisions to be completed by 1977. Consult current catalog for details, as they are being released one at a time.

Lists of Lights and Fog Signals $5.00 each

111A Greenland, east coast of North and South America (excluding continental U.S. except east coast of Florida), and West Indies

111B The west coasts of North and South America (excluding continental U.S. and Alaska), the Hawaiian Islands, Australia, Tasmania, New Zealand, and the islands of the North and South Pacific Ocean

112 Western Pacific and Indian Oceans, including Persian Gulf and the Red Sea

113 The west coasts of Europe and Africa, the Mediterranean Sea, Black Sea, and Azovskoye More (Sea of Azov)

114 British Isles: English Channel and North Sea

115 Norway, Iceland, and Arctic Ocean

116 Baltic Sea, with Kattegat, Belts, and Sound, and Gulf of Bothnia

Radio Aids

117A *Radio Navigational Aids:* Atlantic and Mediterranean Area $5.00

117B *Radio Navigational Aids:* Pacific and Indian Oceans Area $5.00

118 *Radio Weather Aids* $6.00

Manuals

9 Bowditch, *American Practical Navigator* $7.00

9-Tables Contains Bowditch Tables only $4.00

150 *World Port Index* $1.50

217 *Maneuvering Board Manual* $1.50

257 *Radar Plotting Manual* $0.35

1310 *Radar Navigation Manual*

Tables

151 *Tables of Distances Between Ports* (40,000 distances) $3.00

214 *Tables of Computed Altitudes and Azimuths,* Vols. I–IX $6.00 each

229 *Sight Reduction Tables for Marine Navigation,* Vols. 1–6 $6.00 each

249 *Sight Reduction Tables for Air Navigation*
Vol. I For Stars $3.75
Vol. II For Sun, etc. $4.50
Vol. III For Sun, etc. $4.50

Pilot Chart Atlases

$3.50 each

106 Central American Waters and South Atlantic
107 South Pacific and Indian Oceans
108 Northern North Atlantic

Current Atlases

236 South China, Java, Celebes, and Sulu Seas $0.30
237 Vicinity of Japanese Islands and the China Coast $0.60
566 Surface Currents, Indian Ocean $2.40
568 Southwestern Pacific Ocean $2.40
569 Northwestern Pacific Ocean $2.40
570 Northeast Pacific Ocean $2.40

British Admiralty Publications

British Admiralty publications are available from the Hydrographic Office of the British Admiralty at Taunton, Somerset, England, and from chart agents in the USA and around the world. For European coasts they often have a greater variety and detail of coverage than American charts. In remote areas they are still based on the surveys and information gathered by the early explorers, such as Captains Cook and Bligh and others, and must be used with caution. The following publications are of special interest.

Catalog

Catalog of Admiralty Charts and Publications

5011 *Explanations of Symbols and Abbreviations used on Admiralty Charts*

Various	About seventy-seven volumes of *Sailing Directions* for all parts of the world.
136	*Ocean Passages for the World* (Sail and Steam, various size vessels, various seasons of the year)
277	*Port Radio Stations and Pilot Vessels*
200	*Admiralty Tide Tables,* Vol. 1: European Waters and Mediterranean
201	*Admiralty Tide Tables,* Vol. 2: Atlantic and Indian Oceans
202	*Admiralty Tide Tables,* Vol. 3: Pacific Oceans and Adjacent Seas

If you order British Admiralty charts in the U.S., make certain that you specify British Admiralty, to avoid confusion of numbers. Likewise, when you order American charts, use prefix N.O. for Naval Oceanographic Office Publications and N.O.S. for National Ocean Survey charts.

Charts from foreign countries other than Britain are usually not available in the U.S., but you can write for information directly to the hydrographic office of the country involved, using the following list.

Members of the International Hydrographic Bureau

ARGENTINA
Head
Navy Hydrographic Service
Avenida Montes de Oca 2124
Buenos Aires, Argentina

AUSTRALIA
Hydrographer
Royal Australian Navy
Hydrographic Service
Garden Island, N.S.W.
Sydney, Australia

BRAZIL
Director General of
Hydrography and Navigation
Ilha Fiscal
Rio de Janeiro, Brazil

BURMA
Commanding Officer
(Hydrographer)
Naval Hydrographic Depot
Burma Navy
Rangoon, Burma

CANADA
Dominion Hydrographer
Canadian Hydrographic Service
615 Booth Street
Ottawa 4, Ontario, Canada

CHILE
Director
Hydrographic Institute of the
Navy
Playa Ancha, Errazuriz No. 232,
Casilla 324
Valparaiso, Chile

CHINA
Director
Chinese Naval Hydrographic
Office

Tso-Ying, Kaohsiung, Taiwan
Republic of China

DENMARK
Hydrographer
Royal Danish Hydrographic Office
Esplanaden 19
Copenhagen, K., Denmark

DOMINICAN REPUBLIC
Head, Dominican Navy Hydrographic Dept.
Ministry of Armed Forces
Santo Domingo, Dominican Republic

FINLAND
Hydrographer
Hydrographic Department
Vuorimiehenkatu 1
Helsinki, Finland

FRANCE
Hydrographer
Naval Hydrographic Office
13, Rue de l'Université
Paris (7e), France

GERMANY
Director
German Hydrographic Institute
Bernhard-Nocht-Strasse 78
Hamburg 4, Federal Republic of Germany

GREAT BRITAIN AND NORTHERN IRELAND
Hydrographer of the Navy
Hydrographic Department
Ministry of Defence
Taunton, Somerset, England

GREECE
Director
Hydrographic Service
Ministry of National Defense
Athens, Greece

GUATEMALA
Director General
National Geographic Institute
Avenida Las Americas, Zona 13
Ciudad Guatemala, Guatemala

ICELAND
Director of Lighthouse Administration
Icelandic Hydrographic Service
Reykjavik, Iceland

INDIA
Chief Hydrographer
Naval Hydrographic Office
Post Box No. 75
Dehra Dun 1 (U.P.), India

INDONESIA
Chief Hydrographer
Indonesian Naval Hydrographic Service
Djalan Gunung Sahari 87
Djakarta, Indonesia

IRAN
General Director of Ports and Navigation Organization
64, Khiyaban Sepah
Tehran, Iran

ITALY
Director
Hydrographic Institute of the Navy
Passo Osservatorio 4
Genova, Italy

JAPAN
Chief Hydrographer
Hydrographic Division of Marine Safety Agency
5-Chome, Tsukiji, Chuo-Ku
Tokyo, Japan

KOREA
Director
Republic of Korea Hydrographic Office
9-15 Namchang Dong
Chung-Ku, Seoul
Republic of Korea

NETHERLANDS
Hydrographer
Hydrographic Department
171, Badhuisweg
's Gravenhage, Netherlands

NEW ZEALAND
Hydrographer
Royal New Zealand Navy
P.O. Box 292
Wellington, New Zealand

NORWAY
Hydrographer
Hydrographic Office of Norway
Stavanger, Norway

PAKISTAN
Director of Hydrography
Hydrographic Directorate
Naval Headquarters
Karachi, Pakistan

PARAGUAY
Director
Direction of Hydrography and Navigation
Don Bosco No. 169, CC.643
Asunción, Paraguay

PHILIPPINES
Director
Bureau of Coast and Geodetic Survey
421 Barraca St., San Nicolas
Manila, Philippines

POLAND
Chief of the Hydrographic Office
Hydrographic Office of the Navy
Gdynia, 19, Poland

PORTUGAL
Director
Hydrographic Institute
Lisboa 2, Portugal

REPUBLIC OF SOUTH AFRICA
Hydrographer of the South African Navy
South African Naval Hydrographic Office
c/o Fleet Mail Office, Simonstown
Cape Province, South Africa

SPAIN
Director
Navy Hydrographic Institute
Tolosa Latour No. 5
Cádiz, Spain

SWEDEN
Hydrographer
Hydrographic Department
Sehlstedtsgaten 9
Stockholm 27, Sweden

THAILAND
Director
Hydrographic Department
Royal Thai Navy
Bangkok, Thailand

TURKEY
Head of Department
Department of Navigation and Hydrography
Cubuklu-Istanbul
Turkey

UNITED ARAB REPUBLIC
Director
Hydrograph Department
Ras El Tin
Alexandria, United Arab Republic

UNITED STATES OF AMERICA
Commander
U.S. Naval Oceanographic Office
Washington, DC 20390

Director
National Ocean Survey
National Oceanic and Atmospheric Administration
Rockville, Md. 20852

VENEZUELA
Director
Hydrographic and Navigational Service
Comandancia General de la Marina
Caracas, Venezuela

YUGOSLAVIA
Director
Hydrographic Institute of the Yugoslav Navy
Split, Yugoslavia

Cooperating Countries (Not IHB Members)

BELGIUM
Administrator-Inspector General
Coast Hydrographic Office
113, Rue Christine
Ostend, Belgium

COLOMBIA
Dirección Marina Mercanta Colombiana
Ministerio de Guerra
Bogotá, Colombia

ECUADOR
Chief of the Hydrographic Office
Hydrographic Service of the Navy
Malecon No. 105
Guayaquil, Ecuador

EL SALVADOR
Director General of Cartography
Cartographic Office
San Salvador, El Salvador

MEXICO
Director General
General Direction of Lighthouses and Hydrography
Ave Coyocean #131
Mexico 13—O.F., Mexico

PERU
Director
Direction of Hydrography and Lighthouses
Saenz Pena 590
La Punta
Callao, Peru

URUGUAY
Head of Service
Hydrographic Office of the Navy
Avenida Agraciada 3080
Montevideo, Uruguay

VIETNAM
Chief of Hydrographic Office
Department of Transportation and Communications
Saigon, Republic of Vietnam

INTERNATIONAL HYDROGRAPHIC BUREAU
President of the Directing Committee
International Hydrographic Bureau
Avenue President J. F. Kennedy
Monte-Carlo, Monaco

B.

Navigation Equipment Aboard Ship

We are talking here about yachts, fishing boats, and smaller vessels where the skipper-navigator must decide what he will try to do without. Large ships are outfitted by professionals and will not be discussed here.

On a motorboat up to 35 feet that operates on short coastal runs, the most important piece of navigation equipment is a good compass, properly adjusted or with a recent deviation table; also important are a good hand-bearing compass for taking bearings, a radio for receiving weather reports, a VHF radiotelephone for use in emergency and for general communications with the shore and other boats, a good chart of the area, and the usual plotting tools: parallel rulers, protractor, and dividers. If a depth sounder can be afforded, it is good for navigating in fog and for spotting fish, and likewise a small radio direction finder in good working condition can be a help. A lead line is handy to have, and a good barometer is insurance against being caught out in a storm. There is very little reason to have any more, unless you like gadgets, in which case only your pocketbook sets the limit.

If the motorboat is larger—from 35 feet to 65 feet—the equipment is usually more elaborate, though it need not be. A small-vessel radar, if you can afford it, is a great convenience for inshore work at night and in fog. Perhaps you will also want a single-side-band radiotelephone. If you expect to navigate out of sight of land, a loran receiver is a great help. Of course, if we are talking about a fishing vessel that makes long voyages at sea, there is a real need for more elaborate equipment, and now the SSB radiotelephone is a must.

The loran receiver, or Decca where there is chart coverage, is a great time-saver for a busy fisherman. Omega is probably too expensive. The depth sounder is a must, and for long voyages out of sight of land, equipment for celestial navigation, as described below, should be aboard. But fishermen are hardy and practical people, and know how to manage well with few tools. The success or failure of a voyage is largely determined before the vessel leaves the dock, and depends on three factors:

1. The skipper
2. The equipment
3. The boat

A seasoned skipper can take a raft through a gale and survive, whereas a neophyte can lose a well-found vessel in a light breeze. If the vessel is ill-equipped and the trip is poorly planned, life aboard can be pure hell, what with lack of food, water, medicine, fuel, proper navigation equipment, inferior fire-fighting and lifesaving gear, breakdowns, and no spares for engine parts, spars, sails, rigging, etc., etc.—let alone the danger of being lost. If the boat is unseaworthy, of course, she ought not be allowed to leave dock.

With the enormous increase in the number of people who would like to sail small boats around the world—at Coast Navigation School we have thousands of students from every country in the world who all have more or less the same thing in mind—boating skills and navigation proficiency have become more important than ever, and the equipment checklist is perhaps the most important document aboard. Since most such voyages are undertaken in auxiliary sailing vessels from 28 feet and up to 50 feet, the following list of navigational equipment has been prepared for general guidance.

Minimum and Essential Navigational Equipment for a Cruising Boat Under 50 Feet

1. A good compass, properly adjusted or with recent deviation table, preferably with built-in magnets; must have a night light for steering and be mounted in a protected, secure, and convenient place.
2. A good hand-bearing compass for taking bearings, preferably with night illumination.
3. A sun pelorus for taking bearings on the sun for deviation checks. It can also be used for taking bearings on landmarks. A place

should be provided for mounting it when in use, such as a small frame on top of the cabin.

4. A good micrometer sextant with illumination on arc and drum for easy reading. Buy the best sextant you can afford.
5. A second, or emergency, sextant, in case something should happen to the regular sextant. Here an inexpensive model will do, as, hopefully, it will not be used.
6. A reliable watch with a good sweep second hand. It need not be expensive, since you can get a time signal as often as you need, and can set the watch just before taking sights.
7. A good short-wave radio for receiving WWV and WWVH time signals and storm warnings.
8. A study, good-quality barometer.
9. A good marine radio receiver for weather reports.
10. Radiotelephone—after 1972 you need both VHF and SSB for short- and long-range communication. Essential for getting help if you run into trouble.
11. A Simex Star Finder.
12. Navigation tools: parallel rulers or equivalent, protractor, dividers.
13. An *adequate* inventory of charts for the voyage, including harbor charts for the places you intend to visit, arranged in proper sequence and properly stowed and protected against water damage. Make sure you include a great circle chart if you are going far.
14. A supply of plotting sheets: either universal or special latitude sheets for the area you will cover.
15. Current *Nautical Almanac* or *Air Almanac;* if your dates are near the end of the period covered by the book, better get the next issue also.
16. A set of sight reduction tables, N.O. 214, 249, or 229 (my preference is using N.O. 249 with the *Air Almanac*) and a good supply of celestial work forms.

17. Copy of coast pilot and sailing directions for the places where you will make landfalls.
18. Tide and current tables for the area (latest issue).
19. Pilot charts for the months you will be sailing: they show prevailing winds and currents, storm frequency, etc.
20. Light lists for area.
21. N.O. 117 (*Radio Aids to Navigation*) and N.O. 118 (*Radio Weather Aids*).
22. Copy of Bowditch *American Practical Navigator* for reference purposes.

These are twenty-two bare-bone items for a long voyage. Now you can add the trimmings according to the budget. Loran can be used almost worldwide. Omega is even better if you have enough electric power to keep it running, but the cost is high. A radio direction finder is useful, and so is a depth sounder. You might add an anemometer, a mechanical speed indicator, high-powered binoculars, and even consider a chronometer, in case the radio fails to function. There could be no end.

However, remember that a good workman can build a palace with few tools. Remember Slocum, the first and greatest single-handed small boat circumnavigator of them all, who navigated masterfully with a broken alarm clock (reduced from two dollars to one dollar because the face had been pushed in). With such major conveniences as a cedar bucket and a wood-burning stove, he carved his niche in the nautical Hall of Fame. So don't worry if you don't have all the latest gadgets. Be sure you have what you need!

With the minimum equipment listed and your own skill as a navigator you can get there safely, so long as you don't do anything foolish. Remember that if you are beginning to wonder if it is time to shorten sail, it is usually too late! If you are in that big a hurry, you should take a plane. The wonderful part of cruising is the incomparable peace to be found in nature, the one-ness with the elements, the chance to contemplate a glorious sunset at sea, the time to meditate under a starlit sky, having a quiet conversation in the cockpit or curling up in a cozy cabin with a good book and plenty of time to enjoy it. And while we are on the subject, let us talk about the ship's library, a very important part of your vessel's equipment. Slocum read Plato and Gibbon, along with many others of the really great writers, and fortunate indeed is the person who enjoys sharing the thinking of the great minds.

I will let you select your own in that department, but for sheer enjoyment in reading about the people of the sea and their boats, I offer here a list of my favorite books, valuable to the sailor from the standpoint of entertainment, romance, excitement, and sharing the knowledge and personal experience of those who have gone "down to the sea in ships." The list is small, and there are probably a hundred or more books that also deserve to be included. As you read on your own, you will discover the rest of the great literature of the sea. But don't miss these:

Sailing Alone Around the World, by Joshua Slocum
Sea Quest, by Charles Borden
Deep Water and Shoal, by William A. Robinson
Around the World Singlehanded, by Harry Pidgeon
Song of the Sirens, by Ernest K. Gann
The Book of the Sea, by A. C. Spectorsky—a superb anthology
Tinkerbelle, by Robert Manry
A World of My Own, by Robin Knox-Johnston
Alone Through the Roaring Forties, by Vito Dumas
Trekka Round the World, by J. Guzwell
The Venturesome Voyages of Captain Voss, by J. C. Voss
The Fight of the Firecrest, by Alain Gerbault
Gypsy Moth Circles the World, by Sir Francis Chichester
Beyond the West Horizon, by Eric C. Hiscock
Around the World in Wanderer III, by Eric C. Hiscock
Cruising Under Sail, by Eric C. Hiscock—excellent on short-to-medium cruises
Voyaging Under Sail, by Eric C. Hiscock—a must for the circumnavigator
Kon-Tiki, by Thor Heyerdahl
The Ra Expeditions, by Thor Heyerdahl
Four Winds of Adventure, by Marcel Bardiaux
Desperate Voyage, by John Caldwell—a fantastic true story
Lonely Victory, by Eric Tabarly
Heaven, Hell, and Salt Water, by Bill and Phyllis Crowe

My Ship Is So Small, by Ann Davison—the story of a woman circumnavigator
Rough Passage, by Robert Douglas Graham
Wind Aloft, Wind Alow, by Marin-Marie
The Saga of Cimba, by Richard Maury
Stornoway East and West, by Marjorie Petersen
Blue Water Vagabond, by Dennis Puleston
Sea Gypsy, by Peter Tangvald
Cruise of the Snark, by Jack London
Moby Dick, by Herman Melville
The Nigger of the Narcissus, by Joseph Conrad
Two Years Before the Mast, by Richard Henry Dana

Cruising in a small vessel is a way of life that for many becomes a complete addiction. Once the sea is in your blood, you feel that there is no greater or more satisfying experience. These books will give you a sense of the greatness of nature, the beauty, romance, and adventure that can be found only on the sea.

Have fun!

C.

Answers to Practice Problems

Chapter 3 •

LOCATION	LATITUDE	LONGITUDE
Hong Kong	22°18′ N	114°10′ E
New York	40°42′ N	74°01′ W
Sydney	33°53′ S	151°12′ E
Ottawa	45°15′ N	75°45′ W
Buenos Aires	34°36′ S	58°22′ W
Singapore	1°17′ N	103°51′ E
Honolulu	21°18′ N	157°52′ W
New Orleans	29°57′ N	90°03′ W
Berlin	47°30′ N	13°21′ E
Johannesburg	26°05′ S	28°00′ E
San Francisco	37°49′ N	122°25′ W
Cairo	30°00′ N	31°05′ E

Chapter 4 •

CC	DEV.	MC	VAR.	TC	TE
075°	10° E	085°	15° E	100°	25° E
195°	5° W	190°	10° W	180°	15° W
260°	10° W	250°	20° E	270°	10° E
008°	5° E	013°	18° W	355°	13° W
197°	8° W	189°	3° E	192°	5° W
050°	12° E	062°	12° W	050°	0°
277°	13° E	290°	20° W	270°	7° W

Chapter 5 •

1. MB = 280° TB = 270°
2. MB = 179° TB = 194°
3. TB = 090° + 25° = 115°
4. TB = 180° − 125° = 055°
5. TB = 050° − 75° = 335°
6. TB = 270° + 100° = 010°
7. TC = 100°; RTB = 100° + 180° − 45° = 235°
8. Distance to abeam position = 1.5 hours × 10 knots = 15 nautical miles
   Distance off = 15 nautical miles
   Time Abeam = 1900

9\. 1612 – 1527 = 45 min.; distance off = $\frac{10 \times 45}{60}$ = 7.5 nautical miles

10\. Speed is 30 miles divided by 5 hours = 6 knots

11\. Required time is 56 hours divided by 6 knots = 9^h20^m

12\. Distance = 4⅓ × 12 = 52 nautical miles

Chapter 6 •

1. Set is 134°, drift is 4.0 knots.
2. TH = 021°, CH = 035°

Note: There is a further application of a current diagram, not often used in practical work, except perhaps on naval maneuvers, and therefore not discussed in the chapter itself. The problem is to determine *the heading and required speed through the water* in the face of a certain set and drift, to make good a *desired effective speed.*
The procedure is as follows:

Step 1. From point of departure, mark desired course on the chart.

Step 2. From point of departure, plot current vector, i.e., set and drift.

Step 3. From point of departure, mark *required speed in miles for 1 hour along the desired course line.*

Step 4. Draw a line from the end of the speed vector in step 3 to the end of the current vector in step 2.

Step 5. The direction of the line drawn in step 4 indicates the true heading to be steered to make good the desired course. The length of this line indicates the *required speed of the vessel through the water* to make good the *effective speed* along the desired course line.

Chapter 7 •

1\. Tides at Kitimat:

TIME	HEIGHT OF TIDE
0047	–7.2 ft.
0626	15.2 ft.
1305	4.9 ft.
1932	16.5 ft.

Height of tide at 1700 is 12.5 ft.

2. Currents at Ripple Point will be as follows:

TIME	FLOOD, EBB OR SLACK	VELOCITY	SET
2350(29th)	F	3.5	105°
0250	S		
0610	E	4.5	285°
0915	S		
1220	F	4.8	105°
1540	S		
1850	E	4.2	285°

Chapter 9 •

1. Power vessel under way, showing starboard running light and two range lights.
2. Same as problem 1, but vessel is showing port side running light.
3. Sailing vessel under way, head-on, showing optional masthead lights.
4. Port side of tugboat towing submerged tow. Towing lights on foremast.
5. Port side of power-driven pilot vessel under way on station. Also will show a flare-up white light at regular intervals.
6. Starboard side of fishing vessel with nets extended over 500 ft. horizontally in direction indicated by white light.
7. Tug with tow not over 600 ft. in length. Tug is less than 150 ft. in length as it does not show an after range light. Starboard side showing.
8. Port side of sailing vessel, any size, showing only red running light.
9. Tug with tow astern, starboard side, towing lights on foremast, and showing also after range light. If in international waters, the tow is over 600 ft.

Chapter 15 •

1. LHA of star is 20°; angle *t* is 20° W
2. LHA of star is 314°; angle *t* is 46° E
3. LHA of star is 275°; angle *t* is 85° E
4. LHA of star is 357°; angle *t* is 3° E
5. LHA of sun is 320°; angle *t* is 40° E
6. LHA of moon is 0°; angle *t* is 0°
7. LHA of Venus is 252°; angle *t* is 108° E
8. LHA of Jupiter is 90°; angle *t* is 90° W

Chapter 16 •

1	2	3
ZT: 18-13-32	ZT: 05-11-08	ZT: 19-42-42
ZD: −8	ZD: −8	ZD: +8
GMT: 10-13-32, July 9	GMT: 21-11-08, July 10	GMT: 03-42-42, May 16

Chapter 17 •

Nautical Almanac

	GHA	Declination
1.	94°24.8′	S 22°59.7′
2.	334°38′	S 7°23.8′
3.	240°58.4′	S 11°11.4′
4.	192°14.1′	N 45°58.4′

Air Almanac

	GHA	Declination
1.	94°24.5′	S 22°59.7′
2.	334°38′	S 7°25′
3.	240°58′	S 11°11′
4.	192°14′	N 45°58′

Chapter 18 •

1. $H_o = 15°47.2'$ 2. $H_o = 23°40.5'$ 3. $H_o = 44°38.5'$
4. $H_o = 27°37'$ 5. $H_o = 21°12.1'$ 6. $H_o = 35°28.6'$

Index